# A DRAMA OF CREATION

Swedenborg Studies / No. 16
Monographs of the Swedenborg Foundation

# A DRAMA OF CREATION

Sources and Influences
in Swedenborg's
*Worship and Love of God*

INGE JONSSON

*translated by*
Matilda McCarthy

Swedenborg Foundation Publishers

Swedenborg Studies is a scholarly series published by the Swedenborg Foundation. The primary purpose of the series is to make materials available for understanding the life and thought of Emanuel Swedenborg (1688–1772) and the impact his thought has had on others. The Foundation undertakes to publish original studies and English translations of such studies and to republish primary sources that are otherwise difficult to access. Proposals should be sent to: Senior Editor, Swedenborg Studies, Swedenborg Foundation, 320 North Church Street, West Chester, Pennsylvania 19380.

Library of Congress Cataloging-in-Publication Data
Jonsson, Inge.
    A drama of creation : sources and influences in Swedenborg's Worship and love of God / Inge Jonsson ; translator, Matilda McCarthy.
        p. cm. — (Swedenborg studies)
    Includes bibliographical references and index.
    ISBN 0-87785-315-0
    1. Swedenborg, Emanuel, 1688-1722. De cultu et amore Dei.
    2. Creation—Early works to 1800. 3.  Adam (Biblical figure)
    4.  Eve (Biblical figure) I. Title. II. Series.

BX8712.W79J59 2004
231.7′65—dc22

                                                            2004014766

Edited by Mary Lou Bertucci
Designed by Sans Serif, Inc., Saline, Michigan
Set in Sabon by Sans Serif, Inc.

Printed in the United States of America.

# CONTENTS

# INTRODUCTION

Ever since Emanuel Swedenborg (1688–1772) abandoned his scientific activities to become a visionary interpreter of *arcana caelestia*, the secrets of heaven, his name has sparked debate in world literature. In his homeland, opinions have oscillated between extremes such as that of his contemporary Johan Henrik Kellgren (1751–1795), who contemptuously stated that Swedenborg was "quite simply a fool," to that of August Strindberg (1849–1912), who a century later deferentially dedicated one of his books to Swedenborg, "the master and the leader."

That Swedenborg is still influential as the inspiration for the New Church has, of course, implications also for secular scholars. Despite the admirable energy that his disciples, particularly those in Great Britain and the United States, have devoted to publishing and translating his works and manuscripts, some of the results undeniably justify Martin Lamm's opinion that its *"oerhörda omfång ej står i riktig proportion till dess vetenskapliga halt"* (there is no ratio between the [amplitude] of international literature regarding Swedenborg and its scholarly value").[1] As to Swedish scholarship, Lamm's learned and well-balanced monograph from 1915 still represents the apogee of Swedenborg research in Swedish. His book, which was translated into English in 2000, served as a general point of departure when I started to write the present one.

Another basic difficulty in Swedenborg research results from the uncommon complexity of its object. Emanuel Swedenborg's writings bear the stamp of a polymath and require different types of studies. A student of letters, with only a superficial education in science, runs an obvious risk of failing to notice essential facts. This becomes obvious if he or she is interested in clarifying Swedenborg's sources of inspiration, the intellectual and cultural environment in which he lived. Despite this risk, I have found such a project to be necessary, not least because investigating the literary milieu might provide a more stable foundation for serious attempts at interpreting Swedenborg's remarkable position, as well as his mental condition.

For my 1961 dissertation, which is the basis for the present work, I

selected *De cultu et amore Dei* (The Worship and Love of God) (1745) as
my topic. One reason was that this work, among Swedenborg's extensive
oeuvre, comes closest to literature in a conventional sense. Written at the
end of his religious crisis, although never completed, it reflects in a fascinating way his transition from three intense decades as a scholar and re-
searcher in the natural sciences to the final period as an interpreter of Holy
Scripture and the wellspring of the New Church. A grand exposition of the
creation of the world and the first human couple, *The Worship and Love
of God* summarizes Swedenborg's scientific outlook on nature, while
heralding what will come.

# A Survey of Swedenborg's Works

New Church scholars look upon Swedenborg's education and scientific activities until 1745 as a preparation for his call as an exegete and the source
of their church. From this point of view, the term *preparation* has obvious
metaphysical meaning; but in a strictly neutral sense, the word can also be
used by a secular Swedenborg scholar. There is indeed a strong coherence
in Swedenborg's production, which makes even early leaflets relevant for
the study of *The Worship and Love of God*.

Emanuel Swedberg[2] completed his studies at Uppsala University in 1709
by defending a small thesis consisting of comments on selected sentences by
Seneca (4 BCE–65 CE) and Publilius Syrus (1st cent. BCE), to which notes by
Erasmus (d. 1536) and J. J. Scaliger (1540–1609) had been added. While
not a remarkable work, it shows that the young respondent was well
versed in classical literature. This was normal for a student of the time: to
quote Hans Helander, who has published three excellent editions of
Swedenborg's Latin poetry, "Latin was still the dominating language in
many fields in Sweden around 1700. All university lectures were held in
Latin. The academic theses were all written in that language. Latin poetry
and eloquence may in fact be said to have flourished as never before during
the last decades of the 17th century."[3] Nevertheless, few students published collections of Latin poetry as "E.S. Svecus" did in Greifswald in
1715, and Helander has shown convincingly that the writer had a predilection for paraphrasing the great Roman poets, particularly Ovid (43 BCE–17
or 18 CE). There can be little doubt that Swedenborg's intimate knowledge
of Latin poetry and his fondness for an allegorical style were important
background factors when *The Worship and Love of God* was written
thirty years later.

These early pieces of Neo-Latin poetry should not obscure the fact that
the young Swedenborg primarily devoted his energy to science and philosophy. This becomes clear in his letters to his brother-in-law Erik Benzelius
Jr. (1675–1743) during his European travels from 1710 to 1715.[4] These

letters overflow with a passion for knowledge and a naive self-esteem that
appear as chaotic prototypes of the writer's future calling. One of them
contains a long list of more-or-less fanciful inventions, such as airplanes
and submarines; but in the middle of these engineering dreams, the reader
is taken unawares by a psychological project, the earliest indicator of the
young man's synthetic ambition: "*Voluntates et affectiones animorum
hominum per analysin conjectandi modus,*" that is, a way of interpreting
the wills and feelings of human minds by analysis.[5] This early variant of
psychoanalysis obviously had its basis in physics, but it is also the earliest
germ of Swedenborg's interest in the contemporary speculations about a
philosophical calculus, which in time was to find its final expression in his
famous doctrine of correspondence.

Similar synthesizing tendencies appear in other early writings. Cosmological and geological works such as *En Ny Theorie om jordens afstannande* (A New Theory on the End of the Earth, 1717), *En Ny Mening om
Jordens och Planeternas Gång och Stånd* (The Motion and Position of the
Earth and the Planets, 1718), and *Om Wattnens Högd, och Förra
Werldens Starcka Ebb och Flod* (The Height of Water and Strong Tides in
the Primeval World, 1718) are not confined to their particular fields of
study but extend their perspectives toward basic philosophical issues. An
early psychophysical application of this multidisciplinary outlook can be
found in an article written in 1719 called *Anatomi af wår aldrafinaste
Natur, wisande att wårt rörande och lefwande wäsende består af Contrem-
iscentier* (An Anatomy of Our Most Subtle Nature, Showing That Our
Moving and Living Force Consists of Vibrations, 1719); and in several
other works prior to his great works of the 1730s, similar tendencies can
be observed. However, Swedenborg became increasingly more interested in
the practical know-how that a civil servant on the Board of Mines (he was
appointed to a position as *assessor ordinarius* in 1724) was expected to
possess, and the works from the 1720s are of less value in this context.[6]

In contrast to these works, Swedenborg's great books on natural philosophy published in 1734, *Opera philosophica et mineralia* (Philosophical
and Mineralogical Works), are essential in understanding his development.
The third volume of the series, *Principia rerum naturalium* (The Principles
of Natural Things), attempts to explain the evolution of the universe by
means of mechanical laws out of the mathematical point that had been created by the Infinite. He then applies this concept in different variants and
compounds until he has reached paradise on the new-born earth: this representation will later be summarized in *The Worship and Love of God*. As
a follow-up to the pamphlets of the 1710s, Swedenborg extended his vision
to the domain of the soul in *Prodromus philosophiae ratiocinantis de infinito et causa finali creationis* (A Forerunner of a Rational Philosophy of
the Infinite and the Final Cause of Creation), or *De Infinito*, also published

in 1734, a short work dedicated to Erik Benzelius that, in many respects, comes even closer to the drama of creation written in 1745.

The mechanistic interpretation of the human soul posited by *De Infinito* evoked accusations of materialism.[7] But an attentive reader would have noticed that the author of *De Infinito* had made an effort to save the Christian conception of the world from the atheistic menace of contemporary philosophy. On the other hand, Swedenborg had not yet reached a position where he could give his supposed materialism a spiritualized form so that his real meaning might be understood; by way of precaution, therefore, he called the book a *prodromus*, a forerunner.

More than any preceding Swedenborg scholar, Martin Lamm should be given credit for having emphasized the continuity of Swedenborg's spiritual development, the connections not only between the scientific works themselves but also between the scientific and the visionary periods of his life. Before Lamm's groundbreaking study in 1915, Swedenborg's entire life was often seen in the light of the late visions, whereas Lamm presented convincing evidence that the contributions of the prophet and preacher had been continuously foreshadowed in evermore daring projects by the scientist, finally forcing him to transgress the frontiers of science. To illustrate that, Lamm selected the relation between *Principia* and the successive works published prior to 1745, particularly *Oeconomia regni animalis* (The Economy of the Animal Kingdom), published in Amsterdam in two volumes (1740–1741), describing the development from *Principia* to *Oeconomia* as follows: "*Mest skiljer sig filosofien i Oeconomia från den i Principia genom att den mekanistiska uppfattningen under inflytande från Aristoteles, Plotinos, Leibniz och den moderna naturvetenskapen fått vika för en utprägladt organisk. Naturen är ett system af ändamål, som betinga hvarandra: den är en lefvande organism, hvars utveckling bäst förstås genom analogier med människokroppen*" (What distinguishes the philosophy of *The Economy of the Animal Kingdom* most clearly from the *Principia* is that, under the influence of Aristotle, Plotinus, Leibniz, and of modern science in general, the mechanistic concept gives way to a clearly organic one. Nature is a system of ends that mutually condition each other, a living organism whose development is best explained by the analogies offered by the human anatomy).[8]

Lamm attributes Swedenborg's change of opinion to the biological research he undertook when he attempted to solve the basic problem of the interaction of body and soul from the organic side. At the same time, Lamm discusses the importance of Swedenborg's dreams and visions during the religious crisis.[9] Precisely when Swedenborg became familiar with the discoveries and speculations of contemporary biology remains a question. As early as in connection with his 1719 article on anatomy and vibrations, Swedenborg writes in a letter to Benzelius that "*jag på thet nogaste giordt mig* Anatomiam nervorum *och* membranarum *bekant, och så wisat*

harmonien *theraf wid then wackra* tremulations Geometrien," referring to
the Italian anatomist Georgio Baglivi (1668–1707) (I made myself thoroughly acquainted with the anatomy of the nerves and membranes, and I
have proved the harmony which exists between that and the beautiful
geometry of tremulations).[10] As Alfred Acton has shown, Swedenborg's
wide reading of anatomical literature is noticeable also in *Principia* and *De
Infinito*.[11] Therefore, during the years between *Principia* and *Oeconomia*,
Swedenborg did not suddenly turn toward a new direction but rather returned to problems already dealt with. This may have also been Lamm's
opinion; but since he focused on Swedenborg's development, he may have
overestimated the novelty of the observations and ideas presented in
*Oeconomia*. It seems more appropriate to understand *Principia* as a prerequisite, before Swedenborg's early psychophysical studies could start
anew from a sufficiently stable basis.[12]

*Oeconomia* was also meant as a basis, however, a starting point from
which it would be possible to penetrate the secrets of the soul, although a
somewhat different one. In this work, Swedenborg studies the human
body, especially the function of the blood, but the published texts are only
smaller parts of a planned series of several volumes. Among other things,
the series would contain works on the physiology of the brain; and, after
they were translated into English by various American Swedenborgian societies, these studies evoked the admiration of modern experts. Swedenborg was tremendously productive in the decade before writing *The
Worship and Love of God*, but most of this extensive material did not become accessible until the twentieth century. Most of the credit must be
given to the Swedenborg Scientific Association (SSA), with Alfred Acton
taking the lead. The SSA even translated into English a collection of excerpts from the early 1740s, KVA Cod Sw 36–110, which has provided invaluable assistance to scholars interested in Swedenborg's possible sources
of inspiration.[13]

Swedenborg's remarkable productivity in these years makes attempts at
a short survey untenable, but I review the content in more detailed analyses
later in this work. Here, I merely touch upon Swedenborg's confusion and
the change of plans, which are characteristic of his activities in the years
preceding *The Worship and Love of God*. While these changes do not
mean that Swedenborg was losing sight of the goal—the disclosure of the
secrets of the human soul—they show that he often hesitated about how to
achieve it and how to present his results.

In the two volumes of *Oeconomia* that he published, there are several
references to later parts of the planned series: part III on the cortical and
medullary substances of the brain, part IV on the blood vessels and nerve
membranes of the cerebrum, part VII on the tongue and the lungs among
other organs, and unnumbered sections on nerves, muscles, and glands.[14]

It seems reasonable to assume that his fervently resumed studies of anatomy were already far advanced when Swedenborg completed the published parts of *Oeconomia* in the autumn of 1740.[15] However, before he presented this all-embracing anatomical foundation on the enigma of the soul, Swedenborg inserted two psychological chapters in the published volumes, "*Introductio ad Psychologiam Rationalem*" (An Introduction to Rational Psychology) and "*De Anima Humana*" (On the Human Soul). It is difficult to look upon this detour as anything but a change of the original plan and as an attempt to arrive at the final goal without further dalliance in the wide anatomical field. Acton has formulated an attractive hypothesis that Swedenborg's impatience could be partly explained by his note in the manuscript *Philosophia Corpuscularis in Compendio* (A Summary of the Corpuscular Philosophy), written in 1740: "*Haec vera sunt, quia signum habeo*" (these things are true because I have a sign).[16]

But the solution to the problem given in *Oeconomia* did not satisfy him. As becomes clear from a comment in *Regnum animale*, the great work that was to become his "*Summa antropologiae*" but that was published only in part, Swedenborg found that he had jumped to conclusions: "*sed re altius expensa, comperi, me justo festinantius & citatius eo contulisse gradum, scilicet ex indagato solo Sanguine & ejus propriis Organis; quod factum, quia ardor sciendi impulit*" (But on considering the matter more deeply, I found that I had directed my course thither both too hastily and too fast, after having explored the blood only and its peculiar organs: I took the step, impelled by an ardent desire for knowledge).[17] However, Swedenborg did not proceed directly from his planned *Oeconomia* series to *Regnum animale*, the three published volumes that appeared in The Hague and London in 1744–1745. Between these works, he outlined a number of smaller psychological tracts, probably because colossal projects such as the *Oeconomia* and *Regnum animale* threatened to overcome even his considerable abilities.[18]

This plan was not realized either, although some minor studies in fair copies were posthumously published. Instead of carrying out the new plan, Swedenborg started writing *Regnum animale*, in which he would apply the new methods of psychic research that he claimed to have found in the doctrine of series and degrees and the system of correspondences. But first he intended to lay the anatomical foundations with utmost care in a partly rewritten work on the brain.[19] Unfortunately, he once again lost his patience. In many places—for example in the epilogue of volume 2 or in the unfinished section on the senses—one notices that he is anxious to attack the core of the subject.[20] These continual changes are closely connected to his ongoing religious crisis, which can be followed in Swedenborg's dream diary.[21] When he felt his eyes opened to the light of truth in dreams and visions, it must have become both painful and meaningless to submit any longer to the severe restrictions of science.

In the autumn of 1744, Swedenborg once again abandoned his plans and started to write *The Worship and Love of God,* a work in a completely different vein from *Regnum animale.* A poetically structured synthesis, *The Worship and Love of God* does not refer extensively to scientific authorities and is less theoretical than his previous efforts. In contrast to both *Oeconomia* and *Regnum animale,* it uses the fundamental ideas of *Principia* and *De Infinito* to formulate psychological and theological theses. Despite this, it has connections to the *Regnum animale* series, as will be shown later. In *The Worship and Love of God,* Swedenborg once and for all yielded to his impatient ambition to represent his ideas in a literary form and to his ever-increasing need to synthesize. But once again, he was unable to realize his plans, since this work, too, remained unfinished. His theological system was not fully developed but still contained contradictory elements, particularly with respect to the role of Jesus Christ. Because of this problem, *The Worship and Love of God* has been given a secondary status in New Church literature. Despite this, its literary intensity reflects a restless intellectual profundity that Swedenborg had not achieved before and would never surpass.

With this background, we can briefly survey Swedenborg's productions in and after 1745. Following *The Worship and Love of God,* Swedenborg wrote an interpretation of Genesis, *Historia creationis a Mose tradita* (The History of the Creation Related by Moses) (1745), which he himself compares to his representation written two years earlier. Next, he devoted almost two years to other Old Testament studies, resulting in *Explicatio in Verbum Historicum Veteris Testamenti* (An Explanation of the Historical Word of the Old Testament) (1746), but neither of these works was published by Swedenborg.[22] He kept the focus on the interpretation of the Old Testament in the first work he published after his entrance into the world of spirits, *Arcana coelestia* (1749–1756), the title of which refers to his celestial experiences, as Sigstedt emphasized.[23] In the *Arcana's* eight massive volumes, Swedenborg applied the doctrine of correspondence for the first time as the leading hermeneutic principle, often in a way that seems far removed from the literal meaning of the texts to a secular reader. The same might be said of the other books, which followed this magnum opus: *De coelo* (Heaven and Hell), 1758; *De ultimo judicio* (The Last Judgment), 1758; *Sapientia angelica de divino amore et de divina sapientia* (Divine Love and Wisdom), 1763; *Apocalypsis revelata* (The Apocalypse Revealed), 1766; *Delitiae sapientiae de amore coniugiali* (The Pleasures of Wisdom Concerning Conjugial Love), 1768; *Vera christiana religio* (The True Christian Religion), 1771; and many more. His diligence as a writer, a trait he had inherited from his father, did not decrease with his illumination. On the contrary, his religious conviction strengthened it to an almost frightening extent.

Swedenborg's historical importance is primarily based on these later works, and no doubt great parts of them, especially the visionary scenes, would be well worth studying from a literary point of view. They will not be part of this study, however, since it would then grow out of all proportion. Anyone interested in Swedenborg's impact on world literature must, of course, concentrate on his later productions. These theosophical volumes have given rise to widely differing opinions, ranging from folly to wisdom and to numerous psychiatric diagnoses.

# The Contents of
## *The Worship and Love of God*

*The Worship and Love of God* opens with a preface. Here the author states that the thought of the changes of the seasons had made him sad when wandering in a grove, which had given him much delight during spring and summer.[24] Now autumn has come, and he has returned to the grove "*cogitationum turbas discutiendi gratia,*" to dispel the anxiety of his thoughts (§1). The setting is a rhetorical *locus communis* to be sure, but considering the anguish of the dream diary, it is probable that Swedenborg intended to represent his melancholy mood during an actual autumn walk in a London park. Although the rest of the preface, which early on strikes the keynote of the doctrine of correspondence, uses the conventional language of the *mundus senescens* topos (aging world), there is still a personal tone, evoking an individual atmosphere filled with the resigned melancholy of autumn and old age, as well as the restrained nostalgia of spring and youth. The elegiac atmosphere lingers like a haze over the sunlit landscape of the first morning of Creation.

After the preface follows the prologue of the drama, for *The Worship and Love of God* has been composed in scenes like a drama, and it proceeds in a series of pictures and sometimes almost ballet-like interludes. The prologue comprises the first section of the first chapter (§§1–2), describing the genesis of our solar system out of the *ovum mundanum*, the great egg of the world, after providing a quick briefing of its actual shape. In a few short passages, the first motions of the planets around the sun are depicted. The first and second sections (§§3–21) show the newborn earth and paradise, in which the *ver perpetuum*, the permanent spring of the ancient myth of the Golden Age, prevails. The third section of the first chapter, "The Home of Living Creatures in Paradise" (§§22–28) explains how the earth produces all species of living beings, because plants and trees have been equipped with the power of laying eggs, microcosmic correspondences of the *ovum mundanum*, out of which animals are hatched. This scene ends chapter or act 1.

The first section of the second chapter (§§29–38) describes the preparations of the entrance of humankind into the world. In the most temperate zone of the paradisiacal earth, there was a *Paradisus in Paradiso*, in which the tree of life brought forth an egg endowed by nature with its most precious qualities. This egg was fertilized by the Lord through initiating *"supercaelestem . . . formam, seu Animam, quae vita esset,"* a supercelestial form or anima—life—and this soul immediately starts building a microcosm in correspondence to macrocosm in it. All nature assists the soul; every creature is full of tenderness and trembling expectancy while the delivery is prepared and accomplished.

"The Infancy of Adam, the Firstborn"(§§39–56) stages the next scene of the drama, in which Adam receives his earliest lessons in celestial didactics, which recapitulates Swedenborg's theory of cognition. *Anima*, the soul, guides Adam's first steps; but after having trained a hierarchy of intellectual powers, the soul retires to its Olympia in the cerebellum, and from then on Adam is able to continue his education by discussing with his "intelligences."

Section 3 of act 2, "The Love of the Firstborn" (§§57–86) opens with a visit of celestial creatures, with whom Adam's intelligences have previously been talking. In this discussion, theological secrets are revealed to him about the position of man between the celestial sun and the natural sun, about the battle of good and evil, about the love of God and self-worship, *amor Dei* versus *amor sui*. In this section, the most extensive one of the book, Swedenborg imparts most of the psychological and theological wisdom of the work. This scene by and large completes Adam's spiritual education, closes act 2, and also ends part 1.

Part 2, "The Marriage of Adam, the Firstborn" (§§87–110), begins with a portrayal of the creation of Eve. In a dream, Adam, fired by lust, beholds a fair nymph, whom he tries to embrace. He feels as if one of his ribs is torn away, but he succeeds in capturing and kissing her before awakening, bitterly disappointed at only having embraced a branch. The tree, however, was a correspondence of the tree of life, of which Adam himself had been born; and by kissing the egg that the branch carries, Adam infuses his own spirit in it. Out of this egg, Eve is born, and the reader now follows her childhood and first education, although in a shorter version than those of Adam. Part 2 concludes when Eve meets Adam: *"dumque Sponsam manu prehensam obviam duceret, finita est haec Scena, quae, in Theatro Orbis, Sexta erat"* (and this scene, which is the sixth in the theater of the world, closes as his bride steps forth to meet him and he takes her by the hand) (§110).

Swedenborg published his drama of creation up to this point, the end of part 2. The unfinished third part of the work is entitled "The Marriage of the Firstborn Couple" and comprises §§111–131. It begins with a wedding night of incomparable serenity and solemnity. Early the next morning, the newly married couple behold a vision of the universe, which they attempt to interpret. But, in the middle of this scene, Swedenborg stopped writing;

thus, his work technically remains incomplete. Still, before abandoning his task, he had presented and fully developed the eponymous ideological foundation of the work. The finale of the vision—the birth of a celestial community in the shape of a universal man out of the greatest of world eggs—concludes the drama in an artistically effective extension of the basic symbolism.

However, the aesthetic perfection did not correspond to an intellectual completeness; on the contrary, Swedenborg himself indicated in a note (§53, note q) that he would discuss the Fall; and referring to *The History of Creation Related by Moses*, the Genesis commentary immediately succeeding *The Worship and Love of God*, Martin Lamm assumed that the original plan for the poetic drama had comprised not only the Fall but also the Redemption through Christ.[25] It is only natural to be reminded of John Milton (1608–1674), the poet who gave shape to both *Paradise Lost* and *Paradise Regained*, but that is hardly a matter of consequence. As we shall see, even a short review of literary works that deal with the six days of Creation soon demonstrates the difficulty of precisely identifying sources for any particular work.

In summary, Swedenborg's *The Worship and Love of God* not only depicts the origin of the universe and its earliest development but also sums up, in a partly obscured and convoluted manner, his outlook on life just before his access to the world of spirits, a synthesis built upon beautiful and expressive symbols. For precisely this reason, the fragmented character of the work has led to varying assessments, which deserve some attention.

# A DRAMA OF CREATION

# 1

## THE HEXAEMERON TRADITION

### The Place of *The Worship and Love of God* in Swedenborgian literature

*"Detta är af alla Swedenborgs verk det enda, hvari skönhets-elementet, såsom sådant, öfverväger; det är skrifvet, icke blott med en glänsande och klangfull latin, utan framförallt med en poetisk inspiration, som, på ett dussin skalder fördelad, vore tillräcklig att fästa dem på Diktens himmel såsom stjernor af första storleken"* (Of all Swedenborg's works, this is the one in which the aesthetic element dominates; it was written not only in splendid and sonorous Latin, but above all with a poetic inspiration, which distributed among a dozen poets would be enough to fix them in the heaven of poetry as stars of the first magnitude).[1] With these panegyric words written in the 1840s, the Romantic poet P.D.A. Atterbom (1790–1855) commented on Swedenborg's drama of creation. Atterbom was one of the first critics to stress the aesthetic value of *The Worship and Love of God*. A well-informed and sensitive reader, he noticed other qualities of the work: its position as a mediator between the two distinct periods in Swedenborg's life, its identity as both a Platonic and a Christian poem, its way of combining didactics and prophetic poetry. Atterbom's emphasis on "the aesthetic element" also shows his profound knowledge of Swedenborg's other works, in which beauty is more to be found in the magnificent visions than in the rationalistically dry expression of them. Atterbom's essay on Swedenborg contains *in nuce* Martin Lamm's view of the intimate connection between Swedenborg's two periods and also stresses the Platonic influences to which other scholars have paid much attention, sometimes maybe too much. Atterbom's great merits as a critic stand out clearly in this long essay, particularly when it is compared with other analyses.

*The Worship and Love of God* has never attracted much attention, neither in its own age nor in posterity. The work was reviewed in at least two learned journals in 1745.[2] One of them has a detailed and partly bantering summary, as well as a malicious tone that is established in the first sentence in discussing the author's eccentric way of thinking and is fulfilled by referring to a previous review of *Regnum animale*.[3] Obviously, the reviewer did not understand Swedenborg's intentions, for, at the end of his essay, he questions if the purpose of the book has been *"faire passer agréablement au Lecteur quelques momens de loisir"* (to let the reader agreeably spend some moments of pleasure) and refers to a somewhat older cosmogonical authority who asserted that the only true version of the story of creation is the one in Genesis.[4] The second review is quite short, but it reveals the writer's complete confusion. In his vacuous conclusion, only the observation of the dramatic structure of the work is of any value: *"Es scheinet aus allen, Herr Swedenborg habe eine Comödie schreiben wollen, wie er es denn wirklich in Szenen eingetheilet hat, und man könnte auch seine Schrift so zum Zeitvertreibe lesen, wenn nur die Schreibart Schauspielmässig wäre"* (it seems that Mr. Swedenborg has intended to write a comedy, as he has divided his text into scenes; and one might very well read his work as a pastime, if only its style had been suited for a play).[5]

The obscure fate that these reviews heralded for the work came to pass, partly because of Swedenborg's silence about it in his theosophic writings. His only detailed judgment is to be found in *Historia creationis*, a work posthumously published in 1847 but written in 1745, the same year as the publication of *The Worship and Love of God*, where Swedenborg wrote:

> *De Telluris ortu, Paradiso, Viridario, et Adami nativitate in Tractatu meo de Cultu et Amore Dei, Parte 1ma, actum est, sed secundum ducem Intellectum seu filum rationis; verum quia Intelligentiae Humanae, nisi a Deo inspiratae, nullatenus fidendum est, veritatis interest, illa, quae in memorato opusculo tradita sunt, cum Revelatis in sacro codice, et heic cum Historia creationis a Deo Mosi revelata, conferre, et sic quomodo coincidant, sub examen mittere; . . . Quum ea jam sedulo contulerim, miratus sum concordantiam*
>
> (The origin of the earth, paradise, the Garden of Eden, and the birth of Adam have been treated in my tract on the worship and love of God, part one, but there according to the guidance of reason or in the manner of reason; but since on no account human reason is worthy of confidence if not inspired by God, it is important that what is told in the above-mentioned tract should be compared with what is revealed in the Holy Scripture, and here with the history of creation that God revealed to Moses, and examined how they coincide. When I carefully compared them, I was surprised at the conformity).[6]

The attitude of the master is reflected in his earliest disciples. In spite of its deficiencies, Rudolf L. Tafel's vast collection of documents in three volumes—consisting of more than three hundred items on Swedenborg and his works together with extensive notes and commentaries—is an invaluable aid to scholars, and here are found testimonies of two early and loyal followers. The oldest of these originates from Gabriel Beyer (1720–1779), senior master of Greek at the upper secondary school in Gothenburg and one of the teachers of the poet Thomas Thorild (1759–1808). Already in 1765, together with his colleague Johan Rosén (1726–1773), younger brother of the famous Pietist Sven Rosén (1708–1750), Beyer had become disposed to New Church ideas from his meetings with Swedenborg and reading his religious writings. In a fairly long letter written in 1776, he informs his addressee that *The Worship and Love of God* does not have any theological significance, even if it contains many profound and beautiful ideas from a scientific point of view. He continues by asserting correctly that Swedenborg made quite different statements in his later writings about many of the issues treated in the drama of creation, but he also maintains that Swedenborg never referred to the work after its publication, an understandable mistake.[7]

A second document in the Tafel collection refers to Christian Johansén (1746–1813), a factory owner in the town of Eskilstuna, who claims to have interviewed Swedenborg himself about this work and its value. Swedenborg is said to have declared that it was founded on truth, but that some selfish concerns had slipped into it: he had used the Latin language playfully because people had previously poked fun at his simple Latin style, and for that reason he would not value it equally with his other works.[8] New Church scholars have questioned the validity of Johansén's testimony, while Lamm accepted it in comparing Swedenborg's poetic representation of Creation with that of *Paradise Lost* by John Milton.[9] The matter deserves some attention, since it may shed some light on the earliest history of Swedenborgianism in Sweden and its support in literary circles.

Rudolf L. Tafel (1831–1893) noticed Johansén's testimony in 1869 among papers belonging to the society "*Pro fide et caritate.*" They came from its secretary, Gustaf Johan Billberg (1772–1844), councillor of the Administrative Court of Appeal. The society had been formed in 1796 as a continuation of "*Exegetiska och Philantropiska Sällskapet*" (The Exegetic-Philanthropic Society), known from Kellgren's bitter attacks in the 1780s, but it was closed down after a short period. However, it resumed its activities in 1814 and became a kind of center for the Romantics' commitment to Swedenborg, which had quite a few influential members, including the writer Carl Jonas Love Almquist (1793–1866). As Henry Olsson and others have elaborated, the society's disparate tendencies and conflicting intentions reduced its influence.[10] But it acquired some importance because of its publications, and among its projects was also the first, although unsuccessful, attempt at publishing a Swedish translation of *The Worship and Love of God* by one of its most prominent members, Arvid August Afzelius (1785–1871).[11]

Billberg, a person of high esteem, had pursued a career as a civil servant and made a name for himself as a scientist, although a somewhat questionable one.[12] Through his first wife, he had come into contact with a direct link to Swedenborg: her father, Dean Arvid Ferelius (1725–1793), from the town of Skövde, had served as a clergyman in the Swedish parish in London from 1758 to 1772, and during this time, he often met the visionary.[13] Billberg's reference to Christian Johansén in Eskilstuna brings us back to the earliest days of the New Church in Sweden.[14] As Harry Lenhammar has shown, Johansén was one of Swedenborg's first disciples in Sweden; in a letter, Johansén dated his conversion to 1767. In January 1770, he noted in his diary that he had paid a visit to Swedenborg in Stockholm; and from the following year, there exists a manuscript in his hand containing a fragment of a translation of *The Worship and Love of God*.[15] With the exception of a remark by Sundelin that he was one of the most fervent believers in animal magnetism in the days of the Exegetic-Philanthropic Society, Christian Johansén appears to have been a sensible and judicious man.[16]

Thus, there seems to be no reason to question the authenticity of Johansén's statement, even if Swedenborg nowhere else expressed a literary opinion like this one. It also corresponds to what Swedenborg indisputably wrote about his work, as quoted above: the work had been written "*secundum ducem Intellectum seu filum rationis.*" Even if he was pleased that it accorded so well with the Mosaic version, the main point is his scepticism of the impulses of reason, "*nisi a Deo inspiratae.*" Of course, the "playful mood" of his style does not necessarily mean that Swedenborg wished to characterize his work as fiction in the modern sense of the word, but it may indicate that an element of sheer narrative joy had slipped in through the half-open gates of the doctrine of correspondences.

The relative silence around *The Worship and Love of God* among Swedenborg's disciples is reflected in the earliest biographies.[17] In his memorial speech to the Academy of Science in 1772, Councillor Samuel Sandels (1724–1784) mentions the work only as one of many, and the small biography written by Abbé Antoine Joseph Pernety (1716–1801) in 1782 does likewise, while *Assessor Swedenborgs levnet* (1806, in Danish) by Frederik Hermann von Walden (1743–1809) does not seem to know about it. More rewarding is a presentation inspired by Romantic radicalism, a short biography written by Lorenzo Hammarsköld (1785–1827), which was published in 1820 by W. F. Palmblad (1788–1852) in his Uppsala journal *Samtidens märkvärdigaste Personer* (Our Most Remarkable Contemporaries).[18] Here the work is presented as the first result of Swedenborg's theosophic studies: "*der han i tvenne delar framställer en slags spekulativ Poesi öfver vår Jords uppkomst, Adams födelse, första utveckling, förening med Qvinnan, och det, gemensamt med henne, genomlefda oskyldighetens tillstånd, utförd på ett sätt, som lätteligen hänför och förtjusar"* (in the two parts, he presents a kind of speculative poem of the origin of our earth, the birth of Adam, his adolescence, matrimony with Eve, and their life together in the state of innocence, which he had given a delightful and enchanting form).[19] The author emphasizes the poetic elements of the work but also its connections with Swedenborg's previous cosmogonic studies. Even if Hammarsköld subsumed this drama of creation in the long line of Swedenborg's theosophic works, he noticed its unique position, qualities that make this early biography superior to the contemporary sketches and the apologetic anthologies of Swedenborg texts.

The German philosopher and historian Joseph Görres (1776–1848) denotes another connection with the Romantic circle.[20] His Swedenborg study of 1827 moves a step forward on the road opened by Hammarsköld, as *The Worship and Love of God* is subsumed under the theosophical works without any reservations. Görres cites its doctrines when analyzing Swedenborg's mature religious views.[21]

A bibliographic survey reveals that the Romantics took a great interest in Swedenborg and showed a remarkable sensitivity to the elusive beauty of his visions. Yet, when proceeding through the history of Swedenborgian research, we should keep in mind Lamm's opinion: the bulk of publications does not correspond to their scholarly substance. It would be unfair to leave out of the account the enormous volume of Swedenborg research published by various New Church societies for two centuries. Keeping in mind that all studies marked by ideological or confessional loyalties must be read critically, such writing may often yield important information.

Regarding *The Worship and Love of God*, New Church literature has relatively little to offer, especially concerning sources, since the writers seldom move beyond Swedenborg's own production, as may be illustrated by a cursory survey. In some of the earliest presentations, by Nathaniel Hobart (d. 1840) in 1831 and J. J. G. Wilkinson (1812–1899) in 1849, *The Worship and Love of God* was placed among the scientific works, closely related to *Principia rerum naturalium*.[22] The same goes for the first biography by William White (1831?–1890), in which the drama of creation is mentioned only in passing, one reason being that it was supposed to have been written "as much for an exercise of fancy, as with any serious intent."[23]

However, this opinion changed completely when White some years later broke with the New Church and published a second voluminous biography.[24] Here, White devotes a whole chapter to a slightly ironical summary of Swedenborg's story of creation. He regards it still as one of the scientific works, even more so because he stresses its connections with *Principia*; but White had now become convinced that it should not be read as a piece of fiction. On the contrary, Swedenborg is said to have believed every word in it "as sincerely as he ever believed anything"; nor can White find it marked

by poetic inspiration or vivid imagination any longer, but only by dry speculations and constructs.[25] The two-volume biography written by White is a
pronounced example of a convert's way of writing history. Unfortunately,
its insensitive approach, particularly in the second volume, influenced
Swedenborg's reputation in Sweden, especially as presented by the historian Anders Fryxell (1795–1881), as observed by Holmquist, and on the
caricature drawn by Emil Kleen (1847–1923).[26]

The great collection of Swedenborg documents, published by Rudolf L.
Tafel from 1875 to 1877, made it possible to write much more comprehensive "lives and letters." Benjamin Worcester's (1824–1922) extensive biography of 1883 should be the result of a diligent study of the documents,
but this work has little to say about *The Worship and Love of God* other
than the conventional New Church opinion of the prose poem: "interesting
as marking the transition period."[27] There are, however, some signs of a
growing interest in *The Worship and Love of God* in New Church circles
at that time. In 1882, Frank Sewall (1837–1915) presented one of the most
penetrating analyses of the work thus far in a New Church periodical, an
article entitled "A Drama of Creation."[28] Sewall enthusiastically summarizes its content, drawing parallels to Dante Alighieri (1265–1321) and
Milton, Plato (c. 428–348 BCE) and Johann Wolfgang von Goethe
(1749–1832), although in very general terms and without any real discussion of the literary background of the book. Regarding its position in
Swedenborg's total production, Sewall puts a stronger emphasis than
White and Wilkinson on the connection with the theories of the origin of
the universe in *Principia*; consequently, he concludes: "In this, the drama of
Creation, which began with the First natural Point in the *Principia*, reaches
its majestic close."[29] In a later work, Sewall gave some indications of the
stylistic background of the work, astutely pointing out that the language
reveals "reminiscences of the author's early studies of the *Metamorphoses*
of Ovid."[30]

Until Stuart Shotwell's translation, the most modern and the best English translation of *The Worship and Love of God* resulted from a collaboration between Sewall and the prominent American Swedenborg scholar
Alfred H. Stroh (1878–1922), who lived in Sweden for some years and
whose meritorious investigations unfortunately came to a premature end.
In the beginning of the twentieth century, Stroh presented the most detailed
and interesting analysis of the drama of creation to date.[31] It compares *The
Worship and Love of God* with *Principia* and *Oeconomia regni animalis*
and pays a great deal of attention to the unfinished third part. It also contains a survey of bibliographical data. What is missing even here, however,
is a discussion of sources: Stroh's analysis keeps itself totally within the
boundaries of Swedenborg's own production, which is typical of New
Church methods, irrespective of well-intentioned but pointless references
to Dante, Shakespeare, Milton, Goethe, and other heroes among the topoi

of confessional panegyric. Still, in Stroh's case, this narrow point of view occurs less frequently than in others: his studies of Swedenborg's philosophy of nature are focused on possible sources to a large extent.

Beside Stroh, one must mention Alfred Acton (1867–1956), indefatigable translator, editor, and commentator of Swedenborg's writings, the scientific as well as the theosophic ones. Although Acton did not write a specific monograph about the drama of creation, he often refers to it in his many outlines of Swedenborg's canon. Acton has put more stress on what makes it different from the rest of Swedenborg's works: "Except that it contains the same physiological and philosophical principles, *The Worship and Love of God* is entirely different from all Swedenborg's other writings. He himself declares this, and notes that it is written from 'an entirely different love,' that is to say, as we understand these words, that it was inspired by the desire to lead men to the knowledge of God by philosophy poetically clothed in the language of theology, rather than by that same philosophy demonstrated analytically and confirmed experimentally for the benefit of those who will believe nothing but what they can prove."[32]

Otherwise, New Church contributions to the study of *The Worship and Love of God* have been of little value in later years.[33] The popular biography by Signe Toksvig (1891–1983), written in 1948, which is very informative in other respects, has little to say about *The Worship and Love of God* itself, but lets it serve as an illustration of a hypothetical biographical development.[34] Cyriel O. Sigstedt's (1888–1959) *The Swedenborg Epic* (1952) is a very ambitious work, the result of primary research as well as a summary of previous studies. It also presents some new material, but its evaluation of the drama of creation is the conventional one: "a half-scientific, half-poetic paraphrase of the story of creation," said to be the fulfilment of *Regnum animale*.[35]

As would be expected, a move from New Church Swedenborg literature to the secular arena implies a transition from a relative homogeneity to its opposite, even if some specimens of zealotry are also found here, although based on the contrasting creed that Swedenborg was insane. Such preaching is of little help when analyzing *The Worship and Love of God*; and as will become clear, the relative absence of discussion of literary concerns is striking even here.

The voluminous article on Swedenborg in *Biographiskt Lexicon* in 1849, partly founded on the first systematic collection of Swedenborg documents, the Tübingen professor Immanuel Tafel's (1796–1863) *Sammlung von Urkunden betreffend das Leben und den Charakter Emanuel Swedenborgs*, proves that its author possessed both knowledge and understanding. It places *The Worship and Love of God* between the scientific and the theosophic periods, as Atterbom had done before, and characterizes it as "a sublimation of S's scientific system."[36] It goes on to assert that the splendor of language and the power of imagination were weakened in the theosophic writings, which were dictated by spirits; thus, the drama of creation achieves the acme of poetry, reached when Swedenborg still stands "*på spången mellan natur- och andeverld*" (on the footbridge between the natural and the spiritual worlds), as the author eloquently expresses it.[37]

In his elaborate portrait of Swedenborg in *Representative Men* (1850), which has had such an important impact on the general reception of the seer in world literature, Ralph Waldo Emerson (1803–1882) does not mention *The Worship and Love of God*. Nor does the ambitious and substantial academy memorial by Bernhard von Beskow (1796–1868) contain anything of interest for this particular work: Atterbom's characterization is respectfully quoted and some indications of literary influences are given, although unfortunately in rather general terms.[38] In a book published in 1863, Jacques Matter (1791–1864) emphasizes the strong links between the drama of creation and the theosophical period, as Görres had done earlier; Matter contends that the work contains "*à la fois le germe et la substance de toute la doctrine qu'il développa plus tard*"(both the germ and the substance of the entire doctrine, which he was to develop later on).[39] Following Matter, Gilbert Ballet (1853–1916) expressed a similar opinion.[40] Of course, there is a kernel of truth in it, but it must be far more balanced than we find here.

Martin Lamm (1880–1950) devoted a chapter to *The Worship and Love of God* in his brilliant study published in 1915, by far the most exhaustive and substantial presentation of the drama of creation. It is also the first attempt at discussing the work in the context of literary history. Lamm points out how often Swedenborg used mythical modes of expression from the beginning of his career, and in the representation of the evolution of the universe, Lamm noticed "*en sällsynt graciös, rent antikt färgad fantasi*" (ingenious imagination and purely ancient coloration).[41] In an extensive summary, Lamm stresses the philosophical aspects, which is natural considering the general intention of his biography; and, along with Stroh and Sewall, among others, he emphasizes the connections with *Principia* and *Oeconomia*.

Moreover, Lamm draws attention to the fact that *The Worship and Love of God* is also a deliberate rewriting of the biblical story of the Creation and that "*trots prosaformen (man) har full rätt att betrakta verket som ett led i den skapelsediktning, som senrenässansen bragt på modet och som här i Sverige haft sin typiske representant i Haquin Spegel*" (it is clear that, although it is written in prose, we are justified in considering *The Worship and Love of God* as belonging to the series of poems about creation that became fashionable toward the end of the Renaissance, and of which Haquin Spegel was, in Sweden, the most characteristic representative).[42] In Lamm's view, Milton's *Paradise Lost* is the closest model. This is the first time that the hexaemeron genre is mentioned in Swedenborgian scholarship, no matter how obvious it would seem to be. For lack of space, Lamm did not present a broader account of this genre, nor did he discuss its aesthetic demarcations. Yet even a quick glance at the evolution of the genre might otherwise have adjusted the picture considerably, as will soon be illustrated.

After the publication of Lamm's book, Swedenborg was granted a room in the pantheon of Swedish literature. Although Atterbom's appreciation was a splendid exception to the rule, Swedenborg had previously been regarded only as a theosopher and a visionary, who had attracted special attention in Kellgren's battle *pro sensu communi* (for common sense) in the 1780s. In a broader historical context, Lamm returned to *The Worship and Love of God* in his masterpiece *Upplysningstidens romantik* (1918), in which he pointed out how the work remained isolated and little noticed in its own age:

> *För den svenska samtid, som betraktade Spegels barnsligt rimmade bilderbok Guds werck och hwila såsom höjdpunkten av religiös poesi och i Dalins Swenska Friheten såg alla rimliga krav på ett stort nationalepos förverkligade, kunde naturligtvis De Cultu et Amore Dei ha föga att säga. Först den tidsålder, som inledes med Menniskans Anlete, kan bli mäktig att fullt fatta den högstämda idealism Swedenborg givit uttryck åt i sin dikt och följa hans poetiska fantasi i dess flykt.*
>
> (To his Swedish contemporaries, who looked upon Spegel's naively rhymed picture book *Guds werck och hwila* as the apogee of religious poetry and who found all requirements for a great national epic fulfilled in Dalin's *Swenska Friheten*, *De cultu et amore Dei* had little to say. It was not until the age which was introduced by *"Menniskans Anlete"* [1793] that people were able to fully comprehend the sublime idealism represented in Swedenborg's work and to follow his poetical imagination in its flight).[43]

Hitherto Lamm's books have been the only major studies of Swedenborg available in the history of literature, and after them, only a few works of independent value have been published. The large Swedenborg biography by Emil Kleen (1847–1923) presents an almost grotesque contrast to the sensitive analysis in Lamm's book, published two years earlier. The contributions to the literature of the Creation by both Milton and Swedenborg are brushed aside as "poetic nonsense." Even so, some important pieces of information are provided in its two volumes, and they offer some entertainment.[44] The German church historian Ernst Benz devoted a rather extensive chapter to *The Worship and Love of God* in his voluminous, partly valuable study of Swedenborg. However, it consists chiefly of a summary, and for the rest the author closely agrees with Lamm, whose book had been published in a German translation in 1922. For his part, Benz puts a stronger emphasis on the elements of classical mythology, particularly the speculations of the Golden Age in the tradition from Hesiod (fl. c. 800 BCE).[45]

Three later Swedish works on Swedenborg should be noted. First is *Svensk litteraturhistoria* by E. N. Tigerstedt, in which *The Worship and Love of God* is said to connect the idyllic serenity of the eclogue with the sublimity of the Holy Scriptures.[46] Then, in *Ny illustrerad svensk litteraturhistoria*, Sten Lindroth offers a perceptive and balanced presentation of Swedenborg's remarkable production. Lindroth takes the Miltonic influence for granted, but he puts less stress on it than Lamm. Instead, he focuses on the classical tradition, especially on Ovid: "*Det är en ovidiansk metamorfos i flera tablåer, i sina alltjämt läsvärda partier en graciös övning i antik, mytisk anda, genomsusad av pastoral grönska*"(it is an Ovidian metamorphosis in several tableaux, in its still-readable parts a graceful exercise of ancient, mythical spirituality, rustling in pastoral verdure).[47]

Finally, in his detailed and perspicacious biography, *Swedenborgs hemlighet* (1999), Lars Bergquist discusses the position of *The Worship and Love of God* in Swedenborg's religious and moral development. According to Bergquist's interesting interpretation, the title of the unfinished work illustrates that Swedenborg had now come close to his main theme in the theosophical writings, namely, that true Christian faith cannot be separated from charitable deeds. Thus, the true worship of God is founded on an unselfish love of one's fellow human beings, which is a reflection of God's own love. Bergquist draws attention to a central aspect of the book that had been disregarded previously.[48]

As even this brief survey of critical analyses of *The Worship and Love of God* shows, literary concerns have seldom had a decisive influence on the research, in spite of the fact that most scholars agree on the poetic qualities of the work; rather, the biographical or psychiatric interest or the philosophical or theological inclinations have been stronger. Since Lamm's hypothesis that Swedenborg wrote his work under the influence of Milton's epic of paradise is the best and nearly only example of intertextual studies of a literary kind in Swedenborg scholarship, it may be appropriate to devote some space to the literature of the Creation before starting the analysis of *The Worship and Love of God* itself. Since some of the relevant works are not readily accessible, I will go into detail on some studies.

## The Hexaemeron Tradition

How is the term "literature of Creation" to be defined? Would it be appropriate to limit it to the term "paraphrase of Genesis," that is, to be restricted to literary works that are based on the story of Creation in the

Bible? Is the element "literature" to be used in a purely aesthetic sense, so that all other texts than those intended to be artistic should be excluded? Such questions soon arise in trying to arrive at an idea of the heterogeneous genre, which in turn is a prerequisite when studying individual texts. Some Milton scholars emphasize that it is important to remember that *Paradise Lost* is part of the hexaemeron tradition since, if you isolate specific possible sources, you risk misjudging their significance.[49]

*Paradise Lost* itself is easy to subsume under the tradition, even if we restrict the genre to cover what the name explicitly says: the term *hexaemeron* refers to the six days of Creation according to the Mosaic version. However, a number of texts that would fit into the tradition reasonably well were not directly inspired by the Bible, and most accounts of the Judeo-Christian ideas of Creation must be assessed in the light of pagan ones in classical antiquity. However, when it comes to Swedenborg's drama of creation, we need not observe such restrictions of content because it has been so strongly inspired by Genesis.

The aesthetic definitions are more complicated. In Lamm's remark quoted above, artistic qualities were emphasized, and his assessment is correct from a formal point of view, since it refers to the late Renaissance literature of Creation of the kind written by both Milton and Haquin Spegel (1645–1714), whether in verse or directly paraphrasing Genesis. Yet when ancient and medieval texts are included, it is impossible to establish strict aesthetic rules; it would be too difficult to decide where an exegetic commentary ends and a deliberate paraphrase starts. In hexaemeron research, one consequently finds more liberal definitions, such as the following:

> Hexaemeron is the title of certain *treatises and series of sermons* written by the Fathers of the Christian church commenting on the story of the creation of the world as told in Genesis, sometimes *a simple exegesis* and sometimes *an allegorical version* of the scriptural story. The use of the name may be extended to cover the whole body of literature dealing with the subject, *including formal or incidental accounts of the creation of the world,* based upon Genesis, and *poetical versions of the narrative.*[50]

Using this wide-ranging definition, Swedenborg's account of Creation must certainly be included among the contributions to this genre, even if Robbins himself argues that it ends with Milton. In my view, it is impossible to draw any stricter limits. After all, not only are we dealing with the fluidity between fiction and nonfiction, but, because of the nature of the topic, the commentaries are often as obscure as the source. In addition, when it comes to Swedenborg, the symbolic doctrine of correspondence gives a further specific cognitive dimension to poetry and myth: when he read texts belonging to the genre, his appraisals were certainly not dependent on any differences between poetry and prose or other formal criteria.

Space does not permit more than a short survey of hexaemeron texts, which presumably were known to Swedenborg. The first author is Hesiod:

> First of all Chaos came into existence, and then the broad-chested Earth, an unmoving seat forever for all the gods who hold the citadel of snowy Olympus, and murky Tartarus in a hollow in the wide-wayed Earth, and Eros, the most beautiful of all the immortal gods, looser of limbs, who overpowers the mind and the prudent counsel in the heart of all the gods and of all humankind.
>
> Out of Chaos were born both Erebos and black Night; and out of Night in turn were born Ether and Day, whom she conceived and bore by mingling in love with Erebos.
>
> And Earth first of all gave birth to the starry Sky, who was like herself, to cover her completely on all sides, to be an unmoving seat for the blessed gods for all time.[51]

This is the vision of creation in the *Theogony*, the earliest literary example of a poetic account of the birth of the cosmos in ancient tradition. In *Erga kai hemerai*, the first instance of another very frequent hexaemeron motive can also be found, that is, the ideas of a Golden Age, so often encountered in the shape of the pagan Elysium or the Christian paradise.[52]

Some of Hesiod's basic ideas have come back in a peculiar mixture of jocularity and seriousness in Aristophanes' comedy *The Birds*. A frequently quoted passage from this classic work is that in which the Orphic speculation about the great world-egg and the birth of Eros is parodied. This passage has been quoted often in cosmogonic literature from the Renaissance on, among others by Swedenborg in *Principia rerum naturalium*: the poetic qualities of the world-egg myth have also been exploited by later poets, in Swedish literature, for example, by Atterbom and Eric Johan Stagnelius (1793–1823). But no one has used its symbolic potential to such an extreme as the author of *The Worship and Love of God*, which will be shown in detail later. In addition, the history of the myth offers some opportunities to elucidate the literary and scientific milieu in which Swedenborg lived.

Plato appears to be the first among the philosophers of classical antiquity to have an impact on hexaemeron literature; Democritus (c. 460–c. 370 BCE) is somewhat older to be sure, but his thinking has been transmitted by Epicurus (341–270 BCE), and particularly by Lucretius (c. 100–c. 55 BCE).[53] From this point of view, *Timaeus* is the most influential dialogue, in which the philosopher describes the creation of the cosmos as an act of a deity. Of course, occasional reflections on the theme have been inserted in other dialogues, but the unique importance of *Timaeus* in the history of the genre is also explained by the fact that it remained virtually the only Platonic text accessible in Western Europe until the Renaissance. In *Timaeus*, the goodness of the demiurge, the god of creation, inspires him to his work, and he follows an ideal plan in his activities—that is, an idea superior to himself. But the story is often vague and mysterious, and it is an open question whether Plato wrote this work in proper philosophical earnest, strongly influenced by Pythagorean numeral mysticism as it is.[54] A second mythical motive in *Timaeus* of great importance in the hexaemeron tradition is the legend of Atlantis, which connects this work with the *Critias* dialogue.

With the goodness of the demiurg and his ideal plan for his act of creation, two of the most frequently used elements were introduced into the tradition, although the latter one led Christian thinkers into conflict with Genesis, which does not recognize a preexistent pattern followed by God when he created the world. In *Timaeus,* the ideal paradigm is an autonomous idea of Goodness, hardly possible to identify with the demiurg himself.[55] This is the beginning of problems for Christian exegetes. From a Jewish viewpoint, they became manifest even to Philo Judaeus (c. 13 BCE–c. 50 CE), and his solution—that God had also created the intelligible world with its paradigmatic ideas—served as a standard for Christian exegesis via Origen (c. 185–c. 254) and—with Neo-Platonic extensions—Augustine (354–430). Still, as Robbins asserts, "The Christians were always loath to say that the pattern is an independently existing idea."[56]

Even Swedenborg took an interest in this issue. Among the great number of excerpts in the manuscript cod. 36–110, the important passage from *Timaeus* can be found under the heading *"Deus."*[57] Swedenborg's way of quoting selections of it suggests that he is also following the tradition from Philo: read in isolation, his version gives the impression that God created the world as an image of himself, and later other Platonic texts are quoted that confirm this interpretation, for example, from *Leges*. He appears to have selected a motive out of *Timaeus*, the very source of much hexaemeron confusion, and given it a Christian interpretation. While the fact that he consulted *Timaeus* is important *per se*, it is even more so in that it provides *The Worship and Love of God* with a closer connection to the hexaemeron genre in a broad sense. Therefore, a word of caution is necessary if one argues for direct influence from *Paradise Lost*, since many conformities can be explained as common elements in the genre in general.

The problem of time is also discussed in *Timaeus*, and Plato concludes that time was created simultaneously with the world; in a similar way, Christian commentaries distinguish between time and eternity, stating that time did not exist before the Creation.[58] The good intentions of the demiurg can only be partly realized because of the inertia of matter; thus, his power has metaphysical limitations, which is also a recurrent idea in the tradition.[59] Even in minor details, *Timaeus* served as a well of wisdom to later writers. One reason that Plato was so highly respected by Christian commentators was an early rumor that he had been influenced by Hebrew literature during a stay in Egypt, an idea which even Swedenborg noted among his excerpts.[60] Some speculative Renaissance philosophers, particularly those inspired by the Cabbala, explained the similarities between Plato and the Bible as an effect of common wisdom that had been lost; this forgotten insight was often connected to Egypt and its mysterious hieroglyphs. In the fullness of time, Swedenborg came to identify this esoteric wisdom with his own doctrine of correspondence, and we will discuss its connections with contemporary interests in the hieroglyphs later in this work.[61]

It is impossible to determine the precise influence of Aristotle (384–322 BCE) on the evolution of the hexaemeron genre, nor can it be limited to any single work by him. This statement relates to both the genre in general and to Swedenborg, whose references to Aristotle are conspicuously frequent, quite often calling him only "the philosopher" as the Scholastics used to do. Some basic ideas obviously have their origin in Aristotle, as the theory of the elements, the division of the soul into different faculties, the doctrine of the substance; all of these are, of course, extremely important. One of the more curious elements belongs to the same Aristotelian heritage: his *Historia animalium* contributed to some of the anecdotes about animals, which appear in the so-called *Physiologus*, a moral compendium in natural history from the early Christian era with descriptions of the life of animals. These were used as a part of the *Hexaemeron* of Basil (c. 329–379) and later appear in *La Semaine* by Du Bartas (Guillaume de Salluste, 1544–1590).[62] In Swedish literature, the zoology of Aristotle is reflected in Spegel's *Guds Werk och Hwila*, for example, some ideas about spontaneous generation, among other things.[63]

The impact of the Stoics on hexaemeron literature can be focused on two aspects: they emphasized the division of the cosmos into active and passive principles, and they were the first to put the concept of *logos* in the center of an extremely complicated and significant philosophizing (although Heraclitus [c. 540–c. 480 BCE] and Plato had paved the way). In this context, the most interesting part of the almost insuperable problem of *logos* is *spermatikos logos*, a force of matter, a law of evolution, but also a birth dynamic that determines the evolution of matter by analogy with the growth of grains of corn. This theory was transferred via Philo to Neoplatonism, and from it to the Greek Fathers and Augustine, both in the more biological version and the theological one, most beautifully expressed in the prologue of the Gospel of John. For example, Augustine maintained that everything in the cosmos was present in God's primary act of creation, in the same way as the fully grown tree is present in the seed. Philosophically, this thesis probably had its origin in Neoplatonism, but terminologically and metaphorically, it is cognate with the Stoic concept of *logos*.[64]

Something quite similar can be observed in Swedenborg's rather eclectic thinking.

Epicurism, the philosophy opposed to Stoicism, also made a significant contribution to the evolution of the hexaemeron genre: *De rerum natura* by Lucretius being, after Hesiod's *Theogony*, the earliest example of what would be seen from a modern point of view as a more literary treatment of the Creation. Among many other things, this fascinating epic, emotionally intensively religious but theoretically atheistic, discusses, or rather preaches, the origin of cosmos; and in the first book, the reader is confronted with the controversial problem of creation out of nothing, *creatio ex nihilo*, to refer to the technical term used by theologians.[65] Of course, the debate on this issue has been extensive even up to modern times; Milton made an important contribution with his heterodox opinion that the Lord's creative act consisted of arranging a pre-existent matter. Swedenborg also participated in the discussion, presenting various ideas at different times, as is discussed below.

Book five of *De rerum natura* treats the creation of the world and provides a good deal of strange information. Here one meets the theory of the origin of life out of the earth that was first advanced by Democritus and then transmitted by Epicurus. In the orthodox Christian tradition, there are many examples of surly polemics against this automatic mechanics of the atoms, but Lucretius' poetic conception of the course of events has been of great importance. Lucretian influences have been observed in such an orthodox poet as Du Bartas in his *La Semaine* (indeed, a contemporary even honored him with the epithet "*le vray Empedocle et Lucrece francois*").[66] In seventeenth-century French libertinism, strong impulses from Lucretius have been discerned, in vulgar versions as well as in scientifically advanced ones, Pierre Gassendi (1592–1655), whom Swedenborg referred to in *Principia*, being the most famous.[67] Athanasius Kircher (1602–1680), Jan Baptista van Helmont (1579–1644), and other scientists who believed in various kinds of spontaneous generation, addressed Lucretius' ideas of the origin of animals.[68] The great influence exerted by the Roman atheist on eigtheenth-century France is best illustrated by a huge, didactic poem written in Latin, *Anti-Lucretius, sive de Deo et Natura libri novem* (Anti-Lucretius, or nine books about God and nature), published by Cardinal Polignac (1661–1741) in Paris. In this hexaemetric encyclopedia, Lucretius symbolizes all the delusions of the modern age, for which the cardinal holds the Roman atheist responsible. Given Lucretius' currency at this time, there are good reasons to explore potential impulses from Lucretius in Swedenborg's drama of creation, as I do later in this work.

Neoplatonism has already been mentioned several times, and it is clear that this line of thought, which is poetically both efficient and applicable, exerted a decisive influence on a succession of commentaries on Genesis. It was first introduced by Augustine and later represented most prominently by John Scotus Erigena (c. 810–c. 877), Bernard Silvestris (fl. around 1150), and John Milton.[69] Christian exegetes have found it difficult to bring the theory of divine emanations into conformity with what the Bible says, not least because the problem of the origin of evil greatly complicates the matter. As will be discussed later, Swedenborg experienced the same difficulty, and since Neoplatonism reached him from several directions, it will be easier to determine its importance when discussing details.

Ovid's famous poetical summary of the ancient ideas of Chaos appears in the first book of his *Metamorphoses*:

> Ante mare et terras et quod tegit omnia caelum
> unus erat toto naturae vultus in orbe,
> quem dixere chaos: rudis indigestaque moles,
> nec quicquam nisi pondus iners congestaque eodem
> non bene iunctarum discordia semina rerum.
> . . .
> utque erat et tellus illic et pontus et aër,
> sic erat instabilis tellus, innabilis unda,
> lucis egens aër: nulli sua forma manebat,
> obstabatque aliis aliud, quia corpore in uno
> frigida pugnabant calidis, umentia siccis,
> mollia cum duris, sine pondere, habentia pondus.

> (Before the ocean was, or earth, or heaven,
> Nature was all alike, a shapelessness,
> Chaos, so-called, all rude and lumpy matter—
> Nothing but bulk, inert, in whose confusion
> Discordant atoms warred: . . .
> But land on which no man could stand, and water
> No man could swim in, air no man could breathe,
> Air without light, substance forever changing,
> Forever at war: within a single body
> Heat fought with cold, wet fought with dry, the hard
> Fought with the soft, things having weight contended
> With weightless things.)[70]  (I:5–9, 15–20)

In this account, the Golden Age is clothed in its classical poetic form; for many readers through the centuries, the elegant Ovidian version was the principal source of knowledge about the speculations of the origin of the universe in antiquity. It has also been of an enormous importance in hexaemeral literature. As has been observed, Ovid included distinct elements in his chaos, in contrast to Plato who identified only traces of the forms of elements in the chaotic sludge; among many others, Du Bartas joined Ovid.[71] When the archangel Raphael describes how the world looked at its birth in *Paradise Lost*, book seven, he is presenting an Ovidian chaos with discernible elements in pre-existent matter; and in a similar manner, Spegel's account of the early morning of Creation must have been partly inspired by Ovid, to whom marginal glosses explicitly refer.[72] In this particular respect, Swedenborg is in a different position, but otherwise Ovid's influence on him seems hard to exaggerate: it can be followed from the Latin poems of his youth, to the commentaries on the concept of chaos in *Principia*, up to the dewy verdure of the newborn earth in the drama of creation.[73]

Besides these classical sources, there are also impulses from Jewish sources in Christian hexaemeron literature, first of all from Philo but also from others, for example, the historian Flavius Josephus (c. 37–c. 100). In Hebrew wisdom literature—for example, in the frequently quoted apocryphon of Jesus Syrach (fl. 190–180 BCE)—Wisdom is sometimes regarded by analogy with the Stoic *logos* as a creative force, but on other occasions only as a spectator when the Lord created his world.[74] A similar hypostatizing is part of various versions of later paraphrases of the story of Creation: book seven of *Paradise Lost* starts with an invocation of the muse Urania, of whom the poet has strange things to tell:

> Before the Hills appeerd, or Fountain flow'd,
> Thou with Eternal wisdom didst converse,
> Wisdom thy Sister, and with her didst play
> In presence of th'Almightie Father, pleas'd
> With thy Celestial Song.[75] (VII, 8–12)

This passage has been the source of heated discussions, some scholars maintaining that it was inspired by rabbinical literature. The idea is of interest also for Swedenborg, since quite a few scholars have argued for the existence of cabbalistic elements in his thinking. As in the case of Milton, such influences have probably been exaggerated; there is sometimes a terminological affinity, but it is hardly possible to trace it back to a specific text. Instead it can be explained as reflecting general knowledge about the rabbinical and Cabbala tradition, which to a certain extent is also part of European culture. In Milton scholarship, attributions to rabbinical literature are examples of how narrowly focused specialists may sometimes be. Regarding Swedenborg, my basic thesis is that he must be studied in the light of the seventeenth-century tradition, his own age, and classical antiquity; and no theories of esoteric sources should be advanced until this intellectual environment has been exhaustively studied.

No complete hexaemera have been preserved from the period between Philo and Basil, only certain fragments of Theophilus (d. 180) and Origen. Based on some references in later writers, however, Robbins concludes that the old church had been very interested in the theme and that, during this period, almost all the interpretative models were invented that were to be applied by the masters of the hexaemeron genre.[76]

There are five such types of exegesis. The first one focuses on the philosophical problem complex, and here Augustine is the great leader. The second type tries to explain the Creation from a physical point of view: Basil belongs to this group as the leading exegete, as well as Renaissance poets like Du Bartas, his Danish pupil Anders Christensen Arrebo (1587–1637), and Spegel who learned from both. In the third model, Genesis is interpreted allegorically as Philo had done; of course, Origen became the leading figure in this group. The poetical versions constitute the fourth group, usually in the shape of more or less original versified paraphrases of Genesis, while the fifth and final one includes accounts of the Creation that some chroniclers used as a kind of prologue: among those who exhibited such a passion for completeness Flavius Josephus may be mentioned in antiquity. In the Renaissance, *The History of the World* (1614) by Sir Walter Raleigh (1554–1618) is typical; his work has been mentioned as one of the sources of *Paradise Lost*.[77]

In Sweden, the Latin chronicle published by Laurentius Paulinus Gothus (1565–1646) in 1636, *Historiae arctoae libri tres*, illustrates this custom; incidentally, the author also made use of the Ovidian description of Chaos in the first book of the *Metamorphoses*.[78] In Swedenborg's age, scientific works in physics and cosmology in which the writers intended to make the biblical version converge with later discoveries and theories should be added to this list. Swedenborg was well read in this particular kind of scientific writing, and he contributed to it with several works in natural history. It may serve as an example of a problem that notoriously engaged European science in the first centuries of the modern age.

In his study of hexaemera from the Renaissance, Thibaut de Maisières has drawn attention to the fact that Basil, as the leading figure of the Cappadocian Fathers, exerted a significant influence on Du Bartas, Torquato Tasso (1544–1595), and Alonso de Acevedo (b. 1550), and through them also on others.[79] Of course, Basil included elements from preceding thinkers and exegetes, Plato, Aristotle, Philo, Origen, and the Stoics. Even if his *Hexaemeron* is mainly an encyclopedia of natural history, as becomes evident from his frequent and paradigmatic references to *Physiologus*, it also deals with philosophical problems that have become part of the tradition. To give one example, he interpreted the commands of the Lord in the act of Creation, as they are rendered in the Bible, to mean the insertion of *logoi* in matter, which will determine its development.[80] He also proposed that, when the spirit of God is said to hang over the primeval waters in Gen. 1:2, it should be understood by analogy with a bird's sitting on eggs, an idea that comes back in later commentaries in an interesting combination with the ancient myth of the great world egg.[81]

Among Basil's followers in the Greek hexaemeron tradition, the Church Fathers Gregory of Nazianzus (c-330–c. 389) and Gregory of Nyssa (c. 335–c. 394) should be mentioned, as well as the Byzantine deacon and poet Georgios Pisides (seventh century). As Thibaut de Maisières has observed, Pisides' influence on Du Bartas was noticed already by an editor in the seventeenth century:

> *Pisidias en vers grecs, des premiers eut l'honneur*
> *De choisir ce sujet et d'en estre sonneur.*

(In Greek verse Pisides was the first to have the honor
Of choosing this theme and ringing its bell.)[82]

In Latin Christendom, Basil's interpretation was introduced by the Church Father Ambrose (339–397), but the great authority of the Latin hexaemeron tradition is Augustine. He expressed his views on Creation primarily in *De Genesi ad Litteram*, but he returned to the theme constantly in his large production, for example, in his best-known works, *Confessiones* and *De civitate Dei*. What is new in his interpretation of Genesis is its metaphysical character: as Robbins has pointed out, Augustine's intimate knowledge of Plato and Neoplatonism has been decisive, but his long sojourn in the Manichaean world of ideas should also be taken into consideration.[83]

In the history of philosophy, the most fruitful parts of Augustine's ideas of the Creation concern the problem of time: outside the created universe, time does not exist. Similarly, a human being's concept of time exists only as a subjective experience of the present moment, in which memory and expectant imagination supply ideas of the past and the future. With respect to the story of Creation, Augustine rejects the naive interpretation that the world was created in six ordinary days, claiming instead that the Creation was an instant act, *in principio*, in the wisdom of God. What happened was that God inserted forms (*rationes*) in the universe, which later gave rise to all natural things. This agrees with Basil and through him with the seminal *logoi* of the Stoics.[84] The six different days of Creation in the Bible are pedagogically justified, according to Augustine, and more than a thousand years later, his opinion echoes in the greatest of hexaemera:

> Immediate are the Acts of God, more swift
> Then time or motion, but to human ears
> Cannot without process of speech be told,
> So told as earthly notion can receave. (*Paradise Lost* VII,
>    176–179)

Swedenborg shared this view, but in *The Worship and Love of God*, he kept the pattern of the six days of Creation as scenes of the great theater of the world, that is, a different arrangement but one warranted pedagogically as well.

In late antiquity and the early Middle Ages, Latin paraphrases were common, although their importance for the evolution of the genre does not correspond to the quantity. An interesting example of this kind of poetry is offered by the large biblical epic from about 500, written by the Burgundian bishop Alcimus Ecdicius Avitus (d. 518).[85] The voluminous work consists of five parts, the first of which deals with the Creation and earliest age of the world and humanity, while the remaining four describe the Fall, the expulsion from Paradise, the Flood, and the escape of the Jews from Egypt. Like so many other ancient hexaemera, this epic was published in a Renaissance edition, first printed in Paris in 1508.[86] As will be shown later, it played a certain part in Swedenborg's cosmogonic thinking in *Principia* and thus indirectly in *The Worship and Love of God.*

The medieval contributions to the genre may be mentioned rather briefly in this context. Among the eclectic hexaemera from this period, *De divisione naturae* by Erigena, which has a considerable value philosophically as well as theologically, occupies a unique position thanks to its relative originality.[87] In the rather uniform pattern, there appears to be a tendency to disengage from the abstract metaphysical exegesis of Augustine along with an increased interest in physical details, which sometimes results in a bizarre degree of concretion.[88]

The renewal of ancient philosophy, particularly Plato and Neoplatonism, in the twelfth century brought forth some new features in the tradition: now the element theories became rampant, the interaction of elements and the collision between active and passive principles, mainly inspired by Aristotelian and Stoic physics. The Platonic Chartres school headed by Bernard Silvestris left the most distinct tracks of this Platonic renascence.[89] Bernard's most important work is *De universitate mundi* (around 1150), which is introduced by an account of the amorphous chaos and Natura's complaints, presented by Nous, a female emanation from the deity. After that, the reader learns about Natura's creation of her world and how she is assisted by Nous, Urania, Genius, and other apocryphal angels and embodiments of Platonic ideas, when the human race is born. The reflection of macrocosm in microcosm is presented in detail, and the work concludes with a song of praise to the genitals, which prevent the return of Chaos by continuing the work of Natura *ad infinitum.* There is an obvious connection to the *Roman de la rose* here. Ernst Robert Curtius, whom I have followed above, has found Bernard's strange combination of cosmogonic speculation and eulogies of sexuality alien to both Platonism and Christianity; but Bernard learned it from the tract *Asclepius*, ascribed to Apuleius (c. 124–after 170?), who was regarded as Platonic at the time.[90]

Some influences of this twelfth-century renascence can also be registered in the contribution to the genre of the Nordic Middle Ages, the huge didactic poem *Hexaemeron* by the Danish archbishop Andreas Sunesen (1167?–1228). It is a dogmatic manual in verse, which summarizes the famous manual *Liber sententiarum* by Peter Lombard (c. 1095–1160) in about 8,000 hexameters; it was not published until 1892.[91] Of course,

Swedenborg is unlikely to have studied any of the medieval hexaemera, but some of their writing may have reached him indirectly. One example is particularly illustrative. In the collection of excerpts, cod. 36–110, he often consulted a text by Augustine called *De Spiritu et Anima*, a false attribution, which Swedenborg also noted.[92] Gilson called it a vulgarized version of Augustine, and in his *Patrologia* edition Migne quoted Erasmus (1466?–1536) in the commentary, who had proved that the text comes close to being simply a compiled commonplace book. Besides Augustine, Boethius (c. 480–524), Cassiodorus (c. 490–c. 585), Isidore of Seville (c. 560–636), Bede (672?–735), Alquin (735?–804), Hugo of St. Victor (1096–1141), and Bernard have contributed to it—in other words, the whole series of famous medieval theologians.[93] One of the most important was Hugo of St. Victor, and the renowned bibliographer Johannes Trithemius (Johannes Heidenberg, 1462–1516) has included the work among Hugo's writings.[94] Be that as it may, the list reveals that, by reading *De Spiritu et Anima*, Swedenborg had been exposed to medieval ideas to a considerable extent. Moreover, the work had been quite significant to his predecessors in the Cartesian tradition.[95]

During the late Renaissance, with its flaring religious zeal, Christian antiquity generally replaced its pagan counterpart as a source of inspiration in literary and cultural contexts. Thus, many works from the first Christian centuries were revived, including the most distinguished representatives of the hexaemeron genre: Basil, who had been totally forgotten in the Middle Ages, was published in a Greek edition in 1532, to which Erasmus wrote a bombastic preface saluting the Church Father as an equal of the Attic classics, as a Christian Demosthenes. In 1560, the collected hexaemera of Dracontius (fifth century), Hilarius (c.315–c.367), Marius Victorinus (fourth century), Avitus, and Cyprian (d. 258) were edited in one volume. Altogether, the editing of old texts was a flourishing business during the whole century, especially in France.[96]

The renewed interest in the hexaemeron genre explains the rise and rapidly growing popularity of newly written poems of Creation, although we should also keep in mind the general endeavors of the French Protestants to create a distinctive literature in which the religiously least-controversial elements of the medieval tradition as well as of the neoclassicism of the Pleiad were to be included and developed.[97] Du Bartas' *La Semaine*, the earliest modern hexaemeron, scored a remarkable success: *La première Semaine* was published in 1578 and, within thirty years, 230 new editions and translations were issued. Imitations, pieces of plagiarism, and original but distinctly Du Bartas-inspired epics were legion: Tasso in Italy, Joost van den Vondel (1587–1679) in the Netherlands, Acevedo in Spain, and Arrebo in Denmark, to mention just a few. As regards Milton, the greatest of hexaemeron poets, there has been a lively discussion for a long time about his relations to Du Bartas. The problem is much more complicated in Milton's case because he was so well read, a fact that makes it probable he was familiar with Du Bartas' epic, poetically so much inferior to *Paradise Lost* that it would be absurd to speak of any plagiarism.[98]

The wide distribution and great popularity of the hexaemeron genre in the period before Milton are easily illustrated by a quick glance at the history of drama. Among medieval hexaemera, some mystery plays enjoy a certain reputation, for example, *Mistère du Viel Testament* from the end of the fifteenth century. In spite of their rather primitive naivety, they may have been a source of inspiration for hexaemeron writers in the Renaissance.[99] It is also interesting to note that the creation theme is represented by quite a few *autos sacramentales*, for example, by Pedro Calderón de la Barca (1600–1681), as has been pointed out by Fredén:

> In his autos Calderon treats with obvious predilection the biblical tale of the creation. He adorns the simple scenes from Genesis with a Baroque abundance of stage properties, light and sound effects, and with a rich torrent of melodious verse. But he is not content with Genesis. Ancient philosophers and Medieval scholastics, St. Paul, David, and Job, apostolic fathers and evangelists—nothing is too remote or too near at hand, everywhere he is able to find fragments of the picture he wants to call forth with the help of allegory.[100]

In Calderón's hexaemeron world of ideas, which Fredén has studied from an Orphic point of view, the reader or viewer encounters a typical constellation of widely different motives. For instance, the concept of wisdom appears in a way reminiscent of the wisdom literature, and the earth has a part in the creation of the human race, recalling the ancient speculations on the Golden Age. Fredén has suggested Hesiod as a model, but we might as well mention more easily accessible representatives of the genre, Lucretius, Statius (c. 45–96), Ovid, or others. On the whole, it is difficult to uncover any genetic connections in Calderón's eclectic thinking without penetrating analyses that are not within the scope of this book, considering the wide ramifications of the hexaemeron background.[101] However, Fredén has given a valuable contribution by focusing on dramatic hexaemera beside the epic ones, especially with regard to Swedenborg who used a dramatic model in his contribution.

As has been stated previously, it has long been characteristic of Milton scholarship to look for a single source for *Paradise Lost*.[102] However, because the results have been doubtful and contradictory, more recent and cautious methods have been applied in attempts to elucidate the intellectual environment in which Milton's epic took shape. Consequently, the task is to establish the best-known sources at the time with which Milton would have been familiar and to find out to what extent these may offer satisfactory explanations.

A typical study has been investigating the numerous Genesis commentaries written at the end of the sixteenth and beginning of the seventeenth centuries as a kind of theological encyclopedia.[103] The glosses in the margins of Bible editions of the Renaissance represent the primitive origin of this genre, which became independent after the Reformation; both Martin Luther (1483–1546) and John Calvin (1509–1564) contributed to it, and Luther's Genesis commentary was a main source of Arrebo's *Hexaemeron*.[104] But after these early works, very little of any importance was published until 1590, and it has been suggested that Du Bartas' epic and its many successors may have inspired the theological commentaries.[105] At that time, the voluminous *Libri commentariorum et disputationum in Genesin* by Benito Pereira (1535–1610) was published (1589–1598), in which there is a great number of references to Church Fathers and scholastics but few to Rabbins; instead, many of those appear in another huge commentary from the same time, *In Genesin Commentarius* by Jean Mercier (c.1500–1570).[106]

These works served both as compendia and as bibliographies, and it is well known that they were consulted by several hexaemeron writers at the beginning of the seventeenth century. Among these, Hugo Grotius (1583–1645) occupies a unique position, as has been observed by Williams, since he wrote both a Genesis commentary, *Annotationes in Vetus Testamentum*, and a poetic paraphrase, *Adamus Exul*.[107] In this respect, he corresponds to Swedenborg, and this may not be a coincidence. With his famous work on the truth of Christianity, which Swedenborg kept in his library, Grotius appears among authors to whom Swedenborg most frequently refers, particularly in *Oeconomia regni animalis*.[108] Consequently, Grotius holds a prominent position in the hexaemeron tradition, primarily as a lexicographer of seemingly boundless erudition.

It is evident that these commentaries have been widely used by hexaemeron writers. When references in Sir Walter Raleigh's *History of the World*, previously mentioned, seem to demonstrate a stunning learning, scholars showed that, in many cases, Raleigh merely translated the Latin text of Pereira without saying so. It remains an open question whether even Milton made use of such sources. Whiting attempts to establish that such potential stimuli were close at hand, with the result that many elements in Milton's thinking, which had earlier been attributed to the most esoteric sources, can be traced back to works familiar in his time.[109] Of course, this does not reduce Milton's literary renown, only that his supposed erudition gets more reasonable proportions.

Because Lamm hypothesized the influence of *Paradise Lost* on Swedenborg's drama of creation, Milton has received considerable attention in Swedenborgian literature, but that does not imply that *Paradise Lost* is the last work in the hexaemeron genre. Some examples of contributions written after the 1660s have already been mentioned above, and in the area of fiction, they could be multiplied up to the Romantic movement. It may be sufficient to follow Fredén in recalling Herder's *Älteste Urkunde des Menschengeschlechts* (The oldest documents of humanity) and the young Goethe's essays in cosmogony and theogony.[110] In addition, the extensive cosmological literature from the Renaissance and up to Swedenborg's own age, half scientific, half occult, should be taken into consideration, some of which will be studied in detail later.

This short introduction to the literary history of Creation had two purposes: to give an idea of the scope and character of this particular genre and the methodical and objective difficulties of its study, and to sketch the background of Swedenborg's contribution to the genre, *The Worship and Love of God*. It seems reasonable to suppose that Swedenborg was rather familiar with this branch of literature; indeed, in some cases, this has been explicitly proved. On the other hand, the very size of the genre makes it a difficult proposition to tie his drama of creation to one single source, as has been done with *Paradise Lost*.

It is always extremely difficult to prove that an author did not read a specific text, citing internal reasons, when its theme as well as other elements correspond so well as they undeniably do in this case. But a study of Swedenborg's intellectual environment should be able to establish the primary sources, at least to the same extent as in Milton's case. Before this line of inquiry has been exhausted, it seems methodologically doubtful to bring forth more distant ones, and in my opinion Milton's *Paradise Lost* should be seen as one of those. Swedenborg's scientific background is a plausible point of departure: to study the ideas of creation in *The Worship and Love of God* means primarily to analyze the literary and intellectual environment of Swedenborg the scientist in order to establish the original contribution made by Swedenborg the poet to the theme. This can only be carried out by reviewing individual motives in the various scenes on the great theater of the world.

# 2

*ى*

## OVERTURE AND ORIGIN
## OF THE EARTH

(§§1–15)

### Sources from Antiquity

The first fifteen paragraphs in *The Worship and Love of God* form an overture, introducing the following six scenes of the world drama. In the shape of a prologue, the overture is conducted partly by creating the atmosphere and sounding the deepest themes of the opus and partly by describing how the great world theater is being built. Since, for Swedenborg, the most essential element was that of the first humans and their upbringing in a state of innocence, all the scenes of the drama are acted out on earth. However, his yearning for synthesis demands that the whole course of world events in some way be given form; thus, the overture also serves as a medium for an account of the birth of the solar system, including earth.

The narrative begins with a description of our celestial body's present revolution around the sun, followed in a similar fashion by an account of the moon, the planets, and the fixed stars. Only after all this does Swedenborg turn his attention to the birthing process. With this presentation, he follows a tradition, the basic meaning of which is revealed by its prominent position at the very beginning of the work: it is the wisdom of the elders, particularly in the belief in a Golden Age at the beginning of time, through which they understood how the development of the whole universe is reflected in the life course of single objects. Swedenborg, thus, announces his allegiance to this ancient view. Once he has sketched earth's revolution in space and that of the wandering stars, the parental role of the sun becomes obvious, and this means that earthly destinies must evolve from the sun:

*Contemplemur & ipsi faciem Universi in Speculis ejus Singular-*
*ium, & ex iis Temporum & Aetatum Fata evolvamus* (§2)[1]
(Let us, too, meditate on the image of the universe as we see
it mirrored in its particulars, and from those particulars let us
unravel the destiny of the ages.)

This basic thought, which is varied within different spheres, is usually
expressed along with an ancient worldview, and this atmosphere, reminiscent of antiquity, is present throughout the entire work. But it is as characteristic that one can sense the affinity with the biblical foundation in the
cosmological introduction. For example, the reflection of the eternal order
in single objects in nature calls to mind the letter to the Romans on how
God's appearance in creation is obvious and clear to every human being:
"For what can be known about God is plain to them, because God has
shown it to them. Ever since the creation of the world his eternal power
and divine nature, invisible though they are, have been understood and
seen through the things he has made. So they are without excuse" (Rom.
1:19, 20).[2] Contrary to both previous and subsequent works, practically
no sources are presented in *The Worship and Love of God*: Swedenborg
obeys the admonition received in a vision and recorded in his dream diary
not to borrow anything from others, even when it comes to biblical quotations, with one or two exceptions.[3]

In describing the origin of the earth, Swedenborg conjures up a vision of
a time when the sun bore all the universe's celestial bodies in its womb. To
illustrate how the nativity may have passed, he uses a comparison with the
great world egg of ancient myth, whose shell broke at the moment of birth.
This, in turn, is identified with chaos. This egg symbol is one of the most
forcefully uniting elements of *The Worship and Love of God*. Introduced
in this macrocosmic context, it returns in the origins of plants, animals,
and humans and reaches a grand fulfilment in the concluding vision, when
the heavenly society is brought forward from the last of the world eggs. To
comprehend the basic meaning of the symbol, an investigation of its genesis is required; and in order to be understood correctly, it also necessitates
insights into Swedenborg's doctrine of correspondence. However, as has
been emphasized in my introduction, it should be interpreted with care and
not taken as some sort of astrophysical hypothesis: Swedenborg states that
he wishes to make a *comparison* with *Maximum Universi Ovum*, the great
world egg, an important term to keep in mind henceforth. In this drama of
creation, we move about in a shadowy world of corresponding images,
which cannot be confronted with everyday reality; already in the preface,
Swedenborg's desire for wholeness works in a system of symbolic conformities that can be translated into the detail of experience only with a great
degree of care, although he himself, in somewhat prosaic notes, made several attempts at explaining the relationship between symbol and reality.

In turn, it is often difficult to determine how intellectually necessary a certain part of the text was for Swedenborg and to what extent narrative elation took over. Perhaps Swedenborg would not have been able to answer this question himself. An illuminating example can be found in the preface. The birth of the planets from the smouldering solar material is sketched in anthropomorphic expressions: they lay like feeding masses of material by the burning bosom of their origin, the sun vomits balls of fire from its swollen mouth, the etheric matter is wound around the celestial bodies like swaddling clothes, and soon the heavenly bodies are playing like children, leaping in dances around the sun (§10). The wandering stars are called brothers, and their moons are described as servants and maids (§11). The unification of ether and air is depicted as a wedding (§14). This whole atmosphere of birth and childhood naturally has a corresponding meaning and offers a hidden knowledge of the solar system's origin from the sun, but it is taken further than theoretically necessary, as if Swedenborg, with evident pleasure, is dwelling on ancient celestial dances and games, which foreshadow the childhood games of competition that the firstborn man will introduce among his intelligences. In this instance, Swedenborg's understanding of totality appears at the basic level of composition; he introduces the original image in the context of the heavens as a reflection of what is subsequently to occur on Earth, in a shape directly alluding to human experience. The unity is conditioned by art and motivated by theory, in a solid and unbreakable association. Even so, aesthetic pleasure played some part, and similar decorative digressions are found in later sections.

Swedenborg's artistic consciousness is also revealed in the composition of the preface, in its inner context. The last sentence—with its depiction of the egg-bearing earth in constant movement away from the sun, its center and origin—connects to the opening sentence of the section:

> *Circum circa Solem, hujus Universi Centrum, Terrestris noster Globus, sicut Orbita, quotannis volvitur. . . .*
>
> (Around the sun, the center of this universe, our earthly globe spins its gyre year by year). (§3)

The conclusion completes the connection:

> *& secundum progressionem in suâ orbitâ a centro recedente, novas continenter involvebat potentias, ex quibus successive explicarentur usus*
>
> (As it went onwards in its receding orbit from the center, it continually produced new powers as necessary consequences, whose uses would be unfolded each in its turn.) (§15)

As well as correlating to the purely astronomical circulation of the opening scene, this sentence summarizes—in a foreboding allusion to the circulation of hidden powers—the context drafted in the preface. We are in the presence of a stylistically sensitive and skilled writer.

The final paragraph of the prologue describes abundant fertility. The virgin earth is strewn with little eggs or seeds, containing its entire future progress, divided into the three groups of mineral, plant, and animal kingdoms; these in turn are incorporated into each other, with the animal kingdom at the inner core. Thus, all is prepared for the continuing birthing process described in the following episodes, and the first sentence of the first scene connects in form and content to the finale of the prelude.

In a manner similar to the way the prologue aesthetically sketches the background ambience in which the drama is being played out, it also introduces essential themes, which will be linked in discernible patterns later on. Two of these require a more thorough discussion at this point: the doctrine of correspondence and the world-egg motif. A brief summary of Swedenborg's philosophy of nature will facilitate greater understanding.

## The Doctrine of Correspondence

As early as the nostalgically beautiful introduction to his drama of creation, Swedenborg uses a theory characteristic of his belief system, usually referred to as the doctrine of correspondence. According to this doctrine, there is nothing in this existence that does not represent the whole development of the universe. This is the conviction articulated in the prelude, and the thesis leads to the exhortation quoted above, to view the face of the universe through the reflection of details (§2). This keynote resounds throughout the whole drama—from the cosmological preface with its corresponding combinations of the times of the year and the day (§3, note a); of the movements of the sun and the moon (§4); of the great world egg with the original seeds of the three earthly kingdoms (§15), to the world egg of the final vision, which fosters human creation and out of which the holy community will arise (§112). The doctrine of correspondence transmits the sense of intimacy between the macrocosm and the microcosm that the author wishes to convey. To a great extent, this is the reason that *The Worship and Love of God* can be regarded as a piece of literary art, a symbolic drama, where the interpretation of images has not yet achieved the dogmatic firmness that makes Swedenborg's biblical studies such lacklustre reading in the eyes of an outside observer. There are attempts at direct translation of the meaning of symbols later on in the drama—for example, in the discussion on the earthly and heavenly paradises (§55, note s) and of the two suns (§64, note g)—but these occur in the mainly didactic, less poetic parts. Swedenborg generally allows symbols to speak for themselves, without creating a discourse that drastically inhibits the aesthetic effect.

Swedenborg never considered the artistic result of the doctrine of correspondence as a primary goal. His teaching was a theoretical instrument, an intellectual aid to facilitate the understanding of ultimate questions, and he attributed tremendous importance to this aspect. It was crucial to all of Swedenborg's religious writings and gave his spiritual crisis and its visions a unique character.

Swedenborg illustrated the meaning of the "correspondence" concept most clearly in the short, incomplete work *Clavis hieroglyphica* (The Hieroglyphic Key), which consists of twenty-one examples. Each example compares sentences from the natural, spiritual, and divine areas, with the central concept from the earthly sphere being related to its corresponding meaning in the spiritual and the divine spheres. This is done in the same manner as in the above-mentioned notes from *The Worship and Love of God*, in one case with the phrasing quoted directly. This treatment connects the drama of creation to the short hieroglyphic key, which was never published by Swedenborg himself, a fact that makes it difficult to date.[4] The possibility thus exists that words can be translated into different levels of meanings—natural, spiritual, and divine—just as an insightful person can see each natural object as a representation of something spiritual and, in its turn, as a part of divinity. One does not need to underline the spectrum of possibilities this reveals, viewing reality as a design of symbols, an ascending series with the divine as the apex. Nor does one need to emphasize the perspectives this would open for the scientist. But how are we to explain the origins of this singular idea?

Martin Lamm, who stresses the Platonic aspects of Swedenborg's philosophy, answers this question with the basic condition in mind: "*Man behöfver ej nämna mer om korrespondensläran för att varsna dess nyplatonska anor. Hos Plotinos är ju det sinnliga tinget en skuggbild af en osinnlig form och denna i sin tur en återspegling af urbilden, idéen*" (There is no need to dwell further on the doctrine of correspondences to discover its Neoplatonic origins. With Plotinus, things perceived by the senses are the reflection of a form imperceptible to the senses, and this is itself the reflection of the archetype, the idea).[5] Lamm deducts the Neoplatonic influence from the so-called *Theology of Aristotle*, which is quoted directly in *The Hieroglyphic Key* and, moreover, often in the manuscript collection cod. 36–110. Furthermore, Lamm traces an influence from Cabbalistic and Renaissance philosophy, noting, however, the important difference that Swedenborg saw the doctrine of correspondence only as an instrument for knowledge, not as a tool of magical power.[6] Lamm obtained his evidence also from the later theosophical writings, up to its finale in *Vera christiana religio* (True Christian Religion).

While there is no denying the importance of Neoplatonism for Swedenborg, it seems rash to attribute all the glory of his complicated system to one source. An overview of the development of the doctrine of correspondence in Swedenborg's writings gives rise to important adjustments to that thesis. At the same time, it shows how Swedenborg's doctrines, seemingly so influenced by mysticism, are intimately connected with problems posed by his contemporaries.

In the context of his psychological and philosophical studies, most noticeably traced in *De infinito* and *De mechanismo operationis animae et corporis* (1734), there is a manuscript with comments about certain paragraphs from Wolff's *Psychologia empirica*.[7] In the midst of irreproachably rational material, a door suddenly opens to fantasy and mysticism, as Wolff, in the fashion of an ancient and widespread tradition, uses hieroglyphical terms when defining an imaginary concept:

> *Si phantasma quoddam ita componitur, ut per similitudinem partium constitutivarum cum determinationibus rei cuidam intrinsecis, hae ex istis colligi possint, phantasma significatum hieroglyphicum habet, ac vi principii rationis sufficientis componitur. . . . Veteres dogmata et historica per figuras hieroglyphicas repraesentarant; quod Aegyptiis familiare; de Sinensibus alii. Comenius exhibet animam Hieroglyphice.*
>
> (If an imaginary concept is thus composed—namely, that through the likeness between its important elements and the inner determinants of a certain object, these can be concluded on by the elements—the imaginary concept has a hieroglyphical meaning and is composed by virtue of the principle of sufficient reason. . . .
>
> The ancients presented dogmas and myths through hieroglyphs; this is well known among the Egyptians; others say likewise of the Chinese. Comenius presents the soul hieroglyphically.)[8]

The reference to the Egyptians is self-evident in the context, but the reference to Comenius (Jan Ámos Komenský, 1592–1670) and his well-known *Orbis Sensualium Pictus* is of greater interest. The pedagogical need to illustrate all things in images drove Comenius to sketch the soul as a collection of dots, which together formed a human shape. This shape was then interpreted "hieroglyphically": the dots, which by definition lack geometrical extension, symbolized the indivisibility of the soul, and the human shape symbolized its substance quality and unity with the body (in the manner of the Scholastics; the soul is at the same time in the whole body as well as in its every part).[9] This reference to Comenius hints at the most important artistic result of the great interest in hieroglyph interpretation, displayed in the Renaissance and the following centuries: emblematics. I shall return shortly to the importance of emblematics in regard to Swedenborg's doctrine of correspondence and *The Worship and Love of God*.

Wolff continues among the paragraphs marked by Swedenborg. There are different degrees of perfection among the imaginary concepts, where the highest degree allows a complete correspondence between the elements of the imaginary concepts and the elements of the signified object. This is a perfect hieroglyph; and if one such represents the concepts that are part of an object's definition, it can replace it.[10] It is also possible to supply knowledge with the help of hieroglyphic figures, says Wolff, if it is done in the manner of the Egyptians. This is illustrated by the Egyptian method of concealing the truth from unworthy eyes, through the alchemists' mnemonically valuable technique of writing in hieroglyphs, and by a hieroglyphical interpretation of the Hebrew alphabet. Wolff refers to an exegesis he did in another context according to the rule that what is said of God in a human fashion must be understood from that which belongs to his essence.[11]

As early as 1734, Swedenborg thus showed his interest for the possibilities of the hieroglyphical way of writing: he wrote down instructions for how images can be used to supply knowledge that does not allow itself to be explained in plain writing, and he even learned the exegetic potential of this method. Thus, several important elements of the doctrine of correspondence have already been produced, and his guide has not been some obscure Neoplatonic source but the rationalist Christian Wolff, so highly esteemed by his contemporaries and by Swedenborg himself. It is true that Swedenborg does not accept Wolff's system of windowless monads, but the affinity with the representative force of the soul can be strongly felt in his doctrine of correspondence, as it is presented in the preface to the current work. An example from the excerpts is illuminating in this regard: *"vis universi repraesentativa animae non modo ad repraesentandum universum quoad statum praesentem, verum etiam ad idem repraesentandum quoad status praeteritos tendit"* (The soul's ability to imagine the universe not only extends to imagining the universe in its current state but also to imagining the same in its past).[12]

This is one of many examples indicating that Swedenborg must be studied in the context of contemporary and seventeenth-century intellectual environments, along with ancient myth and poetry, which was obligatory for any learned person. In my opinion, many critical analyses of Swedenborg exaggerate his knowledge of Renaissance philosophy, a criticism that can be levelled also against Lamm's monograph. Swedenborg indirectly obtained knowledge about many authors from older periods, most of it probably from relatively contemporary sources. Nothing else seems plausible given his extensive ambition.

Swedenborg read Wolff in 1734, but this experience did not leave any immediate traces on a developed doctrine of correspondence. Over the next few years, Swedenborg studied anatomy and physiology, which he applied with great fervor to his fundamental object of research, the soul. In this context, Wolff appears anew, this time, among other instances, with a characteristic project that was crucially important to Swedenborg's extremely high esteem for his own doctrine of correspondence. The main

problem was how to formulate knowledge that cannot be expressed in ordinary language: it is the old dream of a universal language of philosophy,
the vision of Raimundus Lullus (Ramon Llull; c. 1235–1316), of Giordano
Bruno (1548–1600), of Georg Stiernhielm (1598–1672), and of so many
others, of the perfect philosophical system of concepts, which Swedenborg
encountered in the mathematic sobriety of rationalism, in Wolff's *Ontologia*.[13] Swedenborg quotes some of Wolff's theorems in *Oeconomia regni
animalis*, for example, in part 1, §651: "*In desideratis est Disciplina, in
qua Principia cognitionis rerum finitarum generalia traduntur; . . . atque
sic demum obtineremus vera Philosophiae & Psychologiae Principia mathematica, Philosophis ad ulteriora & promiscue omnibus ad praxin accu-
ratam profutura*" (Among the wishes is one branch of science in which the
general principles for knowledge of finite things were to be expressed; . . .
and only then would we obtain the true mathematical principles of philosophy and psychology, to the benefit of philosophers in their aim to reach
further and common to all, to scrupulous thinking).[14]

Swedenborg enthusiastically embraced this presumptuous dream of rationalism in his *Oeconomia*, where he too interpreted it as a sort of philosophical calculus, even though he primarily focused on its psychological
utility. In a manner typical of his eclectic working method, he quotes (besides Wolff) John Locke, the leading proponent of the opposing school of
philosophy, who in *Essay on Human Understanding*, deemed by Swedenborg to be a golden treatise, also discussed the science of sciences. In his
notes, Swedenborg quotes Locke from a French translation:

> *Peut être, que si l'on consideroit distinctement, & avec tout le
> soin possible cette derniere espece de science, qui roule sur les
> Idees & les mots, elle produiroit une Logique, & une Critique
> differentes de celles, qui on a vues jusqu'a present. L:IV.C:XXI.
> Et alibi, Les idees, sur qui roule la morale, étant toutes des
> essences reelles, d'une telle nature, qu'elles ont entre elles, si je
> ne me trompe, une connexion, & un convenance, qu'on peut
> decouvrir. Il s'ensuit de la, qu'aussi avant que nous pouvons
> trouver les rapports de ces idees, nous serons jusque la en pos-
> session d'autant des verites certaines, reelles & generales; & je
> suis sure, qu'en suivant une bonne methode on pourroit porter
> une grande partie a un tel degre d'evidence & de certitude,
> qu'un homme attentif & judicieux n'y pourroit trouver plus de
> sujet de douter, que dans les propositions de Mathematiques,
> qui lui ont été demontrees.L IV.C:X*

> (And perhaps if they [ideas and words] were distinctly
> weighed, and duly considered, they would afford us another
> sort of logic and critic than what we have been hitherto ac-
> quainted with. Book IV, chapter XXI. And in another place: For

the ideas that ethics are conversant about, being all real essences, and such as I imagine have a discoverable connexion and agreement one with another; so far as we can find their habitudes and relations, so far we shall be possessed of certain, real, and general truths; and I doubt not but, if a right method were taken, a great part of morality might be made out with that clearness, that could leave, to a considering man, no more reason to doubt, than he could have to doubt of the truth of propositions in mathematics that have been demonstrated to him. Book IV, chapter XII:8).[15]

In order to reach this obscure aspiration, one must, in Swedenborg's view, develop the doctrine of series and degrees, which was implicit already in the cosmology of his 1734 work *Principia* and which in *Oeconomia* laid the foundation for the study of physiology.

The theory of the interior coherence of the universe in a continuous series without leaps returns when Swedenborg again shows his interest in the "science of sciences": this is done in a note on the hierarchy of the academic disciplines, which has been collected from the Swedish philosopher Andreas Rydelius' (1671–1738) *Nödiga Förnufts-Öfningar* (Useful Intellectual Exercises) in the excerpt collection cod. 36–110.[16] Rydelius' definition is broad and imprecise; he seems to have imagined a sort of combination of history of ideas and theory of science.[17] But in Swedenborg's list, the message is clear: "*Scientia Scientiarum. Mathesis universalium. Doctrina ordinis, serierum et graduum*" (The science of sciences. The mathematics of universal concepts. The doctrine of order, series, and degrees).[18]

When Swedenborg made this notation, he had in all probability already undertaken his sole documented attempt at creating a philosophical artificial language, which could realize this titanic dream. On some manuscript papers with the headline "*Philosophia universalium Characteristica et Mathematica,*" Swedenborg attempted to express his physiological findings in a sort of algebraic formulas: "S" means the blood in its purest form, that is, the spiritual fluid; "SS," a lower degree of blood, the so-called *sanguis medius*; "SSS," the red blood, etc.[19] He attempted to replace higher correspondences of an object with letters and symbols in order to be able to describe them at all. In fact, Swedenborg posed a complicated series of symbols to this end; but he never got passed the initial stage, and the attempt concluded in a number of rules for the investigation of objects, which are entirely connected to the doctrine of series and degrees.

Swedenborg did not easily abandon the hope of solving the riddle of universal science. In the psychological treatise *De anima*, probably written in 1742, he returns to the question in the last chapter, in the form of a commentary on quotations from John Locke, of which, incidentally, the first two had already been used in *Oeconomia*.[20] The last one is very significant for Swedenborg's development:

> *Le plus haut degré de notre connoissance est l'intuition sans raisonnement . . . car connoissance certaine, à l'abri de toute doute, qui n'a besoin d'aucune preuve, et ne peut en recevoir aucune, parceque c'est le plus haut point de toute certitude humaine . . . tel que celui que les anges ont présentement, et que les esprits des hommes justes parvenus à la perfection auront dans l'état à venir, sur mille choses, qui à présent (échappent) tout-à-fait à notre entendement, et desquelles notre raison, dont la vue est si bornée, ayant découvert quelques foibles rayons, tout le reste demeure enseveli dans les ténèbres à notre égard; L.IV.C.XVII.*
>
> (Our highest degree of knowledge is intuitive, without reasoning . . . which is certain, beyond all doubt, and needs no probation, nor can have any; this being the highest of all human certainty . . . such as angels have now, and the spirits of just men made perfect shall have, in a future state, of thousands of things which now either wholly escape our apprehensions, or which our short-sighted reason having got some faint glimpse of, we, in the dark, grope after. Book IV, chapter XVII:14.) [21]

Locke's famous but—in a strictly empirical context—rather strange doctrine of intuition is thus brought in to support Swedenborg's view on the science of sciences. But universal science cannot be learned, a realization to which Swedenborg has resigned himself. Rather, it is congenital with pure intelligences and is known by angels and souls liberated from their corporal form, such who are not bound by words—these material forms and signs whose meaning we know only through the process of learning. If we were not inconvenienced by the worries of superficial learning, of sensual life and such things, we would also be able to experience truths in this *a priori* manner, simply because higher forms contain all that the lower forms can hold.[22]

Despite the fact that it cannot be learned, universal science appears to be subject to calculation, and this must be done through observing what happens in the inner organs of sense and intellect, as all our thoughts are equal to changes of status in different parts of the brain. These changes can be understood if we describe their forms.[23] Thus, Swedenborg still imagines something akin to his theory, sketched earlier, and it is likely that this is what he refers to when he claims to have found the possibility to execute the operation: *"compertus quidem sum possibilitatem"* (I am indeed certain of the possibility).[24] But the extraordinary difficulties have induced him to give up the attempt, not however without offering a replacement of the highest interest: *"loco ejus proponere volui quondam clavem arcano-*

*rum naturalium et spiritualium per viam correspondentiarum et repraesen-
tationum, quae compendiosius et certius nos in veritates absconditas ducit,
quae doctrina, quia hactenus orbi non innotuit, aliquantum diutius ei
immorari debeo"* (in its place I have aimed to produce a sort of key to natural and spiritual secrets with the aid of correspondences and representations, which lead us to hidden truths faster and more reliably; since this
doctrine so far has been unknown to the world, it beholds me to dwell on
it somewhat longer).[25] This is almost the exact subtitle used to explain the
doctrine of correspondences in *Clavis hieroglyphica*, whether or not he had
already completed it or commenced work on it after having written *De
anima*.[26]

Thus, the intimate connection between Swedenborg's doctrine of correspondence and the elusive dream of a universal science of the age cannot be
questioned, nor can its relationship to speculations regarding hieroglyphs
and emblems. Still, references to these two sources cannot fully explain its
specific character; other important elements have to be added. The cerebral-physiological base, which Swedenborg claims to use for his calculus
and which he partly used in sketching his theory, underlines the psychophysical background of the doctrine of correspondence. A study thereof
can be undertaken among other things with the help of the excerpts kept in
cod. 36–110, which deal mainly with the problems of the soul.

While the psychology of *The Worship and Love of God* will be studied
more thoroughly later in this work, I will put forward here only that
Swedenborg bases his argument on three answers to the classical problem
of the interaction between body and soul: the theory of influx, occasionalism, and pre-established harmony. He attempts to surpass them all and
reach a definitive answer, as the excerpts show. During his studies of relevant literature, he encountered terms such as *analogy, harmony, representation*, and *correspondence*, and he wrote a number of notes under a
heading signifying these terms.[27]

One of the earliest is taken from an opus by the didactic Professor G. B.
Bilfinger (1693–1750) of Tübingen, which illustrates Swedenborg's characteristic method of working. Bilfinger had compiled different theories on the
interaction problem, based on Leibniz's pre-established harmony, and so
wished to prove its validity.[28] Bilfinger's work is systematic and lucidly
written, providing a number of examples and quotations; it came to be a
rich source of knowledge for Swedenborg, as he aimed to acquire a quick
but thorough overview of the problem. Under the heading "Correspondence," Bilfinger provides, early on, a supposed quotation from Leibniz:
*"Si l'union de l'ame avec le corps ne consiste, que dans une simple con-
comitance des pensées & des mouvemens, c'est correspondance plûtot,
qu'Union"* (If the union of the soul with the body consists only of a simultaneous occurrence of thoughts and movements, then it is a correspondence rather than a union).[29]

Despite Bilfinger's quotation, Leibniz's view is a different one, indeed. But under the same heading, we also meet another authority, who embraces this very view on correspondence. He is Nicholas de Malebranche (1638–1715), a thinker who will appear several times later in Swedenborg's works, especially in its theological sections. Swedenborg quotes frequently from Malebranche's *Recherche de la vérité*, a book that Swedenborg possessed in his library (in Latin translation). Malebranche sparked important intellectual impulses for Swedenborg, particularly in several crucial cases. For example, Malebranche explains the connection between soul and body in the following manner:

> *Unio mentis cum corpore, quantùm quidem illam cognoscere possumus, consistit in mutua & naturali analogia & ut ita dicam, correspondentia cogitationum mentis cum vestigiis cerebri, & affectuum mentis cum motibus spirituum . . . si per relationes rerum materialium possis explicare relationes rerum spiritualium, eas certè (relationes) clarissimas dabis eásque ita menti imprimes, ut non modò fidem certissimam obtineant, verùm etiam facillimè retineantur.*
>
> (The soul's unity with the body, so far as we may know it, consists of a mutual and natural analogy, and if I may call it so, a correspondence between the soul's thoughts and the tracks of the brain and between its feelings and the movements of the vital spirits. . . . If one could explain the relations between spiritual things through the relations between material things, one would be able to define them in the clearest manner and imprint them in the soul, so that they would not simply gain the firmest belief but also be more easily preserved).[30]

These theses were preceded by extensive descriptions of the relationship between, for instance, the power of imagination and the cerebro-physiological foundation. Certainly, Malebranche maintains a simpler Cartesian hypothesis on vital spirits, which renders his view biologically more primitive than Swedenborg's, but in basics the two are very close. The research program, which Malebranche sketched in the excerpt above, proves to be something Swedenborg actually attempted to carry out, as we shall see later.

Even more important is the intimate connection between Malebranche's psychophysical speculations of correspondence and his idea of God. The most important issue for Malebranche is the relationship between man and God, scientific theories being only elements within the key to this puzzle. One finds this most clearly in his answer to the question concerning the interaction between body and soul, "*la vision en Dieu.*" God was the only one existing previous to the creation of the world, which could never have taken place had God not imagined it. Thus, God's vision of the world cannot be separated from himself, and all created things, including the material, exist within God.[31] This view is then connected to Descartes' anthropological verification of God. Our soul senses the infinite, even if we do not understand its meaning, and we have a distinct idea of God, which cannot stem from anything else but our union with God: how else could our idea of an infinite and perfect being appear in the imperfect world of the finite? This idea of the infinite exists in our soul, before we have acquired knowledge of the finite, and we experience nothing else except in this idea of the infinite.

Malebranche does not deny our normal experience of a world of finite and apparently separate objects, but he sees the experience of God as an epistemological necessity:

> *Nihil quicquam itaque amamus, nisi per amorem necessarium quo erga Deum movemur, nihil videmus nisi per cognitionem naturalem quam de Deo habemus; atque omnes ideae speciales quas de creaturis habemus, nihil aliud sunt quám limitationes ideae Creatoris, ut omnes motus voluntatis erga creaturas nihil sunt praeter determinationes motûs versùs Creatorem.*
>
> (Therefore, we do not love anything except through the necessary love, through which we are taken toward God, nor do we see anything except through the natural knowledge we have of God; and all the single imaginings we have of creatures are nothing but restrictions to the idea of the Creator, as all movements of will toward creatures are nothing but limitations of the movement toward God.)[32]

This view of a world filled with God leads to an experience of reality in which all particular objects point above themselves towards the universal and to a vision that, better than many other candidates to the title, deserves the name symbolism. Indeed, this term has been used by scholars writing about Malebranche, which further highlights the fundamental similarities between Swedenborg and him.[33] Not only was humanity created in an image of God, but literally everything stems from a divine origin. A consequence of this is that objects carry two meanings, one if observed on their own and another if observed as emblems. These different kinds of meaning are interpreted by different disciplines, namely, science and faith:

> *Malebranche a reçu le grand livre du monde dans l'édition de M. Descartes; il s'est réjoui d'y lire des formules mathématiques à la place de vains discours; il n'a pas songé un instant que ces heureuses nouveautés pussent altérer le sens religieux que tous les philosophes chrétiens ont reconnu dans la nature; il n'a donc pas fermé l'autre grand livre qui est toujours ouvert devant ses yeux.*

(Malebranche received the great book of nature in the edition of M. Descartes. He was delighted at reading mathematical formulas in it instead of vain talk, but he did not for a moment imagine that these fortunate novelties could change the religious meaning that all Christian philosophers had recognized in nature. Thus, he did not close the other great book, which was always open to his eyes.)[34]

Of course, this is not new in the history of Christian thought. The symbolic discourse on the testimonies of nature and Scripture is as ancient as Christianity, existing in its core as early as in the passage from the letter to the Romans, quoted above. But with regard to Swedenborg, the crucial aspect is that Malebranche does not display the Scholastics' rigid doctrine of conformity, nor their fantastic *faiblesse* for examples, but a basic understanding of the idea that all of existence is an *imago Dei* to different degrees and that we experience everything in God and God in everything. This experience offers an answer to the psychological question Swedenborg himself pondered so often. Malebranche's symbolism bears the hallmark of Cartesian sobriety and not that of some sensual warmth or delight in detail, clearly different from Swedenborg, which can be partly explained by the points of origin. Malebranche's faith in God is primary, and his philosophy is inspired by theology, while Swedenborg begins in natural philosophy and from there approaches his prophetic mission. Add to this analysis a psychological divergence, insofar as Swedenborg in the midst of his accomplished systematics felt a need for concrete and lucid examples, which in practice reveals a sensual temperament. This tendency is reflected most strongly in *The Worship and Love of God* and—in painful nakedness—in his dream diary. In a profound sense, the future prophet's spiritual visions stem from the same need.

Even this difference in temperament cannot conceal Malebranche's great importance to the doctrine of correspondence. All the impulses we have encountered have a psychological connection: the hieroglyphical notes from Wolff's *Psychologia empirica*, the speculations on a universal language—especially those based on quotations from Locke, which are applied psychophysically—the excerpts from Malebranche under headings that deal with the communication between body and soul. This psychological genesis is also reflected in the constantly recurring tripartition of the doctrine of correspondence, undoubtedly connected to the spiritual triad of *animus* (sensual consciousness), *mens* (intellect), and *anima* (soul). Natural things belong to *animus*, spiritual to *mens*, and divine to the immortal *anima*.

Thus, one should explain the origin of Swedenborg's doctrine of correspondence chiefly on the basis of this psychological background and not, as Lamm does, in the light of a more conjectural philosophy of nature. Lamm sees the so-called *Theology of Aristotle* as an important source, for instance, because it is mentioned briefly in *Clavis hieroglyphica*. But this work, from which Swedenborg often excerpted passages in cod. 36–110, does not appear once under the most relevant headings where the terms of correspondence are found. Of course, Swedenborg was aware of Neoplatonism; Malebranche is, as an Augustinian disciple, strongly influenced by Platonic ideas, as Lamm, among others, has noted.[35] I believe the pseudo-Aristotelian *De divina sapientia secundum Aegyptios*, which Swedenborg used sparingly before 1740, is significant in this context as an ancient confirmation of ideas he already knew. That he mentions this work and not Malebranche fits in with his predilection for finding ancient corroborations, even if he picked them out of a contemporary source.[36]

In the manuscript cod. 36–110, the first part concludes with excerpts about different theories on the problem of interaction, where the previously quoted extracts from Malebranche can be found, and the following pages contain numerous notes on correspondence.[37] All of these comprise biblical texts, grouped in different categories: "*correspondentia harmonica, parabolica, typica, fabulosa et somniorum; representatio oraculorum; correspondentia actionum humanarum et divinarum.*" Lamm observed that Swedenborg here follows contemporary Bible exegetics, of which Samuel Glassius (1593–1656) was the greatest proponent.[38] The information seems reasonable; in any case, this categorization cannot be traced back to Malebranche or any of the other factors discussed previously. Moreover, it is unnecessary to establish the exact source—a fact also clear to Lamm—since the categories play only a minor part in the drama of creation.

The group *correspondentia fabulosa* is most significant in this regard. In *Clavis hieroglyphica*, it is described thus:" *Quarta est* fabulosa, *apud antiquos in usu, qui res gestas suorum Heroum fabulosis figmentis involverunt, tales sunt repraesentationes Poetarum; et tales sunt* Somniorum" (The fourth is *fabulosa*, which was used by the ancients who covered their heroes' feats with glory in fantastic fables; such are the poets' representations, and such are those of the dreams).[39] The notes under the same heading in the collection of excerpts include numerous biblical examples of this kind of correspondence. In connection with the drama of creation, the interpretation of Genesis is the most interesting. The texts that are noted are 2:21–23, the creation of woman from the man's rib; 3:1, the snake interpreted as the devil or as sensuous desire; 3:15, the antagonism between woman and the snake after the Lord's words; and 3:24, the cherub guard at the closed gate of Paradise and the flashing sword, after some hesitation, interpreted as heat. Thereafter follow some less interesting texts. These excerpts are commented on as follows:

> *Haec per repraesentationes, quales antiquis in more fuere, qui res gestas et facta simulachris adumbraverunt; satis est, quod Deus revelaverit illa quae corpori et animae necessaria sunt,*

*historiam vero similibus signis involvere placuit, quae tamen
veritates rerum continent.*

(These things are expressed by such representations used by
the ancients, which only indicated remote acts and deeds in
parables. It is enough that God has revealed such things as are
necessary for body and soul; it has pleased Him to cover the
history under similar signs, which nonetheless contain the
truths about things.)[40]

Equating the central parts of the biblical Creation with the fables of ancient poetry allows plenty of space for poetic imagination, and Swedenborg
took advantage of this freedom so much in *The Worship and Love of God*
that he belongs to those hexaemeral poets who are furthest removed from
the model. Without actually entering the extremely rich theological literature on this subject, I emphasize that he is by no means unique among his
contemporaries in this interpretation.[41] But the combination of elements
becomes original by virtue of the doctrine of correspondence; among the
building blocks of the opus, few are picked from the actual biblical text,
and those that are have been given other tasks in the total story. Several of
them carry a central symbolism, but this symbolism is found through radical reinterpretations.

The text's composition illustrates both the distance from and the closeness to the biblical text. Although it appears rather vague to begin with,
due to the abundance of more or less digressive information, a division into
scenes can be discerned as a basic pattern. There are six scenes, their association with the days of Creation being obvious; however, a glance at the
scene content also reveals the distance from Genesis:

| *Days of Creation in Genesis* | *Scenes in* The Worship and Love of God |
| --- | --- |
| 1:1–5. In the beginning God created heaven and earth; the making of light; the difference between day and night. | Introduction (§§3–15). Planetary systems and firmament; the birth of earth and the planets from the world egg; earth's first movement away from the sun. |
| 2:6–8. God separates the waters above and below the skies and creates the sky. | Scene 1 (§§16–21). The newborn earth's constant springtime; the creation of plant life; paradise. |
| 3:9–13. God divides earth and sea and lets plants of different species grow and bear fruit. | Scene 2 (§§22–28). The animal kingdom grows out of the world of plants; examples of different species of animals being created. |
| 4:14–19. The creation of the sun, moon and stars. | Scene 3 (§§ 29–38). Preparations for the arrival of man; God impregnates |

|  | the human egg, and the soul builds its body. |
| 5:20–23. God creates birds and the fish of the sea and gives them powers of fertility. | Scene 4 (§§39–56). Man's birth and first fostering; the soul and its different properties are delved into. |
| 6: 24–31. God creates the more advanced animals, wild and tame, and shapes man in his own image. | Scene 5 (§§ 57–86). Continuation of the human education in a more theological course; God, the Son, and evil; premonitions of sin and redemption. |
|  | Scene 6 (§§87–110). Eve's creation and education. |
|  | Epilogue (§§111–131). The wedding of the first couple; the concluding vision (never completed). |

Even if one adds to the account of Genesis 1 the supplementary (and sometimes conflicting) information from other biblical texts, Swedenborg's liberal reinterpretation stands out clearly, although the Creation as a whole proceeds along the same lines.

Other biblical motifs appearing in *The Worship and Love of God* are also liberally interpreted: paradise with its two trees, the trees of life and of knowledge, Adam, Eve, the prince of the world, the Only-begotten Son, all of which will be discussed in their own context. In several respects, the influence of ancient writers is more evident than that of Christians, even if it too is reinterpreted in correspondential terms. The best way to describe the relationship between antiquity and Christianity is to call it a synthesis and we have already seen this blending early in the work in the cosmological prelude that introduces the drama, which Swedenborg himself calls an antique motif (§2). After this overture follow the six scenes with their hexaemeral inspiration.

The doctrine of correspondence thus gave Swedenborg a free hand in the relationship between the biblical and ancient originals, and it was crucially important to his spiritual development. The last question then is to what extent the doctrine or its sources influenced the style of *The Worship and Love of God*. The most important style element in this opus is the use of images, introduced in the division of scenes. Those scenes are in their turn constructed with series of images, from the death-tinged autumnal landscape in the introduction to the blindingly brilliant final vision of the purpose of existence: God's honor manifested in the heavenly community. *The Worship and Love of God* thus becomes a collection of corresponding and yet illustrative paintings. It is appropriate to connect this to the contemporaneous visions of Swedenborg's dream diary, as the similarities sometimes are striking. But in doing so, one strays further into the psychological sphere than into the literary, even though Swedenborg's interpretation of his dreamed images is another expression of the same conviction that lies behind the drama of creation: dream and poetry are placed in the same category in the correspondence system, "*correspondentia fabulosa et somniorum.*"

Again, we must consider the theoretical background. In the brief note from 1734 on Comenius' method of hieroglyphical description of the soul, we are already near the compositional principle of *The Worship and Love of God.* But Wolff's dry definitions and examples of hieroglyphical discourse reflect a widespread tradition, which has been of great importance in the history of literature.[42]

The literary genre of greatest interest to this study is the art of emblematics, but this field has widened to encompass the entire trend of allegory, which concerns especially the seventeenth century and of which emblematic poetry was but one of many expressions. Scholars have seen the rise of emblematics as a result of the humanistic interest in Egyptian hieroglyphs, which, in turn, was motivated by its philosophical orientation; Neoplatonic writings, which were studied so fervently, showed a deep awe of Egyptian wisdom. This could already be glimpsed in the overview of hexaemeral poetry.[43] Both Plato and Pythagoras were introduced to this ancient wisdom hidden in hieroglyphs, according to *De mysteriis Aegyptiorum*—supposedly written by Iamblichus (c. 250–c. 330)—and under the influence of this wisdom, these great thinkers realized that ultimate knowledge can only be acquired through intuitive vision.[44]

Similar speculations—philosophical, cabbalistic, linguistic—flowed together with an interest in hieroglyphs and became a strong stream of esoteric science. In Pythagoras (c. 580–c. 500 BCE), contemporary syncretism was most evidently foreshadowed, as was evidenced by Johannes Reuchlin (1455–1522), for example, as Friberg has observed.[45] Pythagorean sentences came to be seen as the verbal equivalent of images of the hieroglyphs, and it was from these two elements that the emblematic combination of image-symbol and word-symbol was born.[46] But the study of hieroglyphs and the direction of interest it reveals entailed even wider implications for the literary baroque style: in the poetic symbol, often emblematically fixed and saturated with mystical submeanings, writers found a means of surpassing the limitations of reason. Friberg illustrates this literary ideal by quoting Francis Bacon (1561–1626), sentences that could have been written by the Swedenborg of the doctrine of correspondence. There is "*poesis parabolica,*" which is the apex of poetry, a genre cultivated in many forms in ancient times and of which Pythagoras' sentences are examples.[47] Interpreting symbolic poetry as a source of knowledge equal to that of philosophy is consistent with the fact that poetic styles of writing were also used outside poetry; according to Swedenborg's notes from Wolff, the alchemists used hieroglyphs, which in this case must be interpreted as an emblematic method.[48]

Thus, even a superficial survey reveals that the little notes from *Psychologia empirica* have a complex and momentous background. But it is another question as to what degree Swedenborg himself was initiated in these obscure contexts. Although we are entitled to assume a rather general knowledge—unavoidable in one of Stiernhielm's fellow countrymen—there is also some more direct evidence. In the list of different sciences, heretofore mentioned, which Swedenborg compiled in cod. 36–110 from Andreas Rydelius, there is also a note about the *"ars emblematica,"* which according to the note writer is exercised through intellectual images.[49] In the *Nödiga Förnufts-Öfningar*, we find the source of this note in a catalogue of the different forms of rhetoric, after information on tragedies, romances, and parables:

> *Men* ars Emblematica, *konsten at smida* Deviser, *eller tecka Sinbilder, brukar ännu en större kortthet, och äfwen större diupsinnighet, under et, tu eller try ord och en bifogad liten målning begripande en tancka och mening, som hafwer ganska myket at innebära: Så at man kan säja, at thenna konsten i en förunderlig kortthet inneholler weltalighetens och* Poesiens *alldraskönaste smycke.*

> (But *ars emblematica*, the art of forging devices, or fair sensual pictures, uses an even greater succinctness, and even greater profundity, with one, two, or three words and a small painting attached comprising a thought and a meaning, which contain much significance: so that one may say that this art expresses with amazing laconism the most beautiful jewel of rhetoric and poetry.)

And the moral value of emblematics and its relatives, *"Symbola, Aenigmata, Proverbia allegorica, Hieroglyphica, and others such"* is praised in a note: *"All thessa sinrika påfund äro myket priswärdig, när the anwendas til sitt retta ändamål, som är, at upegga sinnen til dygd, och gifwa anwisning til en rett försichtighet"* (All these ingenious inventions are worthy of great praise when used for their just purpose, which is to induce virtue in people's minds and to provide advice on proper caution).[50]

Rydelius' appreciation of poetic allegory and symbolism corresponds with his own attachment and that of many other eighteenth-century critics to the *ut pictura poesis* theory, as Friberg has pointed out. However, it contrasts with his brusque rejection of what he calls "the allegorical philosophers," among which Robert Fludd (1574–1637) and Jacob Böhme (1575–1624) are held to be the worst offenders.[51] In a later context, I will show that Rydelius' thoughts on these mystics return in a central episode of Swedenborg's theological thinking before his crisis of conversion. It is of great importance to our assessment of *The Worship and Love of God* as a work of poetry that Rydelius accuses the allegorical philosophers of misunderstanding the metaphorical aspects of the Bible and of interpreting these aspects too literally, which lead to serious errors: Rydelius' Cartesian clarity of mind could not be disrupted by his infatuation with symbolic poetry.

The same observation can be made to a great extent regarding Swedenborg. His early comparison between the myth of the world egg and the origin of the solar system is one of many examples of this, and the extensive and extremely prosaic footnotes confirm this. Swedenborg was fully aware that his discourse should be read as a poetic vision, a fable with a morally edifying purpose, yet at the same time as a *liber divinus*, an inspired work on God and the soul. The footnotes provide a philosophical and scientific exposition for the symbolic poem. Rydelius would not have misunderstood him and lumped him together with Fludd or Böhme, as sometimes happens in Swedenborg scholarship, but would probably have perceived his manner of writing as metaphorical in a philosophical and symbolic sense or hieroglyphic in a poetic sense.

These literary similarities, which can be extended to encompass more central parts of the world of thought, underline the fact that Swedenborg represents—to a great extent—the part of the eighteenth century that, for all its rich heritage in mysticism, primarily stands for rationalism in thought and deed. But the excerpts, whose point of departure, by the way, is Rydelius' *Nödiga Förnufts Öfningar*, also contain another interesting feature in this context—a book title, which can be found under the headline "*correspondentia typica*": *Mundus Symbolicus* by Fillipo Picinelli (c. 1604–1667).[52] We cannot find excerpts from it here, since it seems to be a memorandum for future use. The work is a well-known and extensive emblematic dictionary, a Latin translation from 1695 from the Italian original, which Swedenborg duly noted.[53]

Swedenborg's knowledge of and interest in emblematics has been established; thus, we may assume a connection between this interest and the structure of his drama of creation. We have already noted the great world theater with its different stages as a well-known emblem, *theatrum mundi*, which also occurs in Picinelli's dictionary.[54] The issue of the immediate influence on *The Worship and Love of God* of sensual imagery art is complex and requires further analysis. To this background, the early and formative impressions of Ovid, especially the *Metamorphoses*, must be addded as an influence from which Swedenborg could have received the first idea for the composition of images used in *The Worship and Love of God*, in the tableaus of transformation and symbolic images; other scholars have also observed these similarities, as previously mentioned. However, Ovid would not have achieved such importance had it not been for the symbolic perception of art, which is part of the doctrine of correspondence.

Thus, the poetic form of Swedenborg's *The Worship and Love of God* rests on theoretical speculation, as would be expected in a writer with greater ambitions as a thinker and scientist than as a poet. The different theoretical elements form an interesting pattern, in which both the poetic details and the grand vision generate the artistic effect. It is significant that Sweden's foremost representative of the Romantic era's syncretistic vision of art, Atterbom, so strongly identified the poetic inspiration behind *The Worship and Love of God*. To see this inspiration, one must have a synthetic outlook, viewing poetry as a form of expression for obscure truths that the clarity of science cannot communicate. Swedenborg achieves this view through his doctrine of correspondence, which was developed around the same time as his research into the human psyche and is intimately connected to contemporary thinking but also contains traditions from Renaissance humanism. Within Swedenborg's oeuvre, *The Worship and Love of God* is the superlative literary effort, conceived of before the doctrine of correspondence was applied exclusively to Bible studies. When this occurs, as can be seen in the works that immediately follow, the system becomes bereft of all poetry, although a poetic impulse struggles to find a place within the visionary encounters. But these *memorabilia* are different from those found in the drama of creation, especially since the preacher tends to manifest his staunch authority. The personal experiences, which no doubt can be perceived behind the drama of creation, are objectified and given a symbolic garment in the visions. At this point, however, revelations had not yet converted the didactic poet to a prophet.

## Swedenborg's Philosophy of Nature

*The Worship and Love of God* begins with the creation of the solar system, but we do not find a detailed dissertation on how the sun and the stars were created. The reason is that Swedenborg had already presented his theory on the first link in the creational chain, namely, in *Principia rerum naturalium* and adjoining works, especially *De infinito*, in 1734. The connection between the drama of creation and the treatise on the infinite is clear already in the first note on *The Worship and Love of God* in his dream diary: "*Elliest berettades något om min bok, man sade at den wore en Liber divinus de Dei cultu et amore, jag tror det war ock något om spiritibus, jag trodde jag hade något derom vti min de Infinito, men swarades intet dertil*"(Furthermore something was told about my book. It was said that it would be a *Liber divinus de Dei cultu et amore* [a divine book on the worship and love of God]; I believe there was also something about *spiritibus* [spirits]. I thought I had something on the subject in my work *De Infinito*, but there was no answer as to that).[55] The connection between the drama of creation and the ideas of *Principia* has, as the overview on

previous research has shown, always been acknowledged; Stroh, for example, gave an excellent synopsis of the relationship between the writings in
philosophy of nature overall and *The Worship and Love of God*:

> These scientific and philosophical works may be divided into
> two grand series, *first,* those dealing with the *macrocosm,* or the
> universe as a whole; and, *second,* those which explain the *mi-
> crocosm,* or man, according to the universal laws formulated in
> the first series. The importance of *The Worship and Love of
> God* is seen when it is known that in it are brought together the
> results of both series; it is the synthesis of all of Swedenborg's
> previous scientific and philosophical studies, epitomized in a
> representative and oft-time correspondential form.[56]

The most important of Swedenborg's universal laws, in the present context, is his teaching on how everything grows out of the first mathematical
point, which has been created through infinity and which later in different
stages of development gives rise to the spiral and vortex movements and
particles, of which nature—to followers of Descartes—is made. This view
comes out in its clearest form in the two first chapters of *Principia.* The
starting point is the three roads that lead to true philosophical knowledge:
experience, geometry, and judgment. For Swedenborg, this is a characteristic conclusion, which shows his intermediary position in the contemporary
philosophical debate. By experience, he means all knowledge of nature
communicated through sensual observations and all knowledge collected
throughout all branches of science during the course of time: in our current
state, this experience constitutes the most important precondition for every
true philosophy, a point of view which comes close to Locke's empiricism,
as Lamm observed.[57] Swedenborg followed up his theory in practice
through very extensive research in a number of areas, which preceded his
enormous productivity during the hectic decade before he was given the *a
priori* knowledge in mysterious ways.

But knowledge based on experience is only a precondition, not an end in
itself. It must be subjected to rational analysis to become something more
than a chaotic mass of information; the best means of doing this is what
Swedenborg calls geometry. The term reflects its Cartesian origin, and the
consistently mechanistic view of nature points in the same direction. Still,
there are reservations: geometry can be applied only to finite matter, and
much in the finite world cannot be studied with the aid of geometry.
Swedenborg mentions for example *"intelligens illud, quod in animali existit, seu anima, quae una cum corpore vitam ejus constituit"* (the observational organ which exists in the animal, or the soul, and which together
with its body forms its life), an important divergence from Descartes'
mechanistic system.[58]

Geometry is thus an aid of limited reach, and to it must be linked a *"fac-*

*ultas ratiocinandi,"* a power of discernment that has been apportioned only to a few. The true philosopher is defined by his ability to detect the real reasons and acquire knowledge about matters that the senses do not comprehend; having reached this insight, he must be able to reason from *a priori* points of departure about our world and attain an overview of reality from a central point (*Principia,* 17). No one can achieve this position fully, although man, in the state of innocence, once held this insight. The motive of this perfect insight in the first inhabitants of paradise is filled with foreboding elements: *"Homo enim integerrimus est summe philosophus factus etiam in illum finem, ut Numen, rerum omnium originem, seu illud, quod omne in omnibus est, eo melius devenerari sciret; nam summe philosophus & scientissimus esse nequit, nisi numinis devotissimus"* (Man in his most perfect state has been created with the greatest wisdom so that he should thus better know how to worship God, the begetter of all things or He who is everything in everything, because no one can possess the highest wisdom and insight who is not also most in awe of God).[59] A man of such perfection, ten years after the writing of the *Principia,* shall become the main character in a drama on the appropriate worship of God.

This numinous perspective provides the Cartesian pattern with a larger space. But the geometric and mechanistic view of this pattern returns continuously in the descriptions of both innocent humankind and fallen humankind; and when Swedenborg—in the second chapter of *Principia*—addresses the deepest origins of the universe (the natural or, in geometrical terms, the mathematical point with its creation from infinity), it becomes even clearer that we are in the midst of the great rationalistic tradition.

The relationship between this mathematical point (Swedenborg identifies it as the point concept of Zeno of Elea [c. 495–c. 430 BCE]) and the infinite had been investigated closely in *De Infinito,* and the theological consequences of this discourse have a direct bearing on *The Worship and Love of God* and will be treated in its appropriate context. The point arises through a movement within infinity, albeit a movement outside of the laws of mechanics, a *conatus,* an endeavor to move. Lamm, and before him Schlieper, are correct in their supposition that Leibniz influenced this view.[60] The pure movement is regarded by Swedenborg as perfect, which means that it possesses the highest form of the spiral. In a note on the forms of nature in *The Worship and Love of God,* a perpetual spiral form is identified, called *"forma vorticalis,"* the highest potency of which is celestial.[61] This means, in other words, that Descartes' theory of the vortex is the basis for Swedenborg's cosmology, as several scholars have pointed out, and consequently this is also true of the drama of creation.[62]

The mathematical point, which is compared to the double-faced Roman god Janus in its position between finite and infinite, thus gives rise to all nature since its movement includes an ambition to produce other units. The first result of the constant vortical movements of these units becomes *"finitum simplex sive primum substantiale"* (*Principia*, 41), the first finite particle, and this particle contains the same active force as in the mathematical point (*Principia*, 45). From this follows the ability to bring about more complex particles in the same manner. As Stroh pointed out, it is never a question of atoms in the ancient or Gassendi understanding, but of Cartesian particles.[63] When Swedenborg then moves on to higher compositions, he introduces the oppositional pair activity and passivity, which becomes so significant for the world-view to follow: *"Sed antequam elementare quid existere potest, necessum est, ut duo principia in mundo sint, unum activum & alterum passivum"* (*Principia*, 80) (But before any elementary particle can exist, it is necessary that there are two principles in the world, one active and the other passive).[64] From the union of these comes the first elementary particle, in which the passive second finites create the surface layer and the active the center. Already in this first element of the universe, we meet the same tension between an active core and a passive surface, which gains its macrocosmic perfection in the birth of the planets out of the world egg.[65]

The original force in the first point, which comes from its constant vortex movement, is transplanted to the higher compositions in the whole chain. Next, the active ones in the second finite point follow, although moving more slowly due to the larger expanse of space through which they have to move, compared to the active ones of the first degree. Together these actives participals form the mass of the sun. The third finite is composed only of the second degree finites in a new union: *"Est consequenter finitum hoc tertium nihil aliud quam simplex sive punctum ter in se multiplicatum, sive ad tertiam sui potentiam elevatum"* (*Principia*, 111) (Thus, the third finite is nothing but the first finite particle or point multiplied thrice in itself, or squared to the third power).[66] Together with the two species of actives, this third finite makes up the second elementary particle, which is a part of the vortex movement of the sun and which helps to create magnetic phenomena. Schlieper supposes that Newton influenced Swedenborg's theory on the role of magnetism in the planetary system.[67] Otherwise, Swedenborg's cosmology is far from Newton's, which follows directly from its Cartesian basic structure.[68]

The problem of magnetism takes up the larger part of *Principia*, and its immensity threatens to implode the work. But in the third part, the thoughts on different degrees of particle unions, with a beginning in the fourth finite, are resumed, the fourth finite being the condition for the primeval chaos of sun and planets. The description is introduced by another of these ekphrases so characteristic for Swedenborg, colored by ancient mythology and strongly reminiscent of the introduction to *The Worship and Love of God*:

*Ergo jam sol gaudet suo vortice, & vortex sole, utrumque simul unus mundus; nam unum sine altero non subsistit. Sed sol adhuc tanquam vacuus in aula immensa regnat: imperium ejus limites habet spatiosissimos, sed adhuc nullos incolas, qui illi ministrent & famulentur; & quibus jussa det, & leges ac jura distribuat: nec vortex aliquid in se aut sinu suo gestat, quod circum solem suum quotannis & perenniter circumferre possit; nihil adhuc cui munia sua offerat. Manet sic Phoebus in sede sua sublimis & illustris; . . . Sed jam in conceptione sua sunt planetae; jamque ovum enascitur, ex quo excludendi sunt.* (*Principia,* 387)

(Thus the sun rejoices in its vortex and the vortex in its sun, and both are at the same time a world because one cannot exist without the other. But the sun reigns still alone in an immense throne hall; his realm has the widest borders but still no inhabitants who serve and obey him and to whom he can give orders and found laws. Nor does the vortex carry anything in it or in its womb that it can bring around the sun yearly and forever, nothing so far to which it can offer its gifts. Phoebus remains aloft and adored on his throne. . . . But soon the planets are created; and already the egg is born from which they will hatch.)[69]

Thus, Swedenborg followed the chain of creation to the hint of the world egg symbol. But the representation of events in *Principia* proceeds all the way to the earthly paradise. In my analysis of the introduction to *The Worship and Love of God,* I stressed the artistic consciousness that colors the description of the planets' solar origin. This responds directly to the episode in *Principia* where the creation of the third elementary particle and of the ether is mentioned. The connection between these two texts is Lamm's, and the observation is correct insofar as both cases are an ancient display of an identical substance.[70] However, the differences are significant. The representation in *Principia* is more overtly mythological: here the sun is referred to as Phoebus, and here Jupiter, Juno, Venus, Flora and Ceres appear, while the author emphasizes his allusions to classical poetry (*Principia,* 398). In the drama of creation, however, no illustrative names of deities are used in this context, nor do allusions to ancient poetry appear; instead, Swedenborg lingers longer in the process of birth, his description being stricter and more in tune with the later moments, which it foreshadows directly. The inner context in *The Worship and Love of God* is far stronger than that of *Principia,* which can be explained partly through the deepening total vision that came with the doctrine of correspondence. At the same time, Swedenborg aims further with this work than with *Principia* and cannot linger too long in the cosmological sphere.

From the ether, the cluster of third-level elementary particles, our attention is turned to the next link in the chain, the fourth element—air. The affinity with ancient modes of expression is marked also in this context:

> *Videamus itaque jam, quomodo aere incincta sit, & Juno suo fratri Jovi nupta: nam veteres philosophi finxere Jovem praeesse aetheri, & Junonem aeri, & sic sua foedera & cubilia non procul a terris sociavisse (Principia, 413)*
>
> (Now we may see the way in which it is surrounded by air and how Juno is given as spouse to her brother Jupiter; for the ancient philosophers imagined that Jupiter reigned over the ether and Juno over the air and that they thus had entered a pact for bed and domicile not far from earth.)[71]

The air is thus closely related to the ether and is composed on its "surface" of the finite of the fifth degree and on the "inside" by the first and second degree elementary particles. The next stage relates in a witty fashion to this by describing how Jupiter still missed his thunderbolts—fire—which then is joined to the system. It consists mainly of the fifth-degree actives. Then follows water or *"finitum pure materiale,"* with which the newborn earth finally inundated herself. During the continuous movement of the orb, this primeval water was covered by a hard crust, and with that Swedenborg had reached the goal of the philosophical volume of his *Opera philosophica et mineralia:* paradise and the first man. In the following parts, technical and mineralogical problems are treated: these parts were the ones to attract, more than anything else, contemporary interest and admiration.

In an appendix, Swedenborg pays tribute to Wolff and declares that they hold unanimous views, although he had not consulted Wolff's writings when conducting his own work.[72] This final chord is in complete harmony with the basic note of *Principia rerum naturalium*: rationalistic themes conducted in different keys. The structure is basically influenced by the Cartesian teachings of Swedenborg's education but has been enlarged with later insights, among others from Leibniz, Newton, and other representatives of the new science, and from empiricism. This eclectic attitude also characterizes Swedenborg's later works, where he attempts to apply his bold mechanistic monism on the areas of biology and psychology.

*The Worship and Love of God* presupposes a knowledge of this complicated cosmology, which has been only hastily sketched here; in his extensive notes Swedenborg tried to repeat its most relevant main themes, even if only in a desultory way. The tendency to cross borders, which we have met in the perspective on infinity in *Principia*, has been strengthened in the drama of creation, however, and the cosmology becomes only one part of the universal context to be described, although remaining a basic component because of the consistent parallelism between the macrocosm and the microcosm. The clearest example of this is found in the symbol of the world egg. I shall treat this rather extensively, since a study of the sources here has importance beyond the actual text, especially when appreciating Swedenborg's learning and relationship to contemporary science. At the same time, the symbolism is of great interest as an example of how poetic vision and cosmogonic theory flow together into an original unity.

## Ovum mundanum

There was a time, outside of all other time, when the sun bore the heavenly bodies of the universe like fetuses in its womb, and at birth it sent them into the ether. However, the sun could not possibly have carried such masses of matter in its burning center; these must have been the product of vapors projected from the sun. Thus, its surface was covered in fumes caused by its rays, and from these liquids, which had been pressed together during the evolution of time, was created a nebulous space, not unlike the white of an egg. This space, with the sun as its core, came to look like *Maximum Universi Ovum*, the great world egg. A shell formed around this egg because the sun's rays were intercepted by the nebulosa. This shell was shattered by the sun through its rays when the time of birth came; the mass of the world egg now formed the heavenly bodies, which can still be seen in the sky, and they have ever since then looked up to the sun as to their father (*The Worship and Love of God* §9).

In a note, Swedenborg comments on his description of the origin of the solar system, pointing out that this world egg is identical to chaos as described in antiquity:

> *Hoc Ovum fuit Chaos illud olim hodieque tam famosum, in quod Elementa rerum congesta fuisse traditur, quae dein in pulcherrimum disposita ordinem Mundum nostrum producerent.*
>
> (This ovum was the "chaos" that has been much talked of both in former times and today. It has been traditionally described as a congested mass of basic elements, which, once rearranged in the most beautiful order possible, produced the world we know.) (§9, note d)

This comment relates directly to the equivalent description in *Principia*, in the chapter *"De chao universali solis & planetarum; deque separatione ejus in planetas & satellites"* (On the universal chaos of the sun and planets; and on its separation in planets and satellites) (387ff). Swedenborg stresses here that the ancients had already reached this conclusion through their speculation, that there had once been a *chaos universale* consisting of both the sun and the planets, and indeed all the elements and seeds, from which matter emanated.

This is exemplified with long excerpts from Aristophanes' *The Birds* and Ovid's *Metamorphoses*; further, Epicurus is mentioned along with the Mosaic story of Creation and the eighth chapter of the book of Proverbs. Although Hesiod is not named, his spirit soars over these waters, too. In Genesis 1:2, on the desolate emptiness of earth and the darkness over the depths, Swedenborg cautiously identifies a Mosaic version of the ancient chaos. From there, he moves on to a detailed investigation into the state of the earth *in ovo* and subsequent to hatching, an investigation that ends in Aristophanes (450–385 BCE) again being quoted as *"ad philosophiam nostram propius"* (closest to our opinion) (*Principia*, 395):

> CHAOS and NIGHT: that was the start of it,
> And black Erebos, and the long nothing of Tártaros;
> No Earth as yet, no Air, no Heaven. There,
> In the untried lap of Erebos, sombre Night
> Laid a wind-egg, whence, with the circling year,
> Erôs was hatched, golden Erôs, wind-swift
> Love, the world's longing. His was the sleight
> Joined Night and wingéd Chaos in that first
> Tartarean marriage and brought the race of Birds
> To the shores of light.      (*The Birds*, Parábasis I, 21–30)[73]

Unconcerned with the fact that this regards the birth of birds according to the Attic comedy, Swedenborg infers that the sun was enclosed in an egg, from which it emerged through the evolution of time.

All these references could be said to be common knowledge, the classic and biblical erudition's *commune bonum*, but great importance has been attached to the Ovidian elements in it, for example, in Stroh's hypothetical remarks, which Lamm alludes to: "Whether Swedenborg received the first hints of his 'nebular hypothesis' from Ovid's *Metamorphoses*, or from some other source than his own original speculations, has not yet been made clear."[74] A closer study of this reference apparatus, combined with the evidence in the final chapter of *Principia*, which deals with paradise and the first man, provides the possibility of a more thorough estimate of Swedenborg's reading and, stemming from this, a reply to Stroh's query.

The world egg myth is immediately associated with Orphicism, even if it can be found in parallel forms within several cultures.[75] According to Neoplatonic sources, the cosmic egg was an important element in Orphic cosmogony, which can be traced to preclassical times, even if the earliest literary evidence is Aristophanes' parody *The Birds*, as quoted by Swedenborg. The difference between the Orphic cosmogony and Hesiod's is insignificant but consists of the very egg symbol. Martin P:son Nilsson claims that the Orphics borrowed it from popular belief:

*Dass die Welt aus einem geborstenen Ei entstanden sei, ist ein durch die ganze Welt verbreiteter Mythus; das Ei, das als ein lebloses Ding, als ein Stein erscheint, aus dem aber rätselhafterweise ein Lebewesen hervorkommt, erschien als der beste Vermittler zwischen dem Stoff und den Lebewesen, zwischen dem Chaos und dem Kosmos.*

(That the world originated from a broken egg is a universal myth; the egg, seemingly a lifeless thing, a stone, out of which a living being comes out miraculously, appeared to be the best intermediary between matter and spirit, between chaos and cosmos.)[76]

We can see from this how close Swedenborg's symbolism is to central mythological motifs, well known to him through the reading of ancient poetry.

However, in order to achieve further progress than such a general statement, we must quickly follow the idea of the world egg in literature from sources that could have been known to Swedenborg. The literary sources for the Orphic egg that were available during his lifetime were all—except for Aristophanes—late-ancient or later; the preserved fragments of a so-called Orphic poetry, which had been published by among others J. J. Scaliger (1540–1609), are normally dated between 100 and 300 CE.[77] Classical Greek literature contains abundant references to Orpheus in several indistinct forms; nevertheless, the role of the cosmic egg in Orphic philosophy has been stressed primarily by Neoplatonic writers. It is, however, noteworthy that this world egg is primarily a theogonic phenomenon, an attempt to describe the birth of the gods, even if this often leads to theories about the creation of the world, similar to those we encounter in Swedenborg's writing.

Thus, an interpreter of one of the Orphic theogonies, Marcus Aurelius' contemporary Athenagoras (2nd century CE), makes the upper half of the god-bearing egg form heaven and the lower half form earth.[78] A similar idea appeared earlier in a fragmented form in Varro (116–27 BCE): "*Caelum est testa, item vitellum, terra: inter illa duo humor, quasi in sinum clusus aeri, in quo calor*" (Heaven is the shell, while earth is the yolk; between these two, there is dampness filled with heat, contained in the air as within a womb).[79] In this form of myth, the thought is often linked to the idea of heaven as a father and earth as a mother, as can be found in a number of varieties within different cultures, to which ethnologists and historians of religion have testified.[80]

Regarding the use of the world egg in Swedenborg's writings, primary interest should be attached to the literary tradition, even if a description hereof must necessarily be fragmented and limited to the sources best known to us. Among these, one of the oldest is Plutarch (c. 46–after 119),

who, in one of his table conversations discusses in a rather humorous manner the problem of the chicken and the egg. Behind the witty dialogue is a
clear insight of the consequences of this question, and the author refers to
Orphean and Pythagorean concepts of the egg as the origin of the universe
and therefore a holy object. He also proposes certain ideas of spontaneous
generation that appear distantly related to Swedenborg's curious combination of cosmogonic and biological elements in his egg symbol.[81] We can
find nearly the same description in the works of the great compiler Macrobius (fl. 400 CE), where there are also long lectures on the identity of the
sun and several different Egyptian divinities, with examples from Orphic
and Egyptian speculation. From this, we may draw comparisons with the
spiritual sun in *The Worship and Love of God*: an explanation can be
found in the common background of Neoplatonic thought.[82]

The Egyptian version of the world egg myth returns in the works of,
among others, Eusebios (c. 264–340), where Kneph, the first god, creates
an egg, which is interpreted as our world, from which the second god, Ph-
thah, hatches.[83] Also the Neoplatonic Proclus (410?–485) writes about the
Orphic text of the egg, while in the works of Achilles Tatius (3rd century
CE), we find a lengthy investigation, which is worth quoting in the Renaissance Latin translation as typical of late-antiquity compilation literature on
the subject and which was well known during the first centuries of the
new era:

> *Caeterum ordo ille, quem in mundi sphaera constituimus ovo-
> rum similis est, ut Orphei sectatores docent. Quam enim ra-
> tionem habet in ovo putamen, eandem in toto universo coelum
> obtinet, atque ut in orbem è coelo suspensus est aether, sic è
> putamine pellicula. Vel, quod aliis placet, quoniam aether idem
> est ac coelum; à quo proximus est aër, erit in ovo membrana in-
> star aëris: caro autem albida, quae in eodem est, si quidem aëri
> respondet, aquae locum vitellus habere potest, tum quod in-
> terius est in medio vitello, terram exprimet. Sin est ut mem-
> branam ovi ad aethera transferre malimus, pro aëre gallinarum
> lac habebimus; & vitelli extremus ambitus aquam exhibebit,
> quod interius est & in medio; terrae instar erit. Ad summam, si
> cum Aristotele quinque sphaeras esse dixerimus, quod intimum
> est in vitello, terrae loco sumetur. Sin quatuor putemus esse;
> quod alii censent; pro terra vitellum integrum, non magnitudi-
> nis, sed situs ratione capiemus.*

> (This order, which we constitute in the spheres of the world,
> is similar to the eggs, as the followers of Orpheus teach. Be-
> cause heaven takes the same position in the whole universe that
> the shell has in the egg, and in the same way the ether is con-
> nected to the heaven in the world, so is the membrane con-

nected to the shell. Or rather, as others suppose, since the ether is the same as the heavens, to which the air is closest, so the membrane contained in the egg will be the equivalent of the air. If the white meat in the egg is the equivalent of the air, the yolk can replace the water and the earth be formed as the innermost of the yolk. But if we would rather place the membrane of the egg in relation to the ether, we shall see the white as a congruent to the air; the surface of the yolk will then equal the water, while what is innermost and in the middle becomes the equivalent of the earth. In short, if we in Aristotle's manner assume that there are five spheres, what is inside the yolk shall take the place of the earth. But if we suppose them to be four, as others believe, we may choose a representation of the earth as all of the yolk, not in terms of its size but in terms of its position.)[84]

Parallel to this pagan philosophical speculation, we find a Christian theological one. As mentioned previously in the overview of the hexaemeral tradition, Genesis 1:2 has been interpreted in association with the world-egg myth as the spirit of God hovering over the depths like a hatching bird; the earliest example of this analogy is found in the works of Basil, with reference to an anonymous Syrian authority, probably Efraim the Syrian (d. 373).[85] The Tremellius-Junius edition of the Bible was found in Swedenborg's library, among other editions, and it contains this interpretation, which is commented on further in the following manner: *"verbum ab avibus pullitiei suae incubantibus mutuatum: quo significatur a Spiritu materiam illam informem fuisse fotam, ut foventur pulli ab incubantibus matribus"* (the word is fetched from the brooding of birds on their chickens: of which becomes clear that formless matter was nursed by the Spirit, as the chickens are warmed by the brooding mothers).[86] The same thought returns in several of the Bible annotations, albeit without further detail.[87] In Spegel's works, where the exegete's and the poet's professions were somewhat united, we encounter the highly poetic image shaped with a rustic objectiveness:

Rät såsom Kyklingar uhr Eggen warda klekte/
Och utaf Skalets Graaf med Hönans Warma wäkte;
Ja som wi kunna see at Soolens liufste Bråna
Gir åt then kalla Säd i Jorden Lif och Fråna/
Så at thet döda Korn får een förnyat Yngska
Och det som ruttit låg upstår i fager Grönska;
Så haar then Helge And och upwäkt Jorden döda/
At hon ward hafwande med mykken herlig Gröda/

(Just as chickens are hatched from their eggs
 And out of the grave of the shell were wakened by the hen's
  warmth;

Yes, as we can see the sun's loveliest rays
Give to the cold seed in the earth life and growth
So that the dead kernel receives a renewed youth
And what was rotten revives in beautiful greens;
So has the Holy Spirit also awakened the dead earth
That she was expectant with much lovely crops.)[88]

However, the similarities to Swedenborg's treatment of the motif are very general: the symbolic contexts are different, and the biological corollaries in Swedenborg's style are almost completely missing. In Renaissance history of nature speculations as well as those of the following centuries, the egg symbol came to be used in a manner closer to Swedenborg's method than that of the ancients. A significant and strident part of the scientific debate during the sixteenth, seventeenth, and eighteenth centuries concerned the question of how the world was created. More precisely, the discussion usually dealt with how to unite the biblical version with the new heliocentric worldview, which was named after Nicolaus Copernicus (1473–1543). The contributions to this often heated debate were different: biblical comments, hexaemera, and dissertations. The quality of the debate varied greatly, for example, between Robert Fludd and Isaac Newton (1642–1727), likewise the motivations.[89] In this dance of arguments, we also encounter the cosmic egg in contexts that may seem both surprising and ridiculous but that, for Swedenborg's contemporaries, were widely known and generally accepted.

Bearing in mind that we encounter the world-egg myth most often in circles close to Neoplatonism, it is reasonable to look for it in the Renaissance within the Platonic school, which—with a varying amount of intermediaries—originates from the Florentine academy. Its greatest names, Marsilio Ficino (1433–1499) and Pico della Mirandola (1463–1494), have little to offer in this regard. Pico was familiar with the speculation of antiquity on the subject, as is clear from references in *Examen vanitatis doctrinae gentium* (Examination of the vanity of the doctrine of the pagans), but he does not provide any views of his own.[90] In his great paraphrase of Genesis, *Heptaplus*, Pico refers nowhere to the cosmic egg; however, there are, as Lamm pointed out, extensive speculations on the human relationship to the universe as a microcosm in relation to the macrocosm.[91]

Among Pico's many disciples and followers was, as one of the earliest and most important, Paracelsus (1493–1541), in whose writings the theory of the cosmic egg holds a significant position, as Lindroth emphasizes.[92] We can read in *Liber meteororum,* for instance:

> dan die andern drei elementen seind in das firmament beschlossen wie ein ei in einer schalen; also ist die erden, das wasser, der luft in disem element verschlossen, wie der dotter, das klar, das heutli im ei ist, das ist in der schalen . . . aber da ist

*ein underscheit zwischen dem clar und dem wasser also, das im*
*clar ein solche chaosische art ist, das nichts dadurch fallen mag.*
*dergleichen ist nun das firmament auch in seinem corpus, das es*
*in der mitten behalt, was da ligt, das es sich unverrucket halten*
*muss.*

(The three other elements are included in the firmament as an egg in the shell; thus the earth, the water, and the air are included in this element, as the yolk, the white, and the membrane in the egg, that is, in the shell; but there is a difference between the white and the water in that respect that there is in the white such a chaotic quality that nothing can fall through it. Now the firmament is similar in its body that it keeps what is in there in the middle, so that it must hold itself immobile there.)[93]

Here is a concrete exposition of the ancient myth, a palpable cosmic analogy with a strong biological nuance; in a more-or-less direct Paracelsic tradition, we encounter the motif early in Swedish, for example, among the works of Sigfridus Aronus Forsius (1550–1624).[94] Nevertheless Paracelsus' philosophy is far more primitive than Swedenborg's, for whom the new science during the seventeenth century was of great significance. Nor do we find the ambition towards a holistic vision, so characteristic of *The Worship and Love of God*, among the works of the strange German scholar and physician.

In England, the cultural sphere to which Swedenborg was most strongly drawn, we encounter an early exposition in the writings of Francis Bacon. In the brief fragment *"De Principiis atque Originibus,"* which has been discussed as a possible source for *Paradise Lost*, the myth of Eros' birth from Night's egg is mentioned.[95] In the tradition of Democritus as Lucretius conveys him, Bacon sees Eros as the principle and power of matter, which to a certain degree comes to identify Eros with the atom.[96] Bacon follows Aristophanes' version of the birth of Eros, thus interpreting this sacrilegious comedy joke philosophically, in a manner similar to how Swedenborg in *Principia* relates the comedy writer's description as *"ad philosophiam nostram propius,"* a symptomatic correspondence in general thought.

The world-egg myth also appears in the numerous writings on ancient mythology that were the result of the great interest in mythology prevalent among especially the Neoplatonic Renaissance scholars. This study peaked in the seventeenth century. One of the most famous mythology scholars, Gerhard Johannes Voss (1577–1649), includes in his work *De theologia gentili* (On the theology of the pagans) an extensive passage on the world egg, where, among other things, the fragment from Varro can be found.[97] Here is an important source of knowledge, which will be discussed more extensively in connection with the mythological allusions more evident later in Swedenborg's drama of creation.

In clear opposition to the empiric Bacon, we find the peculiar school of thinkers known as the Cambridge Platonists, who constitute an independent branch of the Florentine academy tree.[98] First and foremost, problems relating to philosophy of religion occupied the minds of these thinkers, understandably considering the Italian models, but occasionally this led to speculations in the field of natural history. Thus, Henry More (1614–1687) in his extensive Genesis commentary, *Conjectura cabbalistica*, reports on matters that are linked closely to the usual neck-breaking allegory of cabbalism, coming closer to the theosopher Swedenborg than to the scientist. More, however, seems to have had no interest in the world egg.[99]

On the other hand, we meet the world egg in the main work of his colleague Ralph Cudworth (1617–1688), whose *The True Intellectual System of the Universe* combs through ancient philosophical literature to dismiss definitively all of the arguments for atheism; this entailed an extremely rich documentation, in which the idea of the egg is included, first in Aristophanes' description.[100] Cudworth refutes Aristophanes' thought, which he—original enough for the literature of its kind—suspects as being a joke; however, he does not wish to deny certain elements of truth in it. Further on, beginning with the works of Aristotle and Epicurus, Cudworth questions how animals and human beings came to be and, as might be expected, decisively refutes the theory that they were hatched from eggs in the earth, a theory found particularly in Lucretius' *De rerum natura*.[101] Given his predisposition, Cudworth must deny this type of materialistic hypothesis, but the fact that it is mentioned at all displays a knowledge of the more modern biological literature, which was united with the cosmogonic ideas of the world egg in Swedenborg's *The Worship and Love of God*, as will be shown later. In this regard, we should become acquainted more closely with Cudworth, whose influence was mentioned only in passing by Lamm.[102]

The egg symbol was used also in emblematic contexts. In Picinelli's *Mundus symbolicus*, there is a short chapter on the emblematic value of the egg symbol, especially from a Christian theological viewpoint, which could have been an inspiration for Swedenborg; we cannot, however, find evidence of any detailed correspondence.[103] It is a reasonable assumption that Swedenborg possessed at least a general knowledge of the literary tradition, sketched above. It may also be assumed that his own symbolism grew freely out of this very rich ground. Indeed, most of the material described here was introduced to him in a readily available work that bore the greatest significance for the development of his cosmological theories.

In a small astronomical tract from 1718, *Motion and Position of the Earth and the Planets*, Swedenborg dedicates one chapter to polite Cartesian polemics with an English cosmologist named Thomas Burnet

(c. 1635–1715).[104] According to the custom of the time, the work by Burnet, which young Swedenborg here criticizes, had a long and awe-inspiring title, of which I will quote only the first section: *Telluris Theoria Sacra: orbis nostri originem & mutationes generales, quas aut jam subiit, aut olim subiturus est, complectens* (A Sacred Theory of the Earth, presenting the origin and general changes of our world, both those which it has already undergone and those which it will meet in the future). It is divided into four volumes, of which the first two are primarily of interest in the present context. These two books deal with the Deluge and paradise in that order, and were part of a volume in the 1691 edition from Swedenborg's library.[105] The two following books discuss the end of the world as well as the new heavens and the new earth, which are presupposed in Christian escatology.

Thomas Burnet, a disciple of Cudworth, holds a significant position in the English history of science of the seventeenth century, thanks to his cosmological works, not least because of their formal elegance; thus, when Richard Steele (1672–1729) dedicates an issue of the *Spectator* to Burnet's *Theoria*, he compares him to no less a writer than Cicero (106–43 BCE). At the time of this *Spectator* article, Swedenborg was, in fact, in England, moving among the very circles that had participated in a heated debate on Burnet's work, for example, that of the great astronomer John Flamsteed (1646–1719) and his colleagues.[106] Swedenborg would have encountered Burnet's name in his discussions with English scientists, and we might even assume that he may have reacted to Steele's essay, where certain lines seem almost prophetic with regard to the author of the work *The Worship and Love of God*: "How pleasing must have been the speculation, to observe Nature and Providence move together, the physical and moral world march the same pace: to observe paradise and eternal spring the seat of innocence, troubled seasons and angry skies the portion of wickedness and vice."[107]

Steele is not alone in remarking on the literary qualities in Burnet's *Theoria*. We encounter the same observation within English Romanticism, in Samuel Taylor Coleridge (1772–1834), who in his famous collection of excerpts wrote down ideas on how to put the work into verse; Coleridge scholars have noted impressions from his reading of this work.[108] This is again proof of the general observation that the intellectual background to Romanticism is often close to Swedenborg's, something that, not surprisingly, strengthened the Romantics' interest in the Swedish mystic. Also, among contemporary thinkers and scientists, Burnet was well known for a long time: Nicolas de Malebranche exchanged letters with him, and Georges-Louis Buffon (1707–1788) analysed and admired his work in his *Théorie de la terre*, a fact that should be noted before one ascribes to Swedenborg the honor of Buffon's planetary theory, as is common in Swedenborgian contexts. In the Nordic countries, the interest in Burnet is reflected, for instance, in *Jödiske Historie* (Jewish history) of Ludvig Holberg

(1684–1754), where *Telluris Theoria Sacra* is discussed in connection with the tale of Creation and the description of the Fall of humankind.[109]

Although Swedenborg directly referred to Burnet, his work has not been observed in Swedenborg scholarship to date, with an exception for passing remarks by Stroh and Nordenmark.[110] One reason for this is an error in Tafel's document collection. In his account of the content in the manuscript volume, which he has named codex 86 (in Ekelöf-Stroh's catalogue no. 53), Tafel claims that there are excerpts on the great Flood as well as Paradise from an author by the name "Roumette."[111] Without any doubt, this is a misreading. Swedenborg's heading reads *"Ex Bournetto,"* from Burnet, and under this heading are notes on Burnet's world-egg theory with evidence on the appearance of antediluvian earth, the locality and lovely features of Paradise, all with quotes from ancient and biblical authorities, which are mentioned in *Principia* and which will be discussed shortly.[112]

Another reason seems to be that the only place where Swedenborg quoted Burnet directly is in a peripheral and critical fashion. Thus, we read, in *Motion and Position of the Earth and the Planets*:

> *Andre hafwa ock funnit at jorden underkastas stora ändringar; har hafft en hel annan lufft förr än nu; har siudit och pårlat af en stark heta, och sedan afkylt och skaffat sig ett Paradis, medels en jemn werma. Orsaken ther til har en lärd Englendare benämd* Burnet *i sin* Theoria telluris *gissadt wara then, at jorden för syndafloden har följt retta Linien, eller* aeqvatorn *effter, tå jemwel sommar och winter hafwa warit som nu en wår: men af en hop ändringar wid syndafloden har jorden förloradt sin förra jemn-wicht och wendt sig til sollinien, thet är* Ecclipticam. *Som thenna meningen giör en del tilfyllest at wisa tidens ändringar, lemnar man at bifallan: doch med förbehåll at the skärskoda huru then stemmer med naturen in: . . . Här af sluter man, at fast mongen tycker sig hafwa skiäl til hwad påfinnas kan, så bör thet doch lemnas under gissning. Ingen ting bör bifallas; som icke Gudz ord och oryggeliga skiäl samtycka til.*

> (Others have also found that the earth has undergone great changes; has had a completely different air prior to the present; has raged and simmered with a strong heat, and then cooled off and created itself a paradise, with the aid of an even warmth. The reason for this, as an English scholar by the name *Burnet* in his *Theoria telluris* guessed, was that the earth before the Deluge followed a straight line, or the *aeqvator*, when summer and winter seem to have been like a spring nowadays: however, through a number of changes in the time of the Deluge, the earth lost its former equilibrium and turned itself towards the sunline, that is *Ecclipticam*. As this opinion contributes some-

what to explain the changes of time, one may accept it: however
with the qualification that one should evaluate, how it relates to
nature: . . . Hereof can be deduced that although many feel they
have reason to explain what can be found, it should nevertheless be left to guess work. Nothing should be acclaimed, which
God's Word and undeniable reasons do not agree with.)[113]

The question at hand is the climate of paradise and the reason for it, and
this question returns later, in *Principia* as well as in *The Worship and Love
of God.*

In Burnet's work, we find the world-egg theory among the many hypotheses on the creation of the earth and its first period, which are described with biblical and classical writers' observations as an entry point
and from speculative deductions based on the present appearance of the
earth. Burnet finds the Greek version of the world-egg myth in Aristophanes, Eusebios, Macrobius, Plutarch, Achilles Tatius, and Varro. Among
these, he especially approves of Aristophanes; the passage from *The Birds*
is the exact translation used by Swedenborg in the *Principia*, a translation
which thus dates back to his excerpts from the end of the 1710s: punctua-
tion and orthography have been slightly but insignificantly changed during
the transcription.[114]

In his account of the history of the myth, Burnet first mentions the Orphic egg with Plutarch and Macrobius as literary references, from which it
can be deduced that in this egg *"omnium rerum ortum & antiquitatem
complectatur"* (the origin and early time of all objects are summarized).[115]
He further stresses how the Orphics saw the egg as a holy object, the symbol of the origin of the world. Then he equates this world-egg doctrine
with Genesis 1:2, where he finds an analogous reference in the episode on
God's spirit soaring over the waters.[116] The Egyptians also used the egg as
a symbol for the world, Burnet states, and quotes Eusebios to prove this
point. He then proceeds to discuss in a more-detailed fashion the reasons
that the ancients made this comparison between our world and the egg,
finding that they attached importance not only to the outer shape but also
to the series of elements connected in the interior, as Achilles Tatius and
Varro pointed out.[117]

But this means, according to Burnet, that the world egg encompasses
more than our earth for these interpreters: Varro's theory would indeed indicate that heaven is the shell of the egg, that the earth is its yolk, and that
the air is its white.[118] Burnet's own theory is that antiquity's idea of the
world egg refers only to our earth and not to the whole of the universe, a
point of view that earlier in *Theoria* is claimed to be relevant to all ancient
cosmogony. In fact, it was a common view in the cosmological literature of
the time that this was also true of the Mosaic story of Creation.[119] Burnet
ends his summary of world-egg theories by mentioning its prevalence in

Persian mythology, which is so often referred to in contemporary literature.[120]

As this short summary shows, Burnet's work contains an excellent encyclopedia of ancient theories of the world egg, and Swedenborg's early use of it is evident from his excerpts and writings from the last years of the 1710s. But the connection can be brought forward to *Principia* and thereby also immediately to *The Worship and Love of God*. The literary documentation in *Principia* is defective, as is common in Swedenborg's writings, and Burnet's name is not even mentioned. However, Swedenborg quotes Aristophanes in the same version as Burnet's, and out of four poetic examples of the eternal spring in early time, three can be found in *Telluris Theoria Sacra* and the excerpts thereof.[121] One of these indeed stems from such an esoteric source as the hexaemeral writer Alcimus Avitus, whose acquaintance Swedenborg made through Burnet's writings. Without doubt, Burnet's work played a significant part in the design of *Principia*, and this fact underscores the intimate connection of this summary of Swedenborg's philosophy of nature to the speculations of his youthful years. But how far can his reading of Burnet explain Swedenborg's vision?

We may observe first that *Telluris Theoria Sacra* rather strictly adheres to the subject named in the title: it is a *geogonia*, presenting a theory on the origins of our earth, its earliest times and its imminent destruction. Thus, one cannot expect to find the biological elements in Swedenborg's ideas of the world egg here, although they are alluded to in certain contexts.[122]

In applying the ancient world-egg theory to our planet only, Burnet follows the custom of his time; however, it marks a difference in relation to Swedenborg. This does not mean, however, that his conception of the origins of the earth is of no interest to the present context.[123] Burnet understands chaos to be the matter of the heavens and the earth as a liquid mass without shape, in which the elements of all things have been merged, as in Ovid's description. His consistency with the author of the *Metamorphoses* has been noted by the editor of one of the Ovid editions in Swedenborg's library, who refers to Burnet in his comments on the description of chaos.[124] This chaos was created by God as a raw material; Burnet, however, does not stress God's direct activity but speaks mostly of the principles that divine wisdom inserted into nature, a scientific view fully in accordance with Swedenborg's.

In this liquid chaotic muddle, certain changes now occur. The heavier particles sink towards the middle, where the gravitational center is believed to be, while the lighter particles float upward. Among these lighter elements are two species, the lighter forming air and the heavier forming water on the surface, which, in their turns, differ in the degree of humidity. There are the oily and lighter liquids, and then there are the heavier, earthbound liquids, which are separated as cream separates from milk. The upper, oily, and greasy liquid united with dust particles in the air and thus formed the shell of the earth: in this way, antediluvian earth was created, its surface being even and uniform, without mountains or seas. It is indeed Burnet's definite and highly original point of view that the present structure of our earth is a result of the Flood, a catastrophe resulting when earth's crust broke and the waters from its depths sprung forth, in accordance with the punishing will of the Creator.

Burnet relates the appearance of the earth in its paradisiacal shape to the world egg of antiquity: *"Dum itidem contemplor hoc Schema novae telluris, venit mihi in mentem memoratissimi illius Ovi Antiquorum, quod celebratur apud* Orpheum, Aristophanem, Plutarchum, Macrobium *& alios"* (While I observe this, the new earth's order in the same way, I find myself thinking of the famous egg of the ancients, which is commonly known in Orpheus, Aristophanes, Plutarch, Macrobius and others).[125] Thereafter, he applies the idea of the egg on newborn earth so that its burning core corresponds with the yolk, the heavy masses around this kernel become the membrane separating the yolk from the white, the waters in the deep form the white, and the earth's crust becomes the shell: this description is illustrated with a sketch.[126]

The thought of the ancients' ideas of the egg brings with it other associations that Burnet mentions in a later context and to which he refers at this point.[127] In the chaos of antiquity, many bizarre things were hidden: one talked of Eris, severance and division, and of Eros, love and unity. Chaos was depicted in the place of parents with Night and Tartaros or the ocean as offspring, subjects that seem poetic dreams rather than philosophy, Burnet explains.[128] Nevertheless, he interprets them in the light of his general theory, and thus they become significant. In the separation of the elements, he sees both the genealogical and the moral aspects as satisfied: the dust-filled air is the Night and the silted waters Tartaros, both of which are the offspring of Chaos and from whose union a daughter—habitable earth—is born. But during the earliest epoch, hate and division reigned in Chaos, only to be replaced by Venus' or Love's rule, when dust was expelled from the air and formed the crust of the earth together with the silted waters:

> Aristophanes *ait peperisse Ovum, unde Amor emersit & genus humanum: quod non minus verè quàm eleganter dictum est, ut infrà videbimus. Nos apertè asserimus Noctem sive hunc Aërem impurum & turbidum genuisse terram ipsam habitabilem, orbem primigenium, cujus figura erat ovalis: eúmque orbem formatum fuisse ex impuriori materia hujus Aëris in pinguem Abyssi spumam subsidente; quâcum concrevit primùm in mollem limum, & dein in firmiorem Orbem habitabilem. Ac utì Ovum Noctis, aliter interpretari non possumus, ità multò minùs alia Antiquorum testimonia, quae has partes Nocti sive Aëri impuro explicitè assignant.*

(Aristophanes assures that [Night] had given birth to an egg, from which Amor and humankind sprung: which is no less true than tastefully said, as shall be shown below. We declare openly that Night or this impure and soiled air had brought forth this habitable earth, the firstborn world, whose outer shape was oval: and this earth had been shaped from this air's even more impure matter, which sinks into the oily foam of the depths; together with which it first became firm as soft mud and then even firmer as habitable soil. But as we cannot interpret the egg of the Night differently, we can interpret even less other observations from the ancients differently, which clearly ascribe these parts to Night or impure air.)[129]

If we return to the chapter in the third part of Swedenborg's *Principia*, where the theoretical grounds for the more artistic description in *The Worship and Love of God* are to be found, we shall meet points of view strongly correspondent. There is talk of the ancients allowing Night and Tartaros to be born out of Chaos, that earth was their offspring, and that they believed the origins of the gods were to be found in this Chaos as well; and further: *"Amorem vero dixerunt illum, qui omnia discrevisset"* (But that which separated all things, they called Love) (*Principia*, 390). In addition, Swedenborg's description of how the sun's chaos is transformed into the cosmic egg readily agrees with Burnet's portrayal of the corresponding development of earth.[130]

This is the great difference between Burnet and Swedenborg: namely, that the latter's ambitions are so much greater. Burnet provides a theory on how the earth came to be, while Swedenborg wishes to explain the origins of the entire solar system. This naturally means that Swedenborg has also used other sources when constructing his hypothesis on the birth of the universe. The basic Cartesian pattern is evident, but it has been modified and developed, as Svante Arrhenius, among others, has noted, especially in two areas, one of which concerns the origins of the solar system: "Not without foundation did it seem to Swedenborg simpler to assume that the planets and moons of the solar system proceeded from the solar mass instead of having wandered in from portions of space lying outside of the solar system. This thought has been taken up by Buffon, Kant and Laplace and is the fundamental thought in the admired hypothesis of Laplace."[131]

I will not investigate Swedenborg's relationship to Descartes' philosophy of nature as a whole; but that he viewed it with criticism after his stay in England is clear from, among other things, a rather contemptuous statement in a letter to Benzelius in 1718, where he mentions that *"förrdömen som man fådt af Cartesio och andra lärer giöra mesta bry och inkast"* (prejudices given by *Descartes* and others may cause puzzlement and objections).[132] Most probable is that Burnet's *Theoria* was of the greatest importance when Swedenborg constructed his modified Cartesian planetary hypothesis; to some degree, it existed *in nuce* in Burnet's work, and it should have been easy to deduce from the presence of the world-egg symbol the relevant consequences that Burnet alludes to in the following passage:

> *Denique cùm omnes Planetae qui in Coelo nostro continentur, atque ejusdem solis alumni sunt, aliquâ cognatione & similitudine inter se conjungi videantur, atq; eadem ferè habere phaenomena generalia; cúmq; ratio quâ planetam nostrum ex suo Chao deduximus, satìs ampla sit, ut ad plures extendi possit, debeátque, ut videtur, ad omnes extendi in quibus eadem elementa reperiuntur, sive partes originariae; Verisimile mihi videtur omnes planetas Coeli nostri processisse ex Chao eodem.*
> . . .
>
>   (Finally when all the planets which exist in our heaven and which are the foster children of the same sun can be seen united with one another out of the same kinship and familiarity and almost simultaneously used to show similar phenomena, and when the theory, from which we have derived our planet from its chaos, seems grand enough for one to be able to extend it to several, and since one as it seems should extend it to all, in which can be found the same elements or original parts, it seems likely to me that all the planets of our heaven came from the same chaos. . . .)[133]

The step from the sun's foster children to its children, as in Swedenborg, is not far from Burnet's approach.

It is time to reach a conclusion about the theories on the cosmic egg in *The Worship and Love of God* and its predecessor *Principia rerum naturalium*. From this summary of ancient and Renaissance cosmogonic speculation on the egg symbol, a multitude of examples and interpretations can be offered: the motif belongs to the common knowledge of the time. In such cases, the reference to sources must necessarily be imprecise, and one may be forced to satisfy oneself with a sketch of the intellectual environment in general. From this point of view, Burnet's *Telluris Theoria Sacra* should be seen as an encyclopedia and dictionary of quotes for Swedenborg. He may, of course, have known the ancient theories of the world egg through his extensive reading of the classics, and he may have taken an interest in contemporary interpreters, such as Bacon, Paracelsus, or Cudworth, or even others who have not been mentioned here. But in Burnet, Swedenborg met a collection of quotes and proofs that, as the excerpts show, were used directly in *Principia*.

However, Burnet's work beyond doubt had a greater impact than that. The manner in which he used the classic world-egg myth differs indeed from Swedenborg's in that Burnet limited the theory's relevance to the earth; but this means little, since his ancient foundation in several cases displays other meanings. The important matter is that Burnet's geogonic application could so easily be transferred to the cosmogonic area by carrying out ideas that he hinted at himself, and this is what Swedenborg did in *Principia*. Stroh's cautious suggestion of impulses from Ovid is reasonable indeed, but can be easily exchanged with a firm statement on the main source, Thomas Burnet's *Telluris Theoria Sacra*.

The microcosmic correspondences to the world egg in *The Worship and Love of God*, however, are not explained through references to Burnet. They require a special inquiry. The lyrical tendency, shown already in *Principia*, especially in the cosmological chapters, and which returns in a far more developed form in the drama of creation, can be linked to Burnet's work: Steele and Coleridge were both fascinated by its artistic structure. In all probability, this stems from the author's view of the poem as a medium of secret insights, a conviction that, in one instance, he stated in relation to a description of the different shapes that divine providence takes in the universe, where our earth with its heaven makes up the third class, the hidden truths of which many wished to reveal:

> *Et intra hunc orbem & in his arcanis eruendis se exercuit omnis antiquitas, omnis Theologia Veterum, omnis Philosophia, omnium gentium Mystae; in his, siqua habere, fabularum fundamenta; Symbolorum sensus; mens Hieroglyphicorum; literatura Sacra in his tota versata est: Denique in hâc palaestrâ certârunt omnis aevi sapientes, & humani generis praestantissimi Animi.*
>
> (And within this sphere, all antiquity strove to solve these secrets, all the theology of the ancients, all the philosophy, all the mystics of all the peoples; in these they found, if anywhere, the bases for the fables, the meanings of the symbols, the implications of the hieroglyphs. The sacred literature has been entirely interpreted in these. Finally, all the wise men of the era and all the foremost spirits of humankind competed in this arena.)[134]

In the light of Swedenborg's later development, the young science enthusiast Emanuel Swedberg's critical reading of the controversial cosmologist is very significant. In Burnet, Swedenborg received impulses that he would bear all the way to the gates of the spiritual world.

# 3

## PARADISE

### (§§16–21)

As the first section concludes, the new-born earth is depicted in the state of a dewy and trembling equilibrium, which had been established by the recently shaped crust of the earth:

> *nam perpetua erat planities, absque mendis, seu clivis & vallibus, una sphaera sine termino, quam rivi & fluenta ex thermis scaturientia, sicut calentes in novo Corpore venae, pererrarent; & undique roscido circumfusa nimbo, qui recentem iniret atmosphaeram, & in calidos Telluris sinus relapsus, illam continuo vapore refocillaret.*
>
> [C]ontinuously smooth and without blemishes—that is, hills and valleys—the earth was one sphere without a break, over which there wandered rivers and water bubbling from hot springs, like warm veins in a new body. It was also drenched on all sides by a cloud of dew that permeated the young atmosphere, and sank over the warm chest of the earth, refreshing it with constant moisture.)    §14

Now we are allowed to accompany this earth, still naked and unadorned as a chaste virgin, in its hastening race towards the birth and seedtime of the vegetable kingdom. The metaphors connect to the conclusion of the first section as this scene evolves the useful powers to which the introduction alluded. Just as this scene is linked to its prelude, the same goes for the motion of the earth away from the sun, which is now proceeding beyond the stage when the earth's crust came into being. In the beginning, the ages passed so rapidly that the centuries were hardly longer than our months; but with earth's increasing distance from the sun, time slowed down. In this section, the earth has reached its first goal when the annual orbit was neither too close nor too far from the sun, at which time the succession of the seasons was so tight that they became simultaneous, a *ver perpetuum,* a constant spring; and in the same way, the hours of the day were united into some kind of everlasting morning.

Not only time and space were engaged in attaining this blessed state but also the stars of heaven, the atmosphere, and the earth itself. No gales stirred the air; not even the tiniest cloud obstructed the stream of sunbeams, but mild zephyrs cooled them. The earth returned the love of the elements by letting her assistants share the delights of spring: "*Ita ad recentem hanc Tellurem, ut ad suum Centrum, cum perpetuo quodam Vere, totum credas descendisse Caelum, & ei tanquam unico, cui faverent, objecto, gratificatum esse*" (You would have thought that all heaven had descended and brought a form of continual spring to this new earth as if it were the very center of heaven itself; it seemed that heaven was lavishing kindnesses on earth because earth was its only favorite) (§17b).

But this state was the result of an order from God: earth had to convey to its offspring the perpetual spring that it had obtained as a fulfilment of the laws of correspondence. Here Swedenborg has phrased his thesis in direct connection to what he had written in more general terms in the introduction: "*nihil non ex simili Vere auspicia sua duxit*" (For everything has a similar springtime in which to make its beginning) (§18). The thesis is immediately clarified by a reference to what happened during earth's first spring: the entire vegetable kingdom was born from its seeds, and later all creatures were hatched from eggs, as still happens, although the pattern now applies only to lower species that do not live longer than one summer, as Swedenborg informs us in a didactic note (k). In the first paradisiacal ages, all creatures were nourished by the bosom of the earth, by the *lac sapidissimum,* the richest milk, flowing from it.

This indication of the origin of the animal kingdom foreshadows the next scene; here it serves to illuminate what providence intended by the perpetual spring in the early morning of the universe. For the present, the main focus is on the vegetable kingdom. The earth's first children were most marvellous flowers brought forth from seeds closest to its surface, displaying the richest variation of forms and colors. The number of species was equal to the multitude of celestial bodies, each one competing with its neighbor for the palm of victory. Swedenborg conveys this beauty in a way typical of the entire work, uniquely combining the abstract and the concrete. He does not dwell on the species still extant but on those that did not survive the state of innocence of the earliest ages. He doesn't try to reproduce the splendor of colors or the beauty of forms themselves, but their power of communicating correspondences: some of them were starlike, resembling heaven and the sun, while others were similar to the spheres of heaven in their distinct play of colors (§19). The aesthetic experience of the senses is valuable for him only to the extent that it communicates an insight of the coherence of existence, which cannot be acquired by other means.

However, in this capacity the part played by beauty is much greater. Swedenborg constantly returns to the youthful grace of the flowering earth. The virgin becomes a young bride, embellished with lovely roses, her beauty so dazzling that she might have invited the inhabitants of heaven as her guests. From bridal metaphors, Swedenborg sketches the earth as a young mother, lavish in her fertility. All the plants produce new seeds in their turn, which they lay down in the womb of their great mother, covered with their own leaves, so that they prepare the birth of new plants. In this way, the fecund earth is covered with humus. As time advanced and the earth extended its orbit further into space, bushes and trees grew out of the soil of the dead flowers. These trees too enjoyed a single perpetually fruit-ful spring and infused their own spirit into their seeds. In note m, the sem-inal power of the plants is compared to the soul in higher creatures.

In this manner, our world was metamorphosed into a wonderful garden, in which everything breathed happiness and joy. This was paradise, situ-ated in the highest spaces of the ether and near the sun. Swedenborg attests that the ancient's locating paradise in the spaces of ether came close to the truth, since in the beginning the earth completed its annual orbit in these spheres (note n). The brooks and streams that welled out of their springs in the recently solidified crust of the earth, as depicted at the end of the pro-logue, and that were compared in passing to veins in a new-born body, reappear towards the finale of this section (§21). Here the image of the earth as a body with fluids as blood-vessels is expanded: the organic circu-lation, in which the streams pass the heart, is the direct model, and blood as the carrier of nutrition is metaphorically used to describe the earth's nourishment to the root systems of plants. Just as the organic metaphor links to preceding parts, it also serves as a natural transition to the follow-ing scene, in which the origin of animals from the vegetable kingdom is presented. The fertility symbolism, with which the prologue concluded, is applied in the same manner here, an echo that emphasizes the importance of this basic motif for the entire work.

When discussing the location of paradise, Swedenborg refers to the wis-dom of the ancients, indicating that the literary model is found in antiquity. The *ver perpetuum* motif is inspired exclusively by ancient poetry, as will become clear below in comparing similar passages in *Principia*; the fertile earth in this constant spring has the same ancestry. Stylistically, the influ-ence of the Bible is less prominent than in the introduction, but is evident in the intellectual content; as Swedenborg himself states (note i), the evolu-tion of nature is determined by providence, a creed strongly expressed even at this early stage and one that goes far beyond ancient learning.

The classical coloring of the style is found in details. In his account of the floral splendor of the new-born earth, Swedenborg abstains almost to-tally from botanical data, with one exception. When thickets were born, he mentions *arbutei foetus*, a species of heath plants called *Ericaceae*. Such precise information is directly connected to ancient ideas of paradise; among many others, Lucretius, Virgil, and Ovid maintained that the fruits of this plant were bigger in ancient times and that the happy humans of the Golden Age subsisted on them and acorns.[1] Nor is there any doubt that Ovid is the closest source: *arbutei foetus* echoes the *arbuteos foetus* in the shortened quotation from the first book of the *Metamorphoses*, which was cited in *Principia* and soon will be discussed.[2] To contemporaries with solid classical erudition, the connection of the arbutus tree to ancient myths of the Golden Age was well known, and the paradise visions of Ovid probably came to his readers' minds before any others.

The description of paradise is one of the most important factors of this section, and it requires a closer study. In addition, this section clarifies how Swedenborg tried to give an artistic application to his scientific theories respecting the origin of the vegetable kingdom and the power of life.

## Paradisus telluris

To study the description of paradise in *The Worship and Love of God*, we must look back to Swedenborg's earlier works, primarily to *Principia*, as we did with the world egg. The final chapter of *Principia* introduces the motif, admittedly in a less detailed manner but nonetheless elucidating to a certain extent.

After the earth had disengaged itself from the solar surface, it surrounded itself first with ether and later with air. Thus far the account in *Principia* agrees exactly with that in *The Worship and Love of God*, but later *Principia* puts more stress on the part played by water. When the ocean of air had arisen, a cover of water was created out of it around the earth, which later gave birth to *terra firma;* this is a more precise statement than in the drama of creation, where only a *liquidus orbis*, a liquid globe, is mentioned in general terms.[3] Consequently, the origin of the earth's crust has been described in greater detail in *Principia*, and it is interesting to take a closer look at that account:

> sequitur sic 1. *Quod formaverit se crusta super aquas per dissolutionem partium in aquis, & finitorum interjectionem, quae versus superficiem emergerent, & crustam super aquas formarent, quae crusta sic continuo partes sub partes addendo cresceret.*
>
> (Thus it follows that a crust took shape above the waters through the dissolution of particles in these and the injection of finite particles, which emerged to the surface and formed a crust which grew continuously as particles were laid beneath particles.)[4]

Lighter water particles thus moved upwards to the surface; and together with other disengaged particles, they formed a firm crust, or membrane, which increased in thickness as the process continued. Swedenborg did not explain his reasoning further here, but what has already been said is enough to bring up Thomas Burnet's name once more: for what is the account of the origin of earth's crust in *Principia* but an independent development of Burnet's *geogonia*, such as we have got to know it in the preceding chapter?

The connection becomes even more evident by examining in detail the two cosmologists' accounts of the new-born earth's crust. As has been pointed out, Burnet believed the present structure of the earth to be a result of the Deluge, while the antediluvian world looked quite different: "*Forma telluris primae sive primi orbis habitabilis erat aequabilis, uniformis, continua, sine montibus & sine hiatu maris*" (The form of the primeval earth or the first habitable world was even, uniform, coherent, without any mountains and without the depth of the sea).[5] As far as I can discern, Swedenborg does not give any precise information about the appearance of the surface of the primeval earth, even if it becomes clear from the context that it should have been perfectly flat and even; yet in the drama of creation, he speaks of a smooth surface "*absque clivis & vallibus*," without slopes or valleys (§14). Unfortunately, *The Worship and Love of God* was never completed, and its implied description of the Flood, which possibly might have put the comparison with Burnet on firmer ground, did not materialize. In the commentaries on the Bible, with which Swedenborg was occupied during the next few years after *The Worship and Love of God*, he did not take an interest in the technical aspect of the Deluge, as far as I have noticed. Otherwise, his interpretations of the Flood and Noah's ark, which is compared to an egg or a womb, the point of departure for the life of the New Covenant after the Deluge, contain quite a few attempts at following up motifs from the drama of creation.[6]

There is, however, an unequivocal statement close to *Principia* in the preface to his treatise on copper in *Regnum subterraneum sive minerale*, which was published together with the *Principia* under the common title *Opera philosophica et mineralia*:

> *Arbitramur, quod nec negari potest, Tellurem nostram formosissimam, varietate delitiosam, & ubivis paradiso similem ante diluvii universalis inundationem; & ipsam ejus superficiem sine praeruptis montibus & scopulis, sine profundis vallibus, sine lacubus & pelagis indisruptam & aequalissimam exstitisse; dein vero faciem ejus deformem, inaequalem & laceram, disrupta per diluvium crusta ejus, factam esse.*
>
> (We are of the opinion, which cannot be denied, that our earth before the inundation of the universal Flood was perfect

in beauty, pleasant in variation and everywhere like a paradise;
and its surface without any cracked mountains and cliffs, without any deep valleys, lakes and seas, even and plain; but that its
surface then became disfigured, tattered, and uneven, when the
Deluge broke its crust.)[7]

Here Swedenborg is trying to explain the causes of the distribution of met-
als in the earth's crust, and he finds them in the revolutions of the Deluge.
Even without such a clear statement, the conformity of Swedenborg's and
Burnet's opinions of the shape of the new-born earth is too obvious to be a
coincidence; as has been pointed out above, the early excerpts from Burnet,
in which among others the Avitus passage is included, have been used for
this very final chapter in *Principia*, and consequently the spirit of Burnet indirectly hovers over the paradisiacal waters in the present work.

In the same chapter, as well as at several preceding places in *Principia*,
the different periods of rotation in the paradisical age and their effects are
emphasized, an exposition that also appears in the drama of creation. How
can these disparities be explained? The phenomenon is part of the general
planetary theory, according to which the earth disengaged itself from the
sun in a spiral movement after its birth; as the earth's orbit was closer to
the sun than now, the period of rotation was shorter and, consequently,
there was less distance between the seasons, so that these could conjoin to
a *ver perpetuum*.[8] In *The Worship and Love of God*, the argument is illustrated by an experiment, in which a thermometer had been fixed to a cylin-
der that can rotate at various speeds and distances from a source of heat.
The result is, at a medium position, an even temperature without any real
variations. Finally, Swedenborg declares in §17, note i:

> *Antiqui etiam Sapientes, eorumque Cantores, similiter quatuor
> Anni Tempora contrahebant. & sic perpetuum illud Ver, cujus
> mentionem faciunt, introducebant; ignari, quod ita provisum
> esset, ut id mediâ naturâ effectum consequeretur.*
>
> (The sages of ancient times and their poets condensed the
> four seasons of the year in the same way, thus introducing the
> concept of perpetual spring that is mentioned in their works.
> They did not know that this effect had been provided for as a
> consequence of a natural mean.)

This is, in fact, a summary of the account in *Principia*, in which the wise
men and poets of antiquity have got the floor to themselves, for example,
Ovid with his beautiful vision of the Golden Age:

> *Ver erat aeternum, placidique tepentibus auris*
> *Mulcebant Zephyri natos sine semine flores:*
> *Mox etiam fruges tellus inarata ferebat;*
> *Nec renovatus ager gravidis canebat aristis.*

*Flumina jam lactis, jam flumina nectaris ibant;*
*Flavaque de viridi stillabant ilice mella.* I: 107–112

(Spring was forever, with a west wind blowing
Softly across the flowers no man had planted,
And Earth, unplowed, brought forth rich grain; the field,
Unfallowed, whitened with wheat, and there were rivers
Of milk, and rivers of honey, and golden nectar
Dripped from the dark-green oak-trees.)[9]

Ancient philosophers assumed that paradise was situated in a higher region than earth's surface, which, according to Swedenborg's interpretation,
implies that they believed the earth to be closer to the sun in that age. The
gods of Olympus were born in this happy era, Flora and Ceres descended
to their flowery beds, Diana was roaming through the woods with her
nymphs, and the gods mixed with men.[10]

But Swedenborg had pondered these issues before, as becomes clear by
the reference to *Miscellanea observata circa res naturales*, published in
1722.[11] Going back even further to 1717, we find in a small manuscript
entitled *En Ny Theorie om jordens afstannande* (A new theory on the end
of the earth) the same experiment proposed to prove the existence of a constant spring in the paradisiacal morning of life: that the earth is losing
speed slowly but inexorably is illustrated in several ways, by the origin of
the earth, by its spherical form, by paradise, by the age of the antediluvians, by the Flood. The proof of the biblical Flood is particularly interesting in this context:

> *At Syndafloden ock bekräfftar wår mening, kan klart theraf*
> *tagas, som then erkommit af remnor och öpningar som jordens*
> *Superficies och crusta terrestris har giordt. . . . At Diluvium*
> *intet erkommit af en distension som hettan har giordt, thet en*
> *god man i England ment, lärer fås theraf, at then skulle sensim*
> *hafwa ökt sig och skutit jorden op, at hon kunnat fålla och*
> *skarfwa sig igen och flyta öfwer; men om watnet siunckte*
> *undan, och en Cavitet wore emellan watnet och jorden, skulle*
> *ett fall giöra, at en stor del af jordenes hwalf, el. snarare sagt*
> *planities skulle följa effter med.*
>
> (That the Deluge also confirms our view is clear because it
> arose out of cracks and openings in the surface and crust of the
> earth. . . . That the Deluge did not originate in a distension
> caused by the heat, as a good man in England believed, may be
> shown thereby that a distension would have expanded the
> earth, so that it might have joined itself together later on; but if
> the water would sink, so that a cavity emerged between the
> water and the earth, then a fall would cause that a large part of

the vault of the earth, or rather its planisphere, would accompany.)[12]

The "good man in England" against whom the young Emanuel Swedberg is here polemizing, is obviously Thomas Burnet, who in his *Telluris theoria sacra* had compared the prediluvian earth with an eolipil, a sphere in which the enclosed masses of water have been brought to a boil by rays of sunlight. In his view, these beams were never alleviated because the solar orbit always followed the equator before the Deluge. Consequently, there were no other seasons than a hot summer.[13]

Burnet's opinion on this particular point is also refuted by Swedenborg in the following year in the booklet *En ny Mening om Jordenes och Planeternas Gång och Stånd* (On the motion of earth and the planets), quoted above. Swedenborg found it unreasonable to assume that the earth was the only one among the planets to follow the equator exactly and further that the Deluge brought our planet out of its equilibrium, since this is connected with the structure of the atmosphere. It is not essential that he argues against Burnet; rather, the important fact is that the British cosmologist appeared already in the very earliest proofs of Swedenborg's speculation on the oldest ages of the world; this gives still another support to the thesis that *Telluris theoria sacra* was the most important source of inspiration for Swedenborg's extensive cosmogonical production, which reached its artistic summit in *The Worship and Love of God.*

A second element of the complex ideas of paradise that appear in Swedenborg's drama of creation deals with the geographical location of the Garden of Eden, a problem fervently discussed in scholarly literature for centuries.[14] In Christian hexaemeral literature, the discussion was based on Genesis 2:8–14, in which the four rivers rising in the Garden of Eden are mentioned: the Pison encircling the country of Havila, the Giron flowing around Kus, the Hiddekel coursing east of Assyria, and the Frat. As becomes clear in Augustine's Genesis commentary, the myth of paradise was a controversial question early on. Augustine refers to three possible interpretations, a concrete one, a spiritual one, and a third variant uniting both, with which he agrees. According to Augustine, the four rivers should be the Ganges, the Nile, the Tigris, and the Euphrates, which results in an extremely vague location. Augustine did not attach any importance to the geographical issue, rather being more anxious to explain the spiritual meaning of paradise.[15]

If you consult any Bible commentary of the Renaissance, you will be offered a series of proposed interpretations: that paradise included the whole earth in the Golden Age of the Adamites; that it was located somewhere beyond our planet; that it signified the church of the Adamites; that it was located in Babylonia.[16] The hexaemeral poets themselves held different opinions; Du Bartas offers his readers wise advice:

*Curieux, cependant, ne recherche en quel lieu*
*Ce parterre fut fait des mains propres de Dieu,*
*Si sur un mont voisin des cornes de Latone,*
*Si dessoubs l'Equateur, si pres de Babylone,*
*Si sur le clair Levant.*

(Curious one, do not seek for the place
where this garden was made by the hands of the Lord,
if it was on a mountain close to the corners of Latonia,
if beneath the equator, if near Babylon,
if in the light Levant.)[17]

Du Bartas himself seems to locate paradise in Babylonia, but only with the greatest caution. Milton, on the other hand, was obviously better informed:

> *Eden* stretched her Line
> From *Auran* Eastward to the Royal Towrs
> Of great *Seleucia*, built by *Grecian* Kings,
> Or where the Sons of *Eden* long before
> Dwelt in *Telassar.*[18]

Later, Milton applies the epithet "Assyrian" to the wonderful garden (IV: 285). In his book on Milton's literary environment, G. W. Whiting has analyzed the contemporary location discussion in detail, and it becomes evident that Milton could have found his information in such a well-known and widely read source as Raleigh's *History of the World*.[19] In accordance with contemporary practice, ancient authors with their Golden Age and Hesperian gardens are also cited in *Paradise Lost*.

With respect to the real location of paradise, Swedenborg believes that the entire new-born earth was a paradise in antediluvian times, but then there was also a *Paradisus in Paradiso*, a marvelous garden that became the birthplace and first home of humankind and that was located somewhere in the northern hemisphere (§21 and §32). This is the testimony of the drama of creation: it has some predecessors in Swedenborg's other works, but they are more diffuse, although pointing in the same direction. In the small treatise on the slowing down of the earth's orbit, he made a statement in passing: "*at första jorden warit lik* Paradiset *ses så wel af* Bibeln som af Poetiska Fictioner, som säjer at Saturni aevum warit ett ver perpetuum, tienligt til all tings producter så örter som fänadz*" (That the earliest earth resembled paradise can be understood from the Bible as well as from poetic fictions, which tell us that the age of Saturn was a constant spring, useful for the production of both grain and cattle).[20] But by the next year, he made a more distinct statement:

> *Gudz ord berettar om ett Paradis, om en Lustgård benemd*
> *Eden, ther* Adam *med* Eva *hafwa blifwit satte uti: all förnöilig*

*lust skulle funnit sig ther in; wexter, frucht och timmelig liu-*
*flighet i största ymnighet. Mongen holler före at hela jorden har*
*warit samma Paradis, tå ock lufften nödwendigt motte stemt in*
*thermed och warit skickelig at bringa alt sådant fram och hollat*
*sedan wid macht.*

(The Word of God tells us about a paradise, of a garden
called Eden, in which Adam and Eve were placed; all kinds of
joy existed there, plants, fruits, and sensual pleasures in abundance. Many people believe that the whole earth was the same
paradise, when the air must have corresponded to it and had
the capacity to produce and uphold all these delights.) [21]

As Lamm noted, Swedenborg refers later in this passage to the ancient authorities whom he will return to in *Principia* and other works, among
them, "*Homerus Poeternas retta Farfar*" (Homer, the true grandfather of
poets).[22] Referring to Plato, Hesiod, and Moses, Swedenborg states, "*sic*
*mediante perpetuo vere totum orbem terraqueum paradiso quodam orna-*
*tum fuisse*" (thus the whole world had become adorned with a paradise
through the agency of a constant spring).[23] Thus, while Swedenborg paraphrases Genesis in *The Worship and Love of God* regarding the existence
of a specific Eden, he evidently was aware as early as 1717 of current speculations on paradise.

Even though it may seem impossible to discern any individual elements
in this jumble of common knowledge, once again *Telluris theoria sacra*
presents itself as a well of wisdom, with respect to both general arguments
and details. From the outset, Burnet rejects two arguments on the location
of paradise. It cannot have been situated "*in locis extra-mundanis*" (in
places outside the world), that is, in the ether, nor in a tiny spot in Babylonia, while the rest of the planet looked the same as now. The basic theme in
his reasoning is also the fundamental idea of his whole work: that the earth
before the Deluge looked quite different and that paradise is to be found in
the antediluvian world, either in its entirety or in some particular place:

> *Sunt enim quaedam Paradisi phaenomena generalia, quae reli-*
> *quae telluri primigeniae cum eo communia erant, atque horum*
> *primò habenda est ratio, cognoscenda origo, & quis status nat-*
> *urae ea omnia complectatur, dispiciendum; dein designanda*
> *regio specialis Paradisi, quantum fieri potest, & quae ad eam se-*
> *orsim spectant, excutienda.*

> (There were certain general phenomena in paradise, which
> were common to the rest of the new-born earth, the situation of
> which should be investigated first and the origin of which
> should become known. Then it should be examined in which
> status of nature all this can be brought together. After that, one
> should indicate the specific position of paradise as exactly as

possible, and one should also separate it from its adjacent areas.)[24]

Burnet called upon a host of ancient authors to determine the location of the garden, since neither his own theory nor the testimony of Scripture could answer the question:

> *Memorat* Homerus *pensiles* Alcinoi *hortos,* Hesperidum Hesiodus, *ultra Oceanum;* Plato *insuper in* Phaedone *terrae cujusdam aethereae meminit, sive loci amoenissimi quem supra imbres omnes, flatus & fulmina ponit, ad modum Paradisi nostri.*
>
> (Homer mentions Alcinoos' pensile gardens and Hesiod the Hesperides beyond the ocean. Moreover, in *Phaedo,* Plato recalls an area in the ether, the most delightful place, which he locates above all rains, gales, and lightnings in the same way as our paradise.)[25]

Swedenborg notes this very passage in his excerpts from Burnet, and in *Principia,* we hear a distinct echo of it:

> *Veteres philosophi hujus temporis mentionem facientes putarant paradisum in altiori situ fuisse, quam hodie est telluris superficies; . . . unde & Plato in Phaedone terrae cujusdam aethereae meminit; & Hesiodus Hesperidum ultra oceanum.*
>
> (In mentioning this age, the ancient philosophers assumed that paradise was located in a higher region than the present surface of the earth. . . . Because of this, Plato recalls an area in the ether in *Phaedo* and Hesiod the Hesperides beyond the ocean.)[26]

The blazing sword, which, according to Genesis 3:24, parted the first human couple from paradise after the Fall, plays a major role in Burnet's argument, and that is reflected too in *Principia.* According to Burnet's theory, before the Fall, earth followed the equator exactly in its orbit; thus, an area on both sides of this line would be uninhabitable, but the rest of the two hemispheres would enjoy a constant spring.[27] Burnet proposed, supported by a number of learned men, that this torrid and barren zone may be identified with the blazing sword of Genesis, which implies that paradise in a restricted sense must have been located in one of the hemispheres. In a later English version of *Telluris theoria sacra,* Burnet preferred the southern zone, with the support of ancient authorities, but he did so after some hesitation.[28] The blazing sword reappears in Swedenborg's text, to strengthen his thesis that earth's orbit ran closer to the sun in paradisiacal times. In his notes from the 1740s about correspondences, after some doubt, he interpreted the sword as heat, which agrees with Burnet's motif as well as with his own *Principia.*[29] The reference to Genesis fits into a pattern emanating from *Telluris theoria sacra,* in which Plato is a classic example of the paradise theories that locate the garden of bliss in a sphere above the earth, Hesiod represents the view that it was situated beyond the ocean, and Genesis represents those who believed Eden was separated from the rest of the earth by a blazingly torrid zone.[30]

Unlike Burnet, Swedenborg locates the garden in the northern hemisphere in *The Worship and Love of God,* although with a most unsatisfactory formulation from a geographical point of view (§32). There may be several reasons for this. To start with, Burnet's location was first presented in an English edition, which might have been unknown to Swedenborg. At any rate, he is more likely to have been interested in revised versions of a book that had meant so much to him, and Burnet's theories were focused in Swedenborg's extensive reading in the 1740s.[31] On the other hand, Burnet's location was not obvious. The most orthodox location of the Garden of Eden was somewhere around Palestine. No doubt the decisive reason was the fundamental difference between Burnet and Swedenborg, namely, that Swedenborg did not share Burnet's opinion of the orbit of the newborn earth. If you accept Swedenborg's view that the orbit was almost the same in the paradisiacal era as it is now, though considerably closer to the sun, then the climatic relations would be reasonably similar, which would make the northern countries even more commendable.

Finally, a trace of the influence of Olof Rudbeck (1630–1702) on the young Emanuel Swedberg can be discerned in Swedenborg's later location of paradise. Lamm emphasized the great similarities between Rudbeck and Swedenborg, not only because, in his youth, Swedenborg explicitly embraced Rudbeck's opinions, but because their general conception of science compared favorably.[32] In my view, many of these similarities can be explained by their common background and therefore are of little interest. On the other hand, the young Swedberg cited Rudbeck as an authority in one of his early, brief treatises; even if this might have been wise for other than scholarly reasons in those days, the reference fits well into his own thinking. The passage observed by Lamm can be found in *Om Jordenes och Planeternas Gång och Stånd* (1719), more precisely in the dedication to Prince Fredrik of Hessen in the printed edition:

> *wil therföre här uti wisa skiäl til andras gissningar, neml. til the som wår salig* Oloff Rudbeck *i sin* Atlantica *framförer, och at thet intet är, som en del oförståndigt mena, dicht- och fabelwerck; at icke Swerje förr har kunnat wara ett Paradis med, och en boning för Gudar: at icke* Pallas, Flora, Venus *och andra Lust-Gudinnor hafwa kunnat här blifwit födde och opammade, och lefwadt med Swenska Fruentimren alraförst tilsamman, och at the sedan här ifrån hafwa flyttadt sig lengre in i södra* Europen.

(I would like to present some reasons for the guesses of others here, namely, for those which our late Olof Rudbeck advanced in his *Atlantica*, and to show that they are not to be looked at as poetry or fables, as some foolish people believe; that in earlier times Sweden also may have been a paradise and an abode of gods: that Pallas, Flora, Venus, and other goddesses of pleasure may have been born and fostered here and have lived together with Swedish women in the earliest times, and that they moved from here further into southern Europe.) 33

It would be tempting to conceive of Swedenborg, suffering from the experiences of a religious crisis in damp and wintry London, making a heroic attempt at summarizing the cosmological speculations of his life into an artistic whole and, compelled by longing for the Nordic spring, making a final contribution to the Gothic tradition of the seventeenth century in his drama of creation. But Swedenborg did not stress this, if he was even aware of his suggested rudbeckianism at all: his locating of paradise in the northern hemisphere in *The Worship and Love of God* is only significant as still another illustration of the continuity of Swedenborg's thinking *de initio rerum*.

While much could be said about details in Swedenborg's account of the new-born earth, it would probably not change the picture. However, it would be worthwhile to illustrate his thinking on this particular point against a general background. One characteristic of the Renaissance's cosmological literature is the lament for the successive decay and ageing of the universe, a process connected to the increasing degeneration of humanity, which will reach its logical end in downfall and Judgment Day.34 Different explanations for this decline appear in various literary forms, from sermons to hexaemera and more scientific treatises. In the second half of the sixteenth and the first half of the seventeenth centuries, the age when these issues were most intensively discussed, the new conception of the world was continuously gaining ground; consequently, anguish arose about the breathtaking perspectives opened by the heliocentric theory and its dethronement of humanity in the universe. In the same period, the religious conflicts in the wake of the Reformation intensified attention on the moral status of humankind and how badly prepared we were for the judgment that could be soon expected, since, according to many calculations, the allotted six-thousand years were rapidly approaching their end. As indicated by Victor Harris in his survey of this literature, there was an enormous contribution *pro et contra* to the discussion of the evolution of the universe and whether it would lead to decay and downfall or to brighter and happier prospects.35 The pessimistic contributions, which are generally the older ones, are filled with a wistful sense of loss of the happiness of paradise and the perfection of the first human beings: "We are scarce our

Fathers shadowes cast at noone" as John Donne lamented.[36] The ageing
earth, *mundus senescens*, no longer bears fruit as it used to in times past,
its bosom wizened by age. This sombre view is often strengthened by a reference to Psalm102: 25–26:

> Long ago you laid the foundation of the earth,
>     and the heavens are the work of your hands.
> They will perish, but you endure;
>     they will all wear out like a garment.
> You change them like clothing, and they pass away.[37]

Among the ancient writers on the thesis of the increasing age of the
planet, Lucretius is one of the most prominent. On the whole, he exerted
considerable influence on that kind of literature, to which Swedenborg's
present work is in some sense affined, as will be shown below.

In his review of the numerous contributions to the debate, Victor Harris
also studied Thomas Burnet since his work belongs to the same genre, even
though his contribution is of a later date.[38] From one point of view, Burnet's work appears to have been obsolete at its publication. On the other
hand, he explains the decay of the earth almost exclusively as a result of
the Deluge: there is no belief in a successive decay, which necessarily will
lead to the end of the world, nor any absolute parallel between the deteri-
oration of the earth and the decadence of humankind, as in the preceding
horrific accounts. Nor did Burnet claim an exact date for Judgment Day.
Still, his outlook on life is closely aligned with classical sixteenth- and seventeenth-century pessimism.

With regard to Swedenborg's opinion in *The Worship and Love of God*,
one should first pay attention to the melancholic account of the changing
of the seasons in the preface, which leads the author's thoughts to the divergent fates of life and the universe: "*Nec solum Aetates, Sed etiam Saec-
ula aut Aeva, id est, Communes Societatum Vitas, quae ab infantiâ,
integritate & innocentiâ, olim Aureae & Argenteae, dictae sunt; & nunc
ultimas seu Ferreas ad ostium affore, brevi in ferruginem aut argillae pul-
verem dilapsuras, creditur*" (And this is the case not only with individual
periods of our lives, but with epochs in general, that is, with the general
history of human society. There was a day when the times were called
golden or silver because of their childlike purity and innocence; now the
final, or iron, times are believed to be at hand, soon to crumble into rust or
the dust of clay) (§1).[39] In the next paragraph, Swedenborg mentions the
wise men of antiquity, who introduced the history of the world with the
story of a paradisiacal Golden Age. In his view, they drew an analogy of
their observations of the offspring of the earth and its innocent childhood
happiness to existence in general (§2).

This description allies Swedenborg with the pessimistic tradition. But
the preface is only a poetical summary of arguments, which have been pre-

sented earlier in a more scientific shape; as Lamm pointed out, the theoretical slow-down of the earth's orbit explains this interpretation of history.[40] The cosmological articles of the 1710s quoted above also contain thoughts on several of the problems, which were discussed in the genre, for example, the question of the age of the antediluvians and the fertility of paradise. But thanks to his general theory of the planets, Swedenborg's theory of the earth's final destruction will differ from and get a better foundation than the one common at the time, which assumed that the sun is approaching the earth to the effect that an increasing heat will finally destroy it. Swedenborg, on the contrary, supposed that earth will come to an end because of frost after its orbit had stopped. This was the opinion he presented in a 1717 treatise, but already in the next year he had come closer to Burnet's cautious attitude: "*Men wid slutet, huru en planet bristar sender uti minsta partiklar och skingras i en eld och faller igen til sin första lufft och oprinnelse igenom ett afstannande; thet wet allena then högsta GUDen, och wore thet en djerf förmätenhet at therom något undersök giöra*" (But in the end, how a planet will break into its smallest particles, and be dispersed in a fire, and return to its primary air and origin by a stop, this is only for the Lord to know, and it would be presumptuous to try to disclose it).[41]

However, in cod. 36–110, the collection of excerpts compiled around the time of the drama of creation, there are notes proving that Swedenborg knew about theories of a future world conflagration; significantly, he has conceived of the process as a return by earth, once born out of the sun, to its origin and its annihilation by solar fire.[42] He also speculates on the number of souls for which there will be room in our planetary system, no doubt in order to determine the date of Judgment Day; and in his biblical commentaries, which were written just after the drama of creation, he interprets the six days of Creation as a parallel to the history of the world, in the sixth and last age of which we have been living since the coming of Christ.[43] In his theosophic period, however, Swedenborg's conception of Judgment Day was totally transformed: from what he heard and saw, he then claimed that the Last Judgment happened in 1757, but only in the world of spirits, which does not imply any visible changes in everyday reality.[44]

At one point—regarding the human relationship to the universe at large—Swedenborg comes close to the early lamenters, who still believed in the geocentric concept of the world, through which they maintained the traditional and astronomically founded view of humanity as the center of the universe and the meaning of creation. Since in the human being, the microcosm, there is now so much sin and imperfection, similar phenomena must appear in the macrocosm, of which Adam is a reflection; as Harris has shown, this is the argument of Godfrey Goodman, the most renowned British contributor.[45] In later commentators, this opinion changes: humanity is dethroned as a ruler of nature, the universe is no longer exclusively seen from the viewpoint of human teleology, and the decadence of the part does not influence the continuity of the whole.[46]

Swedenborg's cosmology is, of course, not geocentric, but nonetheless he enthusiastically embraces the analogy between humankind and the universe, an opinion represented early in his production and reaching its climax in his theosophic works, in which the world of spirits will be populated by the souls of deceased human beings and structured on the model of the human body. As has been pointed out above, Lamm regards this conception of humanity as the primary link between Pico della Mirandola and Swedenborg; however, his reference to the great Renaissance philosopher must be amplified by recalling the long line of disciples in the tradition of microcosm doctrines.

In *The Worship and Love of God,* Swedenborg successfully avoids the difficulties his heliocentric cosmology might have provoked by making the entire heaven descend to the new-born earth *"ut ad suum Centrum"* (§17), as to its center. Thus, earth becomes the favorite child of the sun and, in accordance with eternal laws, the place on which life will grow and the first human will enter into creation, the crown of which the species is to become. By doing this, Swedenborg advanced a geocentric theory of a higher dignity: the heliocentricity of the planets and the world egg have been superseded by a more significant geocentricity, inspired by traditional microcosm ideas together with his own theological and psychological notions. This is a matter primarily for the more concrete aspects of his natural philosophy, such as it has been poetically rendered in *The Worship and Love of God*: by virtue of the doctrine of correspondence, the sun will regain its central position through its celestial correspondence—the Lord himself.

We should now summarize the status of the new-born earth in the drama of creation. In his analysis of Swedenborg's spiritual ancestry, Martin Lamm emphasized how much Swedenborg depended on contemporary Swedish learning, represented by a varied collective at the University of Uppsala of his youth.[47] However, by European standards, Swedish academic culture was provincial, at least regarding the level of ambition and its disposition to fanciful speculations. This approach, which should not be exaggerated as sometimes is the case in Lamm's brilliant book, agrees with the observations above of Swedenborg's account of paradise. The tradition to which it belongs regarding the decay of the universe was by and large outmoded by the middle of the eighteenth century, its heyday being a hundred years before, and the Rudbeckian fragments only strengthen the impression. Indeed, this assessment may be extended to include Thomas Burnet's *Telluris theoria sacra.* In spite of being widely read and held in high esteem, which gave rise to several reprints during the eighteenth century, Burnet applied methods that, already at its publication, were obsolete. The great astronomer John Flamsteed, a prominent representative of modern science, did not share the respect and admiration that Burnet's book aroused in many readers; on the contrary, Flamsteed whom Swedenborg met in 1711, is said to have claimed that he could refute Burnet "on a single sheet of paper."[48]

Viewing Swedenborg's account of paradise as merely a symptom of his obsolete way of thinking or as a belated descendant of Renaissance cosmology leaves several essential aspects out of the account. In his traditional form, Swedenborg presents a theory of the origin of the solar system—inspired by Burnet, it is true—that is new and far-sighted. Besides, the paradise account is only a part of a magnificent comprehensive view that sheds its poetic lustre on the spring of the new-born earth. In this respect, a comparison with Burnet's work is informative. *Telluris theoria sacra* is clear and well-arranged, according to the testimony of such a competent Latinist as Richard Steele formally elegant and far superior to most contemporary treatises on similar subjects. It bears witness to great erudition and audacious combinations, and it draws parallels between the evolution of nature and the will of providence in a way that must have appeared extremely attractive to Swedenborg. Burnet's view of poetry as a medium of hidden knowledge equal to philosophy and theology probably also impressed him. However, Burnet's work is primarily a theoretical treatise on the origin of the earth and its further development, without any profound theological or poetical intentions.

From the very start, the spiritualized tone of Swedenborg's drama of creation creates a completely different atmosphere. The extensive notes with their learned commentaries—formally a sign that the work is part of the *Regnum animale* series—cannot totally change the impression that the account of the new-born earth and its paradise serves a higher purpose than similar parts of the English cosmologist's treatise. The message of the unity of the cosmos, introduced in the preface, becomes more intensive through an increasing number of correspondences, when Swedenborg is hastening forward through the first ages of the earth to reach the true goal as soon as possible—the first human beings and their spiritual upbringing, the central point of the book. The ideas hitherto discussed take up only a small part of the drama of creation, even though they are of vital importance to attaching the microcosm to the universe.

Thus, *The Worship and Love of God* was meant to be a much more independent and far-reaching work than Burnet's treatise; but in spite of that, Swedenborg obviously got the basis of his cosmology and his notion of paradise from Burnet, although for the most part indirectly, because the drama of creation is chiefly a summary of his previous conjectures on the subject. *Telluris theoria sacra* seems to have been a source of inspiration to such a degree that one might be tempted to assume a connection to the annotation in the *Dream Diary* for October 26 and 27, 1744: "*detta betyder alt det arbete jag nu för hender tager i Gudz namn, frammanför de cultu Dei, på sidan de amore, och at jag intet bör taga af annars kram, vtan mitt"* (This refers to all the work I now enter upon in the name of God, first of all *de cultu Dei*, on the side *de amore*, and that I should not draw upon others' notions, but of mine).[49] This refers to the composition of the present work; contrary to the recently published parts of *Regnum animale*, this book is not to be built on a lot of quotations from other writers, nor to contain voluminous amounts of references, as did *Principia*. Swedenborg conformed to the directions of the dream vision. Still, he may have had such a basic source as Burnet in mind; in any case, this is a more probable explanation than that the sentences refer to Milton's *Paradise Lost*, as proposed by Sigstedt.[50] As far as we have hitherto followed Swedenborg's drama of creation, there is no reason to assume any reading of Milton. But if Swedenborg did think of Burnet's book, it was not only because of its own ideas but also for its sample of traditional opinions, which *Telluris theoria sacra* presents as a summary and adaptation of a material largely familiar to the time and to Swedenborg himself: a résumé of essential elements in the intellectual environment, out of which *The Worship and Love of God* viewed as a cosmogony emerged.

## The Birth of the Vegetable Kingdom and the Force of Life

The plants that grow out of the new-born soil vary in forms and colors, and they are also divided into annual and perennial species. All of them bring forth new seeds according to their purpose, which they let fall into the bosom of the earth and cover with their own leaves to procreate new offspring. However, some of them rise again themselves in a long series:

> *Alii foetus aliter; vel enim ex stirpe suâ iterum & denuo excitati, flores suos, longa serie renovabant; vel ex cinere suo seipsos resuscitabant; succus enim, quem a matre extractum in suas venas diffundebant, non nisi quam ex meris principiis gravidus, & sic ex innumerabilibus sui inchoamentis faecundus erat.*
>
> (Other offspring were produced in different ways. They might be woken into existence from their own rootstock again and again and so repeat their flowers in a lengthy series. Or they might revive themselves from their own remains: the sap they drew from their mother and diffused into their own veins was heavily laden with pure elements, and so was teeming with uncountable incipient forms of the plants themselves.) §19

This statement recalls a passage in *Oeconomia regni animalis*, where a similar representation illustrates the immortality of the human soul:

*Id ut testatum in mundo etiam infimo & crassiori comperimus;
nam beneficio similis perfectionis in aethere tertii ordinis, &
similitudinis inter partes, post cineres suos etiam arte resusci-
tantur inanimata, ut plantae, flores, formae arboreae, in ipsissi-
mam suam effigiem, tanquam ex quodam amore entium ipsum
compositum constituentium.*

(We regard this as testified also in the lower and coarser
world; for by means of a similar perfection in the ether of the
third order and of the similarity between the parts, inanimate
things are resuscitated out of their ashes, even artificially, as
plants, flowers, forms of trees, to their own images, as if there
was a kind of love in the substances which constitute the
unity.)[51]

This association with the *Oeconomia* reflects the new basis on which the
description of organic life in the drama of creation is founded. The cosmological motives could be studied in the light of the *Principia rerum naturalium*, but for the biological ones the answers must be searched in later
productions, from the *Oeconomia* to the *Regnum animale*.

As was previously pointed out, this does not mean that a totally new
phase started in 1734. On the contrary, the macrocosmic philosophy of
*Principia* is a manifest forerunner of the microcosmic one. This becomes
clear in the composition of the drama of creation, in which the introductory
cosmological parts have been intimately connected to the following biological ones by correspondences and consistent symbols, but what happens
there is only an artistic summary of a basic pattern in Swedenborg's systematic thinking. This has been somewhat obscured in Lamm's opinion of the
intellectual background of *Oeconomia* and subsequent works:

*Då Swedenborg öfvergaf de matematiskt-mekaniska studierna
för de zoologiskt-medicinska, hade han faktiskt öfvergått från
ett område, där den exakta forskningen vunnit fast fot, till ett,
där lösa hugskott och fantasier ännu ostördt frodades och där
en mängd aristotelisk skolastik och medeltida magi ännu
förkunnades under vetenskapens namn.*

(When Swedenborg abandoned his mathematical and mechanical pursuits to dedicate himself to medical and zoological
studies, he in effect abandoned a field where exact science had
advanced considerably for one where the most extravagant and
most fanciful theories still flourished in complete freedom and
in which a fully Aristotelian scholasticism and medieval medical
magic were still honored in the name of science.)[52]

In the light of the inquiries above, according to which the work of Thomas
Burnet appeared to be most influential, such a distribution of more or less

"scientific" sources seems to be too simplistic. Among the authors quoted in *Oeconomia*, there are quite a few of the men of distinction in the early history of modern biology.[53] In my view, the continuity and the early determined goal of Swedenborg's thinking should be emphasized instead. He often selects the boldest system-builders and even the most daring hypotheses of more "scientific" predecessors, for example, his fascination with the doctrine of intuition and the universal language of the angels in Locke's work, as observed above.

Swedenborg's conjectures on the vital forces are a clear illustration of that. The mother plants infuse their own nature or soul into the seeds produced by the first-born herbs; here Swedenborg comments, mentioning these vital forces:

> *Prima Vis genitrix seu plastica penitus ipsis seminibus faetuum vegetabilium innata, Animae assimilanda est; . . . Qualis vero ipsa haec Vis seminalis sit, non cognoscitur nisi ex enucleatis Formis prioris naturae, tam quae vires referunt activas, quam quae passivas, tum etiam quomodo Solares radii ad eas copulandas operantur; quod pervastum nimis foret, jam ab ultimis ad prima evolvere.*
>
> (The primary creative or formative force that is deeply innate in seeds that come from the offspring of plants must be compared to a soul. . . . However, what this force in seeds is like cannot be understood without an explanation of the forms nature took beforehand, both those that relate to active forces and those that relate to passive forces, and then too of the way the solar rays work to join them, which would be far too broad a topic to explain now from beginning to end.) §20, note m

Such an evasive attitude is conspicuous in a writer who normally does not hesitate to make digressions, but it may be explained by the fact that he had studied the vital force extensively in *Oeconomia* and that the atmosphere of sincere devotion in the drama of creation reduces the interest of this technical issue. But Swedenborg did not refrain completely from introducing the *vires seminales* in his system. The commentary in *The Worship and Love of God* goes back to a passage in *Oeconomia*, where it is said *inter alia*:

> *Est quaedam Substantia aut Vis formatrix, quae a primo puncto vivente ducit stamen, & ductum usque ad ultimum vitae continuat: quae aliis vocatur Vis plastica, Archaeus, & nonnullis simpliciter natura agens, sed intelligibile magis, uti reor, si illa, respective ad formationis opus, audiat vis aut substantia formatrix . . . ita in animalculis minimis & imperfectis; ita in majoribus; ita in homine aut perfectissimis.*

(There is a certain formative substance or power that draws a file from the first living point up to the highest level of life. Some call it *vis plastica*, or *Archeus*, others simply acting nature, but I think that it will be easier to understand if it is called the formative force or substance with respect to its generative function. . . . In such a way it is active in the smallest and most imperfect animals, in bigger ones, and in man or the most perfect ones.)[54]

However, the innermost quality of this force, which has been applied to the animal kingdom in *Oeconomia*, cannot be captured in words because it lies above the sphere of ordinary language. To be more exact requires a philosophical language of universals.

Thus, an investigation of the *vis genitrix* would lead very far, and there could be no room for it in *The Worship and Love of God*. However, the terminology that Swedenborg referred to in both texts is of interest to the study of sources. After quoting the statement of *Oeconomia*, Lamm noted that Paracelsus and Jan Baptista van Helmont called the natural force *archeus*, while the term *vis plastica* was used by the Cambridge Platonists Ralph Cudworth and Henry More. Lamm found that Swedenborg's terminology comes closest to that of Helmont.[55] Clearly, Swedenborg knew of these terms and their meaning in the mystical philosophy of nature, but that does not mean that he studied it profoundly. On the contrary, it was probably common knowledge at the time, particularly because of its far-reaching theological consequences. This can be illustrated by an example of Swedenborg's reading, from around the same time as he was writing the *Oeconomia*, in any case earlier than the drama of creation.

In the important preface to his theodicy, from which Swedenborg made many excerpts in the 1739 edition, Leibniz discusses Cudworth's *vis plastica* in seeds and eggs. It is a question of the generation of living creatures, an argument that will end in the conception of God. Recapitulating what he had published in learned journals in the beginning of the eighteenth century, Gottfried Wilhelm Leibniz (1646–1716) declares that one does not need to resort to any formative forces but that the birth of organisms can be accounted for within a mechanistic system, provided that there exists a preformation in seeds and eggs, a formation that has its origin in the Creator himself: "*Il n'y a point de chaos dans l'interieur des choses, & l'organisme est par tout dans une matiere dont la disposition vient de Dieu*" (There is no chaos in the interior of things, and the organism exists everywhere in matter, the arrangement of which comes from God).[56]

The doctrine of preformation, with which Leibniz agrees and which had its greatest significance as an explanation of humanity's procreation, gained support until 1720, especially among the microscopists.[57] It has a long history with wide ramifications: some scholars assumed connections between the doctrine that the organism-to-be exists in the egg or the sperm as an infinitesimal image of its mature shape and the *spermatikos logos* concept of the Stoics, through the agency of, among others, Augustine but also the Neoplatonic emanation doctrine of the Cabbala, traces of which have been found in van Helmont, Leibniz, and others.[58] As Jan Swammerdam (1637–1680) noted, the theological advantage of the preformation doctrine is that it offers a simple explanation for the concept of original sin: according to him, all humankind existed in this form in the genitals of the first human couple.[59]

In *Oeconomia*, Swedenborg compares the state of the egg immediately after the conception with chaos and rejects the idea that there should be an infinitesimal image of the mature organism, which would then expand (I, §§248–249). That might mean that Swedenborg subscribed to an opposing doctrine, the so-called epigenesis theory, which was first presented by Aristotle and later held by René Descartes (1596–1650), William Harvey (1578–1657), and others in different versions.[60] But neither in Swedenborg's own text nor in his selection of authorities does one meet any explicit references to epigenesis; on the contrary, Harvey appears at the side of preformationists like Marcello Malpighi (1628–1694) and others.[61] In this respect, he seems comparable to theorists like Georg Ernst Stahl (1660–1734), in whom the mechanistic epigenesis of Descartes was transformed into a vitalistic one and the dividing lines between the two theories virtually erased.[62]

But more important than the embryologically technical issue is the total system of which it is a part. In *Oeconomia*, the intention is to achieve a synthesis, a universal model, rather than to solve minor problems. To illustrate, we continue our examination of the preface of Leibniz's theodicy: "*Comme pour expliquer cette merveille de la formation des animaux, je me servois d'une harmonie préétablie, c'est-à-dire du même moyen dont je m'étois servi pour expliquer une autre merveille, qui est la correspondance de l'Ame avec le Corps, en quoi je faisois voir l'uniformité & la fecondité des principes que j'avois employez*" (To explain the miracle of the formation of animals, I made use of a pre-established harmony, that is to say, the same method I used to explain another miracle, namely, the correspondence between soul and body, by which I proved the unity and fertility of the principles that I had applied).[63] The concordance could hardly be more complete: Swedenborg also uses a system important for solving the problem of commerce between soul and body. Furthermore, he named it after Leibniz's *harmonia praestabilita*, although with a significant attributive modulation. The formative force is leading beyond itself; and, in order to fairly assess it, we will linger for a moment on the main ideas of *Oeconomia*.[64]

The physiological studies in this work start with the blood, and by doing so, Swedenborg attaches them to the physical investigations in *Principia*, as is explicitly indicated in the important preface:

*Ex his facile intelligitur, quas simul scientias ponit unica Sangui-nis: scilicet, omnem Anatomicam, Medicam, Chymicam & Physicam: Imo etiam Physiologicam; nam patitur animus se-cundum statum Sanguinis, & Sanguis agitur secundum pathe-mata animi: Verbo, nullam non, quae versatur circa substantias mundi & vires Naturae. Idcirco ultimo seu non nisi perfectis regnis exstitisse Homo; & mundus & natura se in eo concen-travisse, videtur; ut ex illo tanquam ex microcosmo totum suum universum ab ultimo fine ad primum comtemplari potuisset.*

(From this it can be easily understood which disciplines can be included in the single one of the blood: namely, the whole of anatomy, medicine, chemistry, and physics, finally also physiol-ogy; for the animus is influenced by the state of the blood, and the blood is pushed by the passions of the animus. In a word, it concerns every branch of science that deals with the substances of the world and the forces of nature. Therefore man came into existence only after the kingdoms of nature had been accom-plished, and the world and nature seem to have concentrated themselves in him so that the whole universe could be contem-plated from its beginning to its end in him as in a microcosm.)[65]

The basic ideas are most clearly presented in the third chapter, the title of which, *"De formatione pulli in ovo"* (On the formation of the chicken in the egg), is typical of the time as well as of the genre. Here is introduced the formative force that determines the development of organisms from their first living point to their final stage; the idea fulfils the concept of power that is to be found in the mathematical point in *Principia* and that scholars have regarded as significant for the change of perspective between that work and *Oeconomia*.[66] Swedenborg combines this *vis formatrix* with a form concept clearly inspired by Aristotle, which had also been part of the philosophy of *Principia* but the more explicit teleological consequences of which have now been brought into focus: purpose, or utility, become value-laden words, themes that will continuously reappear later in *The Worship and Love of God* as a reminder of the fact that, in spite of all its poetic qualities, we are still close to Leibniz and in the middle of the utili-tarian Age of Reason.[67]

The teleologically determined connection, which arises in Swedenborg's hierarchy of organisms, finds its specific expression in the doctrine of series and degrees. In a more detailed form, it was first presented in the final part of the first *Oeconomia* volume, *"Introductio ad Psychologiam Ratio-nalem"* (Introduction to Rational Psychology), a significant location, since it indicates that the theory emerged from his attempts to solve the problem of psychophysical interaction. *"Per Serierum & Graduum Doctri-nam intelligimus illam, quae docet modum, quem natura in rerum suarum*

*Subordinatione & Coordinatione observat, & quem sibi in agendo obser-*
*vandum praescripsit"* (By the doctrine of series and degrees, we understand
the doctrine that teaches us the way that nature follows in subordinating
and coordinating things and that she has laid down for herself in acting).[68]
These degrees, which are not relative but distinct links in the chain of the
universe, constitute coherent series, of which there are several types, some
higher and some lower. The most universal series is the cosmos itself,
which contains all the subordinate ones; to support this, Swedenborg refers
in the *Oeconomia* §584 to the presentation on monadism by Christian
Wolff (1679–1754).

There are six major series of subordination, three higher ones compris-
ing the surrounding space and three lower series belonging to the earth and
constituting its three kingdoms of minerals, plants, and animals; their level
of perfection is occupied by humankind. This pattern comes very close not
only to the cosmological scheme in *Principia* but also to the numerical
structure of the hexaemera; undoubtedly, the six days of Creation are behind the number of series, and here you may already find a sketchy sub-
suming of cosmological, geological, and biological phenomena under a
common heading, which will come back in *The Worship and Love of God*
with its hexaemeral distribution of scenes. While its specific character did
not allow any detailed parallels between the six series and the scenes, there
is a manifest connection.[69]

The greater series also has subordinate ones down to the lowest organisms, the only exception being the first substance of nature. Consequently,
all knowledge of nature will depend on an understanding of series and degrees. But this, in turn, can be achieved only by analogy with the universe
as a whole; it is impossible to get a clear picture from the evidence of the
senses, although conjectures have to be founded on experience, here as well
as in *Principia*. The first substance of each series depends on the first substance of nature; this must be regarded as a development of the mathematical point of *Principia*, loaded with *conatus*. Some writers call these first
substances of the series *monads*, while others refer to them as *elements*; but
Swedenborg cannot accept the idea of their absolute simplicity (*Oecono-*
*mia* §592). Here he enters into a rather modest argument with monadism;
he seems to have tried to conceal his criticism by referring to Wolff's *Cos-*
*mologia* as a conclusion, but nevertheless his reservation is significant:

> *Quare si substantia prima cujusvis seriei assumatur ut qua exis-*
> *tentiam a prima mundi dependens, tunc secundum Clar: Woll-*
> *fium, "Status cujuslibet elementi, quilibet relationem ad*
> *mundum integrum involvit. Quod in elementis & substantiis*
> *simplicibus contineantur rationes ultimae eorum, quae in rebus*
> *materialibus continentur. Quod nexus rerum materialium a*

*nexu elementorum pendeat. Quod a punctis Zenonicis, interque
se similibus extensum oriri nequeat.*" (*Oeconomia* I, §592)

(If therefore the existence of the first substance of each series
is supposed to depend on the first substance of the world, then
according to the famous Wolff, the state of every element, whatever it may be, involves a relation to the world as a whole. In
the elements and the simple substances, the final causes of those
elements, which the material things contain, are included. The
connection between the material things depends on that of the
elements. From Zeno's points or similar ones, nothing extended
can emerge.)[70]

What is declared impossible in this passage happens in *Principia*; one may
speculate that the reason Swedenborg remains silent about this change is a
desire to attach himself as much as possible to the famous Leibniz and
Wolff, suppressing differences of opinion. Nonetheless, Swedenborg does
not allow the first substances of the series, as in monadism, to be created
directly from infinity but through the agency of the simple substance of nature. One reason for this is the theological consequence: otherwise the Creator himself would be responsible for the imperfections in existence. This
argument, full of future implications, demonstrates that the philosophical
structure of *Principia* is still valid.

The first substance of the series is now creating and determining the development of the whole series and, consequently, is the *vis formatrix* of the
series. Out of this force, complex substances are formed that are causally
related to each other, so it follows that everything in nature belongs to a series. With a clear reference to Leibniz and Wolff, Swedenborg calls this intensely interconnected system *harmonia constabilita*; and the more
distinctly the differences between complex and simple substances appear,
the more perfect this harmony becomes, a veritable *varietas harmonica*
(*Oeconomia* §593).

There is a moment of motion and successive growth in the attribute *constabilita* that is missing in the preestablished structure of monads; but
Swedenborg also wants to see the same *varietas harmonica*, which emerges
out of the activities of the formative substances in their respective series, in
the simple substance of nature, once again referring to Wolff. Unfortunately, imprecise language does not enable him to describe it. Thus, he
strives to connect himself indirectly to monadism: the perfect harmony already exists *in nuce* in the simple substance of nature, but it will be realized
by a successive development in the system of series and degrees. After having mobilized a number of ancient authorities, Swedenborg then draws the
expected conclusion: both macrocosm and microcosm are in a state of perfect harmonic variation, although the final proof can only be given in a
philosophical language of universals. His doctrine of series and degrees

should be seen as a first step towards such a language, an idea that will come back in the collection of excerpts cod. 36–110 (§§650–651).[71]

Lamm interprets Swedenborg's doctrine of series and degrees as a late application of Aristotle's idea of the hierarchy of organisms.[72] This is a well-founded and important observation, but it has to be pointed out that the closest source of inspiration is Leibniz-Wolff rationalism, which Swedenborg studied exhaustively during the years after the publication of *Principia*; as the excerpts show, he also took a great interest in Augustine's psychological doctrine of degrees in *De quantitate animae*.[73] He obviously aimed at constructing a philosophical system of the rationalistic character, which made Wolff so admired by his contemporaries, but a mediating and more dynamic one. This system was to include quite a few elements from different sources, and there were conspicuously many ancient philosophers, headed by Aristotle, among those who were cited. The reason is the same as it was in *Principia* and as it will be in *The Worship and Love of God*: the ancients lived closer to the golden age of truth (*Oeconomia* §605). He used the same method in cod. 36–110 when taking notes from Aristotle, the Neoplatonic *Theology of Aristotle*, and Leibniz under the proper headings; from the great German, he wrote down some speculations about the philosophical language of universals.[74]

This is the background of the short note on *vires seminales* among the references in *The Worship and Love of God*. The terminology proves that Swedenborg knew of the conjectures on the origin of organisms in the philosophy of nature, presented by predecessors like Paracelsus, van Helmont, Johann Marcus Marci von Kronland (1595–1667), Cudworth, Stahl, Andreas Rüdiger (1673–1731), and many others. This is not essential, nor is the battle between preformation and epigenesis in contemporary biology, which can also be traced in the short note. The context in which the formative forces appear for the first time makes it clear that Swedenborg is not interested in the technical issue but in its consequences for the philosophy of life at large; in this respect, he agrees completely with Leibniz. The crucial point is that the formative forces go back to the simple substance of nature and from it to the Creator himself. Thus, they become instruments for God's plan of the Creation, and with their assistance, this plan will be successively realized in a *varietas harmonica*, which existed as a kind of preformed prototype in the simple substance.[75] In this way, Swedenborg's outlook was more dynamic than that of Leibniz, and it was also linked more strongly to the biology of his day, as he had got to know it from quite a few of the masters in the field. Still, Swedenborg and Leibniz are very much alike.

Swedenborg never succeeded in constructing the philosophical language of universals that was required to describe the *vires seminales*, but as was pointed out above, he looked upon his doctrine of correspondences as a substitute for it. Lamm observed the connection between this doctrine and the idea of a *vis formatrix*. In this force, he identifies a correspondence to the *logoi*, with which the demiurg is forming matter according to Plotinus, and via this link he believes that other Neoplatonic elements invaded Swedenborg's thinking with the doctrine of correspondence as a result: "*Den kraft, som formar stoffet, är i sin tur endast ett stoff för den verkliga formen, en spegelbild af tingets urbild i den intelligibla världen*" (The formative force of matter is itself only stuff for the real form; in the intelligible world, it is a mere reflection of the archetype).[76]

Considering what has been demonstrated above of the growth of the doctrine of correspondence and the sources of the idea of a *vis formatrix*, I question whether Lamm exaggerated the direct influence of Platonism. Both correspondences and formative forces are attempts at solving problems, which were formulated by Leibniz and Wolff, and it seems more appropriate to look upon the Neoplatonic elements, which no doubt exist, as a result of Swedenborg's intense reading of Leibniz; the so-called *Theology of Aristotle* is not significantly present in Swedenborg's writings until after 1740, when he had studied *Tentamina theodicaeae* thoroughly. A reference to the Neoplatonic background of Leibniz's preformation theories, which scholars have elucidated, reinforces the impression. It also accords with Swedenborg's general view of antiquity: he sought direct support from the ancients after they had been brought in focus for him by his study of leading moderns.

It will be necessary to return to the question of Leibniz and Neoplatonism in the theological parts below. However, it is characteristic that the author of the *Tentamina theodicaeae* appears already when the period of transition is just beginning, a period that will end with the drama of creation. Among many other things, *The Worship and Love of God* is also a theodicy, and some essential parts of that theme have been perceived in the little note on the seminal forces. Their full significance will appear when we move on to the birth of higher organisms.

# 4

᠅

# LIVING CREATURES IN PARADISE
## (§§22–28)

The previous section on paradise closes with a *theatrum mundi* metaphor, as does each scene in this drama. As an immediate echo of this metaphor, the introductory line of the third section describes how the earth lay open in its splendor like a stage, on which everything was set for the entrance of the actors. Only one prerequisite was missing: life. By the creation of the vegetable kingdom, nature, emanating from the sun, had exhausted its powers and completed its final circle. After its birth out of the great world egg, nature first created the three atmospheres, of which the air was the last; and then nature combined these active forces with the passive ones of the earth. In this way, new forms were born; enclosed in seeds corresponding to the world egg, they in turn were to become the life-giving principles of new fetuses. But these were hatched in inverted order, as appears from the series of flowers, bushes, and trees, and thereby the circle was closed (§22, note o).

Nature's emanation from the sun represents the crust of the earth in a more restricted sense, the mineral kingdom, the branch that exhausted its powers in creating the vegetable kingdom. Now the earth ceases to bring forth new seeds of its great ovary, so that it may receive and tend what was sowed by its own offspring. In obedience to eternal laws, a new and quite different generation was to sprout from the vegetable kingdom, *"Regnum . . . ex solis Animatis consistens"* (§23, a kingdom consisting only of living creatures). Faithful to his basic views, the author lets life develop successively according to its conditions, which had been established in the vegetable kingdom. From eternity, all flowers, bushes, and trees were given a purpose beyond themselves, a principle of use encoded in the depth of every specimen. From this scene onwards, the teleological keynote, which had been struck in the introduction of the work, will be sounding at increasing strength. Every plant yearns to create from itself new wombs for living creatures: the process is described as instinctive, which is accounted for by the relations between two principles that now stand out more and more manifestly. They are the natural principle, in itself dead and originating from the natural sun, and the spiritual one, alive and generated by the fountain of life, the spiritual sun, which is the Lord himself (§24, note q).

At first, flowers gave birth to microscopic offspring, caterpillars and earthworms, which constitute a transition between the two kingdoms. They too contain a hidden purpose, the power of which will transform them into butterflies and various species of insects, and this double birth gives an excellent illustration of the successive development (§25). Swedenborg's conviction that all insects serve a fixed purpose, even if still not discovered by our imperfect senses, appears to reflect contemporary enthusiasm about the potential of microscope studies.

But the world of insects is only a glimpse of life, an ignoble genus, even though paradise's blazing color becomes more intense by its birth, aglow with the reflection of life. The next phase is the birth of birds; just as the insects were created by the flowers of the ground, the arbutus bushes and the low-rise groves give birth to this higher species. Thus, the animal kingdom comes forth in exactly the same order as had the lower species. After the first generation was born, the thickets ceased carrying eggs, for now the birds could produce their offspring themselves. To the subsistence of the genus of birds, both the fruits of the earth and the countless bugs were assigned, the increase of which would be kept within limits in this way: "*Ita universalis Providentia in singularissimis efficienda & effecta dirigebat (s), ut sicut una causa ab alterâ in alteram, etiam usus ab uno in alterum, ex lege constante & aeternâ, flueret*" (This was the way universal providence was directing what was effected and what remained to be effected—so that just as one cause flowed from another into still another, each useful purpose could arise from one and flow into another, by a constant and eternal law) (§26).

The structure of this second scene parallels that of the first one, not only in the number of sections, which is identical, but also in the composition at large. An essential detail is found at exactly the same place in both scenes, certainly not by chance but by purpose emphasizing the general thesis of the close connection between the vegetable and animal kingdoms. This passage describes the beauty of the newborn genus of birds, a text impressive for the symbolics of the doctrine of correspondence:

> *Haec decore superba proles, caelestibus suis & flammeis coloribus totum & aerem & orbem collustrabat; erant enim Species, quae in vertice suo pro cristâ coronas quasi gemmis distinctas, ac diademate praecinctas, quae circum collum monilia cum suis pretiis, in caudis & talaribus sidera, auroras, & futuras irides, quaeque in suis remigiis ignes Solis in purpuram*

*versos, gestabant; quaedam etiam ipsum Paradisum, aut ali-*
*quam ejus pompam, pennis suis designabant.*

(This offspring, so proud of their beauty, lit up all the air and
the earth with blazing, celestial colors. Some species had what
looked like crowns on their heads instead of crests, set off with
gems and ringed with jewelled bands; some wore costly neck-
laces around their necks, and on their tails and ankles had stars,
sunrises, and the rainbows to come; and some wore purple sun-
fire in the oarage of their wings. The feathers of others even depicted paradise itself, or a part of its spectacular scenery.) §26

When the jubilant choir of birds climbs toward the rosy dawn of creation,
a pattern of colors and shapes will thus be formed as an aerial correspondence of the symbolic tapestry of flowers on the ground (§19). The gem
metaphors used here will return in a still more sublime context later, when
the soul and its abode are depicted (§§51 and 67). The flight of the swift-
winged birds in the mild air of spring may be a premonition of the redemption of the souls, as so often in religious symbolics.

Finally, quadrupeds enter this splendor, although not until the groves
had brought forth their birds, so that their nutrients should not be consumed or downtrodden. The higher animals are born in the same manner
by egg-carrying forests, but these are of a more sublime character. They un-
fold their innermost wombs, fertilize the small eggs that hang down from
the branches with semen, and lower them then into beds of flowers and
plants. Here the eggs wrap themselves up in fetal membranes, and the door
is sealed by a placenta; the sap that was purified in it is sucked through
small veins to the liver for further purification, and then it is united with
the blood as lympha and transported to the heart and the brain (§27).
Thus, the trees act as mothers for the mammals, and Swedenborg gives an
account of their function with abundant embryological details that reminds
the reader of his previous biological works.

This matter-of-fact style may appear incompatible to the rich symbolics
in the description of the beauty of the birds, but it is a tension that characterizes the entire drama of creation. From a modern point of view, it would
be regarded as its major aesthetic deficiency. However, at least on this
stage, it is hardly a matter of inability and a defective sense of style. On the
contrary, Swedenborg is here describing in minute detail what later will
happen also to the first man (§33ff). In that account, he does not stay at
the biological level, but instead focuses on the activities of the soul in the
egg, of which Adam will be born. Much of what appears to be digressions
or excessive exactitude may derive from a desire to present a comprehensive view later on. Of course, this does not eliminate the difficulties for a
modern reader, but it calls for caution in making assessments.

As living emblems, most of the animals born of trees carry branch-like horns bearing witness of their origin; in the wandering herds of the woods and fields, we are thus constantly reminded of the generative power of the forests of the ancient dream of the Golden Age and of the profound continuity of existence that Swedenborg learned to honor in Aristotle and Leibniz.[1] But the animals have even more to tell. In all of them, the nature of their senses is reflected in their bodies, and altogether they create a variable assembly of conflicting temperaments; there was even a kind of inherent social order here in that the warning signs of the senses made it possible for everyone to read the disposition and intentions of the others on their facial features. No creature knew its destiny yet: the horse did not know that a bridle would be put into its mouth and a saddle on its back, nor did the sheep imagine that its fleece would be cut and used for clothes. Nonetheless, the purpose of each animal had been set from eternity. Even the banks and depths of the rivers contribute to making this harmony perfect, as they give birth to their offspring in the same order as the *terra firma*.

The conclusion of the section completes the hierarchy of the organic stages, which is the basic theme of the entire chapter. Here the author points out that every individual is a picture of all its descendants and that this in a way corresponds to the globe, which in turn reflects the world egg; thus, the birth of animal life is part of an all-embracing universal context. The perspective is finally broadened to a song of praise of the universal divine intellect in which everything existed before the beginning of time. With this jubilant chord, so well attuned to the eponymous basic idea of the entire work and representing a natural culmination of the organic hierarchy, the scene closes. The cheerful play of animals forms a final vignette.

Of course, the account of the origin of the animal kingdom must be studied in further details. With reference to the conclusion, even the providential creed, the outlines of which have been presented here, should now be discussed as a background to the more detailed theological exposition in the consecutive scenes.

# The Origin of the Animal Kingdom

In the series of which the animal kingdom is an essential part, concepts of seeds and eggs constitute the strongest connections. The plants were born out of their seeds in the earth's crust, and the leaves of herbs and trees swelled out to ovaries enclosing the eggs, out of which the first individuals of the different species were born; the innermost purpose of the seed had fertilized it (§25). Obviously, Swedenborg's description must not be perceived as a biological theory of the origin of life on earth; it is a symbolic fable primarily devoted to praising the power and the glory of the Lord. Still, his exposition is as closely linked to the scientific climate of the age as it is in the cosmological parts.

Stroh employed the term "spontaneous generation" to define Sweden-borg's conception of the origin of the vegetable kingdom.[2] As Lamm noticed, spontaneous generation (*generatio spontanea sive aequivoca*) is also mentioned in a previous outline of a study of the intercourse between the soul and the body, and as applied to the lowest species, even in the theosophic writings. In this outline, one finds, for example, the frequent al-legation that a carrion spontaneously gives birth to myriads of new ani-mals.[3] The hypothesis of spontaneous generation has certainly played a significant role in the history of biology. The term applies to the idea that living creatures would by themselves be born in and by lifeless matter. This theory can be followed from antiquity far into the nineteenth century, and it is still alive as an explanation of the origin of life on earth, partly as an alternative to the so-called panspermi hypothesis. In an article on sponta-neous generation, Sten Lindroth argued that there is a dividing line in the development of the doctrine occurring around the middle of the seven-teenth century, when its primitive variants had been definitely disproved; yet, after that time, it was revived in more sophisticated versions.[4]

In biological works written in the century before 1650, Aristotle held a totally dominant position because of the general neoscholastic trends of the Reformation era; as a consequence of his authority, the theory of sponta-neous generation of lower animals attracted great attention, particularly in combination with the concepts of form and matter in Aristotelian meta-physics. According to Aristotle, all organisms—indeed, all things—consist of form and matter; in other words, matter is potential form, which has to be given an actual existence by unifying itself with a finite form in order to produce an organism. In a biological context, this implies that the problem of the origin of forms becomes a central issue for those who believe in spontaneous generation. As Lindroth points out, this problem could be solved in a Platonic setting by presupposing an emanation of forms from the lowest celestial sphere, when new bodies were created (as, for example, in Avicenna [980–1037] and his later followers) or, more often at the time, by having the form emerge out of matter by means of some intermediary cause, for example, the solar heat that has such importance for the birth of the Swedenborgian organisms. This is a variant represented, for example, by Averroës (1126–1198) and his numerous disciples.[5]

Several authors tried to find an explanation on a third track, however, by ascribing to the form a perpetually actual existence in matter. According to this theory, a form can arise only from another form, which according to the well-known scholar Daniel Sennert (1572–1637) meant that a multi-tude of subordinate forms, which had been previously hidden under the specific form of the organism, would be released at the death of that organ-ism: "*Överallt finnas i naturen kringspridda dylika befriade former eller frön—semina eller åtminstone semini analoga—som bara vänta på ett läg-ligt tillfälle för att träda i organismbildande verksamhet*" (Everywhere in nature such released forms or seeds are scattered—semen or at least analogies of semen—which are only waiting for the right time to start producing new organisms).[6] But this implies that no spontaneous generation can occur out of lifeless matter, as Lindroth also pointed out: all generation requires seeds of life from previous organisms.[7]

Similar seminal ideas are represented in many contemporary quarters. With respect to Swedenborg, Athanasius Kircher's paracelsistic development of the seminal hypothesis seems to deserve some attention.[8] Controversial but nonetheless often referred to, Kircher believed that God at the beginning of time had inserted a seminal force in chaos, which since then appears both in magnetic and formative shape in matter; together with the bodies of dead organisms, it can generate new individuals. There are several references to Kircher's studies of magnetism in Swedenborg's *Principia*, although most often in a critical tone; and in *Regnum animale,* there are comparisons between magnetism and the attractive forces in the human body, which are part of the same synthetic ambitions as in Kircher.[9]

But other masters had a greater impact. During his student years in Uppsala, Swedenborg was probably exposed to ideas of spontaneous generation going back to Descartes, the philosopher who had inspired young Emanuel Swedberg more than anyone else; Lindroth has observed that the Cartesian doctrine of a mechanically working spontaneous generation was taught by Olof Rudbeck Jr., among others.[10] The basic structure of Swedenborg's presentation can already be found in Descartes. In his *Principia Philosophiae,* Descartes first made a general reservation as a good Catholic's concession to his church that his hypotheses of the origin of the universe were to be seen as expressing what he *would have* believed if the dogma of creation had not given an absolutely true account of what really happened. After establishing his alibi, he proposes that one should look upon our world as a result of a development out of seeds: everything had emerged from these, in a series from the stars in the firmament to the lowest organisms. Even humankind would have been part of this series, the philosopher maintains, if *fides Christiana,* our Christian creed, did not teach us differently.[11] In all its systematical rigidity, this presages the way of thinking in Swedenborg's drama of creation, although its author did not let any dogmatic misgivings prevent him from making the most of the theme in a poetic fable. Even concerning biology, we must keep in mind Descartes' decisive influence on Swedenborg's general thinking, an impact that stayed active in his studies of more recent authorities.

In the mid-seventeenth century, the continental debate on the generation problems was altered. In his *Exercitationes de generatione animalium,* the great William Harvey had formulated the thesis that Carl von Linné (1707–1778) called "the first article of faith in natural history" in his famous speech on insects in 1739—*omne vivum ex ovo* (everything alive comes from an egg). According to Harvey, the thesis applied also to animals and human beings, but he did not grasp the full implications of it. On the contrary, with regard to lower animals, he embraced a belief in spontaneous generation of the scholastic type, which let forms exist potentially in matter.[12] However, Harvey's theory could serve as a starting point for a more modern conception of the nature of generation, and soon such an opinion appeared, supported by "*det beviskraftigaste av alla argument, experimentet, den moderna vetenskapens triumferande medel*" (the most powerful of all arguments, the experiment, the triumphant instrument of modern science).[13] Above all, the Italian Francesco Redi (1626–1697) and the Dutch microscopists Antony Swammerdam and Anton van Leeuwenhoek (1632–1723) are to be given credit for the new outlook, the progress of which to Sweden Lindroth has studied in his dissertations. These biologists completely dismissed the idea of spontaneous generation, maintaining that birth can only be accomplished from existing life through different kinds of intervention by parents.

Among the extensive references in *Oeconomia* and *Regnum animale*, several works by these modern scientists are cited. Harvey is frequently quoted, once from his work on the generation of animals, as are Leeuwenhoek and Swammerdam.[14] In the third chapter of *Oeconomia*, entitled *De formatione pulli in ovo* and one of the most significant parts of the book, one of the favorite themes of the modern biology—the formation of the chicken in the egg—is treated at length, as was already noted above. Thus, Swedenborg was well informed about the recent refutations of the doctrine of spontaneous generation, and the origin of the genera in his drama of creation must obviously be sought in some kind of egg or seed: *omne vivum ex ovo*.

Despite this, one cannot link Swedenborg's account of the origin of life and the outlook of modern biology without considerable qualifications: on the contrary, the drama of creation stands out as a compound of old and new thoughts also in this respect. The role played by the vegetable kingdom in the birth of organisms is primarily determined by the doctrine of series and degrees and its successive continuity. However, it is difficult to disregard completely the fantastic ideas of how certain animals could be generated by trees, an idea that appeared quite frequently in older biological literature.[15] The best-known story tells about the Scottish barnacles, which was an article of faith so highly valued that a bibliographical list of relevant works would be quite comprehensive. Spegel has given a vivid presentation of the strange notion in his hexaemeron *Guds Werk och Hwila*, III:995–1004:

> *Än större Under är at ther i Scotland finnes*
> *Een Siö (men si hans Nampn iag ej så hastigt minnes*
> *Som Pennan löpa wil) af honom skal upfaara*
> *Een sådan Dimba som så kraftig menas wara*

*At Träden ther omkring heelt rara Fruchter bäära*
*Ty thet är ingen Nött/ej Äple eller Pära*
*Men små Ank-Ungar/si man wil för wist betyga*
*The wäxa ther på Trää til thes the orka flyga;*
*Och tå så sökia the först til sit Hemman rätta*
*Och plaska need i Siön; Een löglig Frucht är thetta!*

(A still greater miracle is reported from Scotland,
where there is a lake [I do not remember its name as fast
as the pencil wants to move] from which such a powerful mist
    emerges
that the trees around it carry rare fruits indeed:
For there are no nuts, nor apples nor pears,
but small ducklings; they grow there in the trees
until they are fit for flying,
and then they search for their true home
and jump into the lake; indeed a ridiculous fruit!)[16]

Paracelsus was one of those who took part in the discussion of these remarkable animals, a discussion that had been going on since the eleventh century. According to Daniel Sennert, he founded his opinion on the statement that Adam's origin had also been a tree.[17] It would be tempting to connect this to *The Worship and Love of God*, with the trees giving birth to animals and humans; and no doubt Swedenborg knew about the ideas of barnacles because they are also fluttering about in Leibniz's theodicy.[18] But they cannot have been of decisive importance, since the atmosphere in Swedenborg's work is so different. Rather, they should be seen as primitive examples of a belief in the deep affinity of organisms, and in that respect as distant relatives.

The teleological mark on the description of the origin of animal genera in *The Worship and Love of God* immediately calls Aristotle to mind, but its strong connections to faith also bring other sources to the fore. As was emphasized in the survey of the hexaemeral genre, Augustine interpreted the creation act of God as an introduction of forms in matter, which then generated things and organisms. Von Lippmann has summarized Augustine's opinion of the organisms as follows:

*Nach ihm schuf Gott zugleich mit der anorganischen Welt auch die organische, jedoch zunächst nur 'potentiell', der Möglichkeit nach: er erfüllte die Erde mit verborgenen Keimkräften (occulta semina, rationes seminales, die logoi spermatikoi der Stoiker), den unsichtbaren, die 'keimhaften Anlagen' in sich schliessenden 'Samen', die unter eintretenden günstigen Umständen 'aktuell' ('wirksam) wurden und nun aus Wasser und*

*Luft Frösche und Vögel hervorbrachten, aus der Erde Pflanzen
und Landtiere.*

(According to him, God created the inorganic world together
with the organic, but primarily only potentially, as a possibility:
he filled the earth with hidden powers of growth [secret seeds,
seminal causes, the *logoi spermatikoi* of the Stoics], with invisible seeds enclosing the growth potential, which, on favorable
occasions, became "actual" (=active, effective) and started to
bring forth frogs and birds of water and air, herbs and
quadrupeds of the earth.)[19]

Augustine, however, did not want to interpret this formative principle concretely as *semina* or *ova*, seeds or eggs, but he expected that plants and animals would emerge fully grown of the earth. As von Hofsten has pointed
out, in that way, Augustine could also solve the problem of insular
animals.[20]

There is all the more reason to pay attention to Augustine in this context, as even contemporary biologists took an interest in him. The mechanically working spontaneous generation proposed by Descartes was not well
received by his disciples in its original version; instead, it was modified into
a preformation theory, according to which the organism grew out of a microscopic prototype in the egg or seed. This idea could more easily be
adapted to the Christian belief in providence. Malebranche may serve as an
example, since scholars have emphasized Augustine's strong influence on
him, even in this biological issue: "*De plus, le mécanisme, réduit au rôle
que la nouvelle théorie lui donne, s'accorde mieux avec les Pères, puisque
la théorie de l'emboîtement des germes est la doctrine augustinenne* des
raisons séminales" (moreover, after the mechanism had been reduced to the
role which the new theory ascribed to it, it was in better correspondence
with the view of the Fathers, because the enclosure of the germs agrees
with the Augustinian doctrine *of the seminal causes*).[21]

Thus, Augustine's theocentric idea is here applied to the most important
generation theory of modern biology, *omne vivum ex ovo*. Even if Swedenborg rejected the preformation theory, as shown above, it came back in his
concept of the first substance of nature, out of which the *vires seminales*,
the seminal forces, of the various series emerged; in this substance, there is
a preformed harmony, which stems from the Creator himself. Consequently, this substance can be said to include Augustine's *rationes seminales*, the *logoi spermatikoi* of the Stoics and whatever else the mysterious
powers have been called; but the effects of these powers are displayed in
seeds and eggs in a way that comes quite close to the Cartesian model.

We could discuss quite many other authors in the rich contemporary
embryological and ovological literature to analyze the theoretical background of the animal kingdom's origin, but that would not change the

eclectic picture. The account of the drama of creation, however, implies much more than theoretical speculations. The poetic element makes a strong impression, often resulting in a classical coloring. As noted in the survey of the *hexaemeron* genre above, one can observe influences from Lucretius' *De rerum natura* among representatives of various kinds of spontaneous generation ideas, for example, Kircher and van Helmont. The great exposé of the origin of life on earth in the fifth book was the main source, and there is good reason to dwell on it in connection with *The Worship and Love of God*:

*Principio genus herbarum viridemque nitorem*
*terra dedit circum collis camposque per omnis,*
*florida fulserunt viridanti prata colore,*
*arboribusque datumst variis exinde per auras*
*crescendi magnum immissis certamen habenis. . . .*
*principio genus alituum variaeque volucres*
*ova relinquebant exclusae tempore verno,*
*folliculos ut nunc teretes aestate cicadae*
*linquunt sponte sua victum vitamque petentes.*
*tum tibi terra dedit primum mortalia saecla.*
*multus enim calor atque umor superabat in arvis.*
*hoc ubi quaeque loci regio opportuna dabatur,*
*crescebant uteri terram radicibus apti;*
*quos ubi tempore maturo patefecerat aetas*
*infantum fugiens umorem aurasque petessens,*
*convertebat ibi natura foramine terrae*
*et sucum venis cogebat fundere apertis*
*consimilem lactis, sicut nunc femina quaeque*
*cum peperit, dulci repletur lacte, quod omnis*
*impetus in mammas convertitur ille alimenti.*

(In the beginning the earth gave forth all kinds of herbage and verdant sheen about the hills and over all the plains; the flowery meadows glittered with the bright green hue, and next in order to the different trees was given a strong and emulous desire of growing up into the air with full unbridled powers. . . . First of all the race of fowls and the various birds would leave their eggs, hatched in the springtime, just as now in summer the cicades leave spontaneously their gossamer coats in quest of a living and life. Then you must know did the earth first give forth races of mortal men. For much heat and moisture would then abound in the fields; and therefore wherever a suitable spot offered, wombs would grow attached to the earth by roots; and when the warmth of the infants, flying the wet and craving the air, had opened these in the fulness of time, nature would turn

to that spot the pores of the earth and constrain it to yield from
its opened veins a liquid most like to milk, even as now-a-days
every woman when she has borne, is filled with sweet milk,
because all that current of nutriment streams towards the
breasts.)[22]

*De rerum natura* also praises the mild spring climate in the youth of the
earth:

> *at novitas mundi nec frigora dura ciebat*
> *nec nimios aestus nec magnis viribus auras.*
> *omnia enim pariter crescunt et robora sumunt.*
>     (Then the fresh youth of the world would give forth neither
> severe colds nor excessive heats nor gales of great violence; for
> all things grow and acquire strength in a like proportion.)[23]

Further on are several instances of the laments of the decrease in growing
power of the ageing earth, so frequent in tales of the Golden Age.[24]

However, the essential part remains the description of the origin of life,
which inevitably leads us to Swedenborg's treating of the theme, for example, in the following combination of summary and foreshadowing from the
first scene of the drama:

> *Tempus itaque fuit, cum Vegetabiles faetus ex Seminum suorum*
> *thecis omnium primo erumperent; cumque ipsa Animalia, tam*
> *quae natant & volitant, quam quae repunt & gradiuntur, ex*
> *primis suis uteris ovisque evolverentur, & dein sapidissimo*
> *lacte, ex florido puerperae sinu, tanquam ubere, emanante,*
> *alerentur, & usque ad illum aevum, dum juris essent sibimetip-*
> *sis prospicere, perducerentur* (k)
>     (And so there was a time when the germ of every plant burst
> forth from the covering of its seed; and when each animal that
> swims or flies or crawls or walks broke free from its first womb
> or egg. Then they were nourished with savory milk that came
> from the flowering side of the laboring Earth, as if from its
> breast, and were raised to the age when they were able to take
> care of themselves (k)) §18

In note k, Swedenborg refers like Lucretius to bugs that are still hatched in
the mild warmth of springtime. Although the deepest motives are different,
the final cause being divine providence rather than atomic automatics, the
poetic conception of the Roman poet had a significant effect on Swedenborg's presentation.

There is all the more reason to focus on Lucretius in this context as the
contemporary interest in Lucretius, outlined above, is reflected in Swedenborg's *Principia*. Here are references not only to writers such as Athanasius

Kircher and Pierre Gassendi, who might have transmitted influences from Lucretius, but also to the poet himself. It is true that most of them are critical, particularly of the atomic theory, but sometimes the Roman is quoted with approval as a poetic illustration of the ideas of the scholar in question. This is important, considering the high value ascribed to poetry in the category labelled as *correspondentia fabulosa*; the passages cited in *Principia* contain statements on the magnetic phenomena in the sixth book of *De rerum natura*.[25]

Swedenborg's excerpts from Burnet also prove that he took an interest in Lucretius when it came to the issue of the generative power of the earth in the Golden Age. In *Telluris Theoria Sacra*, Burnet cites Lucretius in a chapter dealing with the ancient idea of paradise—incidentally without any criticism—and Swedenborg made a note of these quotations.[26] In the Latin text, there is also a suggestion of the spontaneous generation of plants and animals, which points to the same passage from Lucretius.[27] Burnet detailed this argument in a later English edition. Even if Swedenborg was unaware of this later edition, we should look at it as an illustration of the intellectual environment.

The point of departure is the account of the origin of life in Genesis. Burnet declares that the birth of humankind was a direct result of an immediate act of God but that all other organisms were brought forth by the earth in the same way as the plants. He is aware that the doctrine of spontaneous generation was a bone of contention, dating back to Epicurus. However, the Greek philosopher extended the doctrine to include humanity, and since this contradicts the revealed truth, it must be false. But the notion of the origin of the animal kingdom was not Epicurus' invention, as Burnet maintains in formulations that appear to be a belated polemic against the too-cautious attitude of Descartes:

The *Stoicks* were of the same Mind, and the *Pythagoreans* and the *Egyptians*, and I think, all that suppos'd the earth to rise from a Chaos. Neither do I know any harm in that Opinion, if duly limited and stated; for what Inconvenience is it, or what Diminution of Providence, that there should be the Principles of Life, as well as the Principles of Vegetation, in the new earth? And unless you suppose all the first Animals, as well as the first Man, to have been made at one Stroke, in their full Growth and Perfection, which we have neither Reason nor Authority sufficient to believe; if they were made young, little, and weak, as they come now into the World, there seems to be no way for their Production more proper, and decorous, than that they should spring from their great Mother the earth.[28]

Burnet abstained from closer inquiring into the technical aspects of this generation process, and he did not make use of any ovological expertise in this context.

Thus, there is great variation among the many important influences for Swedenborg's account of the birth of the animal kingdom. Of course, both intention and form differ between Lucretius and Descartes. Actually, Descartes' outlook on this process summarizes Swedenborg's whole development as a student of nature. Descartes had already formulated the fundamental theme with all the rigidity and callousness of a rational system: his well-known view of animals as automata logically follows this argument. At this point, Swedenborg protests, most explicitly in *Oeconomia*; the doctrine of series and degrees makes it impossible for him to accept the Cartesian mechanics: "*sunt etenim eis affectiones, prout ira, invidia, timor, odium, amicitia, tum & diversi generis appetitus; verbo nulla non adjuncta quae animo attribuuntur, ut totidem incitamenta & calores vitae, nobiscum communia, proinde non authomata machinis inanimatis assimilanda*" (For there are also feelings in them [the animals], like anger, envy, fear, hatred, friendship, and even different kinds of desire; in one word, all qualities belonging to the mind, as an equal number of impulses and heats of life, and common to ours; thus they are not automata comparable to soulless machines).[29] Instead, Swedenborg's anatomical studies familiarized him with the modern idea of the egg as the origin of all living creatures. He was undoubtedly also struck by the great possibilities of uniting science and the Scriptures, which this doctrine offers; Malebranche, one of the most brilliant of Cartesian thinkers, had made good use of them in combination with impulses from Augustine.

At the same time, Swedenborg's reading of embryologic works reminded him of the phantastic fables of tree-born animals, some of which could be found in classical poetry, which had meant so much for him since his youth and was about to be given a significant position in the system of correspondences, as was mentioned previously. From these elements, Swedenborg built an original whole, in its spiritualization of the universe, an effect of his consequent teleological view, characterized by a religious reverence for the life of nature. The human species is not allowed to ruthlessly tread down animals and vegetation or to look upon other organisms as machines. Although everything serves humanity as the crown of creation, in our turn, we must give voice to the praise of all nature to the Creator, give words to its mute yearning for emotional expression.

## Creation and Providence

This particular sensibility, which appears in the vision of the origin of the animal kingdom, differs considerably from that of Swedenborg's closest sources; in fact, it seems partly similar to the Romantic animation of nature, although the pantheistic elements are missing and the background differs significantly. Actually, the shifting religious emotions of the eighteenth century can be observed earlier in Swedenborg than in other Swedish writers. When the well-known hymnologist Emil Liedgren (1879–1963) examined texts proposed for a new hymn book from the decades around 1800, he found a view of nature and a concept of God that come strikingly close to those of Swedenborg; but Liedgren was probably right in interpreting them in the light of James Thomson's (1700–1748) descriptive poetry of nature and the Savoyard confession of Jean-Jacques Rousseau (1712–1778).[30] It may serve as a perspicuous illustration of Lamm's statement that "De Cultu et Amore Dei *är ett isolerat verk inom svensk litteratur, ett halvsekel före sin tid*" (De cultu et amore Dei is an isolated work in Swedish literature, half a century ahead of its time).[31]

The issue of God's presence in his creation is later raised in the drama, and Swedenborg starts with specific aspects of the infinite: providence's organizing and surveying the origin of the vegetable and animal kingdoms (§18), the infinite as the supreme being (§24), providence called universal because it is present even in the smallest units (§26), and creative providence as an obscure image in our minds (§28, note t). Early in the text, there is a close connection to *De Infinito* in several respects, as Swedenborg himself pointed out in his dream diary.[32] Talking of the enormous multitude of forces and potentials that had been inserted into the first finite point, Swedenborg had stated in *De Infinito*:

> *nam a nullo negatur, quin omnia Deo in prima creatione praesentia fuerint, pariter quin omnia praeviderit, & quin statim etiam in omnibus providerit; & consequenter sic omnia formaverit, ut ad ipsissimum finem quasi sponte fluerent: nam non potuit quam perfectissimum esse, quod immediate produceret;*
>
> (For it is denied by nobody that all things were present to God at the beginning of creation, nor that he foresaw everything and also exerted his providence in everything; consequently, he formed all things in such a way that they turned to their real goal as of their own will: for nothing could be anything else than perfect which he created immediately.)[33]

The last sentence resounds in the drama of creation, when Swedenborg depicts how the newborn earth puts on a marvelous clothing of flowers in §19: "*nam non potuit non perfectissimum esse, quod ab ipso Creatore, omnium perfectionum Fonte, immediate producitur*" (After all, everything that the Creator himself, the source of all perfection, acts directly to produce cannot be anything but absolutely perfect). While there is a clear connection, superficially it seems to create a problem: how can Swedenborg let the antediluvian flora grow directly out of the hands of the Creator? The problem is how to interpret the word *immediate*: its use in *De Infinito* did not cause any difficulties because the author was writing about the primary products of infinity. However, the herbs that were created "immediately" by the fountain of all perfection are the primary effects of the traits and potentials inserted by the infinite into the first substance of nature (or point, to refer to the usage of *Principia*). In the first scene of the drama of creation, we are still in a state where the numerous intermediaries between the idea of the Creator and its final result have not been able to obscure the profound connection. By and large, the entire work is marked by this tone, but in detail one may see it most clearly in this reminder of *De Infinito*.

The issue of the providence of God and its role in the creation of the world has wider implications. In the third scene, when Swedenborg deals with the relation between God and the human soul, he introduces a motif of great importance. The soul is forming the human egg into a body comparable to what happened when God inserted his idea of creation into the great egg of the world, thus emphasizing the correspondence between macrocosm and microcosm (§35). There is a significant difference, however; the soul has access to a natural stuff already in existence, while this material had been created out of nothing, as Swedenborg explicitly states: "*Anima hoc desiderio flagrans, sicut Mens, ad imaginem Supremae, etiam quendam Mundulum seu Microcosmum, ad effigiem Maximi, condere, sed non ex nihilo, ingressa est*" (The soul burned with longing. As a mind modeled after the Supreme Mind, she too began to build a kind of little world, a microcosm in the likeness of the greater world, though not out of the void.). In *The Worship and Love of God*, there is a *creatio ex nihilo* before all time, although only briefly indicated in a general phrase.[34] Swedenborg was not interested in this theoretical problem in the drama of creation, but the passage above clearly indicates that he was aware of its consequences. Because of that, we should examine this controversial issue, which has implications for the interpretation of his religious view during his transitional period when the drama of creation took shape.

Swedenborg's writings, not only the theosophic ones but also works such as *Principia,* were put on the *index librorum prohibitorum* of the Roman Catholic Church in the beginning of the nineteenth century. Clissold, the English translator of *Principia,* suggested that the reason was Swedenborg's heterodox opinion of the Creation, both with respect to the idea of a *creatio ex nihilo*, which according to orthodox creed is proclaimed in Gen. 1:1, and to the possibilities of adjusting "such a process of creation with the literal interpretation of the first chapter of Genesis."[35] While the latter difficulty is obvious, the problem of *creatio ex nihilo* is different.

The short statement in Gen. 1:1, "In the beginning . . . God created the heavens and the earth," has given rise to countless interpretations, and each word in it has led to fundamental theological problems.[36] It would be impossible to summarize the discussion here; but, because Lamm argues for Milton's impact on *The Worship and Love of God,* it may be of some interest to take a look at the discussion among Milton scholars of Creation in *Paradise Lost.*

In book VII of *Paradise Lost,* the archangel Raphael tells the inquisitive Adam about the process of Creation, coming somewhat late in the epic because Milton wanted to start with the tremendous battle in heaven between Lucifer and the faithful angels as a prerequisite for the universal drama of creation, fall, and redemption. Our world is created after the victory of the angels of light, and the decisions of the Lord are carried out by his only begotten Son as Word and Spirit; but as already pointed out above, the angel emphasizes that what he says will be poetically and pedagogically adjusted to the intellectual powers of human beings. The point of departure of Creation is chaos, the violent waves of the abyss, which are subdued by the Son through his breathtakingly beautiful imperative "Silence, ye troubl'd waves, and thou Deep, peace" (VII:216). After that follows the famous scene in which the golden pair of compasses in the hands of the Son sets out the limits of the sky and the earth. Milton then paraphrases the first and second chapters of Genesis, keeping a close correspondence to the biblical original. Thus, the Creator is depicted as building our world out of pre-existent elements in a way that calls to mind human planters and master builders.

According to Hebraists, the verb *bara,* to create, which is used in Gen. 1:1, has to be put under considerable semantic pressure to be translated "to create out of nothing," an observation used by Thomas Burnet to support his own heterodox interpretation of Creation. The American scholar G. N. Conklin concluded that Milton was compelled to reject the *creatio ex nihilo* dogma by his own hermeneutics and replaced it by a belief in a creation "from a preexistent matter which proceeded somewhere in time out of God Himself."[37] However, we should not disregard all literary impulses on Milton's exegesis, taking into particular consideration that the problem had been so intensely discussed in Christian tradition and by his contemporaries. Such a heresy had been held by many Christian thinkers and their ancient masters, and probably Milton cannot be pinned to a single source. Whiting, an older and more cautious scholar, maintains, "His relation to contemporary thought is an extraordinarily complicated one that persistently evades dogmatic description and definition. Whatever his specific indebtednesses were—and perhaps it would have been difficult for Milton himself to indicate some of these—it is obvious that his account of creation curiously blends the Neoplatonic and the Christian."[38] To that must be added a poetic inspiration, which cannot be completely mapped out by a study of sources, however scrupulous, a point often neglected in the abundant Milton literature.[39]

In many ways Swedenborg is in a similar situation, and there is no reason to presuppose any influences from Milton on *De Infinito*. The only connection would be the only begotten Son as an intermediary between infinity and the finite world, but partly this is a commonplace of Christian theology, partly Swedenborg's account of paradise is completely devoid of Milton's concrete imagery. Nor can I find that the drama of creation needs to be linked to Milton at this point. Here the problem of *creatio ex nihilo* is a crucial issue. Milton's world has been created out of preexistent matter, which at one time emanated from the essence of God; while this reminds one of Neoplatonism, what about Swedenborg's world according to *The Worship and Love of God*? God created the first finite point, out of which the universe was developed later on, but was this point created *ex nihilo* or was it an emanation from the substance of God? Referring to *De Infinito*, Lamm speaks cautiously of *"grundstommen till ett emanatistiskt system"* (the fundament of an emanation system); however, in the chapter on *The Worship and Love of God*, he brings Milton and Swedenborg together without reservation as representatives of a Neoplatonic doctrine of emanation.[40]

Although the emanation problem is a subtle one, and a modern reader may feel irritatingly uncertain of the actual implication of it among the discussants, it exerted a significant intellectual as well as emotional influence. First of all, the Neoplatonic tradition is heterogeneous and contains a number of rather bizarre offshoots; even if Swedenborg followed Neoplatonic ideas in his vision of Creation, this would not make him a disciple of Milton. While not advocating any influences from the Cabbala, I feel that, in this case, the cabbalistic tradition may come considerably closer to Swedenborg's opinion than does that of Milton:

> *Dans le Zohar, aussi bien que dans les écrits hébreux de Moïse de Léon, la transformation du Néant en Etre est souvent expliquée en employant un symbole particulier, celui du point primordial. Déjà les kabbalistes de l'école de Gérone se servaient de la comparaison du point mathématique, dont le mouvement crée la ligne et la surface, pour illustrer le processus de l'émanation à partir de la 'cause cachée'. . . . Étant lui-même sans dimensions et pour ainsi dire placé entre le Néant et l'Etre, le point sert à illustrer ce que les kabbalistes du XIIIe siècle appellent 'l'Origine de l'Etre', ce 'Commencement' dont parle le premier mot de la Bible.*

> (In the Sohar, as well as in the Hebraic writings of Moses of Léon, the transformation of nothingness into being is often explained by using a particular symbol, the point. The kabbalists of the school of Gerona made use of the comparison with the mathematical point, the motion of which creates the line and the surface, to illustrate the emanation process out of the "hid-

den cause." . . . Being itself without dimensions and located between nothingness and being, as it were, the point is used as an
illustration of what the thirteenth century kabbalists called "the
origin of being," this "beginning" of which the first word of the
Bible speaks.)[41]

Despite the striking similarities, it is difficult to prove any direct connections because the tradition is so widely ramified. Swedenborg must have
had a general knowledge of the mysticism of the Cabbala, since he had
grown up in an erudite milieu in which Johannes Bureus (1568–1652) and
Georg Stiernhielm were still revered.[42] This era of Pietism held a particular
interest in the Cabbala caused by the strong syncretistic tendencies in the
wake of the Thirty Years War. As Ernst Benz has pointed out, both Philipp
Jacob Spener (1635–1705) and August Hermann Francke (1663–1727)—
not to mention Leibniz—were among the readers of the big compilation
*Cabbala Denudata*, and Leibniz made a special note of the inner connections between Jewish and Christian theology.[43] In light of this, we should
pay more attention to the Cabbala at this point than to Milton, since we
do not know whether Swedenborg had read the English poet or not: the
only established fact is that he mentions Milton's name in a letter from
England but only as one in a list of famous English writers.

Even more important is whether we can talk of any natural emanation
at all in Swedenborg's drama of creation. Some excerpts from Leibniz
under the heading *"Deus"* in cod. 36–110 shed light on the problem, while
simultaneously demonstrating once more that Swedenborg's practice of
making notes is most unsatisfactory from a scholarly point of view. He is
obviously jotting down what strikes him as interesting at that moment
without concern for the context, which sometimes will distort the real
sense of the reference; consequently, his excerpts must be checked and used
cautiously.[44] In this particular case, Leibniz has quoted statements made by
Augustine and Baruch Spinoza (1632–1677), which Swedenborg reproduced so defectively that Leibniz's view has been completely reversed. Despite this, the passage is illuminating.

The quotation from Augustine goes back to *De libero arbitrio* and declares that nothing but God himself can emanate from the substance of
God; therefore, all living creatures must originate from nothing. Later
Leibniz quoted other Augustinian texts, which account for the imperfection and corruption of the world as effects of this very *creatio ex nihilo*.
This connection with Augustine by itself calls for caution about interpreting Swedenborg's ideas of the Creator and his work in terms of emanation
at this time. As pointed out above, *The Worship and Love of God* indicates
a creation out of nothing; and when it comes to the view in *De Infinito*, according to which the Infinite caused or created the first finite point through
his only begotten Son, there is no reason to see this as any emanation

process. On the contrary, it has to be explained as a creation out of nothing, in a manner similar to Augustine's view of the process. In addition, this is explicitly stated in *Oeconomia*, with exactly those complications which can be inferred from the Leibniz excerpts. Here Swedenborg has given the following, partly ritual answer to the question of the origin of nature: "*satisfactum sibi credet etiam sciendi avidissimus, arbitror, si dixero, quod sit Dei omnipotentis ex nihilo opus, a quo omnia, propter quem omnia, qui est quod est; ultra ire non datum est: Sapientissimus enim mortalium est, qui certo scit, quod in Divinis nihil, praeter quod revelatum est, sciat*" (I presume that even the most inquisitive reader will be satisfied if I say that nature is a work made of nothing by the Almighty God, of whom and for whom all things exist and who is what he is. It is not allowed to proceed further: for the wisest of mortals is the man who is firmly convinced that he does not know anything else in divine matters than what has been revealed).[45]

Later those very difficulties appear, which the Leibniz excerpts display in the attempts at elucidating the relations between God and his creation. A significant summary of the issue is given in some excerpts from "*La cause de Dieu plaidée par sa justice*":

> Les actuels dépendent de Dieu et dans l'existence et dans l'action; et ils dépendent, non-seulement de son intelligence, mais encore de sa volonté. Ils en dépendent quant à l'existence, en ce que toutes les choses ont été créés librement par Dieu, et même sont conservées par lui; et ce n'est pas sans raison qu'on enseigne que la conservation divine est une création continuée, comme un rayon qui émane continuellement du soleil; bien que les créatures ne procèdent point de l'essence divine, et n'en sont point des émanations nécessaires.
>
> (Living creatures depend on God both for their existence and their actions; and they depend on him not only for their intelligence but also for their will. They are dependent for their existence in the respect that all things are created by the free will of God, and also preserved by him; and it is not without reason that one teaches that the divine preservation is a continuous creation, like a beam that emanates continuously from the sun, although the creatures do not proceed from the divine essence, being no necessary emanations from it.)[46]

Thus Leibniz employed the ancient comparison between God and the sun, in a way close to Swedenborg's practice in *Oeconomia* and in *The Worship and Love of God*. Since this is a commonplace, Lamm believed that it "*knappt lönar mödan att närmare efterfråga, hvarifrån Swedenborg fått denna konception*" (it is hardly worth the effort to seek the source of this Swedenborgian conception).[47] But Lamm may have resigned a little too early. Some texts and excerpts offer at least a prospect of restricting the emanatistic implications, which Lamm seems to have taken for granted. At the same time, some light will be thrown on an important aspect of Swedenborg's scientific thinking and of Leibniz's rationalism as well.

In the second part of *Oeconomia,* Swedenborg extensively compares the natural and the spiritual sun; and in one place, he turns sharply against those who look upon the natural light as *"materialium atomorum affluxum,"* an emission of material particles.[48] With his corpuscular theory, Newton was the leading representative of this view, and the polemics in *Oeconomia* echo the discussions in England thirty years prior, when Swedenborg sided with Descartes' vortex theory against Newton's ideas of corpuscles moving in a vacuum.[49] In the light of Swedenborg's deep-rooted conviction, a commentary on Leibniz's text made by the Latin translator and cited by Acton is illuminating: "The old Platonists held that 'the world flowed from God like a perennial ray from a perennial sun.' The simile is somewhat dangerous, for according to the Epicurean and Newtonian doctrine, the rays of the sun are emitted particles of the solar body, and it might therefore be inferred that all creatures are particles of divinity. In view of this danger, Leibnitz affirms that 'creatures do not emanate from God's essence' etc."[50]

An emanation of this kind implies that evils in the world have also emanated from the essence of God, which is an absurd consequence for Christian rationalists. No doubt this commentary, which Swedenborg probably read, brought up an issue that was essential to him and that accompanied him into the theosophic system; particularly in view of the account of the origin of the planetary system from the sun, where the radiation of the sun is regarded as solar matter, the theological implications must have proved problematic.[51] In *The Worship and Love of God,* Swedenborg has not yet renounced this belief, which emerges from the Leibniz excerpts and corresponding Augustinian view, namely, that the presupposed emanation in the moment of creation is only an image, a symbol. Such an interpretation is supported by a statement in the second part of *Oeconomia,* where Swedenborg compares the natural sun and the sun of life: "*Non prohibemur ad Sanctuarium hoc per viam comparationis accedere; . . . Ergo insistamus viae comparationis; sed comparatio aliquantum illustrat, non vero docet, quid id est, cum quo comparatur*" (We are not forbidden to approach the sanctuary by means of comparison. . . . Thus let us proceed on the track of comparison, even though a comparison only illustrates something and does not teach us what that is, with which it is compared).[52]

Not surprisingly, Swedenborg's formula reflects a view identical to that of his contemporary Andreas Rydelius, when he discussed the ancient comparison between God and the sun. Rydelius assumes that the basis of it is an overly literal interpretation of what is said in Genesis about the light that God created before the sun. This light has been regarded as an emission of the essence of God by the cabbalists Fludd, Böhme, and others, Rydelius maintains, and he proceeds:

> Jag twiflar ock icke, at ju then slemma meningen om alla crea-
> turs emanation af GUDS egit wäsende, som alla tider warit så
> gångbar, härifrån hafwer tagit sin första uprinnelse. Thet är alt
> för swårt och ledo-samt at disputera med sådana Allegoriska
> Philosopher; emedan the icke wilja förklara sina figurliga idéer
> med andra enfaldigare ord, hwaraf man kunde giöra sig för-
> nuftigt begrep; utan the stanna aldeles wid sina figurer, och
> gifwa ther på figurliga förklaringar.

> (Nor do I doubt that the bad view of the emanation of all
> creatures out of the essence of God, so frequent in all times,
> originated here. It is difficult and boring to debate with such al-
> legorical philosophers, because they do not want to account for
> their figurative ideas with other and more simple words, which
> could make sense, but stay with their figures of speech and offer
> only figurative explanations).[53]

Rydelius' surly polemics against mysticism is interesting in a context so close to Swedenborg's statement in *Oeconomia* in other respects. In *The Worship and Love of God*, there are no other signs of a change of opinion about nature's emanation than those springing from the more detailed and theoretically better founded comparisons of the doctrine of correspon-dence. As far as I can see, there is no reason to trace Swedenborg's thinking back to Milton at this point.

This does not mean, however, that one can dismiss the importance of Neoplatonic ideas and symbols for Swedenborg's development, but here we are only concerned with their impact on the drama of creation. In his theosophic period, one confronts a more extended system of ideas on a Neoplatonic fundament, as shown by Lamm, but that was not in place when the drama of creation was in preparation. As will be discussed later, the matter comes to the fore in discourses on principal theological issues such as evil and redemption.[54] Swedenborg was exposed to Neoplatonic influences from several sources. One of them is the so-called *Theology of Aristotle*, a Neoplatonic work that probably dates back to Porphyry (c. 234–c. 305) and from which Swedenborg excerpted many statements in the 1740s, even if he was not convinced that Aristotle really had written it, "*quia sublimius est*" (because it is most sublime).[55]

His doubt did not reduce his great appreciation of the work. Sweden-borg wrote a note about God and his creation taken from a chapter of this work, which is a kind of summary of previous lines of argument on the issue: "*procreavit deus substantiam unicam, nempe intellectum agentem, quem exornavit lumine inter caetera quae procreata sunt, clarissimo et ex-cellentissimo . . . hoc intermedio supremus orbis procreatus est, qui intelli-*

*gentias et animos continet. ac per eundem innovata sunt inferiora in sen-*
*sum cadentia, illis contenta et aliqua ex parte similia, nisi quod ea quae*
*supremus orbis continet, pura sunt et perfecta et omnis mixtionis experta"*
(God created the single substance, i.e., the active intelligence, which he
adorned with the clearest and excellent light among all the rest of the creation. . . . Through its agency, the supreme world, which contains intelligences and souls, was created. And from that world, all the lower things
have been brought forth as new, which things are perceived and contained
by the senses and partly similar to them, only that the things of the
supreme world are pure and perfect and free from all mixture).[56]

Although the Neoplatonic structure is evident here, the passage does not
contradict the idea of an original creation out of nothing. Shortly before
Swedenborg put a summary of "Aristotle's" system in italics: through the
Word, God created the active intelligence and through it *animum com-*
*munem*, the soul of the world; this soul formed the world of the senses and
was also inserted into plants and animals.[57] Swedenborg did not himself
point out the obvious correspondence to the prologue of the Gospel of
John, so essential to all Christian theology influenced by Platonism; but the
editor of *De secretiore parte divinae sapientiae secundum Aegyptios* underlines it in his scholia to another passage, from which Swedenborg made excerpts, where the divine light is presented in the image of a sun.[58]

None of these extracts contradicts the belief in a creation out of nothing. Before his final vocation, Swedenborg seems to have been in a situation similar to Augustine's struggle to free himself from the Manichaean
song of sirens. In this period, the Church Father embraced a radical materialism, which went as far as the concept of God: God is light but in the
shape of an extended substance, of which humankind is a part. This belief
results in a kind of pantheism close to the ideas of Spinoza, which caused
much commotion among Swedenborg's contemporaries.[59] Augustine found
the alternative to this Manichaeism in a creation out of nothing, which
makes it possible to avoid the unacceptable consequence that evil also
comes forth from the essence of God. Thus, even Swedenborg encountered
the strong Augustinian influence in the rationalist tradition from Descartes:
"*C'est par saint Augustin que le cartésianisme deviendra une philosophie*
*pleinement chrétienne*" (it is because of St. Augustine that Cartesianism became a totally Christian philosophy), as a French historian maintains.[60] As
is well-known, philosophic interest in Augustine's doctrines, of which
Swedenborg had both direct and indirect acquaintance, was also supported
by contemporary trends of theology.[61]

Hence, the small piece of information about *creatio ex nihilo* in *The*
*Worship and Love of God* uncovers a complex background of philosophical and theological considerations. At the same time, it is a well of discord,
which, together with views of evil and redemption, is to become the deluge
that causes the synthetic structure of the drama of creation to crumble. In

Swedenborg's new world of religious conviction, the Neoplatonic emanation theory, the supposed presence of which in the drama of creation has
been attributed to Milton, is a crucial part, and there the *creatio ex nihilo*
dogma has been abandoned.[62] But before that, he tends in this direction,
which could be interpreted without referring to *Paradise Lost*: the rather
few similarities depend on common sources, for example, Augustine.

To fairly assess these early Platonic tendencies, one has to stress Swedenborg's proximity to Leibniz in this respect too; it has already been observed
in connection with the formative forces in *The Worship and Love of God*,
and the aspect can be logically extended to include the idea of creation and
to the belief in providence, which has emerged in the utilitarian and teleological message of the first two scenes but will appear in its most elaborate
form in the account of evil. Here we witness Swedenborg's wrestling with
the theodicy problem that Leibniz brought into focus. Looking at the excerpts dealing with this difficult issue, we meet *Tentamina theodicaeae* as
the most frequently consulted source, hardly surprising in a period when
this work served almost as a supplement to Holy Writ. In it, Swedenborg
found a historical survey containing most of the important contributions to
the debate, and he made use of this to get to know his predecessors.

Swedenborg's Creator, *numen universi*, for whom he proposed a series
of qualities in a manuscript strongly reminiscent of the drama of creation,
"*Omnipraesentia, Omniscientia, Omnipotentia, Providentia, Esse, Agere,
vivere*" (Omnipresence, Omniscience, Omnipotence, Providence, Being,
Action, Life) appears as a providence acting even in the most insignificant
details.[63] Thus, the experience of the series and purposes of nature even in
the smallest species inevitably leads to the discovery of the Divine, an idea
that was formulated more explicitly in *Clavis hieroglyphica*, with reference
to Rom. 1:19, 20.[64] Such a conception of providence implies that God
must have known from the beginning about the arrival of evil into the
world: thus, the early statements point toward the essential account of the
prince of the world and his entourage, and these links were probably evident to contemporary readers. For the well-informed, the resemblance to
Leibniz would also have been obvious, although it is not a simple proposition to discern all different opinions in the *Theodicy*. Judging by his excerpts, Swedenborg too might have agreed with the opinion of a
present-day biographer: "*Es ist gar nicht so leicht, aus dem Gewirr der ver-
schiedenen Ansichten des 'Theodizee'-Problems, die Leibniz im Lauf der
Untersuchung frei entwickelt, die eigentliche und letzte Meinung des
Denkers herauszulesen*" (It is definitely not easy to infer the real and final
opinion of the philosopher himself from the confusion of views of the
theodicy problem, which Leibniz enlarges upon during his investigation).[65]
To be able to ascertain this opinion, Swedenborg noted important passages
in which the providence problem was simplified by linguistic distinctions.
A case in point is that he took down Leibniz's terminology with respect to

the different kinds of necessity—metaphysical, moral, physical—as well as the divergence between destination and predestination.[66]

Like Leibniz, Swedenborg uses a terminology implying that God allowed evil to appear, an action that can only be understood from the essence of divine omnipotence. He does not present any theoretically elaborate analysis of the theodicy problem in his extant works before the theosophic period, but there are indications suggesting that he might have thought of something similar to Leibniz's model. In the nature of omnipotence, there is a capacity to conceive of the opposite of the divine law and even to allow these contradictions to become finite realities to a certain extent. This means that God permits an opponent to arise in the finite world—that is to say, evil will be born. But in this optimistic worldview, the birth of evil will be transformed into something good, by virtue of the complimentary qualities of omnipotence—namely, omniscience and divine goodness—so that the opposites will be straightened out to a perfect harmony, far more beautiful than what it would have been without the presence of evil.[67]

This comes close to the *varietas harmonica,* which has been studied above in light of Swedenborg's reading of Leibniz regarding the generative force, and Lamm has also noticed that Swedenborg's psychological applications of the *Oeconomia* pattern in *Regnum animale,* vol. VII, or *De anima,* are based on Leibniz's *principium identitatis indiscernibilium* (the principle of the identity of indiscernible things).[68] This will become obvious to anyone who observes the Leibnizian terminology in a section on the relation between Adam's fall and the order of God, the basic theme of *The Worship and Love of God,* which was sounded as early as the introduction:

> *et plura, quae clare demonstrant, quod providentia fuerit quod potuisset peccare, et praescientia quod peccaret, et quod integritatem suam pristinam amitteret, et sic quod inde ut a suo principio proflueret, quod animae inter se mutuo distinguerentur, et omnis varietas, quae usquam dabilis est, animarum potuisset existere, et sic finis creationis seu regnum Dei obtineretur, cujus seminaria sunt societates terrestres; quae similiter coelestem illam repraesentant; nam nihil non in huc mundo datur, quod non contineat repraesentationem mundi futuri.*

> (Many other things clearly prove that it was foreseen that he might sin, and known in advance that he would do so and lose his original innocence, and by that, as from its beginning, would appear that the souls were mutually separated; and that every potential variation of souls would be able to exist and the purpose of the creation be fulfilled, the kingdom of God, the seminaries of which are the terrestrial societies; in a similar way these represent the heavenly one, for there is nothing in this

world that does not contain a representation of the world to come.)[69]

The basic condition of this vision of divine providence can be found in the conception of the Creation: evil arises indirectly, through nature, since nothing else than what is good can emerge directly from the essence of God; this is a view Swedenborg shares with Leibniz. Consequently, the song of praise of providence in the second scene leads to the idea of *creatio ex nihilo*, which is presented in the third scene, and this in turn to the account of the powers of evil in the following parts. Thus, Leibniz's theodicy has been of utmost importance theoretically, but among the excerpts from it, one can also find notes that appear to have exerted a more personal attraction than the purely intellectual one. Regarding the idea of God and providence, there is good reason to quote two passages from the famous preface of *Tentamina theodicaeae*: "*Manifeste hinc conficitur, veram pietatem, immo veram felicitatem, consistere in amore Dei, sed in amore illuminato, cuius ardor comitem habeat lucem*" (This indicates clearly that true piety, as well as true happiness, consists of love of God, an illuminated love, the ardor of which is accompanied by light).[70] The same claim to understanding is varied in a second note: "*Nequit amari DEUS, nisi ejus perfectiones cognoscantur, haecque cognitio sincerae pietatis principia includit*" (One cannot love God without knowing his perfection, and this knowledge includes the principles of a sincere piety).[71]

In these notes, the intellectual's firm belief in the light of reason comes forth but also a pious man's confidence in God's love, and we can feel how close this comes to the purpose of this book, which is to show the way to the true worship of God. Even if Swedenborg's drama of creation is more strictly structured, and in its very form strives to express the synthesis conceived by his intellect, there is no denying the impression of profound affinity, in details as well as in its general intention. This impression will be reinforced by the polemical discourse on the harmony theory of Leibniz and Wolff, which we will meet in a psychological context from the years after the publication of *Oeconomia*.[72]

# 5

⁓

# THE BIRTH OF ADAM

(§§29–38)

The eulogy of providence, which closed the previous scene, is characteristically complemented with a psychological analogy in a note, a comparison with what happens in the human soul before it makes a decision and carries it out (§28, note t). This reference serves as an appropriate transition to the current section, in which Adam is to be born, putting forth a fundamental motif that will now be the focus of the account. But first the preceding scenes' pictures of the new-born earth are summed up, the playground for the cheerful games of the animals that became the final vignette of the previous scene.

The plants and the animals transformed the naked earth into a beautiful garden of flowers, fruits, and living creatures. The biblical account of the Promised Land, flowing with milk and honey, and the ancient dream of the Golden Age are metamorphosed in Swedenborg's paradise, with milk gushing from the maternal branches after they have weaned their progeny and streaming back into the roots of the mother trees. The grassy bedrooms are joined together with honey trickling from the honeycombs of colonies of bees (§29). Now there are abundant blessings ready for all senses: touch rejoices in the mild warmth of spring mixed with the moisture of the earth; to delight the sense of smell, the leaves perfume the air with balmy odors, which together with the air enlarge the fine web of the lungs; taste is stimulated by the most exquisite fruits; hearing transmits the warbling of birds, so that the inner parts of the brain are harmoniously activated; and sight revels in viewing the integrated whole, which is pedagogically represented in the system of correspondences (§30).

In this sensual panorama, Swedenborg once again creates his characteristic union of scientific objectivity and poetic insight: the Golden Age vision of pagan and Christian antiquity and the conjectures of natural history have been refracted in prisms, supplied by the age of utility, the eighteenth century, which manifested its delight at exact pieces of information. Utilitarianism is more easily brought to mind as the author's consistently teleological thinking recurs even in small details.

However, this beautiful and joyful atmosphere, the height of the earth's orbit when it reaches the culmination of spring, is marked by expectant yearning. Sensual beauty lacks significance before the first human has arrived, the one who will transmit external impressions to a rational consciousness and behold the coherence of the universe. All nature is yearning for this being, whose duty it will be to convey its eulogistic thanksgiving to the Creator.

In the garden of paradise, completed last of all and located in a region with the mildest climate, the tree of life now carries the most precious egg in which nature had concentrated its highest potential. Like a bride adorning her chamber before the arrival of the bridegroom, nature has supplied this egg with its most superb gifts. When its work is finished, fertilization takes place by means of *Suprema Mens*, who meets nature halfway to breed the soul in the guise of the sun of life with its concentrated rays, and afterwards to implant it in the egg:

> *Hoc primum erat omen connubiale Essentiae Spiritualis cum*
> *aurâ supremâ Naturae; ex constituto, ut fluens causarum orbis*
> *ab Infinito in Maximo Mundi Ovo conceptus, & ad hoc mini-*
> *mum perductus, intra naturam absolveretur, sed postmodum*
> *per nexum cum Infinito infinitus redderetur; utque per talem*
> *copulam Terrestre atrium Caelesti committeretur aulae.*
>
> (This was the first sign of the union of spiritual essence with
> the uttermost aura of nature. It followed upon the decree that
> the flowing cycle of causes, conceived by the Infinite in the
> Great Ovum of the System and extended into this least little
> ovum, should be completed within nature, though it would af-
> terward be rendered infinite by forming a bond with the
> Infinite—and it followed also that through this connection an
> entryway would be made from earth to the halls of heaven.)
> §33

In a preceding note, Swedenborg implies that the relation between the soul and the body, as a reflection of the relation between God and nature, will be a basic theme henceforth; so far he confines himself to stating the actual course of events—that the soul has been created by Supreme Reason out of its own essence. A more detailed treatment would exceed the prescribed expository limits, to which this new scene, as the last one, has been adjusted, but what has already been said should be enough to reveal the unique position of the human soul in nature.

As soon as the soul had been implanted in the egg, it starts to form a universe or a body, which is then formed by nature according to its wishes. The parallel to what had been told earlier about the senses of animals, which can only imagine nature, reminds the reader of Swedenborg's previous comparison of the generative forces with souls (§20, note m). However, at the same time, it is emphasized that the human soul also conceived of the heavenly universe. This happens in an anticipatory vision of the soul's longing for wings to glide down to the world of senses, seen through the gates of the body, and afterwards to return to heaven to tell about the joy and beauty of this world. The traditional symbol, the wings of the soul, is employed with Swedenborg's unique concrete power of imagination to describe the double identity of the soul, and in the light and gliding motion he summarizes the oscillation of the entire drama between the wondrous joy of science and the comfort of faith. We can also identify here the central problem of his religious crisis, metamorphosed into an airy and transparent image.

Nature was expressly present to realize the yearning of the soul, for it had been created out of nothing to be subject to souls and intelligences in the same way as these are obedient to their Maker, thus to carry out the decrees and aims of providence; all the intermediate purposes, which are stages on the road to the end of the series, the will of providence, or the order of God, are called *usus*, "uses" (§34). The reader is constantly aware of the proximity to the formative activities of the generative forces in seeds and eggs, which lends new weight to the message of the profound unity of the universe.

But Swedenborg economized on details. He confined himself to showing how the soul emits its radiation in the chaotic mass of the egg—*rudis indigestaque moles*—and first builds a grand edifice for the intelligences and their servants to live in; from here—that is, from the brain and the abodes of reason in it—the soul then extends the slenderest threads, which are the beginnings of the fibres. This account poetically describes a controversial embryological background, namely, whether the brain is the first organ to take shape in the egg, as Swedenborg maintained in *Oeconomia* (vol. I, §241ff) and *De fibra* (§128), supported by Malpighi and others, or the heart plays this part, as claimed by Harvey and others, but no theoretical aspects are applied. On the contrary, the presentation retains the persistently symbolic tone: the soul's forging of wings to satisfy its yearning to descend into the garden of paradise makes the lasting impression. In this scene, Swedenborg abstained from scientific discourses, which also gave it an artistically more coherent form than most of the others.

The focus then returns to the hold of the human egg, the tree of life, standing as a crowned center of the paradisiacal garden. The egg-carrying branch grows into a gentle womb, which is covered with a thin bark and soft leaves. The golden fruit is nourished by the juice of the tree together with the nutritive fluids of the neighboring trees; the rays of the sun are allowed to approach it only after they had been softened by passing through transparent fruits and their light has become like the color of a flower. Air is permitted to flutter in the vicinity of the tree but not to penetrate deeper, so that the frail lungs will not expand prematurely. The surrounding arbutus trees, the classical plant symbol of the Golden Age, push out long shoots, which help the tree of life carry its burden and will receive the child at his birth. Other trees and herbs prepare cradles covered with cotton that the mild zephyr has carried from the cotton plants. The entire narration breathes a touching tenderness and care, a restrained breath of yearning waiting for the miraculous union of heaven and earth, which the slowly gleaming light and the mild breezes will soon witness.

But Swedenborg also presents the other part of the union. The inhabitants of heaven, the pure spirits, guard the sacred grove to prevent wild animals from coming too close. In a faint reflection of a conventional hexaemeron motif, the animals of the earth humbly kneel in front of man, their prince. Not all of them, however: some are paralyzed with fright and run away into the dark of the forests. Although the holy peace around the couch of birth must not be disturbed, the contrast serves not only to intensify the serenity but also to remind one of the powers of darkness, which one day will struggle for the soul of the race now to be born. This scene heralds the appearances of evil in the shape of wild animals that are encountered in a later scene.

For now, the power of celestial spirits is strong, and when they keep guard, no harm can be done. In the child's delivery, the branch of the tree of life slowly descends and finally lays its burden on the bed of flowers. In their robes of white clouds, the celestial spirits assist at the birth of Adam, as they one day will guide his offspring into the Promised Land. When the months of the pregnancy—by virtue of the cosmology of the introduction as many years—are over, the human child breaks his fetters and receives the fragrant air with a kiss, which permeates his breast to give him a new and different life. The marvelous scene then concludes with honors of the heavenly choirs, and the darkness of the midnight hour is illuminated by their trembling lights, symbols of joy and grace (§38).

Significantly, the only direct references to the Bible in *The Worship and Love of God* are to be found in this scene (note y). Although the events described in this work are far removed from those of Genesis, with respect to the atmosphere, we approach the Bible more closely than in preceding scenes, as would be expected, since the unique position of the human soul between heaven and earth demands an immediate act of God, even in Swedenborg's system. The series of organisms are generated from seeds and eggs in accordance with the immanent principles of the first substances, which clearly indicate divine providence as their origin. This is insufficient in regard to the human being because he is something greater than body and senses. With this scene, Swedenborg reaches the nucleus of the drama, where humanity's relation to God will be treated with a fullness and sophistication that far exceeds the fixed scheme of the first scenes and also changes the literary execution: with the arrival of man, the mere description of scenery is replaced by the actions and dialogues of *dramatis personae.*

Although biblical inspiration can be seen in faith and thinking, classical influences appear as clearly in form. The scene emits the atmosphere of the Golden Age, steeped in ancient poetry, and the central symbol of the tree of life comes close to classical mythology in spite of its formal connections to Scripture. To elucidate this, it will be necessary to study the sources of *arbor vitae* and *ovum humanum* in light of the previous observations of the cosmology and biology of the drama of creation, after which Swedenborg's representation of the relation between God and the human soul will be examined in detail.

## The Tree of Life and the Creation of Humanity

With the birth of Adam, the cosmological egg symbol from the introduction achieves its microcosmic consummation. The reason Swedenborg allows the first man to be created in this way is his wish to establish a synthesis, his tireless attempts at classifying all natural phenomena in common categories. This ambition was given a free hand because important aspects of the Genesis text had been interpreted according to the concept of *correspondentia fabulosa,* as was pointed out previously. When Swedenborg the exegete returned a short time later to the domains of the hexaemeral poet in *Historia creationis,* he adopted a similar position:

> *Num ille immediate ex terra formatus fuerit, et sic non aetates suas ab infantia, ad juventutem percurrerit; vel num mediate ab ovo, et sic porro, fides sit penes Lectorem; quandoquidem unus dies significat integrum temporis spatium, seu plurium annorum praeterlapsum, ille etiam ex ovo potuit nasci, et ovum non immediate ex humo telluris, sed mediate per fibras cujusdam objecti vegetabilis seu arboris, per quas essentiae in sanguinem transiturae rectificarentur; si hoc, nihilominus ex terrae pulvere efformatus est, nam ex terra est quicquid percurrit radices seu fibras vegetabilium.*
>
> (Whether he was created immediately from the earth and thus did not pass his ages from infancy to adulthood, or whether he was formed indirectly out of an egg and so on is left to the reader to decide. However, since a single day means an

> entire period of time, or a process of many years, he might also
> have been born of an egg, which was not produced immediately
> of the earth but indirectly through the agency of the fibres of
> some herb or tree, which would purify the essences that were to
> be transmitted into his blood; if so, he would nonetheless have
> been shaped by the dust of the earth, for everything flowing
> through the roots or fibres of plants emanates from the earth.)[1]

It seems clear that, even after his spiritual tumult, Swedenborg wanted to adhere to his version in *The Worship and Love of God*, although he did not find the issue more important than that the reader may believe as he or she likes. This implies that Swedenborg understood the part played by poetic imagination in his presentation of the birth of Adam. This essential scene is partly an aesthetic play on the somber ground of meditation.[2]

Of course, an internal motivation does not exclude external impulses. Swedenborg might have encountered the motif in contemporary natural history as well as in ancient mythology. Even such a well-known work as Grotius' book on the truth of Christianity, which Swedenborg often quoted—for example, in *Oeconomia* and in the collection of excerpts— contains numerous references both in the text and the commentaries to ancient authors who might have steered Swedenborg's thoughts in the direction of the drama of creation.[3] A second work by Thomas Burnet, *Archaeologiae Philosophicae: sive Doctrina antiqua de rerum originibus libri duo*, includes several Asian myths about men being born out of eggs, illustrating that an interest in the motif was present in contemporary literature that attracted Swedenborg, as well as a general adaptation of mythological phenomena to modern science.[4]

The same interest can be demonstrated in contemporary dissertations. In its preface, a German thesis from 1672 called *"Homo ex ovo, sive De ovo humano"* conveys a respectful amazement of the circle of nature, which is represented by the egg: *"ex vegetabilibus, ex animalibus ova, ex ovis vicissim animalia, ex ovis vegetabilia"* (out of plants, out of animals eggs, out of eggs in turn animals, out of eggs plants).[5] As Harvey maintained, the human being is also part of this very circle. The rest of the dissertation consists of a survey of relevant literature with numerous examples, introduced by a general description of the Orphic egg, before the author proceeds *"ab ovo mundano ad humanum,"* from macrocosm to microcosm.[6] In this context, the author mentions the myths of Castor and Pollux, as well as Helen and Clytemnestra, who were born out of eggs, and he also reports on Syrian and Egyptian gods of similar birth. But all this information is given in passing, and the author soon moves to anatomical discourses with mostly modern references, among others to Harvey, Thomas Bartholin (1616–1680), and Nicolaus Steno (1638–1686); incidentally, he also mentions the fantastic homunculus project of Paracelsus.

Some twenty years later, the same writer came back with a longer work on a similar subject, something like a calendar of ancient and modern knowledge called *Oologia curiosa*.[7] This treatise also opens with a survey of the mythic and mystic egg concepts, which we have already met in Burnet's *Telluris theoria sacra*, but in a considerably more extensive form: even conjectures of Renaissance chemists on the elements of the earth and their presence in the egg are reported.[8] In the second part of the book, the author presents more detailed ideas of the egg, and he combines the mythical vision of the spontaneous generation of human beings out of the mud of the Nile with an account of Leda in the guise of a swan laying eggs, out of which Pollux, Castor, Helen, and Clytemnestra were born. Further on, he illustrates the ideas of Democritus and Epicurus about the birth of the human race out of the earth *"vermiculorum modo,"* like worms, with reference to the Lucretius passages quoted above. Finally, other literary theories are reported, according to which the origin of humanity like that of the insects should be looked for in marshes and woods.[9]

Thus, Swedenborg had models of his thesis on human birth from an egg, as well as works discussing the important connection of macrocosm and microcosm. The most conspicuous element of his representation, however, is that he uses the biblical tree of life as the hold and fundament of the egg. To a certain extent, even this motif can be traced back to ancient myth and poetry, and *Oologia curiosa* contains some suggestions, for example, a reference to Hesiod's *Erga kai hemerai*:

> Kronos now shapes another generation of human beings, the third one; he makes it of copper, totally different from the previous one of silver. Strong and irrepressible, it is made of ash-wood. This race loves acts of violence and fights, the clamorous games of the god of war; but they do not eat bread.[10]

And further on Virgil is quoted:

> *Haec nemora indigenae Fauni Nymphaeque tenebant*
> *gensque virum truncis et duro robore nata,*
> *quis neque mos neque cultus erat, nec iungere tauros*

> (In these woodlands once
> Dwelt native Fauns and Nymphs, a race of men
> From tree-stocks sprung and stubborn hearts of oak,
> Who had no rule, no art of life, nor knew
> To yoke the steer . . . .) [11]

Garmann refers to several other ancient stories of humans born out of trees, even if he, as a true adherent of Harvey's thesis *"omne vivum ex ovo"* does so to exemplify wrong ideas. Even so, his negative attitude attests to contemporary knowledge of the varied ways in which the motif had been treated in ancient times.

As significant a source as Leibniz's theodicy supports this general knowledge. One of Swedenborg's extracts from it offers an example of the importance of considering the whole context, out of which Swedenborg has picked his quotation. Just before the sentence Swedenborg copied, Leibniz referred to the Scottish barnacles mentioned above and made a quotation of a Latin hexameter passage:

> . . . *populos umbrosa creavit*
> *Fraxinus, & foeta viridis puer excidit alno.*

(The shadowy ash has created people, and a flourishing boy jumps forth from the fertile alder); this is Statius speaking in his *Thebais* (IV: 280–281).[12] In this epic, the Theban civil war is in preparation; one of those who are rallying around the flags is the hero Parthenopeus, of Argive origin but here said to come from Arcadia. The hexametric lines are part of the description of the entourage of the hero, alluding to the ancient Arcadian paradise, the inhabitants of which are "*astris lunaque priores,*" older than the stars and the moon, and born of the trees of the forest in the distant Golden Age. Here an important source of inspiration has been found, which Swedenborg most probably knew well, even without being reminded by Leibniz. The interesting fact is that Leibniz has quoted Statius in a context, the biological fantasy of which comes close to the drama of creation.

There are also mythological parallels for the human-breeding egg. Both some ancient and old Norse myths had the first human couple being born of an oak or an ash.[13] Trees as divine abodes also appear in mythological contexts, for example, in the shape of dryads and of the holy trees of Zeus, the oaks of Dodona. But Swedenborg's description is more precise than these general ideas, as is his use of the biblical *arbor vitae*, which exceeds the Genesis text. Of course, this tree of life appears in alchemical speculations still flourishing in the seventeenth century.[14] The versatile Paracelsus occupies a prominent position in this tradition also. Ideas of *arbor vitae* are represented in his writings, although mostly in the sense of elixirs of life or more correctly as an element of such magic mixtures.[15] The apocryphal *Liber Azoth*, which was attributed to Paracelsus at the time, comes closest to Swedenborg when it implies that Adam was born out of a tree. The theory is, however, shrouded in speculative mystery, and it is combined with ideas of *arbor vitae* in a way that permits both symbolic and grossly concrete interpretations; as pointed out above, the biologist Daniel Sennert had noticed that the belief in the existence of barnacles could be supported by a reference to Paracelsus' representation.[16] Thus, no detailed information about the birth of Adam can be found in *Liber Azoth*, only some general thoughts and references in passing to Ovid's use of tree motifs in his transformation tales.[17]

This reminder of Ovid is justified, if we leave the strict plan for a moment to move forward to the description of the birth of woman in the sixth scene of the drama, in which Swedenborg links the biblical version to his comprehensive view by means of the *correspondentia fabulosa* pattern. In Gen. 2:21, the Lord had Adam fall into a deep sleep and then stripped him of a rib, from which God formed Eve. Instead, Swedenborg has Adam dream of a rendezvous with "*venustissima facie & corpore Nympha,*" a nymph with the most beautiful face and body, whom he tries to catch in midair: the excitement and the hunt seem to tear off a rib from his breast (§87). In actual fact, however, Adam has caught and embraced a branch to which the egg from which Eve is to be born is attached; by kissing it passionately, he fertilizes this egg by inserting a soul of his own *anima.* Swedenborg's description of the birth of Eve is steeped in a glowing sensuousness, which is totally missing in Genesis, and recalls the divine love of classical mythology. It also suggests an erotic man's personal experiences of youthful dreams and his bitter disappointment on awakening to loneliness and yearning.

In rather cautious terms, Lamm advanced the theory that Swedenborg got the idea for his biblical paraphrase at this point from *Paradise Lost.*[18] The situation is indeed identical. Adam thinks he is seeing Eve in a dream, and his awakening is marked by the same bitter sense of loss, until the Creator invisibly leads her to him. But for the rest, the differences in *Paradise Lost* are more conspicuous. In his dream, Adam sees the act of Creation in a way closely connected to the Genesis text; the Creator shut his eyes but allows his inner sight to be open:

> by which
> Abstract as in a transe methought I saw,
> Though sleeping, where I lay, and saw the shape
> Still glorious before whom awake I stood;
> Who stooping op'nd my left side, and took
> From thence a Rib, with cordial spirits warme,
> And Life-blood streaming fresh; wide was the wound,
> But suddenly with flesh fill'd up and heal'd:
> The Rib he formd and fashond with his hands;
> Under his forming hands a Creature grew,
> Manlike, but different Sex, so lovly faire,
> That what seemd fair in all the World, seemd now
> Mean, or in her summd up, in her containd
> And in her looks, which from that time infus'd
> Sweetness into my heart, unfelt before,
> And into all things from her Aire inspir'd
> The spirit of love and amorous delight. (VIII: 461–477).

The fact that the Creator comes forth in this direct way makes quite a different and much more biblical impression, as the naively grandiose vision of Genesis has been sublimated into poetic mastery. In Swedenborg's description of the creative act, however, the persistent and often-observed intermediation of natural forces and spiritual powers between the will of the Creator and its outcome is fulfilled, which leaves a veiled and airy abstraction much stronger than Milton's concrete paraphrase. With reference to literary models, the sensuous tone of Swedenborg's description is reminiscent of Ovid rather than of Milton, first to the myth of Apollo and Daphne, in which the defeated hopes of the divine youth are expressed in a parallel situation "embracing the branches tightly, as if they were limbs."[19] The association comes even more easily in recalling that the young Emanuel Swedberg once treated a similar motif in one of his Ovid paraphrases, a *"Fabula de Perillae & Nerei Amore,"* in which a nymph hunted by the god of the sea was protected by and enclosed in the laurel of Minerva, a metamorphosis that comes near to the situation in *The Worship and Love of God* thirty years later.[20]

There is a possible trace of an Endymion motif in this scene, perhaps also a faint echo of Plato's androgynous myth, which Swedenborg noted among his excerpts.[21] Thus, there appears to be no ground for a reference to Milton; all the similarities can be accounted for by a common reading of ancient poetry and myth, as even Lamm suggested.[22] In comparison with Swedenborg, Milton is more faithful to the biblical source regarding the birth of human beings. Milton's first human couple were created as adults, but Swedenborg, as well as Burnet, introduces Adam and Eve into the drama of the world as infants.

However, the symbol of the tree of life has also a more specific background than the one outlined here, a significance connected to the extremely complicated psychophysical processes in the following scenes. In the studies of the anatomy of the brain, which are a logical consequence of Swedenborg's Cartesian education and the results of which have been perceived already in *De Infinito*, the concept of *arbor vitae* also appeared. It happens in the first detailed discussion on brain anatomy in Swedenborg's *Oeconomia*, as well as in the very extensive collection of manuscripts from the early 1740s, on which Swedenborg's reputation as a cerebrologist is founded. A description of the cortex of the cerebellum, the primary source of which is Malpighi, serves as an example:

> *Alia compositio & insinuatio hujus substantiae Corticalis apparet in Cerebello: insinuatur enim circellis & plicis, & penetrat distinctissime; & ubique promit ex se fibrillas, tam visibiliter, ut arboris formam, dum tota compages perpendiculariter scinditur, repraesentent: in qua arbore vitali se pulcherrimo ordine & unanimo consensu refert truncus ad ramos, ramus ad frondes, frons ad quemlibet oculum seu particulam tam mirabiliter,*

*ut communis actio sit eadem cum singularum particulari, &*
*vicissim.*

(Another composition and compound of this cortical substance appears in the cerebellum. For it twists and turns into
small circles and folds and penetrates in a particular way, and
everywhere it sends out small fibres of itself in such a visible
manner that it is represented in the form of a tree, when the
whole compound is cut at an angle. In a beautiful order and
concord, the trunk of this tree of life is related to the branches,
the branch to the leaves, the leaf to every eye or particle in such
a wonderful way that the common action will be the same as
the specific action of the single parts and vice versa.)[23]

This tree of life comes forth at an adequately performed dissection: *"Ideo
si scindatur compages per medium usque ad quartum Ventriculum, apparet
forma arbusculi, Arbor vitae nonnullis vocati"* (If therefore the compound
is cut through the middle down to the fourth ventricle, the form of a little
tree will appear, by several people called the tree of life).[24] The same piece
of information is varied in some other neurological contexts from the period before *The Worship and Love of God.*[25]

Thus this tree of life appears primarily in the cerebellum, although similar forms can also be found in other parts of the brain. In combination
with Swedenborg's psychological system, this opens wide perspectives. The
task of the cerebellum is to house *anima*, the soul, and consequently the *a
priori* knowledge, which is distinctive of the soul, in contrast to *mens*, the
reason, with its empirical knowledge. In the Genesis commentaries, which
Swedenborg wrote during the next few years after *The Worship and Love
of God,* he interprets the trees of paradise according to a psychological and
theological scheme close to the line of thought found in his drama of creation. In *Historia creationis* he wrote:

> *Cum itaque effectus naturales sint symbola rerum caelestium,
> Ipsa arbor vitalis in medio horto collocata Sapientiam ex caelo
> seu per viam superiorem, in mentem ejus, defluentem, arbor
> vero scientiae boni malique Intelligentiam ex mundo ejusque
> natura, per viam inferiorem, seu per sensus animumque, in ean-
> dem mentem, influentem, significabat.*
>
> (Since then natural effects are symbols of heavenly things, the
> tree of life, placed in the middle of the garden, signified the wis-
> dom, which was pouring into his intellect from heaven, or on
> the higher road, while the tree of knowledge of good and evil
> signified the knowledge, which came pouring into the same in-
> tellect from the world and its nature on the lower road, or
> through the senses and the mind.)[26]

As Martin Lamm observed, in the same work Swedenborg indicates that the story of creation must be connected to the Messiah and the kingdom to come. Even in this pattern, the symbol of the tree of life is included, for the first time in the Genesis commentary next to *Historia creationis* in correct order, in which the spiritual meaning of *arbor vitae* is said to be "*Princeps caeli, unicus Amor et Filius Dei*" (The Prince of heaven, the only love and Son of the Lord), while the tree of knowledge represents the prince of the world and the love of self.[27] However, these interpretations appear after his great calling in April 1745; in the present work, this firm theological scheme is not evident. Nevertheless, the drama of creation is a chaos of potentialities, primarily from a theological point of view, in which the germs of later motifs abound. The symbol of the tree of life illustrates this. Of course, Swedenborg was familiar with the Christian interpretation of the tree of life as the Old Testament *figura* of the cross; among many others, the identification goes back to Augustine, who extended the symbol even further: "*er setzt den LB gleich mit der Frucht des LB, mit Christus selbst.*"[28]

Still more important is the correspondence between the tree of life in paradise and *arbor vitae* in the abode of *anima*, the cerebellum. The soul builds up its body in the same way as the Creator made his world come forth out of the *ovum mundanum*. Having noticed in his studies of the anatomy of the brain, how the symbol of the tree of life has been used to describe the nervous system of the cerebellum, which represents the first result of the activity of the soul in the embryo, Swedenborg must have found it natural to have the image of the tree of life as the womb of the human being embody his conviction of the universe as a web of correspondences. *Arbor vitae* becomes a medium of the divine influx into nature as the nervous system of the cerebellum transports the *fluidum spirituosum* in the human body. The picture of the tree of life in *The Worship and Love of God* draws essential inspiration from this anatomical background; in this way, it becomes even more significant to call the soul Adam's mother and *arbor vitae* the mother tree.

At the same time, this interpretation enforces the artistic connections between this scene and the following ones that take place in Adam's psyche so that the borders between that and the terrestrial paradise are sometimes blurred. An anatomical correspondence in the brain explains this erasure. Swedenborg did not emphasize this correspondence in his drama of creation; instead, he uses the trees of paradise as symbols of the two ways of attaining knowledge. There may be several reasons for that, but the most important one must be the theological orientation that dominates the latter part of the drama, particularly the issue of good and evil. Nonetheless, the symbol of the *arbor vitae* is genetically connected to the background outlined here; the studies of the anatomy of the brain, which preceded *The Worship and Love of God*, were aimed toward the same goal as this work: to retrieve and spread the immediate knowledge of God and the soul, which Adam, born of the tree of life, possessed in the state of innocence. Thus, the episode of the tree of life exemplifies how a scientist's knowledge is metamorphosed into significant symbols when his literary creativity had been stimulated by the *correspondentia fabulosa* theory and the experiences of the religious crisis can no longer be handled within the boundaries of science.

As one could expect, a study of the biological themes of Swedenborg's drama of creation has so far resulted in a number of scientific and literary sources of inspiration. Nevertheless, the lasting impression is one of profound originality. When it comes to the idea of *homo ex ovo*, in which the various egg concepts reach their intellectual and artistic climax, one may find superficial resemblances among the authorities of the epoch, one may point to the ovological orientation of contemporary biology inspired by Harvey, one is reminded of paracelsic and alchemical speculations and ancient myths of the tree of life, one meets the term of *arbor vitae* in the writings of the brain anatomists, yet it is difficult to establish any precise conformities. No writer known to me displays such an extended combination of macrocosm and microcosm as in Swedenborg's ovological thinking. In the egg, he found a point where the birth of the infinitely small life and the infinitely great one could be brought together in accordance with the principle presented in the introduction *"Repraesentationes enim particulares sunt totidem Specula Communium"* (§2), particular phenomena are reflections of the general ones. In *The Worship and Love of God*, this concept is given a higher dignity than in contemporary science, and the egg becomes a symbol of the convergence of nature and spirit at different stages, at the highest one a *receptaculum* of the influx of the spirit of God into nature. The result is a strange and daring union of sensuous lucidity and abstruse spiritualism, of biblical inspiration and classical mythology, of the accuracy of science and the aesthetic play of poetry.

Swedenborg's classical erudition played the main part in giving his visions a literary shape; there are clear traces of Ovid and the juvenile poems inspired by him; Lucretius may have influenced the description of the earth as the great mother, while Virgil, Statius, and others may be traced behind the tree motifs. This classical background explains enough, so there is no need to assume any reading of Milton at this stage of the drama. Finally, Holy Writ is the firm ground: it stands to reason that it makes itself particularly felt in a staging of the creation of the image of God in nature.

## God and the Soul

After the birth of Adam, the focus shifts from God in nature to God in the human soul. This means considerable changes, intellectually and emotionally, since Swedenborg here approaches his most pressing problems, which are drifting along toward their final solution during the preparation of this remarkable work. To get a more complete impression of that, it will be necessary to take a closer look at the religious problem complex in his previous production.

De Infinito (1734) is the first systematic attempt at harmonizing philosophy and Christian faith in Swedenborg's *oeuvre*. It is dedicated to Eric Benzelius Jr., Swedenborg's brother-in-law, who became bishop of Linköping at the time. In ornate Latin, Swedenborg conveys his gratitude to Benzelius, who once led his inquisitive but indecisive mind *ad haec et similia*, towards the ultimate foundations of human knowledge.[29] Although conventional, these phrases should be taken seriously. Scholars have credited Benzelius for influencing the scientific orientation of Swedenborg in his youth, a view supported by their correspondence in the 1710s, showing that the brothers-in-law took a common interest in the progress of science at the time.[30] Professionally Benzelius belonged to a humanistic and theological tradition of learning; even with due consideration for the rather broad-minded manner of recruiting bishops in historic times, it is remarkable that Benzelius ended his life as archbishop elect of Sweden.[31]

Perhaps Swedenborg chose to dedicate De Infinito, an essay on the relation of God to the finite world, to his brother-in-law in order to emphasize his particular harmonizing influence. Even if it seems reasonable to attest, as so many have done, that Swedenborg's development into a seer can be psychologically explained to a great extent by the legacy of his father and the atmosphere of belief in spirits and angels around him, Benzelius probably exerted a stronger influence on Swedenborg's intellectual career up to the religious crisis, because of his broad education and his power of combining passion for science and Christian faith.[32] There is also evidence that he supported the young Swedenborg in conflicts with his domineering father, who portrays himself in his memoirs as a man of very little understanding of purely theoretical studies.[33] This dedication to his brother-in-law stands as a portal to a new phase in Swedenborg's production, starting with De Infinito; and the union of science and faith in The Worship and Love of God comes closer to Benzelius' views than those of Jesper Swedberg.[34] Still, the appearance of his imposing father in the religious chaos of the dream diary seems symptomatic, and we may summarize the inner tensions of the drama of creation by the changing of the guard between Swedenborg's spiritual fathers.

De Infinito is intimately connected to Principia, in which work a concept of divinity is used in an essential context. When Swedenborg discusses the origin of the nucleus of nature, the natural or mathematical point, in the second chapter of the first part of Principia, he employs the concept of the infinite. This concept of God is, however, not a personal one. On the contrary, the infinite functions in Principia as an active divine power less than as a practical postulate—in Aristotelian terms an unmoved mover.

When the first natural point has emerged from infinity, Swedenborg transfers all his attention to the following phases of the development of nature. He reveres the Word of God: *"Ipsae literae sacrae etiam nos in eo informare volunt, quod mundus a Deo & ab infinito creatus sit: quod successive creatus; quodque tempore creatus sit; & quod infinitum sit ens in se, sit esse quod est, sit omne in omnibus, sit universum"* (The Holy Writ also wants to teach us that the world was created by God and from the infinite; that it was created successively; that it was created in time; and that the infinite is an entity of itself, an *esse*, that it is all in all, is universal).[35] The first man in his state of innocence is praised for his power of immediate contact with God and for his knowledge of the right worship of God, and Swedenborg eloquently depicts the humble awe of a wise man for infinity, about which qualities we cannot know anything: *"ergo illud profundissime & devotissima anima devenerabitur; & per venerationem illam ex sola cogitatione corpus seu totum systema membranaceum & sensitivum ejus quasi ab uno extremo ad alterum timide sed etiam dulce contremiscet"* (therefore, he shall venerate it with the profoundest awe of the soul; and at the simple thought of it, his entire body or system of membranes and nerves will oscillate in terror but at the same time in delight from one extreme to the opposite one by this veneration).[36] Thus far, however, the veneration and the humility lack a personal tone, seeming merely ornamental and rhetorical phrases suitable for the genre.

Swedenborg's aspirations are excited by the unknowable, and in *De Infinito,* he approaches the problem of God and his relations to the finite world. The essay consists of two parts, the first of which is about exactly this problem, while the second section discusses the commerce between body and soul under the heading *"De mechanismo operationis animae et corporis."* This combination—as well as its phrasing—immediately subsumes the book in the Cartesian tradition, focusing on the psychophysical interchange problem.[37] How then is the contact between the two worlds established?

Following Descartes even here, Swedenborg declares that such a question is both unnecessary and arrogant, since in Holy Writ we can find the only true answer—faith. The first two paragraphs of the text are therefore devoted to defending the reason that the issue was brought up: that there is a law of human thinking that forces the human being constantly to penetrate the unknown. To a secular reviewer, the expression sounds almost ironic in the light of Swedenborg's own future development.[38] A thinker wants to find a philosophical answer to the question to convince sceptics about the truth of Revelation and to protect them from heresies. This purpose also belongs to the recurring elements in the post-Cartesian tradition—not least as it was represented in those Uppsala circles that both Benzelius and Swedenborg knew so well—that had been alarmed by the problems caused by Descartes' sharp distinction between spirit and matter.

At the same time, it is another portent of what will determine all his later production.

Swedenborg, then, has to start from the bottom, beginning by asking if the infinite exists at all.[39] He finds the answer in the particular physico-theological proof of God's existence, according to which "the need for a constructor is established by the ingeniousness and perfection of the mechanism," to use Lamm's phrasing.[40] This line of reasoning is typical of the time, but its specific shape offers a psychologically interesting example of Swedenborg's excessive joy of learning. As it has been practiced in this genre since Cicero's *De natura deorum*, he substantiates his proof of God's existence with examples from the human body. He collected an enormous amount of data from a manual of anatomy, the well-known *Compendium Anatomicum* by Lorenz Heister (1683–1758), and became so enthusiastic that the examples threaten to exceed all limits. The renewed interest in anatomy bespeaks the zeal of a convert and reveals the intimate links between *De Infinito* and *The Worship and Love of God*, as is also indicated in the dream diary. In *The Worship and Love of God*, Swedenborg returns to the ultimate foundation after a decade of intense anatomical studies; and although he did not succeed in keeping himself within the limits of his theme this time either, he forced his way deeper into the land of the unknowable in this project, guided not least by the studies of the physiology of the brain, the preliminary stages of which can be observed in *De Infinito*.[41]

As is well known, the physico-theological proof of God's existence was used since Plato and Aristotle. Swedenborg's next attempt at proving the existence of God is a similar case, for it is a variant of the argument, which is often called "*consensus gentium*." It argues that since different peoples share a principally similar belief in the existence of a higher being, such a being must exist. Aristotle and Cicero are mentioned as the most prominent advocates of the argument, while Locke, to whose epistemology Swedenborg comes close, for example, in *Principia*, refuted it.[42]

After referring to these two proofs, Swedenborg discusses various notions of God. He starts with the naively pious view, the anthropomorphic character of which reduces the *esse* of the infinite to finite proportions and makes God into some sort of a transcendent despot. Swedenborg, of course, dissociates himself from this belief, most often in a cautious and conciliatory tone, but in some cases with scorn and sarcasm: "*cui sententiae eo libentius favent illi, qui putant se Infinito propinquiores & amiciores esse, & illum sic ad suas partes & pro arbitrio posse flectere, & sub autoritate quasi divina animis & societatibus humanis imperare*" (This opinion is favored by people the closer to and more loved by the infinite they believe themselves to be, and who think that they can bend him arbitrarily to their side, and thus make it possible for them to rule over the souls and societies of men as it were by divine authority).[43] The statement is unfortunately too general to identify any precise targets; otherwise, it would be tempting to interpret it as a late protest against his home as a child, in which he had been exposed to a man who indeed regarded himself as "closest to and most loved by the infinite," but there are, of course, too many members of that category to select just Jesper Swedberg, for example, the pharisees in the Scriptures, perhaps the Roman Catholic Church, or some sectarians. The crucial difference between Swedenborg's notion of God and that of naive piety is the process of creation. The childish belief in a celestial gardener planting earthly objects one after the other is unacceptable to Swedenborg, who held a view inspired by Augustine according to which everything came into existence at once as seeds and determined potentials.

After that follows an account of how different philosophers have tried to establish the *esse* of infinity, but as usual Swedenborg is very reticent, and the only name mentioned is Aristotle. "The philosopher," as he is called according to the practice of Scholasticism, holds the first place among references in Swedenborg's production, which may seem surprising in view of its Cartesian background. Descartes and his disciples, for example, Malebranche, who exerted an important influence on Swedenborg, looked upon Aristotle as their major opponent.[44] Swedenborg lived in a different situation ideologically, particularly after the synthetic contributions by Leibniz, in which Aristotelianism no longer constituted any danger to the freedom of thought. Therefore, he could let his general conviction of antiquity as an epoch versed in knowledge of essential truths determine his choice of references. In this theological context, Aristotle had an advantage over many thinkers. The main objection against the philosophical attempts at solving the problem of infinity is that they tried to squeeze the infinite into the framework of finite thought, identifying infinity with macrocosm, for instance, and also with microcosm, with the atom. Thus, they ended up in pantheism or nature worship.

But by rational thinking, Aristotle had reached the principally correct view that God is not finite and that neither the universe itself nor its largest or smallest parts can be God, since they are natural and finite. The Philosopher and some of his disciples tried to solve the problem by extending the natural universe to infinite dimensions, which they did by depriving it of all limits and giving it the shape of a circle. Thus, nature would be without an end and time without a beginning.[45] However, the line of argument dissolved in a series of contradictions, according to Swedenborg, since these philosophers were forced to discern finite parts of the infinite universe: even if you put together such parts in all eternity, you will never get an infinite sum, and there will always remain a decisive difference between finite and infinite. The finite world emerged out of infinity, and so we face—or return to—the fundamental question: how does this happen?

The infinite is the immediate cause of the first finite object. By definition, this could not have happened without a link, a *nexus*, which must also be infinite for logical reasons. The intentional cause, *causa finalis*, exists for the sake of the first cause, and everything is related to this first cause by the *nexus*: consequently, everything has been created for the infinity, the first cause of all.[46] Thus argues the intellect. But is there no revealed truth that can make the picture complete? Did not the Lord declare that he had brought forth a Son by eternity, who is infinite and God, and that "*nexum esse finiti & Infiniti per unigenitum infinitum & Deum, & patrem & filium esse unum Deum, utrumque infinitum, utrumque creatorem universi finiti; in creationis opere utrumque concurrisse, sed tamen ita distinctos esse, ut ille sit pater hic filius* (the connection between the finite and the infinite is achieved through the only begotten infinite and God; that the Father and the Son are one God and both infinite; that both are the creator of the finite universe; that both cooperated in the act of creation but that both are nevertheless apart, so that one is the Father and the other the Son).[47] Since the two are one, the *nexus* role of the Son does not imply that the universe should have been created mediately by the Lord, as Lamm also noticed.[48]

Behind Swedenborg's philosophical concepts, a particular biblical passage is easily recognizable, the famous prologue of the Gospel of John, and it is only natural that one will meet a commentary of the salvation act of the Son further on in *De Infinito*, of which more will be said in its proper context later in this study. After having given some positive determinations of the relation between the infinite and the finite world by referring to Revelation, Swedenborg transfers his attention to humankind, the last effect within the sphere of nature, by which the intention of the creation can be fulfilled. By virtue of the Aristotelian concept of causality, there must be something in this finite effect that has a part of the Infinite—namely, our recognition of God's existence and our rejoicing at his love. Therefore, humanity's worship of God and the experience of his love become the noblest qualities of the human species.

It is not only on these verbal grounds that one is reminded of *The Worship and Love of God*. The title of the drama of creation and its philosophical and theological implications are directly portended in a following passage of the text, when Swedenborg describes humankind's situation, in which the understanding of the meaning and end of the creation has been obscured by sin and imperfection. Obviously, he intends to regain this lost knowledge. To succeed, it is necessary for people to constantly keep the divine ends in sight; earthly incentives and blessings must not be experienced in isolation but as parts of universal harmony and elements of the proper worship of God. Although mentioned in passing here, an exhaustive presentation is promised: *Sed de his in philosophia ratiocinante de culto divino* (but [more] on this in a philosophical discussion on divine worship) or earlier: *ex hoc fonte dein venit omnis cultus divinus, de quo alibi, quia vastissimi operis est, sed revelatum habemus* (from this fountain comes all divine worship, on which somewhere else, since it is an enormous work, but it has been revealed to us).[49]

Thus, the keynote of the drama of creation has already been set in *De Infinito*, but the thematic handling of it is still missing. If one tries to penetrate the symbolic world of *The Worship and Love of God* from *De Infinito*, one is struck by the greater complexity of the drama of creation, both in general and in theological details. While there is an essential distinction between finite and infinite in *De Infinito*, the author attempted to bridge the gap within the framework of the mechanistic system; he did not introduce the problem of evil. In spite of all endeavours to express the profound unity of existence, the complexity of life is emphasized in *The Worship and Love of God*, where the issue of evil could not be kept out of the text. The emotional tone also changed: *De Infinito* employed purely theoretical arguments, while the drama of creation conveyed an atmosphere of urgent personal commitment.

The altered emotional atmosphere, which in its way reflects the religiously turbulent decade between the two works, is particularly noticeable in the concept of God. The problems of emanation and *creatio ex nihilo* have been discussed above starting from the origin of material objects and living organisms, and so far Swedenborg does not seem to think in terms of any emanation of nature. But the situation changes when the human soul is initiated into nature. In the third scene, the reader will see the connection, *nexus*, between finite and infinite in action, when the divine intellect creates Adam's soul out of itself and inserts it into the egg that had been produced by nature as the ultimate end of providence. But this *suprema mens* is also compared with the sun of life, the concentrated rays of which create the soul, and this metaphor links the text with a passage in *Oeconomia*, where Swedenborg attempted to capture symbolically the relation between God and the world:

> *Sed scire, quâ haec Vita & sapientia influit ratione, est infinite supra sphaeram mentis humanae: nulla est analysis & nulla abstractio, quae eo pertingit: nam quicquid est in Deo, & qua ratione agit, est Deus. Sola est repraesentatio ejus per viam Comparationis cum Lumine. . . . Sed ultra in comparationis partes exire non licet, quatenus unum est intra naturam, & alterum est supra: unum est physicum, alterum est pure morale: & unum cadit sub philosophiam mentis, alterum autem se recipit intra Sacra Theologiae; inter quae sunt fines, quos transcendere ingeniis humanis impossibile est.*

> (But to know, how this life and wisdom flows in is far above the sphere of human intellect. There is no analysis and no abstraction that can reach so far, for whatever is in God and how he ever acts is God. The only representation of that can be given

by a comparison with the light. . . . But it is not allowed to proceed any longer into the details of the comparison, since one is
within nature and the other is above it: one is physical, the
other is purely moral: one falls within the philosophy of mind,
the other retires into the sacred domains of theology. Between
those are boundaries that it is impossible for human intellects to
cross.)[50]

For obvious reasons, this cautious attitude, which corresponds to that of
Leibniz, is not as clearly portrayed in *The Worship and Love of God*. The
symbolic form of representation allows the author greater freedom in details, since the theses can be translated to their different levels of significance by virtue of the correspondence system. By all appearances, the
account of the creation of the soul contradicts the concept of *creatio ex nihilo*, and it foreshadows the emanation idea, to which there are some allusions in the final scenes of the drama of creation and which will be fully
developed in the theosophical works. From his general argument against
the *harmonia praestabilita* model, Swedenborg clearly rejected Wolff's notion of the creation of the soul *ex nihilo*.[51]

But it remains an open question whether the vision of the encounter between godhead and nature in the human egg should be interpreted as a theoretically elaborate idea. In a symbolic context of this kind, it seems
doubtful that Swedenborg wanted to express his conviction of the human
being as the image of God in nature, as it is written in Genesis, and he
chose a metaphoric language in excellent correspondence with the keynote
of the work. Once again, he may be compared with Augustine, whose importance for the Swedenborgian psychology becomes the more evident as
one studies his sources. The partition of the human psyche in three areas,
which Swedenborg presented in *Oeconomia*, can be found *in nuce* in the
works of the Church Father and the pseudo-Augustinian *De spiritu et
anima*. Swedenborg agreed with Augustine's ideas in the excerpts, as will
be shown below. As regards the creation of the soul, Swedenborg's excerpts
from Augustine convey hesitancy. It seems reasonable to interpret the symbolic account of that event as portrayed in *The Worship and Love of God*
in light of the following illustration from Augustine's *De anima et ejus
origine*: "*Quod enim de ipso est, necesse est ut ejusdem naturae sit cujus
ipse est, ac per hoc etiam immutabile sit. Anima vero, quod omnes fatentur,
mutabilis est. (Non ergo de ipso, quia non est immutabilis sicut ipse.) Si
autem de nulla re alia facta est, de nihilo facta est procul dubio, sed ab
ipso*" (For whatever is of [God] must necessarily be of the same nature as
he, and therefore also unchangeable. But the soul is variable, as all recognize. [Thus, it is not of him, since it is not unchangeable as he.] But if it
was not created out of something else, it was undoubtedly created out of
nothing, but by him).[52]

The link with *Oeconomia* can also be supported by theoretical arguments. When Adam embraces his bride in his dream, in reality he kisses the egg out of which Eve will be born, and in that way inseminates his soul in it (§87). There is a specific theory behind this metamorphosis, which is explained thus in *Oeconomia*: "*Quod Anima cujuscunque prolis a Parente suo traducatur, & sic omnium ab Adamo, qui suam immediate acceptam tulit Creatori Universi, id sequitur ex nuda Animae descriptione*" (It follows from the mere description of the soul that the soul of every descendant comes from his or her father, and thus the souls of all from Adam, who was given his soul directly by the Creator of the universe).[53] Later in *Oeconomia,* Swedenborg outlines the general intellectual background, and Lamm interpreted his conception as a combination of Aristotle and Tertullian, which is also characteristic of the theosophical writings.[54]

The close connection with previous conjectures becomes evident in another issue. The references to Genesis, which are listed in a note to this scene, are based on the interpretation of what happened when the Lord infused a "spirit of life" into Adam after having shaped him from the dust of the earth (Gen. 2:7). It is clear to Swedenborg that "spirit of life" mentioned here must mean air, and the reasons are, first, biological, that the body is vivified by breathing, and, second, hermeneutic, that the air at other places in the Scripture has been called "spirit of life" or "spirit of God." The Bible passages given are Gen. 6:17, 7:15, 22; Ex. 15:8, 10; 2 Sam. 22:16; Psalms 104: 29, 30; and Job 27:3 (§38, note y). All these texts, except the one from Job, have been registered in cod. 36–110, the collection of Swedenborg's excerpts, which means that the author consulted his notes when he was about to explain the birth of Adam in the drama of creation: all of them are collected in the final part of the manuscript, that is, among the notes on correspondences.[55]

But Swedenborg had noticed this problem even earlier. In two excerpts from Augustine under the heading "Anima, soul," Gen. 2:7 is discussed. The Church Father devoted a chapter in *De civitate Dei* to refuting such interpretations of this passage, which imply that the Lord only called a soul to life that already existed in the newborn man. However, the interpretation depends on the meaning of the concept "soul," and in another place, Augustine makes an analysis based on a distinction between soul and spirit, his point of departure being the Greek terms of the *Septuagint*.[56] Swedenborg agrees with him: "*multis locis in sacris distinguunt inter animam et spiritum. ibid. distinguenda sunt secund. meam theoriam*" (At many places in Scripture, soul and spirit are separated. They should be distinguished according to my theory).[57] This adherence to Augustine is also noticeable in *Oeconomia*, where several quotations are taken from him, "*illuminati judicii Patrem*" (vol. II, §282) (a Church Father of enlightened judgment), as he is called.

This distinction is the basis of his own exegesis in *The Worship and*

*Love of God*: the soul has already been inserted in the human egg, and the "spirit of life" in Gen. 2:7 cannot be interpreted as *mens spiritualis*. But this means that, because of Swedenborg's original opinion of the creation of humanity, his position will be a kind of compromise between Augustine and the exegetes whom the Church Father opposed. God immediately inseminated the soul in Adam—so far Swedenborg agrees with Augustine—but the "spirit of life" in Gen. 2:7 should be understood as an arousal of the soul in accordance with the interpretations, which had been commented and refuted in the excerpts from *De civitate Dei*. It is typical of Swedenborg's often unscholarly and misleading way of making excerpts that he confined himself to writing down Augustine's report of their ideas but abstained from making any notes of his exhaustive criticism of them.[58] However, under the same heading, there are also other excerpts from Augustine, which give the impression that the Father had lost hope of his ability to solve the problem of the creation of the soul. Excerpts from *De Genesi ad Litteram* come close to the caution recommended in *Oeconomia*.[59]

The significant Augustinian impact on this psychotheological issue makes the previous comparison between the concepts of emanation of the two thinkers even more relevant. From his Neoplatonic period, Augustine harbored strong impressions of the idea of the divine emanation into nature, and Swedenborg became particularly interested in that very aspect of his thinking, which was also in line with contemporary philosophy. But as a dauntless rationalist, Swedenborg did not share the dogmatic care that restrained the Father from being consistent enough to conceive a complete emanation system. When he had found the ultimate religious truth, he no longer stayed with Augustine. It is interesting that the affinity with the Church Father is so strongly felt in *The Worship and Love of God* in the small image of the meeting of the Supreme Mind with the human egg. This theme will lead away from Augustine when it is carried through in the variations of the theosopher. It is significant that this happens in a symbolic context, one impressed by correspondences. The doctrine of representations and correspondences opened the gate to a world in which the borders between images and reality would be blurred and everything could be adjusted to the revealed pattern. In the drama of creation, the gate is only ajar, and the thinker is staying on the threshold: the bright light of the new world is illuminating the scientific and philosophical background that he has not yet abandoned. But the departure is approaching as he is about to portray the position of humankind in the cosmic context, the outlines of which we have seen developed in the first three scenes of the drama.

# 6

༄

# THE INFANCY OF ADAM

(§§39–56)

The shimmering lights of the heavenly choirs, which glimmered around the scene of birth at the end of the previous scene, receive a celestial equivalent in the introduction to the fourth scene when the stars throw flaming sparks; they wish to remain and observe the child waking up, but the rosy morning light forces them to yield. The rays of the sun, however, are not allowed to shine on the bed, so that the heavenly lights may be his eye's first experience. The child rests, his hands lifted in prayer and thanksgiving, a position in which the invocation of the soul is reflected in the stature of the body.

Already in this introductory scenery, where the meeting between nature and spiritual world at the birth tree of the firstborn is vividly described, we can sense the correspondential background. Dawn's forcing away the midnight stars symbolizes a new era in the universe's development, and a study of the sources uncovers a clear connection with the Genesis interpretation in the *correspondentia typica*-category of the excerpt collection:

> *Exstitit ex* vespere *et* mane dies. *Dies significat* primum periodum, aetatem, *non diem, quia ante solis ortum; nec diebus alligata sunt opera divina.* Vespera *est quando adhuc non factum, res creanda in rudimento obscuro, ut homo in ovo, utero;* mane *vero est prima, infantilis, puerilis et lusilis aetas, seu periodus in suo ortu et primogenitura.*
>
> (The day originated in evening and morning. Day signifies the first period, the age, not a day, since [it arrived] before the sunrise; divine work is not bound by days. Evening signifies that something has not yet happened; that which shall be created is still in its dark beginnings, as the human in egg and womb. But the morning is the first, infantile, childish and playful age, or a period in its rise and birth).[1]

Such direct applications of the doctrine of correspondence in the introduction of the scene implies that the doctrine will be crucial to the shape of the motifs; that this occurs after the human soul has been introduced into the world drama is natural given the background of the doctrine, which can be found within psycho-physical investigations, as was stated earlier. Immediately after the introduction's emblematical scene of devotion, the carefully structured anticipation of Adam's coming is replaced by the first results of the soul's activities. In the little body, the soul (*anima*) releases all the actions, until the intellect (*mens*) has been able to fill its empty dwellings; the tripartite psychological division that first appeared in the *Oeconomia* now appears in concrete form.[2] In the description of the newborn's first movements, Swedenborg allows his nature-observing inspiration free roam, and we see how the infant learns to feed on the mother-branch's teats and to swallow its milk. But the soul is supported in her upbringing by the protective heavenly beings, whose actions fill the following two passages (§§41, 42). They enter the newborn's innermost area, especially the Olympus of the brain, where the intellect is to be seated. Here they find, to their joy, images of the macrocosm in its two symbols, the starry sky and the world egg; Swedenborg provides a prosaic interpretation in notes, where the former is said to correspond to the *glandulae corticales* of the *cortex*, the latter to the brain as a whole (§41, notes a and b).

Thus, the physiological stage has been introduced in sketches by the heavenly beings, to whom no physical barriers make an anatomical study difficult; however, the didactic purpose of the work requires extensive factual information in notes for readers who do not possess angelic omniscience. This heavenly guidance is an artistically efficient tool, which has introduced the knowledge of cranial anatomy necessary for the rest of the drama in a natural fashion, emphasizing the particularity of the newborn between heaven and earth. To the psychological observer, it also reveals how Swedenborg claims to have won the *a priori* insight, which belongs to the angels and the first man in *regnum innocentiae*.

The description in the following paragraph (§42) of the paradise game, the angels' manner of celebrating humanity's birthday, completes the motifs. The paradise game is an equivalent of the movements of the finite points and the celestial bodies on a higher plane, a concentric spiral movement that, in three repetitions, achieves a successively higher perfection until it represents the supercelestial harmony, where *Numen Supremus* himself reigns. Into this game, they also bring with them the newborn's intellect, in which the Highest joyfully sees the final purpose of his creation. Rejoicing, the angels then return the heavenly child to earth, to the outermost circle, and the child's tiny lungs, which had ceased breathing during the ecstasy of the vision, again do their work. In one of the exquisite little details so abundant in this drama, Swedenborg allows the heavenly game to end in the excited movements of the tender lobes of the lungs. The observation serves as an excellent illustration of how intimately connected the human body is with the spirit, but it is also associated to Swedenborg's own experiences of respiratory arrest and visionary ecstacy, as will be shown later. We shall also find that the numerous descriptions of play in *The Worship and Love of God*, introduced by the dance of the planets around the sun in the first scene of chapter one, have a theoretical background in *Oeconomia*'s psychological argumentation.

After the end of the game, we leave the heavenly beings for a moment, and instead the soul's upbringing is brought into focus. The newborn child differs from his successors by his ability to move suitably from the earliest days; in this sense, Adam was closer to the animals, which can also master their limbs from birth. The reason for this is that the newborn allows his soul to lead him in everything, as the animals also do, whereas his successors depend on their intellect (*mens*), which runs the body's muscles, which is not present at birth but which grows with the aid of the senses (§43, note c). Swedenborg attaches the greatest importance to this difference and promises a clarifying treatment of the relationship between the soul (*anima*) and the intellect (*mens*): our present state is an obvious symptom of our imperfection.

Swedenborg now seeks to spread this promised clarity through a detailed description of how Adam's intellect grew. But before this, he dedicates some graceful passages to images of the soul's toil with the child, how it first makes him get up and walk, something it achieves through awakening his desire for fruit high up in the trees. The groups of heavenly beings take part in this playful zeal, for instance, by supplying him with ideas of tiny winged brothers as playmates (§44). Although this is another example of pure narrative joy, the imaginative idyll has a serious background for its visionary author: "*Caelicolae enim, coram oculis puris, ac mentibus, a terrenis amoribus, vacuis, quidvis repraesentare, & simul eas, quo, lubet, studio & ardore, incendere queunt*" (Those who live in heaven can show anything to eyes that are pure and to minds that are free of earthly desires; they can fire them with whatever zeal and enthusiasm they please) (§44).

This is only a prelude to true humanization, and our attention is now turned to the brain, where the mansions of the intellect are described in terms of ancient temple symbolism. The innermost chamber of Olympus, its most holy abode, is the soul's own dwelling, whereas the other, the sacristy, was hallowed to the intelligences, who together form the intellect. The third becomes a vestibule that houses remembered knowledge (§§ 45, 47). This is poetic embroidery on a previous cerebro-physiological fabric.[3] Into these dwellings, the intelligences would be brought like brides into bridal chambers when the time comes, and the soul longs for this time as she would no longer be bound to obedience to the body. The intellect would become her deputy in that task, to be the kind of power that "*ex affectione boni comprehenderet verum, & ex intellectu veri desideraret bonum, quaeque Caelestia conjungeret terrestribus, ac utraque in se, sicut trutina balances, juste libraret"* (could understand truth through a feeling for what was good, and that could desire what was good through an understanding of what was true; and could unite the heavenly and the earthly and fairly balance both in itself, like the pointer of a set of scales) (§45).

The theme Swedenborg is developing here belongs to the most difficult conceivable: he attempts to treat, within the framework of the fable, the physiologically based psychology, which his studies of the previous decade had led to. This meant that the note apparatus grew to unfeasible proportions; nevertheless, there are no other signs of doubt or fatigue. Indeed, he continues the description with a successively bolder and more energetically applied symbolism. Sight becomes the first sense to aid in the education of the intellect.

Already the crawling infant's eyes perceived the flowering paradise, then the different species of plants and finally remarkable flowers in a more thorough observation; the purpose is said to be to teach the child through his senses about creation, which was developed from the great world egg into species and individuals (§46).

The same procedure occurs with the trees and animals after the child learns to walk; again we are reminded of the hexaemeral topos in which the animals pay tribute to their lord, the human being, perhaps even a reminder of Adam's general regard and classification of the animal species, which we can find in the works of Philo, among others.[4] The eye conveys its experiences through the fibers to the as-yet-uninhabited Olympus, and the soul descends to meet them, dressed in a shading robe and simple adornments made of crystal: thus, the soul's gradual transformation into lower forms is symbolically portrayed, as the spiritual descent many times from now will be described in the manner of dressing and covering. The simple images of the eye, formed by sunlight, are transformed when embraced by the soul and are given life by her kisses, so that they become representations—ideas—that *anima* leads by the hand to the dwellings of memory. But the soul, who has now again disrobed, soon calls them forth to the bridal chambers; once more they are transformed through her life-giving breath, this time into intellectual ideas in a celestial form, provided with limbs and organs, so that they are similar to bodies. In this manner, they are now sent back, under the name of truths, to the memory, and from these *veritates* the intelligences are conceived (§47).

This anthropomorphic symbolism provides Swedenborg with the opportunity to give concrete shape to a complicated psychological process. At the same time, it also agrees with his general conviction that all spiritual essences and qualities possess or can assume human forms. The passage demands attentive reading, as it is at times unclear on which level of meaning one finds oneself. It is immediately used to depict another one of the basic themes—the union of truth and love. At the motherly bosom of the soul, the newborn intelligences feed on life and love, conceptually compared to the glimmer and warmth of the spiritual light, and love as the spiritual fire is molded into their bodies like a sort of blood (§48). Swedenborg then outlines rather extensively the cerebral correspondence to Adam's earliest existence in paradise, and we are told of the intelligences' fast growth under the influence of the natural harmonies, which stream through the senses and which are transformed into beauty and goodness.

From these experiences, the maturing intelligences are allowed to understand how all joy and all bliss flow forth from love, and a union with this love becomes their utmost desire. The soul has waited for this insight before it could leave the reign of the body in the hands of the intelligences: "*His apperceptis, piissima Mater, omnibus laetitiis quasi exultans, infantes suos, quod fines ex desiderio vellent, & intuerentur, prorsus ut sui imagines, in summis delitiis habere caepit, ac inter suaviationes, illas non amplius suas Intelligentias, sed Sapientias, salutabat*" (They had come to this perception; and inasmuch as in some sense she exulted in all joy, their mother, already deeply devoted to them, began to regard her infant children as among her greatest delights, because, like close images of her, they eagerly willed the ends and kept them in view. She no longer called them "Understandings" by way of endearment between her kisses, but "Wisdoms") (§48).

This salutation is given in the following passages during a farewell speech to the wisdoms, which Adam perceives in a dreamlike state, just as he awakens (§52). In this long speech, Swedenborg summarizes his view on the relationship between soul and intellect, *anima* and *mens*, in a theological perspective, and the monologue acquires the form of a teary farewell: the soul warns her daughters not to strive toward any other goal than the love of the Highest:

> *ex illo sunt omnia, quia ille est omnium; inde vestrae faustitates,*
> *& faustitatum felicitas; ex amore vestro amamini, & ex amore*
> *Ejus amatis; inde lux vestrarum intuitionum, & sacer vestrarum*
> *actionum calor; ejus enim luminis radii sunt totidem veritates,*
> *& ejus radiorum ignes sunt totidem bonitates.*
>
> (All comes from it, because it is a part of all—from it comes
> your bliss and the blessedness of your bliss; because of your
> love you are loved, and because of God's love, you love. From
> his love comes the light of your seeing and the sacred heat of
> your doing; for the rays of God's light are each a truth, and the
> fires of his rays are each an act of goodness.) (§49)

This passionate prayer is rich in omens: it alludes to the fight between good and evil, the main theme of the fifth scene, and also with the later motif of God's Son and his salvic act in the human intellect. It also alludes to the following scenes' coming identification of the soul with God, the intellect with the Son, and the sensuous consciousness (*animus*) with the prince of the world.

If the soul's farewell speech thus introduces the coming theological problems in hasty allusions, it also contains in its second part a multitude of information on the position of the intellect in the body; this twofold task of the *mens*—to view the divine goal and to lead the body after its will—is kept compositionally apart, because both the soul and its children momentarily weep with the pain of parting. When describing the reign of the intellect in the body, Swedenborg is forced to use the note apparatus for extensive commentary; this is reasonable considering that he also needs to deal with matters that are directly ruled by the soul in this body—in the nomenclature of science both the autonomous and the central nervous systems (§50). In a peculiar combination of objectivity and metaphor, the wisdoms are told that they may not rule over, for instance, the sexual organs and have limited rule over the lungs. Furthermore, the psychological faculties' physical situation is somewhat different from before: the throne and seat of the intellect is the *cerebrum*, while the soul has dedicated a little homestead for herself underneath the beautiful castle, an inconspicuous place, whose name is the "little brain," *cerebellum*.

Thus, the previous temple symbolism (§45) has been replaced by an anatomically precise description; the metaphors are gathered this time from the sphere of courts and palaces, and this transformation later corresponds also with a change of names when Adam calls the mansion of the wisdoms Helicon instead of Olympus (§54). Swedenborg used the different images to underline the difference between the stadium, where the soul immediately ruled the whole body during the education of the intellect, and the present state, when the intellect has taken power. In his choice of symbols, he displays an acute sense of literary style since the emphasis on the power and the reign is congruent with the throne and the palace, while the earlier state, ruled by the God-begotten *anima*, was better suited to temple symbolism.

However, the sun has started to rise, and the senses of the body awake: the farewell can no longer be postponed. The wisdoms hurry into their court, there to find a magnificent throne, a hearth of diamonds and gold, and a roaring fire burning with forked flames. The author promises in a note to explain this symbolism at a later stage, and this promise is fulfilled, after the psychological teaching has been tied firmly with a theological pattern in the next scene (§67). In this briefly sketched image, Swedenborg himself thus underlines the observation, so often made in the previous analyses, that the composition constantly points forward to new elements in the same way as creation itself develops from the chaos of the world egg toward the final end, the holy communion.

This interpretation is postponed; instead, the soul's farewell speech is succeeded by three monologues, spoken by Adam to his wisdoms. From the point of view of verisimilitude—in itself somewhat inappropriate—this situation is most irregular: with what part of himself does Adam speak to his own intellect? Swedenborg has apparently foreseen this question since he answers it at a later stage (§53, note p) by implying that Adam was thinking. To begin with, this common-sense consideration has to yield to the symbolic message. When the author allows Adam to talk to his wisdoms, he wishes to give concrete form to the process in which the newborn's intellect rose synthetically, as described earlier (§52, note n). The first monologue is otherwise parallel to the soul's first farewell speech, and Adam declares his love of the mind, which with its two characteristics, intellect and will, makes him a true human being with all the possibilities of free will, which are his and his alone among all created beings.

In his second monologue, preceded by the wisdoms' dressing him with the attributes of a king, Adam is close to the last part of the soul's farewell. The setting is different: Adam and his wisdoms have moved down to the world of the senses, to an amphitheatre of paradise games, and the content becomes the testimonies of the senses and their interpretation. The firstborn is on his way to the same insight that preceded the intellect's takeover of control. He sees in all the alluring objects only the particular purpose and goodness hidden deep inside them, another proof of his unique position. Swedenborg does not miss an opportunity to show didactically how different the situation has become for Adam's offspring after the Fall, which forced us to struggle toward true goodness on the laborious road of experience and with the help of science, while the firstborn, whose intellect lived in the love of God, could experience both truth and goodness in his inner self, in the same manner that the mindless animals through their souls have an insight into what is good for them (§53, note q). Adam repeats over and over how the experience of goodness is crucial to his existence and that there is nothing that is not connected to goodness. The long speech ends with a vision in which the heavenly congregation guards a tree nearby; still ignorant of evil, the youth calls it the tree of good knowledge, the fruits of which he may not pick.

Adam does not yet possess the knowledge that the author permits us to take account of in note q, but the changing scenery is a sign that he will now attain it. Among the birth scenes of the curtains of yet another theater in paradise, built with arbutus leaves, vines and ivy, Adam establishes his wisdom school (§54). In a competitive game, he attempts to impel his wisdoms to reveal where the inner experience of goodness stems from, an insight gained during their education by the soul, but he does not succeed. Only when his enthusiastic search for knowledge brings him visions does he realize the connection: he observes his wisdoms in the womb of the highest love, the source of all wisdom and goodness. The passion for knowledge spurs him on further, to experiencing this love in a new vision, where we receive confirmation that the birth scenes of the new arena correspond with a spiritual message. Adam is told how everything is born from love, how everything is maintained through love, and how goodness stems from love. He is then allowed to experience that this love envelopes him also:

> percipe jam, quod amor, quo me amplecteris, de meo sit; facio, ut tu eum in te sentias, & ex meo eum percipias, & sic ex tuo meum; proinde, ut videas Parentem & Meum & Tuum; per Me es Ejus instar & imago: & quia sic ambo sumus ex Eodem, meus eris non filius sed frater.

> (See now that the love with which you embrace me comes from mine. I make you feel that love in yourself and perceive it from my love, and in that way feel my love from your own. This is how I can make you see my Parent and your own as well. Through me you are his likeness, his image: and because we are thus both from the same One, you will not be my son but my brother.) (§55)

This allusion to Hebr. 2:11 reveals who this love is, but Adam's vision, as Lamm pointed out, also corresponds with the Christ visions in the *Dream Diary*.[5] In this instance, Swedenborg has used his visionary experience directly, not just in the content but also in order to describe how the vision appeared; it is an intense intellectual contemplation on the foundations, which leads to a visionary answer. Together with the paradise game in the earlier passage, this vision is an example of an observation, which will be repeated in the next scene, that the intensity in the description of the firstborn man has a personal basis: Adam has become a portrait of Swedenborg's own reborn self.

In Love's speech, there is also a warning of ungodly love, and in this context the tree of knowledge get its interpretation. There is so far no emphasis on the problem of evil, however; Swedenborg wished to conclude Adam's first education by teaching him the deepest message of the revelation. The vision is fulfilled when Adam's eyes are opened to the beaming heavenly paradise, where everything shadowy in earthly paradise is removed. But then Love draws a veil over the clear eye, and the youth is confused: has he fallen down from the heavenly halls to his own paradise? The answer to that question, asked with tearful eagerness, forms the finale of the scene, and it is provided in two different ways: by Swedenborg himself in an explanatory note (§55, note s) and by Adam's wisdoms. Both are essential.

In §55, note s, we encounter the first completely verbal application of the doctrine of correspondence in direct quotes from *Clavis hieroglyphica*.[6] Adam's wisdom is less systematic. There has been no change of situation, Love says, but his eyes have become veiled after the moment of grace. In reality, God's love is always present in his innermost self, and there he can also find God's kingdom. Adams learns he has not fallen from the highest to the lowest but has returned from the innermost to the outer limits, where as a natural being he lives his existence. As soon as the intellect opens its gates inwards, the spiritual light from the Highest and his love streams forth, and it is on this road that Adam was earlier admitted into heaven. In this intellect, nature and spirit are united, and through this, the divine intelligences will always pass when they wish to visit earth: accordingly, the temple symbolism from the introduction of the scene reappears. The scene concludes with the arrival of the heavenly guests, a scene introduced by the same angelic beings' flickering lights and the glistening beauty of the starry sky during the night of the birth.

This analysis shows that the composition has now become more difficult to encapsulate: the space is much wider and the firm macrocosm-microcosm system from the earlier scenes is found only in details. Instead, the system of correspondence seems to be more directly applied than before. All this is reasonable enough considering that Swedenborg here reaches highly subtle materials, evasive of simple description, and that the psycho-theological theories had not yet gained the firmness of dogma; thus, the numerous repetitions are motivated both didactically and autobiographically. Despite this, a compositional pattern is still obvious. After the wonderful birth scene, we follow, in five passages, the soul's and the heavenly beings' education of the tender child, and thereafter ensues six passages of the soul's work creating Adam's intellect, concluding with her abdication. Only after his intellect has been educated can the firstborn be said to be a true man, and it is indeed said outright (§52) that he is no longer a child but a youth. The last five passages describe this youth's education under the guardianship of the God-enlightened intellect, concluding with the visionary experience that wisdom interprets in the scene's finale. Thus, we can differentiate between three groups of motifs, which form stages on the road of knowledge and which contain for all intents and purposes the same amount of space.

The psychological background requires particular attention, since it is the precondition for this scene as well as the following. In connection with this, the description of the kingdom of God within the human being, given in the finale, presents an opportunity to study the intimate relation between soul analysis and religion, in the light of the sources. Despite the appearance of many biblical references, the coloring is still in the classical manner, and it is in this context interesting to give a survey of Swedenborg's view of antiquity against the background of "*la querelle des anciens et des modernes.*"

# The Psychological Background

It would be a fascinating task of intellectual history to give a detailed description of how Swedenborg's theoretical psychology developed during decades of study, and it would be particularly valuable to look into the anatomical background. However, this is a matter that would require an entire dissertation in itself, so in this context, we need to limit ourselves to an overview, an indispensable requirement for understanding Swedenborg's ideas.

In a note to the fourth scene in the drama of creation, all unnecessary discussion on the question of whether the soul is material and extended (§53, note p) is dismissed; this is a futile task, since the "realm of literature" now has reached its highest peak. The expression appears rather often in Swedenborg's production, but the question of the essence of the soul refers to a particular text. In conjunction with *Principia* and *De Infinito*, there is among his manuscripts a brief sketch with the title *"De mechanismo animae et corporis,"* where Swedenborg declares with optimism that we shall eventually gain knowledge of the interaction between the body and the soul, if only *"orbis literatus,"* the learned world, gradually grows in knowledge, as has happened since a few centuries back.[7] A little later in the same draft, we find the road of research mapped:

> *de corpore animali et anima omnia probanda sunt per philosophiam primam sive metaphysicam, per analysin rerum naturalium, per geometriam et mechanismum, per figuras et calculum, per experimenta, per anatomiam corporis humani, per effectus, per passiones corporis et animae, per scripturam sacram, sic investienda est haec theoria.*
>
> (Regarding the living body and the soul, all should be proven through a first or metaphysical philosophy, through the analysis of natural objects, through geometry and mechanics, through figures and calculus, through experiments, through the anatomy of the human body, through effects, through the passions of the body and the soul, through the Holy Scriptures; thus, should we investigate this theory.)[8]

This program has been the fixed star for a decade of intense speculation, and Swedenborg evidently claims to have reached the peak of literature, which was his aim, in the drama of creation. The relatively simple psychology of the mechanistic *Principia* system was soon to become far more complicated. As Lamm pointed out, Swedenborg practiced in *Principia* a traditional division of the psyche into *animus*, the vegetative soul, and *mens*, the intellect.[9] In *Oeconomia*, he observed three elements instead: *anima*, the soul; *mens rationalis*, the intellect; and *animus*, the sensory life or the vegetative soul as before. Thus, together with the body's collaborating sensory organs this becomes a series of four degrees.[10]

As previously discussed, the doctrine of series and degrees is, as we discerned with the description of the creation of organisms, Swedenborg's biologically inspired contribution to the rationalist collection of philosophical systems. Psychologically, this was initially applied in the final chapter of *Oeconomia*'s first part, *"Introductio ad Psychologiam Rationalem"*[11] and was motivated primarily by the fact that the research into the soul cannot be undertaken with direct methods, since the soul leads such a withdrawn existence. The only way is to follow where *anima* herself walked when it formed and descended into its body. Without this aid—Lamm uses the excellent term "conclusion of analogy"—we end up with hasty conclusions, for instance,

> *quod Anima vel a principiis sibi propriis, vel a se superioribus immediate in corporis sui effectus influat; unde necessum est, ut communicatio operationum vel per* Influxum Physicum, *vel per* Causas Occasionales, *explicetur: & si nequeat per Illum, nec per Has, se subinsinuat & substituit tertia quasi necessario assumenda, hoc est,* Harmonia Praestabilita.

> (that the soul, either from its own principles or from such as are above it, immediately flows into its body's effects; from this follows with necessity that the interaction must be explained either with the doctrine of influx or through occasionalism: or if neither will do, a third will inveigle itself as a replacement and as a necessary alternative, namely, the pre-established harmony.)[12]

None of the classic interaction models satisfies him, but Leibniz is regarded with the highest esteem.

The walk on the road of the soul is extensively described in the drama of creation, but Swedenborg himself has been in her company for a long time. Given his Cartesian education, he sought her in veins and nerve fibers, a reasonable starting point for one who in his years of study had picked up the idea that interaction was triggered in the *glandula pinealis* through the meeting of the soul and the spirits of life, which were "born out of the finest particles of the blood—from the *partes sanguinis subtilissimae*—only to race through the organism as kinds of vaporous warm streams through the veins and nerves."[13] He calls to his aid modern anatomy, especially its study through microscopes; and on the basis of this, he supports the idea that the blood can be analysed not only as visually observable substances, but also in a higher degree of purity, *fluidum spirituosum*, which is the active force of the spiritual life. Before others, Leeuwenhoek forms the essence of this account with his investigations of the cerebral venous system, and we shall meet his and other anatomists' professional language in the most concrete description of the soul flow available in Swedenborg's writings, namely, in Wisdom's speech to Eve in the sixth scene of the drama of creation (§95ff; *Oeconomia* II, §122ff.). The doctrine of correspondence and the fable have now annulled the reservations found in *Oeconomia*: "*Sed quia hoc intra Naturam tam penitus latet, nulla iniri cogitatione*

*potest, nisi per Doctrinam Serierum & Graduum junctam Experientiae;
nec describi, nisi beneficio Philosophiae Universalium Mathematicae"* (But
since this lies hidden so deep within nature, one cannot penetrate it with
the help of any idea, but through the doctrine of series and degrees in
union with experience; nor can it be described without the aid of a mathematical philosophy of universals).[14]

This soul flow is the formative substance in relation to its body, although this does not mean that it should lack a form itself. From the doctrine of series and degrees, Swedenborg deduces its form *"ab aethere
meliori, quem Antiqui Auram Caelestem appellarunt"* (from a finer ether,
which the ancients called the heavenly aura).[15] Since this aura is at its
closest under the substance created first, Swedenborg in his *fluidum spirituosum* achieved a connecting link between *primum finitum*—the metaphysical basic concept of natural philosophy—and later links in the life chain
(*Oeconomia* II, §226). Thus, as early as the *Oeconomia*, we find the synthetic life philosophy of the drama of creation *in nuce*; and even in the details, one notes astonishing correspondences. The operations of the soul
flow are ruled by three principles: one that relates to the natural, through
which it can exist and move around in the world; one that relates to the
spiritual, through which it may live and attain wisdom; and, finally, one
that is the *anima*'s own, to determine itself to actions, answering to the
final purpose of the universe (II, §269). At the stage of *Oeconomia*,
Swedenborg identifies the soul with the *fluidum spirituosum*, and he quotes
in support of his bold rationalism Locke's doctrine of intuition. This is
characteristic of his eclecticism, but the quote also shows how his spiritualism has been inspired by the most respectable examples. Although the ideas
of faith were in themselves, at least in the main, common to most great
contemporary thinkers, the ruthless concrete application is unique to
Swedenborg.

Locke's influence is noticeable also in other respects.[16] The *anima* is separated from the intellect, which means that Swedenborg was able to pass
the problem, posed by congenital ideas; *mens* develops in time from nothing in the fetus, just as we saw it happen in the first man. However, after
the Fall, its education—in the same way as in Locke's *tabula rasa* theory—
is completely dependent on experience. The soul exists, however, with all
its wisdom already from the beginning, and is never-changing. The connection between *anima* and *mens* decides what the intellectual capacity of the
individual will be.[17] The lines thus drawn bring with them the idea that we
may never have a clear idea of the *anima* as long as we live the life of the
body (II, §277). The firstborn is indeed privileged in this regard, but not
even he may grow up to be a man under the care of the soul since divine direction leads his education after his infancy through the intellect.

Another *Oeconomia* argument points to the conflict that is the starting
point for the description of evil in *The Worship and Love of God*:

*Quod Mens sit distinctum quid ab Anima, praeter ex argumen-*
*tis supra collatis, apparet etiam ex conflictu mentis quasi cum*
*seipsa; ex conscientia quadam intimiore, quae mordet & sollici-*
*tat ex principiis etiam ignotis; persaepe etiam in rebus mere nat-*
*uralibus, altam originem ex amore sui trahentibus. Quod saepe*
*ignarissimi ut a quâdam Parcâ feramur in eventus secundum*
*quoddam filum, ut bombyx per suum; unde nomina, scilicet*
*Fatum, Fortuitum, Casus, Fortuna. Mens enim alte ignorat, qua*
*ratione Anima Rempublicam suam disponit & gerit.*

(That the intellect is differentiated from the soul is evident,
except from the arguments drawn up above, also from the internal conflict within the intellect; of a kind of inner conscience,
which torments and worries us from even unknown principles:
often even in purely natural matters, which derive their deep
origins from self-love. [It is also clear from the fact that] we are
often directed in the deepest ignorance as if by some goddess of
destiny to events along a kind of life thread, as a silk worm after
his [thread]: hence names like Destiny, Circumstance, Chance,
Fortune. For the intellect is deeply ignorant of the way in which
the soul organizes and administers her state.)[18]

Immediately hereafter Swedenborg quotes Augustine, as pointed out
earlier.

The localization of the psychic processes, so illustratively described in
*The Worship and Love of God*, also falls back on the anatomical studies.
As early as the essay "*De mechanismo operationis animae et corporis*,"
published in *De Infinito* in 1734, Swedenborg had discussed the cortex as
the seat of consciousness—as Stroh noted—although still within the frame
of *Principia*'s division of the psyche.[19] In *Oeconomia*, the portrayal becomes more precise, so that *mens* is located in the cortical substance, which
moves like a heart in expansions and contractions and in this manner
brings the finest essences of the blood to the fibres and nerves. The soul
flow thus exists in this blood together with the most flexible particles of the
body, and the proportion between *fluidum spirituosum* and the bodily elements of the blood now dictates what quality the intellect will have; the
heavier and the more polluted the blood, the more physical the intellect becomes and to the same degree the soul's force of action is diminished, that
is, the activity in the *fluidum spirituosum* (II, §305).

However, between *Oeconomia* and the drama of creation lie intensive
studies on the question of locality, and it is hardly surprising that Swedenborg declared in the later work *Regnum animale* that he had made rash
deductions in *Oeconomia*, although this statement, as Acton pointed out,
applied more to the method than the results.[20] In principle, Lamm's discovery of a correspondence between the psychology of *Oeconomia* and the

drama of creation is correct; nevertheless, from the point of view of source study, the research from the period in between also needs to be taken into account.[21]

Before that can be done, however, the third component of the psyche, *animus*, remains. In order to solve its task correctly, *mens*, the intellect, must receive *a posteriori* information from the senses and simultaneously be enlightened by the *a priori* light of the soul, but the *animus* is a step lower in the development or is placed further in the periphery, to use the common terminology in *The Worship and Love of God*. That this organ really exists is easier to see than is the fact that *anima* does, says Swedenborg, and the foremost proof of this is the difference between such ideas that the sense organs transmit from the outer world (*ideae materiales*) and the transformation these undergo in order to become intellectually manageable. The metamorphosis, which the simple pictures of the eye undergo during the soul's embrace in the recently analyzed fourth scene, thus corresponds immediately to the theoretical structure of *Oeconomia*: "*Dictae illae ideae non sunt absimiles imaginibus oculi, nam sub forma limitata, seu cum figura, magnitudine, situ, loco, tempore, apparent; quae mox ut intrant sphaeram mentis circumciduntur, & abstracte a limitibus versantur*" (These ideas mentioned are not dissimilar to the pictures of the eye, for they appear in a limited form, or with the shape, size, position, room and time, which, as soon as they appear in the area of the intellect, are cut and appear freed of limitations).[22] This *animus* is seated in the cerebrum, while *mens* is thus placed in its cerebral cortex. It is characterized by the emotional life: its ideas are sensual, as are its imagination and its lust.

Close at hand to this psychological triad pattern is the moral deduction that there is an inner and an outer person, in constant struggle with each other. Just as *animus* can come into conflict with *mens*, so the intellect can struggle with the soul, and the soul with the life, which flows of God's Holy Spirit (*Oeconomia* II, §281). These questions are indeed alluded to in the fourth scene, but they are not developed until the fifth scene with its theodicy problem. We shall return there to *Oeconomia*, for example, in connection with its theologically important discussion of the freedom of the will and love.

In this context, one more motif will be stressed. During the education of the child, a road between the soul and the intellect is opened in Adam's later heirs, and in *Oeconomia* the reciprocal action is interpreted in the terminology of soul flow, the *fluidum spirituosum*, which from itself created the most subtle membrane in the nerve thread. This membrane transmits the nerve reports from the senses to the soul flow, but the stream also goes in the opposite direction. This soul flow is identical to *anima* itself, whose very being is order, truth, and wisdom. From this follows that the *a posteriori* nerve reports, which are coordinated with the principles of science and order, are the easiest to transmit; this means that it is important to shape the child's general concepts correctly, since these determine his or her intellectual development. The communication between *anima* and *mens*, interpreted in this physiological manner, is made easier by curiosity and joy in knowledge, and for this very reason the Creator in his wisdom allowed the childhood years to be happy and filled with play (*Oeconomia* II, §296). Thus, another everyday experience has been integrated, in Swedenborg's characteristic manner, in the all-encompassing metaphysical perspective. So, even though Adam's education is conducted under special and privileged circumstances, it fulfills this theoretical view that the firstborn is raised under the sign of paradise games and competitive plays.

After the *Oeconomia*'s psychological chapter provided a rather rashly concluded starting point, Swedenborg fulfilled his promised anatomically detail studies.[23] Acton's view that the excerpt material in cod. 36–110 had been collected after *Oeconomia* was published seems well founded, and we find it in use for the first time in a great opus on the fibres, *De fibra*, which was never published by Swedenborg.[24] This work is closely connected with *Oeconomia*, which is incessantly quoted, and it gives a detailed neurological completion of *Oeconomia*'s greater outlines. As in the mighty cerebral-physiological works from the same incredibly productive decade, *De fibra* is, because of its anatomically technical focus, of less interest to *The Worship and Love of God*, although the drama contains passages that directly refer to the earlier work, especially the neurology lessons Eve is given in the sixth scene.[25] In his earlier scientific works, Swedenborg so often stressed the correspondence between the structure of the brain and the macrocosm, as well as with the shapes of living nature, such as eggs and trees, that we see how long the intimate symbol connections in the drama of creation lived a potential existence before they were realized there.

Nevertheless, for a historical study with a focus on the sources of a literary work, these great works must be given a secondary value, an evaluation made easier by the fact that they make extremely difficult reading. More important, on the other hand, are some psychological treatises from the beginning of the 1740s, where Swedenborg debates the theories of several of his great masters.[26] First, a controversy, kept only in fragments, with Leibniz and Wolff catches our interest. Acton dates this at 1742; it was intended to be part of a series of smaller studies, announced in the second edition of *Oeconomia*.[27] I have previously stressed correspondences in detail and in the general purpose between the monadologists and Swedenborg, yet even where the differences are striking, as in the doctrine of series and degrees, Swedenborg was apparently careful to avoid polemics. The study of Wolff's and Leibniz's writings was extremely important to Swedenborg's development and was conducted with the utmost awe for these great learned men.

But now we find Swedenborg for the first time engaged in a thorough debate with his rationalistic precursors, a polemic that sometimes became grimly ironic and irritable: "*est enim Harmonia praestabilita hodie ad instar responsi irreprehensi a tripode emissi, inque vatum et sapientum ore plurima volvitur, et per illam, quid significet anima, et quid harmonia, pariter quid actiones, leges, series et vires in regno toto animali, explanari allaboratur*" (For today the pre-established harmony is like an irrefutable answer from the tripod, and it is the foremost in the mouths of prophets and wise men, and through it is achieved an explanation into what is meant by the soul, by the harmony, and at the same time what [is meant by] the actions, the laws, the series and the powers in all of the animal kingdom).[28]

Thus, through this refrain, we now hear that the terms are oracular and unintelligible, and the knowledge they convey trivial. Instead Swedenborg praises empirical research, which has helped us in dispersing the delusions of the elders. The doctrine of monads is much too static, it chains the thinking to the prestabilizing pattern, and it makes all speculation on the final and most important questions impossible.

This same criticism was behind the more careful phrases of *Oeconomia*, and it seems to have been made even more focused by Swedenborg's intense reading in the works of the great anatomists, which he presented in the neurological investigations. The polemic ends with a eulogy on the science of modern times; Wolff still enjoys a place of honor here, despite the sharp criticism, because he liberated rationalistic philosophy from a multitude of trivialities. However, a thinker who can unite empirical science with a rationalism purified from dogmatism and ignorance is required to reach the deepest insight:

> *exspectat jam e nostro saeculo virum ingenii per experientias exacti, perque scientias et cultum subacti, et facultate causas investigandi perque nexum argumentandi et secundum seriem determinate concludendi, praepollentis, cui se hodie, ut reor, despondebit; succumbet, auguror, telis, et foedera et lectum sociabit: exoptem, ut nuces spargere, et faces praeferre, mihi liceret.*
>
> (Already [nature] expects from our century a man with an intelligence perfected with experience, disciplined by science and studies, and capable of investigating the causes, to follow the arguments through associations, and to make decisive conclusions in accordance with the series; a man with whom she, as I believe, today wishes to be betrothed and to whose love deceptions she will fall prey and with whom she will be united in bed and stead: I long to spread the nuts and lead the torchbearers).[29]

Swedenborg's ambition toward achieving synthesis, or his eclecticism, was seldom presented so frankly as in this Ovidian allusion to the Roman wedding ceremonies, while he also revealed his burning aspiration and the vast dimension of his self-esteem, which in the coming religious crisis will appear as the hardest obstacle to his soul's salvation. The dream of becoming the first to solve the riddle of the soul is characteristically enough presented as a conclusion to the criticism of Wolffianism, which provides new evidence that Swedenborg must be read primarily with a contemporary perspective in mind.

The passionate dream can be followed in other variations until the drama of creation and as well as in the later theosophical system, where it becomes true with a sometimes disheartening concretion. In the psychological treatises of the 1740s, we keep approaching *The Worship and Love of God* in motif and atmosphere, although the gray theories have not yet achieved the distinction of the fable. The soul's retreat to the cerebellum—which unsurprisingly does not mean that its *fluidum spirituosum* ceases to flow although it is not stressed until the sixth scene—is given a wide-ranging anatomical motivation, as seen, for example, in the little essay *"De actione"*: *"Cerebellum non ita in toros, articulos et congeries distinctim mobiles est divisum, qualiter est cerebrum, quae est ratio, quod cerebelli actio sit naturalis, cerebri autem voluntaria"* (The cerebellum is thus not divided into mobile calluses, groups, and masses as is the brain, which is the reason for the cerebellum's activity to be natural, while the brain's is run by will).[30] The transformation of the intelligencies into wisdoms, when they manage to perceive the spiritual purposes, is also described abstractly in this treatise.[31]

According to Acton's dating, during 1742, Swedenborg also wrote an extensive investigation into rationalistic psychology, which Immanuel Tafel published in 1849 under the title *Regnum animale, pars VII, De anima.*[32] In its preface, we encounter again the proud dream of finally capturing the soul in the net of knowledge, this time materialized in concrete reality:

> *Sic demum licet de anima ex principiis seu synthetice agere: orbis Eruditus a primo aevo usque ad hoc tempus, ubi foetus conceptus excludi et nasci debet, ei jugi incubuit, ut ad genuina principia eniteremur, . . . talis enim est perfectio angelica, talis est scientia caelestis, et prima naturalis, talis ideo est innata nobis ambitio; scilicet ut ad integritatem primi parentis enitamur, qui a priori conclusit omnia posteriora, et sic universam naturam non solum sub se vidit, sed etiam sibi subjectae imperavit.*
>
> (Thus it is at last allowed to treat the soul on the basis of principles or synthetically; from the first era to today, when the conceived fetus will be brought forth and born, the world of learning has always strived to reach the same principles, . . . because such is the perfection of the angels, such is the celestial

science and the first natural, such is therefore our instinctive
ambition—namely, to reach the innocence of our first parent,
who deduced everything posterior *a priori* and thus did not only
see all of nature under himself but also ruled it, as it was subjected to him.)[33]

We find little here of the inebriated self-esteem present in the criticism of
Wolff; rather, a sense of humility before this superhuman task and a fear of
the inconceivable are evident. Swedenborg stresses the similarity between
the psychological insight sought after and that of Adam. This view exists
already in the *Oeconomia*, but it is elaborated in the present work, and
evidently Swedenborg was able to comply with what one of Malebranche's
interpreters stated: *"Faire la psychologie d'Adam avant la chute n'est pas
une fantaisie de métaphysicien; c'est l'introduction nécessaire à la connais-
sance de soi-même"* (To learn about Adam's psychology before the Fall is
not a metaphysicist's fancy; it is the necessary introduction to one's self-
knowledge).[34] Malebranche's influence can be felt strongly in *De anima*,
which strives to unite in several ways Cartesian and Wolffian theories on
the interaction of body and soul through the practice of terms of correspondence used by the two schools.[35]

There is, however, a long road to travel before Swedenborg reaches the
direct discussion on the psyche of the first man. His enormous production
of the early 1740s is partly due to the fact that the same material appears
under new headings and that investigations already written are placed in
different contexts. Through this method, we see reflected the same ambition found in *The Worship and Love of God*, where the basic themes established before *Oeconomia* attained a place. In other words, we observe
an attempt at conclusion and synthesis; but it reveals at the same time
problems of design, which are solved momentarily in the shape of the
fable. How close to this solution Swedenborg had been in *De anima* is
made clear from what he says about the pure intellect's possibilities of expression, the intellect that is the soul's first offspring: *"sed intellectus purus
suas analyses simplices et universales per simulacra, qualia visuntur in
somniis, tum etiam per parabolas et similitudines, imo per fabulas quales
antiqui in aevis aureo proximis, repraesentat"* (But the pure intellect reports its simple and universal analyses through images, such as they are
viewed in dreams, and also through parables and similes, even through
such fables as were used by the ancients in times closest to the Golden
Age).[36]

With the same undaunted systematic procedure as always, Swedenborg
attacks the problems of rationalistic psychology in *De anima* and begins
with the sensory organs, after which he step-by-step ascends to the soul
and its eternal existence. It becomes an extensive catalogue over separate
psychological characteristics, which in detail continues the attempts from

*Oeconomia* and to which a general reference can be made with respect to the psychology of the drama of creation.[37] There is not room here to investigate this fully, so I limit my research to the most important elements, love and will.

To live without love is impossible in Swedenborg's intellectual world, since it would entail the severance of the part from the entirety. This means that he counts on many variations of love, sensual, rational and spiritual, as well as countless subdivisions of these: love is not only the bond of union between the part and the whole, but it is also the driving force behind all actions, *"ipse calor vitalis, et ipsa vis vitae"* (the very warmth and force of life).[38] With great care, Swedenborg analyses first the *amores* belonging to *animus*, that is, sexual love, conjugal love, parental love, self-love, and many more. In this series, we also find variations of hate, which are not seen as the absence of love but as negative passions springing from evil. The view, explained by his idea of love as the driving force of all actions, is made clear in a description of the lust for revenge: *"Vindicta ex odio et invidia profluit; odium quidem est contrarium amori, sed non est privatio amoris et sic vitae, sed est amor contrarius, et cumprimis amor mali; datur enim amor boni et amor mali"* (Vindictiveness stems from hate and jealousy. Hate is on the one hand love's opposite; however, it is not the absence of love and thus of life, but it is an opposite love, primarily a love of evil; for there is a love of good and a love of evil.)[39] This is the psychological effect of the theological view introduced later in the treatise, in the same way as the tree of knowledge in the fourth scene of the drama foreshadows the extensive description of evil in the following scene.

Love's dominance becomes ever more evident the higher we reach in the human psyche. To Swedenborg, the intrinsic value of reason lay only in the possibility to choose between a higher and a lower love, and the didactically structured account of how the intellect is educated toward creating this role is the basis for the corresponding chain of events in *The Worship and Love of God*, down to the minutest detail.[40] The ages of the world are parallel to the psychological scheme. During the Golden Age, *animus* was completely subjected to the intellect, and during the Silver Age, both ruled with the same righteousness. The later Bronze Age bore witness to how sensuality began to combat sensibility for the throne, while, in the Iron Age, *animus* was victorious and made *mens* its slave.[41] The note of melancholy in the preface to the drama becomes, in the light of this pattern, something more than a historical convention and a personal feeling of sadness. Indeed, it becomes an expression of deep despair at the human condition. The Golden Age would not suit mortal beings, however, since it would mean psychologically that the soul could reign alone, without the aid of the intellect. The Silver Age, when the higher and lower loves are in equilibrium, thus becomes the ideal state. Evidently this symbolism was crucial to Swedenborg's view of antiquity, which will be discussed presently.

The intellect would thus not be able to exist without love, neither as intelligence nor as will. This partition of the intellect was carried through in the *Oeconomia* and belongs to the conventions of faculty psychology; among Swedenborg's notes, we find excerpts from several contributors, among others, Rydelius, Malebranche, and Leibniz. From Leibniz's theodicy, Swedenborg quotes Bayle, characteristic of rationalistic psychology:

> On enseigne constamment dans les Écoles que comme le vrai est l'objet de l'entendement, le bien est l'objet de la volonté; & que comme l'entendement ne peut jamais affirmer que ce qui se montre à lui sous l'apparence de la verité, la volonté ne peut jamais rien aimer qui ne lui paroisse bon. . . . Il y a dans l'entendement une détermination naturelle au vrai en general, & à chaque verité particuliere clairement connue. Il y a dans la volonté une détermination naturelle au bien en general: d'où plusieurs Philosophes concluent que dès que les biens particuliers nous sont connus clairement; nous sommes necessités à les aimer.
>
> (It is constantly taught at schools that as what is true is the object of the intelligence, what is good is the object of the will; and that as the intellect can never affirm anything but what appears in the shape of truth, the will can never love anything but what seems to be good. . . . In the intellect there is a natural determination toward truth in general, and toward every particular truth, which is clearly known. There is a natural determination in the will toward goodness in general, and therefrom many philosophers conclude that, as soon as particular goodnesses are known clearly to us, we are forced to love them.)[42]

In this Socratic optimism, the intellect's judgment becomes crucial to the will, an opinion that Swedenborg shares. But of greater importance is the fact that both the intelligence and the will are dependent on love; in order to shed light on these relationships, we must dwell for a moment on the *Oeconomia*'s and *De anima*'s discourse on the intellect's freedom of choice.

Swedenborg compares will to the struggle towards action: his term, *conatus*, is taken—as Lamm points out—from Leibniz.[43] However, this will is completely connected to the intellect, since the result of its operations is a deduction that forms the will: the distinction between the intellect's freedom of choice and that of the will, which Clissold believed existed in *Oeconomia*, has been carried through in *De anima*, but this leads to hardly any substantial differences.[44] This concept must lead to a situation where the freedom of will becomes as great as that of the intellect, which depends on the intellectual capacity; the more intelligent and mature a person is the greater is that person's freedom.

This freedom will primarily consist of choosing the best and rejecting the evil.[45] The intellect has great possibilities to acquire the necessary insight—through the soul's influx of divine wisdom, the senses' reports on the outside world, the results of science, and above all *mens'* ability to isolate itself from *animus'* chaotic passions. The premises are advantageous, but it is important to make the intellect turn to the right sources. For Swedenborg realizes that it is one matter to understand something intellectually and another matter to will it, and metaphorically he speaks of a separation between intelligence and will, which certainly was experienced by the author himself: "*& persaepe in intelligentioribus separatius toro vivant, quam in simplicioribus; nam illi beneficio intellectus accedunt tanquam persuasi ad partes inferiorum, & ipsissima vitia sub forma virtutum speciose recondunt*" (And very often do they live more apart in intelligent persons than in simpler ones, for the former are persuaded with the aid of the intellect to take the lower senses' part and deceptively conceal the very vices under the shape of virtues).[46] Can will then be regarded as free in relation to the decisions of the intellect? The answer is a hesitant yes, since a decision already made can be changed in the face of a higher justice, that is, after a renewed inquiry into its reasons (II, §328).

However, all this concerns mundane conditions. Regarding the primary issues, *mens* can will the means but not the aim: *mens* must allow *anima* to influence it, which means that the spirit of God will guide it. To a certain degree, the intellect can raise itself freely to these altitudes, above all through the guidance of the Scriptures, but can it choose freely? Freedom of will depends on love for the purpose, a love resulting in a desire to achieve it, and we do not manage to generate such a love of the highest from our own intellectual power. Knowledge of the meaning and purpose of a desire may not be absent, but a love strong enough is missing. Here we encounter for the first time a recurrent image in *The Worship and Love of God*: "*Talem ignem sacrum non valemus ipsi exsuscitare, vix desiderare nisi ex quodam voto per se non activo: proinde nequimus ea, quae superiores hos fines spectant, ut essentialia a judicio in conclusum aut voluntatem vi propria electrice inferre*" (We cannot light such a holy fire ourselves, hardly desire it with more than a passive wish: therefore we cannot through any power of selection in ourselves introduce something that views these higher aims as the essential, from the judgment to the deduction or the will).[47] The fire can only be lit by God himself. In order to explain how it happens, Swedenborg accepts Malebranche's view of the relationship between God and humankind, as observed by Lamm.[48] Our ambition to reach the final aim of creation, which cannot be fulfilled through ourselves, results in God's own will to bring us forth. It seems to be a law that our will shall give rise to his.[49]

In *De anima*, we encounter turns of phrase that use terms of providence and reveal a firmer view. A text on *Prudentia Humana*, human wisdom, is enlightening:

> *Ut prudentia summa sit, requiritur ut respiciatur finis optimus, ut conservatio societatis, patriae, religionis, gloriae Divinae, et similia, tunc quando homo proponit, Deus disponit, seu providentia Divina cum providentia humana concurrit: mens in hoc casu nullum finem respicit nisi ut intermedium, nec usque ultimum, nisi in ultimo est qui est primus; qui ad eum collimat, et sic respicit fines omnes ut intermedios, ejus prudentia non requiritur activa ex se, sed activa redditur ex amore superiore; et se media ex se praesentant.*
>
> (In order for wisdom to be perfect, it is required that it views the best aim, such as the conservation of society, of the nation, of religion, of the glory of God and the like; thus, when man proposes, God disposes, i.e., divine providence cooperates with human providence. In this case, the intellect regards no purpose, not even the final one, as anything but intermediary, unless in the final there is present that which is the foremost. He who strives towards this and thus views all purposes as intermediary, his providence need not be active in itself, but it becomes active by a higher love, and the means produce themselves.)[50]

This statement should be understood in light of the extensive quotations from Malebranche among the excerpts, and that point can be widened to encompass the doctrine of love, which is characteristic of the psychology of *De anima* and which forms an important stage on the road to the theosophic sermon of *amor regnans*. The intense studies of *Recherche de la vérité*, where every conscious act becomes a divine mystery inspired by God's love, gave Swedenborg some crucial impulses; this has already been stressed concerning the doctrine of correspondence, and it will be repeated in the theological parts. In the freedom of intellectual activity—and its inevitable result in the Fall—Swedenborg sees the preconditions for humanity's eternal well-being and a richness in the variation of existence, as well as the motivation for the final aim of creation, the infinitely varied heavenly community. Also in this regard, we can see the relationship to Malebranche: "*Il suit de ce principe que pour établir cette variété de récompenses, qui fait la beauté de la céleste Jérusalem, il fallait que les hommes fussent sujets sur la terre, non seulement aux afflictions qui les purifient, mais encore aux mouvements de la concupiscence qui leur font remporter tant de victoires, en leur livrant un si grand nombre de combats*" (It follows from this principle that to establish this variation of rewards, which forms the beauty of the heavenly Jerusalem, human beings had to be bound to the earth, not only to the sorrows that purify them but also to the impulses of lust that give them so many victories in such a great number of battles).[51]

The ever-present divine perspective in these theoretical investigations is naturally of greater interest than only from the aspect of sources. I will not attempt here to solve the complicated problem of Swedenborg's religious crisis—its reflections in the motifs of this present work are discussed in their contexts—but I refer to Lamm's excellent account.[52] There is, however, every reason to emphasize his opinion that a psychiatric study ought to be undertaken primarily from the viewpoint of the patient himself and his knowledge of the diseases of the psyche and his view of human life as a whole. We encounter a person who for decades lived in a world where the theocentric pattern was taken for granted and where the reality of a spiritual existence was regarded as self-evident by respectable thinkers. We also encounter an anatomist of the soul who learned from his predecessors that every psycho-physical act indicated a divine presence or revealed a pre-established harmony. That pondering on these problems should result in religious visions is hardly surprising in the light of a psychology of role-taking: Hjalmar Sundén has shown in an immensely interesting study how well this can be applied to religious phenomena. This does not in itself seem to require any psychiatric explanation, at least not at the time when *The Worship and Love of God* was written. A work of such synthetic and symbolic power could hardly have been written by a man suffering from a mental disorder.

This does not mean, however, that Swedenborg lacked certain neurotic characteristics, which in a crisis situation could deepen into a serious psychosis. His solitary life in the civil service and in his chamber of study; the coldness of heart that allows him to assume a hell in order for the rationalistic richness of variety to be fulfilled; the self-assuredness evident in the juvenile boasts of the early letters, in the dream of finally solving the riddle of the soul, and in the theosopher's identification with the Messiah; the overbearing and crude sexuality in the dream diary; the constant repetitions in different contexts of recurring, almost fixed ideas—all these are characteristics concurrent with the schizoid type.[53]

But these must also be nuanced after studying the writings. The ideas of inferno belong to the contemporary Christian convention, and the fixation with certain ideas is the scientist's method of processing his hypotheses from different angles. The sexuality in the dream notes, interpreted by the visionary himself in serene symbolism, must partly be viewed in the light of his studies of the human sexual organs conducted for the benefit of the anatomical science. The boasts and the proud dreams can be seen as a mask behind which we can catch a glimpse of insecurity, which had wavered under the pressure from his dominant father, a stuttering inferiority complex corresponding physically with his faltering gifts of speech.[54] Indeed, self-esteem had been a problem for him as is evident from the dreams, where love of oneself is viewed as the crucial obstacle. This belongs to the normal pattern of Christian religious crises, but the intensity of the feeling seems to be motivated foremost by his ambition for glory, which we encounter in the writings.

In regard to *The Worship and Love of God*, the religious crisis is interesting mainly as an expression of a fruitful literary atmosphere. We have seen how the psychological theories from the beginning were placed in a theological structure, but its form is changed from the abstractly intellectual to the concretely religious, reaching successively closer to the central Christian beliefs: *De anima* has in this regard accomplished much more than *Oeconomia*.[55] This development continues in the dream notes, but in order to render the new experiences a new form is required: it becomes a *liber divinus*, where *"annars kram,"* the trash of others, cannot be given room.[56] From the close contact with the symbolical world of the Bible, the literary creativity is unleashed that has always existed, but the harsh methodology allowed only limited room to maneuver. It will become the main task of the following analyses to show how Swedenborg handles the central Christian beliefs in his drama of creation.

## "The Kingdom of God Is within You"

The vision of love that Adam experiences in the fourth scene is interpreted at the conclusion by one of his wisdoms: heaven is constantly within him, and God holds him most intimate, *"Is intimum te habet"* (He holds you innermost) (§56). Cooperation between heaven and earth also takes place through our innermost being, as the spiritual beings must always pass through this Helicon when visiting earth. This idea is essential to Swedenborg personally, who for so long had searched for the secret of the soul and of heaven. Here lies *in nuce* the entire work of the spiritual visionary since what happens in Adam's intellect with its task of transponding the earthly visits of the celestial beings will also happen to the person who returns to the state of innocence enjoyed by the firstborn. This underlying personal euphoria lends such intensity to the strangely concrete symbolism; what appears to a modern reader as the most abstruse speculation was an experienced reality.

But from the theological point of view, the text is a paraphrasing extrapolation on a central biblical quote, about the kingdom of God within us. We also find that Swedenborg in his excerpt collection underlined an important paragraph: *"Divinum regnum intra vos est dicit Christus. Luc. XVII:21."*[57] In *The Worship and Love of God* §56, we find a sentence uniting the two designations, the headline *Caelum* of the manuscript and the *divinum regnum* of the Bible text: *"sed est Caelum, quod etiam Regnum Dei dicitur, penitus intra nos"* (But there is a heaven, which is also called the Kingdom of God, deep inside us.) The interpretation of the divine kingdom of the New Testament follows the Augustinian tradition: the drama of creation manifests a correspondence in atmosphere, down to purely verbal reminiscences with *Confessiones* lib. IV, a text that has also been exploited in the excerpts under a different headline.[58] Augustinian research has stressed the psychological experience of the divine in the Father, and a modern Catholic scholar ascertains the following:

> *Le génie d'Augustin se plaît en ces profondeurs (ou en ces hauteurs, car les deux images expriment la même réalité) et c'est ici le moment de rappeler le mot célèbre d'un livre des Confessions relatif à une époque bien antérieure de sa vie, où le saint dit à Dieu: 'Tu m'étais plus intime que le fond de mon âme et plus élevé que son sommet'(Conf. III, VI, 11). Ce comparatif, qui situe Dieu dans un au-delà, n'exclut pas une certaine présence effective, et voilà pourquoi l'auteur dit plus loin, au positif: 'Dieu est au fond du coeur' (ibid, IV, XII, 18). Le fond, intimum, désigne ce qu'on découvre en soi spécialement par la voie de l'observation intérieure, et le sommet, summum, est le principe de l'activité de l'esprit la plus simple, la plus proche par là de l'infini. C'est dans le mens, le nous des Grecs, qu'il faut la chercher, et au delà des intuitions courantes qui dirigent l'activité mentale."*

> (The spirit of St. Augustine felt at home in these depths [or on these heights, for the two images express the same reality], and here it is time to recollect the famous word of a book of the *Confessiones* which refers to a much earlier period of his life, where the saint said to God, "You are deeper in me than the bottom of my soul and much higher than its peak" [*Conf.* III, VI, 11]. This comparative, which places God beyond everything, does not exclude a certain real presence, and this is why the author later on used the positive: "God is at the bottom of the heart" [ibid. IV, XII, 18]. The bottom, *intimum*, denotes what one discovers especially by introspection, and the peak, *summum*, is the most simple principle of the soul's activity and the one closest to infinity. It is in the intellect, the *nous* of the Greeks, where His presence must be sought, and beyond the flowing impressions which rule mental activity.)[59]

The nearest example of an Augustinianism of this kind among the excerpts does not stem from Augustine himself, however, but from the apocryphian *De spiritu et anima*. From this book, the influence of which on the Cartesian tradition has already been mentioned, Swedenborg noted a description of the relationship between the soul and God, which is the abstract pattern behind the concrete portrayal in the drama of creation:

> *Mundus est exterior, Deus autem interior: nihil enim eo interius,*
> *nihil eo praesentius. Interior est omni re, quia in ipso sunt*
> *omnia: exterior est omni re, quia est super omnia. ab hoc ergo*
> *mundo ad Deum revertentes et quasi ab imo sursum ascen-*
> *dentes per nosmetipsos transire debemus; ascendere enim ad*
> *Deum est intrare ad seipsum, et non solum ad se intrare, sed in-*
> *effabili quodam modo in intimis seipsum transire. qui enim in-*
> *terius intrans et intrinsecus penetrans seipsum transcendit, ille*
> *veraciter ad Deum ascendit etc. . . .haec enim est requies cordis*
> *nostri, cum ( . . . ) Deum suum contemplatur; et ipsa sua con-*
> *templatione suaviter reficitur.*

(The world is exterior, but God is interior. For there is nothing more interior than he, nothing more present. He is more
interior than everything, because in him is everything; he is
more exterior than everything, because he is above everything.
When we return from this world to God and ascend from the
profound upwards, we must travel through ourselves. For to
ascend to God is to enter oneself and not only enter oneself, but
also to surpass oneself in the innermost in an unspeakable manner. For he who transcends himself by entering the innermost
and penetrating himself in the interior ascends truly to God. . . .
For this is the peace of our heart, when it looks upon its God,
and wonderfully it is strengthened by its vision.)[60]

All knowledge of God must come through penetrating the innermost of the
soul, and the ascension is made through a penetration; this experience of
God in the soul is also a remedy for its worry and torment.

But the image of God in *The Worship and Love of God* is shaped in
greater detail, and the excerpts under the heading "*Deus*" soon leave Augustine.[61] The Church Father was not primarily interested in the ontological
issue of God and the world, but rather in the belief in God as will and of the
problem of salvation: the great and important difficulty for later theology, especially the theology Swedenborg had come to know, is to unite the Platonic
view and its incomprehensible God outside all conceptual definitions with
the thought of dominant will in the biblical divine image.[62] Augustine's way
of interpreting the idea of God in psychological analogies ought to have been
of far greater importance to Swedenborg than his expositions on God's
essence, and many more Augustinian excerpts in cod. 36–110 appear under
psychological headlines. The correspondence with Augustinianism in its
widest meaning is underlined in a quote from *De spiritu et anima:"summa*
*sapientia est ipse Deus; sapientia hominis est pietas seu cultus Dei*" (The
highest wisdom is God himself. Man's wisdom is piety, or the worship of
God).[63] In this psychological analogy, we are very close to the original
thought that gave its name to *The Worship and Love of God*.

Like Augustine, Swedenborg also experienced the anguish in *cor nostrum inquietum*. The visionary experiences from the time of his crisis are reflected in the fourth scene of the drama of creation, especially in two moments, the paradisiacal games of the spirits and Adam's vision of Love. After the heavenly beings return Adam to earth, the lungs resume their work, which had ceased during the visionary ecstasy (§42). Evidently this is an allusion to the experiences of respiratory arrest, which Lamm has drawn from the *Dream Diary* and *Spiritual Diary*.[64] Lamm is of the opinion that "*det här är fråga om ett fenomen, som är kändt och beskrifvet af en mängd olika mystiker. Det är en respirationshämning, som ofta åtföljer de mystiska själstillstånden, kontemplationen eller den ordlösa, 'mentala' bönen*" (we here have a phenomenon that is known and described by a number of different mystics. It is a suspension of breathing that often accompanies mystical states of mind, contemplation, or inarticulate "mental" prayer).[65] In Tor Andrae's *Mystikens psykologi*, Swedenborg's experiences are compared to the respiration techniques of the Indian yoga system; Sundén has posed a hypothetical question that is interesting in this context: "*Leder t.ex. den andningsteknik, som är ett för yogaövningarna utmärkande drag, till ett aktualiserande av hjärnstrukturer, som de i sinneskontakternas upplevelsevärld bundna människorna aldrig aktiverar eller utnyttjar*" (Does, for instance, the respiratory technique, which is a characteristic of the yoga practices, lead to an actualization of cerebral structures that men who are bound to the world of experiences of sensual contacts never activate or use?).[66]

The brain anatomist Swedenborg would have appreciated and acknowledged this question. In the respiratory pauses of the newborn, we encounter not only a personal experience but also a theoretical view, although as always strangely enmeshed. The connection between the respiratory movements in the lungs and the rhythm of the brain appeared, as Lamm points out, as early as the *Oeconomia*, and Swedenborg alluded to his own ecstatic experiences in *De fibra* against this background.[67] In *Regnum animale*, the development of which can be followed in part in the *Dream Diary*, the connection is emphasized, for instance, in the following: "*Respiratio Pulmonum non solum in Corporis truncum, sed etiam in Caput, inque ejus motuum & sensuum Organa influit (x); & quidem ad ipsum fontem sui motus seu Cerebrum, ad quod per infinitos rivos, sicut per maeandros & circulos, redit, & se cum ejus respirationis vicibus, quae Animationes dicuntur, consociat*" (The pulmonary respiration does not only flow into the trunk of the body but also to the head and to its motor and sensory organs; and more precisely to the brain, the very source of its movements, to which it returns in infinite streams like meanders and circles and reunites with its respiratory changes, called animations).[68] The text is further commented upon in a note: "*ut dum Mens intensime cogitat, & animas suas tacite & lente reciprocat, eo momento apparent etiam Pulmones ad certam libram elevati, similiter silentia agere, & vix sensibiliter flabra emittere & haurire, ne aliquo motu analyses mentis rationalis turbent"* (As when the intellect is thinking intensively and is breathing silently and slowly, in the same moment even the lungs, elevated to a certain height, seem to remain silent in a similar way and exhale and inhale the air almost unnoticeably, so that they do not disturb the analyses of the intellect by any motion).[69] In Adam's respiratory arrest, we have an excellent example of how the physiological theories and the practical experiences cohere in an artistic depiction.

As for the other ecstatic moment in the fourth scene, the vision of Love has an even more profound basis in personal experiences. Lamm has shown convincingly how this depiction corresponds to the *Dream Diary*'s vision of Christ at Easter 1744.[70] That the drama of creation was written under the influence of contacts with Christ, which are part of Swedenborg's religious crisis, is also clear from the fact that it was begun because of such a vision, which occurred the night between October 26–27, 1744.[71] However, these visions have their place in the development toward central Christian beliefs, which we can observe in the psychological writings: as they emphasize a longing for a faith without reasoning, earlier alluded to, they also form a comprehensible outcome of a successively more concrete way of thinking.[72]

That this vision of Christ, depicted here as a divination of divine love, should occur in a context where the Augustinian influence is manifest is interesting not only because of the source issue but also for a psychological evaluation. This Church Father, admired by Swedenborg even in early days for his enlightened judgment, is not only one of the most important theoretical influences in the rationalistic, especially the Cartesian tradition, but also—in addition to Paul—a classical icon in the history of conversions: the suggestive power in the self-analysis of the *Confessiones* has exercised an almost immeasurable influence in widely differing times and confessions. Against the background of the excerpts' witness statement of the Augustinian studies of the early years of the 1740s, it is not unreasonable to assume that Swedenborg's "conversion" to a certain degree depends on such reading; a detailed investigation, for which there is no room here, could perhaps lead to some interesting results. In this context, we note that the godly kingdom in the innermost of the soul has been depicted by the imaginary power schooled in brain physiology, which we encounter in Swedenborg's drama concerning the creation of the world.

## The Ancient and the Modern

Adam's conversations with his intelligences are said to mean that he is thinking (§53, note p). Through the discourse of this text, Swedenborg explains that the kingdom of literature has reached its highest peak. This is thus an echo of the hymn of praise for the modern era, a few strains of which we have listened to in the fragmentary treatise about the harmony between body and soul. At the same time, one is constantly struck by the strong influence from ancient myth and poetry as well as of the *encomium temporis antiqui,* which is so often brought forth in *The Worship and Love of God.* In the tempestuous *"querelle des anciens et des modernes"* of the time, Swedenborg apparently held an intermediary position. How shall we interpret his point of view?

As for understanding ancient thinking, Swedenborg is quite clear in his treatises on harmony: it would be work akin to Sisyphos' attempt to develop these half-forgotten systems, and it would also signify to roll the same stone as did our modern authors and especially our parents, *"qui veterum urnas et cineres adoraverunt et exosculati sunt"* (who adored the urns and ashes of the ancients and covered them with kisses).[73] Evidently, Swedenborg here wishes to represent a more modern tradition than those he alluded to: he is irritated by the devoted admiration of antiquity, especially in the predecessors to the tradition he adheres to, which should mean philosophy prior to Descartes. However, this rejection must be seen in the light of the summation. While one ought not to adore antiquity, it is nevertheless inappropriate for the followers of pre-established harmony to boast of superiority to the ancients, since what they ought to say is *"quod monadas illorum exterminaverimus, et plura aeque occulta substituerimus"* (that we have expelled their monads and replaced them with many equally obscure items).[74] In their speculation, the ancients and the moderns are in an equally precarious position, although the moderns have a greater burden of guilt, as they have had access to the immense knowledge gathered by empirical science during close to two thousand years.

The time data come from the prologue to *Regnum animale* (§23), where Swedenborg drew the most far-reaching empirical consequences. Experience must be the basis for all search for the truth, and any attempt to achieve the highest principles of the synthetic path to knowledge without its aid will lead to the birth of *"faetus cumprimis mendosi, id est Monstra Hypothetica,"* in particular these freaks, that is hypothetical monsters (§9). This sounds like an echo of Newton's famous *"hypotheses non fingo,"* and it shows clearly that the development of empirical science is the basis for Swedenborg's position in the treatise of harmony. He praises the great astronomers, Copernicus, Kepler, Flamsteed, and others, and he pays tribute to the technology of telescopes and microscopes, physics, chemistry, and experimental psychology. Newton appears side by side with Leibniz and the Bernouilli brothers—Jacques (1654–1705) and Jean (1667–1748)—but they must as mathematicians share their place of honor with the ancient genii.[75] It is not surprising that these modern researchers form a procession in the dream notes, written while *Regnum animale* is being created: *"Såg en process af manfolck,som war magnifique, vtsmyckad, så wackert, at jag intet wackrare sett, men försvan snart; war, som jag tror, experiencen, som nu är i stort flor"* (Saw a magnificent procession of men, so adorned that I never saw anything finer, but it soon disappeared. It was, as I believe, [empiricism], which now is in its heyday).[76]

The strong rejection of all hypothetical speculation *a priori*, which we encounter in the *Regnum* prologue, partly affects the author himself negatively: the hasty penetration in *Oeconomia* to the domains of the soul had been insufficiently founded (§19). The difference in atmosphere between these two works, which Lamm has clearly shown, also impinges on the view of antiquity.[77] In the prologue to *Oeconomia*, we find the clearest evaluation of ancient and modern in Swedenborg's writings. Rash generalizations are used. Ancient wisdom was greater than ours, since philosophers managed to reach as high as, for instance, Aristotle, Hippocrates, Galenos, Archimedes, and Euclid without any other education than they managed to find themselves; one is struck by the fact that all names were chosen from a list of natural scientists. However, our time surpasses antiquity with our greater knowledge of facts. Changes of nature are reflected in the world of learning: *"Illuxit enim dies & floruimus ingenio; subiit nox & multis saeculis obstupuimus; jam Aurora adest & floremus experientia; ab hac iterum in diem & aevum ingenii forte tenditur"* (For the day dawned, and we were greatly endowed with wisdom; night fell, and we were petrified for many centuries; now approaches the rosy morning, and we pride ourselves on experience; perhaps the direction from here is again to the day and the age of wisdom).[78] He who now knows how to use modern science correctly shall be able to surpass the ancients: Swedenborg's personal hopes of becoming this man are obvious, and the optimism is close to the far-reaching ambition from the harmony essay.[79] However, in *Regnum animale*, joyous confidence has been transformed into something bordering on resignation, an atmosphere portended already in the prologue to *De anima*. It seems as if intensive studies in modern anatomy strengthened the insight that empirical foundations are necessary, while ancient wisdom had been clouded by a longing for the true knowledge, only available through the grace of God.[80]

Thus, Swedenborg's view of antiquity modified regarding the ancients' scientific knowledge. These modifications however hardly apply to his use of elements of style in the antique manner, which appear almost everywhere in Swedenborg's writings, giving them character. We find the culmination of this tendency in *The Worship and Love of God*, although the antique components have a wider significance here. The highest ascension, now reached by the kingdom of literature, no doubt refers mainly to modern empirical science: this is clear from the polemic in the note against a misguided rationalism's empty speculations on the soul's material or ideal essence. The attempt throughout the work to give empirical evidence in the notes for the symbolic descriptions indicates the same.

At the same time, the connection to ancient wisdom is far stronger than elsewhere: the whole preface praises the wise ancients, whose sensibility was closer to heaven, and the following drama is explicitly written in their fashion (§2). The context reveals the reason: the doctrine of correspondence has now under the pressure of the religious crisis been made current and capable of rendering the highest wisdom, described in *De anima* as the content of *"fabulas quales antiqui in aevis aureo proximis"* (fables such as the ancient from the ages closest to the golden one). During the time of the crisis, Swedenborg experienced—in pain and delight—the correspondential function of the dream life, while fables now become the second element of the fourth category of the doctrine of correspondence, *"correspondentia fabulosa et somniorum."*[81] The ancients, both heathen and Christian, inserted their esoteric wisdom into this pattern, as appears from both the hieroglyphical key and the excerpts, but their intellects were in the radiant equilibrium of the Silver Age between *anima* and *mens*, as we surmise from the short allusion in the preface to the Golden Age, a reflection of the excerpt notes on the mythical encounters between men and gods, and in quotes from both Jewish and Greek documents.[82]

These excerpts show that Swedenborg is not unique among his contemporaries as regards his view of myths: *"Dass die griechischen Mythen eine Entstellung der biblischen Überlieferung enthalten, war am Anfang des XVIII. Jahrhunderts die allgemeine Überzeugung geworden und wurde auch während der ersten Hälfte des folgenden Jahrhunderts sowohl von Altertumsforschern wie von katholischen und protestantischen Theologen in unzähligen Schriften vorausgesetzt oder durch vermeintlich neue Gründe gestützt"* (That the Greek myths contained a distortion of the biblical tradition had become a general conviction at the beginning of the eighteenth century, and it was also taken for granted during the first half of the following century by scholars of antiquity as well as Catholic and Protestant theologians in countless writings or supported by supposedly new arguments).[83]

Behind this consensus, shared by Swedenborg, lies a long development. When Senator Gaius Velleius in Cicero's important *De natura deorum* provides a critical exposé on the battling philosophies of his time, he mentions among the aspects characteristic of Stoicism its allegorical interpretations of myths.[84] Stoic interpretations were important for Christian theology through Origen, but also for the history of mythology. This type of interpretation can be found as early as the Carolingian Middle Ages, including a beginning insight that it goes further than the ancient myth poets had intended: *"nicht sie wollte man auslegen, sondern die geheimnisvolle Absicht Gottes ergründen, der sie so hatte sprechen lassen"* (one did not want to interpret them, but to ascertain the secret intention of God, who had allowed them speak in such a way).[85]

The Platonic current of the twelfth century—represented by, for instance, the Chartres school, whose hexaemeral importance has already been discussed—includes new impulses in mythological writing and interpretation. An interest in literature was a hallmark of this century's renascence of the classical education, and among the poets most in fashion were Virgil and Ovid, on whose works were written both allegories and morally edifying commentaries.[86] This is especially true of Ovid, who through the *Metamorphoses* became the foremost transmitter of ancient mythological knowledge.[87] With his obligatory presence in the curricula, Ovid kept this position for a long time, and his tales of transformation form, in this regard, the common basis for the goliards' of the twelfth century and a later assessor of the Royal Swedish Board of Mines possessing an unusual sensitivity to symbolism.

The connection between mythological studies and Platonism is repeated during the fifteenth century Renaissance, when both poets and philosophers showed great interest in mythology. However, it rarely went beyond enthusiasm and minor attempts. Pico della Mirandola's grand attempt at proving esoteric doctrines of wisdom in ancient poetry was never finished.[88] With humanism came an interest in the correlation between the myths of different cultures, for instance, between the tradition of Egypt and that of Greece, a line of study that has existed since late antiquity and that reaches its culmination in the comparative mythology of the seventeenth century.[89]

This mythological study does not continue undisturbed, however. The religious fanaticism of the Reformation sometimes results in something close to a medieval anticultural stance. In Luther, for instance, we find an energetic opposition to allegoric interpretations of mythology, called *"eine schmeichelnde Buhlerin, eine Erfindung des Satans und fauler Mönche, die auch die Metamorphosen ausgelegt und z.B. Apollon auf Christus, Daphne, den Lorbeer, auf Maria bezogen haben"* (an ingratiating courtesan, an invention of Satan and lazy monks, who have also interpreted the Metamorphoses and e.g. related Apollo to Christ, and Daphne, the laurel, to Mary).[90] Nevertheless, as Lutheran orthodoxy releases its hold, mythological interest grows also in Protestant countries, a growth characterized during the seventeenth century by comparative views. When studying the submissions of Grotius, Burnet, and Leibniz, one is struck by the examples from Egyptian, Persian, and Indian mythology, all used in order to extract an original vision corresponding with Christian beliefs.

These submissions stem from scholarly accounts. One of the most important was written by Gerhard Johannes Voss, who unites a euhemeric and a symbolic interpretation of myth in an eclectic whole, so typical for his era.[91] He also entertains a belief in the original vision; however alongside this vision and elements of truth manifested in Greek mythology, Voss also finds demonic ingredients: *"Auch er nimmt mit einzelnen Kirchenvätern an, dass sich die abgefallenen Engel als Götter verehren liessen. Er rechnet zu ihnen Typhon, Ahriman und in gewisser Beziehung selbst Apollon"* (Even he supposes with some fathers of the church that the fallen angels let themselves be venerated as gods. He counts among them Typhon, Ariman and in a way Apollo himself).[92] Voss was followed by a multitude of disciples in different countries, all of whom contributed to the situation in Swedenborg's era. Even this sketchy overview is a reminder of what I stated earlier regarding the genesis of the doctrine of correspondence: the erudition of the seventeenth century and of his contemporaries is often sufficient to explain Swedenborg's inspirational environment. In analysing a later scene in *The Worship and Love of God* with its demonology inspired by mythology, this overview will be supplemented by a more detailed study.

The high esteem for ancient myth and poetry gives *a priori* reason to be sceptical towards Lamm's theory of an influence from Milton. The general similarities that he examines seem both exaggerated and general in the extreme: Lamm evidently based his view of the hexaemeral genre on Du Bartas, Spegel, and the like.[93] Of the similarities in detail examined by Lamm, I have already shown one to have a common precursor in classical poetry, Ovid, and the same is probably true of the others. In the light of the rich excerpt material, one must also emphasize the importance of Swedenborg's never once having referred to the English poet, except in a list in a letter to Benzelius from 1711, which Lamm submits.[94] Through excerpts and quotations, there are however good possibilities of tracing the point of origin, but that this has not been possible as regards Milton should act as a caution when it comes to methodology, especially as Swedenborg himself has been given a divine charge not to use *"annars kram,"* the gee-gaws of others, in this particular work.[95]

Of course, it can never be proved that Milton held no importance for Swedenborg. Indeed this would seem rather improbable, considering his English orientation and the influence of Milton on, for instance, Spegel and Olof von Dalin (1708–1763), as Lamm has pointed out.[96] But it is still a long step from the obvious influence that Lamm urges. Since it is clear that the similarities in question regard the ambience of antiquity, it would seem more appropriate to assign these to the common classical basis, in particular as Swedenborg stated his theoretical esteem for it. That the biblical tale of Creation should become subject to Swedenborg's rewriting in a classical style is so evidently explained in his other writings that we do not need to assume that his possible reading of Milton was of importance to the project. The influence from antiquity regards the form, not the theme; and the correlation between Genesis and ancient fables does not mean that Swedenborg viewed the content of classical poetry as equal to the Word of the Bible.

Direct allusions to ancient mythology in *The Worship and Love of God* are almost exclusively to be found in descriptions of the powers of evil.[97]

This fact is an evaluation, underlined by a note at the end of his collection of excerpts: *"nec scio an totus Seneca valeat uni sententiae Davidis aut Salomonis"*(Nor do I know, if all of Seneca is worth one single line of David or Solomon).[98] Although a conventional statement, it is significant through its position in Swedenborg's development: it serves as an apology for the study of the ancients, reflected in his juvenile dissertation where the *Selectae sententiae* from Seneca and Publilius Syrus appear, which influenced his style so greatly. It also presages the journey to the land of biblical exegesis. First, however, remains the culmination of classical influence in *The Worship and Love of God*. Given this background, we might read in Swedenborg's statement on the ascension of literature an evaluation of his own work, where modern empirical science is given the same form that the ancients used to spread their wisdom.

# 7

*ۈ.*

# THE LOVE OF THE FIRSTBORN

(§§57–86)

The fifth scene in *The Worship and Love of God*, "The Love of the First-born," is the most extensive of them all and also the boldest attempt at depicting, with the aid of the doctrine of correspondence, the faith that had developed during the time of crisis, even as Swedenborg's scientific views deepened. To a greater extent than before, Swedenborg used the possibilities of the fable to move between the sublime and the grotesque, while the links with earlier scenes are less evident than before. Tensions in the intellectual content also correspond with this compositional change. Most representative of the view presented here is the pattern of emanations—which earlier had not been prominent and which is contrary to the idea of a *creatio ex nihilo* evident in the third scene, "The Origin of Adam, the Firstborn"—now being used in far-reaching parallels between the spiritual and the natural suns and in relatively precise theses of the neurological interaction in the body between the soul and the rational mind.[1]

To evaluate this "emanationalism" in relation to the previous sections and with regard to the theoretical background, we must stress that *The Worship and Love of God* first and foremost is not a philosophical treatise but a symbolic fable. Thus demands for intellectual stringency must not be too harsh: the introductory remark on the world egg is essential to evaluating the entire drama, and it must be remembered that this is where the doctrine of correspondence was first applied in a thorough manner. That Swedenborg had not attempted theological exactitude in his view can be deduced from a warning contained in a dream in the spring of 1744, *"at jag intet borde besmitta mig med andre böcker, som angår theologica och dylika satzer: ty det har jag i Gudz ord och af then Helge Anda"* (that I should not contaminate myself by reading other books on theology and related theses, because this I have in the Word of God and from the Holy Spirit).[2] Of central importance to him was to give form to a message of the love of God in our life, after its theoretical motivation in his scientific writings had deepened during the fellowship with Christ in the crisis period. In the attempt to unite these intensely experienced Christian thoughts with the scientific system, tensions and paradoxes are made fairly evident.

Regarding background sources, we know that the precursors mentioned above have not been used solely in *The Worship and Love of God*, which follows from its expressly synthetic character, and the excerpts referred to have also been written earlier. This fact is relevant especially when evaluating the theoretical consequence of the drama as regards theological questions: what we find in this regard is an extension of earlier attempts, and our studies of the sources can in several cases illuminate the background to these sketches. However, the literary form that they acquired during some hectic autumn and winter months in 1744 and 1745 seems to have been created without any profound study of the sources. The feeling of fellowship with Christ in God, experienced in visions and reading of the Scriptures, is in itself enough of an explanation for the emanation symbolism so often used by Christian thinkers such as Augustine and Malebranche, and it does not in itself justify labelling *The Worship and Love of God* as a Neoplatonic work. However, this tendency is important because of what will happen when symbolism turns into dogmatism.[3]

The complicated intellectual background presents a stimulating challenge to literary analysis, and the fifth scene is inspiring from a literary point of view. In its introduction, the divine intelligences, which appear at the end of the previous scene (§48ff), perform a dance, another one of the geometrically inspired ballet intermezzi that we have met several times before: they appear as little girls, with their hair braided and their foreheads beautifully adorned with jewels, but otherwise in natural nudity. Their lovely faces, characterized in the wonderful ecphrasis *"sicut picti risus imagines,"* as images of smiles in a painting, spread a brilliant shimmer of light on the garden of paradise. However, the dance is not simply an aesthetic delight, and the young man's suspicion of a hidden message is soon confirmed by his eldest wisdom. Through actions such as these, the heavenly beings express all the ideas that humans can only articulate in conversations, bound as they are to words. Heavenly language is thus images conveyed by correspondence, and the person who can interpret these images can also follow a heavenly conversation (§57, footnote u). With the aid of visions like this, Adam is thus educated in the basics of the doctrine of correspondence, and he will be given the opportunity to demonstrate his insights in the drama's finale. Biographically the vision is an important stage in the journey toward a relation with the spirits, where thoughts are expressed similarly in changes of positions.[4]

The vision has yet another task: to teach the young man that love rules his life, that he himself is nothing, that the Highest is everything. Adam at first regards this lesson as a crude jest and is incensed. His questioning has the usual role in a Platonic dialogue: it gives rise to a didactical address, which is now provided in the wisdom's response (§58). The scene is entirely structured on this collaboration between the young man and his wisdom, which gives the author an opportunity to distance himself from the physical situation, the lonely man in paradise. The wisdom represents pure intellect, which during the state of innocence is in direct contact with the soul and which is thus aware of what eventually will happen, an insight the wisdom presents to its eager listener with the same methodology that was described in *De anima*, *"per parabolas et similitudines, imo per fabulas quales antiqui in aevis aureo proximis"* (through parables and similitudes, in fact through fables such as the ancients used in times close to the Golden Age).[5]

Thus, both a future sinful race and Christ's sacrifice can be depicted in terms of anticipating visions, even prior to the existence of others besides Adam. In the wisdom's answer, the development of the understanding of love is fulfilled, a process that has been displayed in the psychological studies conducted down through the years previous to this work. It reaches its zenith when the soul's light for a moment is dimmed: it becomes a tangible demonstration of the thesis that human life is the divine light that enters us through *anima*, the soul. The human being is thus a passive recipient of the life that flows from the Highest: *"Unus est modo, qui vivit, ex Quo quia vivimus, ex Eodem etiam agimus; sique ex Eo vivimus & agimus, in Eo sumus"* (Only the One lives; because we get our life from him, our actions too come from him; and if we get our life and actions from him, we are *in* him) (§58).

The wisdom's allusion to Paul's famous areopagus sermon, a Bible text significant both to Swedenborg's personal situation and to the environment reminiscent of antiquity, ends in a discussion of free will and its relationship to this love. The motifs in *De anima* are developed further: love rules will, since the purpose is always some form of love, a thesis illustrated with the image of a dove, the conventional bird of love, flying past on his way to his mate, driven by his love for her. The bird experiences his flight as a conscious act of his own will, but the wisdom refers the bird's behavior to a deeper reason.[6] Swedenborg provides an anatomical illustration of the will's passivity in extensive notes (§58, note y; §59, note z).

However, love's dominance also means, in the wisdom's description, that the perspective is opened towards the evil forms of love. Before allowing these to appear on stage, Swedenborg must provide an accumulated picture of the role of divine love in the human psyche, and this is done in the form of dialogue and demonstration in the following six paragraphs (§§61–67). Within the divine emanation, we find light, giving knowledge of the truth, and also love, allowing us to feel goodness. The wisdom instructs Adam through comparisons between the spiritual sun in the heavenly paradise, where his soul may enter, and the natural sun in *paradisus telluris*. Although these two kinds of light chase one another away, they are still united in friendship (§64). The wisdom illustrates this relationship by reminding Adam of how the soul created his intellect, as we saw in the fourth scene, "The Infancy of Adam, the Firstborn." For the sake of credibility, the author has the wisdom disclose that it was able to witness this creation since it is the eldest of the wisdoms, a piece of information characteristic of Swedenborg's almost comical exactitude in the midst of the fantastic and outlandish display.

Withholding a laugh, the wisdom recounts how the visual impressions are transformed into intelligences and wisdoms during the soul's life-giving embrace. However, it extends this familiar motif by showing how these wisdoms have been bestowed with a kind of bodies, ruled by *anima* itself like a soul. In this image, Swedenborg differentiates between degrees of intellectual purity, while the coming anthropomorphic pattern for the spiritual world has come one step closer to its perfection. Again the symbolism of correspondence compels him to use an ever bolder degree of concretion. Within the psychology of the drama of creation, the language of symbols permits a clearer motivation, why the *mens intellectualis* is the place where heaven and earth meet: divine light and life flow into the intelligences' souls, which are *anima* itself, while the impressions from nature's light stream into their bodies. Thus the psychological triad's borders are erased, and the concepts are enmeshed. This tendency was already present in *De anima*, but it is taken further here, and this would seem to be motivated by theological reasons, soon to be presented.

However, it is of the utmost importance that this influx occurs to fulfil the order of the Highest: the meaning of this will henceforth become a constantly recurring theme both in text and commentary. The influx must flow from the higher to the lower, from the soul to the intellect and from there to sensory life and the body—an emanation program with a heavenly correspondence in the influx of divine life into the universe, revealing its proximity to the Platonic world of ideas. This fact is reflected in a commenting note, where God in syllogisms of correspondence is relieved of all responsibility for folly and hate in the world, which only result from taking away his intelligence and love (§64, note g). This deduction is a direct quote from *Clavis hieroglyphica* with its reference to *Aristotle's Theology* and its systematic attempt at translating natural terms into spiritual and divine ones.[7] To understand the deepest atmosphere of the drama of creation, we must observe how this view is shaped into a stronger emphasis than before on human passivity and humanity's role as recipient of the divine light. The tendency appeared in the theoretical doctrine structure, but that it appears so oppressively in this work is a result of the religious crisis, when the ego's need for salvation ends in submission and a sense of divine presence leads to an experience of self-obliterating passivity.[8]

This is most clearly expressed in the notes. In the fable, the philosophy is depicted in symbolic episodes, of which the nearest one describes what happens in Adam's intellect, when the divine order is suspended for a moment. The wisdom allows the sensory perceptions, the servants of the intelligences, to rush into the Olympus whichever way they like. Great confusion ensues, where the intellectual jumble is symbolized by the slaves' ruffled hair and wandering lanterns, as they search for the wisdoms' mansion; they involve themselves in heated and divergent debates, and it all ends in quarrels and riots (§66). This grotesque tableau is interrupted when the soul barges into the holy room driving the wild flock back with flashes from its light; no more than the first human couple can stand watching the divine light with an unshaded eye can disorganized ideas endure *anima*'s blazes. Swedenborg the rationalist depicts disorder through an image of contradictory and ignorant quarrels; behind the blind slaves, one may detect a harsh narrator's transformation of the obstructive polemic, of which Swedenborg so often expressed disdain in his scientific works, and they also foreshadow the descriptions of the mortals' blind search for the truth of the Highest, with which this scene ends (§85).

Wisdom interprets this dramatic episode in a lengthy monologue, and her speech ends in a new sermon on the superiority of love in Adam's life, which appears in §67: *"nam Amor imperat Menti, & Mens Corpori"* (Love rules the mind, and the mind rules the body). These educational homilies suffer from the weakness of all didactic poetry; however, this is irrelevant to a man who claims to possess truth and who wishes to save the ignorant reader from a vain search. In order to be reminded constantly of the dominance of love, the sacred fire described in the previous scene is now present in the Helicon of the intelligences (§51), and its symbolism is explained. Focus, the hearth, represents the truths and their intelligences, the gold surrounding its rings signifies the goodnesses and their wisdoms, and the melt-down of the hearth into gold as hard as diamonds through the fire of love indicates the union of goodness and truth. The numerous colors show the different ways of interpreting this union, as the intelligences and the wisdoms are not completely identical but form a harmoniously varied community (§67). Even in this respect, the intellect is the image of heaven, as will be explained later.

The discourse on divine love concludes with the interpretation of the symbol, with which it was introduced. Now follows a portrayal of the essence of evil love, taking up the ten following paragraphs. It begins with the wisdom's stressing to Adam that there are several kinds of love, all attempting to mimic the love of the Highest; therefore, it is most important that one become familiar with one's love, as it is crucial to human existence, the time bound and the eternal. We now come one step closer, as Lamm pointed out, to the theosophical *amor regnans*.[9] At the same time, however, Swedenborg refers back, in a note of commentary, to his anatomical studies, when he provides a quick repetition of his theories on the origin of the fibres in the brain's *glandulae corticales*, a passage referring mainly to *De fibra*.[10] In this context, he asserts that it is easier to gain insight into the accuracy of his belief through phenomena themselves, rather than *"per obscuram & spatiosam viam Anatomicam & Philosophicam"* (from the obscure and lengthy route of anatomy and philosophy) (§68, note m), although it will be completely proved in this manner. Clearly this indicates his impatience in reaching the goal, as well as displaying the didactic motivation of the form of the book, since it obviously does not require the same kind of readers, educated in anatomy and philosophy.

Ironically, this assurance is illuminated by the fact that we here encounter the strongest tensions in the intellectual background. The wisdom is forced to reveal to the young man that against the love of the Highest stands an evil power, a black love that hides itself to assure that its victims believe it does not exist: *"sic etenim Lucem Caelestem extenuat, & Sacrum Ignem exstinguit, quem exosus, interponit tale umbraculum, ut post id ludos suos instituat; quapropter nusquam alibi plus & securius vivit, quam penes quos, se non vivere, fidem facit"* (He dims the light of heaven and douses the sacred fire. He hates that fire so much that he blocks it with a screen and starts his games behind the thing. And so there is no place where he thrives as much or lives as securely as among those whom he convinces that he does not exist at all) (§68, note m). The Christian belief in the devil is thus incorporated into the emanatic monism, and the tension between these extremely disjointed elements is expressed, as usual, in a paradox: *"Non est nisi Unicus Amor, omnium Bonitatum & Veritatum Fons; sed datur etiam & existit alius, qui quia omnium malorum, etiam omnium falsitatum, origo est"* (There is only the One Love, the source of good and truth; but another has arisen that exists along with it; it is the origin of all falsity, because it is the origin of all evil) (§69).

This "prince of the world" was also produced by the Highest because of his love for his creation; thus, the first part of the paradox is fulfilled. The prince was, however, created to act as intermediary between life and nature, so that the most perfect order would be produced. But having power over all the universe corrupted him, so that the prince of the world wished to usurp the rule over heaven as well. He lapsed through insurrection against the only Son and became the love of division; and thus the second element of the paradox is explained. The prince of the world lives by the beams from the Highest's life, like all other beings; but celestial love is denied to him, and he is consumed by the dry flames following his making himself a god. At the same time, he is still bound by necessity, which the Highest introduced to counter the prince's expected defection.

To assure the surprised listener, the wisdom immediately provides a psychological application of this theological program, where *anima*, the soul, takes the place of the Highest, the intellect takes the place of the Son, and *animus*, the lower mind, takes the place of the prince of the world. Given her *a priori* knowledge, the wisdom has the opportunity to journey the opposite way compared to the thinker and natural scientist Swedenborg, who in his scientific works followed the tiresome *a posteriori* path. With soothing words, the wisdom assures the young man that *animus'* evil spirit is harnessed and is in itself incapable of causing any damage, as long as everything happens according to the law of order; a human being can indeed force his or her intellect away from the sensual temptations (§70).

Yet the prince of the world is a constant danger to weak intellects. He cannot reach the higher road, that of the soul, with his large and obese body, but he can manage to crawl onto the road of the senses (§71). The disdain expressed in this contemptuous wording is fulfilled with a furious description of what happens in the intellect, where the prince of the world has attained power. Again for credibility's sake, the wisdom explains how she can know anything of this matter, as such a human intellect does not yet exist: she recounts what has been told to her (§72). An order is introduced there, mimicking the celestial. The prince delegates the government to a deputy, *Animus*, who resides in the lower mind, and he offers him the power to choose any love at all, as long as it is of the flesh and the world. Thus human freedom ends, as the intellect is run by its own slaves.

Despite all this, the confused intelligences can be reached by reproaches from the wisdoms of heavenly love, who have fled to the innermost abodes of the soul: these are the qualms of a bad conscience, which Swedenborg so vividly depicts (§73). However, the chilling moments of insight are fleeting; they are sent flying by sensual temptations, and the small doorway into the kingdom of the soul is shut and locked. This observation on the mechanism of hardening, which Swedenborg has depicted with his curious impulse, seems to be inspired by reshaping the Apollonian hierarchy into images of different lusts. That modern humans cannot appreciate such symbols as the ancients could is now explained by the blindness of the intellect, which the worldly prince has achieved (§70, note o).

Thus far we have been inside an imagined human psyche, where certain criteria for the demands of probability have still been met. It would seem, however, as if the reference to ancient myth has inspired Swedenborg to liberate himself from any remaining restrictions. Wisdom in her next episode refers to what she has heard and seen: *ex auditu et visu*, a customary subtitle for his theosophical writings. She has once followed some heavenly wisdoms who were traveling throughout the world to investigate the attempts of the evil one, and they chanced to meet a flock of evil intelligences. The stage is a town square, the natural meeting place in an environment styled on antiquity (§74). The evil ones stroll in brilliant festive costumes on their way from their Pythian games, dissimulating emotions of joy.

The tableau is evidently an extension of what has been recently said of the intellects, where the prince of the world has taken power, and the heavenly wisdoms repeat faithfully the earlier homily, although this time in concrete and painful reproaches. We see here a detail parallel to Swedenborg's spiritual development, in which theoretical insights were transformed into dream visions. The wisdom, who is Adam's narrator, appears to be Swedenborg's alter ego, when it speaks *ex auditu et visu*. The episode when the sensory images rush into the intellect in a disorganized fashion is now repeated, but this time in a terrifying metamorphic motif: "*ac illico apparebant eis omnes genii, sicut colubrae, circum capita illarum flexae ac sibilantes, saniemque suam in Corporis illarum venas, viis per morsus apertis, infundentes (s); ac totidem sibi visae sunt facies Gorgonicae; illae externatae aufugere volebant, sed ex jactatu Corporis, comae illae infernales, sinus ac facies illarum, pulsabant*" (Instantly all the daemons appeared to the understandings as snakes, twisting and hissing around their heads, laying them open with bites, and injecting venom into the veins of their bodies (s), making the understandings think that they had become Gorgons' heads. Terrified, they wanted to run away, but the writhing of their bodies made their hellish locks lash them in the breast and face) (§74). This horrific description is perfected in an escatological perspective, when it is said that the eternal life of the confused intelligences shall be like a beaten and tormented body without a head and with its feet upward (§75). The visionary experienced this thesis in his own dreams during the hectic period around Easter 1744.[11]

That the wisdom has been speaking of human intellects becomes ever more evident when it broadens its description to encompass the darkness that surrounds the evil intellects: the truths escape and must be traced in vain through convoluted sciences. One cannot ascertain whether life is anything but nature, one fights and kills, all during the broad-jawed laughter of the prince of the world (§§75–76). The evil kinds of love among human beings are innumerable, but above them all stand two captains, *Amor sui* and *Amor mundi*. Under these generals of the devil, there is a classical hierarchy of mixed descent: "*duces, satrapae, primores plebejorum, centuriones, cum innumeris lictoribus*" (rulers, satraps, leaders of the masses, captains, and countless lieutenants) (§77). In the imaginations of these misguided intellects, one variety will take the lead. They invent all kinds of names for the laws governing their lives, such as fate, chance, circumstance; the evil love has so confused them that they cannot discover the guidance of providence. Indeed, they find their destinies so complex that they can be compared, as Swedenborg expresses it in a chillingly suggestive metaphor, to "*glomeres lumbricorum, qui coacervati capita sua vel humo infodiunt, vel ipsi acervo implicant*" (a ball of earthworms, which when they are piled together either dig their heads into the soil or work them back into the heap) (§77).

This dark portrayal of an evil breed naturally gives rise to the theodicy problem, and the final main section of the scene deals with this question in different variations. It begins with a picture in which the three spiritual powers of the drama of creation are set against one another: the Highest once armed himself with the flashes of justice and anger to overthrow the tyrant prince and his rabble in Orcus. However, at the very moment when the lightning was about to hit the raging devil, the Son threw himself into the fray, embracing the misguided intellects. And rather than letting his Son suffer his righteous anger, God promised to spare his world, until it had lived through its ages (§78). This image must be interpreted with some care, and we shall study it in more detail later against an emblematic background. Nevertheless, to a certain degree it can be viewed as a symbol for Christ's act of redemption. Swedenborg was obviously aware that he extended beyond the frame in the wisdom's monologue, since Adam asks the wisdom to retreat a bit on the same road and explain to him how he could experience his union with the divine love as thoroughly as possible (§79).

This means a renewed application of the theological program within the human psyche, when the wisdom shows, through forcing the captured prince of the world into different acts of transformation, how harmless the evil one is for those who live under the protection of the Highest. The devil appears here in the shape of an enormous dog, a wolf, a lion, a dragon, a flame of fire, all frightening and often-used symbols for the devil, which have appeared in Swedenborg's dreams, as Lamm noted.[12] We carry this awful enemy with us in our sensual life, and humanity's essence is therefore disintegrated. Although the prince of the world appears in our sensual lusts in the shapes just exhibited, as long as the Highest's love reigns in our intellects, these lusts are innocent and harmless. The wisdom does not preach a gospel of asceticism but one of order bound by law (§84). And after the disjointed speech, as it is characterized by the wisdom itself, it reaches the main point: how we shall be able to enjoy love forever (§85).

This has been the purpose of the wisdom's whole narrative, as it is the center of our entire lives: inside the human being is heaven, earth, and hell, but inside there is also free choice. Little do we understand of where the goal is! Using the image of a race in an ancient stadium, the wisdom depicts the innumerable ways in which humanity will look for the meaning of life: here we find symbolized different religions and sects, different seekers, and mobs confused by the devil. It is a melancholy scene of discord and pointless zeal, which in the last episode is contrasted against the wisdom who revels in the joy of the true goal, where the love of the Highest is situated (§86). The heavenly wisdoms, who initiated the scene, have been ordered never to abandon Adam's intelligences, and we are allowed one last glimpse of them as they pay tribute to their lord and master.

The many strange and didactic speeches that comprise this scene confuse the reader; certainly, in this scene Swedenborg did not carry through the same relatively stringent composition as in the previous scenes, and the didactic purpose diminishes the aesthetic qualities. However, the systematizer reveals himself again in a format reminiscent of the fourth scene's pattern, which was divided in three: first, a discourse on the superiority of love in the psyche and the order instituted by God; second, an extensive narrative on evil love culminating in the dramatic meeting between the three spiritual powers in §78; and finally, the theodicy problem presented in a psychological light, mainly involving the righteous task of evil love in human beings, who fulfill the order of God.

Thus, the drama moves closer its basic theme. The union with love, like the different forms of human adoration of God in §85, correlates to its first appearance in *De Infinito* a decade earlier. In that work, *The Worship and Love of God* is foreshadowed after a description of the contemporary sinful race and its ignorance of the purpose and meaning of life.[13] In this composition, Swedenborg attempted to give form to so much of his newly won knowledge that he was forced to exceed the frame; the narrative joy inspired by mythology was given new wings by the eagerness of a preacher. An investigation of his teachings on different aspects of the doctrine of love and the view on evil will help unravel his ideas.

## Love, Free Will, and Christ

Analysis of motifs and a study of the genesis of *The Worship and Love of God* reveal that few texts in the hexaemeral tradition are conceived in such a psychological fashion. The main purpose of the Christian contributions to this genre is to preach about the soul's salvation; however, this is often obscured by accumulated pieces of cosmological and biological science, prompted by Genesis. Swedenborg uses the Creation as his starting point, but he keeps in focus the aim articulated in the title.

In discussing the previous scene (§§39–56), we stressed that the discourse on freedom of will is intimately connected to the view of love as the life of the intellect. In the *Oeconomia*, just as his rationalist colleagues maintain, Swedenborg asserts that freedom of will is primarily motivated in the relationship between God and the world. God wishes to be loved by human beings with a love materializing from free will, not from some kind of instinct, akin to the desires of the senses. Swedenborg quotes this idea from Malebranche among the excerpts, a view that Swedenborg made his own. Characteristic expressions of it appear in the second part of *Oeconomia*:

> *quid omnipotentiae obstaret, nos cogere, si vellet; potuisset per fulmina & tonitrua compellere nos ad aras; ipsa nostra genua inflectere, ut adoraturi procumbamus: Angelos & Manes mortuorum per singulas societates sub forma humana, distribuere; aut quovis instanti ore tenus, uti olim Judaeos e monte Sinai, al-*

*loqui & terrificare; verbo perpetuis miraculis voluntates nostras frangere: sed an sic respiceretur quid ut nostrum in ipsa necessitate? & annon sic usque penitius aestuaremus in culpam?*

(What could prevent the Almighty from forcing us, if he wished to? He could drive us with thunder and lightning to the altars, and bend our knees so that we fall down in prayer. He could have distributed angels and the spirits of the dead in human form to different societies, or he could have spoken to us with all manners of threats and made us frightened, as he did with the Jews from Mount Sinai in olden days. He could with one word crush our will with constant miracles. But what would be our own under such oppression? Would we not smoulder with hatred in our innermost selves?)[14]

Thus, our own ambition is of the utmost importance to our salvation, and in our supreme efforts of the will, we have the opportunity to arouse divine grace. In support of this view, Swedenborg quotes Hugo Grotius and, through him, Lactantius (c. 240–c. 320).[15]

Lamm pointed out that Swedenborg at this stage had already distanced himself from the Lutheran orthodox doctrine of redemption through faith alone; this is especially evident in a little essay called *"De fide et bonis operibus"* (On faith and good works), which was probably written around the same time as *Oeconomia*.[16] The discourse, which directly attacks Luther's translation of Romans 3:28, contains the same character of conceptual analysis as the final chapter of *Oeconomia* and differentiates between salvation bringing faith, which is a direction of the will and a union of faith and love, and the "historical" faith, which is mere knowledge, possessed even by the devils.[17] This distinction, a recurring motif in Jesper Swedberg's harsh criticism of Protestant solifidism, belief in salvation through faith alone, is one of the unifying ties between Pietism and him; at the same time it is, as Swedberg states with sorrow in his travel memoirs, a long tradition in Catholic orthodoxy and orthopraxis.[18] Lamm points out, however, that Swedenborg cannot be identified with any specific theological view but that he expresses his opinion philosophically as the natural consequence of his belief in free will. This is clearly illustrated in the excerpts in his notebook, where we find under relevant headlines common authorities such as Augustine, Malebranche, Leibniz, and Bible texts, notably from Paul.[19]

In the fullness of time, Swedenborg's view on the freedom of will and the act of salvation leads to a break with the Christian doctrine of atonement, but this occurs after he wrote *The Worship and Love of God*.[20] Prior to that, Swedenborg attempts to unite the revealed faith in Christ with his thinking. The holy fire in the temple of the intellect cannot be lit without the aid of the Highest. Love of the final purpose must be inspired by the grace of God, and this happens according to the law of irrefutable order, which is God himself (*Oec.* II, §331). Lamm seems to have exaggerated somewhat Swedenborg's scepticism to Malebranche's *"l'ordre immuable"* (unchanging order) in this passage; what he feared most was that this law of irrefutable order was superior to God himself, like the pre-existent creation pattern of the demiurg in Plato's *Timaeus*, which would suggest a limitation in God's omnipotence.[21] This was never Malebranche's intention; indeed, to avoid all anthropomorphic deviations, he refers to God's self-love, which enables God to constantly follow *"l'ordre immuable,"* which is himself.[22] In the writings prior to *The Worship and Love of God*, it is difficult to deduce that Swedenborg subscribed to this logically clear motivation; however it does appear in several places in the Malebranche excerpts in Swedenborg's notebooks. The most probable explanation for this is his anthropocentric focus, which prevented him from definitively describing the divine mystery.[23] This does not change the fact, however, that the doctrine of God's order in the universe so essential to *The Worship and Love of God* must be seen in the light of Augustinian philosophy, as will be discussed in greater detail later.

In *Oeconomia*, Swedenborg refers to the fountain of grace that will assist us so that our intellects can distance themselves from sensuality and the body and draw nearer to the Highest: *"Imo ut Libra stet a parte Illius, clementissime providit, ut per Mediatorem, qui in homine unitus Deo Legis Divinae ipsissima essentialia ad amussim implevit, adiri, & per Illum super gentem humanam reflecti posset"* (Yes, in order for the scales to weigh in his favor, [God] has in his clemency provided that he should be reachable and that he (as with a candle) should be reflected over humankind through a Mediator, who is united with God in our human nature and who has fulfilled the essence of the divine law in everything).[24] This statement recalls an earlier passage: in *De Infinito*, the Son, as was pointed out previously, became the unifying link between the eternal and the finite existence. While there is no extensive discussion of the problem here, we find a philosophically stylized description of the Son's act of salvation. God's creational intention to refer all finite beings to himself through humanity as an advocate *ad majorem Dei gloriam* would have been impossible if the Son had not taken human form and thus consolidated the connection between finite existence and infinity, which was broken through the Fall. Through the Son, we may regain our knowledge of God's infinity, and through him we are led to the true faith and become God's children.

With these generalizations, the dogma of incarnation is thus glossed over. However, Swedenborg deals somewhat with the complication that hardly one-third of humankind knows of Christ's becoming man: how then can God's ambition be achieved? In his answer, Swedenborg develops the thesis that, since the Father and the Son are one, a faith in God encompasses a belief in the infinity of God's being, that is, also in the Son. Without the Son's involvement, the creational plan could not be realized and no one saved, yet heathens are allowed the provision of the Savior through the grace of God.[25] For those who believe in the arrival of the Messiah, however, the demands are higher:

> *Dico . . . at qui illum sciunt, vel scire possunt, illos fieri per adventum ejus, & ad fidem illis necessariam esse notitiam adventus ejus, nam per notitiam qualitas fidei elucescit, & distinctior & plenior ejus perceptio sit, quae sic in sciente separari nequeunt. Sed de his in philosophia ratiocinante de cultu divino; hic tantummodo tradere volui, qui finis creationis fuerit, & quod primarius fuerit propter Infinitum seu creatorem; & quod nihil sit in mundo creato, quod illuc non tendat.*
>
> (But for those who know the Messiah or have the opportunity to learn about him, I say that they will also participate by his advent, but the knowledge of his arrival is necessary for them, for their faith; for the quality of faith emerges through the knowledge, and the conception of it becomes more genuine and distinct, which [qualities] cannot be separated in those who have knowledge. But on this in a philosophy on the worship of God; here I have only wanted to convey the final purpose of the creation, that it occurred primarily for the Infinite's or the Creator's sake; and that there is nothing in the created world that does not lead to him.)[26]

How, then, did Swedenborg fulfill his promise to deal further with the relationship between faith in and knowledge of Christ? In the present scene of the drama of creation, the inquisitive Adam learns that God created the world for his own love's or his Son's sake; it is of importance that this occurs in conjunction with the sketchy presentation of the intermediary function of evil (§69). This is restated even more obviously later, when the theological didactics are repeated from other starting points to Eve in the sixth scene, "The Marriage of Adam, the Firstborn." A *Diva caelestis*, an educational spirit, describes to the virgin how God of eternity, before the world was made, gave birth to a Son, through whom spiritual and natural things could be united and through whom God could rule his world: "*Is itaque natus est Unio & Mediatio inter Superiora & Inferiora, seu immediate inter Supremum, suum Parentem, & ipsum Caelum, id est, Caeli Indigenas; quare Ille solus est, per quem omnis Ordo instituitur & absolvitur, seu per quem via a Supremo ad ultima naturae, & retro, sic prorsum & rursum, ducitur*" (And so he was born to be the unifying and mediating element between the higher and the lower, or directly between the Supreme One, his parent, and heaven itself, that is, those who dwell in heaven. Which is why it is he alone through whom all order is established and brought to completion, or to put it another way, he is the one through whom the way leads from the Supreme One to the farthest elements of nature and back again—forward and backward) (§91). This intermediary role in God's world order is further emphasized in the interpretation of the final vision, where the Son is depicted under the image of a flaming ring of purple around the blinding light of the kernel; through the Son, the life of the Highest eventually can flow into humanity: "For through Him we both have access in one spirit to the Father."[27]

The philosophical treatise on the worship of God, which Swedenborg promised in *De Infinito* in 1734, became a drama about creation, and the changed plans brought consequences also in details; we do not encounter any profound treatment of the advent of the Messiah and his act of salvation as incarnate explicitly in the completed part of *The Worship and Love of God*. The parallel between the macrocosm and the microcosm has meant that the Christ of the Scriptures above all appears as the divine love in the human intellect. This is a far-reaching consequence of the psychological direction, which the discussion on the connection between infinity and our finite existence has taken in the tradition of Descartes. However, we find also important impulses from antiquity here. An illuminating case can be found in a context important to the development of the drama of creation, in *Clavis hieroglyphica* and its ninth example structured as a mathematical analogue: "*Perfectus ordo constituit harmoniam, haec parit pulchritudinem, quae naturam redintegrant et conservant: imperfectus vero ordo producit disharmoniam, haec parit deformitatem, quae naturam pervertunt et destruunt*" (Perfect order creates harmony; this gives birth to beauty, and together they awaken nature and maintain it. However, an imperfect order produces disharmony; this gives birth to deformity, and together they pervert and destroy nature).[28]

This sentence from the natural arena is then provided with spiritual and divine correspondences; and in his *confirmatio propositionum*, Swedenborg bases his theses on the laws of physics, on the experiences of the senses, on love that unites the intellects and thus matches harmonies, "*quae est ratio quod Pythagoras omnia harmoniis adscripserit, et quod vetustissimi Philosophi quendam amorem cuncta formavisse, consociasse, et conservare dixerint*" (which was the reason Pythagoras ascribed everything to harmonies and the ancient philosophers said that a kind of love had formed and united everything and now maintained it).[29] In an extensive quote from Plato in Swedenborg's notebook of excerpts, this view of love held by the ancient philosophers is related to a mythological background; there can be no doubt that Swedenborg was greatly influenced by Plato's description of cosmogonic love and the divine power that reigns in the soul.[30] The ancient elements in *Principia*'s cosmology, which were analyzed earlier in the light of the Burnet studies, have now reached their psychological peak; even the physiological correspondence between the evil love in the *animus* and diseases of the body, hinted at in *The Worship and Love of*

*God* using *De fibra* as a foundation, can partly be referred to these Plato excerpts.[31]

With this pattern taken from antiquity and rationalist philosophy, the evidence from the Bible will now be united, and it is natural that our first thoughts are led to the prologue of the gospel of John, as its *logos* sermon was one of the most important influences from philosophical speculation in the Christian tradition.[32] Naturally, Swedenborg knew this text well, and it would have occurred to him repeatedly during his studies, for instance, when reading of the origins of life on earth, where the *logos* theme so typical for the Stoical view on nature recurs frequently. As previously pointed out, the commentary of *Aristotle's Theology* in one central passage that Swedenborg copied stresses the correspondence to John's prologue. However, the scribe has nothing to say for himself regarding this issue, and it is also striking that the notion of the Word, *Logos*, is not used anywhere in *The Worship and Love of God*.

The gospel uses the term for the Son, born from eternity, which is why Swedenborg's restrictive practice cannot be explained alone with reference to the incarnation dogma; one remembers also that Milton's Creator merely issues general commands,

> and to what he spake
> His Word, the filial Godhead, gave effect (VII: 174–175).

The short notes in cod. 36–110 under the headline "Messiah, Christ, Jesus" do not refer to John's gospel either, which is the more conspicuous, as there are plenty of Bible references here.[33] Among the correspondence excerpts, the text contains notations, albeit without comment, and it seems as if Swedenborg was more interested in the gospel's talk of the Word as life and light, a reading that clearly reveals its connection to the studies of Malebranche's psychology.[34] These terms, the only Son as transmitter of the life of the Highest and the True Light, are common in the illuminated symbolic world of the drama of creation; thus, John's prologue must have been significant. However, more important than this self-evident conclusion is that Swedenborg in his search for the truth in the Bible found a guide in *Recherche de la vérité*.

This observation is confirmed by other hidden biblical references in *The Worship and Love of God*. A summarizing passage in the next scene speaks of the Son's role in the order of creation:

> *ita Ordinis hujus Gyrus volvitur, scilicet a Supremo, qui est Ip-sissima Vita, per Unicum suum Amorem, & sic per Vitam Cae-lestem; & ab hâc per vitam naturalem, in ipsam Naturam: & tunc rursum ab hâc, per eandem Vitam naturalem ad Cae-lestem, sed per continuas exuitiones, & sic per unicum Amorem, ad Supremum, seu ad ipsissimam Vitam: Ita vertitur*

*omnium cardo, & panditur janua a Vita & ad Vitam, atque Or-*
*dinis hujus perpetuatur gyrus, per solum Amorem seu Unigeni-*
*tum Supremi; per Quem, & propter Quem, omnia.*

(This is the revolving course of the cycle of this Order—
specifically, from the Supreme One, who is truly Life itself;
through his Only Love, and therefore through the heavenly life;
and from this through the natural life, into nature itself; then
back from this latter, through the same natural life to the heavenly, but by a process of continually shedding elements; and
thus it goes through the Only Love to the Supreme One, which
is to say, to what is truly life itself. This is the turning of the
hinge of all things, and the opening of the door out of life and
into life, and the continuation of the cycle of the Order through
the Only Love, or the Only-Born of the Supreme One; through
whom, and because of whom—all things.) (§105)

The final line directly alludes to the Bible: the origin can be read in the epistle to the Hebrews 2:10, a text which in the version used by Swedenborg
reads like this: "*Decebat enim ut ipse propter quem sunt haec omnia, &*
*per quem sunt haec omnia, multos filios in gloriam adducendo, principem*
*salutis ipsorum per perpessiones consummaret*" (It was fitting that God,
for whom and through whom all things exist, in bringing many children to
glory, should make the pioneer of their salvation perfect through suffer-
ings).[35] The Christ of the Bible text does not shy away from calling these
children of his brothers (2:11), in the same way we have found Love calling Adam "*non filius sed frater*" (not son but brother) in the fourth scene
(§55).

The epistle to the Hebrews, with its partly Alexandrian Christology, is
one of the biblical texts that Swedenborg refers to most frequently in his
excerpts.[36] His excellent knowledge of its special world of symbols can be
illustrated with a detail that is also of interest with regard to the conception of his intellectual environment. An extract from Grotius' *De veritate*
*religionis christianae* refers to Psalm 110, with its talk of Sion's king as a
high priest after the order of Melchizedek; here Swedenborg writes the
word "Messiah" over Grotius' text.[37] In fact, the epistle to the Hebrews
emphasizes this Messiah prophecy more strongly than in other places, naturally enough given the addressee: "*Der Gedanke 'Christus der wahre Ho-*
*hepriester' steht in keinem anderen Buch des NT so sehr im Mittelpunkt*"
(The idea of Christ as the true high priest is in no other book of the New
Testament so much in focus).[38]

Swedenborg notes this priesthood of Christ in several places in cod.
36–110, especially under titles of correspondence, the reason being that he
found among them examples of his own developing doctrine of correspondence: the tabernacle, the veil, the Holy of Holies, the entire ritual of the

ancient covenant has a correspondence with Christ's new testament, where the true high priest after the order of Melchizedek once and for all entered the sanctuary and achieved eternal salvation with his own blood (Heb. 9). Through this act of sacrifice, Christ revealed the Holy of Holies and in his flesh showed a way through the curtain (Heb.10:19–22). In these and similar sentences, Swedenborg found his own view of existence as a web of symbols predicted in a Christological program, and the temple images in Adam's psyche are also similar to the world of the epistle to the Hebrews.

The excerpts from Hugo Grotius are important since he has been quoted relatively frequently in the previous writings, as indeed in the entire cod. 36–110; however, it could have been done mainly as an encyclopedia of religious history.[39] When it comes to the basic philosophy, one is again forced to assume influences from Malebranche. In his works, we may find a similar Christology that partly underlines the same Bible texts. In *Entretiens sur la Metaphysique,* Malebranche lets his mouthpiece Theodore give a description of God's relationship to his creation, where Christ's role is depicted in terms of priesthood and the Bible references in the margin allude, among other sources, to the epistle to the Hebrews:

> *Aussi est-ce dans la vuë du culte que nôtre Souverain Prêtre devoit établir en l'honneur de la Divinité, que Dieu s'est resolu de se faire un temple dans lequel il fust éternellement glorifié. . . . Dieu se plaist dans ces sacrifices spirituels & divins; & s'il s'est repenty d'avoir étably un culte charnel, & mêmes d'avoir fait l'homme: il en a juré par luy-même, jamais il ne se repentira de l'avoir réparé, de l'avoir sanctifié, de nous avoir faits ses Prêtres sous nôtre Souverain Pontife le vray Melchisedech. . . . C'est par luy qu'il nous donne accès auprès de sa Majesté Suprême. C'est par luy qu'il se complaist dans son ouvrage. C'est par ce secret, qu'il a trouvé dans sa sagesse, qu'il sort hors de luy-même, s'il est permis de parler ainsi, hors de sa sainteté qui le separe infiniment de toutes les creatures; qu'il sort, dis-je, avec une magnificence dont il tire une gloire capable de le contenter.*

> (It is also with reference to the worship which our high priest would establish in honor of the Divine that God decided to make himself a temple in which he was to be glorified in eternity. . . . God found delight in these spiritual and divine sacrifices, and if he had regretted having established a worship in flesh, and even having created man, he swore that he would never regret having restored man, having consecrated him, having made us his priests under our high priest, the true Melchizedek. It is through the high priest that he gives us access to his Supreme Majesty. It is through him that God finds delight in his own work. It is through this secret, which God has found

in his wisdom, that God comes out of himself, if it is permitted
to say so, out of his holiness which separates him infinitely from
all creatures; God comes out, I say, with a magnificence from
which he derives a glory capable of satisfying him.)[40]

I will not dwell on the possible influence within this particular passage
from Malebranche, as there are naturally differences; nevertheless, we are
very close to the basic motif in Swedenborg's work, the worship of God. In
the title itself, with its reference to the connection between cult and love, he
expresses a thought that has an undeniable correlation to the high priest
after the order of Melchizedek in the epistle to the Hebrews—and in Malebranche's writing.[41] There is every reason to study this sketched background also as regards the *nexus* term in Swedenborg's texts. The only Son
appears in *De Infinito* as a transmitter between the finite and the infinite in
a context that directly points to *The Worship and Love of God*, although
the author did not exceed this general program, completely analogous to
Malebranche's philosophy: "*La mission du Médiateur commence avant la
chute, car une première médiation est nécessaire pour rendre possible le
mystérieux passage du néant à l'être*"(The mission of the mediator starts
before the Fall, for a primary mediation is necessary to make the mysterious passage from nothing to existence possible).[42] This mediation is fulfilled in the final vision of the heavenly community, the escatological
culmination of the world egg; the background to this idea will be investigated in that context.

Psychologically, this *nexus* term is used in ever larger contexts in *The
Worship and Love of God*. When love is of God, which means the only
Son, Swedenborg defines it as affection in the union of the two forces of
nature, or between the acting and the receiving (§80). This task of love explains its unselfishness: "*idque solum ut suum existimans, quod ex altero
in se reflectitur*" (Considering as its own only what is reflected into it from
another) (§80). When Swedenborg attempts to exemplify this affection, he
chooses an earthly couple in love, who in their sweet caresses try to achieve
a complete union within the same life, although divided in two individuals.
This is a new instance of the curious combination of theoretical
speculation—in this case, a reminiscence of Plato's androgynous myth and
anatomical studies of humanity's procreation—and the sensuality that appears so strongly in his own diary written at this same time.[43]

To reach this love, be united with it, and enjoy it in eternity are the goals
of Adam's education and that of his race: "*quid caetera! nisi volatiles
plumae, flocci, & stercora; in nos enim Seipsum, & universum suum
Caelum transcripsit, similiter etiam Mundum, ipsumque Infernum; &
quasi optionem dedit, unum aut alterum eligendi*" (What else is there? The
rest is drifting feathers, motes of dust, clods of dung. He has transcribed
himself and his entire heaven into us, along with the world and hell too;

and he has, in a manner of speaking, given us the option of choosing one or the other) (§85). In the final vision, which follows after Adam has finally become a complete man through his experience of earthly love, Swedenborg's theology of love achieves its goal before definitively entering the spiritual world. The vision's brilliant center of light cannot be endured by the watching eyes: "*ut si absque Mediatione Vitae Caelestis, ob Unigenito Ejus eradiatae, in Mentes influeret Humanas, vitam earum & visum, sicut splendor solaris nudos perstringens oculos, in mortis redigeret umbram; nulla est Infiniti communio cum finitis, nisi per Eum, qui mediat; quare vita absque Eo, non vita est, sed mortis & umbrae imago*" (If the Infinite were to flow into the minds of humans without any mediation from the life of heaven—if that mediation did not radiate forth on behalf of his Only-Born One—their lives and their power of vision would be driven back into the shadow of death, just as the splendor of the sun dazzles the naked eye. The Infinite has no contact with the finite, except through him, the one who mediates; so life without him is no life, but a picture of death and shadow) (§118).

Besides the essential speculations on divine light, which are part of the inspiration for this vision, we also encounter the Christology of the gospel of John in the reading discussed previously: "*In eo vita erat, et vita erat lux hominum*" (In him was life, and the life was the light of all people) (John 1:4). However, Swedenborg also attempts a psychological precision of the life-giving flow, and here he reaches the final motivation for the title of the work. In the manuscript, it is underlined twice:

*Vita enim Divina, ex quâ Intelligentia Veri, per candidam Lucem repraesentata, Amori per purpuream Flammam effigiato juncta, facit ut Intelligentia sapiat, scilicet ut non solum ex Vero quid Bonum, sed etiam ex Bono quid Verum sit, percipiat, et sic ex Veris et simul ex Bonis, Optimum, id est, Supremum, et colat et amet (b): quare absque intercedente aut mediante Vita ipsius Flammae seu Amoris, Optimus aut Supremus, nullatenus adiri Cultu, quia nullo coniungi Amore, potest; talis enim est accessus per Cultum, qualis est coniunctio per Amorem.*

(For it is divine life—from which arises the understanding of what is true—that makes the understanding become wise. It is represented by the brilliant light and is linked to love, which in turn is symbolized by the blush-red flame. Divine life makes the understanding perceive not only the good that arises out of what is true, but also the truth that arises out of what is good. And so we come to worship and love the Best, that is, the Supreme One, out of what is true and at the same time what is good. [b] As a consequence, without the life of that flame, love, interceding and mediating for us, the Best or Supreme One utterly cannot be approached in worship—because there is no love with which to form a connection with him. And *the quality of our approach [to God] through worship matches the quality of our connection [with him] through love.*) (§122)

The separation of the intellect into the psychological faculties of understanding and will, combined with the true and the good as respective objects, which we have studied previously from the point of view of the contemporary optimistic intellectualism, has now been melted down to form a higher unit in the melting pot of love. The finale summarizes a tendency that can be followed through the entire drama. When the soul in the previous scene aims to install a viceroy in the newborn's brain, there is talk of an intellect that from love of goodness would realize truths and because of this insight long for goodness (§45).[44] However, the precondition for this state is the love of the Highest, in the soul's speech to the wisdoms called the goal of all ambition: *"ejus enim luminis radii sunt totidem veritates, & ejus radiorum ignes sunt totidem bonitates"* (for the rays of God's light are each a truth, and the fires of his rays are each an act of goodness) (§49).

During the psychological speculations of the 1740s, Swedenborg became fascinated by love's governing role in the human, a tendency that can be observed also in contemporary psychology, for instance, in a characteristic context in the following statement by Rydelius:

Perceptio tantum lucens *är then, som intet går oss til hiertat, utan lemnar wår siäl alldeles i sin kallsinnighet, af orsak at thes* objectum *är et sådant blott* verum, *som intet för oss wisar sig under* boni *eller* mali *hamn, antingen något* bonum *eller* malum *sticker sig therunder, eller ej . . . Men then* Perceptio, *som här heter* ardens, *hafwer* bonum *eller* malum *til sitt* objectum, *antingen thet är så i sanning eller ej, och altså går oss til hiertat. Jag bekenner, at* verum *och* bonum *ofta äro så tätt förknippad uti et* objecto, *at the icke kunna åtskiljas; Ty somliga* veritates *hafwa uti sig en sådan fägring och teckhet, at the på en gång röra både förståndet och hiertat hos en menniskio, som hafwer uplyst förstånd.*

(A perception which is just shining does not go into our hearts, but leaves our soul completely in its callosity, because its object is only such a truth, which does not show itself to us in the shape of good or evil, whether something good or bad hides there or not. . . . But the perception, which is here called burning, has good or evil as its object, whether it is so in truth or not, and therefore goes into our heart. I confess that truth and goodness often are so closely connected within an object that they cannot be separated. For some truths contain within them such splendor and beauty that they at once touch both the understanding and the heart in a man who has an enlightened intellect.)[45]

It is tempting to see the fire in the Helicon of the intelligences as poetical embroidery on Rydelius' canvas, especially as we find among the excerpts that Swedenborg noted Rydelius' discussion of the concept of wisdom. He identifies three kinds of knowledge in the intellect: *scientia*, science; *prudentia*, cleverness; and *sapientia*, wisdom. Among them wisdom is the greatest, which as its aim has *summum bonum*, the highest good, and which unites truth and goodness. In the excerpt collection, Swedenborg also identified his *amores* with these imaginative ideas, which in his account of Rydelius' great summation of the senses he called *boni imago*, image of goodness, which is *ardens*, burning, like *veri imago*, image of truth, is *lucens*, shining.[46]

However, the excerpt material is in itself a warning against making too decisive an attribution. We are without doubt within the great rationalist tradition: following the ancients, the most extensive quotes under the title "*Verum, Bonum, Felicitas*" in cod. 36–110 are taken from Leibniz and Malebranche. We find here theses about the union of truth and love as the only objective of divine will from Leibniz, and significant summaries of the knowledge of truth and love of goodness from Malebranche. Clearly Swedenborg's thoughts have developed from here.[47] The religious elements have been crucial in this development. The deepest precondition for Adam's ability to understand truth from goodness, in his state of innocence, is the presence of divine love in the intellect; this is the premise for the true worship of God, as well as for the development of wisdom, as we learn from, for example, §122 and note b. The highest knowledge is the insight of how the human being can approach God, but "approach" means in spiritual matters "to unite with." Union can come about only through love, which in turn means that, as the height of knowledge is to approach God, the sum of wisdom is to unite with God through love.

In this manner, the text, which clearly expresses the basic thought giving name to the work, is commented upon in an extensive note where the psychological and theological motifs are united one last time. Love signifies both the human love of God and God's love, the only Son. Humanity's approach toward God, the adoration, depends on our love, our predominant inclination: thus far we move within the psyche in the same pattern, which had begun in *De Infinito* and *Oeconomia*. However, the prerequisite for our true worship is that God's love exists in the human intellect; thus the theological attempts that can be found in the above-named works are fulfilled in close proximity to a Christology of the New Testament. The most relevant Bible text is John 14:6: "Jesus said to him, 'I am the way, and the truth, and the life. No one comes to the Father except through me.'"

Swedenborg himself wrote down a text, which is part of the same totality but which comes even closer to his own symbolism: *"quod amor sit conjunctio tanquam palmitis in vite, vide* Johan.Evang.XV.8,9 etc." (That love is union, like that of the branch with the vine, see St. John 15:8, 9 etc.).[48] We might also consider his interest in the view of Christ expressed in the epistle to the Hebrews, which we observed previously: the thought of God's Love as the only prerequisite for the true worship of God, *cultus*, is a natural association with the true high priest after the order of Melchizedek, whose acts of sacrifice were anticipated in the intermediation of the Son, when God sent his flashes of flame against the prince of the world.[49]

However, this biblical background does not appear ostentatiously in *The Worship and Love of God*. On the contrary, it is striking that it takes up so little space, both generally and specifically in the Son-of-God motif. The psychologically conceived only Son of the drama of creation is a short step from the theosophic writings, where the second divine person is brought together with the first and where Christ becomes a human incarnation of God himself, *Divinum Humanum*: Love becomes a characteristic of God besides wisdom. This development is fully understandable against the background of his previous speculation. Indeed, we might say that the Christocentric piety that characterizes *The Worship and Love of God,* despite its lack of direct biblical references, to a far greater degree than any of his other works, was a decisive factor in Swedenborg's final illumination. To shed light on this, we will turn for a moment to Swedenborg's religious crisis.

# The Longing for Salvation and Dreams of Christ

*The Worship and Love of God* is interesting not merely as a synthesis of Swedenborg's scientific writing and as a late contribution to the hexaemeral tradition, but also as a symptom of the spiritual climate in the mid-1700s. Its Christocentric atmosphere raises the question about the influence of Pietism. Pietism in its conservative Halle variety penetrated Swedish conformity around 1700 and reached its peak during the 1720s. The radical element in Pietism broke out during the 1730s, to a certain degree due to the sojourn of Johan Conrad Dippel (1673–1734) in Stockholm in 1727. The 1740s saw the breakthrough of Herrnhut.[50] Educational journeys to foreign countries played an important role in the entry of new ideas into Sweden during this time as well as previously. During the 1690s, these journeys were often directed toward the newly founded university at Halle. Among the young Swedes who eagerly sought knowledge there was Erik Benzelius the younger, who visited colloquia and in all probability became acquainted with August Hermann Francke, an assumption that explains Benzelius' respect for Pietism.[51]

This relative sympathy for the new piety also characterized Jesper Swedberg. In all essential aspects, the bishop shared Pietism's view of Christian living and its emphasis on good deeds as opposed to the orthodox doctrine of *sola fides*, as was discussed previously. In his memoirs, Swedberg often describes high-church efforts to combat Pietism's popularity, without offering any image of Christian virtue worth following. A country priest preaches one Whitsunday against the movement, after which a generous feast ensues in the house of *pastor loci*: "*Then samme presten låg sedan om morgonen på gaton, at alle som then dagen gingo i ottsongen . . . sågo honom ther liggia som ett so i orenligheten. Thet war icke allenast med orden och predikan, vtan ock med gierningarna weldeligen wederleggia Pietisterna*" (The same priest was then lying in the morning in the street, so that everyone who went that day to morning prayer . . . saw him lying like a pig in the dirt. This was not only with words and sermons, but certainly also with deeds to confute the Pietists).[52]

Little is known of Swedenborg's own relations with Pietism. However, the already sketched influences of his early environment ought to have been reinforced by the fact that his own administrative agency's younger members often played an important part in the spread of the new ideas in Sweden. It has also been questioned whether the radical Pietist Dippel's visit to Stockholm in 1727 was not in fact significant to Swedenborg's development; but, like Lamm, I cannot see any traces of Dippelianism until later, although his name does appear in the excerpts.[53] The battle that broke out around Dippel went on for a long time; as always Dippel left behind him shaken minds, who made their anguish public in a rich polemical literature.[54] One of these was Erik Benzelius. Dippel claimed that, during his stay in Sweden, among other things he had been offered a position in the Board of Mines, a claim that Benzelius denied vigorously: "*Sannerligen, thet förnäma rummet, som wardt ledigt i högbemelte* Collegio *wid 1727 åhrs Riksdag, war intet at blifwa fylt och ärsatt af* Christiano Democrito" (Indeed, the noble room, which became vacant in the dignified *Collegio* during the session of parliament in 1727, was not to be filled and replaced by *Christiano Democrito*.).[55] Perhaps Dippel, as has been asserted, gave this incorrect information in good faith, having taken his admirers' praise too seriously. Regarding the vacancy, it may depend on the aspirant at the Board of Mines, Erland Fredrik Hjärne (1706–1773), who was among Dippel's admirers.[56]

Radical Pietism, which became more organized in the wake of Dippel's visit, differed greatly from the older kind. A movement like the socalled *gråkoltarna* (grey robes) in Stockholm with their apocalyptic disposition was part of it, and separatist tendencies grew stronger the more energetically the ecclesiastic authorities used their spiritual and judicial powers. A sentence of exile was issued against the Eriksson brothers (Jacob, 1689–1737; and Erik, 1695–1761), who headed a Finnish separatist movement; and an accountant at the war college named Abraham Breant (d. 1756) followed them voluntarily into exile, among others.[57] No doubt Breant's exile and resignation from public service aroused great attention within the bureaucracy. Swedenborg returned to Stockholm during the summer of 1734 after a long period of travel abroad, just two weeks prior to the expulsion of the dissenters, and it is implausible that he would have remained uninformed of their fate.[58]

During the two years Swedenborg now spent in Sweden, the radical movements became ever more radical and fanatical; Linderholm finds that it seemed as if "a kind of cultural fear arrested the minds" and bases that assertion, for instance, on contemporary assessments about the above-mentioned Erland Fredrik Hjärne, among others.[59] Benzelius' contribution to the Dippelian controversy, from which is clear that the bishop did indeed meet Dippel during the German study trips of his youth, dates from April 17, 1736. From the same time comes the only direct evidence of Swedenborg's attitude toward sectarianism (although perhaps not toward Dippel himself) at this stage. It is a note in his travel diary for the years 1736–1739; on the atmosphere in Copenhagen, the following judgment is striking: "*Är också* inficierad *af* pietismo *el.* quakerismo, *med den galenskap, at de tro behaga Gud at giöra af med sig el. andra, hwarpå monga exempel förspörjes*" ([The city] is also infected with Pietism or Quakerism, with the folly that they believe they please God by doing away with themselves or others, of which there are many examples).[60] It seems reasonable to think that experiences in Stockholm lie behind his judgmental attitude towards the Danish counterparts.

The importance of the Board of Mines for the spread of these new movements, which ties in well with the agency's intellectual recruitment and international orientation, is obvious when we focus on the last branch of the Pietist tree. In the catalogue of Swedenborg's library, we encounter the title of the first extensive description of the history of Herrnhut, written by a Swede.[61] This account, originally given to Archbishop Johannes Steuchius (1676–1742) in Uppsala in 1741 by an official delegation from Herrnhut, was published in London in 1743 in a somewhat extended version. It becomes clear that Sweden enjoyed an early connection with this congregation of Brethren. The association came about at the official investiture in 1727, when the mining official Carl Henrik Grundelstjerna (1701–1754), aspirant at the Board of Mines in 1722, visited Herrnhut.[62] Through Grundelstjerna, knowledge of the Brethren congregation was spread to Pietist groups in Stockholm in the midst of the consequent events surrounding the Dippel controversy. Among the names noted in previous research are all the leaders: Carl Michael von Strokirch (1702–1776), Sven

Rosén, Erland Fredrik Hjärne, his brother Carl Urban Hjärne (1703–1766), the vicar Erik Tolstadius (1693–1759), and many more.[63] Without confirming any personal influence, this information is valuable since it reveals a significant interest in the new religious movements among the younger members of Swedenborg's own agency. It serves as a concrete illustration to Lamm's assessment on an environment of overheated religious atmosphere at the time, which *"ej kunnat undgå att påverka äfven en så utpräglad studiekammartyp som Swedenborg"* (could not fail to act upon even such a genuine closet-scholar as Swedenborg and which perhaps even hastened his own development).[64]

A hasty sketch of the most interesting person in contemporary sect religion, Sven Rosén, illustrates this. The youngest of the famous brothers, Johan, became senior master in Gothenburg and one of the country's first Swedenborgians: but in Johan's relations with Swedenborg, there is, as far as I can see, no reference to Sven.[65] A social failure, Sven Rosén has nevertheless become renowned in later research as *"en af den svenska religiositetens ädlaste och renaste gestalter"* (one of the noblest and most genuine personalities of Swedish religiosity).[66] The word *multi-talented* could also be applied. During his studies in Uppsala, Sven Rosén developed an early interest in philosophy and was one of the first in Sweden to apply the Leibniz-Wolff philosophy to theological problems.[67] This effort was prompted not only by a desire for theoretical clarity but also from a religious need to safeguard the certainty of belief, an effort that lost its attraction when, in late 1729, Rosén underwent a personal crisis of conversion inspired by Pietism.[68] Even at this early stage, we can see a parallel to what would occur with Swedenborg a decade later: philosophical speculation also lost its meaning to him once intuitive insight had been attained internally.

Rosén's spiritual development can be traced in extensive diary notes, which have been used frequently in the Linderholm biography.[69] In these notes, Rosén, after his Wesleyan, exactly dated conversion, observed his own thoughts and feelings with the utmost care, leading to many heartrending expressions for the struggle for certainty of faith and purity of behavior. We also find detailed observations on the bodily location of religious emotions, as well as dietary scruples of the same kind as the ones contained in Swedenborg's *Dream Diary*. There are also visionary elements, although they can hardly be compared to Swedenborg's. And, despite the strong focus on sexual ethics, we do not find, as Linderholm emphasizes, the erotic dreams that are such a noticeable element in Swedenborg's account of his dreams.[70]

In the diary, we also find information on Rosén's reading, of interest because of what it may say of the literary background to Swedish Pietism. Besides older and well-known edifying books by Luther, Johann Arndt (1555–1621), Christian Scriver (1629–1693), and others, we also meet representatives of different kinds of mysticism, such as Jacob Böhme, Paracelsus, and Madame Jeanne Marie Guyon (1648–1717). The last's book on prayer was published by Rosén in a Swedish translation in 1739; in conjunction with his membership in Strokirch's Philadelphian Society, this led to a sentence of exile, issued in the beginning of 1741.[71] After a couple of years in Germany, Rosén arrived in London in the autumn of 1743, where he joined the Moravians and thus reached the end of his spiritual development.

Rosén's entry into the congregation of Brethren took place at roughly the same time as Swedenborg set out on the journey that sealed his entry into the spiritual world. Prior to reaching his crucial insight into its secrets, Swedenborg encountered the same Moravian Brethren in London. In the *Dream Diary*, a note dated May 20, 1744, announces this fact:

> *igenom åtskilliga skickelser fördes jag vti kyrkian, som* Moravianske Bröderne *hafwa, som beretta sig wara de rette Lutterske, och känna den heliga andans wärckan, som de beretta hwarandra, och endast anse Gudz nåd, och Christi blod och förtienst, och enfaldeligen gå til wercka; derom betre en annan gång, men mig lärer ännu intet wara tillåtit at foga broderskap med dem: derass kyrckia repraesenterades mig 3 månader förvt, som jag henne sedan såg, och alle der wara klädde som prester.*
>
> (By various providential dispensations, I was led to the chapel of the Moravian Brethren, who claim that they are the real Lutherans; that they are conscious of the operation of the Holy Spirit, as they tell one another; that they look only to the grace of God and the blood and merit of Christ; and that they work in innocent simplicity. Concerning this, I shall speak more fully another time, but I may not yet be permitted to join their brotherhood. Their chapel was represented to me three months ago, just as I afterwards saw it, and all who were there were dressed as clergymen.)[72]

The little church in Fetter Lane thus received visits within some six months from the two major figures of Swedish religious life in the eighteenth century. For one of them the acquaintance with the Brethren became crucial and led him to join their circle, but what importance did this resting place have for the other one?

The question of Swedenborg's attitude towards the Moravians at the time of his spiritual crisis has been dealt with by Lamm and Pleijel, among others. In New Church literature, the debate has been somewhat distorted by the spiteful attitude towards the Brethren that Swedenborg displayed in his theosophic writings and by the accusation of Swedenborg's insanity instigated by the Brethren. But one must state with some surprise that theologians have shown little interest in Swedenborg generally and in this important issue.[73] Lamm finds certain connections between "*den Zinzen-dorfska 'hjärtereligionen' med dess afvoghet mot alla metafysiska sub-tiliteter och dess koncentrering på det inre upplefvandet af Kristus*" (the "religion of the heart" of Zinzendorf, with its aversion to any metaphysical subtleties and its concentration on the inner life of Christ) and Sweden-borg's religiosity during the period of crisis.[74] In a diary entry dated Octo-ber 10–11, 1744, Swedenborg interprets a dream thus: "*betyder den moravianska kyrckian, at jag är der och intet antagen . . .*" (signifies the Moravian Church, that I am there yet not accepted).[75] Lamm sees this—in a passage written with great caution—as a sign that Swedenborg was or-dered by God to refrain from joining the Moravians. Pleijel suggests, on the contrary, that Swedenborg may have received a negative response to an application for membership, something that often occurred at this time and that would offer a psychological explanation to the animosity later dis-played by the visionary.[76]

There are possible confirmations of this interpretation in the *Dream Diary* itself. In a passage from July 1744 , the dreamer sees a congregation he wishes to join, as he sits in an empty pew, covering himself with a cloth; Swedenborg's interpretation is as follows: "*betydde at jag med egen om-sorg wille komma i den församlingen, och at jag wille holla mig för andra obekant. . .*" (This meant that I wished on my own to come into that con-gregation, remaining unknown).[77] In the beginning of the same text, he has seen another congregation, this time evidently the Assembly of Holy Men, the victorious congregation in heaven, so often spoken of by Jesper Swed-berg: "*Såg en församling, der hwar och en hade en liten Crona på hufwudet, och twå som stodo fremst, med ganska stora och härliga Cronor, en talte med glädie, som war halft fransyska, halft tyska.* betydde de som fådt martyr Cronor, *dem jag tenckte på dagen förvt; men hwilcka de twå woro, om det war Huss, wet jag ei*" (I saw a congregation where everyone had a little crown on his head, and two of them stood out front with quite large and magnificent crowns. One of them spoke joyfully, half in French and half in German. This signifies those who have received the crowns of martyrs, which I thought about the day before, but who the two were, if one was Huss, I do not know.)[78] The name *Hus* serves as a keynote, as he belonged to the Moravian saints. In Gradin's short overview of the history of the Brethren, Johan Huss (c.1370–1415) appears at an early stage, along with another pre-Herrnhut martyr. Gradin sums up Hus' life and work up to the Council of Constance: "Here he sealed the sacred Testimony to the Truth of God and the Apostolical Discipline, with his own Blood, being burnt at *Constance* the 6th Day of *July*, 1415. *Jerom* his Collegue was honour'd with the same Martyrdom the 30th Day of *May*, 1416."[79]

That Swedenborg in his rather ill-equipped library had several books re-lating to Herrnhutism-Gradin's history, a *Gesangbuch der Evangel.*

*Brüder-Gemeinden 2.ter Th.*, and *A Manual of Doctrine* (London 1742)—
is from a strictly methodical point of view insufficient evidence to support
the view that he wished to join the congregation; he may have acquired
these tomes later with a polemic purpose in mind, or he may have received
them from his Moravian landlord.[80] However, in conjunction with all the
other notes related above, we probably should view these texts as evidence
of Swedenborg's interest in the congregation of Brethren. Indeed, one could
interpret the crucifix cult, which Lamm and others regarded as inspired by
Catholicism, as another Herrnhut feature.[81] This supports the interpretation of the mysterious notes in the *Dream Diary* as proof that Swedenborg
actually did apply for membership but was denied it, perhaps for the very
reason that he wished to keep his membership secret: that would have been
an understandable wish from the son of a bishop and a royal assessor,
being acquainted as he was with several members of Sweden's highest
clergy.[82]

But even if this were the case, Swedenborg had no reason to keep such a
rejection a secret from his diary. The question seems to require some study
to be answered; however, that would be to digress too far from the subject
at hand, and furthermore it is of little value to the understanding of *The
Worship and Love of God*. It is more important that Herrnhut be recognized as one source of inspiration since it had probably strengthened the
trust in the Savior's merit, which appears in more orthodox forms in other
passages in the *Dream Diary*.

Another illuminating example of how images from the earlier writings
appear in Swedenborg's dream notes, as a contrast to their ecstatic tone,
occurs in connection with the great vision of Christ at Easter 1744.
Swedenborg comments on the tension he feels at the thought of Christ as
experienced during the previous night and the dark undercurrents, which
suck him towards evil depths, a conflict bringing him close to the brink of
madness:

> *jag kan likna det wid twenne wichtskålar, på ena ligger wår
> wilja och arga natur, på den andra Gudz kraft, hwilcka wår
> Herre steller således i frestelse, at han låter det ibland komma til
> ett aeqvilibrium, men så snart det wil wäga ned på den sidan,
> hielper han det op; således har jag funnit efter werdzligit wis at
> tala, hwaraf följer at det är så litet wår kraft, som den drager alt
> ned, och är opposit snarare, än medhielpande til andans kraft;
> och således, at det är endast wår Herres werck, det han så
> disponerar.*

> (I compare this to the two scales of a balance. In one of them
> is our own will and our evil nature; in the other, the power of
> God. In temptation, our Lord so arranges these that at times
> they come into an equilibrium, but as soon as one of them

weighs down, he helps it up again. This is what I have found to be the case, expressing it in a worldly manner, from which follows: that this is very little by our own power, which draws everything downwards and is opposed rather than cooperating with the power of the Spirit, and consequently it is the work of our Lord alone, which he thus disposes.)[83]

This explanation had been referred to previously in *Oeconomia*, albeit it is our passivity in the face of God's grace that is emphasized now. Later in the same diary note, his self-love—in the aspect of a foolish group worshipping him as a saint—wrestles with faith in Christ. During these battles against the temptations and sneers of his rebellious ego, Christ's cross becomes his weapon.[84] The dreams of Easter 1744 show many examples of this trust in Christ; of course, the timing of these dreams can be explained by the liturgy. One example bears on his future drama of creation:

> . . . *doch i andanom, war en inwertes och kenbar öfwer hela kroppen glädie, tychte alt på öfwerswinnerligit sett huru alt abouterade, flög likasom op, och giömde sig vti ett oendeligt, som ett centrum, der war amor ipse, och at derifrån extenderade sig omkring och så ned igen, således per incomprehensibilem circulum, a centro, som war amor, omkring och så dit igen, denna amor vti en dödelig kropp, hwaraf jag tå war full, liknade then glädien, som en kysk man har då han är i werckelig kiärlek och in ipso actu med sin maka, sådan amaenitas extrema war suffunderad öfwer min hela kropp.*
>
> (. . . as to the spirit there was an inward joy that could be felt all over the body. Everything seemed in a consummate way to be fulfilled, flew upwards as it were, concealing itself in something infinite, as a center, where love itself was, and it seemed as if it issued thence round about and then down again, thus moving around in incomprehensible circles from a center that is love, and back. This love, which then filled me, in a mortal body is like that delight a chaste man enjoys when he really is in love and makes love to his spouse. Such an extreme joy was suffused over my whole body, and this for a long while.)[85]

At the end of this journal entry, this *amor* is identified with Christ as *finis ultimus*, the highest goal.

This vision is characteristic of *The Worship and Love of God*: the geometrical structure, clearly revealing the dreamer's philosophical and scientific education, the parallel positioning of the love of the flesh and that of the spirit, which is Christ—this stuff consistently recurs. The last aspect is the most salient. Among the psychological indications, which have been raised respecting Swedenborg's supposed psychosis, the obtrusive and sometimes vulgar sexuality in the *Dream Diary* has been given a prominent position.[86] Even if Swedenborg, as has been suggested previously, interprets the female dream figures symbolically as spiritual beings representing sciences and truths, thereby creating what one is tempted to call an inverted Freudianism, it is inevitable that the sublime eroticism of *The Worship and Love of God,* as it is portrayed in the sixth scene, stems from a strong and rebellious carnality.

However, this sexuality in itself does not bring feelings of guilt; the doctrine of correspondence and the system of series and degrees allow Swedenborg serene possibilities of interpretation. When he experiences intercourse in his dreams in Leyden during the morning of April 24, described in detail, he sees it as a symbol of love for *"den helge"* (the Holy One): *"ty all kierlek har derifrån sitt vrsprung, är en series, i kroppen är den werckeligen i projectione seminis"*(for all love originates from that source [the Holy One], constituting a series, in the body manifest in the projection of semen).[87] This is in principle the same extremely extenuated union of physical and psychological matters included in *The Worship and Love of God,* albeit in a level of artistic sublimation, where the secretions and exhalations of the body only serve to transmit the intensity of the dream life to certain scenes.

In the midst of such characteristic dream visions, dogmatic remarks can sometimes be found, differing only slightly from Lutheran conformism: a *summa summarum* from May 1744 is representative of this phenomenon: *"det är intet annat än nåd hwarigenom wi blifwa saliga. 2 nåden är vti Jesu Christo, som är nådastohlen. 3. kiärleken til Gud i Christo är som saligheten befodras igenom. 4. Och at man då låter föra sig af Jesu anda. 5. alt hwad af oss sielf kommer är dödt, och intet annat än synd, och wärdt ewig fördömelse, 6. ty intet godt kan komma än vtaf Herran"* (only grace can save us. 2. Grace is in Jesus Christ who is the throne of grace. 3. It is the love of God in Christ by which salvation is effected. 4. And that one then allows oneself to be led by the spirit of Jesus. 5. Everything that comes from ourselves is dead and is nothing but sin and worthy of eternal damnation. 6. For nothing good can come except from the Lord).[88] Thus, in the chaos of the religious crisis, there are examples of several different aspects of the same basic ambience: the longing for wholehearted and spontaneous faith, trust in the grace of God and fear of self-love and the temptations of evil. There is often talk of visits to churches and holy communion in the Lutheran congregations; however these cannot keep him from temptation, and the calls for grace and salvation sometimes echo with an anguish *de profundis.* Love, the Son of God, appears in a succession of forms from a geometrical center to the crucified Christ. In this confusion, the Jesus cult of the Moravians may have seemed a refuge for a mind torn apart, irrespective of how far any plans of membership had materialized.

The Brethren could have offered him only a temporary escape from the deepest problems, which for a system builder like Swedenborg must be solved within the limitations of his own world of ideas. The titanic ambition of gaining definitive insight into the secrets of the soul and life became a part of his personality that could not be sacrificed. Nor did his Lord demand that of him, but allowed him after the crisis and its literary harvest to flee into the world, which to a nonconfessional observer only too easily can be regarded as an effect of mental illness. For general psychological reasons, the simple Uppsala student and preacher Sven Rosén and the royal assessor Emanuel Swedenborg could not have been joined in any permanent brotherhood. There is in Swedenborg's personality, as I see it, a trait of aristocracy, displayed in a sense of civic duty, in conventionalism, and a chilly *noli me tangere* in personal relations, as well as in a rationalist aloofness, which provides his "mysticism" with intellectual overtones.[89] Those traits would probably have distanced him from the powerful emotions of Herrnhut, once the crisis had calmed down.

Clearly, the similarities to the Moravian Brethren during the crisis must not be exaggerated. When Swedenborg looks for expressions of his religious feeling in a lyrical form, he does not choose one of the congregation's songs but a hymn from the official Swedish hymn book of 1695, which in its sensibility is strongly Christocentric without suffering from *"den svärmiska överspändhet, som den pietistiska Jesuskärleken ofta visar"* (the romantic highly strung character, so often displayed by Pietist love for Jesus).[90] Jacob Arrhenius' (1642–1725) hymn number 245 with its Pauline vision of Christ is the text he selects:

*Jesus är min wän den bäste,*
*Hwilkens like aldrig är;*
*Skal jag då så med de fläste*
*Öfwergifwa honom här?*
*Ingen skal mig kunna skilja*
*Ifrån den mig har så kär:*
*En skal wara bägges wilja,*
*Altid här och ewigt där.*

*Jag är wiss och där på liter,*
*Hwarken lifwet eller död,*
*Mig ifrån min JEsu sliter:*
*Änglar, höghet eller nöd,*
*Djuphet eller annat mera,*
*Ware kommand' eller när,*
*Skal mig från Guds kärlek föra,*
*Som i JEsu Christo är.*

(Jesus is my closest friend
Whose like is not to be found.
Shall I then as most others do
Abandon him here?
No one shall part me
From him who holds me so dear:
One shall be the will of both,
Always here and for ever there.

I am certain and trust therein,
Neither life nor death
Will tear me from my Jesus:
Angels, powers or misery,
Depths or other things to come,
Be they far or near,
Shall take me from God's love,
Which is in Jesus Christ.)[91]

This traditionally pious trust in Christ is also a significant element of the inspiration behind *The Worship and Love of God*. In the end, the work becomes Swedenborg's way of battling demons. The longing for salvation has been fitted into the theoretical pattern, although he begins to sense increasingly the tensions within his thinking during this process. These tensions lead to the work's never being completed, but they also contribute to the final clarity of the great vision in 1745, when he experiences divine presence anew: a man appears at night, as Lamm pointed out following Robsahm's account:

> Han sade sig då vara Herren Gud, verldenes Skapare och Återlösare, och att han utsett mig att förklara Skriftens andeliga innehåll för människorna samt att han skulle sjelf för mig förklara hvad jag borde skrifva i detta ämnet, mig blef då samma natt till öfvertygelse öppnad Mundus Spirituum, infernum et caelum, der jag igenkände mångfaldiga bekanta af samma stånd. och ifrån den dagen öfvergaf jag all verldslig vitterhets öfning och arbetade in spiritualibus efter hvad jag af Herren befaltes att skrifva.

> (He then said that He was the Lord God, the Creator of the world, and the Redeemer, and that He had chosen me to explain to men the spiritual sense of the Scripture, and that He Himself would explain to me what I should write on this subject; that same night also were opened to me, so that I became thoroughly convinced of their reality, the worlds of spirits, heaven, and hell, and I recognized there many acquaintances of every condition in life. From that day I gave up the study of all world science, and laboured in spiritual things, according as the Lord had commanded me to write.)[92]

It is no longer a vision of Christ, but of the Creator and the Savior in the same person. Thus Swedenborg reached a child-like submission under God the Father, a predominant trait in the dream notes, when he began writing *The Worship and Love of God*: during the night of October 8–9, 1744 , he dreamed of a little beautiful and innocent child, whom he views as "*sjelfwa innocentia*" (innocence itself): "*af det wardt jag ganska rörd, och önskade wara i ett sådant rike, der all innocence wore*" (I was quite touched by [the child] and wished I were in such a kingdom, where all is innocence).[93] The firstborn in *The Worship and Love of God* is indeed in this *Regnum Innocentiae*, this realm of innocence, and the child in the dream seems to be a reflection of Adam as depicted in the sections on Creation, a figure who at the time would have taken up much of the visionary's thoughts. During his work with the theodicy problem, the author expressed his own longing for the realm of innocence. The struggle between love and evil, which Adam's wisdom allows the terrified young man to experience, is impossible from a point of view of outward consistency; however, against the background of the *Dream Diary*, these descriptions become the psychologically crucial ones, the nucleus of the battle against the demons. The furious force with which this motif is treated reflects the power of the experience. After this excursion into the fascinating but frighteningly impenetrable jungle-like world of the *Dream Diary*, the treatment of the motif calls for a revisit to the original text.

## The Prince of the World and the Demons

The first hints of evil rush like cold shadows over a sunlit landscape in the fourth scene's allusion to the tree of knowledge and its meaning (§§ 53, 55). In the present scene, the tree's symbolic function has been taken over by the prince of the world, who like the tree has been created by heaven but who has perverted himself with vain ambition and whose love originates from within himself. The worldly prince plays his greatest part in *The Worship and Love of God* of all Swedenborg's writings; for the theosopher, there is no specific personification of evil, which relates to the altered Christology.[94]

The prince made an earlier entry in the psychological *De anima* with its metaphysical extrapolations. A chapter on the providence of God summarizes the origins of evil, where we encounter another version of the thesis from *De Infinito* and *The Worship and Love of God* on God's immediate creation: "*quicquid enim immediate a Deo profluit, id non potest non optimum esse, et perfectissimum*" (for whatever is immediately streaming forth from God cannot be other than perfect and superior). Despite this, evil has indeed come about:

> *at vero quod oriundum sit malum, imperfectum, id originem aut causam immediate non a Deo sed ab ipso subjecto creato, in quo natura est, ducit. Ita ab ipso diabolo quod insurrexerit contra suum Deum, et rebellis fuerit: ipso Adamo quod contra mandatum divinum fecerit, ambiente, se perfectiorem et superiorem existere. Quod providentia divina Adamum non immediate duxerit ad istud malum, sed quod permiserit, id admodum clarum est ex scriptura sacra, /—/ et plura, quae clare demonstrant quod providentia fuerit quod potuisset peccare, et praescientia quod peccaret. . . .*

> (But that evil and imperfection should come about does not originate immediately from God but from the very created subject, in which nature exists. Thus from the devil, who revolted against God and became a rebel: from Adam, since he acted contrary to God's command in his ambition for a higher and more complete existence. That divine providence did not lead Adam immediately to this evil, but only allowed it, is quite clear

from the Holy Scriptures, . . . and much else, which clearly
shows that it was providence that he could sin, and foreknowl-
edge that he would do so).[95]

This distinction was well known to Swedenborg's contemporary readers,
and the excerpt collection reveals its background: Leibniz's theodicy, primarily, but also the other authorities prevalent in that manuscript.[96] The
written evidence that Swedenborg refers to here reflects the theodicy problem, and the interpretation aligns with Leibniz's own: "*Mais toutes ces expressions & autres semblables, insinuent seulement que les choses que
Dieu a faites servent d'occasion à l'ignorance, à l'erreur, à la malice & aux
mauvaises actions, & y contribuent; Dieu le prévoyant bien, & ayant dessein de s'en servir pour ses fins; puisque des raisons superieurs de la par-
faite sagesse l'ont déterminé à permettre ces maux, & même à y concourir.
Sed non sineret bonus fieri male, nisi Omnipotens etiam de malo posset
facere bene, pour parler avec Saint Augustin*" (But all these expressions,
and other similar ones, imply only that the things that God created provide
opportunities for ignorance, mistake, wickedness, and evil deeds, and contribute to these. Since God foresaw this and planned to use them for his
own purposes, higher reasons of a perfect wisdom determined him to permit these evils, and even to contribute to them. But he who is good would
not allow anything to occur in an evil manner, unless he as omnipotent
could make good also of evil, to speak in the manner of St. Augustine).[97]
In this quotation, two of the most prominent authorities converge, subsequently reminding the reader of their similar views on evil, not least as regards the final consequences of Adam's Fall, which will be discussed later
in this study.

Other details within *De anima* reveal that it is an important forerunner
to the demonology of *The Worship and Love of God*. The discussion on
hell and its ruler is a systematically structured foundation for the description of the battle between heaven and hell found in the Creation story. A
stylistic kinship is evident: the antique portrayals of the devils are partly
explained by a theoretical pattern introduced in *De anima*: "*Veteres tam
philosophi quam physici, sacerdotes pagani communi consensu confir-
marunt cruciatus infernales, illorum poenas, Tantali caeterorumque, tum
Erebum, Styga, Erinnyes, furias describunt: Pythagoras, Plato caeterique
adhuc plura de illis cogitarunt; lumine enim suae naturae conspicati sunt,
quod nequaquam felices potuissent esse, qui non in hac vita sibi viam per
virtutem ad felicitatem praeparaverint*" (The ancients, whether philosophers, physicists, or pagan priests, have confirmed with one voice the existence of hellish torment, and describe its punishments, Tantalus' and
others, and besides Erebus, Styx, the Erinnyians and the Furies. Pythagoras, Plato, and others have furthermore thought on these [matters]; for in
the light of their own nature, they realized that those who had not pre-

pared the way to happiness through virtue in this life could never be happy.)[98] The publisher of the latest English translation refers to the excerpt edition, which also leads to Leibniz.[99]

The struggle between good and evil is fought in the human intellect, where God's Son and the prince of the world are present as different kinds of love; this is the central psychological thesis in the description of evil in *The Worship and Love of God*. However, in the world of fable, this can be illustrated with great freedom, and Swedenborg used these possibilities to the utmost. I shall return in the next chapter to the basic theological problem, but first I wish to illuminate the inspiration from antiquity. One is immediately struck by the use of myths surrounding Apollo and the muses, inspired by the doctrine of correspondence. I have several times already pointed out that Swedenborg had great insight in classical mythology and indeed a lively interest therein, and this is also evidently true for this significant detail: in the Ovidian style exercises of his youth, for instance *Ludus Heliconicus*, one can find almost all the relevant figures mentioned.[100]

In this early poetic work, mythic figures are employed conventionally, without original interpretation or unusual application, although he sometimes invents his own; this displays knowledge and interest but not yet independence, and it is of little value in tracing sources. I need not emphasize how common a motif Apollo and the Muses were within the contemporary convention in Latin poetry, especially with poems of homage, which constitute the major part of Swedenborg's lyrical production.[101] Swedenborg's usage becomes different as early as in *Principia*, where several ancient myths are used to illustrate cosmological theories, as earlier chapters in this study have shown. The drama of creation is somewhat similar to *Principia* in terms of the origin of the universe; otherwise, its mythological allusions—explicit statements are few indeed—signify a new developmental stage, explained by the doctrine of correspondence.

In Swedenborg's manuscripts of excerpts, there are hardly any traces of systematic studies in mythology. A few notes can be found from Abbé Villars' (1635–1673) already quoted book *Comte de Gabalis ou Entretiens sur les Sciences Secretes* (Count de Gabalis, or conversations on the secret sciences), closely connected to demonological speculations. In conjunction with these, there are also some excerpts from *Aristotle's Theology* and from some dialogues of Plato, although not very detailed.[102] In connection with the correspondence investigations in *Clavis hieroglyphica* insignificant elements of mythological interest appear.[103] Despite all this, one ought to be able to assume that Swedenborg knew of such basic works of comparative mythology as that of Gerhard Johannes Voss, which was referred to above. Voss, a great scholar, belonged to the polyhistorians who were constantly invoked. When Erik Benzelius gave lectures on the history of learning beginning in the spring of 1704 and during the course of the five following terms, he used among other works a chronological volume by the same Voss, albeit accompanied with critical disaffection. Despite this, Voss was still associated with a giant like Isaac Casaubon (1559–1614), whom the young Emanuel Swedberg had praised highly.[104]

Another reason to give attention to Voss in this context concerns the sources for the portrayal of Apollo and the muses in the drama of creation. The prince of the world launches hallowed games among his followers. The primary games are Apollonian, devoted to the honor of the snake Pythos (§73). Such *ludi* interested Swedenborg at an early stage, as is clear from notes probably stemming from the dissertation preparations, where among others the Pythian games are mentioned.[105] They appear in the dissertation, however, merely as information, while *The Worship and Love of God* displays a more lyrical inspiration. The first book of Ovid's *Metamorphoses* also describes the origins of the Pythian games, which should be noted; it follows the portrayal of the flood, which ensued when Jupiter abstained from using his lightning blasts against the evil race of the Iron Age. After the waters receded, earth gave birth to beings of different species:

> *Illa quidem nollet, sed te quoque, maxime Python,*
> *Tum genuit: populisque novis, incognita serpens,*
> *Terror eras. tantum spatii de monte tenebas.*
> *Hinc Deus arcitenens, & nunquam talibus armis*
> *Ante, nisi in damis capreisque fugacibus usus,*
> *Mille gravem telis exhausta pene pharetra,*
> *Perdidit effuso per vulnera nigra veneno.*
> *Neve operis famam possit delere vetustas;*
> *Instituit sacros celeri certamine ludos;*
> *Pythia de domitae serpentis nomine dictos . . .*

> (She [Earth] bore unwanted, a gigantic serpent,
> Python by name, whom the new people dreaded,
> A huge bulk on the mountain-side. Apollo,
> god of the glittering bow, took a long time
> To bring him down, with arrow after arrow
> He had never used before except in hunting
> Deer and the skipping goats. Out of the quiver
> Sped arrows by the thousand, till the monster,
> Dying, poured poisonous blood on those black wounds.
> In memory of this, the sacred games,
> Called Pythian, were established. . . .) (I: 438–447).[106]

To apply the fable of the Pythian snake to biblical demonology with its reptile figures is obvious: the prince of the world is said by Swedenborg to have launched games in the snake's honor, that is, as a kind of black mass. Therefore, it is interesting to note that the commentary of the Ovid edition in Swedenborg's personal library, which was quoted previously, among other things refers to Voss' great mythology, *De theologia gentili* (On the theology of the pagans), and to the chapter where Apollo becomes an example of the demonic character of ancient myth.[107]

Beside Apollo and Python, Swedenborg also recounts a hierarchy of the muses, for which the *Metamorphoses* had been the main, although not the only, literary source.[108] The prince of the world crowns his nymphs and gives them the name of muses, Olympiades, and Heliconides; the first can be traced to the commentary for I:212, where the name is said to refer to Hesiod's *Theogonia*.[109] The second form does not appear in Ovid; however, various Heliconiades are there as a synonym for the muses; mount Helicon and its muse inhabitants are mentioned several times in the *Metamorphoses*.[110] The term Parnassides as a name for a lower race of muses is given two synonyms by Swedenborg, Aganippides and Pierides. This mythological confusion requires some commentary.

The association of the Pierides with the heliconian source Aganippe can be found in the fifth book of the *Metamorphoses*, where a singing contest between the muses and the nine daughters of Pieros is depicted in a conversation between Pallas and a muse. The goddess discovers nine chattering magpies in a tree, complaining of their bitter fate, and the muse tells her that these birds are the daughters of the mighty Pieros of Pella; arrogant because of their number, they had arrived at the muses' mountain and challenged them to a singing contest

> *Desinite indoctum vana dulcedine vulgus*
> *Fallere. nobiscum, si qua est fiducia vobis,*
> *Thespiades certate Deae. nec voce nec arte*
> *Vincemur; totidemque sumus. vel cedite victae*
> *Fonte Medusaeo, & Hyantea Aganippe:*
> *Vel nos Emathiis ad Paeonas usque nivosos*
> *Cedamus campis. dirimant certamina Nymphae.*

> (They said, 'Quit fooling silly ignorant people
> With your pretence of music! Hear our challenge!
> We are as many as you are, and our voices,
> Our skill at least as great. If you are beaten,
> Give us Medusa's spring, and Aganippe:
> Or, if we lose, we will cede you all Emathia
> From plains to snow-line; the nymphs shall be the judges.')
>
> (5:308–314)[111]

The Pierides appear here as a group of usurpers, a lower kind of muse, and they are accordingly transformed into birds, chattering magpies.[112] Thus far Swedenborg's description corresponds with Ovid's fable; perhaps it seemed important that these Pierides provide a vile counterpart of the

Olympic mythology, paralleling the work done in spiritual darkness by the genies of the prince of the world.

However, in other details Swedenborg differs from the *Metamorphoses*. He states that the Aganippe fountain sprung from the earth by the force of Pegasus' hoof, whereas in Ovid—like the commentator—this context differentiates between Aganippe and a higher heliconian fountain, Hippocrene, which the winged horse had conjured.[113] More serious are Swedenborg's allusions to the Parnassos fountain; this probably constitutes confusion between the temple in Delphi devoted to Apollo and the muses, and the fountains of Helicon. This misuse cannot be found in Ovid, but possibly in the commentator; referring to Statius, Lucan (39–65) and Seneca the Younger (4–65), he views Helicon as one of the twin mountains of Parnassos, which would explain a synonymous use of the names.[114] However, it seems more likely, given the fact that the names Aganippides and Parnassides (as identical with Pierides) cannot be traced from the *Metamorphoses* or its commentary, that Swedenborg himself was responsible for this mythological digression: it is the memories of an intense reading of Ovid that we encounter here, as Sewall noted, rather than direct studies of the text for this special purpose. That a certain edition of Ovid's works should have been in his library does not mean that Swedenborg brought it with him on his journeys; nevertheless, there is good reason to assume that he had once actually read and studied this very edition.

The same goes for a seventeenth-century manual that might have contributed to the confusion among the muses. In P. Gautruche's *L'histoire poétique* of which Swedenborg possessed the third edition (Paris: 1695), the following information was offered about the muses: "*On les appelloit de divers noms, selon la diversité des lieux qu'elles avoient coûtume d'habiter: car on les nommoit tantôt Pierides, à cause de la Forest Pieris en Macedonie, le lieu de leur naissance; tantôt Heliconiades, à cause du Mont Helicon, assez proche de leur Parnasse tant cheri, d'où elles prenoient le nom de Parnassides, comme celuy de Cyterides, à cause du Mont Cythéron; celuy de Castalides ou Aganippides, au sujet des fontaines de ce nom, qui leur étoient consacrées*" (One called them by different names because of the diversity of places where they used to live; for one named them now Pierides because of the Pieris Forest in Macedonia, the place of their birth, now Heliconiades because of Mount Helicon, close to their beloved Parnassos, from which they had taken the name Parnassides, as Cyterides from Mount Cytheron; Castalides or Aganippides came from the names of the fountains, which had been devoted to them).[115]

The most important aspect in this mythological context is not to discern exactly which sources were used, but what purpose Swedenborg had in choosing the fables pertaining to Apollo, Pallas, and the muses. Evidently, these divinities were mainly active in the area of knowledge: scientific insights and intelligences are symbolized by Pallas and her nymphs, experiences are symbolized by men with Apollo as their leader (§73, note q). However, it is a question of empirical knowledge, attained through the senses, thus the connection with the prince of sensuality. Usurping muses have indeed appeared before in Swedenborg's writings; the important epilogue to the second part of *Regnum animale* describes among other things the false truths transmitted by the senses to intellects, which are not independent enough of the body:

> *sed sunt modo Veritatum spectra & impurae larvae, quae fines ultimos in seipso & amore sui intuentur, quaeque firmiter & cum fide persuadent, quod sint Virgines Delphicae & Gratiae, quibus quia ipsi applaudimus, totam Parnassicam cohortem etiam applausuram esse, credimus: sed longe abest, ut Veritates sint, nam tantum distant, quantum phasmata (!) corporis & ludibria mundi, a caelestibus essentiis & formis.*
>
> (But they are but images of truth and impure masks, which view the final purposes in themselves and in the love of themselves and who decisively and trustfully convince that they are Delphian virgins and graces. Since we honor them ourselves we believe that the entire cohorts of the Parnassos will honor them: but they are far from being truths, for they differ [from them] as much as the imaginations of the body and the illusions of the world differ from heavenly beings and forms).[116]

The connection between Apollo and the oracle has also been an influence: the fact that the text refers to the Pythian games in all probability alludes not only to the great snake but also to the Pythia, whom Swedenborg has shown an interest in before in different contexts.[117] We find oracular answers in several places in the excerpt collection cod. 36–110, for instance in an important polemic by Augustine against the Neoplatonist Porphyry's speech on the Apollinian oracle, or in Abbé Villars, who refers the oracle's answers to demons in a position between angels and men. This is pointed out in Swedenborg's own account, which stresses that the oracle's statements, according to this author, did not come from the devil.[118] To Swedenborg the juxtaposition of the oracle with the devil probably seemed plausible, which is significant with reference to the demonology in this particular work. Finally, it is important to note that the Apocalypse uses a similar name for a prince of darkness. In Castellio's version, which is the one Swedenborg used in this instance, the text about the swarm of tormenting spirits that flew over the injured human race after the fifth angel had blown his horn reads as follows: *habentque sibi praefectum regem, angelum tartari, cui nomen est hebraice Abbadon, graeco autem sermone Apollyon"* (They have as king over them the angel of the bottomless pit; his name in Hebrew is Abaddon, and in Greek he is called Apollyon).[119] Apollo's role in *The Worship and Love of God* as a subordinate demon fits well with this biblical text, although this does not completely explain Swedenborg's use of the myth but must be seen as an element in a complicated background.

The mythical motifs in Swedenborg's writings treated so far have not pertained to the prince of the world himself, but only to his followers. When he appears, the illuminating possibilities of mythology are applied. The prince of lies appears in a number of disguises, a classical Christian formula, but Swedenborg first illustrates this fact with a reference to Pomona's eager suitor Vertumnus, the fable of which can be found in *Metamorphoses* XIV:642–771, even if it had been used by several Roman poets, for instance, Propertius (c. 50–c.15 BCE).[120] Later we read about more sinister masks, when the prince of the world transforms into a dragon, a wolf, Cerberus, a panther, a bear, and a flame. These appearances also belong to ancient mythology rather than the Bible, even though most of them can also be found among the metaphors of the New Testament.[121] All of them can be traced to the master of metamorphoses, as can be seen in a few examples.

The vain rage Cerberus displays when Adam's wisdom demonstrates her power over him recalls his frame of mind when Hercules heroically forces the beast to come with him from the underworld:

> . . . *rabida qui concitus ira*
> *Implevit pariter ternis latratibus auras:*
> *Et sparsit virides spumis albentibus agros.* VII: 413–415

> (While the great dog, fighting, turned his eyes away
> From daylight's flashing radiance. All three throats
> Bayed in his fury, and from his triple jowls
> White foam dripped on the fields of green.)[122]

This rage occurs in both texts; however, Swedenborg, being a systematic man, fills his portrayal with biological color when depicting the gall-filled black veins. The contrast between the horrid shapes of the devil and his real harmlessness appears in a manner similar to Macareus' account of the arrival in Circe's castle:

> *Quae simul attigimus, stetimusque in limine tecti;*
> *Mille lupi, mistique lupis ursaeque leaeque*
> *Occursu fecere metum; sed nulla timenda,*
> *Nullaque erat nostro factura in corpore vulnus.* (XIV:254–257)

> (Within her courts, . . . a thousand wolves and bears
> And lionesses met us, and we feared them,
> For no good reason, for, it seemed, they would not
> Make even a single scratch upon our bodies.)[123]

In addition, the prince of the world's deeds in the human intellect are described with the aid of mythology. The encounter between the heavenly wisdoms and the evil intelligences has been discussed in the analysis of the scene: it is ended with a terrifying metamorphosis motif, in which the evil geniuses of sensual life are transformed into snakes and intelligences into Gorgon heads (§74); a little later, this passage is interpreted and the synonym Medusa heads is used (§76). The concept of the Gorgons is so common that it has become a sort of topos, and Swedenborg's application of it reveals no deeper knowledge. In Ovid, the words *Gorgo* and *Medusa* are used with derivations in many instances; however, in this context, the episode where Perseus answers the question why Medusa alone of the Gorgon sisters wears the horrid hair ornament is the only applicable one:

> *Accipe quaesiti caussam. clarissima forma,*
> *Multorumque fuit spes invidiosa procorum*
> *Illa: nec in tota conspectior ulla capillis*
> *Pars fuit. inveni, qui se vidisse referrent,*
> *Hanc pelagi rector templo vitiasse Minervae*
> *Dicitur. aversa est, & castos aegide vultus*
> *Nata Iovis texit. neve hoc impune fuisset;*
> *Gorgoneum turpes crinem mutavit in hydros* (IV:793–800)

> (She was very lovely once, the hope of many
> An envious suitor, and of all her beauties
> Her hair most beautiful—at least I heard so
> From one who claimed he had seen her. One day Neptune
> Found her and raped her, in Minerva's temple,
> And the goddess turned away, and hid her eyes
> As it deserved, she changed her hair to serpents. . .)[124]

Here we encounter a motif of punishment by transformation, where a superior divine power is the active cause, in the same way as in Swedenborg's text: the crime is in both cases committed within the same sphere, the sensual life. If this general image were to be attributed to any specific source at all, it ought to be Ovid.[125] Also the chilling cold and rigor mortis that affect the evil intelligences could be connected to the Gorgon myth, while it also fits into Swedenborg's psychological thinking: Medusa's head, even when decapitated, could petrify those who looked upon it.[126]

The ancient character appears in this demonological context also in details outside of mythology: the devil's competition schools, "*ludi,*" with their false education and the demoniacal hierarchy.[127] However, even a thorough investigation into these details would provide little new information. Swedenborg chose figures from classical mythology to portray his conception of the prince of evil, who is seated in the flesh and whose sin it was to have broken the connection between nature and heaven and to have instituted a condition among his followers where sensual pleasure became a purpose in itself. Swedenborg employed well-known motifs, easily identified by his classically educated contemporaries, and gave them a personal interpretation; in his view of the demonic meaning of the ancient world of gods, he had support among his contemporaries, as has been shown above. He did, however, not strive for detailed profundity in using classical mythology; it seems more likely that he used his considerable knowledge of ancient literature—primarily Ovid—that he had acquired earlier in life, without any repeated reading of the texts.

In his excellent chapter on *The Worship and Love of God* in his Swedenborg study, Lamm debates Stroh's view that the spiritual beings of the drama of creation—not only Adam's wisdoms and intelligences but also the heavenly beings—had not been intended as "real spiritual beings" but as poetically personified abstractions.[128] Even though Lamm admits that the heavenly wisdoms in several places are interpreted as divine powers, thoughts, and purposes, he argues against the background of the doctrine of correspondence, as this does not require any limitation of their super-sensual reality; his argument is supported by references to Philo, Plotinos (203–270), and *Aristotle's Theology*.[129] Lamm's point of view appears to be correct, even though the fable character of the drama gives reason to apply the term *reality* with caution, a fact underlined by the mythological study. Besides, there is reason to place the nuances somewhat differently as regards the sources behind the spiritual doctrine.

Neoplatonic demonology, as it is depicted in *De divina sapientia secundum Aegyptios* and—for the theosophic writings—Milton's spiritual "materialism" form the basis of Swedenborg's spiritual world, according to Lamm, although he also points out that the belief in angels and spirits was indeed part of most of Swedenborg's contemporaries' faith.[130] When studying the evidence that Swedenborg used in his earlier works and excerpts, difficulties in determining the crucial sources soon appear, although certain tendencies can be found. In the psychological final chapter of *Oeconomia,* a number of authorities on the question of the angels' status are recounted: Apuleius, Origen, Ambrose, Lactantius, and others said that the angels have natural bodies, while Dionysos Areopagita (c. 500), Philo, Athanasius (c. 293–373), John Chrysostom (c. 347–407), and Thomas Aquinas (1225?–1274) with their scholastic followers believed that they lacked bodies—a list that seems to reveal an almost incredible erudition but which in fact is a hidden quote from a seventeenth-century manual, as I have shown in another context.[131] However, there are mediating points of view, and it is significant that Swedenborg attempts to fit their views into his own system: Augustine's hesitation as to whether the angels possessed bodies made of air is interpreted as a precursor to his own theory about the soul as *fluidum spirituosum,* and the agreement among the moderns that we shall become purified bodies after death—that is, spirits without flesh and bone—is regarded in the same manner (*Oeconomia* II, §356).

Although this mainly relates to the souls of the deceased, Swedenborg's joining Augustine and "the moderns" seems significant; it is furthermore striking that *Aristotle's Theology* does not play a particular role in the published parts of the *Oeconomia* series, as was discussed previously. In the excerpts with which Swedenborg prepared for the continued publication of *Oeconomia* and which are reflected first in *De fibra*, the situation changes insofar as this Neoplatonic source takes up a relatively large space. We also encounter it under a contextually significant title together with Abbé Villars and Plato, and its description of the spirits' bodiless existence in the transcendental world was of great importance to Swedenborg's conception of the spiritual society.[132] Nevertheless, one must recall and stress Lamm's reservation on the spirits in *The Worship and Love of God* that they "are not unrelated to the Neoplatonic demonology."[133] Against this, other impulses must be weighed, primarily that of Augustine, whose importance to Swedenborg's psychological image of God so often has been pointed out above.

Among the excerpts, there are a number of angelologic reflections: Swedenborg has written down a characteristic catalogue of angels, demons, and human souls collected from *De definitionibus fidei*, and it need hardly be stressed how close we are here to the correspondentially constructed spiritual doctrine of the drama of creation: "*creatura omnis corporea est. angeli et omnes caelestes virtutes corporeae, licet non carne subsistant: ex eo autem corporeas esse credimus, quia localiter circumscribuntur, sicut et anima humana, quae carne clauditur; et daemones qui per substantiam angelica natura sunt*" (Every created being is corporeal. Angels and all heavenly virtues remain corporeal, although not of flesh: we see them as corporeal, since they are limited spatially, like the human soul, which is incorporated in the flesh; and also the demons, who in their substance are of the same nature as angels).[134] From the important hexaemeral source document *De Genesi ad litteram*, we note speculations on the question of whether the soul was made from the angels, something which Augustine rejected. From the apochryphal *De spiritu et anima* comes information about how the soul acquires knowledge in different ways through its gifts of cognizance: "*cognoscit siquidem Deum supra se, angelos juxta se, et quidquid coeli ambitu continetur infra se*" (since it becomes acquainted with God above itself, the angels beside itself and whatever is contained in the heavenly cycle under itself).[135] I could exemplify further with references to Augustine's assertion that the feelings of the angels could be revealed by their ethereal bodies and other ideas characteristic to Swedenborg; however the already-quoted material suffices in showing Augustine's great influence in yet another area.

But also the modern disciples of Augustine, whom Swedenborg had studied, require our attention in this context. The prince of the world, who constantly aims to deceive the human race and lead us astray, reminds one in his general function of Descartes' supposed evil spiritual power. As will be discussed later, it is from Leibniz's theodicy that Swedenborg received his biblical and poetical impulses for the description of the fallen angels; the Neoplatonic view, which Lamm found behind the interpretation in the drama of creation of the heavenly beings as divine forces and thoughts, corresponds well with a passage from Malebranche found among the excerpts. This text ends with a quote from Paul's Areopagus sermon, the passage we found paraphrased above in the introduction to the fifth scene:

> *Stet igitur illa sententia, Deum esse mundum intelligibilem, aut locum spirituum, ut mundus materialis est locus corporum. Ab ipsius potentia illos (spiritûs) suas accipere modificationes; in ipsius sapientia suas omnes reperire ideas, atque per ipsius amorem illos agitari omnibus motibus ordinatis; quia autem ipsius potentia & amor ab ipso non differunt, credamus cum Divo Paulo, ipsum ab ùnoquoque nostrûm non esse longinquum, nósque in ipso habere vitam, motum, & esse. Non longè est ab unoquoque nostrûm, in ipso enim vivimus, movemur & sumus.*

> (Let therefore the belief remain that God is the intelligible world or the place of spirits, as the material world is the space of bodies. From the force of the Same the spirits receive their modifications; in his wisdom do they find all their ideas, and from his love they are all encouraged to make their ordered moves; and since his power and love do not differ from himself, we believe with St. Paul that he is not far from any of us, that we have life, movement and being in him. He is not far from each and every one of us. For in him we live, we move and we have our existence.)[136]

It shall be shown below that the structure of the spiritual societies are most evidently connected to these modern thinkers, especially Leibniz.

The excerpt material thus gives the impression that Swedenborg in his ruminations on the spiritual world sought advice among the entire group of his psycho-theological authorities; the interest in the world of angels, which can be detected already at the time of *De Infinito*, has so far not been given any startling expressions.[137] However, in the works for which the excerpts are preparations, we approach the later demonological system. As late as in *De anima*, Swedenborg does not talk with certitude about the heavenly forms of the angels and the souls of the deceased; he doubts, however, that it will be a human form, since he cannot understand what function the physical limbs—of which, among others, the sexual organs are named—would have in heaven. Still, he does not deny another possibility: "*proinde non videtur anima illam formam, quae imperfectior est, non autem caelestis, adeptura esse: nisi nova tellus, nova atmosphaera crearetur, et in novam hanc tellurem ut incolae novi mitteremur, sicuti quorun-*

*dam est opinio*" (Therefore, the soul does not seem to have to acquire the form, which is less perfect and not celestial: unless, as is the opinion of some people, a new earth and a new atmosphere were to be created and we were to be sent to this new earth as settlers).[138] There are also traces of such thoughts, showing a kinship with the early cosmological writings, in cod. 36–110.[139] We are still at a stage, however, where such speculations lack any real concretion and are to be regarded as conjectures brought forth by the systematics.

To a certain degree, the *Dream Diary*, at least initially, is characterized by the same indecisive view of the spirits. The religious crisis experienced by the dreamer focuses on witnessing Christ, as well as on the evil temptations that threaten to hide God's love from him. These temptations are often adapted, as Lamm pointed out, into the animal forms in which the prince of the world reveals himself to Adam.[140] However, we do not meet other than occasionally angelic beings—and then only as a word—neither any named demons other than in some conventional terms towards the end of the notes, when the dragon of the Apocalypse appears and humankind is said to be *"soldater at strida emot Satan continuerligen"*: soldiers to fight Satan continuously.[141] Otherwise, it is a striking feature in Swedenborg's dream world that the doctrine of correspondence is constantly used to interpret the various people, mainly women, who thus cannot be equalled with Christ as experienced in direct visions. They instead become symbolic representations of, for instance, wisdom, sciences, or piety; and they can therefore hardly be called spiritual visions in the earlier stages of the dream crisis, but exemplify instead the secret insight that is transmitted in the category *correspondentia fabulosa et somniorum*.[142]

Toward the end of the dream notes, the situation changes, however, as Lamm also concluded: Swedenborg has now realized that there are spirits of different kinds, *"den ena anden som är Christi, är den enda som har all beatitudinem med sig, af de andra lockas man på 1000 sett at gå in med dem, men olyckelig den som det giör"* (The spirit of Christ is the only one that carries all beatitude with it. The other spirits entice us in a thousand ways to follow them, but unhappy is the one who does).[143] Korah's and Dathan's rebellion against Moses in Num. 4:16 is the biblical background for the dreamer's vision, and even if it is hardly justified to perceive these symbolic figures as particular spirits, as Acton does, the demonological concretion appears clearly.[144] It is significant that the next dream vision introduces *The Worship and Love of God*: *"man sade at den wore en Liber divinus de Dei cultu et amore, jag tror det war ock något om spiritibus, jag trodde jag hade något derom vti min de Infinito, men swarades intet dertil"* (It was said that it would be a divine book on the worship and love of God; I believe there was also something about spirits. I thought I had something on the subject in my work *De Infinito*, but there was no answer as to that); the interpretation of this dream intensifies the warning for the spirits' seduction, "*hwilcke repraesentera sig efter hwars och ens amour, ty amores repraesenteras med andar*, jemwel i sielfwa wercket som fruentimber i dra—" (which are represented according to the love of each, since loves are represented by spirits, furthermore, in fact, by women in dra—).[145]

Obviously, this note is important in understanding the doctrine of spirits within *The Worship and Love of God*, and there can be no doubt that the spiritual beings of the dream visions return there in literary form: this makes Lamm's objection to Stroh all the more justified.[146] This does not mean, however, that the celestial beings in *The Worship and Love of God* were to represent some sort of angelologic system. With their general classical and biblical shape, they unite unique Swedenborgian correspondence characteristics, but the essential matter is their symbolic function. *The Worship and Love of God* is not a theologically elaborate treatise, but primarily a didactic fable about God, humanity, and the universe, written under the living impressions of the world of the dream visions, rich in correspondences, but not from the dictation of systematized spirits.[147]

Regarding Milton's importance to Swedenborg's world of spirits, it leads beyond the work treated here: Lamm supposes that Milton's view on the angels' physical functions, expressed for instance in diffuse ideas on heavenly marriages in *Paradise Lost*, has influenced the spirit doctrine of the theosophist.[148] Given my general scepticism regarding influences from Milton, I must conclude also in this instance that Lamm's arguments seem weak and constitute an unnecessary multiplication of explanations. The theory of marriages in heaven is the natural consequence of the anthropomorphic symbolism, contained *in nuce* in the microcosm-macrocosm parallel that Swedenborg developed in the extreme. The doctrine of correspondence has, as Lamm himself emphasized, offered his imagination countless opportunities to expand, and his increasing focus on love during the 1740s demanded its celestial fulfilment.[149] For anthropomorphizing the world of spirits, the drama of creation was an important developmental step: that is clear already from the analysis of the symbolic portrayal of the psychic functions, and it shall be further discussed below. However, to assume an influence from Milton because of this seems unnecessary.

Understanding *The Worship and Love of God* as a work of art, however, does not depend on the sources for the doctrine of spirits, but rather on the personal manner in which it is used to convey the message that grew from the scientific writings and was given a concrete form during the chaos of the dream crisis. With regard to this, it is certainly important that Adam as a representative of the race to come be given descriptions of the encounters of good and evil spiritual powers; that he sees the chained prince of the world in his own sensual life; and that he is educated concerning the seductive powers of evil in weak intellects through anticipative images. However, the important matter is not the encounters between subordinate demons and angels: these are but varieties of the two main contestants, the Only

Son and the prince of the world, who battle in the human intellect with an absolutely crucial intensity that Swedenborg himself experienced during his struggle for certainty of faith. The rendering of this motif in *The Worship and Love of God* will now be examined.

## The Son of God and the Prince of the World

When the Messiah theme in *De Infinito* is combined with Swedenborg's philosophy of nature, it is done through the use of the term *nexus*, the intermediary between the infinite and the finite; as has been previously stated, Swedenborg was unable to express his idea with much precision. In order to incorporate the evil world power into the pattern of Creation without disrupting the classical solution to the theodicy problem, he uses the *nexus* concept again: the prince of the world was created as a second *nexus* between infinity and nature and became a source of life in the midst of rigid matter. To aid him, he was provided with a set of servant spirits of different rank (§69). Through these, divine life was to stream into nature since otherwise the most perfect order could not come about.

However, the prince of the world was not content with this assignment and rebelled against God's only Son; nevertheless he still lives as part of the Highest's life, the source of all living things. But his love stems from himself, and thus he becomes the fountain of the evil love stream, just as the good one stems from the Son. Thus, the Son and the prince of the world become the antagonists of the drama of creation, and their battle in the human intellects will cease only when time ends. This view is close to the one in the New Testament, expressed for instance in John's first epistle 3:8: "Everyone who commits sin is a child of the devil; for the devil has been sinning from the beginning. The Son of God was revealed for this purpose, to destroy the works of the devil."

Despite the vivacious clarity with which the devil and his followers are portrayed in *The Worship and Love of God*, there is as little hesitation as to the deepest powerlessness of evil as there is in the gospels or in the epistles of the apostles. The trust in omnipotence and in love does not fail; therefore, the attitude toward evil becomes similar to that shown by Malebranche when he haughtily dismisses the horror stories of demonography: "*Il faut mépriser les démons comme on méprise les bourreaux; car c'est devant Dieu seul qu'il faut trembler; C'est sa seule puissance qu'il faut craindre. Il faut appréhender ses jugemens & sa colère, & ne pas l'irriter par le mépris de ses Loix & de son Evangile. . . . Mais quand les hommes parlent de la puissance du démon, c'est une foiblesse ridicule de s'effrayer & de se troubler*" (One must despise demons as one despises executioners; for it is only before God that one must tremble with fear. It is only his power that one should dread. It is imperative to fear his judgments and wrath, and not to infuriate him through the contempt of his Laws and Gospel. . . . But when people are talking about the power of the demon, it is a ridiculous weakness to be afraid and to be concerned).[150]

The reference to perfect order as the reason for the creation of the prince of the world connects with the belief in providence, which we previously studied in light of the Leibniz's excerpts and which will return in the final vision of the heavenly society and God's order. The same theoretical background appears in "The Love of the Firstborn" when Swedenborg describes the world that is subordinate to the prince of the world. In the wisdom's foreboding description, it is not hard to recognize the superficially rationalistic world of ideas prevalent in the eighteenth century, nor its Stoicist fatalism (§77). The intellects conquered by evil are ruled by evil passions to different degrees, and they build up their own worlds: evidently ideas about existence and philosophies are referred to here, but also the kind of life provided by social position or way of living.

Swedenborg compares these small worlds of the intellects with orbs or universes, all subjected to the one power, God and his love, an image that is strikingly similar to Leibniz's monadic system, without being identical in content. These worlds run through their times, the years and the days: the changes of the year they call their life's destinies (*Fata suae Vitae*), the day's they call whims of fate (*Fortunas*), and the shift between storm and sunshine they associate with chance. All this is due to their ignorance. They do not realize that the rule of the world, which they recognize, must stretch its power down to the smallest units in order to exist at all. Indeed, this spiritual darkness is the deed of the prince of the world: he wants the human race to ascribe all that happens either to blind chance or to merciless fate, for the very reason that he knows well that nothing—not even himself—exists because of chance or luck.

He shares this conviction with Swedenborg. In the collection of excerpts, there is a special section incorporated among the notes on providence and predestination, with the title *Fortuna fortuitum Casus*.[151] Here we encounter quotes from Augustine, Aristotle, Plato, and Leibniz, who all insist that chance does not exist as some kind of independent being; an excerpt from Augustine is representative: "*fortasse quae vulgo fortunam nominant, occulto quodam ordine regitur, nihilque aliud in rebus casum vocamus, nisi cujus ratio et causa secreta est*" (Perhaps that which is commonly called fate is ruled by some hidden order and therefore we call only those matters chance the reasons for which are secret).[152] Blind belief in fate is also rejected among the excerpts, especially in those from Leibniz; indeed it is discarded in several varieties, "*fatum mahometanum,*" the Stoical determination theory, the merciless fate, which Bayle wished to regard as binding even to God.[153] But Swedenborg has also found support from the great rationalist in depicting these evil intellects as fatalistic; there is a note from a letter to Michael Gottlieb Hansch (1683–1749) in 1707 illustrating this: *"Nec illud inelegans providentia nos regi, qua rationem se-quimur, fato et instar machinae, dum affectibus ferimur"* (Nor is it unreasonable to say that we are ruled by providence, through which we follow the intellect, by destiny as a machine, when we are ruled by emotions).[154] The dependence on bodily senses and their passions is, of course, distinctive of the intellects led astray.

Nevertheless, this view in *The Worship and Love of God* does not lead to any kind of asceticism, any more than it did before. The battle between the inner and outer person, which is part of the psychological pattern of *Oeconomia*, must not lead to the rejection of all earthly reasons for joy. We hear an echo of the disdainful reference to the Copenhagen Pietism in the diary from 1736 in a sentence where Swedenborg calls those men mad who draw this conclusion: nature is in itself harmless and dead, so it is only important not to let the enjoyment of its goodness become a goal in itself (*Oeconomia* II, §323). Regretfully, this happens easily. The body's desires are only means to reach an end the soul has defined, yet they are like rivers, gathering clay during their course. Besides, they can encourage a hedonistic lust in the intellects of weaker individuals. Here is the reason that Adam constantly certifies that he in his earthly paradise experiences only matter as a means of reaching the ends, how the outward beauty of things is nothing, their inner usefulness everything.

This relationship between the intellect and the body is symbolized in the drama of creation in the battle between God's love and the prince of the world. The description reaches its artistic culmination in the episode, when the three spiritual powers are placed against one another in the flaming light from the heavenly bonfires (§78). This concrete picture of zealousness, as it has been described in *De anima*, is also a problematic scene from the point of view of intellectual consistency.[155] The portrayal cannot be characterized as a biblical paraphrase without some difficulty. When the Lord's wrath is mentioned in the Bible, it is usually done with images of embers or fire and the verb *to be infuriated*, but the flashes of lightning rarely occur in connection with anger; the only text that could fit this description is Job 36:32, but this is far from *The Worship and Love of God*.[156]

Indeed the image of Jupiter *tonans* from classical mythology comes much closer, and the excerpts contribute in this regard with certain information on the background. Under the headline *Malum, vitia, crimina, peccata*, Swedenborg wrote extensive notes from, among others, Leibniz's theodicy. He refers in the part called *"De bonitate Dei"* (On God's Goodness) to §271 with its text on the devil voluntarily remaining in a state of damnation and to §273 with its rich references to the Bible.[157] The numerous excerpts indicate an intensive study, and it is interesting that Swedenborg, in the intermediary §272, was reminded of the lightning-hurling

Zeus. This happens in conjunction with Leibniz recounting the fable about how Gregory the Great liberates Emperor Trajanus' soul from hell:

> *Selon cette fable, les prieres de saint Gregoire avoient la force des remedes d'Esculape, qui fit revenir Hippolyte des enfers; & s'il avoit continué de faire de telles prieres, Dieu s'en seroit courroucé, comme Jupiter chez Virgile:*
>> *At Pater omnipotens aliquem indignatus ab umbris*
>> *Mortalem infernis ad lumina surgere vitae,*
>> *Ipse repertorem Medicinae talis & artis*
>> *Fulmine Phoebigenam Stygias detrusit ad undas.*
>
> (According to that fable, the prayers of St. Gregory had the strength of the drugs of Aesculapius, that made Hippolytos return from the underworld; and if he had continued to say such prayers, God would have become furious with him, like Jupiter in Virgil:
>> Then, wroth that mortal should from shades of hell
>> Rise to the light of life, the Almighty Sire
>> With his own levin-bolt to Stygian wave
>> Thrust down the finder of such craft and cure,
>> The Phoebus-born.)[158]

The situation in the *Aeneid* is, as one might expect, completely different, and its image of Jupiter is only one of innumerable classical examples of the deeds of the wrathful lord of the skies. We shall momentarily study another, more relevant ancient poet, but the text from Virgil can all the same have been relevant to Swedenborg since it had been brought forth in connection with a discussion, central to him, on evil in Leibniz's influential theodicy.

In the following §§273–276, Swedenborg also noted a number of biblical texts that deal with the battle between good and evil powers. First comes the devil's defection and the Son's mission to "destroy the works of the devil" (1John 3:8), followed by John 8:44, where the devil is called *"homicida à principio,"* a manslayer from the beginning. God has not spared the sinning angels either, but throws them into the abyss to dwell there until doomsday (2Peter 2:4), a piece of information varied in the letter of Judas 6. Leibniz had also observed the mutual dependence of these passages.[159]

More significant than these, however, is the reference to Revelations 12:7–9, which Swedenborg had recorded first. Leibniz says here that it seems to him that the author of the Apocalypse wished to clarify what the other canon writers left obscure, by describing a battle in heaven between Michael and his angelic army against the dragon: the ancient snake, devil, Satan was hurled with his angels down to earth, to the joy of heaven and its people but to the horror of the inhabitants of earth. This is how Leibniz interprets this mysterious text, which must have seemed attractive to the Swedenborg of the doctrine of correspondence: *"Car quoiqu'on mette cette narration après la fuite de la femme dans le desert, & qu'on ait voulu indiquer par-là quelque révolution favorable à l'Église; il paroit que le dessein de l'Auteur a été de marquer en même temps & l'ancienne chute du premier ennemi, & une chute nouvelle d'un ennemi nouveau"* (For as well as one places this story after the flight of the woman into the desert and by that has wanted to indicate some revolution favorable for the Church, it seems that the plan of the author has been to suggest at the same time the old fall of the first enemy and a new fall of a new enemy).[160] To a certain extent this is just what happens in Swedenborg's drama of creation. Even he goes far beyond the Bible text in order to clarify an obscure ancient tale, and he also pulls together several different elements into an intense scene: the devil's being hurled into Tartaros (in Swedenborg's Latin Bible this very term is used in 2Peter 2:4), which is postponed; Christ's act of redemption; the prince of the world subjected to the Son; doomsday—all is contained within a symbolic whole.

Besides this contemporary inspiration, other elements must also be taken into consideration regarding the literary form. First and foremost, Swedenborg's deep familiarity with Ovid must be viewed as an important factor. In the first book's description of the different eras of ancient time, there is a celestial deliberation with Jove presiding, where the subject is what to do about the evil race that fills the earth during the Iron Age. It is not only the dreadful Lycaon's house that shall be punished: all are offenders and shall receive their punishment according to Jove's decision. Nevertheless, the gods hesitate:

> Dicta Iovis pars voce probant, stimulosque frementi
> Adjiciunt. alii partes assensibus implent.
> Est tamen humani generis iactura dolori
> Omnibus; &, quae sit terrae mortalibus orbae
> Forma futura, rogant: quis sit laturus in aras
> Thura? ferisne paret populandas tradere gentes?
> Talia quaerentes, sibi enim fore cetera curae,
> Rex Superum trepidare vetat; sobolemque priori
> Dissimilem populo promittit origine mira.
> Iamque erat in totas sparsurus fulmina terras;
> Sed timuit, ne forte sacer tot ab ignibus aether
> Conciperet flammas, longusque ardesceret axis.
> Esse quoque in fatis reminiscitur, affore tempus,
> Quo mare, quo tellus, correptaque regia coeli
> Ardeat, & mundi moles operosa laboret.
> Tela reponuntur manibus fabricata Cyclopum.
> Poena placet diversa; genus mortale sub undis
> Perdere, & ex omni nimbos dimittere coelo. (I:244–261)

(Part of them approved
With words and added fuel to his anger,
And part approved with silence, and yet all
Were grieving at the loss of humankind,
Were asking what the world would be, bereft
Of mortals: who would bring their altars incense?
Would earth be given the beasts, to spoil and ravage?
Jove told them not to worry; he would give them
Another race, unlike the first, created
Out of a miracle; he would see to it.
He was about to hurl his thunderbolts
At the whole world, but halted, fearing Heaven
Would burn from fire so vast, and pole to pole
Break out in flame and smoke, and he remembered
The fates had said that some day land and ocean,
The vault of Heaven, the whole world's mighty fortress,
Besieged by fire, would perish. He put aside
The bolts made in Cyclopean workshops; better,
He thought, to drown the world by flooding water.)[161]

The situation does indeed display significant similarities, even if its inner attitude is different. In Swedenborg's text, the Godhead does not hesitate, but he is moved by his love to refrain from administering his justice. Several motifs are, however, present in Swedenborg's drama: the promise not to deprive the earth of its human inhabitants, the concern for the human race. This Ovidian background could also explain the inconsistency in *The Worship and Love of God*: there is a degenerated human race here, which does not exist when Adam has the scene described to him, since the Iron Age, which according to the preface of Swedenborg's drama is about to occur, has already begun in Ovid's text. Thus, the Ovidian metamorphosis anticipates a series of events that will occur in the final deluge of Swedenborg's unfinished work and that has already been decided upon in God's eternal wisdom. To the many earlier pieces of evidence of an Ovidian influence can thus be added yet another very important example.

However, the lack of regard for the demands of superficial consistency has other more important explanations. In Adam, Swedenborg not only described the first man in *regnum innocentiae* but also the symbolic predecessor to the future humankind, which in his intellect, enlightened with divine illumination, is capable of imagining the past and future states of the world, which Swedenborg noted among his excerpts from Wolff, as was pointed out previously in the chapter on the doctrine of correspondence. Finally the scene relates to a literary genre, the art of emblematics. The actors in this picture—the angered Lord of the skies who hurls his flashes of lightning against the enraged dog of hell, while the only-begotten Son throws himself in between in order to save the misled human race—and their positions form an emblem under which several mottos would be suitable.[162] In the monumental work of emblematics, Picinelli's *Mundus Symbolicus*, the title of which Swedenborg wrote down among his correspondence excerpts, we find the flash of lightning.[163] Among the applications in its scope of meanings, we find both *ira divina* (divine wrath) and *gratia Dei* (the grace of God), *Christus judex* (Christ the judge), and *Mors Christi* (the death of Christ), *superbi puniti* (punished arrogance) and *virtus & sanctitas* (virtue and holiness).

Of course, caution is recommended when dealing with such varying meanings. Nevertheless, it seems as if Swedenborg was influenced by Picinelli's joining of Christian and ancient motifs in his image of God, for instance, in the following passage on *ira divina*:

> *Vindicta Divina longè clarissimè in fulminis Emblemate dignosci potest, cui hanc inscriptionem praefixi: NULLA VIS CONTRA. Fulminis violentiam sequenti disticho exprimit Ovidius:*
>> *Nil adeò validum est (adamas licet alliget illud)*
>> *Ut maneat rapido firmius igne Jovis.*
> *Enimverò fulmen aptissimum est irae Divinae instrumentum, teste ipsomet Deo: Si acuero ut fulgur gladium meum, & arripuerit judicium manus mea, reddam ultionem hostibus meis.*
>
> (God's punishment can in the most clear manner be depicted under the emblem of the flash of lightning, to which I have attached the following sentence: *No power resists.* Ovid expresses the violence of the bolt in the following distichon:
>> *But nothing is so strong, even if aligned by diamonds*
>> *That it can resist the rapid fire of Jove.*
> Indeed the flash of lightning is a very suitable instrument of divine wrath, according to the words of the Lord Himself: *If I whet my glittering sword, and my hands takes hold on judgment, I will take vengeance on my adversaries* [Deut. 32:41].)[164]

Another of the figures in the scene can also be illuminated by Picinelli: the hellish dog, which was to be thrown into the depths of Tartarus, can be identified among the applications of the dog symbol.[165] However, a combination of elements in Swedenborg's typical manner cannot be supported by Picinelli's dictionary.

Within the incredibly rich emblematic literature, previous research has stressed that the innumerable Renaissance symbols for erotic love were transferred to the religious sphere to a great extent during the seventeenth century: "Ovid has been succeeded by Saint Augustine" wrote one illustrious scholar.[166] Collections such as *Amoris Divini Emblemata* (1615) and

*Pia Desideria Emblematis, Elegiis et affectibus SS. Patrum illustrata* (1624) became immensely popular and had many successors all the way up to the eighteenth century; indeed, Madame Guyon wrote the preface to a French edition of *Pia Desideria* from 1717.[167]

The prevalence of these collections can partly be connected to the renewed cult of the child Jesus, who appears among certain emblematical writers in entire series of images. In *Cor Iesu amanti sacrum*, the human heart is the scene where Jesus enters and drives away all the snakes and slimy reptiles of profane love with his light; finally, he mounts a throne in the heart, which is crowned with victory's wreath. All this is interpreted as stages on the road of mystical life.[168] In another collection, *Jesus en de Ziel* by the Dutchman Jan Luyken (1649–1712), the child Jesus and the soul are the actors. One of its pictures, the text of which comes from the famous Messiah sermon in Isaiah 53:4–5, depicts the soul slouching in a state of desperation before lightning bolts from heaven, while Jesus in the shape of a wreathed boy stands between her and the bolts and protects her not only from these, but also from hellish monsters who threaten to engulf them both with their dragon jaws or Cerberus maw.[169] This is a scene of great intensity: "storms of oceanic grandeur, lightnings cross the immeasurable space, and one seems to breathe the ozone in the shuddering air,"as Praz suggestively stated.[170]

This scene relates immediately to the encounter between the spiritual powers in *The Worship and Love of God*: the lightning of justice, the Son of God, humankind, the dog of hell are all there (§78). Nothing would contradict the assumption that Swedenborg was influenced by this very emblem from *Jesus en de Ziel*. Nevertheless, the popularity of emblematic literature must force us to be careful in making too firm an attribution, requiring wide-ranging specialist investigations, including the visions of the theosophic writings, to establish in detail the possible emblematic background. Such an investigation seems likely to be able to provide very interesting results, important also to the evaluation of Swedenborg the visionary. However, it may suffice to point out the obvious similarities in theory and practice, which make it highly probable that the writer of the drama of creation had been thinking in emblematic categories: its symbolism is in spirit related to emblematic art, which appears to be a possible intermediary between biblical and ancient studies and the illustrative power in Swedenborg's description of the battle between good and evil.

This struggle continues until the end of time within the human being, and Swedenborg underscores this opinion when the wisdom describes the mediating function of the prince of the world. Love interfered to reestablish the connection between nature and heaven, the bridge demolished by the defection of the demons; through Love, heavenly life is again infused, and thus humanity is saved from death, the heirloom of the prince of the world, as described in §82:

*Hoc Divino beneficio, hostis hujus anima subigitur, & sic ipsum ejus caput conteritur, & truncus ejus corporis, unà cum caeteris inimicis similiter affectis, ejus scilicet geniis, sicut transversus limes, aut scabellum, pedibus nostri Amoris, qui in Olympi sui solio residet regnatque, subjicitur: in simili effigie Amor noster in Mentium nostrarum Olympis, subjugato Animo, repraesentatur; nam effigiem totius Caeli in nobis portamus.*

(By this Divine blessing, the soul of the enemy is brought into subjection, and thus his head is beaten; and the trunk of his body, together with the other foes who are similarly inclined [that is, his daemons], is cast down as a boundary stone across the way, or as a footstool beneath the feet of Our Love, who sits on a throne in his Olympus and rules. Our Love is represented by a similar likeness in the Olympus of our minds, with the lower mind in subjection to him; for we carry a representation of all of heaven inside us.)

Biblical allusions are evident: the woman's seed, which tramples the snake's head according to Genesis 3:15 and the footplate, *scabellum*, in front of which the enemies lie according to Psalms 110:1, the same text that introduces the Melchizedek motif, as I pointed out previously.[171] And the Son's power over the evil powers naturally refers back to Bible reading from other texts: one thinks of 1Corinthians 15:24–28, where this state is to appear after the end of time.[172] These biblical allusions undeniably strengthen the impression that Swedenborg, in his vision of the Son's interference, combined a Messianic prophecy with an idea about a heavenly battle before the creation of time, in a manner corresponding to what Leibniz says about the Apocalypse writer in his theodicy.[173] There is all the more reason to remember this, as the encounter of the spiritual powers also contributes to the theodicy debate. Love's ability to force the prince of the world into carrying out his role in God's order of creation means a temporary solution to the problem, although the definitive solution cannot be presented until the world has lived its predestined time. In those parts of the drama of creation that Swedenborg finished, the question of the end of time is treated only in allusions, and we will return to this when analyzing the vision of the finale.

This heavenly struggle between good and evil reminds one of *Paradise Lost*, and Lamm also talks of Swedenborg's drama containing a description of *"ett stort fältslag mellan Guds och världsfurstens trogna, där Kristus till sist fäller utslaget"* (a great battle in which Jesus Christ provokes the final decision between those loyal to God and those loyal to Satan).[174] He probably is referring to §§76–78 in *The Worship and Love of God*, compared to *Paradise Lost* VI:680 on. Unfortunately, this comparison is forced. In Milton's epic, it is God's Son, the Messiah, who runs Satan and his rabble out of heaven and throws them into hell, whereas in Swedenborg's drama, the Son throws himself between God's wrath and the prince of the world and is almost torn apart by him, while the planned descent into Tartarus is postponed. Of course, Christ takes decisive action also in Swedenborg's vision, but with the motive of forgiving love, not as the executor of God's anger and justice. The prince of the world is indeed depicted with a classically tinted language of symbols, but this similarity is too superficial to allow a theory of influence, especially in the light of the difference between the two Messiahs. Swedenborg's work is completely different in its design; it is acted out in the human mind to a far greater degree than Milton's heavenly epic and is a tapestry of symbols woven with much finer material. If threads from *Paradise Lost* appear in *The Worship and Love of God*, which one can always imagine but never disprove, they are at least difficult to differentiate in connection with the only Son and the rebellious spirits.

However, it may be that one of Milton's contemporaries had a certain effect when Swedenborg sketched the wandering of humankind: namely, John Bunyan (1628–1688) and his work *Pilgrim's Progress*, a text that is vividly created despite its rigorous allegorical scheme. Such episodes as Christian's encounter with the evil Apollyon and the lurking lions and dragons spring to mind, and the image of the different ways of reaching the goals of life also raise associations; the blind mobs running past the narrow road are reminiscent of the episode when Christian and Hope are lost and reach Doubting-Castle, before they are forced to return, as well as their encounter with Atheist and its conclusion: "*As for this man, I know that he is blinded by the God of this World*" contains general similarities to the confrontation between good and evil spiritual powers in *The Worship and Love of God*.[175] However, correspondences that cannot be explained against the common background of Bible studies, religious allegories, and emblematics are impossible to establish in the scope of this study. Indeed, Swedenborg probably read *Pilgrim's Progress*, but its importance ought primarily to have been as a practical demonstration of an emblematically inspired allegory and its capacity to convey a religious message, which would have appealed to him through its emphasis on the significance of a Christian way of life.[176] This would have fulfilled Bunyan's own hope, and the didactic Swedenborg would no doubt have agreed with the instruction in the final poem:

> Now Reader, I have told my Dream to thee;
> See if thou canst interpret it to me;
> Or to thy self, or Neighbour: but take heed
> Of mis-interpreting: for that, instead
> Of doing good, will but thy self abuse:
> By mis-interpreting evil ensues.
> Take heed also, that thou be not extream,

*In playing with the outside of my Dream: . . .*
*Put by the Curtains, look within my Vail;*
*Turn up my Metaphors, and do not fail:*
*There, if thou seekest them, such things to find,*
*As will be helpful to an honest mind.*[177]

If one is to summarize "the out-side of my Dream" in Swedenborg's drama of creation, the most striking aspect is again the antique style, primarily the similarity to Ovid, the favorite poet of his youth. Elements from modern thinking and the biblical world are incorporated with this style in strange images, for which emblematic inspiration probably had some significance. Finally, one must also accentuate that the Adam of the drama of creation finds himself in a situation closely reminiscent of Swedenborg's own condition in the hard school of the dream crisis. He has himself become assured of the supreme power of divine love over the demons, but his conviction is still fragile and trembling: the extended demonstration of the metamorphoses of the prince of the world appears to be a conjuring game between laughter and tears with demons, who still have teeth to bite with and claws to tear tender flesh.

# 8

ﻋﻠﯽ

## THE WEDDING OF ADAM AND EVE

§§87–131

The fifth scene ended with an image of humankind's confused striving toward the divine goal, of which they knew nothing in their ignorance, and in contrast to this Adam's wisdoms, who were already in a state of joy within the goal: "*intrabimus jam Olympum tuum, ut sponsae thalamum; en video, Amor noster ipse praefert taedam; & Sapientiae Ejus applaudunt*" (We will now enter your Olympus, as brides enter the marriage chamber. See there! Our Love himself leads the way, carrying the torch, and his Wisdoms show their approval with applause) (§86). This symbolism of bridal mystique is motivated both theologically and aesthetically and dovetails with the previous scene's confused mobs, a prelude to our present scene, where Adam's development into a human being is fulfilled with his marriage: man's intimate union with God's love is given its earthly correspondence in Adam's and Eve's wedding, which accords with the imagery used heretofore. The previous, more generally sketched description of man's ability to go astray when divine order is not kept is individually applied in this sixth scene to the narrative of the confused youth who in a dream experiences the birth of his wife, an episode that has been analyzed previously. He has subconsciously sought after love, and a divine impulse has led his steps without his knowing it, in the same way as providence leads the ignorant masses.

After the two dramatically vivacious introductory episodes, Adam leaves the stage to return again in the last one (§§87, 88, 110). Otherwise, the focus turns toward Eve's education under heavenly supervision. This means that the contents to a certain extent run parallel to the end of the fourth and all of the fifth scene—the extensive account of Adam's development—since, after the education of the intellect, he had become a youth. Swedenborg evidently wanted to avoid repetition, and he used the parallel situation instead to illuminate his philosophy from other points of view. The emphasis is now placed upon the bodily reflection of the spiritual life, and this theme is carried through in a multitude of didactic variations. One may find far less in this scene of the narrative and symbolic joy, inspired by myth, than was evident in previous ones; instead there are extensive lectures on the relationship between the spiritual and the natural, given by a heavenly intelligence to the patiently listening girl. The difference in expression is also clear from the fact that the author had less need than previously for explanatory notes: Eve's lecturer is generally explicit enough.

This does not preclude Swedenborg from dwelling, with obvious pleasure in several lovely scenes, on the beautiful maiden's outward appearance. The introduction to the wide-ranging discussions on body and spirit is one such scene. In her first bloom of adolescence, in the state of laughing playfulness that we found above to be a precondition for the educational aptitude of youth, Eve sets out on a walk in paradise and reaches a well, in the crystal waters of which she can see her own image appear (§90). After the initial surprise, she understands what she sees, but is again astonished when she realizes that she can tell from her own reflection what goes on in her intellect. She cannot solve this riddle on her own; and in accordance with her prayer, the divine intelligence appears, who will later explain all of the diffuse circumstances to her.

Lamm relates this episode to inspiration from the famous scene in *Paradise Lost* where Eve tells Adam how she awoke to life in the garden of Eden. She becomes clear of her own existence through viewing her own reflection in a well, a reflection that at first frightens her but that later pleases her with expressions of love and affection; whom the image reflects is disclosed by a disembodied voice:

> What thou seest,
> What there thou seest fair Creature is thy self,
> With thee it came and goes:   (IV: 467–469)

Lamm correctly states that there is no correspondence to this episode in Genesis; the similarity with *Paradise Lost* is also more significant than in the other examples.[1] Nevertheless, the arguments are hardly convincing. In relation to the narrative, the situation is much more momentous in *The Worship and Love of God* than in *Paradise Lost*, and it introduces a long theoretical discourse on the theme of the face as the mirror of the soul, the background of which in the anatomical writings shall be investigated later. In order to introduce this motif—a crucial element in Swedenborg's thinking and one that was foreshadowed in the drama in the second scene in reference to the physiognomies of the wild animals reflecting their temper—he chooses a well, the only mirror available in paradise.

In addition, the well is an important reminder, as Lamm himself pointed out, that Ovid's Narcissus myth is often assumed to be Milton's inspiration.[2] When looking at the different descriptions in more detail, it is evident that Milton focused on Eve's surprise; nothing is said about her face, quite naturally as she herself is the narrator. However, Swedenborg dwells with sensual pleasure on the girl's limbs, her ivory-white neck, her bosom, arms, and hands, which is totally in the spirit of Ovid. In the description of the beautiful Narcissus' image in the waters of the well, we encounter the same manner of lingering over every feature separately, and also the same color impression—the ivory white—in an attractive detail: "*eburnea colla*" echoes in Swedenborg's "*eburnei candoris pectus*" (III:422 and §90).[3] Even if this example does not suffice as final evidence, taken together with other Ovidian elements in style and motifs, it strengthens the impression that classical inspiration was crucial to *The Worship and Love of God*. This particular case could be an issue of a background common to both Milton and Swedenborg.

Nevertheless, for the narrative purposes, this episode serves merely as an aid: it provides the opportunity to account for the divine order in the human body. Once this order reigns, the changes within the higher functions of the psyche correspond clearly to shifts in Eve's appearance, and this is a sign of the state of innocence. However, the girl possesses as little insight regarding what is not *integritas* as did Adam in the preceding scene, and this forces her heavenly guide to broach the subject of evil. The theological background is obviously regarded as well known to the audience, and instead its psycho-physical application appears as the subject for the education given in the following episodes. It begins with a description of how the three spiritual principles give rise to the fibers and blood vessels of the body (§92). In order for Eve to get a clear picture of this, the series of principles must be equated with the corresponding forms, from the highest, *Supra-Caelestis*, which is the form of the soul, to the lowest, *Angularis*, the material form (§93). The hierarchy of forms, which is introduced here, entails an extended application of a macrocosmic pattern stemming from the first section of the drama (§6, note b), and thus it becomes another reminder that man is a *typus mundi*.

This theme is subsequently developed in the form of both demonstrations and lectures. The heavenly intelligence, who can adopt any human form she wishes—as has been pointed out previously, this is an important piece of angelologic information that shows the closeness to the theosophic system—provides a neurological demonstration with the aid of her own body. Eve is now permitted to experience the anatomical dream coming true, which was so fervently desired by Swedenborg's predecessors as well as by himself. With great care and precision, the divine being undresses the coverings of a nerve and exposes a fiber; however, not even she can abstain from using the technique of magnification that meant so much to Swedenborg's and his contemporaries' hopes for admission to the arcana of biology: "*sed ne plurium aspectus distinctas opacet ideas, unicam modo fibram latici suo perviam, a vicinarum nexu decerptam, simplicius lustremus, quam etiam arte meâ amplificatam tibi sistam*" (But looking at so many things is going to obscure the individual concepts. Let's simplify our search, and examine just one fiber that is permeable to its own fluid, detached from its connection with the neighboring fibers. I even have a technique for showing you this enlarged) (§95).

In this wonderful microscope, we are allowed to follow the fiber back to its origin in one of the glands of the cortex; with this description, a promise from the fourth scene is fulfilled, namely, that the author would show how these *glandulae corticales* correspond with the universe, at the same time employing the egg symbol (§41, note a, and §95). First, the sphere appears, in which the sensual consciousness, *animus*, dwells. Then another and higher sphere is opened, in which intelligencies and wisdoms have their abodes, characterized by the heavenly shape and thus the divine love. In the very center of these vortical spheres, the gate is opened to the innermost temple of the soul, from the super-celestial form of which divine life saturates the human body.

Thus, the celestial being has led her listener from the outer organic forms to the innermost, and in doing so has brought to fruition the research program that her author battled with for a decade. At the end of this episode, we encounter a dichotomy, which lacks meaning within the context of the drama but which is crucial to Swedenborg himself: "*Tu, mea Filia! quae in ipsum hunc Ordinem, & ejus vitae Lucem, nata es, tametsi adhuc puella sis, clare tamen, sicut video, contemplaris; aliter, qui a fatuo naturae lumine, sapiunt; iis nihil, praeter extremorum sensuum dictamina, persuadet*" (My daughter—you who were born into this very order and the light of its life—this is the way things are; and although you are still a very young woman, I see that your thinking on this matter is clear. Those who live by the deceptive light of the material world think differently. Nothing persuades them except what they are told by the farthest outlying senses) (§95). The dream of the perfect anatomical map of the human psyche, the one that will finally convince even those who demand empirical verification, could only be made true by a heavenly being. Resignation to the impossible has long been forecasted, as in the recurring reflections on the universal language, but Swedenborg did not abandon his ambition to convince the sceptics. Thus he allowed the definitive proof to be given by a spirit, who with her anatomical skill united the insight of intuition in the universal language, which he once—quoting Locke—declared was the property of the angels, as we have already discussed.

The dissection is carried on to the *fluidum spirituosum*, which converts the psychic decisions into physical action and transmits the reports from the senses to the center. At the beginnings of the fibers, in the cortex glands, there is a source of life, from which the spiritual fluid flows. And from there it flows through fibers of different caliber to the blood; then it returns to its source after having completed the cycle. This model immediately reminds one of Descartes' mechanism of reciprocal action in the *glandula pinealis*, but the pattern is far more complicated than that of the first mentor; the soul fibers are not seen as organic tissues other than in an analogous sense, and the presentation must be read figuratively. The attentive Eve also receives her education in this manner. Deep in thought about what she has learned, she experiences something flashing passed the light of her intellect: *"& eo ipso instanti, in interius Caelum quasi illapsa, omnia, quae hactenus in typo, in ipsa conspiciebat ideâ"* (and in that instant, everything that up to that point had been merely a representation penetrated into her deeper, inner heaven, and she saw it as an actual Idea) (§98). As he had done previously, Swedenborg applied his mysterious experiences to a situation parallel to his own; his pondering of the deepest problems has taken him past the border to the brilliantly shining spheres of heaven, where all is revealed.

Eve too must return from the fields of the blessed, and the next question is whether divine order could not appear in a shape visible to the senses. According to the heavenly intelligence, this occurs in the human face, where she can distinguish a series from the natural form, which is called spheric, up to the supra-celestial one, the form of the soul, which illuminates all parts of the face with light and life (§99); to this Swedenborg adds a long note with detailed information on the facial muscles (note a). Since this order is reflected in the human face, it must follow that the heavenly beings, God's images, cannot clothe themselves in other appearances than the human form when they live in the flesh. It is an important step toward the anthropomorphic world of spirits within the theosophic system, and it grows accordingly from the neurological theoretics, which reaches its peak in this sixth scene of the drama of creation.

The beauty of the face thus stems from God's order. However, Eve realizes that this is only a correspondence with a higher perfection, which she calls that of life, *perfectio vitae*, and which encompasses the state of innocence. Her celestial teacher develops this theme with some eloquence in the remaining sections. This is done in repeated summaries of the theological pattern, with which we have become familiar in the two preceding scenes and its now accomplished psychophysical application. There is little new to tell; it is primarily a varied emphasis on fundamental theses, a format that now and then suffers from verbosity. Nevertheless, the psychological triad *anima, mens,* and *animus,* corresponding to the three spiritual powers, approaches becoming just two, which is significant to theosophy: *animus* is frequently called *mens inferior,* and the division between *mens* and *animus* thus becomes less distinct than before. No doubt this has to do with the neuro-physiological inspiration, which forms the basis for this scene to a greater extent than in previous ones.[4]

On the whole, the gradual progress toward the later writings can be sensed more strongly at this stage. The many didactic repetitions end in a contrast between the happiness of those who live according to God's order and the bestial misery of those who have been led astray. Although this motif is not new, it relates more clearly to the visionary inspiration of the author; the relationship between these happy ones and the heavenly beings is an important precondition for their bliss: "*Cum Caelicolis, seu Nobiscum, perpetua jungunt consortia, nam mutuos sociamus sermones; sumus iis oracula, dum consulimur, & iis perspicuas de Caelo mittimus sortes: in summâ degunt luce, quam nulla interpolat umbra*" (They interact constantly with us, the Heaven-Dwellers; we converse together. When they consult us, we are oracles to them, and deliver clear responses from heaven. In a word: they live in a light that no darkness can mar) (§106).

In contrast to this, we find furious metaphors used to describe those who live the life opposed to divine order: wild slaves—one is reminded of their hasty entrance into the intellect in the previous scene—take over and rule, the prince of the world puts out the heavenly light, and mud is mixed with the clear well water. They become like night owls and will-o'-the-wisps, fluttering across the marshlands (§107). We are provided with an anatomical illustration according to the previous neurological pattern (note b). Whereas the earlier descriptions of the world of evil focused more on the deceitfulness of the prince of the world, the emphasis is this time on the evil people themselves. With their dissembling, we have come one step closer to the motif so often developed in the theosophic writings—that all deceitful disguises and masks will be unmercifully revealed in the sharp light of the spiritual world and the innermost truth will be unveiled.[5]

The possibilities of variation must however dwindle in the end, even to so didactic a writer as Swedenborg, and he is satisfied hereafter simply to refer to the more extensive discourses in the two previous scenes (note c). Thus, this sixth scene ends in the encounter between the two first humans, an episode that, in its poetic shimmering, contrasts with all of the long lectures given by the celestial being, which were necessary for the symbolic language of this finale. While the celestials adorn her as a bride, Eve glances at her groom: her blushing, the purple hue of the tissues, becomes a clear picture of love, which streams through her fibers in the manner with which we have become familiar through the celestial classes (§109). The complicated symbolism allows for a certain amount of sensual infatuation, although the divine order demands that decorum be followed and keeps sensuality on a close rein. The passionate hunt for love in the dream image of the introduction reaches fruition in the ritual meeting between the first humans (§110).

Even if this scene, the last one in the book published by Swedenborg himself, seems to be structured more in a didactic than in an artistic fashion, there is a clear compositional pattern. Following the two initial passages, where Adam's dream experiences are depicted (§§87, 88:2) are Eve's childhood and the episode of the reflection in the well (§§89, 90:2); this exposition and the one on the state of innocence are carried through in different varieties in an extensive text (§§91–98:8), after which a vision provides a transition to an exposition on the reflection of divine order on the human face (§§99, 100:2). This, however, is mostly a detailed repetition of what has already been said, and the same is true of the next large section, where the subject is the perfection of life (§§101–108:8); then follow the wedding arrangements of the final paragraphs (§§109–110:2). This is indeed evidence of a formal disposition, but its correspondence in content is less obvious than in the previous scenes, and the repetitions are plentiful.

This scene, which was published separately as a second part of *The Worship and Love of God*, was evidently intended as a preface to the exposition on humankind, the Fall of which the author had promised to treat in §53, note q. The subtitle, "*de conjugio primogeniti seu Adami*," is inadequate, since neither Adam's wedding nor his married life is described in the published part but only in the incomplete third section. Its publication, which according to a letter to the envoy Joachim Frederic Preis (1667–1759) in the Hague could not have occurred before March 11, 1745, could be an indication that Swedenborg again hesitated with regard to his gigantic ambitions, as happened both with the *Oeconomia* series and *Regnum animale*. He may have wished to start publishing smaller parts, since he had not been able to keep the immense material and the overall picture together.[6] This interpretation fits with the tensions in composition and content, which are visible in the fifth scene and even more so in the sixth. With their many repetitions, they convey an atmosphere of confusion and tiredness, even indecision at times: how far should the plans be realized and the fable transmit the message of God's order and the salvation of humankind? How long would the preacher be able to hide behind his symbolic personae?

This impression is strengthened by the unfinished third part. The main section of this part consists of a vision that appears to the first human couple the morning after the wedding night. Even without the interpretation, which Adam had been able to present to his wife to a certain extent, it clearly symbolizes the turn of events in the world from the Creation to the end. However, at the same time, its summarizing character is evident. It is structured in six sections and a finale: this is the hexaemeral number returning, but also the division into scenes of the complete work, exemplifying what Augustine called the perfect number.[7] It appears that this monumental ecphrasis was an attempt to create a dignified end to the emblematic drama: the symbol of the great world egg is used here, the interaction between the three spiritual powers is depicted in a consequent sun-and-light imagery, there is a reference to the defection of the prince of the world and a foreboding of the holy society, which shall be built by the future human race. Hadn't Swedenborg already presented his view, as far as it could be molded into the shape of the fable, through this vision and the anticipatory episodes in the previous scenes? What function could the vision have that would not result in the continuation's becoming nothing more than a realization of events already predicted? A note on a loose page of the manuscript about what the third part was to contain seems to support this conception: "*De vita Conjugii Paris Primogeniti, seu Adami & Evae, et inibi de Animae immortalitate, ejus statu post mortem, Paradiso cealesti repraesentato in terrestri, fine universi in hoc pari, sicut in suo ovo*" (on the firstborn couple's or Adam and Eve's married life, and also about the immortality of the soul, its state after death. the heavenly Paradise imagined in the earthly, the purpose of the universe in this couple, like in its egg.).[8]

The fact that Adam, in his interpretation of the vision, is allowed to formulate the main theme of the book, which has given it its name, points in the same direction (§122). Its importance is emphasized by its having been underlined twice in the manuscript, and compositionally its effect ought to have been noticeable if placed in a summarizing finale. Against this, it can be said that Swedenborg, in note a of the third part, still adhered to his promise to treat sinful humanity in our state of confusion: the reservation "*volente Deo*" belongs to the rhetorics of the genre and the epoch and cannot support any conclusion, although it proved to be a premonition in the light of later developments. The essential fact is, however, that the author did interrupt his exposition on the vision; this must certainly have been done under the influence of the spiritual experience in mid-April of that same spring. After this initiation, there was no possibility of lingering within the pattern of a fable, when all hesitation had been replaced by certainty.

From an artistic point of view, it is fortunate that this illumination did not occur until after some test prints and manuscripts of the third part had been completed. It provides the drama of creation with the coherence of the unfinished symphony, and it is doubtful whether the work would have gained from a completion of the promised motifs. As a pastoral idyll of the most serene coloring, the introduction of the third part is close to the sensual atmosphere of the conclusion of the sixth scene. The firstborn couple wander around Eve's garden, where all nature's wedding joy in springtime overwhelms them as an outward correspondence of their own love. The time is also motivated correspondentially, since, according to the hieroglyphic key, the midday hour means "*intellectus consummatus, seu judicium maturum, quale est in aetate adulta*" (perfect intellect, or mature judgment, such as it is in adult age).[9]

In this love-filled paradise, the union of matrimony is sealed, and the couple is united in a higher bliss where all their joy is multiplied because it is experienced together. Swedenborg uses the beautiful metaphor of one heart divided into two champers (§11). For the reader, coming from the chaos of the dream diary to life according to God's order in this work, the chaste sensuality of the first nuptials starkly contrasts to the callous sexuality of the dream life. In the world of fable, the author's "lust for women," which he called his *"hufwudpassion"* (main passion), is transformed into a subtle fabric woven from dreams of love, sense of community, and innocence.[10] The symbolism of correspondence endows the sensual atmosphere with a chaste shimmer; and when the golden arrows of dawn witness the awakening of the bride and groom, it culminates in the prophetic vision.

A brilliant kernel of light appears on the heavenly orb, forcing the couple to close their eyes. A purple, flaming belt develops around this center, adorned with little human forms, images of the enchanted audience. Then a girdle of fire forms around this belt, assuming the color of bronze and iron and beating like a heart. Surrounding these two belts, a multitude of innumerable little eggs appears, from which fetuses are born; the human forms move their cycles inward, while the animal forms distance themselves from the belts. Thereafter, the viewers see a circle being closed around this entire world, so that everything appears in the shape of an enormous egg enveloped in swaddling clothes. As these dissolve, a human body rises from the center and subsequently floats up toward heaven. Finally, the two belts separate, and the circle forms a pyramid-shaped spiral, which unceasingly continues its movement (§112).

The didactic purpose of *The Worship and Love of God*, which is all the more evident the nearer we come to the end, requires an exposition on the grand emblem, the peak of this symbolic work and of early Swedish eighteenth-century literature as a whole. First, Eve provides her humble interpretation: she has understood that the universe is a collection of means to achieve one single end, but her intellect does not manage to interpret the deepest meaning *"quae tam leviter & strictim summas rerum percurrit"* ([because it] skimmed too lightly and rapidly over the surface of things) (§113). Touched by a deepened love for his wise wife, Adam refers to her interpretation in his answer: the highest purpose of the universe is *"Sapientissimi Creatoris Gloria,"* the glory of the Lord, the wisest Creator, about which the society of the holy shall bear witness (§115). Understanding this is necessary to comprehend correctly the details of the vision, to which Adam then proceeds. These details, however, do not add anything new—apart from the expression of the main theme of the work—but vary motifs already carried through, often with reference to previous parts, especially the physiological applications which his wife was shown in the sixth scene.

In these peculiar final scenes, where the departure to the world of spirits is coming closer, there is scope for many detailed investigations. However, considering that several motifs have already been treated, we shall look at only three important themes: the discourse on the fibers and nerves of the body, God's order, and the society of the holy.

# Fibers and Spiritual Flow

*Fibrae, quae Glandulas Conglomeratas integrant, sunt quadru-
plicis originis, inde etiam naturae, usus, determinationis. Prima,
quae omnium fibrarum est principium, forma, potentia, est
Fibra Cerebri late sumti, ex substantiis, ut matriculis, ejus Cor-
ticalibus seu Cineritiis exclusa: haec in Cerebro dicitur
Medullaris, in Corpore Nervea. Altera, est Fibra inferioris sys-
tematis seu Corporis, ex priore seu Cerebri principiata & infor-
mata, estque Vasculum sanguineum, seu Arteria & Vena (z).
Tertia, est utriusque tam Fibrae Cerebri, quam Fibrae Corporis;
seu Fibrae Nerveae & Vasculi progenies, & vocatur Fibra Mus-
culi seu Motrix. Quarta, est Fibra Glandulae conglomeratae, ex
grandinibus & acinis ejus enixa, continuata, adunata (a).*

(The fibers, which form the conglomerate glands, are of four
origins, therefore also in nature, use, and determination. The
first, which is the principle, form, and force of all fibers, is the
fiber that belongs to the brain in general, hatched from its cortical and cinereous substances like little mothers; it is called the
marrow fiber in the brain, the nerve fiber in the body. The second one is the fiber of the lower system or the body, directed
and created by the first or the brain fiber, and it is the blood vessel or artery or vein. The third one comes both of the brain fiber
and the body fiber or is an heir to the nerve and blood vessel
fiber, and it is called muscle or movement fiber. The fourth is the
conglomerate gland's fiber, born, collected, and fulfilled from its
grandines and acinae.)[11]

In Swedenborg's works, this is one of many attempts to distinguish the
basic elements of the body. Stroh has pointed to the general similarities—
also in these psychophysical matters—between Swedenborg and Descartes,
"whose psychology, it may be added, carried off the prize in a famous discussion in the spiritual world."[12] This is correct with regard to the starting
point—the metaphors of mechanisms and machines, which we encounter
on so many occasions in Swedenborg's earlier writings, for instance in *"De
mechanismo operationis animae et corporis,"* and which will still appear in
the drama of creation, revealing their origin. Lamm also paid attention to
this fact and clearly showed the Cartesian background of the short physiological essays on tremulations and contremiscences from the late 1710s—
Swedenborg's first attempts to create a uniform explanation of the world
with the aid of mechanical theories on the origins of sensory perceptions
and psychic activities. Moreover, Lamm linked them to Polhem's similar
ambitions.[13]

In the same manner, Lamm interpreted the physiological applications of the cosmology in *Principia*. The soul is the most subtle substance of the body and is subjected to mechanical laws. However, the Cartesian life spirits and their task of transmission are seen primarily as an expression of theoretical despair, and Swedenborg appears at this stage to be even more mechanistic than the master himself; the ignorant division of the soul from the context of nature is furthermore dangerous, as it leads many down the path of atheism.[14] He seems to have envisaged the soul as a kind of refined and immortal body that, like material things, would be influenced by movements. In these early works, the term *membrane* is used when describing sensory organs and nerves, and it is not until *Oeconomia* that the fibers, blood vessels, and *fluidum spirituosum*, the soul flow, take over from these psychic machine parts. The view of the soul as a subtle body can nevertheless have been an inspiration even after the mechanical theories became transformed into a more organic thinking. It is particularly significant for the anthropomorphic pattern, the primary quality of Swedenborg's world of spirits.

Swedenborg's psychophysical system raises concerns regarding materialism, and he has indeed noted a passage from Wolff's *Theologia naturalis* in his diary as an allusion to this problem.[15] It is interesting to see how Swedenborg used another text book of the same authority, *Psychologia empirica,* among other works in his efforts to progress from the cosmological *Principia* pattern toward a psychophysical direction.[16] The excerpts from this work are in the shape of a discussion of Wolff's definitions and theses, while his own system is being extended. There are also combinations of the parts of the soul membrane with the elements of *Principia*, which are illustrated graphically; in the center of its spirals we find the active of the first finite particle, while outside we find the next membrane containing the first element. There then follows another one with the second element; and, in the next, we find ether, which can stream forth as in a small canal. Thereafter, we find yet another two membranes, of which the one farthest out contains blood.[17]

The tremulations of these membranes are described with terms used in harmony: "*Omnia trement harmonice, ut ad octavum, vel simile; nam membranae omnes different octavis*" (All things vibrate in harmony, as in the octave or a similar one; for all membranes are differentiated in octaves).[18] The reason that nature has set out so many graceful things for our senses is also explained in these categories: everything must contribute to the harmony of the soul, all membranes from the largest to the smallest. Using this as support, these notes begin the thesis about the face as the mirror of the psyche, which became so important later on; the destructive influence of the Fall of humanity on the different membranes is also mentioned.[19]

The hieroglyphical way of writing, which we noted among these excerpts in the section on the doctrine of correspondence, is also interpreted according to the same pattern of harmonious tremulations: "*Quod tale hieroglyphicum plus valeat in memoria, patet ex eo quod plures suppeditet tremores, qui concurrant. . . . Unde talis scriptura adinveniri potest quae exhauriat fere omnia; et plus scribere liceat in una linea, quam explicari potest per aliquot folia; sed qui intelliget, erit scius*" (That such a hieroglyphical [description] means more in the memory is clear from the fact that it provides more tremulations, which concur. . . . Thus such a way of writing can be invented, which can comprehend almost everything, and in which it would be possible to write more in one line than can be explained in several pages. But he who can understand this must be wise).[20] The life of the will is also included in the vibrations of the membranes, and the nerve fibers are seen as a chain of microscopic membranes through which impulses are propagated in both directions through movements. The interaction between soul and body thus becomes a mechanical tremulation transport, and the organism appears as an extremely intricate system of harmonically tuned instruments.[21]

Swedenborg thus forces into Wolff's sober definitions a fantastic attempt to apply the cosmologic elements on the microcosm—a radical extension of the contemporary idea, inspired by Newton, of the identity between the powers of the universe and those working on earth—which is far bolder than those he published.

The aim at uniformity in these excerpts can be seen as a brave engineer's sketch of what is to return later in a different format. The purely technical concretion of the Wolff commentaries has been replaced in the drama of creation with a lucidity achieved by correspondence symbolism, and the sketch of soul membranes and natural elements, which Swedenborg hastily drew in these early notes, reaches its perfection in the angel's self-dissection in *The Worship and Love of God* and her combination of psychic elements with the forms of the universe. This connection will presently be further discussed.

However, much has changed during the decade between the two attempts to create a synthesis, and this can be most distinctly studied regarding the spiritual fluid and the life spirits, whose role has been reduced as far as possible in the mechanical model. It has already been stressed how the investigations of the blood, which open *Oeconomia*, have been connected to the physical system of *Principia*. These studies were conducted on the basis of works by great contemporary authorities, Leeuwenhoek, Giovanni Maria Lancisi (1654–1720), Herman Boerhaave (1668–1738), Malpighi, and others, for whom Swedenborg expresses the greatest respect. We have observed traces of anatomical studies in his earlier writings, but it is only at this stage that he displays intimate knowledge of the field.[22]

From what the great scientists have reported of their microscopic studies Swedenborg deduces in the introduction to *Oeconomia* that the blood can be subdivided into several kinds: first, the red blood; thereafter, a purer, transparent blood; and then a yet subtler liquid, which is invisible even to the eye armed with a microscope—some call it *spiritus animales*, "life spirits" (I, §37). To begin with, Swedenborg assumes a cautious attitude and promises a later discussion on the issue, but he soon abandons this attitude and finally regards the soul flow as a given fact, determined by the highest aura: thereby he connects it to the cosmology of *Principia* (I, §635). This model was most consistently formed in the little fragment called "*Philosophia corpuscularis in compendio*," which ends with a phrase frequently quoted in Swedenborg literature as characteristic of his particular sources: "*Haec vera sunt quia signum habeo*" (These things are true because I have a sign).[23] As I have shown in another context, this must be regarded as a reply to Leeuwenhoek in a kind of posthumous dialogue, when Swedenborg was making notes from his *Arcana naturae detecta* in Amsterdam in the beginning of 1740.[24] It means that, although a genetic study is undeniably made rather complicated with more or less "mystical" references like this one, it is still necessary to ascribe great importance to the anatomical authorities as guides. Lamm has probably overestimated somewhat the role of Neoplatonic ideas as incitements, as they must have been familiar to Swedenborg much earlier, in the same way as "mysticism" in general. In the symbiosis of ancient wisdom and modern experiential science, which he claimed so often to aim for, contemporary science was in all probability the primary source.[25]

In discussing the doctrine of correspondence, I stressed how Swedenborg, in order to perfect his psychological theorizing, was forced into facing the problem of the philosophical language of universals, so often discussed among his masters. The draft for such a language, which has been preserved, is interesting mainly in connection with the fibers and *fluidum spirituosum*. Here he wished to construct a series of signs through which he aimed to determine the objects of sensory perception in their higher correspondences. The example given in the fragment deals with signs for the blood, the arteries, the muscles and the nerves: "S" signifies the blood in its highest subtlety, that is, the soul flow; "A" signifies the highest artery or the simple nerve fiber; "M," the highest muscle, that is, the motor determination of the simple nerve fiber; and "N" also signifies the simple nerve fiber.[26]

This means that "N" and "A" are the same, but in different forms of appearance: when brought together in bundles and shrouded in membranes, the nerve fibers become a nerve thread; but when wound in rings, they form blood vessels, and twisted together a motor fiber or a muscle thread. Thus, the same general terms give rise to a number of particular correspondences. In order to describe the visible substances, determinations are added, which are also expressed with initials: "Sa," "Na," etc., in a successively higher degree of complexity.[27] We encounter an attempt at mapping the nature of fibers with a universal language in this fragment. In the world of senses, this proved impossible, but in the fable constructed on the foundation of the doctrine of correspondence, it could be done by an angelic being. This is another expression of how the literary form of the drama of creation made possible certain attempts that had earlier been thwarted. At the same time, it underlines how intimately the doctrine of correspondence is connected to the problem of interaction between soul and body.

The question of the nature of the fibers was a major problem for Swedenborg, and their promised investigation appears as a draft on a third volume in the *Oeconomia* series.[28] I will not be discussing Swedenborg's contributions to the anatomy of the brain, both because of lack of competence and for reasons of space, but some reflections on the sources are nevertheless necessary in order to interpret the intellectual background of the drama of creation. It has been stressed several times by scholars, and it is evident also to the layman, that Swedenborg's method was primarily to compile the actual discoveries made by anatomists and then interpret them in the light of his synthetic view.[29] There are numerous examples of how he attempts to achieve a union between ancient wisdom and modern empirical science also in this anatomical context: in *De fibra*, for instance, where he describes the brain and its different parts as an extremely developed chemical laboratory or a colossal gland, consisting of innumerable small glands, it is done with a significant combination of authorities: Hippocrates' and the ancients' view is in accordance with Malpighi's and other modern scholars' (§80).

At the same time, the goal remains to unite the world of ideas of *Principia* with the study of organisms in different ways. As early as the second volume of the *Oeconomia*, Swedenborg quoted among others Boerhaave in describing the role of the cortex substance in a way that foreshadows both the cosmological imagery and the accounts of the circulation in *The Worship and Love of God*:

> *Ergo est Corticea substantia in medio sita, seu in termino ultimo Arteriarum & primo Fibrarum Cerebri, ut bicipitis Jani instar retrorsum & antrorsum respiciat, a parte nimirum Arteriarum ipsum sanguinem crassiorem, a parte autem fibrarum fluidum spirituosum, quae se in Corticea ut in communi & principali substantia quasi uniunt; ut nimirum per mirabilem circulum redeant toties effectus ad suas causas, quoties causae tendunt ad suos effectus; & vicissim.*
>
> (Therefore the cortex substance is situated in the middle or at the outer limit of the arteries and the first one of the brain fibers, so that it observes backwards and forwards like a two-faced Janus on one side the arteries and the coarser blood, but on the side of the fibers the soul flow, which in a way unite in the cortex substance as in their common principle; [this occurs]

because the effects must return to their causes through a wonderful circle, as often as the causes strive toward their effects,
and vice versa.)[30]

This is the same symbol that was used in *Principia* to indicate the mathematical point with its position between infinity and the finite existence.
Indeed, the cortex substance of the brain takes the same position between
spirit and matter, which is stressed by the structure of the brain often being
compared to that of the universe, a motif that reaches its culmination in
the drama of creation, for instance, in the following passage from the third
part, §124, note e: "*Ex inde patet, quod ex nobis ipsis, si modo Facultates
nostras distincte rimari velimus, clare perspicere queamus, quale sit Universum, tam Caelum, quam Mundus*" (Thus it is obvious that we can
clearly perceive from our own selves [provided only that we wish to investigate our own faculties] what kind of thing the universe is, as well as what
heaven and the world are).[31]

In the cortex substance of the brain, *fluidum spirituosum* or the life spirits are produced: this had been asserted previously in the physiology of the
brain in the published parts of *Oeconomia*, and it is treated in various
ways in later investigations. In *Oeconomia* II and in the fragment on the
universal language, the soul flow and the purer blood are distinguished; in
the little essay "*De spiritu animali*" (On the life spirit), Swedenborg seemed
set on identifying them for a moment but then changed his mind, and this
is what finally happened in the angel's speech in *The Worship and Love of
God*.[32] The starting point for these speculations was the anatomist
Leeuwenhoek's microscopic investigations of blood, according to which
the blood liquid could be analyzed in coarser and finer particles. The most
subtle ones form the life spirit in Swedenborg's view, and thus it becomes a
question of judgment to a certain degree where the dividing line between
middle and spiritual blood should be drawn. In the angel's exposition, the
life spirits flow forth in the shape of the purer blood down through the
body; but even in the theoretical works, the distinction is of little interest,
as the two species move together.[33] More importantly, Swedenborg is completely clear and consistent that these life spirits are only the purely technical, unifying link between body and soul and that their existence in itself
does not solve the problem of reciprocal action. Thus far, he does not accept the Cartesian solution to the problem.[34]

However, the precondition for solving the riddle is as thorough a mapping as possible of the physical basis. In the treatise on the fiber, Swedenborg makes a welcome, although entirely theoretical, purge of the
terminology before starting his discourse. He states that he will use the
term *fiber* for that which originates in the cortex. Its continuation in the
body is called "nerve fiber," as is the case in the anatomical theater of paradise. From these nerve fibers, we should distinguish, among others, the

veins, even if they have in common that they are hollow like a species of small canals.[35] These distinctions are important to Swedenborg, since they make it possible for him to create some order among the contradictory information emanating from the authorities. As Acton noted, he quotes a number of authors after Thomas Bartholin, among them Aristotle, who regarded the heart as the origin of the nerve fibers and these as a kind of vein. Swedenborg views this as the restricted experience of the ancients.[36]

The same problem recurs in the question of the hollowness of the fibers: the peripatetic school and especially its master denied that the fibers were penetrable, and thus it may seem to those who judge only by the evidence of the senses: *"sunt certe valde crassi et a musis alieni"*—they are indeed very uneducated and distant from the muses. He supports his opinion with Plato's *Theaitetos*, which he excerpted in cod. 36–110. If this was a serious matter to the ancients, it becomes yet graver in modern time, when the information from the microscope must be denied. After a long collection of quotes from a number of anatomists, of whom Bartholin, Raymond Vieussens (1641?–1715), and Leeuwenhoek appear to come closest to Swedenborg's own view, he concludes that modern empirical scientists have been able to confirm the doctrines of Hippocrates (c. 460–c. 377 BCE) but not those of the philosophers.[37]

If this could be regarded as a certain dissociation from philosophical speculations, Swedenborg is soon forced to make some himself. The angel's dissection in *The Worship and Love of God* had as its object a nerve, which was uncovered, stripped of its membranes, and followed into its kernel, a fiber that thereafter was investigated up to its origin in a cortex gland (§95). The account completely accords with what is said in *De fibra*: *"Fibra est principalis nervi substantia: fibrae simul coagmentatae ipsissimum nervi corpus aut medullam constituunt"* (The fiber is the main substance of the nerve: several connected fibers together form the very body or marrow of the nerve).[38] However, there are fibers of different degrees, and while it is true that the innermost simple fiber can be uncovered in the angel's super-sensual microscope, empirical research still cannot reach all the way with available earthly instruments. So, the concepts of philosophical rationalism are called in to assist, and, as expected, Wolff and Aristotle reappear.[39] Following Swedenborg's recurring tendency to exceed boundaries, the anatomical studies pass on to lengthy reflections on the scale of forms. This is the background to the hierarchy of forms, which is introduced to Eve in a brief overview by the angel before the dissection begins. The reverse order in the drama of creation indicates in its own way the altered starting position, along a path of synthesis, as this knowledge was transmitted to the first human couple (§93).

The overview of the scale of forms, which is provided in *De fibra*, is an attempt at realizing a project that had been mentioned often as an extension of the doctrine of series and degrees, such as it is encountered in

*Oeconomia* I.[40] The doctrine of forms is also clearly connected to the blood investigations, the beginning point of the *Oeconomia*. We see this from an observation in an essay on the red blood, probably written in 1742: "*Quod sanguis in se contineat omnes formas organicas a prima spirituali ad ultimam angularem, sic ut sit compendium et complexus omnium formarum naturae*" (the blood in itself contains all organic forms from the first spiritual to the outermost angular, so that it is the summary of all natural forms).[41] Since knowledge about the simple can be gained by studying its conglomerates and the true essence of such conglomerates is only their *essentia prima*, Swedenborg draws conclusions about the finest essence of the blood based on the study of its complexity—that is, about the life spirits in their perfection. However, he also realizes that such conclusions cannot provide insight on the true character of the invisible beings and that such an insight would demand a *doctrina formarum*.[42]

This doctrine was intended with the hierarchy of forms in *De fibra*: the angular, the circular or spherical, the spiral, the vortical, the celestial, and the spiritual (§§251–273). During the course of this theorizing, the natural philosophy of *Principia* is often called upon, and Swedenborg compares his own point of view with that of others—for example, Plato, Aristotle, Leibniz, and Wolff. He emphasizes the similarities between his celestial form and Plato's "The One," the Neoplatonic *Aristotle's Theology*, Leibniz's monad, and Wolff's simple substance. This means that the discourse is not only one of many attempts to intertwine the cosmological system with the biological and psycho-theological, but also one of the numerous compilations of ancient and modern (§266). In organic application, the veins are then described as having a spherical shape, the nerve fibers a spiral one, and the beginnings of the simple fibers a celestial form (§275).

Swedenborg never published *De fibra*; instead he planned an account of his doctrine of forms in the *Regnum animale* series.[43] Since this gigantically planned *Summa antropologiae* could not be finished, a doctrine of forms was never part of the works of natural philosophy. However, in the synthetic intention of *The Worship and Love of God*, we encounter a compressed presentation of the doctrine of forms, at first in notes to the cosmological passages where it completely corresponds with *De fibra*, and the proximity to *Principia* is apparent (§6, note b, and §24, note q). The organic application in the angel's lecture is, however, somewhat different: the vortical form, which in both works follows just after the heavenly one, is now called "sub-celestial" and belongs to *animus* and the prince of the world; its closest equivalent in *De fibra* would be the second organic form, which is the brain's form in its function as a general sensorium (§93). No doubt this is connected to the consistent psycho-theological distinction between *mens* and *animus* in *The Worship and Love of God*, which has widened the gap between the spheres of the body and of the soul to a certain extent. However, this is a point of view that can be held only with regard to the theories behind the description, since the entire atmosphere in the drama of creation is otherwise characterized by the spirit flowing in as the only living matter into the passively receptive nature.

One could follow Swedenborg's various wrestlings with the problems of fibers and soul flow much further, but this is best left to experts. This brief sketch illustrates how complicated is the background to the angel's dissection. We have encountered the basic element of the Cartesian education, the vortical motions—Swedenborg is well aware that he holds an outdated opinion, as is illustrated by a passage in *De fibra* (§265)—and the life spirits. We have studied an early attempt at a mechanical model of soul membranes and nerve fibers, a factual engineer's hypothesis, which is prophetic in its innermost structure. We have seen how the modern microscopists inspired Swedenborg with their own enthusiasm for the breathtaking new perspectives in natural science, primarily Leeuwenhoek with his blood investigations and his other uncovering of *arcana naturae*. Imitating them, Swedenborg follows a path that will lead him to secrets of a higher kind, *arcana coelestia*. And we have found many examples of an ambition to unite ancient wisdom with modern experimental science, which reaches its culmination in the present work. Furthermore, through these studies, Swedenborg realized that it would be impossible to advance to the kernel with observational instruments and ordinary language as the only available tools. His reflections regarding the philosophical language of universals emanate from the analysis of the blood and fibers; while they indicate a transition to mystical speculations, respectable masters were his guides.

The crucial difference is, however, that Swedenborg does not stop at the border of the incomprehensible, nor does he satisfy himself with the hope of an enlightened future. The desire for the deepest form of insight—which is something far more than intellectual curiosity, indeed a struggle to achieve clarity regarding the meaning of life—drives him toward a point of view which has nothing in common with science except for terminology. From this particular perspective, it is understandable, although regrettable, that Swedenborg has been of such little interest to historians of science. He distanced himself ever more from scientific ideals of objectivity and exactitude of expression; from a theoretical point of view, one is forced to characterize the doctrine of correspondence as a monumental collection of examples of the fallacy commonly called *quaternio terminorum*.

However, for the purposes of a literary study, such theoretical objections are insignificant, since sharpness of thought is not necessarily a guarantee for a first-rate piece of art. More important are descriptive power and independent thought with which the common human—almost *archetypal*—need for synthesis has been satisfied. In that respect, the angel's dissection—like the drama of creation as a whole—should be regarded highly. In condensed symbolism, it summarizes the author's progress through decades of study from the grosser bodily tissues, from a mechanistic world model, up to the super-celestial life beams that allow themselves to be viewed only analogically as fibers. Thus the discourse combines the anatomical and philosophical sources, of which the most influential ones have been quoted, in an original whole in the light of the divine illumination, which is the basic motif of this work.

# Divine Order

The description of fibers and soul flow contains as little intrinsic value as the other factual information in *The Worship and Love of God* but serves to illustrate God's order as reflected in the human body. This motif forms a foundation for the entire demonstration of world events from the beginning: the Lord, the rightful worship of whom Swedenborg wishes to teach with his opus, has established an order in eternity to which everything in the universe is subject. However, under the influence of the fallen prince of the world, humankind has broken this law in refusing to understand God's glory as *finis omnium finium*, the highest purpose. Instead, we have put ourselves in that position. To Swedenborg this constitutes a crime against the very law of existence, which for a man of his technical and scientific learning is incomprehensible. This fact does not, however, alter God's plans, in which world events have been predicted for eternity. God is not harmed by human actions, but humanity's fate becomes desperate due to this very conformity to law. The insistent and beseeching tone, which appears ever more forcefully in the message of God's order as depicted in this work, can be regarded as an attempt to awaken those led astray and urge them to change their ways. It is characteristic both of the period and the person that such a sermon begins with a description of the origins of nature and man in fulfilment of evolutionary laws established within them.

The motif of divine order is accomplished in several different ways in *The Worship and Love of God*. They are all philosophical ones, easily referred to authorities with which we have become familiar in other contexts. The concluding vision in the third part is a final attempt to symbolically summarize the motif. The nucleus of the vision is "*Candidissimae Lucis Centrum*," a central point of the most brilliant light, the beams of which darken the sun and the stars. Adam and Eve are unable to endure its brilliance and are forced to close their eyes. Despite this, the divine light still penetrates all the fibers and surprises the senses with darkness. Later when Adam interprets this part of the vision to Eve, he starts with the symbolic character of this divine revelation: "*Ut oculis nostris, per naturae effigies, caelestes intueremur formas, Suprema Mentium Vita se per Candidissimam repraesentare voluit Lucem, quae ex spatioso Centro, sicut ex Sole, se in Universi effudit fines*" (To enable us to see heavenly forms with our eyes in a simulation of nature, the Supreme Life of Minds willed a representation of itself to appear in an intensely bright light, which poured forth to the bounds of the universe from an extensive center, as though from a sun) (§117).

This light is intelligence, wisdom, righteousness, and honor, for the divine light contains truths from which emanate intelligences, goodnesses, and wisdoms, in the same number as its beams. From its flow comes the order bound by the law of the universe, which is called *Justitia*, righteousness, justice. The gleam of the light is called honor, which encompasses all the other characteristics and which therefore is the purpose of purposes. But the infinite God, represented by this light, cannot enter into direct contact with mortal beings, since that would blind and kill them. All communication must be carried out through the mediation of the Only Son; for that reason, the viewers' eyes close until the light had been circumvented by a belt, which is the image of the Son. Despite this fact, the infinite light penetrates the closed gates of the senses, which signifies that nothing can be hidden from God; however, the senses cannot endure the presence of the light even in this form, so they are put into a state of vertigo and darkness (§§117–120).

This is the last and most extensive presentation of Swedenborg's ideas of God before his definitive entry into the world of spirits, where so much was to change, both in theological theory and psychological practice. "On the footbridge between the natural and the spiritual worlds," he transmits in stronger words here rather than later both the anguish involved when facing God's burning light and also the marvelous certainty and trust that are the other side of pious people's awe before the face of the Lord. From a theoretical point of view, this vision is primarily a concrete symbol for a thought that we have encountered several times before. In *Oeconomia* I, there is a passage that appears in identical form in part II—in itself a good illustration of how the anatomical studies lead to the psychological and how both are united in the theological perspective—where Swedenborg describes in some detail the impossibility of defining God's essence with our finite thinking and our incomplete language; despite this, there are those who try to achieve the unthinkable:

> *Qui itaque hoc abydum ductrice mentis philosophia tentare audent, eos devovet sua audacia; redeunt quasi impotes succiduo poplite, uti qui spectarunt profundissima; aut quasi lumine cassi, uti qui intuitum fixere in Sole: imo quod saepius indoluit, volat dein macula aut umbra etiam eorum ante visum per se hebetem rationalem, ut mediâ luce caecutiant, & in mera re animi pendeant: sic temeritatis poenas luunt.*
>
> (Those who therefore dare to investigate this abyss with the aid of the philosophy of reason are condemned by their boldness to death; they return impotent and bending their knees,

like those who have viewed the deepest; or they return blinded, like those who have looked at the sun. Furthermore a stain or a shadow, which often irritates them, flies in front of the vision of their mind, in itself blunt, so that they are blind in the midst of the light and restless in their minds regarding this situation: thus they are punished for their thoughtlessness.)[44]

The burning light of the divinity is primarily a biblical motif. The obvious example is Exodus 33:20, where the Lord speaks to Moses: "But," he said, "you cannot see my face; for no one shall see me and live."[45] But there are also other texts: John 1:18, 1Timothy 6:16, 1 John 4:12 are some examples. The well-read Swedenborg also noted a passage with the same content from Plato's *The Sophist* among his excerpts.[46] However, this talk of our inability to view God's face characteristically enough also involves a philosophical difficulty, and here we return to the intellectual environment.

Again, it is Malebranche whom we encounter in the annotations; it is surprising that his importance to Swedenborg, which Lamm observed, has not been the subject of further research. One of the more recent scholarly works on Swedenborg, Ernst Benz's extensive monograph, has to my knowledge not acknowledged Malebranche at all, despite the fact that there was a natural reason, as the author in as many words describes Swedenborg's encounter with the famous Oratian fathers Abbé Jean-Paul de Bignon (1662–1743) and Jacques Lelong (1665–1721)—members of the same order as Malebranche—in Paris in 1713.[47]

Malebranche is probably best known for his contribution to the classical debate on the interaction between body and soul, the theory which he calls *"la vision en Dieu"* (the vision in God). His solution, which from a rationalist point of view acts somewhat as a precursor to Berkeley's empirically inspired one, stems from his concept of God, as was emphasized in the section on the doctrine of correspondence. Aspelin summarizes: *"Vi kan inte direkt uppfatta de fysiska tingen, och vi får intet verkligt vetande genom sinnesintryckens förmedling. Men vår ande är delaktig av de idéer eller eviga mönsterbilder, enligt vilka Gud har skapat den yttre världen. Genom dem får vi vår kunskap om tingens geometriska struktur och om deras lagbundna samband. Vi skådar alla ting i Gud"* (We cannot directly comprehend the physical objects, and we get no real knowledge through the mediation of the sensory impressions. However, our spirit has part in the ideas or eternal images, according to which God has created the external world. Through them we receive our knowledge about the geometrical structure of the objects and their connections bound by law. We view all things in God).[48] Among the numerous excerpts from Malebranche, in this context one is struck by a characteristic of both the note taker and the source, that is, the almost technically precise meaning they both infer from the Bible. Swedenborg observed this on the basis of 1Timothy 6:16, while

Malebranche found the Pauline lecture on God's dwelling in a light unendurable to human beings difficult to swallow, since it complicates the theory of *"la vision en Dieu."* Swedenborg also noted Malebranche's solution, which in opposition to Paul mobilizes John's gospel with its sermon on Christ as being the true light and quotes several Church Fathers who called the human soul a light lit by eternal wisdom.[49]

Furthermore, Swedenborg partly took down a similar Malebranche idea in the same context. In reply to the challenge, which is posed also by Exodus 33:20, Malebranche emphasizes that the human being comes closer to God the more he distances himself from his body, which means that death is a prerequisite for a perfect view of God (the obvious Bible reference is 1 Corinthians 13:12); however, there are people who, already in this life, have managed to tame their bodies and distance themselves from them so that they are nearly united with God—among the possible examples Paul is mentioned.[50] Paul is now Swedenborg's most venerated biblical authority, whose statements are allotted a philosophical significance; in one of the excerpts Swedenborg declares that Paul in Romans 8:29 speaks in accordance with the theory of the pre-established harmony.[51] The entire approach is closely related to the preaching about how a man must open himself to the influx of the divine, a central theme with Swedenborg. It is not a sermon of asceticism, but it means that man must distance himself from his body, which is but a passive recipient of forces from the outside, a means of fulfilling the purpose of creation.

In the final analysis, the position of the sensual bodies is defined by divine order, and we unsurprisingly find Malebranche's influence also at the center of the theological problem. Gouhier has summarized Malebranche's ideas of creation with admirable clarity:

> *Dieu a créé le monde pour sa gloire; le monde glorifie Dieu parce que l'Incarnation d'une personne divine le sanctifie; cette personne divine est la première pierre d'un Temple spirituel qui est l'objet réel de la création; les esprits, c'est-à-dire les êtres faits à l'image de Dieu, sont les matériaux de ce Temple et parmi eux se trouvent les hommes dont l'âme est unie à Dieu par la volonté et la raison; quant aux choses matérielles qui disparaîtront lorsque le Temple spirituel sera achevé, elles célèbrent a leur manière la gloire de Dieu en figurant la vie du Christ; enfin; puisque Dieu n'a pas fait surgir d'un seul coup de baguette l'édifice de sa gloire, puisqu'il a voulu qu'il y ait un temps, son intuition créatrice contient l'histoire du monde: Dieu a donné un contenu aux siècles et les jours qui passent racontent la construction du Temple éternel.*
>
> (God has created the world for his glory, and the world glorifies God because the Incarnation of a divine person sanctifies

it. This divine person is the first stone of a spiritual temple that is the real object of the creation. The spirits, that is, the beings created as images of God, are the materials of this temple, and among them are those men who are united with God in will and reason. As to material things, which will disappear when the spiritual temple is completed, they celebrate in their way the glory of God by symbolizing the life of Christ. Finally, since God did not make the building of his glory appear as if by a stroke of magic, since he wanted time to exist, his creative vision contains the history of the world: God has given a content to the centuries, and the days that pass tell about the construction of the eternal temple.)[52]

Thus, the aim of creation is the glory of God, and it is molded in the spiritual temple, the *civitas Dei*, which is the real object of the act of creation. Among the building blocks are those whose souls are connected with God in will and reason; however, these people are part of a greater context of beings created in God's image. The connection with Swedenborg is undeniable: "*Splendor hujus Vitae, seu Intelligentiae & Sapientiae, & ab his Justitiae, vocatur Gloria, quae quia in se omnia ista concludit, est, sicut dictum, Illa, Finis omnium finium*" (The splendor of this life, or rather the splendor of understanding and wisdom, and of the justice that comes from them, is called glory, which, because it contains and includes all those things in itself, is, as I have said, that purpose of all purposes) (§117). Thus Swedenborg follows Malebranche in letting the glory of God become the purpose of purposes. But glory keeps company with several essential concepts, which are also part of Malebranche's world of ideas. From the divine symbol in the final vision of the drama of creation flows the order bound by law, called *Justitia*. This order, "*l'ordre immuable*" (the unchangeable order), is in God himself, and should God reject his own righteousness, it would amount to self-denial, as was expressed in the dramatic meeting between the three spiritual powers in the fifth scene (§78).[53]

In that episode, order that was seemingly being destroyed through the fall of the prince of the world is restored, and the Son is given power over the evil forces so that they are made to carry out their appointed task. This scene has been interpreted above as a symbol of Christ's act of salvation, among other things. The question is, however, whether there is an influence from Malebranche also in this instance. While it is true that the drama of creation does not treat the Fall other than in the prediction of its psychological consequences, some conclusions can be drawn from previous works where providence and theodicy problems have been discussed rather extensively, especially *De anima*.[54] The line of argument here begins with the fellowship of holy men, which is the aim of creation. In order for this *societas animarum*, this society of souls, to exist, it must have a perfect government, which means that the souls are separated from one another and form a harmonic abundance of variations. In agreement with Lamm, I have emphasized above that there is a clear similarity to Leibniz in this instance, but this eschatological pattern can also be referred to the varied harmony of the organism, as is often described in the anatomical writings.

Of course, the Almighty could have created such a society directly, without taking the detour around our earth, but the result of such an act would have been entirely different. Omnipotence is limited insofar as it cannot be imperfect, changeable, or evil, which means that it could not have been able to directly create a spiritual society of the most perfect form since such a society must include the presence of all conceivable variants, from purity to impurity, from love to hatred, from highest perfection to greatest fault. God was only able to let evil appear indirectly, from the nature he had created; this thesis is supported by references to the devil's rebellion and Adam's Fall, both of which were necessary for the realization of the plan of creation.[55] The description in *De anima* is completed with a kind of infralapsarian view, closely connected to Augustine's as it is quoted in Leibniz's theodicy: "*Providentia tam singularissime quam universaliter etiam regnat in eligendis prospiciendisque illis, qui felicitatem caelestem consecuturi sunt, genus enim humanum est ipsum seminarium, et Dei civitas aut Ecclesia per universum orbem est sparsa, indeque caelestis societas collecta: ideo peculiari Dei providentia reguntur omnes illi qui electi dicuntur esse*" (Providence rules also in the smallest parts and in the greatest wholeness through choosing and predicting those who will enjoy heavenly bliss; for mankind is a nursery, and God's state or church, from which the celestial society is collected, is spread over the entire earth. Thus all those who are called the chosen ones are governed through a special providence of God).[56]

It would be a mistake to view this as if Swedenborg assumed predestination to damnation or bliss. What he refers to is a previous knowledge about how certain people will use their free will, the freedom to choose which is a *conditio sine qua non* in his—and Malebranche's and Leibniz's—theological system; moreover, during the theosophical period he will make very harsh judgements regarding the doctrines of predestination.[57] By virtue of the fact that *The Worship and Love of God* never did discuss the Fall, we do not encounter any discussion regarding the role of evil in the world harmony, except where it is forced to carry out the divine decisions against its will. Nevertheless, we find behind its entire vision the geometrically structured system of *De anima*. Evil is a necessary precondition for the perfection of the whole; without the devil's rebellion and Adam's Fall, maximum variation could not have been achieved. One remembers the paradoxical beginning of the anonymous Catholic hymn: "*O felix culpa! quae talem ac tantum meruit habere Redemptorem!*" (O, happy that fault which won for us so loving, so mighty a Savior!). With the thought of the happy consequences of the Fall, there is already *in nuce* the view that Lamm identified in *Historia creationis*, that *"skapelsehistorien bör sättas i närmare samband med Messias och hans tillkommande rike* ([the story of] Genesis should be more particularly related to the Messiah and his future realm).[58]

Without a doubt, Swedenborg is very close to Malebranche's view in this regard. Also for him, the Fall plays an essential part in the sense that it was predicted (but not predestined or carried out because of a divine act of will) before the Creation. Its consequences would be *ad majorem Dei gloriam*. The glory of God, the purpose of creation according to Malebranche as well as *The Worship and Love of God*, would become greater through the redemption than through the creation of a world where salvation was not needed: *"Ce qui fait la beauté de l'édifice spirituel de l'Eglise, c'est la diversité infinie des grâces que celui qui en est le chef répand sur toutes les parties qui la composent"* (What makes the beauty of the spiritual building of the Church is the infinite diversity of grace which he who is its head distributes to all the parts of which it is composed).[59]

While it is true that Malebranche's Creator does not have any interest in what happens with the finite world and its inhabitants, nor any need for its existence or the adoration of its human beings, God does love himself and his own glory. God's love of glory is the motif behind grace: *"Parmi tous les mondes possibles, ce monde sali par le péché est encore le meilleur qui soit. Toute la philosophie consiste à donner un sens au mot meilleur et dans la philosophie chrétienne la valeur du monde se mesure à la gloire que Dieu en tire: or rien ne peut rendre plus d'honneur à Dieu qu'un Dieu sauveur"* (Among all the possible worlds, the one sullied by sin is still the best that can be. The entire philosophy consists of giving a meaning to the word *best*; and in Christian philosophy, the value of the world is measured against the glory that God can extract from it. But nothing can give more honor to God than a God Savior).[60] Swedenborg, being a natural scientist, could not agree with this theocentrically inspired disregard for created nature, least of all in his drama of creation where a main theme is the divine influx into the world and its reflection of the eternal laws of this order. Nor does he go that far in the theosophical works, where—as Lamm has shown clearly—he otherwise followed the concept of *l'ordre immuable*, which appears all the stronger the nearer one comes to the end in *The Worship and Love of God*.[61]

However, as early as the *Oeconomia*, Swedenborg indirectly sketched the happy consequences of the Fall in a psychological context. In a general state of innocence, the human being would immediately after birth have possessed all the knowledge and perfection of *anima*, the effects of which are painted in the darkest colors. *Anima* would become arrogant and attempt to raise itself above God, its mistakes could not be repaired, and there would be no room for grace since evil would grow from the soul itself and not, as now, from the intellect. Finally, the world would become uniform, all opposites equalled, and there would be no societies on earth or in the life to come: "*& innumera plura, quae indicant placuisse Numini, quod perfectio totius resultaret ex Varietate singulorum, quae ideo respicienda est ut medium necessarium ad finem ultimum creationis*" (and innumerous other [conditions], which show that it has pleased God that the perfection of the whole should emerge from the variation of the parts, which thus must be seen as a necessary means for the final purpose of the creation).[62] One is immediately reminded of the *felix culpa* view, which has been expressed more definitely in *De anima*, although the interest in *Oeconomia* has been concerned with the psychological question of the freedom of will rather than with the eschatological consequences.

Given this background, it is easier to understand one of the difficulties entailed in the description of the two first human beings' growth *in statu integritatis*: Adam and Eve are expressly in this state of innocence (§§108, 109). Nevertheless, we have been able to follow a development in them, ruled by the celestial instructors to be sure, which in principle corresponds with their later successors; the intellect gains its illumination gradually, and only then does its bearer become a true human being.[63] It is obvious that the author himself was aware of the problem, not least from a commentary note in the introduction to the fourth scene (§43, note c), where the following is stated:

> *in integerrimum enim statum & in ipsas perfectiones, natus est; quapropter non potuit non, ejus Animae, plena potestas in ipsos Musculos & Sensoria Corporis, absque hujus Secundariae Mentis ejusque Voluntatis mediatione, a primis vitae horis, esse data: quod vero in ejus posteris aliter obtineat, evidentissimum imperfectionis signum est. Verum absque clarâ perceptione, quid Anima, & quid Mens intellectualis, & quomodo una alteri juncta, & una ab alterâ, distincta sit, non facile rationum veritates, in his perspicere licet; ob quem finem, his elucidandis, opera, in sequentium serie, impendenda est.*

> (He was born into a highly integrated and advanced state; full power over his muscles and the sensory organs of his body must have been granted to his soul from the very first hours of his life, without any need for the mediation of his secondary mind and its will. It is a very obvious proof of our imperfection that things are different for his posterity. However, without a clear understanding of what the soul and the cognitive mind are—how they are joined to one another, how they are separate—we cannot readily see the reason and truth of this matter. With this purpose in mind, we must work to elucidate this topic in what follows.)

The motivation is not a change of view but simply a respect for the chosen fable and its didactical purpose: Swedenborg gains the educational effect that Adam and Eve are more easily perceived as symbols of humankind since their growth so closely resembles the *tabula rasa* education of their successors, and he has also repeatedly exceeded the frame in his anticipating descriptions of a fallen species. This has been done in the spirit of education but in opposition to a formal consequence, which had been broken from the start.[64] At the same time, the theoretical philosophy must have been difficult to unite with the basic note of paradisiacal purity and bliss, which characterizes this work: how could this atmosphere match an interpretation of the Fall as a precondition for the harmony of the universe?

Together with other elements in the theoretical background, which also entail difficult opposites, such as evil and the symbolism of emanation or the relationship between God the Father and his Son, this could be another reason that Swedenborg abandoned his plan—or was forced through a vision to abandon it, which perhaps means the same—to treat even the Fall within the frame of the fable. The stiff and inhuman geometrical program, which was provided in *De anima* and which was inspired primarily by Malebranche and Leibniz, could not be included in the overwhelming vision of the influx of life and love in the rigid mass. This vision has its personal basis in the dream experiences of what the kingdom of innocence really is: he has himself been allowed to sense the bliss that a life in accordance with the divine order brings, and he is still terrified of breaking this order. He wishes to convey this personal experience with his didactic poem, at least as far as the yet-not-perfected certitude can lead him. Because of that, the intellectual impulses that can be identified behind the work have been given a different coloring, an intensity and a beseeching importance that they almost always lack in their origin. They have turned from theoretical models to experienced reality.

An evaluation of the sources behind the image of God in *The Worship and Love of God*, which is finally expressed in terms of the order of God and which is ultimately molded in the burning kernel of light in the final vision, gives in principle the same results as the cosmological and the psychological discourses. Although a multitude of influences is discernible, the strongest connection is with the great rationalist tradition from Descartes to Leibniz and Wolff, and in the final sections Malebranche must be seen as the primary source with the basic terms so often used by Swedenborg—*Gloria Dei, justitia seu ordo immutabilis,* and *amor Dei*—as well as his intimate correlation of the psychophysical problem of interaction with the concept of God.

Moreover, important impulses from the poetry and philosophy of both the Bible and antiquity are present. Swedenborg used a wide definition of antiquity, which included patristic studies, and the importance of Augustine has been emphasized above. Swedenborg's rationalist masters, as well as the Pietists, are close to this Church Father in theological and sometimes also philosophical issues. It is quite clear from the excerpt material that the teachings of Augustine had been imparted to Swedenborg through his own studies as well as through the mediation primarily of Malebranche and Leibniz. Placing *The Worship and Love of God* within a wider Augustinian tradition is also supported by the Neoplatonic language of symbols. While it is true that the numerous consultations with *Aristotle's Theology* have left significant and portentous traces in the drama of creation, Swedenborg is essentially close to the already strongly Neoplatonically colored but centrally Christian chain of ideas, the main links of which are Augustine, Malebranche, and Leibniz. The image of God as the spiritual light after the testimony of the excerpts can be related partly to Malebranche's psycho-theological reasonings on certain Bible quotes in the commentary to *Recherche de la vérité*. Thus the handing over of the ancient symbol can be partly identified.[65]

The image of God seems to be preconditioned by a reading of Milton to as little an extent as the cosmological and biological parts. The heavenly majesty that appears in *Paradise Lost* is not Swedenborg's God. In the drama of creation, we do not meet the celestial king in person as in Milton, but rather we encounter Augustine's indeterminate infinity, symbolized by the light of the sun and present in the human heart, and Malebranche's *"l'ordre immuable"*; the purpose laws, according to which God's order is developed during the course of the creation of the world, are indeed reminiscent of Aristotle and other ancients but must be seen primarily as a result of Leibniz's influence. Barely a century separates *Paradise Lost* and *The Worship and Love of God*, but this period saw, among many other things, the introduction of new scientific and philosophical ideas, the traces of which we so often have been able to discern in Swedenborg's works and the influences of which have also determined the development of the image of God.

## The Celestial Society

In the important manuscript volume cod. 88–93, included in one of the covers is a list of the works that Swedenborg planned for the years 1740–1747; it is introduced with a work called *De cerebro* (On the brain) and finished with the title *Civitas Dei* (The city of God).[66] The catalogue is a very general sketch and is but one of numerous examples of plans and rearrangements. In one instance, Acton compiled Swedenborg's different works, printed, written, or sketched, with a published plan of the gigantic synthesis *Regnum animale*, and in this process he claimed that almost all of the parts in this disposition are covered by the works produced. This conclusion—perhaps somewhat exaggerated because of the author's New Church disposition to see a divinely inspired pattern behind the visionary's "preparation period"—is given an important complement: "To the above Parts may be added an eighteenth part with the title, listed in all the earlier plans, 'The City of God.' By this title, we understand Swedenborg to mean the contemplation of the universe as the theater of Divine Wisdom, and the dwelling place of the most High. It was to attain the heights from which alone he could contemplate this City of God that Swedenborg pursued his arduous toil and labor; it was the hope of this vision that inspired him in his studies and meditations; and it was the vision itself that he finally describes in that poetic fruit and crown of his philosophical works, the *Worship and Love of God.*"[67]

When Swedenborg widens the psychological perspective across the border of death in the finale of *Oeconomia regni animalis*, the Augustinian term *civitas Dei* appears as a description of the earthly society, which is the correspondence to and the nursery for the heavenly kingdom:

> *Quod exsolutum a vinculis & laqueis terrestrium in omnem sui Corporis formam coaliturum sit, & victurum vitam omni imaginatione puriorem. Tum quod nulla sit actiuncula ex consulto, & nulla vocula ex consensu, in vita ejus corporea, edita, quae non affulgente luce sapientiae, inhaerenter designatae, tunc ante ejus conscientiae judicium, distincte compariturae sint. Demum, quod Societas Animarum sit in Caelis, cujus seminarium est Civitas Dei in terris, in qua & e qua respicitur finis finium.*
>
> (The soul after having been liberated from the ties and chains of earthly things will grow together to the whole shape of its body and live a life purer than can be imagined. Furthermore not even the smallest act in its corporeal life has been done consciously and not the smallest word been uttered with the approval of the will, which will not then appear clearly in the brilliant light from a wisdom imperviously arranged, that is in front of its conscience's court of law. Finally there is a society of souls in heaven, the nursery of which is the city of God on earth; in this society and through it the end of ends is viewed.)[68]

In his exposition of this thesis, Swedenborg refers to Paul's Areopagus sermon among other things, the text of which we have earlier found traces in the drama of creation and which has evidently been an important Bible reference for him. The apostle's speech to the people of Athens about an unknown God echoes in the treatment of the *civitas Dei* concept, which we encounter in *De anima*, also in this instance with the same meaning as in *Oeconomia*, although somewhat more specific.[69] As would be expected, the city of God is not identified with any particular religion or church, but God selects its citizens from all faiths, as long as the essential demands of

Christianity are met—to love God above everything and one's neighbor as oneself, since this is the law of all laws—while different churches are seen only as means to fulfil them. Paul describes his view in a similar manner, when he identifies *Deus ignotus* to the sceptically listening people of Athens: temples and rites are *adiaphora*; from an eschatological perspective, only the message of Christ and the demand for human improvement are essential.

Lamm tentatively suggests that a Pietistic influence is discernible in this syncretistic dream, and he stresses that Dippel had preached the same doctrine about the communities' entering into one single "*Geisteskirche*" (church of spirits).[70] It is also evident that the historical growth of Pietism provides it with a different attitude toward confessional disparities than orthodoxy; syncretistic tendencies appear early and have become very strong in Zinzendorf, for instance.[71] However, these trends were also present within the orthodox tradition: during his travel abroad in the 1690s, Erik Benzelius Jr. came into contact with several advocates of syncretism, both in its older form at the University of Helmstedt, and in its modern, unionist version for which Leibniz was a key inspiration.[72] I have pointed out above that contemporary interest in the Cabbala is connected to these syncretistic ideas, the precondition of which is weariness with battles of doctrine and religious persecution; Leibniz himself was also inspired by this cabbalistic reading.[73] Given how Swedenborg conceived of his celestial society, it would seem more relevant to refer to Leibniz primarily with regard to its ecumenical character; a brief overview of *societas animarum*, such as it is introduced in *De anima*, will strengthen the argument.

When studying Swedenborg's understanding of providence, I emphasized—in agreement with Lamm—the importance that Leibniz's *principium identitatis indiscernibilium* (the principle of the identity of non-separable phenomena) had on the harmonically varied heavenly community in *De anima*. So important is this *varietas harmonica* that it motivates the tempter's evil deeds and the Fall of Adam, since a state of innocence makes every difference between the souls impossible; the term *antiquitas*, which is used here, must be interpreted in the light of the idea discussed above of the Golden Age and the general state of integrity. However, one can simultaneously discern a combination of the allusion to antique poetic ideas of the heroic era in the prologue to the drama of creation and the theosophical allegory on Genesis behind the view, which was compelled by the system.[74] In any event, the holy community cannot appear in its perfect form until all possible variations have been used up: "*hanc suam ecclesiam Deus ex universo orbe colligit, usque dum omnia loca occupata sint, seu dum aliqua differentia supersit, quae in forma regiminis necessaria sit, ut perfectissima evadat*" (this church of God collects from the entire globe, until all its places are occupied, or as long as any difference remains, which is necessary for the form of government, so that it can become the most perfect.).[75]

The celestial society must have a governor, a man without sin, a vanquisher of the temptations of the senses, but also a divine being: Jesus Christ, *salvator et conservator noster* (our savior and protector), is the name Swedenborg uses. Through faith in Christ and through love, human beings have the only possibility of approaching God's throne; it is the same idea that there is no salvation except through Christ, which we have encountered before. In *De anima*, we also find a similar complement that even non-Christians could apply to the merits of the Savior.[76] In the name of consistency, *societas animarum infelicium* (the society of unhappy souls) or hell, which is the biggest sector, is placed as an opposite; however, after doomsday, it will fall apart since it is held together only by fear of its leader, the devil, and not by any mutual love as is the case with the celestial society.[77]

The connection between these eschatological ideas and the doctrine of series and degrees, where the influence from Leibniz is similarly evident, seems obvious. Nevertheless, the image of God's kingdom on earth and its heavenly correspondence do not bring us very far outside views held within confessional Christianity.[78] Nor has Swedenborg achieved any concretion in his view of the society of souls, even if the description in *Oeconomia* is more original than the Bible paraphrase in *De anima*. I have emphasized previously that the concept of *varietas harmonica* has been used to underline the parallel between microcosm and macrocosm in *Oeconomia*. This pattern can be studied in direct neurological application in *De fibra*, for instance, in the following conclusion of a chapter on the variation of the fibers and nerves:

> *Varietas singulorum entium in omnibus mundi regnis, animali scilicet, vegetabili et minerali, imo in mundo circumfluo seu atmosphaerico, est universae naturae necessaria qualitas seu attributum, quae omnem aequalitatem et identitatem tanquam sui destructivam aversatur et horret, nam sine varietate nihil datur in natura aliquid et quale.*
>
> (The variation that exists between the separate beings in all the realms of the world—that is to say, the animal, plant, and mineral kingdoms, yea in the fluent world or the atmosphere— is a necessary quality or an attribute in the universal nature, which with abhorrence turns away from all similarity and identity and fears them as something destructive to her; for without variation there is neither matter nor quality in nature.)[79]

After this accomplished anatomical harmony, there may easily follow a transformation of the human figure to the heavenly community: perhaps Plato's image of society as a correspondence to the human soul in the *Re-*

*public* was also influential.[80] Most important is the liberation of the imaginative power, which the doctrine of correspondence brought about. There is a significant note in the excerpt collection cod. 36–110 among the sketches of a continuation of *Oeconomia* and *Regnum animale*, which were written after the extensive Bible references under correspondence headlines:

> *Societas caelestis comparanda est cum corpore unanimi, quod licet infinitis constat partibus, usque tum ita unitae sunt, ut una sentiat et quod altera patitur et agit, sic ut omnis sit communio. Verbo societas caelestis comparanda est cum corpore, cui praeest caput, quod est Jesus Christus. Plura sunt in corpore membra, ita plures societates, quae conspirent.*
>
> (The heavenly society is comparable to a unanimous body that consists of an infinite number of parts; however, these are so closely united that the one part can sense what the other feels or does, so that everything forms a community. The heavenly society is in one word comparable to a body that is ruled by the head, which is Jesus Christ. There are many limbs in a body, likewise many congregations, which all harmonize.)[81]

In the concluding vision of the drama of creation, this image is extended to become a human body with the Only-Begotten as its intellect: the fable has opened the possibility for Swedenborg to use the correspondential speech of the biblical writers, which he wished for among the excerpts when lamenting the straitjacket of contemporary language.[82] In all probability, reading the Bible was also important. Again it is Paul who is quoted most frequently, and among the excerpts under the headline *Correspondentia typica*—the art of correspondences, which according to *Clavis hieroglyphica* are to be found in the biblical parables that in the New Testament represent the kingdom of God and the heavenly community, *"regnum Dei & societas caelestis"*—we find several examples of Paul's image of the Christian congregation as a body where Christ is the head (among others, 1Corinthians 6:15; 12:12, 14, 27; Ephesians 4:12, 15, 16; Colossians 1:18).[83] However, the annotator has also accepted the idea of the human being as a temple of God: *"vos templum estis Dei viventis"* (for you are the temple of the living God, according to 2Corinthians 6:16, and in the more concrete shape of the body as a temple of the Spirit [1Corinthians 6:19]).[84]

The image of the heavenly kingdom as a temple belongs to the permanent patterns of Christian eschatology; it has been exemplified above from Malebranche. Naturally this symbol was as familiar to Swedenborg as, for instance, the idea of the heavenly Jerusalem; this much is obvious from his eager reading of the epistle to the Hebrews. That Swedenborg instead chose the human form as a symbol of the holy community is easily explained by means of the theoretical background sketched here; the doctrine

of correspondence gave the skilled physiologist and anatomist the authority to interpret, for instance, the following Pauline text in that direction:

> *There are* also celestial bodies, and bodies terrestrial; but the
> glory of the celestial *is* one, and the *glory* of the terrestrial *is* an-
> other. *There is* one glory of the sun, and another glory of the
> moon, and another glory of the stars: for *one* star differeth from
> *another* star in glory. So also *is* the resurrection of the dead. It is
> sown in corruption; it is raised in incorruption: It is sown in dis-
> honour; it is raised in glory: it is sown in weakness; it is raised
> in power: It is sown a natural body; it is raised a spiritual body.
> There is a natural body, and there is a spiritual body. And so it
> is written, The first man Adam was made a living soul; the last
> Adam *was made* a quickening spirit. Howbeit that *was* not first
> which is spiritual, but that which is natural; and afterward that
> which is spiritual. The first man *is* of the earth, earthy: the sec-
> ond man *is* the Lord from heaven.[85]

The Bible excerpts provide an opportunity to tie together Swedenborg's
human-shaped heavenly community with, for instance, Malebranche's spiritual temple, since Paul's sermon on the body as a temple of the Spirit is in
itself an example, a parable, that falls under Swedenborg's category *Correspondentia typica*. In light of the author's own practice, such speculative
interpretations become not only justified but indeed necessary.

As is well known, this correspondence between the human body and the
heavenly kingdom is extended in sometimes provocatively concrete form
during the theosophical period, and even God is given a human shape for
the visionary.[86] Lamm has mentioned a number of mystics as parallels, if
not predecessors, primarily ones inspired by the Cabbala: the names comprise a series from Plato to Pico della Mirandola and Paracelsus, and many
more could be added, for instance, Cicero (106–43 BCE) with his important
*De natura deorum*, a text that Swedenborg certainly drew from.[87] It would
be a hopeless mission to determine one precise model in such a varied tradition, which must have influenced Swedenborg's general education to a
greater or lesser degree. Lamm desists from such a venture and emphasizes
instead the seer's originality in connecting the remarkable building blocks,
of which the most significant ones are to be found in monadology and the
author's own application of its principle of harmony on the organisms.

Artistically this originality perhaps comes across most forcefully in *The
Worship and Love of God* where the idea of *maximus homo*, the Grand
Man, appears as a suggestion and an image. It provided the poet with the
opportunity to tie together the different scenes of the enormous drama into
an interconnected entity, both theoretically and aesthetically. The
reader/viewer is allowed to follow the preparations for the Creation up to
the arrival of Adam in the three first scenes, while the following three de-

scribe the education and union of the human couple. In the last passage, which falls outside of the hexaemeral scene division, we experience the summarizing vision, which prophetically depicts how the offspring of this human couple form the heavenly kingdom, which still only appears in human shape. Its terrestrial breeding ground, *civitas Dei in terris*—the City of God on earth—as it was called in *Oeconomia*, is in this vision the multitude of human souls, molded in the last of world eggs, and the qualities of these souls decide their place in the spiritual community.

For natural reasons, Swedenborg did not find space for any detailed description of the nursery of the heavenly kingdom in his rather compressed series of images, nor did he terrify the firstborn bride and groom with any harbinger of the haunted inhabitants of the opposite society: in the shimmering vision in the sky, only exultation at God's order and its utmost end are featured. Perhaps it is reasonable to interpret this as a sign that the poet at last managed to capture the dreamer's ambivalence and disruption in a symbol that had not yet been petrified by the certainty of the prophet. From the world egg symbol—which expresses in the clearest manner the moment of an organic birth process that is such a central motif for Swedenborg's drama of creation from its beginning to the finale, and in which so many influences were joined in a personal synthesis, such as the ancient parallel between microcosm and macrocosm, the apostle Paul with his figurative speech on the congregation as a body with Christ as the head (1Cor.15:40–47), the Church Father Augustine with his *civitas Dei* symbol creating a pattern for millennia, Malebranche's "*l'ordre immuable*," Leibniz's and Wolff's perfect harmony, and the microscopists' humble awe in front of the wonders of nature—is hatched the society of holy men, in which the loneliest and most disharmonious human shall once and for all find peace and the communion of souls.

# 9

৯৮

# CONCLUSION

The analysis of Swedenborg's *The Worship and Love of God* has illuminated the research problems initially traced. Although several less important themes have been only touched upon, it should be clear how this work
summarizes the author's entire development, scientific, literary, and personal. Almost all the published works and manuscript drafts, in which the
seeker put down his thoughts during thirty-five arduous years, are reflected
in one form or the other in *The Worship and Love of God*. We have been
able to follow Swedenborg's journey from the Seneca studies of his dissertation and the mechanistic psychoanalysis of the England traveller, via cosmological essays of the Polhem assistant to the grand system structures of
the natural philosopher in *Principia rerum naturalium*, *Oeconomia regni
animalis*, and *Regnum animale*. A survey of such a comprehensive production, which is somewhat removed from the usual fields of literary history,
must by its nature involve extensive documentation, and in addition the
motif study has also at times led to lesser-known sources. For these reasons, it is appropriate to summarize the most significant results.

The synthesizing nature of the drama of creation immediately strikes the
reader. However, just as the work encompasses so many basic motifs from
his previous writings, this feature again represents a higher concentration
of a characteristic present in all the works. The need for a comprehensive
view, a synthesis, is a prime mover in all of Swedenborg's activities, as he
expressed as early as in his youthful correspondence with Benzelius. In the
young enthusiast, we find a naïve and boastful joy of knowledge, for which
no details are too insignificant. This feature lingers throughout in the mature writings, but it cannot overshadow the underlying goal. Swedenborg
does not conduct unbiased research in the modern sense—that would have
been an anachronism—nor could he be regarded as a member of the large
group of contemporary scientists whose dedicated observations of details
with primitive instruments gave them honorary seats in the history of science. He earned his contemporary fame primarily with geological and min-

eralogical studies, connected to his profession; and posterity's admiration for his neuro-physiological works do not relate to his own discoveries but rather to an ability to compile and apply the observations of others. This does not involve any criticism in itself, since Swedenborg himself viewed his contribution in this manner. Nonetheless, it is important to recall when conducting a fair evaluation.

The need for synthesis is expressed in several forms. Among the earliest, we find the ambition, so typical for the age, to bridge the gap between spirit and matter, and thereby to overcome the principal dualism of Cartesianism. Given the orientation toward science and technology, which the twenty-year-old almost programmatically acquired during his long stay abroad, it is natural that the first attempts at solutions were based on mechanistic theories: the life of the soul can be explained in a pattern of tremulations and can be calculated in geometrical categories. In principle, the same view remains right through the mid-1730s, although in a modified shape, like a harmonically tuned membrane system to which the macrocosmic elements of *Principia* have been connected. However, the complications are successively more strongly felt, and it is symptomatic that in this very context we encounter the great philosophers of his time in an eclectic combination of Malebranche, Locke, Leibniz, and Wolff. The proximity to Leibniz and Wolff is perhaps what comes across most strongly in this psychophysical context; at times there is an almost servile tone when Swedenborg, while suppressing the differences, strives to associate himself with the great rationalists. On one or two occasions, the reverse is apparent: now the differences take the form of a rebellious irritation, which incidentally returns in the celestial debates of the theosophist.

The combination of philosophical authorities in itself displays the need for synthesis, as does the intense biological studies conducted after *Principia*, which in their turn contributed new points of departure for the discussion on interaction between soul and body. The renewed interest in this research is expressed partly in an enthusiasm for knowledge of details, like that of the young student, but also in a hectic eagerness to reach quickly the illusive goal, the solution to the riddle of the soul. The humble awe felt by the microscopists confronted with the abundant life in nature strengthens Swedenborg's conviction that the Divine is revealed in the material world, as Paul taught. This is the same faith that his kinsman Linnaeus combined with his scientific objectivity, but Swedenborg's need for a holistic view cannot be stopped at the frontiers of science. As Lamm pointed out with such admirable clarity, in the frenetic speculation during the decade before *The Worship and Love of God*, we encounter an increasingly profound impulse toward religious certainty and an insight that the analytical method of science cannot reach all the way. This leads to a strange antiphon changing between a systematic fulfilment of gigantic writing plans and confirming signs from guiding powers, signals that at last also permeate the manuscripts.[1]

The fascinating notes in the *Dream Diary* conclude with a notice that *The Worship and Love of God* is being written, and it is a tempting, albeit unfortunately an uncertain, hypothesis that the work had engaged the visionary so much that the crisis was temporarily overcome. When the theoretical tensions became more forceful toward the end, the poetic imagination no longer managed to channel the psychic unrest, and the fable was interrupted in the middle of the exposition of a prophetic vision on the fate of the universe. Swedenborg can no longer hide behind the Adam of the fable, but is given a divine command to dedicate his life to openly preaching a message close to the one in *The Worship and Love of God*, but from which the most conflicting elements have been removed. The yearning after a whole and indivisible truth to replace Cartesian dualism reached a goal far removed from the theoretical starting point but close to the heritage of spiritualism and biblicism that Jesper Swedberg passed on to his progeny. Through the religious crisis, in which the figure of the father appeared to warn and admonish, the circle had been closed.

In the early works, another element appears that also reflects the longing for synthesis and that in itself portends what will come. In support of his different hypotheses, the young Emanuel Swedberg preferred to call upon the fables of ancient poetry together with the words of the Scriptures, and there is no doubt as to the familiarity the Latin amateur poet felt with ancient verse. In itself, this characteristic could be seen as rhetorical ornamentation to contemporary taste, but that interpretation is insufficient in the long run: the ambition to unite the wisdom of the ancients with the experience of the moderns becomes stronger and more significant with time and reaches its peak in *The Worship and Love of God*. It is a characteristic of the age, a reflection of the *"querelle des anciens et des modernes,"* which can be traced in the reading during the visit to England. However, for Swedenborg, it will acquire a mystical dimension through the doctrine of correspondence.

One of the most important pervading symbols in the drama of creation is the egg, in the shape of the ancient world egg, of eggs hatching animals or humans, or of the imaginary origin of the heavenly community. Behind this symbol, the analysis has observed a rich flora of scientific theories. With regard to the cosmological egg, I have argued that Swedenborg was inspired by Thomas Burnet's *Telluris theoria sacra* and that this source must be regarded as significant for his entire orientation. It is a telling testimony both about Swedenborg's need for a comprehensive view and his poetic imagination that the strongest impressions he gained from the visit to the English intellectual environment of the 1710s were not collected from the great Newton but from a scientifically obsolete yet stylistically elegant theory builder like Burnet. In this instance, it is primarily his survey of the ancient cosmological poetry so rich in quotes that acted as a symbol-covered well of wisdom.

Among the esoteric sources of knowledge, Burnet also mentions the hieroglyphs. The cosmologist thus conjures up a primordial tradition, but its affluent ramifications are impossible to trace in detail. At a first glance, it would seem futile to try to determine how Swedenborg's hieroglyphic speculations relate to this tradition. However, in his *Clavis hieroglyphica*, he referred to a work supposed to be written by Aristotle in support; and on the basis of this work, which is Neoplatonic in origin, Lamm regarded Swedenborg's conception, the doctrine of correspondence, as a result of studies in Neoplatonic metaphysics. Without wishing to deny—or indeed being able to do so—the Neoplatonic inspiration that Swedenborg received both on this work and from so many of his other masters (Augustine, Malebranche, and Leibniz, to mention just the most significant ones), I felt it appropriate to emphasize another aspect of his thinking.

When studying the excerpt material that applies to *The Worship and Love of God*, one receives the definite impression that the origin of the doctrine of correspondence should be examined against the background of the psychophysical interaction problems. From hieroglyph notes, which caught his interest in Wolff's *Psychologia empirica*, there is a connection with Wolff's and Locke's reflections on the philosophical language of universals. This imaginary thought instrument of antiquity and the Renaissance acquired a mathematically logical character through Descartes and Leibniz. When Swedenborg attempts to realize his diffuse plans of constructing such a language, a project that further underlines the ever-more urgent need for synthesis, it is evidently done with these thinkers as his models. After the self-evident failure—it is significant that its basic elements are the blood and the fibres, the immediate physical foundation of the psyche—Swedenborg declares that he wishes to replace it with a doctrine of correspondence and representation, which is the key to natural and spiritual *arcana*. From what I believe can be discerned from the excerpts, this substitution is due in large part to the influence from Malebranche, whose theocentric psychology of correspondence left profound traces on Swedenborg's thinking, in several cases crucial to his entire outlook on life.

The theoretical background of the doctrine of correspondence in the hieroglyph tradition is interesting not only for the ideas of the drama of creation but also for its form. The basic element of the composition is the image, and stylistically the work can be characterized as a number of symbolic pictures and scenes, which are explained and commented upon in notes and by spiritual beings who explain their significance. This mode of expression in itself should give association to the *"ars emblematica,"* the art of forging devices, or fair sensual pictures, to quote Andreas Rydelius, an idea that seems all the more apt as emblematic research has emphasized the connection between the interest in hieroglyphs and the taste for allegory. In this tradition, symbolic poetry becomes a bearer of wisdom that cannot be expressed with scientific explicitness. This idea has been found in Francis Bacon's works, but one could as easily quote Thomas Burnet.

Therefore, it is not surprising to find a note among Swedenborg's correspondential excerpts regarding an emblematical dictionary with the attractive title *Mundus symbolicus*. From the textual analysis, it is extremely tempting to pinpoint a specific influence behind the dramatic battle between the three spiritual powers; given the enormous extent of emblem literature, however, I have chosen to look upon Swedenborg's scene as a parallel occurrence, kindred spirits rather than a direct imitation. This view seems to be more generally applicable as well. In *The Worship and Love of God*, I have seen a work that had been imagined emblematically and that has an obvious connection with the emblematic and generally allegorical tradition, vis-à-vis basic atmosphere and intellectual background. However, the detailed execution must be explained with regard to the author's previous production.

This is particularly clear if one considers the poetic impressions behind Swedenborg's drama of creation. Martin Lamm viewed the work as a part of the hexaemeral epics, a movement that flourished in the late Renaissance and that reached its peak in Milton's *Paradise Lost*, a hypothesis that has been generally accepted. In my evaluation of Lamm's reasoning, I have argued that it is impossible to establish any binding proof that this theory is incorrect; only probability arguments can be used, as is so often the case when discussing influences. To begin with I have attempted to provide a picture of how complex the hexaemeron tradition really is and how difficult a study of sources becomes because of this fact. Lamm has only touched upon the peak of the genre, and not its broad and somewhat obscure base. What may seem like direct influences when fleetingly comparing two works within the same genre can often be referred to a common source, a difficulty present when making a comparison between Milton and Swedenborg (this is incidentally clear also from Lamm's discourse). In my opinion, the motifs that Lamm believed to be imitations of Milton can all be interpreted as the result of hexaemeral studies conducted by both authors. This is true in the case of the creation of the first humans, Eve at the well mirror, and the battle between the spiritual powers. As regards Milton's supposed influence on Swedenborg's development toward a doctrine of emanations and an anthropomorphic world of spirits, I cannot see any imperative reason to presuppose such an influence, since Swedenborg's philosophy is consistently determined by the basically synthetic character of the system.

In addition, Swedenborg quoted and referred to only ancient poets in his previous works as is also the case in *The Worship and Love of God*. This in its turn is explained by the theoretical foundation, the interest in hieroglyph concepts, and the doctrine of correspondence, ancient poetry being an expression of the philosophy of the epoch, both of which are determined by a wisdom that was later lost. The combination of Genesis myths—for instance, Eve's creation—and the fables of ancient poetry seems crucial to me. The purpose of the didactic drama of creation is to represent a synthesis of the experience of modern science and ancient wisdom, and the form has been adapted to the latter of these two elements. When interpreting the symbols of the Apollonian myth, Swedenborg states that the inability of the moderns to understand their meaning must be ascribed to the darkness in which the prince of the world has managed to envelop their intellects. Evidently Swedenborg had the same kind of people in mind as in the prologue to *Regnum animale*, where he spoke of those who can accept only reasons apparent to their intellects; theses about the soul they view as fantasies and fables, and therefore they kneel in prayer to nature (§22).

By using a fable structure as the ancients did in a work about the worship of God, not nature, and in this manner shaping his comprehensive vision of nature, humanity, and God, while simultaneously quoting modern empirical science in footnotes, Swedenborg strives to awaken the contemporary intellectuals (writing in Latin limited the number of readers to an educated elite) and make them realize that they were led astray by the devil. This amounts to the same method as the one Thomas Burnet used in his *Telluris theoria sacra*, where the fables of ancient poetry are reinterpreted to support a natural philosophy, although the cause is far more important in Swedenborg's case. In such an exclusive intellectual milieu, there is hardly any place for *Paradise Lost*. Of course, this does not mean that Swedenborg was unaware of the great epic's existence. He would certainly have been familiar with Spegel as well as Milton and many other hexaemeral predecessors, but that is far from saying that there was an immediate influence.

The apparently dramatic form given to *The Worship and Love of God*, which was observed by a confused contemporary critic, could in itself be seen as a hexaemeron characteristic beyond Milton, since the tradition also encompasses works of drama. However, as far as I can see, the scene structure was not caused by any direct impulses from other dramas of creation but rather by the classical *topoi* originating from Plato, called "*theatrum mundi*": it has been combined with the perfect number, according to Augustine, that of the six days of creation. While Swedenborg showed an interest in scenic art and theaters in his travel notes, the main stress ought to be put on the symbolic world theatre motif, which has been used so often in religious allegory and to which incidentally Jesper Swedberg alludes when he describes his autobiography as a "*theatrum providentiae divinae.*"[2] Thus, even this motif points toward antiquity in a wider sense. All these impulses from the ancients go far beyond Ovid; but in an environment of allegory like this one, it is reasonable to feel the presence of the *Metamorphoses* poet more strongly than that of other masters, especially since the young Emanuel Swedberg published metrical Ovidian paraphrases. The essential issue is, however, that the doctrine of correspondence dissolved the borders between poetry and philosophy to a greater degree than heretofore in the general hexaemeron tradition.

This does not mean that this wisdom of the ancients—the *sapientia veterum*—is accepted without further notice. On the contrary, it is evaluated in the light of modern empirical science and is adjusted to it. This happens already in the cosmological works, but it becomes even more evident in the biological ones, where the sources are introduced more explicitly. The sources contain most of the modern champions of anatomy, primarily those who pioneered the use of the microscope. Swedenborg was one of many contemporaries who were fascinated by the new possibilities of observation, and the revelations of the microscopists regarding the presence of life in the most insignificant contexts in nature had great importance for the change of focus after *Principia*. For the comprehensive view, the anatomists' studies of fibers, nerve threads, and blood veins were the most important, since they could be attached to the Cartesian life spirits. Tremendous perspectives regarding the solution of the psychophysical interaction problem suddenly appeared. Leeuwenhoek's analysis of blood is used to support Swedenborg's theory of the cycle of the soul flow, which nonetheless could not be displayed in the categories of everyday language. The attempt to grasp it in the philosophical language of universals failed, but in its place an angelic being appears in the drama of creation like a heavenly Leeuwenhoek, and now there are no limits to the enlarging powers of the lenses: in the anatomical demonstration in Eve's garden, the titanic dream is realized. When the author speaks in a preceding note of literature's now reaching its highest peak, it can be regarded as a general contribution to the modernity debate; but against the background of his hopes of becoming the one to unite the two streams into a greater whole, it sounds rather ominous. In *The Worship and Love of God,* Swedenborg has a being who possesses the wisdom of the ancients to an eminent degree conduct a demonstration according to a modern method, and thus—*mutatis mutandis*—his ambitions become a reality.

However, the need for synthesis is not satisfied only through this union of ancient and modern. In addition, we find the testimony of the Scriptures and the Christian faith. In itself, this ambition is not original; in fact, Swedenborg had been raised with it. Concordance with the Word is a necessary precondition for all scientific truths, he assures us in the works of his youth, and biblical quotations are often used to support even quite peculiar remarks, in a similar fashion to Burnet, for instance. Up to and including *Principia*, it is most often about biblical ideas on Creation, and only seldom does any profoundly personal tone sound in these references. Nor are the ideas of Christ, with the help of which Swedenborg attempts to tie together the infinite with finite existence in *De Infinito*, anything more than intellectual hypotheses; from that point of view, it is illuminating to compare this treatise with *The Worship and Love of God*, which was foreshadowed within it.

The atmosphere gradually changes in the psychological theorizing from *Oeconomia regni animalis*, in which it ends in fundamental theological problems. From the brooding about psychophysical interaction grow the essential questions about our salvation. How shall the innermost knowledge be found? How can the soul regain communion with God, which the first humans could enjoy *in statu integritatis*? In order to find answers to such questions, the personal urgency of which the systematics cannot conceal, Swedenborg resorts to the Christian idea of salvation: *salvatio non sit nisi per Christum*—without the intervention of the Son, there cannot be access to the Father. In the dream crisis, these ideas of Christ reach a visionary culmination, and they occasionally turn to an ecstatic cult of the crucifix, which may be seen as one of several Moravian elements. In the interpretations of the dreams, Swedenborg sometimes quotes his published statements on the Christological problem and confirms them with his visionary experiences.

The fundamental synthetic attitude comes across strongly in these ideas of Christ. As Lamm and others emphasized, Swedenborg opposed most vigorously the Lutheran doctrine about justification by faith alone, *sola fide*, and he could not accept the orthodox dogma of the church any more than his father, the bishop, could. In its place, he puts a syncretistic view, according to which the ignorant gentiles can also become members of the divine kingdom. The terrestrial nursery of this kingdom, *civitas Dei in terris*, is not fenced in by any confessional barriers. It is possible that his temporary attraction to the Moravian Brethren can be partially explained by their relative syncretism; however, one ought to connect his view primarily with Leibniz's unifying ambitions. The links with the rationalists Malebranche and Leibniz become even more obvious due to efforts to bind the idea of the Messiah with the story of Creation: it is the pattern from *De Infinito*, which returns in the Christological nexus ideas in the works leading up to the drama of creation, but at the same time it is a reflection of a rationalist theology.

In light of this, it is quite natural that the most important biblical authority in the excerpts is the Apostle Paul and that the references to the Church Father Augustine are so numerous. In *The Worship and Love of God*, where there are almost no quotations, there are clear allusions to both these authorities. However, due to the synthetic endeavor, the biblical basis seldom emerges strongly. The Son is not called the Messiah, neither Christ nor the Word, but God's love and the Mediator; and the reader will often associate these names with ancient mythological ideas rather than

276 ❀ A Drama of Creation

with Christian ones. The battle between the Son and the prince of the world recalls the battle between Eros and Eris in ancient mythology and philosophy more readily than it does biblical spiritual powers in the sky. The doctrine of correspondence gives a reasonable explanation for this. The lack of biblical references is all the more striking, as Swedenborg's writings immediately following the drama of creation consist entirely of Bible exegesis with visionary comments. Since the fabled opus could not be completed, and its theoretical tensions could not be settled in a mythical synthesis, merciful providence provided the seeker with the Bible exegesis mission, through which he would attain the peace of certainty. He was well prepared for this task through his scientific work, which largely consisted of analyses of different texts, and he was liberated from the superhuman work of summarizing the collective wisdom of humankind without assistance.

In his intense search for a comprehensive view, Swedenborg must have encountered the same difficulties as other monists before and after him: an all-embracing system always encompasses opposing elements and theoretical tensions to different degrees. When comparing Swedenborg's world of ideas with the great contemporary philosophical systems, we see that his aspiration for synthesis was problematic from the beginning. His scientific interests made it impossible for him to accept the negative assessment of the reliability of sensual impressions held by radical rationalism, but he was too firmly rooted in a Cartesian tradition to be able to agree with a pure empiricism. Therefore, he sought the solution in an eclectic compromise between Descartes, Malebranche, Leibniz, Locke, and Wolff, and in addition in a quite understandable association with Aristotle, the general orientation of whom corresponds so well with his own. It is hardly surprising that such an eclecticism led to inconsistencies; however, his bold attempt at uniting rationalism and empiricism is an interesting forerunner to what Immanuel Kant (1724–1804) half a century later claimed to do, with all the consequences that led to the synthetic philosophy of Romanticism.[3] From a professionally philosophical point of view, this kind of comparison is hardly meaningful: Swedenborg was never a sharp thinker—on the contrary, he displays many logical absurdities, such as, for instance, the uninhibited use of the *quaternio terminorum* for the doctrine of correspondence.

The theoretical difficulties are felt most forcefully in *The Worship and Love of God*, since it summarizes so many thoughts and motifs spread throughout the previous writings. In my analysis, I have dwelled particularly on the contrast between the symbolism of emanation and the belief in a creation from nothing, with which the theodicy problem is closely connected. The tensions are extremely forceful here; however, they are common property to all Christian theology with a Platonic character. The excerpt material offers a specific possibility about the background: a characteristic note from Leibniz's theodicy speaks of the central comparison between God and the sun, for which Newton's corpuscular theory implied a further complication. On the problems of theodicy, Swedenborg sought advice primarily from Malebranche and Leibniz, but he added a Christian demonology, which took up very little space in their thinking, to their patterns of harmony and perfection. The prince of the world becomes powerless against the Almighty also in Swedenborg's thinking, but the very real existence of evil appears much stronger in *The Worship and Love of God* than in the philosophical treatises of his predecessors.

Swedenborg's drama of creation is a work of completely different character than those philosophical texts, and therefore its contradictions, illusive and real, cannot play any significant part for the evaluation of this piece. Its didactic character is indeed noticeable; however, the element of pedagogy is not limited to details but encompasses the basic philosophy: the order of God, such as it comes to light in nature and human lives. The author wishes to convert the reader to this attitude toward life; to this end, he allows his fable to include as much theory as is necessary for the understanding. Intellectual analysis is also fitted into the teleological perspective, which is so significant for the entire opus. The lengthy descriptions of evil beings and of people led astray amount to a widening of the epic frame, which would hardly be justified in itself except that they clearly reveal the didactic function. His contemporaries hide behind the confused mob of fatalists and worshippers of nature, and the purpose of these demonic episodes is to warn them of the temptations of the prince of the world and self-love.

The preaching voice resounds more and more forcefully the closer one comes to the finale: this is partly explained by the structure of the fable but also by the fact that here Swedenborg speaks the language of experience. With anguish and pain, he has witnessed the struggle between good and evil powers during his dream crisis, and it is tempting to interpret *The Worship and Love of God* as a continued conjuration of the spirits, as a confirmation of a still frail insight: that the preacher's calls to revival are also directed at himself. When the young man in paradise experiences the contrast between the horrid appearances of the prince of the world and his inner powerlessness with fearful joy, it seems to me to be a poetic reflection of the exalted state between jubilation and horror, which the *Dream Diary* sometimes reveals with regard to the fascinating visions.

The study of *The Worship and Love of God* has mainly been limited to sources and motifs, such as they appear when analysing the present text. The problem of Swedenborg's mental status has been touched upon only when the text has made it inevitable; however within the chosen frame of the monograph, I have not considered myself as being able to take a definitive position on the sensitive issue of whether Swedenborg's development ought to be interpreted using models of abnormal psychology or not. Lamm is the primary secular scholar who has taken the latter view, whereas a number of psychiatrists have considered themselves qualified to declare Swedenborg mentally disturbed. How to define his disease is apparently a contentious issue, but the more general view seems to be that it was some form of paranoid psychosis. The varying interpretations are confusing to the layman. An unambiguous diagnosis seems hardly possible based on the available material, and this calls for caution and some modesty: the patient—if he indeed deserves this title—was nevertheless a brilliant talent of rare dimensions and whoever tries to follow his footsteps must be filled with admiration for his wide reading and his intellectual scope. Besides there is a much more important matter of principle: the question of whether mental disease was present or not is obviously significant to those who, for whatever reason, interest themselves in the truth value of Swedenborg's teaching. For a study of sources and texts within the tradition of intellectual history, a psychiatric analysis is of little consequence.

On the other hand, such investigations could lend support to the psychiatric diagnosis. The analysis of *The Worship and Love of God* seems to have confirmed Lamm's opinion that Swedenborg's development up to the gates of the spiritual world cannot be explained through readings of mysticism but must be put in context with a personal disposition, which ruthlessly drew the most farfetched consequences from the doctrines of very respectable masters, after pondering them over many years, culminating in an acute religious crisis, when the Word became hallucinatory flesh. Of course, the studied excerpt material in no way encompasses the total reading conducted by the author; nevertheless, it provides a sufficient basis, together with his previous production, for an exploration of the main motifs in the drama of creation. The selection of sources displays a scientific fastidiousness, an aristocratic ambition to keep company only with great thinkers, and this is a characteristic that follows him into theosophy. Swedenborg never becomes a sectarian revivalist; on the contrary, he continues his debate with the famous spirits in the celestial academy.

However, in the most profound sense, his search in nature and literature is determined by his longing for synthesis. It appears almost with the force of a natural instinct and cannot be stopped by anything; indeed for the satisfaction of this instinct, elementary principles of logic are sacrificed, and Swedenborg is led by its star to a dream world that is clearly connected with his previous theorizing to be sure but where the layman finds it difficult to accept a dogmatism, the consistent but frightening culmination of which is the visionary's claim that his own work is the second coming of the Messiah. Together with other characteristics, this intense holism seems to reflect a schizoid disposition, the inherent splitting tendencies of which have been driven on the verge of what is unbearable during the dream crisis. To a secular observer in our time, it becomes only too natural to interpret Swedenborg's later production as the result of a pathological development inherent in this type of personality.

But even if this conjectural interpretation were correct, it contributes little to an understanding of *The Worship and Love of God*. Without any doubt, the religious crisis left its traces, but they are easily incorporated into the overall structure, and the author has transformed and made objective his own personal experiences in the same fashion as any other poet. If a work of that kind of synthetic force has to be explained psychiatrically, it would seem to follow that deep down all religion and religiously inspired poetry are products of disordered souls. While this view is held by some, it is entirely without consequence in this case. Swedenborg conveys his message within a traditionally chosen frame of fiction and speaks through his protagonists; he does not appear directly other than in the commenting footnotes. This is a significant contrast to the theosophical works with their preaching from what he has heard and seen, *ex auditu et visu*. There we often encounter the visionary himself in authoritative debates on various issues, with heavenly beings awarding him the palm branch of victory and confirming his comments with brilliant lights. The formal structure of these visions has indeed been inspired by literature, but still we are far away from the world of poetry: they are reports from the existence beyond and not symbolic crystallizations of a philosophic and religious view, like the scenes of the drama of creation.

"The idea is more than the deed—higher than the issue": Strindberg's wisdom from *Ett drömspel* (A Dream Play) comes to mind, when trying to evaluate *The Worship and Love of God* aesthetically. Naturally enough, the ambition behind this singular work is greater than its realization; however the pondering dreamer succeeded in transferring much of the beauty of his thinking in the fable about the origin and purpose of the universe. From the initial macrocosmic process of birth to the final vision of the heavenly kingdom of God, a symbolic consistency is fulfilled in which the comprehensive view has been expressed with grandeur: the planets are hatched from the great world egg, the plants and trees of the ground grow from seeds, birds and quadrupeds grow from the plant eggs, Adam is born from the fruit of the tree of life, the celestial community is developed from countless human eggs, which are brought together to become an immense counterpart to *Maximum universi ovum*, the great egg of the world. The forms of nature ascend in a series from the lowest to the supracelestial, spiritual one: thus nature and spirit become degrees on the same scale, and the unity is underlined by the emanation symbolism inspired by Plato.

The composition of the drama corresponds to this succession of series. The origin of the earth is depicted in an introductory passage, then follows the origin of the world of plants in the first scene, that of the animal kingdom in the second, and the birth of Adam in the third. Thus far the formal balance is excellent, and the connection between the scenes extremely consistent. After the arrival of the first man, this picture is altered, however; and for a modern evaluation, the third scene and the introduction to the fourth appear to constitute the artistic culmination, to which all heretofore aspired. During the description of Adam's education, the theoretical tensions begin to appear most forcefully, and this tendency has not been propitious to the formal execution: the footnotes have grown beyond proportion, the lengthy monologues tend to become too didactic, the symbolic images are fewer, and the frames of the fiction are transgressed in an increasingly uninhibited manner.

All this is explained by the task, so detrimental to the system, of drawing a picture of a man in the Golden Age of innocence, under the immediate influence of the soul and thus of heaven, and at the same time allowing him to represent symbolically his sinful progeny, whose development is completely different according to the author's psychological theories. While it is true that one can observe an ambition to refer to the comprehensive view, for instance, through comparing the parts of the brain with the world egg and the firmament, and while it is also true that the description of Adam's upbringing is of great interest to the study of Swedenborg's personal situation, it nevertheless disrupts the composition. This does not mean that it could be dismissed as completely inartistic. On the contrary, certain episodes are indeed more intense than those of the previous scenes. The seduced intelligencies' ostentatious swaggering in the square is horribly contrasted by their innermost poverty, revealed in celestial mirrors; the terrible metamorphoses of the devil are grotesquely efficient illustrations of the powerlessness of evil; Adam's dreamed encounter with Eve is depicted as a storm of passion, the swells of which can still be felt in the sublime paradisiacal scenes during the wedding day; the vision in the sky in the third part is a magnificent emblem, in which the birth and light symbolism has been ingeniously reset.

From the intention of the work, it follows that one cannot expect any individualized description of persons or milieus: we constantly find ourselves in an environment rich in symbols, where people and spirits are representatives of psychological characteristics and religious concepts. In Swedenborg's opus, we do not find any such powerful portrayal like that which we encounter in Milton's image of Satan. Nevertheless, there are certain attempts at adding personal nuances. The firstborn youth is a passionate character, flaring up fiercely at what he regards as unreasonable in the wisdoms' sermons and becoming excitedly sensual in the love hunt of his dream. His wife, meanwhile, instead appears quietly humble in front of the mysteries of existence and yet with an intuitive ability to understand matters of vital importance, giving an impression of prudence and balance. The different spiritual beings are not completely alike either: Adam's wisdom recounts what it has seen or heard of, sometimes laughing, sometimes sighing, while Eve's celestial pedagogue directly divulges the innermost knowledge, at the source of which it finds itself. In the midst of all airy abstraction appears an ambition for individualizing concretion, which could hardly have been imposed by the theoretical conceptions but which seems to bear witness to a narrative joy.

The poetical inspiration behind *The Worship and Love of God* was strongly admired by Atterbom, and it is natural that the synthetic conception of the world of this work attracted the romantic outlook of this poet. Indeed, Lamm emphasized that the drama of creation is half a century before its time in many respects, a point of view that is strengthened when comparing the work with the symbolic fairy tales of Romanticism. There are obviously many features in common as regards the sensibility, but they must not be exaggerated. The description of the influx of divine love into the human being and nature, the anthropomorphic symbolism, the sincere feeling for the profound unity of the universe, all create an atmosphere close to the romantic "*Weltanschauung*," but this has to do with a common Platonic influence. However, the subjectivity of romantic poetry never appears in Swedenborg. On the contrary, the core of the drama is the preaching of God's order, the geometrically inspired world order, which is so essential to the natural philosopher's idea of God, and human beings fulfill their calling when they submit to the eternal laws. Purpose and usefulness are basic ideas in the work, Aristotle's and Leibniz's teleology expressed in eighteenth-century terms of utilitarianism, and the different scenes emerge out of one another in accordance with the plan of creation. Instead of the romantic fairy tale, the drama could be compared to the strictly regular fugue of contemporary church music, composed within the firm structure of staircase dynamics: ancient themes are contrasted to modern melodies, which will in time be varied in the subjective timbres of Romanticism. The music alternates between ethereal heights to grotesque depths, from curious effects to the sublime. Indeed, it is a remarkable hymn *ad majorem Dei gloriam,* to the greater honor of the Lord, which rings in the midst of our poor 1740s, an unfinished symphony expressing the yearning for the fullness of truth, love, and innocence in one of the most fascinating and elusive Swedish geniuses.

# APPENDIX
## THE QUESTION OF COD. 36–110
## AND THE DATING OF
### *CLAVIS HIEROGLYPHICA*

The extensive manuscript material that is Swedenborg's legacy was left to and is kept for the most part in the library of the Royal Swedish Academy of Sciences. It has been subjected to intense research and publication activities from members of the New Church, as has been mentioned previously. Despite this, the manuscripts have been insufficiently examined; the misreading I observed regarding the Burnet excerpts in the Tafel document collection is not an isolated phenomenon. On many occasions, the dates are uncertain and the sequence likewise.

With regard to cod. 36–110 and *Clavis hieroglyphica*, both predate *The Worship and Love of God*, a determination sufficient for the monographic study of this work. However, cod. 36–110, the manuscript of excerpts, makes dating possible, which will be important in a broader context. It exists in a small hard-cover volume of 276 pages and cover pages in the format 9, 6 × 31, 2 cm; the pagination is Swedenborg's own, and he has also provided an index. This incurable systematics is a great help in dating, since it reveals that Swedenborg used the manuscript in different ways. The first 203 pages include relatively coherent psychological and theological excerpts, which conclude with an extensive collection of quotations illuminating the problem of interaction between body and soul (194–203). After these pages have been partially filled under headlines, which obviously had been prearranged, an index has been made.

The latter part is less systematic, although there is a clear and significant pattern in this context. It appears in the positions of the different headlines regarding correspondences: *Correspondentia harmonica*, page 205 (just fewer than five pages); *Correspondentia parabolica. allegorica*, page 220 (one page); *Correspondentia typica*, page 235 (seven pages); *Correspondentia fabulosa et somniorum*, page 250 (two pages); *Repraesentatio oraculorum*, page 267 (half a page); and *Correspondentia actionum human. et divin,* page 270 (one page). The last category falls outside of the schedule and must be characterized as an unfinished draft. Swedenborg did not include it in his index, which may not prove anything in itself since it is found on the page just before the list of contents. If one disregards this draft, there are thus fifteen pages between every headline except for the last two, where the difference is seventeen pages. The empty spaces between the categories are filled with disparate excerpts, plans for the *Oeconomia* and *Regnum animale* series, and numerous drafts.

In his English edition, Acton concluded the following regarding the question of dating: "To sum up our conclusions, the first 203 pages of Codex 36 were written in 1741, in preparation for *The Fibre,* and perhaps for other small psychological tracts; the sketches of the anatomical works were written in 1741, 1742, and 1743; while the rest of the Codex was written in 1744."[1] The result is therefore almost the same as in Stroh and Ekelöf's chronological catalogue, in which the years 1740–1744 have been proposed.[2] *Terminus ante quem* is 1739 according to the Latin translation of Leibniz's theodicy, which has been used in the manuscript; and partly with the support of the different drafts for *Regnum animale, terminus post quem* should be determined as being 1744. Acton appears to be correct in his supposition that the excerpts up to page 203 had been made as preparations for the sequels to *Oeconomia, De fibra,* and the small psychological treatises following it.[3]

Regarding the relationship between the drafts for the biological works and the correspondence excerpts, Acton seems, however, to have ignored one crucial point, something that led him onto the wrong track. According to his estimation, Swedenborg would have written down the plan for the sequels to *Oeconomia* first on page 268 in the manuscript, after which he rewrote it on page 269; thereafter, he turned back to the pages 262–263, where the most detailed disposition is to be found.[4] The same sequence of pages can be observed with regard to the drafts for *Regnum animale:* first a short draft after the plan for *Oeconomia* on page 269, thereafter a more detailed one on page 265, and finally the most extensive one on pages 253–255.[5] This procedure is quite remarkable for such a systematic person. The simplest explanation is that Swedenborg used available spaces between pages that had already been filled: pages 267 and 270 include correspondence notes in the manuscript's present condition. If Acton's dating of the disposition drafts for the *Oeconomia* series to 1741 is correct, which does not contest known facts, these biblical correspondence excerpts would thus have been added before or during this particular year.[6]

However, Acton wishes to date it differently, and this must be due to his general ambition to make Swedenborg's course up to the spiritual visions completely consequential and unbroken. In his view, they were added during 1744 as a sequel to *Clavis hieroglyphica,* written immediately before them.[7] According to an earlier opinion, held by Lamm among others, they were instead preparations to this opus and like it written in 1741.[8] The manuscripts thus seems to support this dating, while the relations between *Clavis* and the Bible excerpts can be more difficult to determine.

In my view, the probable turn of events was as follows. In the chapter on the doctrine of correspondence, I emphasized the connection between this doctrine and the philosophical language of universals. The demands for such a language emerged from the doctrine of series and degrees, especially with regard to the psychophysical interaction. When the attempt to construct such an artificial language failed, Swedenborg sought to replace it with a doctrine of correspondence, which in my view must be regarded partly as inspired by Malebranche and which is clearly connected to the psychological triad pattern of *Oeconomia*.[9] From references in *Clavis hieroglyphica*, it seems evident that the treatise fulfills the promise given in *De anima* for a more extensive treatment of the correspondence doctrine.[10] In that case, the Bible notes must have been a preliminary study, something that may be supported by an addition to the headlines in cod. 36–110.[11]

According to the plans for the finalization of the *Oeconomia* series, made after the Bible references, the doctrine of correspondence should be included in the psychophysical transaction V after brain-physiological and neurological studies; however, in the later drafts to *Regnum animale*, it has been placed in a fundamentally similar—although with regard to interior sequence different—context in tome III.[12] Even Acton admits that the basic theses of the doctrine of correspondence were completed by the beginning of the 1740s. That they were never quoted from *Clavis* until *The Worship and Love of God* is explained by the fact that the drama of creation is a synthesis of the entire scientific production, only details of which had been published previously.

The question of the dating of the excerpts and *Clavis* is not a crucial problem, but it does illustrate the need for an unconditional examination of Swedenborg's manuscripts.

# NOTES

## Introduction

1. Martin Lamm, *Emanuel Swedenborg: The Development of His Thought*, translated by Tomas Spiers and Anders Hallengren (West Chester, Pa.: The Swedenborg Foundation, 2000), xxiv. The original Swedish edition is *En Studie över hans Utveckling till Mystiker och Andeskådare* (Stockholm: Hugo Gebers Förlag, 1915), viii. All quotations from this work are referenced to both the 1915 Swedish edition and the 2000 English translation.

2. Swedenborg's family name, Swedberg, was changed to "Swedenborg" in 1719 on the ascension of Ulrika Eleonora to the Swedish throne. According to George Dole and Robert Kirven, "[I]n a move which strengthened her position in the parliamentary House of Clergy and increased the number of her supporters in the House of Nobles, she ennobled the families of Sweden's bishops" (*A Scientist Explores Spirit* [West Chester, Pa.: Chrysalis Books, 1997], 24). Since Emanuel's father, Jesper Swedberg (1652–1735), was bishop of Skara, his family was raised to the aristocracy.

3. Hans Helander, ed. and trans., *Emanuel Swedenborg: Festivus applausus in Caroli XII in Pomeraniam suam adventum, edited, with introduction, translation and commentary by Hans Helander* (Uppsala: Uppsala University. Acta Universitatis Upsaliensis, 1985), 26. Helander has also edited *Camena Borea* (Acta Universitatis Upsaliensis, 1988) and *Ludus Heliconius and Other Latin Poems* (Acta Universitatis Upsaliensis, 1995).

4. Swedenborg's correspondence from his European tour has been published (mainly by Alfred H. Stroh) in *Opera quaedam aut inedita aut obsoleta de rebus naturalibus, nunc edita sub auspiciis Regiae Academiae Scientiarum Suecicae* I (Stockholm, 1907) (hereinafter *Opera*); see the preface by G. Retzius, viii. These letters are also available in English translation: R. L. Tafel, *Documents concerning the Life and Character of Emanuel Swedenborg* (London: Swedenborg Society, 1875), I:197ff (hereinafter *Documents*); and more completely in A. Acton, *The Letters and Memorials of Emanuel Swedenborg* (Bryn Athyn, Pa.: Swedenborg Scientific Association, 1948).

5. Letter of September 8, 1714; *Opera* I:226. See also Ernst Benz, *Emanuel Swedenborg: Naturforscher und Seher* (München: Hermann Rinn, 1948), 74; or its English translation, *Emanuel Swedenborg: Visionary Savant in the Age of Reason,* translated by Nicholas Goodrick-Clarke (West Chester, Pa.: Swedenborg Foundation, 2002), 66. All quotations from this work are referenced to both the 1948 German edition and the 2002 English translation.

6. In *Technology on Trial: The Introduction of Steam Power Technology into*

*eden, 1715–1736* (Uppsala: Almqvist & Wiksell International, 1984), 118, ₅58–170, S. Lindqvist explains that Swedenborg was responsible for the first technology assessment in Sweden. Lindqvist has also made a penetrating study of Swedenborg's efforts to become accepted as assessor ordinarius by the Board of Mines.

7. *Acta eruditorum* 1735, 556ff.; see Lamm 1915, 47ff.; 2000, 48ff. (*Prodromus . . . de Infinito*, hereinafter *De Infinito*).
8. Lamm 1915, 110; 2000, 110.
9. See especially chapter 6.
10. November 3, 1719; *Opera* I, 292; *Documents* I:310.
11. Alfred Acton, ed., *Psychologica, Being Notes and Observations on Christian Wolff's Psychologia Empirica by Emanuel Swedenborg* (Philadelphia: Swedenborg Scientific Association, 1923), xviff.
12. I agree here with Acton 1923, xvii.
13. Codex 36 is the sign given to it in the list of Swedenborg's manuscripts produced about 1790, currently being housed by the Royal Swedish Academy of Sciences; see *Documents* III:797ff. These documents are identified as number 110 in A. H. Stroh and Greta Ekelöf, *Kronologisk förteckning öfver Emanuel Swedenborgs skrifter 1700–1772* (Uppsala, Sweden: Almqvist & Wiksell, 1910; appendix 3 to *The Yearbook of the Academy of Sciences*), 31. Since both numbers have been inscribed in the manuscripts, it seems practical to use the sign cod. 36–110. Alfred Acton published these works in English translation under the title *A Philosopher's Note Book* (1931; Philadelphia: The Swedenborg Scientific Association, 1976). Parts of it have been photolithographically reproduced in volume III of the series edited by R. L. Tafel, *Em. Swedenborgii autographa: ed. photo-lith.* (Stockholm, 1869–1870) (vol. III, 1870, 180–196; hereinafter *Photolith.*) and also phototypically in *Em. Swedenborgii autographa: ed. phototyp.*, edited and published by the Swedenborg Society in London (Stockholm, 1916), vol. XVIII, 72–83; hereinafter *Phototyp.*). For a review of these manuscript editions, which are wide-ranging indeed, although not altogether satisfactory from a scholarly point of view, see S. C. Eby, *The Story of the Swedenborg Manuscripts* (New York: The New Church Press, 1926).
14. *Oeconomia regni animalis in transactiones divisa* I–II (Amsterdam, 1740–1741) (hereinafter *Oeconomia*); English translation by A. Clissold, *The Economy of the Animal Kingdom* (London: W. Newbery, H. Ballière, 1845–1846): see I, §147 (Clissold trans, 112), §157 (Clissold, 120–121), §50 (Clissold, 43), §279 (Clissold, 254); II, §115 (Clissold, 138), §127 (Clissold, 149), §146 (Clissold, 165). Compare Acton's preface in *A Philosopher's Note Book*, vii–viii.
15. Compare A. Acton's introduction to his translation of Swedenborg's manuscripts on the physiology of the brain, *Three Transactions on the Cerebrum* (Philadelphia: Swedenborg Scientific Association, 1938), I:xviiff.
16. *Opera* III:268; *Three Transactions on the Cerebrum* I:xxvi: "For my own part, I think it highly probable that under the influence of the illumination of which this sign was the representation, Swedenborg decided to undertake at once a treatise on the human soul." As I showed in my book on Swedenborg's doctrine of correspondence, *Swedenborgs korrespondenslära* (Stockholm: Almqvist & Wiksell, 1969), the mysterious phrase seems to have been a posthumous answer to the Dutch microscopist Antony van Leeuwenhoek (1632–1723); see Inge Jonsson, *Visionary Scientist: The Effects of Science and*

*Philosophy on Swedenborg's Cosmology*, trans. Catherine Djurklou (West Chester, Pa.: The Swedenborg Foundation, 1999), 65ff.

17. *Regnum animale anatomice, physice et philosophice perlustratum*, I–II (The Hague, 1744); III (London, 1745) (hereinafter *Regnum animale*); English translation by J. J. G. Wilkinson, *The Animal Kingdom Considered Anatomically, Physically and Philosophically by Emanuel Swedenborg* (1843–1844; Bryn Athyn, Pa.: Swedenborg Scientific Association, 1960), 12.

18. See *A Philosopher's Note Book*, viiiff.

19. See *Three Transactions on the Cerebrum* I:xxvii–xxviii.

20. *Regnum animale* II, Epilogue, §§394–404; Wilkinson translation, 554–575; Im. Tafel (ed.), *Em. Swedenborgii Regnum animale. . . . pars quarta* (Tübingen and London, 1848), 172–227 (hereinafter *De sensibus*); English translation by E. S. Price, *The Five Senses* ( 1914; Philadelphia: Swedenborg Scientific Association, 1976), 215–282.

21. There are four Swedish editions of Swedenborg's dream journal, which was published posthumously in 1859, the latest one by Lars Bergquist, *Swedenborgs drömbok. Glädjen och det stora kvalet* (Stockholm: Norstedts Förlag, 1989). This edition has been translated into English as *Swedenborg's Dream Diary*, translated by Anders Hallengren (West Chester, Pa.: The Swedenborg Foundation, 2001). All translations of the dream diary hereinafter are taken from this edition and page numbers will be cited for both the English and Swedish editions. The manuscript was published in *Phototyp.* XVIII:590–618.

22. See A. Acton, *An Introduction to the Word Explained: A Study of the Means by Which Swedenborg the Scientist Became the Theologian and Revelator* (Bryn Athyn, Pa.: Academy of the New Church, 1927), 6ff.

23. Cyriel O. Sigstedt, *The Swedenborg Epic* (1952; London: Swedenborg Society, 1981), 225.

24. I have used the edition in *Photolith.* VII (Stockholm, 1870); English translation throughout by Stuart S. Shotwell, from a first draft of his forthcoming edition of *The Worship and Love of God* (West Chester, Pa.: The Swedenborg Foundation, 2005). Parts of the Latin work were translated into Swedish by J. Boyesen and A. H. Stroh, "Om gudsdyrkan och kärleken till Gud," *Nya kyrkans härold* (1902–1903), and by H. Bergstedt, *Emanuel Swedenborg, Religiösa skrifter i urval* (Stockholm: Hugo Gebers förlag, 1925). A complete translation into Swedish has been done by Ritva Jonsson Jacobsson, *Om Guds dyrkan och kärleken till Gud* (1961; Stockholm: Natur och Kultur, 1988).

25. Lamm 1915, 175–176; 2001, 174–175.

# Chapter 1

1. P. D. A. Atterbom, *Svenska siare och skalder* (Upsala, 1841), I:46. Translation by Inge Jonsson.

2. See Sigstedt, 200, and note 311.

3. *Bibliothèque raisonnée des ouvrages des savans de l'Europe* XXXIV (Amsterdam: 1745): 371.

4. Ibid., 383–384. The anonymous cosmologist seems to be Abbé Pluche, *Le spectacle de la nature, ou entretiens sur l'histoire naturelle et les sciences* (1732). See G. Lanson, *Manuel bibliographique de la littérature française moderne*, nouv. éd. (Paris: Hachette, 1925), 730. Translation by Inge Jonsson.

5. *Neue Zeitungen von gelehrten Sachen* (Leipzig, 1745), 658. Translation by Inge Jonsson.

6. Im. Tafel, ed., *Em. Swedenborgii Adversaria in libros veteris testamenti* (Tübingen and London, 1847), I:7; English translation by A. Acton, *The Word of the Old Testament Explained* (Bryn Athyn, Pa.: Academy of the New Church, 1928), I:10.

7. *Documents* II:427. On Beyer, see *Svenskt Biografiskt Lexikon* 4, 120–127, and also O. Herrlin, "Religionsproblemet hos Thorild" (Ph.D. dissertation, Uppsala, 1947), 95ff.

8. *Documents* III: 710.

9. For examples of New Church critics, see F. Sewall, "A Drama of Creation," *The New-Church Review* 3 (Oct. 1882): 167–195; A. H. Stroh, "Analysis and Review of *The Worship and Love of God*," *The New Philosophy* 5 (April 1902): 70–71; and C. T. Odhner, "The Worship and Love of God," *New Church Life* 34 (1914): 331. Lamm, 1915, 193–194; 2000, 192–193.

10. H. Olsson, "C.J.L. Almquist före Törnrosens bok" (Ph.D. dissertation, Stockholm, 1927), 42ff.; Greta Hedin, "Manhemsförbundet" (Ph.D. dissertation, Göteborg, 1928), for example, 200–201.

11. Hedin, 28; Stroh, "Analysis and Review," 71.

12. *Svenskt Biografiskt Lexikon* 4, 346ff.

13. *Documents* I:704–705; see also S. Evander, *Londonsvenskarnas kyrka* (Lund: Berlingska boktryckeriet, 1960), 80ff.

14. *Documents* III:1246–1247.

15. H. Lenhammar, "Tolerans och bekännelsetvång. Studier i den svenska swedenborgianismen 1765-1795" (Ph.D. dissertation, Uppsala University, 1966), 256 and 380.

16. R. Sundelin, *Swedenborgianismens historia i Sverige under förra århundradet* (Upsala, 1886), 217. Incidentally, Johansén translated §§1–28 of *The Worship and Love of God* in 1771; the manuscript is kept in the Royal Library in Stockholm (Teol.Swedenb. No A 616).

17. For a survey of earlier Swedenborg scholarship, see Hj. Holmquist, "Ur Swedenborgsforskningens historia," *Kyrklig tidskrift* 15 (1909): 97–132.

18. About the identification of the anonymous writer with Hammarsköld, see H. Olsson, "Den svenska romantikens litteraturforskning," *Finsk tidskrift* CXII (1932): 63–64.

19. *Samtidens märkvärdigaste personer, Biographisk tidskrift* (Upsala: 1820), I:128. Translation by Inge Jonsson.

20. Compare Olsson 1927, 94ff.

21. J. Görres, *Emanuel Swedenborg, seine Visionen und sein Verhältnis zur Kirche* (Strassburg, 1827), 56ff.

22. N. Hobart, *Life of Emanuel Swedenborg, with Some Account of His Writings, together with a Brief Notice of the Rise and Progress of the New Church* (Boston: Allen and Goddard, 1831), 32–33; compare Sigstedt, note 310; J. J. G. Wilkinson, *Emanuel Swedenborg: A Biographical Sketch*, 2nd edition (London: James Speirs, 1886), 62ff.

23. W. White, *Swedenborg: His Life and Writings* (London, 1856), 22. The first American edition of this work appeared in 1866.

24. W. White, *Emanuel Swedenborg: His Life and Writings,* I–II (London: Simpkin, Marshall, 1867).

25. Ibid., I:172, 182–183.

26. Holmquist, 112. In the portrait of Swedenborg drawn by Fryxell in his *Berättelser ur svenska historien,* part 43 (Stockholm, 1875), 149ff., *Worship and Love of God* is not mentioned. E. A. G. Kleen, *Swedenborg, en lefnadsskildring,* I–II (Stockholm: Sandbergs, 1917).

27. B. Worcester, *The Life and Mission of Emanuel Swedenborg* (Boston: Roberts Brothers, 1883), 207.
28. *The New-Church Review* 3 (1882): 167–195.
29. Ibid., 194–195.
30. F. Sewall, *Swedenborg and the 'Sapientia angelica'* (London: Constable, 1910), 46.
31. In *The New Philosophy* 1902; see note 9 above. See also Lamm 1915, 161, note 1; 2000, 338, note 1.
32. Acton, *Introduction to the Word Explained*, 108.
33. See, for example, a title that looks very promising, H. Lj. Odhner, *Swedenborg's Epic of Paradise and Its Literary Sources* (Bryn Athyn, Pa.: Academy of the New Church, 1945); unfortunately, Milton's *Paradise Lost* is the only specific source analyzed, and it adds nothing of value to Lamm's argument.
34. Signe Toksvig, *Emanuel Swedenborg, vetenskapsman och mystiker* (Stockholm: 1949), 159ff. In English, Signe Toksvig, *Emanuel Swedenborg: Scientist and Mystic* (1948; New York: The Swedenborg Foundation, 1983).
35. Sigstedt, 195.
36. *Biographiskt lexicon öfver namnkunnige svenska män* (Upsala, 1849), 16:301.
37. Ibid., 319.
38. R.W. Emerson, *Representative Men* (Boston, 1850), 93–145; *Svenska akademiens handlingar* 31 (Stockholm, 1859), 61–226. On Swedenborg's influence on Emerson, see Anders Hallengren, "The Code of Concord: Emerson's Search for Universal Laws" (Ph.D. diss., Stockholm University, 1994), esp. 66–84.
39. J. Matter, *Emmanuel de Swedenborg, sa vie, ses écrits et sa doctrine* (Paris, 1863), 76. Translation by Inge Jonsson.
40. G. Ballet, *Swedenborg. Histoire d'un visionnaire au XVIIIe siècle* (Paris, 1899), 28ff.
41. Lamm 1915, 167; 2000, 166.
42. Lamm 1915, 186; 2000, 184.
43. M. Lamm, *Upplysningstidens romantik* I (1918; Stockholm: Hammarström & Åberg, 1981), 119. Translation by Inge Jonsson.
44. Kleen, 263–264.
45. Benz 1948, 264–283; 2002, 241–257.
46. E. N. Tigerstedt, *Svensk litteraturhistoria*, 3rd edition (Stockholm: Natur och Kultur, 1960), 176.
47. *Ny illustrerad svensk litteraturhistoria* (Stockholm: Natur och Kultur, 1956), II:188. Translation by Inge Jonsson.
48. L. Bergquist, *Swedenborgs hemlighet* (Stockholm: Natur och Kultur, 1999), 215–229.
49. See, for example, G. C. Taylor, *Milton's Use of Du Bartas* (Cambridge, Mass.: Harvard University Press, 1934), xiv; and A. Williams, "Commentaries on Genesis as a Basis for Hexaemeral Material in the Literature of the Late Renaissance," *Studies in Philology* 34 (1937): 191. Two of the primary sources for this section are also among the references of these two important studies: F. E. Robbins, *The Hexaemeral Literature* (Chicago: University of Chicago Press, 1912) and M. Thibaut de Maisières, "Les poèmes inspirés du début de la Genèse à l'époque de la renaissance," *Recueil de travaux* (Louvain, France: Université de Louvain [Librairie Universitaire], 1931).
50. Robbins, 1 (italics added); see Lamm's statement, on page 161 (2000): "There is no question here of an allegorical commentary on the creation story found

in Genesis, but rather of a partly scientific and partly poetical paraphrase of that creation—a sort of creational fiction."

51. Hesiod, *Theogony* I, 116–128. Translation by Stuart Shotwell.
52. See W. H. Roscher, ed., *Ausführliches Lexikon der griechischen und römischen Mythologie* (Leipzig and Berlin, 1925), vol. 6, col. 375ff (Weltalter). A short summary of this speculative tradition is given by P. Svendsen in his *Gullalderdröm og utviklingstro* (Oslo: Gyldendal Norsk Forlag, 1940), 13ff.
53. G. Rudberg, "Antika urtidsteorier," *Samtiden* 32 (1921): 96.
54. R. G. Bury, ed., *Plato*, The Loeb Classical Library (London: Harvard University Press, 1952), 7:3ff.
55. See, for example, ibid., 8:7–8.
56. Robbins, 5–6.
57. Cod. 36–110, p. 120; Acton, *A Philosopher's Note Book,* 243.
58. See, for example, Augustine, *Confessiones* XI:XII, edited by P. Labriolle (Paris: Desclèe de Brouwer, 1947), II:306; Du Bartas, *La premiere sepmaine,* I:31ff., a critical edition with introduction, commentary and variants by Urban T. Holmes, John C. Lyons, and Robert W. Linker (Chapel Hill, N. C.: University of North Carolina Press, 1938), II:196. Haquin Spegel gave the thought a pithy turn in his *Guds Werk och Hwila* (Stockholm, 1685), 31:
> Dock Frågewiser kan et richtigt Swar få höra
> Hwad Gud haar giordt förr än han wille Werlden göra
> Han haar tå Helfwetet uptent och börjat skapa
> Åt the nyfikne som Lön-Saker efter gapa. . . .

(Curious people may get a correct answer to what the Lord did before the creation of the world: he prepared hell for those anxious to uncover secrets.) Translation by Inge Jonsson. See also Robbins, 6–7.
59. Ibid., 6.
60. Ibid., 12–13; in cod. 36–110, Swedenborg's source is G. Carreri, *Voyage autour du monde 1693–99,* of which he has made a note on page 134; Acton, *A Philosopher's Note Book,* 289.
61. Lamm 1915, 98ff.; 2000, 99ff.
62. Robbins, 13–14; see also E. von Lippmann, *Urzeugung und Lebenskraft* (Berlin: Julius Springer, 1933), 24.
63. See, for example, 193 and 237–238; the most frequent reference is to Plinius' *Naturalis historia,* as would be expected.
64. Robbins, 14ff.
65. *Titi Lucreti Cari De rerum natura libri sex* I:146ff., edited by C. Bailey (Oxford: Oxford University Press, 1947), I:182ff.
66. G. Hocke, *Lukrez in Frankreich von der Renaissance bis zur Revolution* (Köln: Kerschgens, 1935), 49.
67. Ibid., 70–71; and R. Pintard, *Le libertinage érudit* (Paris: Boivin, 1943), 477–504. See also *Emanuelis Swedenborgii Principia rerum naturalium, phototypice ed. Swedenborg Institut* (Basel, Switzerland: Swedenborg Verlag, 1954), 188–190, 223, 229, 239. Even Molière is said to have translated Lucretius in his youth: see D. Mornet, *Molière,* 4th ed. (Paris: Hatier, 1943), 18–19.
68. Hocke, 118.
69. Robbins, 19ff.
70. P. *Ovidi Nasonis Metamorphoseon libri* XV, ed. by H. Magnus (Berlin, 1914), 5–6. English translation: *Metamorphoses,* translated by Rolfe Humphries (Bloomington & Indianapolis: Indiana University Press, 1955).

Reprinted by permission of publisher. All subsequent translations from Ovid's *Metamorphoses* are taken from this edition and will be cited in the text.

71. Robbins, 8, note 1.
72. See *Paradise Lost* VII, 192ff.; Spegel, 33.
73. See *Principia*, 389ff.
74. Robbins, 24–35.
75. All quotations from *Paradise Lost* are taken from *Great Books of the Western World* (Chicago: Encyclopedia Britannica, 1952), 32, and will be cited in the text. Concerning potential rabbinical influences on Milton, see, for example, H. F. Fletcher, *Milton's Rabbinical Readings* (Urbana, Ill.: University of Illinois Press, 1930); his argument has been criticised, among others, by G. N. Conklin, *Biblical Criticism and Heresy in Milton* (New York: King's Crown Press, 1949), 52–66.
76. Robbins, 36–37.
77. See, for example, G. W. Whiting, *Milton's Literary Milieu* (Chapel Hill, N. C.: University of North Carolina Press, 1939), 15ff.
78. L. Paulinus Gothus, *Historiae arctoae libri tres* (Strengnes, 1636), 8.
79. Thibaut de Maisières, 15ff.
80. Robbins, 45.
81. Ibid., 48–49; see Thibaut de Maisières, 35. Even Spegel uses a similar metaphor referring to Basil; see Spegel, 33.
82. Thibaut de Maisières, 23. Translation by Inge Jonsson.
83. Robbins, 64ff.; see E. Gilson, *Introduction à l'étude de Saint Augustin* (Paris: J. Vrin, 1929), 242ff.
84. Robbins, 67.
85. *Alcini Ecdici Aviti Poematum* VI, ed. by R. Peiper in *Monumenta Germaniae Historica* VI:2 (Berlin, 1883), 203ff.
86. Thibaut de Maisières, 19.
87. Robbins, 73ff.
88. Ibid., 77.
89. Ibid., 84; on the so-called renaissance of the period, see C. H. Haskins, *The Renaissance of the Twelfth Century*, 4th impr. (Cambridge, Mass.: Harvard University Press, 1939), especially 341–365.
90. E. R. Curtius, *Europäische Literatur und lateinisches Mittelalter* (Bern, Switzerland: Francke Verlag, 1948), 116ff. See also G. Fredén, *Orpheus and the Goddess of Nature*, Göteborgs universitets årsskrift LXIV:6 (1958): 23ff.
91. See the article by H. Koch about Anders Sunesen in *Dansk Biografisk Leksikon* XXIII, 144.
92. Cod. 36–110, back cover; Acton, *A Philosopher's Note Book*, 508.
93. Migne, *Patr.lat.* XL (Paris, 1887), col. 779–780: *Admonitio in librum de Spiritu et Anima*. See also Gilson, 55, note 1.
94. "*Joannes Trithemius abbas recenset hunc librum in catalogo lucubrationum Hugonis a sancto Victore*": *Patr.lat.* XL, col. 779–780.
95. See Robbins, 73–91. Descartes' closest disciples frequently refer to *De spiritu et anima*, an important fact with respect to the interest in Augustine at the time and to Swedenborg's intellectual background; see H. Gouhier, *La vocation de Malebranche* (Paris: J. Vrin, 1926), 75.
96. Thibaut de Maisières, 18–19.
97. Ibid., 11–12.
98. The debate had already begun in 1750 with W. Lauder's *An Essay on Milton's Use and Imitation of the Moderns in His Paradise Lost*, a contribution that

distorted the discussions for a long time, however, by its bizarre and falsified arguments; see Taylor, passim.

99. Thibaut de Maisières, 9ff.

100. Fredén, 70.

101. The quotation from Fredén is an excellent example of the scope of the hexaemeral genre.

102. For ample evidence of this trend, see R. M. Adams, *Ikon: John Milton and the Modern Critics* (Ithaca, N.Y.: Cornell University Press, 1955), 128–176.

103. See, for example, A. Williams' study in note 49, above.

104. V. Lundgaard Simonsen, *Kildehistoriske studier i Anders Arrebos forfatterskab* (Khvn, Denmark: Munksgaard, 1955), 116–117.

105. Williams, 195.

106. Ibid., 197.

107. Ibid., 197. The fact that Grotius used the classics with more freedom than other commentaries seems also to be of interest with regard to Swedenborg.

108. A.H. Stroh, ed., *Catalogus bibliothecae Emanuelis Swedenborgii* (Stockholm, 1907), 5 (hereinafter *Cat.bibl.*).

109. Regarding ideas about Creation, Whiting focuses on three works as particularly significant: Raleigh's *History*, Samuel Purchas' *Pilgrimage* (1626), and Mercator-Hondius' *Atlas* (Amsterdam 1623); see Whiting, 15.

110. Fredén, 119ff.

# Chapter 2

1. As is customary in Swedenborgian studies, the numbers following extracts refer to paragraph or section numbers, which are uniform in all editions, rather than to page numbers.

2. The Scripture quotations contained herein are from the New Revised Standard Version Bible, copyright © 1989 by the Division of Christian Education of the National Council of the Churches of Christ in the U.S.A., and are used by permission. All rights reserved.

3. See dream of October 26–27, 1744; *Swedenborgs drömbok*, 287–290: "*at jag intet bör taga af annars kram, vtan mitt*" (that I should not draw upon others' notions, but of mine: *Swedenborg's Dream Diary* §278, 313–314).

4. See the appendix below.

5. Lamm 1915, 95; 2000, 95–96.

6. Ibid., 1915, 96ff.; 2000, 96ff.

7. Wolff, KVA Cod Sw 88–93, 159–206; *Photolith*. III:102–136; published by A. Acton in 1923 (complete title given above, in "Introduction," note 11, hereinafter referred to as *Psychologica*). See also Toksvig, 161 (Swedish edition; in English edition, see 125); her argument is built on Acton's dating of *The Hieroglyphic Key*. See the appendix below.

8. C. Wolff, *Psychologia empirica* (Frankfurt and Leipzig, 1732), §152, p. 105ff.; *Psychologica*, §97, p. 91 (English translation, 90). Translation by Matilda McCarthy.

9. Pointed out by Acton, *Psychologica*, 90–91 (footnote).

10. Ibid., §§99–100, pp. 92–93.

11. *Ibid.*, §101, footnote, 92–93.

12. C. Wolff, *Psychologia rationalis* (Frankfurt and Leipzig, 1734), §183; KVA cod. 36–110, p. 38 a; Acton, *A Philosopher's Note Book*, 75. Translation by Matilda McCarthy. Moreover, the future state of the world is also included in this representative power, even more important in understanding the applica-

tion of the doctrine of correspondence in the fifth scene of *The Worship and Love of God.*

13. Contemporary interest in the problem can be studied among others in Leibniz; see G. Aspelin, *Tankens vägar* (Stockholm and Uppsala: Almqvist & Wiksell, 1958), II:89 (in general terms); B. Russell, *A Critical Exposition of the Philosophy of Leibniz*, 2nd ed. (London: George Allen & Unwin, Ltd., 1949), 169ff.; and A. Wedberg, *Filosofins historia*, vol. 2 (Stockholm: Albert Bonniers förlag, 1959), 49–59. For Descartes' ideas on the subject of a universal language, see E. Cassirer, *Descartes* (Stockholm: Bermann-Fischer, 1939), 39–68. Swedenborg could learn about this dream in a tone of ironical scepticism in Th. Baker, *Reflections upon Learning* (London, 1708), 21ff., which Swedenborg had found well worth reading, as he told Benzelius in a letter from April 1711; see *Opera* I: 209. Like John Norris, Baker was influenced by the philosophy of Nicholas de Malebranche; see Lamm 1915, 88; 2000, 88. It should also be noted that even Christopher Polhem, the idol of Swedenborg's youth, had plans for a universal language; see S. E. Bring, *Bidrag till Christopher Polhems lefnadsteckning* (Stockholm: Svenska Teknologföreningen, 1911), 98–99.

14. The quotation from Wolff is taken from *Philosophia prima, sive ontologia, methodo scientifica pertractata* (Frankfurt and Leipzig,1730), §755, p. 560 (rather inexactly reproduced; for example, *traduntur* in Wolff has become *tradantur*). Translation by Matilda McCarthy.

15. *Oeconomia* II, §212; Swedenborg's reference to IV:X is a mistake for IV:XII. Swedenborg is responsible for the reproduction of the French text, of course. Locke's original English is taken from the Great Books edition (Chicago: Encyclopedia Britannica, 1952), 35:395, 360.

16. A. Rydelius, *Nödiga Förnufts-Öfningar*, 2nd ed. (Linköping, 1737); cod. 36–110, p. 4; Acton, *A Philosopher's Note Book*, 9. Acton notes that Rydelius is the source; see 7–8, footnote.

17. Rydelius, 28–29.

18. Cod. 36–110, p. 4; Acton, *A Philosopher's Note Book*, 9.

19. *Photolith.* VI, 265–269; English transl. in A. H. Stroh, ed., *Scientific and Philosophical Treatises by Emanuel Swedenborg* (Bryn Athyn, Pa.: 1905), 2:49ff. (the example in the text can be found on pages 265 and 52, respectively). The terminological affinity to Leibniz's *Characteristica universalis* is underscored by Swedenborg's quoting an extract from Leibniz on the same subject in cod. 36–110, p. 118; Acton, *A Philosopher's Note Book*, 239–240.

20. See above note 15.

21. Immanuel Tafel, ed., *Eman. Swedenborgii Regnum animale . . . pars septima de anima* (Tübingen and London, 1849), 255–256 (hereinafter referred to as *De anima*); English translation by N. Rogers and A. Acton, *Rational Psychology* (Philadelphia: The Swedenborg Scientific Association, 1950), §562, pp. 318–319 (hereinafter referred to as *Rational Psychology*). [Once again, Swedenborg quotes Locke from a French edition.] For Locke's original text, see note 15 above.

22. *De Anima*, 256–257; *Rational Psychology* §563ff., pp. 319–320.

23. *De Anima*, 257; *Rational Psychology* §566, p. 320.

24. *De Anima*, 257; *Rational Psychology* §567, p. 321.

25. *De Anima*, 258; *Rational Psychology* §567, p. 321.

26. See Appendix below.

27. See cod. 36–110, p. 157; Acton, *A Philosopher's Note Book*, 336ff.

28. G. B. Bilfinger, *De harmonia animi et corporis humani, maxime praestabilita, ex mente illustris Leibnitii, commentatio hypothetica* (Frankfurt and Leipzig, 1723). A review of Swedenborg's *De Infinito* in *Acta eruditorum* (1735) called his attention to Bilfinger.

29. Cod. 36–110, p. 157; Acton, *A Philosopher's Note Book*, 336–337; Bilfinger, §206, note c, 207. Translation by Inge Jonsson.

30. N. de Malebranche, *De inquirenda veritate libri sex* (Genève: 1685), 117, 120; both pages are referred to in the English translation of cod. 36–110, pp. 334–335, but only the latter one was noted in this context by Swedenborg (p. 156), while the former was registered under another heading (p. 194); Acton, *A Philosopher's Note Book*, 400–401. According to Acton (4), Swedenborg used a Latin translation of *Recherche de la verité* from 1691. In his library, Swedenborg owned a Latin edition from 1689 (*Cat.bibl.*, 4), but it was a reprint of the same translation, "*assez médiocre.*" See D. Roustan's edition, *Oeuvres complètes de Malebranche* (Paris: Boivin, 1938), 1:394. Translation by M. McCarthy.

31. *De inquirenda veritate* III:II:V; noted by Swedenborg in cod. 36–110, p. 195; Acton, *A Philosopher's Note Book*, 404.

32. *De inquirenda veritate* III:II:VI, 211; cod. 36–110, p. 196; Acton, *A Philosopher's Note Book*, 407. Translation by M. McCarthy.

33. H. Gouhier, *La philosophie de Malebranche et son expérience religieuse*. Bibliothèque d'histoire de la philosophie, 2nd ed. (Paris: J. Vrin, 1948), 32ff.

34. Ibid., 34. Translation by Inge Jonsson.

35. Lamm 1915, 87; 2000, 87.

36. Although Lamm (1915, 182, footnote; 2000, 338, note 174) argues for Neoplatonism as the inspiration for the doctrine of correspondence based on a terminological observation in *The Worship and Love of God*, it should be pointed out that Swedenborg's use of the word *idea* is more closely aligned with Augustinian reasoning on idea and form, as he wrote it down in cod. 36–110, p. 17; Acton, *A Philosopher's Note Book*, 37.

37. See appendix below regarding cod. 36–110.

38. Lamm 1915, 103–104; 2000, 104.

39. *Phototyp.* XVIII:123; R. Hindmarsh, ed., *Clavis Hieroglyphica* . . . (London: 1784, 24); this is an unreliable edition. A. Acton, trans., *Psychological Transactions and Other Tracts, 1734–1744*, 2nd ed. (1920; Bryn Athyn, Pa.: Swedenborg Scientific Assoc., 1984), 155–213 (the quoted passage, 193); hereinafter referred to as *Psych.trans.*

40. Cod. 36–110, p. 250; Acton, *A Philosopher's Note Book*, 478.

41. See L. Diestel, *Geschichte des Alten Testamentes in der christlichen Kirche* (Jena, 1869), 483ff. and 724ff. A more detailed study of sources follows below.

42. This tradition has enjoyed ever-increasing attention; a fine Swedish example can be found in Axel Friberg's research on Stiernhielm's *Hercules*. See A. Friberg, "Den svenske Herkules," Studier i Stiernhielms diktning (Ph.D. diss., Stockholm University, 1945).

43. Ibid., 14.

44. Ibid., 16–17.

45. Ibid., 23–24.

46. Ibid., 25. It is notable that Jesper Swedberg's dissertation in 1682 was a commentary on some Pythagorean sentences (*Commentarius in Demophili Similitudines et Sententias Pythagoricas*); see G. Wetterberg, ed., *Jesper Swedbergs Lefwernes Beskrifning* I (Lund: Vetenskapssocieteten, 1941), 57; see also H.

W. Tottie, "Jesper Swedbergs lif och verksamhet" (Ph.D. diss., Upsala University, 1885), I:20.

47. Friberg, 30.
48. Ibid., 31.
49. Cod. 36–110, p. 3; Acton, *A Philosopher's Note Book*, 8.
50. Rydelius, *Nödiga Förnufts-Öfningar*, 23–24. Translations by Inge Jonsson.
51. Friberg, 31.
52. Cod. 36–110, p. 241; Acton, *A Philosopher's Note Book*, 466. Swedenborg mistook the name for "Pinicellus."
53. D.Phil. Picinellus, *Mundus symbolicus, in emblematum universitate formatus, explicatus, et tam sacris, quam profanis eruditionibus ac sententiis illustratus,* I–II (Cologne, 1695). See also M. Praz, *Studies in Seventeenth-Century Imagery* (London: The Warburg Institute, 1939), 1:190: "Picinelli's *Mondo simbolico,* that encyclopaedia of emblematics."
54. Lib. XVI, cap. XXI, §212; II:81: "*Orbis terrarum theatrum visus est vanitatum mundi detectori Ecclesiastae, cum dicit:* Generatio praeterit & generatio advenit, terra autem in aeternum stat. (I:4) *Ut enim theatrum sub tanta prodeuntium varietate ac vicissitudine firmum semper consistit; ita Mundus theatrum est, in quo hujus vitae fabula peragitur, homines scenae serviunt. hic comicam, ille tragicam personam sustinet*" (The world is shown as a theater by the expositor of the vanity of the world, Ecclesiastes, when he says: One generation comes, another leaves, but the earth will last for ever. (1:4) For as a theater stands firm during a great variety and change of performers, so the world is a theater, in which the play of this life is staged, and men aim at playing a part, one a comic role, the other a tragic one.). Translation by Inge Jonsson. E. R. Curtius has traced the frequent *theatrum mundi* symbol to Plato and a great many followers on the one hand, to Paul and Church Fathers such as Clemens Alexandrinus and Augustine on the other. For later applications, he attached great importance to the *Policraticus* by John of Salisbury (d. 1180); see Curtius, 146ff. The frequency and the various origins of the symbol make it impossible to establish any exact sources Swedenborg might have used.
55. October 6–7, 1744; *Swedenborgs drömbok*, 266; *Swedenborg's Dream Diary*, 290.
56. Stroh, "Analysis and review," 33–34.
57. Lamm 1915, 28ff., 44–45, and 66ff.; 2000, 29ff, 45, and 66ff. As in many other respects, assessments of Swedenborg's philosophy of nature differ widely. Many New Church scholars have been primarily interested in proving how far-sighted the master's theories were and how well they can be adjusted to modern models in physics, while rather few experts outside the New Church have analyzed his works. However, there are some older investigations of value, for example, H. Schlieper, "Emanuel Swedenborgs System der Naturphilosophie" (Ph.D. diss., Berlin, 1901); N.V.E. Nordenmark, "Swedenborg som astronom," 1933, and S. Arrhenius, "Emanuel Swedenborg as a Cosmologist," *Opera* II: xxiii–xxxv; but also a well-informed and objective Italian investigation of recent date, F. M. Crasta, *La filosofia della natura di Emanuel Swedenborg* (Milan: Franco Angeli, 1999); see my review of this work in *ISIS* 93, no. 2 (June 2002): 312–313.
58. *Principia*, 15. Translation by Matilda McCarthy.
59. Ibid., 20. Translation by Matilda McCarthy.
60. Lamm 1915, 38; 2000, 39, and 331, note 61; and Schlieper, 10: "*Aber Swedenborg trennt sich weit von Descartes und nähert sich Leibniz bis zu*

*einem gewissen Grade, indem er dem Punkt den Substanzwert verleiht. Die Punkte, denn überall ist Punkt, erzeugen durch selbstthätige Composition das mechanische Weltall, ohne erneuten Eingriff des nur hypothetischen Infinitums; darum darf man diese Philosophie wohl im Ganzen monistisch nennen"* (But Swedenborg differs widely from Descartes and comes closer to Leibniz to a certain extent, because he ascribes substance value to the point. The points—for there is a point everywhere—generate the mechanical universe through independent composition without any further interventions by the only hypothetical Infinity. For that reason, one may call this philosophy monistic on the whole). Translation by Inge Jonsson.

61. §6, note b.
62. Arrhenius, xxvi–xxvii; Nordenmark, 74. Stroh has even argued that Descartes' system was the only one with which Swedenborg was intimately linked; see his series of articles entitled "Swedenborg's Early Life, Scientific Works, and Philosophy," *The New-Church Magazine* (1915): 542 and passim.
63. "The Sources of Swedenborg's Early Philosophy of Nature," *Opera* III: xxxiv–xxxv.
64. Translation by Matilda McCarthy.
65. See *The Worship and Love of God* §9, notes d and e.
66. Translation by Matilda McCarthy.
67. Schlieper, 16.
68. Nordenmark, 73–74: *"Swedenborgs spekulation är en naturfilosofi som ej tar någon hänsyn till Keplers, Galileis och Newtons upptäckter och matematiska analys"* (Swedenborg's speculations constitute a philosophy of nature, which does not take Kepler's, Galilei's, and Newton's discoveries and mathematical analysis into account); translation by Inge Jonsson. See also Arrhenius, xxviii.
69. Nordenmark has noticed (62) the connection to Ovid in this description. Translation by Matilda McCarthy.
70. Lamm 1915, 162–163; 2000, 161.
71. Translation by Matilda McCarthy.
72. *Principia*, 451–452. Swedenborg has obviously been anxious to emphasize both his independence of and his adherence to the great authority, whose extensive philosophical production in many ways resembles Swedenborg's future program in which the cosmology is a preliminary stage to the psychology as in Wolff.
73. Aristophanes, *The Birds,* translated by Dudley Fitts (New York: Harcourt, Brace & World, Inc., 1936, 1960), 242.
74. *Opera* III:324; Lamm 1915, 162; 2000, 161.
75. See, for example, O. Gruppe, *Die griechischen Culte und Mythen in ihren Beziehungen zu den orientalischen Religionen* (Leipzig, 1887), 612ff. Fredén (10–11) gives a short overview of the theogony and cosmogony of Orphicism.
76. M. P:son Nilsson, *Geschichte der griechischen Religion* I (Munich: Beck Verlag, 1941), 648. Translation by Inge Jonsson. Thus, Lamm's reference to Hesiod (1915, 20; 2000, 22) seems to be precipitate. Fredén (10) puts more emphasis on the differences between the Orpheans and Hesiod.
77. W. K. C. Guthrie, *Orpheus and Greek Religion,* 2nd ed. (London: Methuen, 1952), 14ff.
78. Pauly-Wissowa, *Real-Enzyklopädie der classischen Altertumswissenschaft,* Halbband 36:I, col. 1350.
79. M.Ter.Varronis. *De lingua latina libri qui supersunt* (Zweibrücken, 1788), I:318. Translation by Matilda McCarthy.
80. See, for example, H. Baumann, *Das doppelte Geschlecht* in *Ethnologische*

*Studien zur Bisexualität in Ritus und Mythos* (Berlin: Reimer, 1955), 175ff. and 268–269.

81. J. Needham, *A History of Embryology* (Cambridge: The University Press, 1934), 50–51. See the selection of Plutarch by H. Conrad, *Vermischte Schriften* (Munich and Leipzig, 1911), I:66ff.

82. *Aur. Theodosii Macrobii Opera*, Saturnal.lib. I, for example, ch. XXIII, lib. VII, ch. XVI; Pontanus-Meursius-Gronovius' ed. (London, 1694), 215ff. and 446–447.

83. Eusebios, *Preparatio evangelica*, lib. III ch. XI; F. Vigerus ed. (Paris, 1628), 115. See also F. Creuzer, *Symbolik und Mythologie der alten Völker* (Leipzig and Darmstadt, 1821), III:313.

84. D. Petavius, *Uranologion sive systema variorum authorum* (Paris, 1630), 127. Translation by Matilda McCarthy.

85. The passage plays a central part in Thibaut de Maisières' argument for an influence from Basil on Tasso; Thibaut de Maisières, 35–36. On the identification of the anonymous author, see D. Zöckler, *Geschichte der Beziehungen zwischen Theologie und Naturwissenschaft* (Gütersloh, 1877), I:171–172, 189.

86. I. Tremellius and F. Junius, *Testamenti veteris Biblia sacra* (Frankfurt, 1579), 3. See also *Cat.bibl.*, 1, 8. Translation by Matilda McCarthy.

87. See F.M. Mersennus, *Quaestiones celeberrimae in Genesim* (Paris, 1623), col. 730 and 919; D. Pareus, *Operum theologicorum exegeticorum* tom. I (Frankfurt, 1647), o. 29–30. See also H. Grotius, *De veritate religionis christianae*, new ed. (Amsterdam, 1669), 40–41.

88. *Guds Werk och Hwila*, 33. Translation by Inge Jonsson.

89. See Katherine B. Collier, *Cosmogonies of Our Fathers: Some Theories of the Seventeenth and Eighteenth Centuries* (New York: Columbia University Press, 1934), 13–24.

90. Ioannis Pici Mirandulae, *Opera quae extant omnia* tom. II (Basel, 1601), 501ff.

91. Lamm 1915, 259–260; 2000, 286.

92. S. Lindroth, "Paracelsismen i Sverige till 1600-talets mitt" (Ph. D. diss., Uppsala University, 1943), 402–403.

93. Theophrast von Hohenheim, gen. Paracelsus, *Sämtliche Werke* I. Abt., Bd 13, ed. by K. Sudhoff (Munich and Berlin: Oldenbourg, 1931), 140–141. Translation by Inge Jonsson. See also *Das Buch Paragranum*, ed. by F. Strunz (Leipzig: E. Diederichs, 1903), 51.

94. Lindroth, 402–403. A general observation of the similarities between Paracelsus and Swedenborg was made by J. Chr. Cuno; see *Documents* II: 478.

95. *The Works of Francis Bacon,* edited by James Spedding, Robert Leslie Ellis, and Douglas Denon Heath (London, 1887), III:79ff.; Engl. transl., ibid. (London, 1889), V:459ff. See also Whiting, 9ff.

96. See *De sapientia veterum, Work*, VI:654ff.; see also Ellis' preface to *De principiis*, III:65ff.

97. G.J. Voss, *De theologia gentili et physiologia christiana* (Amsterdam, 1642), I:V, 33–34.

98. E. Cassirer, *Die platonische Renaissance in England und die Schule von Cambridge* (Leipzig and Berlin: Cassell & Co., 1932), 6: "*Vor allem ist es jenes Bild der platonischen Gedankenwelt, das Marsilius Ficinus und die Florentinische Akademie gezeichnet hatte, das auch für die Denker der Schule von Cambridge als schlechthin-gültig, als eigentlich exemplarisch erscheint*" (Above all, the picture of the Platonic thinking, as it had been sketched by

Marsilio Ficino and the Florentine academy, appeared to be totally valid, actually exemplary, even to the Cambridge philosophers). Translation by Inge Jonsson.

99. *Henrici Mori Cantabrigiensis scriptorum philosophicorum* (London, 1679), II:461–643.

100. R. Cudworth, *The True Intellectual System of the Universe: The First Part; Wherein All the Reason and Philosophy of Atheism Is Confuted; and Its Impossibility Demonstrated* (London, 1678), 120ff.

101. Ibid., 688ff.

102. Lamm 1915, 69; 2000, 70.

103. *Mundus symbolicus* IV:LXXII, I:335–336. Mario Praz pointed out that, in some of the numerous emblem books, the egg symbol was used in a great many variations, for example, in "the very quaint *Ova Paschalia sacro emblemate inscripta descriptaque* by Father Georgius Stengelius, Munich, 1635, in which all the emblems are egg-shaped and the conceits derived from the egg" (Praz, 180).

104. *Opera*, III:283–298 (sketch) and 299–320; Burnet is mentioned on 297 and 319–320.

105. *Cat.bibl.*, 8.

106. *Dictionary of National Biography*, III:408ff.

107. *The Spectator*, vol. II (London, 1797), 350–353 (no. 146, August 17, 1711). Steele chiefly paraphrased the final chapter of the fourth book, and his way of placing Burnet together with Cicero is characteristic of the contemporary debate on modernity; see Collier, 69, note 5.

108. J. L. Lowes, *The Road to Xanadu: A Study in the Ways of the Imagination*, 2nd ed. (London: Constable, 1951), 612.

109. See *Oeuvres complètes de Malebranche*, introduction by D. Roustan, I:xviii; L. Holberg, *Jödiske Historie,*(Copenhagen, 1742), I:5–6 and 18–19. On Burnet's position in the history of learning in Great Britain, see B. Willey, *The Eighteenth Century Background: Studies on the Idea of Nature in the Period* (London: Chatto & Windus, 1940), 27ff. See also Zöckler, 143ff. Because he was so well known, Burnet is referred to only with initials in Thomas Baker's 1708 work *Reflections upon Learning*, 101 (together with William Whiston [1667–1752], to whom Benz has attached great importance for Swedenborg, although for rather weak reasons; see Benz, 1948, 46ff.; 2002, 42–45).

110. Stroh, "Swedenborg's early life, scientific works, and philosophy," 396; Nordenmark, 47.

111. *Documents* III:871.

112. KVA Cod Sw 86-53, 165–171. Ekelöf and Stroh's dating of 1719 might be too late, since Burnet was mentioned in a text published in 1718. In general, the huge manuscript collection has not been satisfactorily dated, commented on, or published. See the appendix.

113. *Opera* III:319–320. Translation by Inge Jonsson.

114. Thomas Burnet, *Telluris theoria sacra* . . . (Frankfurt, 1691), 220ff. This is the duodecimo reprint (of the original London edition ten years before) that Swedenborg owned and used (this passage appears on page 235ff.). The original edition is quoted in the text; but in the notes, references are given to both, although the differences are unimportant. See *Principia*, 389.

115. Duodecimo ed., 270; original ed., 285.

116. Ibid., 270 and 286, respectively.

117. Ibid., 270–271 and 286–287, respectively.

118. Ibid., 271–272 and 287, respectively. Burnet wants to modify the geocentri-

cally inspired interpretation of Varro, so that the sun becomes the yolk, the ether up to the fixed stars becomes the white and what is above the shell, but he does not wish to commit himself.

119. Ibid., 217 and 232, respectively. See also E. Dickinson, *Physica vetus et vera* (Hamburg, 1705), v; and W. Whiston, *A New Theory of the Earth* (London, 1737), 3.

120. Duodecimo ed., 273–274; original ed., 289–290. Contemporary interest is even reflected in Swedenborg's excerpts from Grotius and Leibniz; see cod. 36–110, pp. 145, 179, and 181; Acton, *A Philosopher's Notebook,* 316–317, 381, and 385.

121. *Principia*, 448; see also cod. 86–53, p. 171. The same quotation from Ovid can be found partially in *Opera* III:300.

122. In Burnet, 138–139 and 153, there are references to Lucretius, which may have been of importance to Swedenborg, since he noted them in cod. 86–53, p. 168.

123. The account is to be found in lib. I, chapter V, duodecimo ed., 33–43, and original ed., 34–48. A more detailed and slightly modified description appears in a later English edition, *The Sacred Theory of the Earth*, 6th ed. (London: 1726), I:71–88.

124. *Publii Ovidii Nasonis Metamorphoseon libri XV*, edited by J.G. Walchius (Leipzig, 1731), 7 (*ad modum Minellii*; cf *Cat.bibl.*, 8, and W. Engelmann, ed., *Bibliotheca scriptorum classicorum*, 8th ed. [Leipzig, 1882], II:447).

125. Burnet, duodecimo ed., 40; original ed., 45. Translation by Matilda McCarthy.

126. Ibid., 41 and 46, respectively.

127. Lib. II, chapter VII; duodecimo ed., 42; original ed., 47.

128. See English ed. I:365ff.

129. Duodecimo ed., 229; original ed., 243–244. Translation by Matilda McCarthy.

130. *Principia*, 391ff., and Burnet, 33ff. and 34ff., respectively.

131. Arrhenius, xxvii.

132. *Opera* I:281.

133. Burnet, 100, and 108–109, respectively. Translation by Matilda McCarthy.

134. Ibid., 287, and 303–304, respectively. Translation by Matilda McCarthy.

## Chapter 3

1. Pauly-Wissowa, *Real-Enzyklopädie der classischen Altertumswissenschaft*, vol. VI, col. 399ff.

2. *Metamorphoses* I:104. The commentary of a 1731 edition of Ovid states, "Arbuteus *ab* arbuto *arbore illa humili, quae poma fert instar cerasorum*" (22) (Arbuteus of arbutus, the humble tree that carries fruit like cherries).

3. *Principia*, 429ff., 445; *Worship and Love of God* §14.

4. *Principia*, 445. Translation by Matilda McCarthy.

5. Burnet, duodecimo ed., 42; original ed., 48. Translation by Matilda McCarthy.

6. *Adversaria* I:79ff.; English translation *The Word Explained* I:102ff.

7. *Emanuelis Swedenborgii Regnum subterraneum sive minerale de cupro et orichalco* (Dresden and Leipzig, 1734); *Opera philosophica et mineralia* tom. III, preface, 3 (not paginated). The passage has been quoted by A. G. Nathorst in *Opera* I:xxvi, note 1, although without observing the connection to Burnet. Translation by Matilda McCarthy. See also *Miscellanea observata circa res*

*naturales* I (Leipzig, 1722), reprinted in *Opera* I: 63 and 82–83. See also excerpts in cod. 86–53, p.168.

8. Swedenborg's planetary theory is also treated in S. Arrhenius, *Människan inför världsgåtan* (Stockholm: Hugo Gebers förlag, 1907), 76ff.; and in Crasta, esp. 240–304.

9. *Metamorphoses* I:107–112; translation by Rolfe Humphries, by permission of Indiana University Press. *Principia*, 448.

10. *Principia*, 448; cf Lamm 1915, 162–163; 2000, 162.

11. See note 7 above.

12. *Opera* III: 276; see also 309ff. Translation by Inge Jonsson.

13. See Burnet, duodecimal ed., 45ff.; original ed., 51ff.

14. A later work by Burnet, *Archaeologiae philosophicae: sive doctrina antiqua de rerum originibus*, II; VII–X, second edition (London, 1728), 375–476, contains an enormous number of references to ancient philosophy and patristics; it offers a good illustration of the extensive genre.

15. *De Genesi ad litteram* lib. VIII, chapter VII; Migne's edition in *Patrologia latina* XXXIV, col. 378.

16. See Mersennus, col. 1141ff.

17. *La seconde Sepmaine* I:123–127; *ed. cit.* III:5. Translation by Inge Jonsson.

18. This precise location has been criticized as disturbingly anachronistic by J. Peter in *A Critique of Paradise Lost* (New York: Columbia University Press, 1960), 87. An interesting analysis of Milton's view of paradise, which among other things emphasizes its emblematic inspiration, can be found in J. B. Broadbent, *Some Graver Subject* (London: Chatto & Windus, 1960), 173–185.

19. Whiting, 45ff.

20. *Opera* III:273. Translation by Inge Jonsson.

21. Ibid., 305. Translation by Inge Jonsson.

22. Ibid., 305; see Lamm 1915, 20–21; 2000, 22.

23. *Principia*, 448. Translation by Inge Jonsson. The list of authorities illustrates that Swedenborg held a synthetic opinion even before the doctrine of correspondence.

24. Burnet, duodecimo ed., 133; original ed., 147. Translation by Matilda McCarthy.

25. Ibid., 245, and 260–261, respectively. Translation by Matilda McCarthy.

26. *Principia*, 448; cod. 86–53, p. 171. Translation by Matilda McCarthy.

27. See Swedenborg's criticism in *Om Jordenes och Planeternas Gång och Stånd*, quoted above.

28. Latin ed., 206ff.; original ed., 221ff. Also see the English ed., I:362–363.

29. *Principia*, 448; see also the correspondence examples there. Philo once interpreted the flaming sword as the sun; see the edition to which Erik Benzelius contributed: Th. Mangey, ed., *Philonis Judaei Opera* (London, 1742), I:143.

30. *Telluris theoria sacra* II, chapter VI, passim; see also *Archaeologiae philosophicae*, 388ff.

31. Leibniz mentions Burnet respectfully in his theodicy, from which Swedenborg made extensive excerpts in cod. 36–110. Hereinafter Leibniz's work will be quoted from the original French, whenever Swedenborg's own excerpts in Latin are not used; *Essais de theodicée sur la bonté de Dieu, la liberté de l'homme, et l'origine du mal* (Amsterdam, 1720), where there is a reference to Burnet in III: 275, §245. In the notes, reference will be given to the Latin text: G. G. *Leibnitii Tentamina theodicaeae . . .* (Frankfurt and Leipzig, 1739), 1006–1007. Burnet is also praised in Leibniz's correspondence; see the edition

used by Swedenborg, Ch. Kortholtus, *G.G. Leibnitii Epistolae ad diversos . . .* (Leipzig, 1742), IV:53.
32. Lamm 1915, 19ff.; 2000, 21–23.
33. *Opera* III:301–302. See also Lamm 1915, 20, and the references given there; 2000, 21; 330, notes 33 and 34. Translation by Inge Jonsson.
34. One example of these ideas can be found in the article by Steele referred to in the previous chapter, note 107, above.
35. V. Harris, *All Coherence Gone* (Chicago: University of Chicago Press, 1949), 86–172.
36. Quoted by Harris, 126. See also the lamentations of Horace in his Roman ode III:6: "*aetas parentum peior avis tulit / nos nequiores, mox daturos / progeniem vitiosorem*" (*Q. Horatius Flaccus Oden und Epoden*, ed. by Adolf Kiessling and Richard Heinze, 7th edition [Berlin: Weidmannsche Buchhandel, 1930], 294); quoted in Swedish translation in Rudberg, 89.
37. See Harris, 184.
38. Ibid., 157–158.
39. See *Emanuelis Swedenborgii Oeconomia regni animalis in transactiones divisa . . .*, III, edited by J. J. G. Wilkinson (London, 1847); hereinafter referred to as *De Fibra*; English translation by A. Acton, *The Economy of the Animal Kingdom . . . by Emanuel Swedenborg*, III (Philadelphia: Swedenborg Scientific Association, 1918), 161–162. Here one may find childhood connected to the Golden Age and the old age with the era of iron from a neurological point of view, which should be compared to the correspondence between the changes of nature and those of life in *The Worship and Love of God*.
40. Lamm 1915, 166–167; 2000, 165.
41. *Opera* III:319. Translation by Inge Jonsson. This is the published version; but in an earlier draft, the author expresses himself differently: "*. . . afstannande; thet är, igenom thet at hela then stora kretsen, som jorden är omgifven med, förlorar sin rörelse, lemnas til en annan gång*" (ibid., 297) ( . . . coming to a standstill: that is, by what the whole big sphere, with which the earth is surrounded, loses its motion will be left to another time). Also in other contexts, the printed version has a more Christian tone.
42. Cod. 36–110, inner front cover; Acton, *A Philosopher's Note Book*, 1.
43. *Adversaria* I:37–38, §19; *The Word Explained* I:48–49.
44. Lamm 1915, 326ff.; 2000, 325ff. See also Inge Jonsson, "Emanuel Swedenborg och Yttersta domen. Ett litterärt 200-årsminne," *Ord och bild* (1958): 417–424.
45. Harris, 22ff.
46. Ibid., 197ff.
47. Lamm 1915, 17–22; 2000, 18–23.
48. *Dictionary of National Biography,* III:409. In J. J. Scheuchzer's encyclopedia of theology and natural history, *Kupfer-Bibel* (Augsburg and Ulm: 1731), one may study the intense debate caused by Burnet's work (see the introductory "*Verzeichnis der Auctorum*") but also the esteem with which it is referred to. Swedenborg's meeting with Flamsteed in 1711 is mentioned in a letter to Erik Benzelius of April 30 the same year; see *Opera*, I:209–210. In his reply to Celsius in 1740, he made a mistake about the year (1710); see *Documents*, I:574.
49. *Swedenborgs drömbok*, 288; *Swedenborg's Dream Diary*, 313, §277.
50. Sigstedt, 203.
51. *Oeconomia*, vol. II, §355. Translation by Matilda McCarthy.
52. Lamm 1915, 53; 2000, 53–54.
53. See Clissold's translation of *Oeconomia*, II:359–369.

54. *Oeconomia*, vol. I, §253. Translation by Matilda McCarthy.
55. Lamm 1915, 69–70; 2000, 70.
56. French ed., xxviii; Latin trans., 414. Translation by Inge Jonsson.
57. Needham, 147–149 and 183: "By 1720 the theory of pre-formation was thoroughly established, not only on the erroneous grounds put forward by Malpighi and Swammerdam, but on the experiments of Andry, Dalenpatius and Gautier, who all asserted that they had seen exceedingly minute forms of men, with arms, heads, and legs complete, inside the spermatozoa under the microscope."
58. Ibid., 48, note, and 61ff.
59. Ibid., 149: "'In nature,' he said, 'there is no generation but only propagation, the growth of parts. Thus original sin is explained, for all men were contained in the organs of Adam and Eve. When their stock of eggs is finished, the human race will cease to be.'"
60. Ibid., 22, 61. See also M. Ramström, "Emanuel Swedenborg as an Anatomist," *British Medical Journal* (Oct. 15, 1910): 2.
61. See Clissold's index of authors, in his translation of *Oeconomia*, II:360.
62. Needham, 161; see Lamm, 1915, 52ff.; 2000, 52ff.
63. French ed., xxviii; Latin trans., 414. Translation by Inge Jonsson. The entire *Essais de theodicée* is polemical, primarily against Pierre Bayle (1647–1706), which means a meeting of two heroes of erudition, throwing quotations and references about.
64. Lamm presented a brilliant survey of this (1915, 69–94; 2000, chap. 4), to which I refer for a general briefing.
65. *Oeconomia,* vol. I, §7. Translation by Matilda McCarthy.
66. See, for example, Schlieper, 19–20, and Lamm, 1915, 69–70; 2000, 69–70.
67. See Lindroth's statement in *Ny ill.svensk litteraturhistoria*, II:197: *"få ord är vanligare i hans skrifter än* usus, *gagn, nyttig gärning"* (few words are more frequent in his writings than *usus*, use, useful action).
68. *Oeconomia*, vol. I, §580. Translation by Matilda McCarthy.
69. See the survey of the content of *The Worship and Love of God* and the formulation in *Oeconomia*, vol. I, §584: *"In his sex Seriebus Natura acquievisse videtur, nam septima non datur"* (In these six series, nature is seen to have come to rest, for a seventh one does not exist). Translation by Matilda McCarthy.
70. Translation by Matilda McCarthy.
71. *"Scientia Scientiarum. Mathesis universalium. Doctrina ordinis, serierum et graduum"* (The science of sciences. The mathematics of universals. The doctrine of order, series and degrees): cod. 36–110, p. 4; Acton, *A Philosopher's Note Book,* 9.
72. Lamm 1915, 72; 2000, 72–73.
73. Cod. 36–110, pp. 6–7; Acton, *A Philosopher's Note Book,* 12ff.
74. Ibid., 117ff.; 236ff.
75. The concept of *varietas harmonica* and its eschatological implications is discussed below.
76. Lamm 1915, 96; 2000, 96.

# Chapter 4

1. I have not been able to find any direct prototype for this motif; it should be regarded as an independent effect of inspiration from Ovidian emblematics and Leibnizian *lex continui* thinking. The idea of the appearance of animals as

reflecting their character is an early parallel to the account in the sixth scene of the face of man as a mirror of his soul.

2. "Analysis and review," 38–39.
3. *Photolith.* III:99; English trans. in *Scientific and Philosophical Treatises* II:27–28. See also in Lamm 1915, 52; 2000, 52–53.
4. S. Lindroth, "Uralstringen. Ett kapitel ur biologiens äldre historia" (Spontaneous generation: A chapter of the older history of biology), *Lychnos* (1939): 159–192; this essay presents an excellent survey of the debate.
5. Ibid., 160ff.
6. Ibid., 166. Translation by Inge Jonsson.
7. Ibid., 167.
8. Kircher has been mentioned, for example, by Wilkinson in his Swedenborg biography, 295, but only in general terms.
9. See the extracts from Muschenbroek in *Principia*, among others, 182, 188, 223; see also *Regnum animale*, vol. I, §162, note g.
10. "Uralstringen," 177–178.
11. *Renati Des Cartes Opera philosophica* (Frankfurt: 1692), *Principiorum philosophiae,* pars tertia, XLV:52. The reference has been made by N. von Hofsten in *Skapelsetro och uralstringshypoteser före Darwin* (Creationism and theories of spontaneous generation before Darwin), Uppsala universitets årsskrift (Uppsala: Uppsala University, 1928), 22.
12. Lindroth, "Uralstringen," 164. See also E. Nordenskiöld, *Biologins historia* (The history of biology) (Helsingfors, Finland: Björck & Börjesson, 1920), 1:161ff., and von Hofsten, 18ff.
13. Lindroth, "Uralstringen," 180. Translation by Inge Jonsson.
14. See Clissold's index in his translation of *Oeconomia*, II:360, and the passages listed there, and Wilkinson's "Bibliographical Notices" in his translation of *Regnum animale*, 706–14.
15. von Lippmann, 38ff.; see also Lindroth, "Uralstringen," 168ff.
16. Quoted by Lindroth, "Uralstringen," 171. Translation by Inge Jonsson.
17. D. Sennert, *De chymicorum cum Aristotelicis et Galenicis consensu ac dissensu* (Wittenberg, 1619), I:85–86; see also von Lippmann, 42.
18. *Essais de theodicée*, §351: French edition, 351, Latin translation, 1126–1127.
19. von Lippman, 23. Translation by Inge Jonsson.
20. von Hofsten, 18.
21. P. Mouy, *Le développement de la physique cartésienne 1646-1712* (Paris: J. Vrin, 1934), 275. Translation by Inge Jonsson.
22. Lib. V:783–787, 801–815; ed. cit.., 472ff.; English translation by H. A. J. Munro, *Great Books of the Western World* (Chicago: Encyclopedia Brittanica, 1952), XII:71.
23. Lib. V: 818–820; ed. cit., 474–475, Munro translation, 71.
24. See, for example, lib. II:1141ff.; ed. cit., 296ff., Munro translation, 29–30.
25. *Principia*, 210, 228–229.
26. *Telluris theoria sacra*, 138–139 and 153; the Lucretius quotations are taken from II:1159–1161, and V:933–935, ed. cit., 296–297 and 480–481; transl. cit., 29 and 73. Swedenborg made excerpts from Burnet's quotations of Lucretius in cod. 86-53, p. 168.
27. *Telluris theoria sacra*, 136 and 150.
28. English edition I:249ff.
29. *Oeconomia* II, §346. Translation by Matilda McCarthy.
30. E. Liedgren, *Svensk psalm och andlig visa* (Swedish hymns and sacred songs) (Stockholm and Uppsala: Diakonistyrelsens förlag, 1926), 441ff.

31. Martin Lamm, *Upplysningstidens romantik*, 2 vols., 2nd ed. (1918–1920; Stockholm: Hammarström & Åborg, 1981), I:119. Translation by Inge Jonsson.
32. October 6–7, 1744; *Swedenborgs drömbok*, 266; *Swedenborg's Dream Diary*, §250, p. 209.
33. *Em. Swedenborgii Prodromus philosophiae ratiocinantis de infinito, et causa finali creationis: deque mechanismo operationis animae et corporis* (Dresden and Leipzig, 1734), 48 (to be referred to as *De Infinito* below); English translation by J. J. G. Wilkinson, *The Infinite and the Final Cause of Creation . . . by Emanuel Swedenborg*, new impr. (London: The Swedenborg Society, 1908), 40.
34. A similar *creatio ex nihilo* conception can also be found in §34; compare *Three Transactions on the Cerebrum*, I:730, §1202.
35. See Clissold's introduction to his translation, *The Principia . . . by Emanuel Swedenborg* (London: W. Newbery, 1845–1846), I:lxxxiii and following.
36. A general idea of the part of the debate of immediate interest for Swedenborg is given by Diestel, 482ff.
37. Burnet, *Archaeologiae philosophicae*, 427–428.; Conklin, 67.
38. Whiting, 35.
39. See the instructive chapter "Milton's Reading" in Adams, 128–176, and its concluding evaluation: "We shall not wholly misrepresent the spirit in which John Milton approached his reading, I think, if we say that for the most part he held up other books, as he held up himself, to the criterion of his own magnanimity; that he approached few authors in the spirit of a man seeking permission to hold an opinion or borrow an expression, but sat over most of his library as a judge, if not as a conqueror." In a less magisterial, somewhat neurotic sense, Swedenborg might have been reading in a similar spirit.
40. Lamm 1915, 44, 189ff.; 2000, 43. See also 1915, 111–112 (2000, 110–111), where the definition of emanation is so extensive and cautious that it must be taken symbolically. I can agree with that, even if I can see no reason for referring to Milton as a support.
41. G. Scholem, *Les grands courants de la mystique juive* (Paris: Payot, 1950), 234; in English, *Major Trends in Jewish Mysticism* (New York: Schocken Books, 1946), 218.
42. See S. Lindroth, *Paracelsismen*, passim, and J. Nordström, "Georg Stiernhielm: Filosofiska fragment," (Ph.D. diss., Uppsala University, 1924), particularly chapter 6.
43. Ernst Benz, *Die christliche Kabbala: Ein Stiefkind der Theologie* (Zürich: Rhein-Verlag, 1958), 10–24 (rev. by Inge Jonsson in *Lychnos* [1959]: 282-283). Among Swedenborg's excerpts from *Essais de theodicée,* there are also notes on the Cabbala pattern; see cod. 36–110, p. 79; Acton, *A Philosopher's Note Book*, 160. This is also the case with the Grotius extracts, in cod. 36–110, pp. 121, 178; Acton, 250, 379.
44. Cod. 36–110, p. 122; Acton, *A Philosopher's Note Book*, 252; *Essais de theodicée*, §284; French edition, 304–305; English translation, 1057. Even the New Church reviewer of Acton's edition emphasizes the unsatisfactory quality from a scholarly standpoint of Swedenborg's way of making notes (*The New Philosophy* [1931]: 441–443).
45. *Oeconomia,* vol. I, §306. Translation by Matilda McCarthy.
46. P. Janet, ed., *Oeuvres philosophiques de Leibniz*, tome II (Paris, 1866), 483; cod. 36–110, p. 122; Acton, *A Philosopher's Note Book*, 253. Swedenborg quoted the Latin translation at hand (1358): "*Actualia dependent a Deo tum*

*in existendo, tum in agendo, nec tantum ab intellectu ejus, sed etiam a volun-
tate. Et quidem in existendo, dum omnes res a Deo libere sunt creatae, atque
etiam a Deo conservantur; neque male docetur, conservationem divinam esse
continuatam creationem, ut radius continuo a sole prodit; etsi creaturae neque
ex Dei essentia, neque necessario promanent"* (French ed., 492). Translation
from the French by Inge Jonsson.

47. Lamm 1915, 74; 2000, 75.
48. *Oeconomia,* vol. II, §260; Clissold translation, II:244.
49. See Stroh, A.H., "Swedenborg's Contributions to Psychology," *Transactions
of the International Swedenborg Congress 1910* (London: Swedenborg Society, 1911), 156.
50. Cod. 36–110; Acton, *A Philosopher's Note Book,* note on 253: Although
Acton did not translate the text exactly, the content has been rendered correctly in all essentials. The translator of Leibniz mentions Spinoza as an example in contrast to Descartes, Huyghens, Leibniz, and Wolff (1358–1359).
51. *The Worship and Love of God,* §63, note c; and also §62, note b.
52. *Oeconomia,* vol. II, §254. Translation by Matilda McCarthy.
53. Rydelius, 278–279. Translation by Inge Jonsson.
54. For example, Lamm 1915, 250-267; 2000; 251–258.
55. J. Carpenter, ed., *Libri qvatuordecim qui Aristotelis esse dicuntur, de secretiore parte divinae sapientiae secundum Aegyptios* (Paris: 1572). See also cod.
36–110, last cover; Acton, *A Philosopher's Note Book,* 508. Lamm (1917,
55–56; 2000, 56, n. 76) refers to *Photolith.* III, where the passage has been included together with minor parts of this manuscript; but otherwise he does
not seem to have used the excerpted material. The so-called *Theology of Aristotle* was published in a German translation by F. Dieterici, *Die sogenannte
Theologie des Aristoteles* (Leipzig,1883); see also his "Ueber die sogenannte
Theologie des Aristoteles bei den Arabern," *Abhandl. und Vorträge des fünften internationalen Orientalisten-Congresses* (Berlin, 1882), 5–6.
56. Cod. 36–110, p. 119; Acton, *A Philosopher's Note Book,* 242. This is an in-
exact copy of Carpenter's edition, spread 150 (should be 151), lib. 14:15.
Translation by Matilda McCarthy.
57. Cod. 36–110, p. 119; Acton, *A Philosopher's Note Book,* 241–242. The summary refers to lib. 13:6, 7. It is a reminder that Swedenborg has rejected the
idea of a world soul, in *Worship and Love of God,* §24, note q; and is a
polemic allusion to Neoplatonism, probably in the form presented in the *Theology of Aristotle.*
58. Lib. 11:4, spread 105.
59. See Gilson, 242ff., and P. Courcelle, *Recherches sur les confessions de Saint
Augustin* (Paris: Boccard, 1950), 60–78.
60. Gouhier, 80.
61. It is also reflected in Jesper Swedberg's autobiographical *Lefwernes Beskrifning;* Benz points out (1948, 6; 2002, 4) the obvious comparison between the
educative zeal of the parents and that of Saint Monica (*Lefwernes Beskrifning,*
22). A case of Augustinian influence outside the notorious Jansenist circles is
offered by Antoinette Bourignon, who was given her final call in a vision of
the Father; see J. Björkhem, "Antoinette Bourignon" (Ph.D. diss., Lund University, 1940), 45ff.
62. Lamm (1915, 250–251; 2000, 249–250) correctly views the emanation doctrines held by Swedenborg. But with respect to the drama of creation, he does
not give attention to its symbolic fable, nor to Swedenborg's capacity for making subtle theological distinctions, probably because Lamm wants to reach

Swedenborg's theosophic phase and consequently reads its consistent systematics into the previous writings. The conformity with Augustine, which Lamm discusses here, is actually noticeable much earlier.

63. *Photolith.* VI:83. Translation by Matilda McCarthy.
64. *Clavis hieroglyphica,* exempel VI, confirmatio propositionum 2; ed. cit., 99–100; *Psych.trans.,* 167–168.
65. K. Huber, *Leibniz* (München: Oldenbourg, 1951), 248. Translation by Inge Jonsson.
66. Cod. 36–110, p. 64ff.; Acton, *A Philosopher's Note Book,* 123ff.
67. Huber, 249ff.
68. Lamm 1915, 93, note; 2000, 93, 335, n. 118.
69. *De anima,* 252; *Rational Psychology,* 314–315. Translation by Matilda McCarthy.
70. Cod. 36–110, p. 123; Acton, *A Philosopher's Note Book,* 254–255 (a misreading in the Latin, *ordo* instead of *ardor,* 255); *Essais de theodicée,* ed. cit., vii, transl. cit., 389. Translation by Matilda McCarthy.
71. Ibid., 123; transl. cit., 255; *Essais de theodicée,* ed. cit, viii; transl. cit., 391. Translation by Matilda McCarthy.
72. A survey of Swedenborg's later opinions of Wolff, based primarily on *Diarium spirituale,* is presented in *Documents,* I:617ff.

## Chapter 5

1. *Adversaria,* I:10; *The Word Explained,* I:13. Translation by Matilda McCarthy.
2. Thus, I regard this biblical commentary as yet another support for the authenticity of the statement by Christian Johansén, quoted previously.
3. H. Grotius, *De veritate religionis christianae* lib. I:XVI, Annotata (Amsterdam, 1669), 38–108. Swedenborg owned the twelfth edition (1662) in his library. See also *Cat.bibl.,* 5.
4. Burnet, *Archaeologiae philosophicae,* 481ff.
5. Chr. Garmann, *Homo ex ovo* (Chemnitz, 1672), "Preface," 1. Translation by Matilda McCarthy.
6. Ibid., 4.
7. Chr. Garmann, *Oologia curiosa duabus partibus absoluta, ortum corporum naturalium ex ovo demonstrans* (Cygneae [Zwickau]: s.a). See also Needham, 157.
8. Ibid., 20–21.
9. Ibid., 138ff.
10. Ibid., 158. I have rendered the text from two Swedish translations by E. Hellquist (Lund: Gleerup, 1923), V:9, ll. 143–146; and by I. Björkeson (Stockholm: Natöur och Kultur, 2003), 95.
11. Ibid., 159. Virgil, *Aeneid,* Book VIII:314–316, translated by James Rhoades, *Great Books of the Western World* (Chicago: Encyclopedia Brittania, 1952), 13:267.
12. Cod. 36–110, p. 65; Acton, *A Philosopher's Note Book,* 127; *Essais de theodicée,* French ed., 350–351; Latin ed., 1125ff. P.Papini Stati *Thebais,* ed. A. Klotz (Leipzig: Teubner, 1908), 128.
13. See, for example, V. Rydberg, *Undersökningar i germanisk mythologi* (Stockholm, 1889), II:70–71; U. Holmberg, *Der Baum des Lebens,* Annales acad.sc.fenn. tom. XVI (Helsinki: Academia scientiarum fennica, 1922–1923),

51–70 (the theological analogy between the tree of life and the cross of Christ is mentioned on pp. 66–67.)

14. See e.g. C.G. Jung, *Psychologie und Alchimie* (Zürich: Rascher, 1944), 103, among others.
15. See J. B. van Helmont, *Opera omnia* (Frankfurt, 1707), 744ff.
16. Paracelsus, *Sämtliche Werke*, Sudhoff edition, XIV: 578, 582.
17. Ibid., XIV:582.
18. Lamm 1915, 187; 2000, 185–186.
19. *Metamorphoses* I:452–567.
20. Emanuel Swedenborg, *Opera poetica* (Upsala: Typis Academicis, 1910), 57–62; Emanuel Swedenborg, *Ludus Heliconius and Other Latin Poems* edited, with introduction, translation, and commentary by H. Helander, 102–109.
21. Cod. 36–110, p. 73; Acton, *A Philosopher's Note Book*, 147.
22. Lamm 1915, 187ff.; 2000, 186.
23. *Oeconomia*, vol. II, §149. Translation by Matilda McCarthy.
24. Ibid., vol. I, §560. Translation by Matilda McCarthy.
25. *Oeconomia*, vol. I, §§505, 561; vol. II, §§79, 135, 140, 150; *De fibra*, §61. See R. L. Tafel, trans., *The Brain Considered Anatomically, Physiologically and Philosophically by Emanuel Swedenborg* (London: The Swedenborg Society, 1887), II:248, §665 (hereinafter *The Brain*); *Three Transactions on the Cerebrum*, I:33, §57a. On Swedenborg's brain research, see M. Ramström, "Hvarpå grundar sig Swedenborgs åsikt om hjärnans funktion, och särskildt om hjärnbarken som själsverksamhetens säte?" (What is the theory of Swedenborg's view on the function of the brain, and particularly on the cortex as the seat of the mind?) (Uppsala: 1910), and idem, "Om Corpora Striatas och Thalami funktion enligt Swedenborg och nutida forskning" (On the function of corpora striata and thalamus according to Swedenborg and present-day research), *Kungl. Vetenskapsakademiens Handlingar* 49, no. 9 (1912); and *Transactions of the International Swedenborg Congress* (London: Swedenborg Society,1910), sect. I; T. Gordh Jr. and P. Sourander, "Swedenborg, Linné och hjärnforskningen" (Swedenborg, Linné and brain research) *Nordisk medicinhistorisk årsbok* (1990): 97–117 (contains a short summary in English).
26. *Adversaria*, I:11; *The Word Explained*, I:I, 15. Translation by Matilda McCarthy.
27. *Adversaria*, I:40; *The Word Explained*, I:51.
28. R. Bauerreiss, *Arbor vitae* (München: Bayerische Benediktineradkaemie, 1938), 4; a similar symbolic application of the tree of life can be found in Stagnelius: see G. Widengren, "Gnostikern Stagnelius," *Samlaren* NF 25 (1944), 164–167.
29. *De Infinito*, A 3; Wilkinson trans., *The Infinite Cause of Creation*, 3.
30. See, for example, Lamm 1915, 17ff, and 2000, 18–20; Benz, *Emanuel Swedenborg*, 24ff, and 2002, 22–25; and Toksvig, 39.
31. A brilliant portrayal of Benzelius, written by Hans Forssell, was published in *Svenska Akademiens handlingar* (Acts of the Swedish Academy) 58 (Stockholm, 1883). Leibniz belonged to the large group of scholars with whom Benzelius corresponded; see Asta Ekenvall, "Eric Benzelius d.y. och G.W.von Leibniz," Linköpings biblioteks handlingar (Acts of the Linköping library) 4, no. 3 (1953): 5–64.
32. The dedication may also be an act of sympathy in the personal crisis that affected Benzelius because of the divorce scandal of his daughter Greta Norrelia, which culminated in 1732–1733; on this affair, during which Benzelius' wife, Swedenborg's sister Anna, showed a conspicuous degree of erotic tolerance,

see an amusing essay by H. Schück in *Från det forna Upsala* (Stockholm: Hugo Gebers förlag, 1917), 113–167; see also A. Nelson, "Eric Benzelius d.y:s eftermäle" (Eric Benzelius Jr.'s reputation), *Donum Grapeanum* (Uppsala: Almqvist & Wiksell, 1946), 86ff. On Swedberg's belief in angels, see, for example, B. Wahlström, "Swedberg och änglarna" in *Psalm och sång* (Lund: Gleerup, 1959), 104–115.

33. See a letter to Benzelius in December 1715, *Opera*, I:234; Lamm 1915, 23ff.; 2000, 24ff.
34. Through Benzelius' lifelong work with an edition of Philo, he is also connected to the hexaemeral tradition: see Forssell, 209–223 and 352–375.
35. *De Infinito*, 28. Translation by Matilda McCarthy.
36. Ibid., 20. Translation by Matilda McCarthy.
37. See L. F. Hite's excellent introduction to the English translation, especially xvii–xviii.
38. *De Infinito*, 25; Wilkinson translation, 19.
39. *De Infinito*, 28–29; Wilkinson translation, 22–23. On the so-called second Cartesian contest that raged at the university of Uppsala and in the estate of the clergy in 1686–1689 and which had long-term effects, see especially R. Lindborg, "Descartes in Uppsala" (Ph.D. diss., Uppsala University, 1965), 223–350. This dissertation has an English summary. Stroh noticed the influence of the contest on Swedenborg's development in many contexts, for example, in "The Sources of Swedenborg's Early Philosophy of Nature," *Opera*, vol. III.
40. Lamm 1915, 43; 2000, 43.
41. *De Infinito*, 55–78; Wilkinson translation, 46–67. The example occupies almost one-tenth of the text; Heister's being the source has been pointed out by Wilkinson in his translation, 47, note. See also Cicero *De natura deorum* II:LIVff, ed. H. Rackham (London: Harvard University Press, 1933), 251ff.
42. Concerning Swedenborg and Locke, see Lamm 1915, 28ff.; 2000, 29–33.
43. *De Infinito*, 88. Translation by Matilda McCarthy.
44. See Gouhier, *La vocation de Malebranche*, 7: "*Avant de rencontrer Descartes, Malebranche n'avait guère envie de devenir auteur; il ne pensait qu'à vivre en bon prêtre de l'Oratoire de Jésus; or il trouve un jour L'Homme de Renè Descartes, et le voilà qui prend la plume, qui attaque Aristote avec plus de violence que ne l'avait fait son nouveau maître, le voilà qui occupe l'Europe de ses querelles pendant quarante années*" (Before encountering Descartes, Malebranche had no desire to become an author, his only thought being to live as a good priest of the Oratorian order. But one day he found *Man* by René Descartes. He then took pen in hand and attacked Aristotle more violently than his new master had. He subsequently engaged Europe in his controversies for forty years). Translation by Inge Jonsson.
45. *De Infinito*, 97ff.; Wilkinson translation, 84ff.
46. *De Infinito*, 115; Wilkinson translation, 99.
47. *De Infinito*, 117. Translation by Matilda McCarthy.
48. Lamm 1915, 43–44; 2000, 44.
49. *De Infinito*, 149; 130. Translation by Matilda McCarthy.
50. *Oeconomia*, vol. II, §251. Translation by Matilda McCarthy. This passage is referred to by Lamm 1915, 74, see also 111ff.; 2000, 74, also 111ff.
51. See J. J. G. Wilkinson "*De anima fragmentum*," in *Emanuelis Swedenborgii Opuscula quaedam argumenti philosophici* (London, 1846), 89–122, esp. 116 (hereinafter referred to as *Opuscula*; English translation by A. Acton in *Psych. Trans.*, 19–71, esp. 56–57).

52. Lib.I: cap.IV; Migne's ed. in *Patrologia latina* XLIV, col. 477. Translation by Matilda McCarthy. For Swedenborg's excerpts of Augustine, see cod. 36–110, p. 12; Acton, *A Philosopher's Note Book*, 27.
53. *Oeconomia*, vol. II, §295. Translation by Matilda McCarthy.
54. Lamm 1915, 80, note; 2000, 334, n. 105.
55. Cod. 36–110, 205–206, 256; Acton, *A Philosopher's Note Book*, 422–424, 484–485. In the excerpts, the Bible references are correct, but in *The Worship and Love of God*, there is a mistake in the Exodus reference (XIV instead of XV; ed. cit., 22). The difference in the reference to Ps. 104 is due to the divergent numbering in the Castellio Bible used by Swedenborg.
56. *De anima et ejus origine*, esp. I:XIV; ed. cit., col. 484ff. See also Acton, *A Philosopher's Note Book*, 27, note; see also A, Nyman, *Själsbegreppets förvandlingar* (The transformations of the soul concept) (Stockholm: Hugo Gebers förlag, 1943), 14–31.
57. Cod. 36–110, p. 12; Acton, *A Philosopher's Note Book*, 27. "Ibid" in the quotation refers, as Acton noticed, to *De anima et ejus origine*. Translation by Matilda McCarthy.
58. See the Acton translation of cod. 36–110, p. 26, note; and *De civitate Dei* lib.XIII:cap. XXIV, B. Dombart's ed. *Sancti Aurelii Augustini episcopi De civitate Dei libri XXII*, vol. I (Leipzig, 1877), 592ff.
59. Cod. 36–110, p. 9; Acton, *A Philosopher's Note Book*, 18ff.

## Chapter 6

1. Cod. 36–110, p. 235; Acton, *A Philosopher's Note Book*, 454–455. Translation by Matilda McCarthy.
2. The triad consists of *animus*, the vegetative soul, the sensuous consciousness; *mens*, the intellect, the reason; and *anima*, the intuitive soul; see also Lamm 1915, 77; 2000, 77.
3. *Photolith.* VI:62; English translation in *The Brain* I:7–8.
4. See Robbins, 33–34.
5. Lamm 1915, 170; 2000, 171.
6. Compare §55, note s, with *Clavis hieroglyphica*, examples XV and XI; *ed. cit.*, 113 and 108; pointed out by Acton in *Psych. trans.*, 201ff (the examples from *Clavis hieroglyphica* translated by Acton, 181 and 175–176.) The rendering in *The Worship and Love of God* is not exact but has been adapted to fit the scene.
7. *Photolith.* III:96; English translation in *Scientific and Philosophical Treatises* II:22.
8. Ibid., 97; English translation, 24–25; Swedenborg wrote "*investienda*," but, like Stroh, I regard this as a miswriting of "*investiganda*." Translation by Matilda McCarthy.
9. Lamm 1915, 77; 2000, 77
10. For the section on psychology, a general reference should be given to Benz 1948, in which the author has attempted to sketch an intellectual background in Böhme, Paracelsus, van Helmont, and others, starting from the dream of the first being's state of innocence and partly following Lamm. However, Benz makes it quite clear that this is a commonly accepted idea (1948, 158–159; 2002, 139); for that reason, I am skeptical of his attributions, which are not supported by any quoted material. Of course, this does not mean that Swedenborg would have been ignorant about the "mystical" tradition, but it seems reasonable to presume that he did not take his point of departure from

it but from Descartes and his many disciples and from modern anatomy. Swedenborg appears to have been a kind of intellectual aristocrat in his choice of mentors, at least for excerpting and quoting in his own works.

11. The title was probably chosen to emphasize the connection to Wolff.
12. *Oeconomia* I, §579. Translation by Matilda McCarthy.
13. This is a translation of Nyman, 56: "*alstrades ur blodets finaste partiklar—ur partes sanguinis subtilissimae—för att sedan som en slags dunstartade varma strömmar genom blodbanor och nerver rusa omkring i organismen.*"
14. *Oeconomia* II, §219. Translation by Matilda McCarthy.
15. Ibid. II, §227. Translation by Matilda McCarthy.
16. Both Lamm (1915, 28ff.; 2000, 29ff) and even more strongly Benz (1948, 171, 177; 2002, 157) look upon the intuitionism of Locke as a partly decisive impulse to mysticism for Swedenborg. But against this argument, we might point out that, through his early interest in Malebranche, Swedenborg had for a long time been living in an intellectual environment where the intimate connection of the psyche to the Divine was a basic idea and that his excerpts from, for example, Augustine give the impression of being much closer to his own thoughts than the annotations from Locke. He may have chosen to quote Locke in his published works because of his ambition to find authoritative support from one of the most famous contemporary philosophers whose empirical epistemology attracted him.
17. See Lamm 1915, 80–81; 2000, 80-81.
18. *Oeconomia* II, §281. Translation by Matilda McCarthy.
19. Stroh, "Swedenborg's Contributions to Psychology," 162–163.
20. See Acton's introduction to his translation of *De fibra*, xv–xvi; see also *De fibra*, §93; ed. cit., 16; Engl. transl., 25.
21. Lamm 1915, 164, 171, 173, 176–177; 2000, 160–194.
22. *Oeconomia* II, §279. Translation by Matilda McCarthy.
23. See Acton's introduction to *De fibra*, x–xv.
24. Acton, *A Philosopher's Note Book*, vii: "And we may assume with confidence that it was in preparation for this work, and also for other contemplated treatises on the relation between soul and body, that he made those extracts from philosophical authors which fill the first 202 pages of Codex 36, and which, consequently, were written at the end of 1740 and the beginning of 1741."
25. The argument on forms in *The Worship and Love of God* stems partly from the relatively extensive section on the degrees of forms in *De fibra*, as is discussed below.
26. For the dating of these, see Acton's introduction to *Psych. trans.*, xvi–xx.
27. "*De anima fragmentum,*" *Opuscula*, 89–122; Eng. transl. in *Psych. trans.*
28. *Opuscula*, 97; *Psych. trans.*, 28. Translation by Matilda McCarthy. See also *Three Transactions on the Cerebrum* I:475, §796.
29. Ibid., 115; *Psych. trans.*, 55. Translation by Matilda McCarthy. This expectation might be interpreted in the light of Augustine's statement on the possibility of combining the mysteries of faith and the evidence of reason, which Swedenborg took down from Leibniz's theodicy: "*Cependant S. Augustin (aussi-bien que M. Bayle) ne desespere pas qu'on puisse trouver ici-bas le dénoüement qu'on souhaite: mais ce Pere le croit reservé à quelque Saint Homme èclairé par une grace toute particuliere*" (However, St. Augustine does not despair [nor M. Bayle] that one might find the solution which one strives for here on earth; but the Father believed that to be reserved for a Holy Man enlightened by a particular grace). Translation by Inge Jonsson; French edition, 67, Latin translation, 559; cod. 36–110, p. 23; Acton, *A Philosopher's*

*Note Book*, 49–50. It is clear from his annotations that Swedenborg's dreams have moved along similar tracks during the religious crisis; once he even dreamt of being adored as a saint (April 7–8, 1744; *Swedenborgs drömbok*, 127; *Dream Diary*, 144).

30. *Opuscula*, 74; *Psych. trans.*, 126. Translation by Matilda McCarthy. See also *De sensibus*, 32–33; Price translation, *The Five Senses*, 41, §84.
31. *Opuscula*, 83; *Psych. trans.*, 138.
32. See Acton's introduction to *Rational Psychology* (his translation of *De anima*), vol. III.
33. *De anima*, 2; *Rational Psychology*, 2–3. Translation by Matilda McCarthy. The state of integrity is discussed below.
34. Gouhier, 103. Translation by Inge Jonsson.
35. See the section "*De Commercio animae et corporis*" in *De anima*, 75–84; *Rational Psychology*, 92–103, §§159–174.
36. Ibid., 63 (§13), and 78 (§135). Translation by Matilda McCarthy.
37. It would be a rewarding task to analyse this work in comparison with Wolff's *Psychologia empirica* and *Psychologia rationalis*, both with regard to the content and the form and intention, but this is beyond the scope of this investigation.
38. *De anima*, 93, §7; *Rational Psychology*, 114, §203.
39. *De anima*, 128; *Rational Psychology*, 160, §270. Translation by Matilda McCarthy. Compare the phrasing in *The Worship and Love of God* §69, quoted below.
40. *De anima*, 143–150, "*De formatione et affectionibus mentis rationalis*"; *Rational Psychology*, 179–188, §§298–314. See also §§39–86 in *The Worship and Love of God*, and Lamm 1915, 179; 2000, 179.
41. *De anima*, 149–150, §8; *Rational Psychology*, 187, §312.
42. Cod. 36–110, 49; Acton, *A Philosopher's Note Book*, 96; *Essais de theodicée*, French ed., 321, §309; Latin ed., 1080–1081. Translation by Inge Jonsson.
43. Lamm 1915, 84; 2000, 83. See also *Clavis hieroglyphica*, examples I–IV, ed. cit., 89–97; *Psych. trans.*, 157–165.
44. See Clissold's translation, II:322, note.
45. See *Regnum animale* II:280, §401: "*At vero ut ipsas Veritates, sive sint Naturales, sive Morales, sive Spirituales (nam omnes unam rem per correspondentiam & repraesentationem agunt (g), in Mentis nostrae sphaeram invitemus, necessum est, ut impuros istos Corporis ignes, & sic fatua nostra lumina exstinguamus, & Mentem nostram a parte corporis vacuam radiis potentiae spiritualis illuminandam subjiciamus*" (But above all to invite the very truths into the sphere of our intellect, whether they are natural, moral or spiritual [for they all deal with the same thing through correspondence and representation (g)], it is necessary that we extinguish the impure fires of the body and thus our fatuous illuminations, and subject our intellect, free from the bodily part, to be illuminated by the rays of the spiritual power). Translation by Inge Jonsson.
46. *Oeconomia* II, §323. Translation by Matilda McCarthy.
47. *Oeconomia* II, §330. Translation by Matilda McCarthy. For an example of this motif, see *The Worship and Love of God*, §§51 and 67.
48. Lamm 1915, 87ff.; 2000, 87ff.
49. *Oeconomia* II, §331: "*Lex apparet esse, quod velit, ut nostrum velle Ipsius Velle, & nostrum posse Illius Posse excitet!* (This law of his ordaining appears to be that our willing should invoke God's willing, and that our power should invoke his).

50. *De anima*, 192; *Rational Psychology*, 239, §405; see also *De anima*, 161 and 186–187; *Rational Psychology*, 201–202, §332, and 232–233, §387. Translation by Matilda McCarthy.
51. Gouhier, 100 (quoted from *Traité de la nature et de la grâce*). Translation by Inge Jonsson.
52. Lamm 1915, 123–160; 2000, 123–159. To map the scope of the debate on Swedenborg's mental condition would demand a whole bibliography, but some examples may be illustrative: A. Lehmann, *Overtro og Trolddom* (Superstition and Sorcery) (Copenhagen, 1894), III:12–23, where Swedenborg is portrayed as *"et Menneske, hvis Nervesystem er fuldstaendigt ödelagt af sexuelle Udskejelser"* (a man whose nervous system is completely destroyed because of sexual excesses) (p. 13); E. Hitschmann, "Swedenborg's Paranoia," *Zentralblatt für Psychoanalyse* (1912), 32ff.: the pathological picture is here interpreted as a regression with homosexual elements: *"Der ganze Wahn erscheint als Erfüllung infantilen, narzistischen Grössenwahns: des Vaters ihn übertreffender Sohn, eine Art Gottes-Sohn, Erlöser zu werden, Reformator des Christentums"* (The whole delusion appears as a fulfilment of an infantile, narcissistic megalomania: the son surpassing the father, a kind of Son of God, a savior to be, a reformer of Christianity), p. 36. E. Kleen has made a list of several assessments of psychiatrists (II:733–763), from H. Maudsley, W. W. Ireland, G. Ballet, B. Gadelius, F. Svenson, and O. Kinberg. All of them are said to have thought that *"Sw-g led af en paranoid sjukdom med hallucinationer"* (Swedenborg suffered from paranoia with hallucinations), p. 733, but there are nevertheless differences of opinion whether hysteria or epilepsy would be the basis of the paraphrenic psychosis (Svenson believes, contrary to Lamm, that epilepsy seems likely). Kleen further quotes A. Herrlin, who as early as 1903 wrote that Swedenborg's condition *"företer en bestämd frändskap såväl med förrycktheten (paranoian) som med hysterien utan att dock fullständigt täckas af något af dessa begrepp"* (shows a definite affinity with the paranoia as well as with the hysteria although without being totally covered by any of these concepts), p. 760. However, Kleen surpasses his authorities, of whom hardly anyone has found a *"steg för steg fortgående progression"* (step-by-step continuing progression), which he claims to have proved was the case. In K. Jaspers, *Strindberg und van Gogh*, 2nd ed. (Berlin: Springer, 1926), 86–95, Swedenborg becomes a textbook example of schizophrenia in an extremely broad sense. The same opinion in a more elaborate version can be found in R. Lagerborg, *Fallet Swedenborg* (The Swedenborg case) (Stockholm: Hugo Gebers förlag, 1924), where the regressive pattern posited in Hitschmann's article is repeated, as well as the hypersexuality assumed by Lehmann: *"vid hans alltid hypertrofiska sexuella konstitution tyder den ångest han utsättes för, när impotensåldern inbryter, på en översekretion från sköldkörtelgruppen; den rubbade biokemien föranleder kristidens överspändhet, både extaser och hallucinationer, bättringsiver och erotomani"* (with his constantly hypertrophic sexual constitution, the anxiety to which he is exposed when entering the age of impotence indicates an overstimulation of the thyroid group; the disturbed biochemistry causes the overexcitement of the crisis period, both ecstasies and hallucinations, zealous penance and erotomania), p. 59. In spite of his adherence to Kleen, however, Lagerborg does not want to look upon Swedenborg as insane in an everyday sense of the word; on the contrary, he believes that the disorder had stopped at an increase of the intoxication of the affects, and he quotes with approval Gadelius' thesis that in psychotic states it is a matter of quantitative change rather than qualitative

ones (p. 62). T. Andrae, in *Mystikens psykologi* (The psychology of mysticism) (Stockholm: Sveriges kristliga studentrörelses, 1926), 367–389, analyses Swedenborg's mental condition during his visionary period, which leads the author to the following conclusion, in spite of his admiration of Lamm's investigation: "*Starka skäl tala alltså för Kleens mening, att Swedenborg led av parafreni, dvs. paranoia med hallucinationer, enligt Kraepelins nomenklatur, eller enligt Gadelius' diagnos av 'en otvetydig sinnessjukdom av förryckt prägel, en paranoia förenad med hallucinationer och religiöst excentriska idéer av megalomanisk natur'*" (Thus there are strong arguments in favor of Kleen's opinion that Swedenborg suffered from paraphrenia, i.e., paranoia with hallucinations, according to Kraepelin's terminology, or in accordance with Gadelius' diagnosis, from "an unmistakable mental illness of an insane character, a paranoia combined with hallucinations and religiously eccentric ideas of a megalomanic art"), p. 380. In his great book *Religionen och rollerna* (Religious roles) (Stockholm: Diakonistyrelsens förlag, 1959), 306–310, Hj. Sundén proposes that Jung's personality categories should be applied to Swedenborg's development—that is, the four basic types of thought, feeling, sensation and intuition—of which one becomes dominant. Regarding Swedenborg the scientist the category of thought would be the dominant function, in combination with intuition, while feeling and sensation would be exiled to the subconsciousness; but these latter avenge themselves during the religious crisis: "*de bortträngda funktionerna bryter in i medvetandet gestaltande drömmar och visioner*" (the repressed functions force their way into consciousness creating dreams and visions), p. 309. In principle, this method of describing the development does not differ very much from the previous ones, since it will also here be a question of a split personality, but there is a hidden metaphysics in Jung, which makes it risky to use his scheme for scholarly descriptions, at least without any expert knowledge. There seems to be a jinx on his obscure terms, and I find it hard to see how a Jungian description could explain anything here. T. S:son Frey has touched upon Swedenborg in a popular survey (*Nytt och nyttigt* 2 [1960]: 9–10), writing about a "*fantastisk paranoisk psykos*" (phantastic paranoic psychosis), possibly caused by "*hjärnlesioner med epilepsi*" (brain lesions with epilepsy). Finally, referring to the evidence from two witnesses in London, Lars Bergquist has discussed whether Swedenborg may have suffered from an acute psychic illness in the summer of 1744, but he does not find it very important: "*I dag kan vi acceptera att Swedenborg en viss tid varit sjuk och förvirrad—saken varken ökar eller minskar värdet av hans insats.*" (Nowadays we can understand and accept that Swedenborg may have been ill and confused for awhile: this does not lessen the value of his contributions). See his commentary on his edition of Swedenborg's dream journal, *Swedenborgs drömbok* 1988, 48–55; *Swedenborg's Dream Diary* 2001, 52–59; quotation in Swedish, 53; in English, 57.

53. The term is used here in its conventional sense with no claim to diagnostic specification; moreover, it appears from Frey's survey that modern psychiatry has overcome the terminological intoxication to a great extent, which still may tax a layman's patience (see, for example, p. 5). The various diagnoses in Swedenborg's case can be traced back to indistinct definitions, but most of them observe a split personality, that is, a schizoid predisposition.

54. In 1724, Swedenborg declined a proposal from Benzelius to apply for a chair, among other reasons, on the grounds that he did not have "*donum docendi, min Bror wet igenom den naturella difficultate at tala*" (the gift of teaching, my brother knows from my natural difficulty to speak); May 26, 1724, *Opera*

I:313. As to Swedenborg's erotically metaphoric style, K. Hagberg has pointed out that it is in line with the conventional usage in scientific contexts in the Baroque age; consequently, it can hardly serve as a basis for an interpretation in psychiatric terms ("Linnaeus, Swedenborg och barocken," *Svenska Dagbladet*, February 18, 1961).

55. *De anima* ends in more extensive reasonings on heaven and hell, on the state of the soul after death, on the role of Christ, and on divine providence; see 224–255 and *Rational Psychology*, 279–317, §§486–560.

56. *Swedenborgs drömbok*, 288; *Swedenborg's Dream Diary*, 313–314, §278, Oct. 26–27, 1744.

57. Cod. 36–110, p. 112 (heading: Caelum, aura, aether); Acton, *A Philosopher's Note Book*, 230: "The kingdom of God is within you says Christ. Luke 17:21."

58. Cod. 36–110, p. 74 (*Amor, affectus*); Acton, *A Philosopher's Note Book*, 147; Labriolle's ed., 79.

59. F. Cayré, *Dieu présent dans la vie de l'esprit* (Bruges: Desclée de Brouwer, 1951), 168. Translation by Inge Jonsson.

60. Cod. 36–110, p. 69; Acton, *A Philosopher's Note Book*, 137–138; *ed. cit. Patrologia latina* XL, col. 791. The quotation is marked in the manuscript. Translation by Matilda McCarthy.

61. A recurrent feature of the system of excerpts is that the extracts from Augustine come first under every heading, where there are such, although not in the beginning where Rydelius' *Nödiga Förnufts-Öfningar* served as the point of departure. The location emphasizes, in a sense, how highly Swedenborg appreciated "*illuminati judicii patrem.*"

62. See W. Pannenberg's article in *Die Religion in Geschichte und Gegenwart*, vol. 3 (Tübingen: JCB Mohr, 1958), col. 1721–1822. (Gott. V. *Theologiegeschichtlich*).

63. Cod. 36–110, p. 16; Acton, *A Philosopher's Note Book*, 35. Translation by Matilda McCarthy.

64. *Diarium spirituale* (Spiritual Diary) was the name given by the first editor of Swedenborg's annotations of his spiritual experiences from the period 1747–1763, Im. Tafel in Tübingen. The second Latin edition, published by J. D. Odhner since 1982, has been given the title *Experientiae spirituales* (Spiritual Experiences); it is of obvious interest for the discussion of Swedenborg's mental condition and for his later writings, but it starts after the work on *The Worship and Love of God* had been interrupted.

65. Lamm 1915, 13–14; 2000, 15.

66. Andrae, 383–384; Sundén, 183. Translation by Matilda McCarthy.

67. Lamm 1915, 62ff. and 116–122; 2000, 62–64, 116–122.

68. *Regnum animale* II:121–122, n. 336; Wilkinson trans., 451. Translation by Matilda McCarthy. The relation between *Regnum animale* and the dream crisis is discussed in Acton's *An Introduction to the Word Explained*, 34–113.

69. *Regnum animale*, II:122; Wilkinson trans. 451. Translation by Inge Jonsson.

70. Lamm 1915, 170; 2000, 169.

71. *Swedenborgs drömbok*, 287–290; *Swedenborg's Dream Diary*, 312. This is Lamm's interpretation (1915, 149; 2000, 149–150), but Acton believes that the work was begun on October 7 with reference to an earlier annotation (October 6–7, *Swedenborgs drömbok*, 265–267; *Swedenborg's Dream Diary*, 290). See *An Introduction to the Word Explained*, 109, note 4. Acton presumes that Swedenborg had erroneously written October 27 instead of 7, which is reasonable in itself, and it would imply that §§1–56 of *The Worship*

*and Love of God* had been completed in less than three weeks (*"på sidan de amore"* I would then regard as referring to the third section of the second chapter, *De Amore Primogeniti*). However, the time between these data seems most probably to have been spent in preparation, during which Swedenborg hesitated about different plans; see the annotations on the dreams of October 9–10 (*drömbok*, 273; *Dream Diary*, 298) and of October 26–27: *"enär jag gick med min wän igenom en long gång, kom en wacker flicka och föll honom i famnen, och som ynckade sig, jag frågade om hon kende honom, swarade intet, jag tog henne ifrån honom och ledde henne wid armen, det war mitt andra arbete dit hon addresserade sig, hwarifrån jag tog henne i detta"* (*drömbok*, 289; *Dream Diary*, 315): "While I went with my friend through a long tunnel, a beautiful girl turned up and fell in his arms, but she was whining. I asked if she knew him, and she did not reply. Then I drew her away from him and led her by the arm. *It was my other work to which she addressed herself and from which I took her in this way.*" To judge by the end of this annotation, the work on the drama of creation did not start seriously until now.

72. See Sundén's Jungian description of the dream crisis: *"Intuitionen dominerar den medvetna tolkningen av drömmarna, men i drömmarna dominerar sensationen i så hög grad att Swedenborg känner Kristus fatta om sina händer, känner sig vara försatt i hans sköte och blickar in i hans anlete, erfar doften av vin, hör märkliga ljud etc."* (309). (The intuition dominates the conscious interpretation of the dreams, but in the dreams *the sensation* dominates to such an extent that Swedenborg *feels* how Christ takes his hands, *feels* how he is sitting in his bosom and *looks* into his face, *smells* the scent of wine, *hears* strange sounds, etc.). Translation by Inge Jonsson

73. *Opuscula*, 96; *Psych. trans.*, 26. Translation by Matilda McCarthy.

74. *Opuscula*, 112; *Psych. trans.*, 51. Translation by Matilda McCarthy.

75. *Opuscula*, 113ff.; *Psych. trans.*, 52ff.

76. *Swedenborgs drömbok*, 92 (March 30–31, 1744); *Dream Diary*, 105.

77. Lamm 1915, 119ff.; 2000, 118ff.

78. *Oeconomia* I, §25. Translation by Matilda McCarthy. See also §23 which evaluates the ancients and §24 which praises the moderns.

79. *Oeconomia* I, §26.

80. See the prologue to *Regnum animale*, esp. §§6–13; Wilkinson trans., 10–13.

81. Lamm 1915, 104; 2000, 104.

82. Cod. 36–110, p. 89; Acton, *A Philosopher's Note Book*, 185: *"Judaei vocarunt omnes substantias medias inter angelos et homines Dadaim, at graeci per transpositionem syllabarum Daimonas"* (The Jews called all substances mediating between angels and men Dadaim, but the Greeks through a transposition of syllables Daimonas); translation by Inge Jonsson. The annotation is taken from *Comte de Gabalis, ou Entretiens sur les sciences secretes*; in the edition used by Swedenborg (Amsterdam, 1715); the passage is found on 71–72. This book against occultism was written by Abbé Villars (M. d'Astarac in Anatole France's *La Rôtisserie de la reine Pédauque*) in 1670 and became quite popular. In spite of its tales of visions, it was of little significance to Swedenborg.

83. O. Gruppe, *Geschichte der klassischen Mythologie und Religionsgeschichte* (Leipzig: Teubner, 1921) (supplement to Roscher, 58). Translation by Inge Jonsson.

84. I:XIV s; ed. cit., 38ff.

85. Gruppe, 10–11. Translation by Inge Jonsson.

86. Haskins, 105–109.

87. Ibid., 108; Gruppe, 16–21.
88. Gruppe, 26.
89. Ibid., 27–38.
90. Quoted from ibid., 38. Translation by Inge Jonsson.
91. Ibid., 47ff.
92. Ibid., 49. Translation by Inge Jonsson.
93. Lamm 1915, 186ff.; 2000, 184ff.
94. *Opera* I:215: "*Här äro ock ståteliga Engelska Poeter, som äro werda för sina inventioner ens igenomläsning som Drydens, Spekers, Wallers, Miltons,Cowleys, Beaumont och Fletchers, Shakespeare, Johnsons, Bens, Oldhams,Benhams, Philips och Smiths etc.* (There are also magnificent English poets here, who deserve to be read because of their inventions, such as Dryden, Speker, Waller, Milton, Cowley, Beaumont and Fletcher, Shakespeare, Jonson, Oldham, Benham, Philips and Smith etc.) (translation by Inge Jonsson). There are probably good reasons to agree with Lamm that Emanuel Swedberg had copied the list from some learned work (1915, 186; 2000, 184–185); however, see a more positive view in S. Rydberg, "Svenska studieresor till England under frihetstiden" (Swedish students in England during the age of liberty) (Ph.D. diss., Uppsala University, 1951), 282–283.
95. *Swedenborgs drömbok*, 288; *Dream Diary*, 313.
96. Lamm 1915, 186; 2000, 185.
97. See especially §73, note q.
98. Cod. 36–110, p. 270; Acton, *A Philosopher's Note Book*, 499 (heading: *Correspondentia actionum hum. et div.*). Translation by Matilda McCarthy. When the young traveller Emanuel Swedberg eagerly read Baker's *Reflections upon Learning* in London, he could come across a very harsh opinion of Seneca quoted from Malebranche, "a Master in the *Art of Thinking*": "there is little more in him, at the bottom, than a Pomp of Words" (op. cit., 52).

# Chapter 7

1. See, for example, §64, note g; and *Clavis hieroglyphica*, exempl. XIV, *msed. cit.*, 112; Acton, *Psych.trans.*, 204 and 180.
2. April 25–26, 1744, *Swedenborgs drömbok*, p. 190; *Swedenborg's Dream Diary*, 217.
3. See the chapters "*Die Lehre von den Entsprechungen*" (The doctrine of correspondences) and "*Die Metaphysik des Lebens*" (The metaphysics of life) in Benz 1948, 387–422; 2002, 351–384. Although the influence from Lamm is obvious, the theological accents are somewhat differently placed.
4. See the chapter "*Rum, tid, minne*" (Space, time, memory) in Toksvig, 264–275; English translation, 250–261, in which Swedenborg's ideas have been connected to parapsychological observations and speculations.
5. Translation by Matilda McCarthy.
6. The example is analysed in Lamm 1915, 177–178; 2000, 176–178, as a "*hänförande vacker liknelse*" (beautiful parable).
7. See note 1 above. The hieroglyphic key was referred to previously in §55, note s.
8. See the interpretation of the religious crisis in Benz 1948, 176–210; 2002, 162–192.
9. Lamm 1915, 178–179; 2000, 177–178.

10. See §68, note m; also *De fibra*, for example, 9–16; Acton translation, 13–25; see *Oeconomia* II, §101–207.

11. April 9–10, 1744; *Swedenborgs drömbok*, 139–149; *Swedenborg's Dream Diary*, 158: "*i samma stånd som jag war, kom jag än diupare i andanom, och fast jag war waken, intet kunde regera mig sielf, vtan kom som en öfwermechtig drift, at kasta mig på mitt ansichte och taga ehop henderne och bedia hwad tilförne, om min owärdighet, och med diupeste ödmjukhet och wördnad bedia om nåd, at jag som den störste Syndaren, får syndernes förlåtelse, då jag merckte at jag war i det stånd, som natten näst för den sista, men widare intet kunde se, emedan jag war waken: det vndrade jag, och så wistes mig i andanom, at menniskia i detta tilstånd, är som en menniskia som wänder fötterne op, och hufwudet ner; och kom för mig hwarföre Moses moste afkläda sig sina skor, då han skulle gå til den helige*" (In the state I was in, I came still further into the spirit; although I was awake, I could not control myself, but there came as it were an overwhelming impulse to throw myself on my face and to fold my hands and to pray, as before, about my unworthiness and to ask for grace with the deepest humanity and reverence, that as the greatest of sinners I may receive forgiveness of sins. I then noticed that I was in the same state as during the night before last, but more I could not see, because I was now awake. I wondered at this, and then it was shown to me spiritually that a human being in this state is like a person who has his head down and his feet up; and it occurred to me why Moses had to remove his shoes when he was to go into the presence of the Holy One).

12. Lamm 1915, 172; 2000, 171.

13. *De Infinito*, 147ff.; Wilkinson translation, 125–128. Generally speaking, the entire treatise can be said to have this intention, with the review of various philosophers' opinions on infinity.

14. *Oeconomia* II, §336; translation by Matilda McCarthy. There is a misprint in the text: "*instanti oretenus*" instead of "*instanti ore tenus.*"

15. *Oeconomia*, §331. The references illustrate Swedenborg's unreliable quotation practice. The authors have been mixed up (corrected in the English translation, II:325); it is understandable, since Grotius refers to Lactantius in an indistinctly phrased note in *De veritate religionis christianae* VI:VII, ed. cit., 392–393. But it bears evidence of Lactantius—"the Christian Cicero"—being quoted from Grotius; both references are given in cod. 36–110 from Grotius but here in right order, 78; Acton, *A Philosopher's Notebook*, 158.

16. Lamm 1915, 87–94; 2000, 89ff. "*De fide et bonis operibus*" has been published in *Phototyp*. XVIII:57–68 and in *Opuscula*, 7–14; English translation in *Psych. trans.*, 11–18. On the dating, see Acton's introduction to *Psychological Transactions*, xivff.

17. "*Fides autem historica, est modo scientia aut notitia, quod ita sit, qua etiam diaboli instructi sunt, qui sciunt Deum existere talem, qualis describitur in sacris;*" *Opuscula*, 12; *Psych. trans.*,15; cf Lamm 1915, 90; 2000, 89–90.

18. *Lefwernes Beskrifning*, 82–83 and 88ff.

19. Cod. 36–110, pp. 21–24 (heading: *Justificatio, Fides, Theologia, Bona opera*); Acton, *A Philosopher's Note Book*, 45–53; see Lamm 1915, 91; 2000, 89–90.

20. See Benz 1948, 513ff.; 2002, 469ff.

21. Lamm 1915, 86–89; 2000, 87–90.

22. See Gouhier 1948, 19–28, 41, 45.

23. Cod. 36–110, pp. 27 and 124; Acton, *A Philosopher's Note Book*, 57–58 and 258–259.

24. *Oeconomia* II, §332. Translation by Matilda McCarthy.

25. *De Infinito*, 144ff.; Wilkinson translation, 124ff. This seems to be a development of the liberal view, which Leibniz quoted from Francis Xavier and François de Sales in *Essais de theodicée*, §95 (French. ed, 139, Lat.ed., 723); in the later excerpts, Swedenborg annotates this passage, cod. 36–110, p. 64; Acton, *A Philosopher's Note Book*, 124. This idea should be balanced by a reference to Dippel's and the general Pietist idea of Christ in the interior; see Lamm 1915, 280ff.; 2000, 277–278.

26. *De Infinito*, 148–149; Acton translation, 127–128. Translation by Inge Jonsson.

27. The epistle to the Ephesians 2:18; annotated under the heading "Messias" in cod. 36–110, p. 178; Acton, *A Philosopher's Note Book*, 379.

28. Msed. cit., 104; transl. cit., 171–172. Translation by Matilda McCarthy.

29. Ibid., 105–106; transl. cit., 173. Translation by Matilda McCarthy.

30. Cod. 36–110, p. 75; Acton, *A Philosopher's Note Book*, 149ff.

31. *The Worship and Love of God*, §74, note s; *De fibra*, 185–191; Wilkinson translation, 261–268.

32. See A. Harnack, *Lehrbuch der Dogmengeschichte*, 4th ed. (Tübingen: Mohr, 1909), e.g., I:697–796. See also F. Sewall, "The Only-Begotten in Swedenborg's Cosmology and Theology," *The New Philosophy* (1914): 89–103.

33. Cod. 36–110, p. 178; Acton, *A Philosopher's Note Book*, 378ff.

34. Ibid., p. 207; Acton, 425–426.

35. Th. Beza's version, quoted from the edition of 1648 of the Tremellius-Junius Bible, 911; see cod. 36–110, p. 178; Acton, *A Philosopher's Note Book*, 380.

36. See Acton, *A Philosopher's Note Book*, Index of Scripture passages, 520.

37. Cod. 36–110, p. 178; Acton, *A Philosopher's Note Book*, 378.

38. G. Sevenster's article (Christologie I) in *Die Religion in Geschichte und Gegenwart* I, col. 1758. Translation by Inge Jonsson.

39. Grotius' synthetizing ambition, such as it manifests itself in his extensive quotations of old masters, was probably what made the most important impression on Swedenborg; as pointed out in note 15 above, Grotius gave Swedenborg, among others, access to patristic material.

40. *Entretiens sur la metaphysique & sur la religion* (Rotterdam, 1688), 327–328; see also 334. Translation by Inge Jonsson. Christ as the true Melchizedek is also included in the Roman Catholic mass text.

41. The excerpts do not include this work itself, but it is mentioned in passing in a quotation from Wolff's *Psychologia rationalis*, §589: cod. 36–110, p. 95; Acton, *A Philosopher's Note Book*, 199.

42. Gouhier, 23; the remark is based on the quoted passage from *Entretiens*. Translation by Inge Jonsson.

43. Cod. 36–110, p. 73; Acton, *A Philosopher's Note Book*, 147; see also Acton translation, *The Animal Kingdom . . . by Emanuel Swedenborg, Parts 4 and 5, the Organs of Generation, and the Formation of the Foetus in the Womb* (Bryn Athyn, Pa.: Swedenborg Scientific Association, 1928), §§208–214, pp. 180–189.

44. Compare to this the important extract from the Augustinian apocryph *De spiritu et anima*, cod. 36–110, p. 16; Acton, *A Philosopher's Note Book*, 35.

45. Rydelius, 83. Translation by Inge Jonsson.

46. Cod. 36–110, p. 38; Acton, *A Philosopher's Note Book*, 72.

47. Ibid., 37, 45–51; Acton, 69–71, 84–100.

48. Cod. 36–110, p.152; Acton, *A Philosopher's Note Book*, 331. Translation by Inge Jonsson.

49. *Worship and Love of God*, §78.

50. E. Linderholm, *Sven Rosén* (Uppsala and Stockholm: Almqvist & Wiksell, 1911), 82.
51. H. Pleijel, *Svenska kyrkans historia* (History of the Swedish Church) (Stockholm and Uppsala: Diakonistyrelsens förlag, 1935), V:163; see also Forssell, 146–147.
52. *Lefwernes Beskrifning*, 114. Translation by Inge Jonsson.
53. Lamm 1915, 58–59 and references given there; 2001, 58 and 332, n. 79. See also cod. 36–110, p. 62; Acton, *A Philosopher's Note Book*, 117.
54. K. F. S. Henning, "Johan Conrad Dippels vistelse i Sverige samt dippelianismen i Stockholm 1727–1741" (J.C. Dippel's Stay in Sweden and the Dippelianism in Stockholm 1727–1741), (Ph.D. diss., Upsala University, 1881), 1–55.
55. Benzelius' preface to A. Rydelius, *Anteckningar öfwer then så kallade Christiani Democriti Demonstratio Evangelica II* (Notes to Demonstratio Evangelica II by the so-called Christianus Democritus), (Linköping, 1736), 4. Translation by Inge Jonsson.
56. *Svenska kyrkans historia* V:320; see Henning, 45.
57. Linderholm, 204–229; *Svenska kyrkans historia* V:345–346.
58. Acton, *Letters and Memorials*, 455; see also Linderholm, 310.
59. Linderholm, 313. Ex-officio Swedenborg must have been in contact with Hjärne on one such occasion; see Wendla Falk, *Bergsrådinnans dagbok* (Stockholm: Diakonistyrelsens förlag, 1957), 81–82.
60. *Photolith*, III:53; *Resebeskrifningar af Emanuel Swedenborg under åren 1710–1739* (Travel Notes by Emanuel Swedenborg, 1710–1739), utg. af Kungl. Vetenskapsakademien (Uppsala, 1911), 65. Translation by Inge Jonsson. Since Dippel severely censured ascetic tendencies in contemporary Swedish Pietism, this statement has little to say about Swedenborg's opinion of him (see Linderholm, 117ff, and Lamm 1915, 59; 2000, 59). On the other hand, John Norris, Malebranche's English translator, rejected the claims of the Quakers to count him among their fellow-believers. They look upon the idea of "the inner light" as identical with "*la vision en Dieu*"; and according to a quote in Baker's *Reflections upon Learning* (1708), Norris also admitted "[t]hat if the Quakers understood their own Notion, and knew how to explain it, and into what Principles to resolve it, it would not very much differ from his" (131). This is yet more evidence of how common these ideas were at the time. Consequently, it becomes even more important to focus on the sources nearest at hand. Swedenborg was certainly aware of the similarities between his views and those of the sectarians, but he probably took the same aristocratic position as Norris in his case to the Moravian Brethren, as will be discussed below.
61. A. Gradin, *A Short History of the Bohemian–Moravian Protestant Church of the United Brethren* (London, 1743). See *Cat.bibl.*, 4. See also N. Jacobsson, *Den svenska herrnhutismens uppkomst* (The Origin of Moravianism in Sweden), (Ph.D. diss., Uppsala University, 1908), xv–xvi and 178–189. As I have shown in another article, Swedenborg met Gradin in Hamburg on his journey to Paris in 1736: "*Köpenhamn–Amsterdam-Paris: Swedenborgs resa 1736–38*" (Copenhagen–Amsterdam–Paris: Swedenborg's Voyage in 1736–1738), *Lychnos* 1967–1968 (Uppsala: Almqvist & Wiksell, 1969), 43–44 and 74.
62. Jacobsson, 51–62.
63. Ibid., 65ff.
64. Lamm 1915, 58; 2000, 58.

65. On these relations, see *Documents* II:237–386. See also *Documents* I:655.
66. Linderholm, 430. Translation by Inge Jonsson.
67. Ibid., 141–156. See also H. Wijkmark, *Wolff's filosofi och svensk teologi* (The Philosophy of Wolff and Swedish Theology), Bilaga till Nya elementarskolans arsredogörelse 1914–1915 (Stockholm: Nya elementarskolan, 1915), passim; and T. Frängsmyr, *Wolffianismens genombrott i Uppsala* (The Breakthrough of Wolffianism at Uppsala University), (Uppsala: Acta Universitatis Upsaliensis, 1972), 90–91.
68. Linderholm, 159ff.
69. The diary has been published by N. Odenvik, *Sven Roséns dagbok 1730–1731* (Stockholm: Filadelfiaförlaget, 1948).
70. Linderholm, 184–203; for the comparison with *Swedenborg's Dream Diary*, see 185, note 2.
71. Ibid., 179–183, 370–371, and 412ff.
72. *Swedenborgs drömbok*, 204; *Dream Diary*, 234.
73. See Sigstedt, 189–190 and 435–439. Pleijel noted the need for an investigation of Swedenborg's relations to Lutheranism, *Svenska kyrkans historia* V:615.
74. Lamm 1915, 145; 2000, 144. The Moravians did not preach the asceticism that Swedenborg censured in Pietism, and this might have made them more attractive to him.
75. *Swedenborgs drömbok*, 275; *Dream Diary*, 300.
76. Lamm 1915, 145; 2000, 145. *Svenska kyrkans historia* V:615; Bergquist agrees with Pleijel in his commentaries on the October 10–11 dream, 275–277; *Dream Diary*, 301–302.
77. *Swedenborgs drömbok*, 229; *Dream Diary*, 258. For a New Church interpretation of similar dreams the month before, see Acton, *An Introduction to the Word Explained*, 88–92.
78. *Swedenborgs drömbok*, 228; *Dream Diary*, 219.
79. Gradin, 7. Unfortunately, there is no other material that can support the tempting hypothesis that Swedenborg's dream reflects a reading of Gradin's *History*.
80. *Cat.bibl.*, 7–8. That *A Manual of Doctrine* belongs to the London congregation is evident from an advertising bibliography at the end of Gradin's book (63 s.p.). Regarding Swedenborg's Moravian landlord (Brockmer) and the information on Swedenborg's mental disturbance that Brockmer attested to, see *Documents* II:581–612 and *Swedenborgs drömbok*, 48–55; *Dream Diary*, 53–59.
81. Lamm 1915, 143ff.; 2000, 144–145; and H. W. Gruhle, "Swedenborgs Träume" (Swedenborg's Dreams), *Psychologische Forschung* (Berlin, 1924), V:314–315. When Gradin sent a report on Herrnhut to Stockholm in 1739, he described the congregation as a "*Korsförsamling, ty den grundar sig på Jesu blod och död*" (community of the Cross, for it is founded on the blood and death of Jesus), as quoted in Jacobsson, 122.
82. In addition to Erik Benzelius, who died as a Lutheran archbishop in 1743, there was Benzelius' son Carl Jesper (1714–1793), court chaplain in 1741, his nephew Lars Benzelstierna (1719–1800), professor of theology in 1747, and others: see *Documents* I:88–95.
83. April 7–8, 1744, *Swedenborgs drömbok*, 124; *Dream Diary*, 140.
84. *Swedenborgs drömbok*, 127; *Dream Diary*, 182.
85. April 9–10, 1744, *Swedenborgs drömbok*, 136–137; *Dream Diary*, 154–155.
86. Lamm 1915, 152–153; 2000, 151–152.
87. *Swedenborgs drömbok*, 186; *Dream Diary*, 212.

88. *Swedenborgs drömbok*, 201; *Dream Diary*, 230.
89. See S. Lindroth's portrait in *Ny ill.sv.litteraturhistoria* II, esp. 197.
90. E. Liedgren, "Jacob Arrhenius," *Svenskt Biografiskt Lexikon* Bd 2, 279. Translation by Inge Jonsson.
91. Quoted from S. Norberg's edition (Göteborg, 1786), 163. Translation by Inge Jonsson.
92. Lamm 1915, 155; 2000, 155; *Documents*, 1:30–48 (quote, 36). The Royal Library in Stockholm has a copy written by C. Deleen (Biogr.Pers. Swedenborg 1:55), in which this passage is found on page 4; A. Hallengren, ed., *Carl Robsahm, Anteckningar om Swedenborg* (Stockholm: Föreningen Swedenborgs Minne, 1989), 37–38. The translation is from *Documents*, 1:36. See also Chr. Johansén's statement above. R. Josefson has strongly stressed the similarities between the Moravian Christocentricity and Swedenborg's theology: "*Han vill ej veta av någon annan gud än Jesus Kristus. Gud själv har gått ned och antagit människoväsen för att frälsa människorna. I hans teologiska produktion möter man gång på gång uttryck för en innerlig Kristustro, vilka icke skulle ha funnits där, om han icke mottagit starka impulser från herrnhutismen*" (He does not want to know of any other God than Jesus Christ. The Lord himself has descended shaped as a man to save humanity. In his theological production, one meets time and again expressions of a fervent faith in Christ, which would not have been there if he had not received strong impulses from Herrnhut.) "Emanuel Swedenborg: En konturteckning till 250-årsminnet," *Ny kyrklig tidskrift* 1 (1938): 11; translation by Inge Jonsson. This agrees with my opinion that the orthodox concept of redemption, such as Swedenborg wrestled with it in *The Worship and Love of God*, had now been replaced by the belief in the Lord as love and salvation. See also Anders Hallengren, "In Search of Robsahm's Memories," *Gallery of Mirrors: Reflections of Swedenborgian Thought* (West Chester, Pa.: Swedenborg Foundation, 1998), 77–88.
93. *Swedenborgs drömbok*, 271; *Dream Diary*, 296.
94. S. M. Warren, *A Compendium of the Theological Writings of Emanuel Swedenborg* (London: Swedenborg Society, 1909), 689; J. S. Bogg, *A Glossary Or the Meaning of Specific Terms and Phrases Used by Swedenborg in His Theological Writings Given in His Own Words* (London: Swedenborg Society, 1915), 30.
95. *De anima*, 252; *Rational Psychology*, §555, p. 314. Translation by Matilda McCarthy.
96. Cod. 36–110, pp. 62–66, 68, 111; Acton, *A Philosopher's Note Book*, 117–131, 135–137, 229.
97. *Essais de theodicée*, §276; French ed., 299 (incorrect note number); Latin ed., 1049; the biblical references are noted in cod. 36–110, p. 181; Acton, *A Philosopher's Note Book*, 386–387. Translation by Inge Jonsson.
98. *De anima*, 249; *Rational psychology*, §548, pp. 310–311. Translation by Matilda McCarthy.
99. *Rational Psychology*, 310, note 6 (cod. 36–110; Acton, *A Philosopher's Note Book*, 382ff).
100. Apollo, Pallas, the Muses, Parnassus, Olympus, Helicon, the Pierides, the oracle, the fountain Aganippe; *Opera poetica*, 43–66; an excellent new edition was published by H. Helander in Uppsala, 1995.
101. An illustrative example close at hand can be found in the Leeuwenhoek edition from the 1720s, which Swedenborg consulted frequently, in its introduc-

tory *"carmen panegyricum"*; A. van Leeuwenhoek, *Opera omnia seu Arcana naturae detecta* (Leyden, 1722), 1:3ff.

102. Cod. 36–110, p. 89; Acton, *A Philosopher's Note Book*, 185ff.

103. *Msed. cit.*, 105–106, and 123; *Phys. Trans.*, 173 and 193.

104. Forssell, 193–209; young Swedberg's eulogy on Casaubon in a letter to Benzelius from London in October 1710, *Opera* I:207 (also printed in *Opera poetica*, 22). In I. Collijn's bibliography of Swedish seventeenth-century literature, fifteen Swedish editions of different textbooks by Voss have been registered (*Sveriges bibliografi, 1600- talet* [Uppsala: Svenska litteratursällskapet, 1946], II:988–989). His son Isaac Voss (1618–1689) belonged to Queen Christina's bibliographic consultants and acquired notoriety by taking the *Codex argenteus* out of the country, when he left Sweden; maybe the university librarian Benzelius extended his disapproval of this outrage to Voss Sr. as well.

105. KVA Cod Sw 37–90, excerpts from Plautus, Terentius, Cicero, and Florus. Acton assumes that they are part of the preparation for the dissertation, and he is probably right (*Letters and Memorials*, 4, note 9). Tafel connects them to cod. 36–110, which seems completely wrong (*Documents* 1:847), while Ekelöf and Stroh dated the manuscript to 1729, which may be correct for its scientific annotations but hardly for these excerpts (*Kronologisk förteckning*, 25).

106. Humphries translation, 16. See Walchius edition of Ovid, 72ff., in which the commentator presents a physical allegorical interpretation of Python (73); see a modern rendering in Magnus' Berlin edition 1914.

107. The reference to Voss appears on page 72.

108. The muses as a term for a race of demons is also used in ecclesiastic polemics against art and artists; see M. Rudwin, *The Devil in Legend and Literature* (Chicago & London: The Open Court Publishing Co., 1931), 252. This usage, however, probably did not mean much to Swedenborg.

109. Walchius edition, 37.

110. See Roscher, I, col. 1986; *Metamorphoses*, e.g., 2:219 and 5:254.

111. Humphries translation, 116–117. Walchius edition, 408 (see Magnus edition, 181); the Walchius commentator connects Hyantea to Boeotia.

112. The Pierides as a lower kind of muse appear also in Cicero's *De natura deorum* III:XXI; ed. cit., 338–339. This is of interest, since the text was somewhat important to Swedenborg, probably even to his theology, as will be discussed below.

113. Ed. cit., 408; but Ovid uses Aganippis as a synonym of Hippokrene in *Fasti* (5:7; see Roscher, I, col. 98). The complexity of these fountain myths can be studied, e.g., in E. Maass, "Untersuchungen zu Properz," *Hermes* Bd 31 (1896): 375–434, where, on page 423, the scholar concluded: *"Zwei Vorstellungen finden wir von den helikonischen Musenquellen bei den Griechen und ihren römischen Nachfolgern vertreten. Die ältere ist die schon bei Hesiod auftauchende, nach welcher die Musen an Aganippe-Permessos in ihrem Haine die Dichter, gleichviel welcher Gattung, begeistern und berufen. Die jüngere sondert zwischen der Kleinpoesie (Elegie, Epyllion im alexandrinischen Sinne u.s.w.) und dem grossen Epos im homerisch-hesiodischen Stile und fixirt zwei Helikonquellen, die kleinere, auch niedriger gelegene Aganippe, ein Nebenwasser (Quelle) des Permessos, und die grössere Hippukrene hoch oben nach dem Gipfel zu, jene für die Kleinpoesie bestimmt, diese für das Epos"* (We find two concepts of the Heliconian muse fountains among the Greeks and their Roman successors. The older one appears already in Hesiod, accord-

ing to which the muses at Aganippe–Permessos call the poets, irrespective of genre, to their grove and fill them with enthusiasm. The younger one separates the minor genres (elegy, epyllion in the Alexandrian sense etc.) from the grand epos in Homeric–Hesiodic style and settles two Heliconian fountains, the smaller and lower Aganippe, a tributary fountain to Permessos, and the bigger Hippukrene higher up near the top: the former is intended for the minor genres, the latter for the epos). Translation by Inge Jonsson. Incidentally, there seems to be only one instance of the form Aganippides in Roman literature, namely, Ovid, *Fasti* 5:7; see *Thesaurus linguae latinae* I, col. 1266, l. 36.

114. Walchius edition, 56.

115. P. Gautruche, *L'histoire poétique*, 3.ed. (Paris, 1695), 24. Translation by Inge Jonsson.

116. *Regnum animale* II, §401; translation by Matilda McCarthy. See Wilkinson translation, §463, p. 571.

117. One of the more bizarre instances is an extract from the anatomist Martin Schurig (1656–1733) who, supported among others by Tertullian (c. 160–c. 230), claimed that the oracles of the Pythia were issued from her genitals: KVA Cod SW 88–93, 132; an echo of this can be heard in *Regnum animale* 4–5; Acton trans., *The Animal Kingdom . . . The Organs of Generation*, §196, p. 176.

118. Cod. 36–110, p. 121; Acton, *A Philosopher's Note Book*, 250; the Augustinian text was taken from Grotius' *De veritate religionis christianae* IV:IX, see ibid., 89; transl. cit., 185.

119. Rev. 9:11 (the chapter noted in cod. 36–110, p. 251; Acton, *A Philosopher's Note Book*, 480). How close at hand this interpretation may be is pointed out in F. Boll, *Aus der Offenbarung Johannis* (From the Apocalypse of St. John) (Leipzig & Berlin: Teubner, 1914), 73. Apollo as the name of a demon is included in the multitudes of terms that are listed in Rudwin, 28. There is also a possible influence from Bunyan, as will be discussed later.

120. *The Worship and Love of God*, §72; *Metamorphoses*, Walchius edition, 1037–1044, Magnus edition, 561–568; Humphries translation, 358–362.

121. Rudwin, 38.

122. *The Worship and Love of God*, §§81, 82. *Metamorphoses*, Humphries translation, 166; Walchius edition, 557–558, Magnus edition, 258.

123. Humphries translation, 346.

124. Ibid., 106

125. Lamm believed the association was to Milton, but he abstained from using the observation as an argument, since he found the similarities too general (1915, 189, note 10; 2000, 339, note 179).

126. See Roscher, I, col. 1695ff.

127. In this context, *Ludi* might be associated with disreputable gladiator schools in Rome; see K. E. George, *Ausführliches lateinisch-deutsches Handwörterbuch*, 8th ed. (Hannover & Leipzig: Hahnsche Verlagsbuchhandlung, 1918) II, col. 721.

128. Lamm 1915, 181–185; 2000, 180–184. Stroh's opinion led him to some doubtful translations in his English version of *The Worship and Love of God*, for example, §57 where "*Diva*" is rendered "holy stranger" and "holy being" (115–116).

129. Lamm 1915, 182–183; 2000, 181–182.

130. Lamm 1915, 10, 183–184, and 191ff.; 2000, 11–12, 183–184, 190ff. See also Benz 1948, 215ff.; 2002, 242–257.

131. See my *Swedenborgs korrespondenslära* (Stockholm: Almqvist & Wiksell,

1969), 96–97; the manual was called *Corps de philosophie contenant la logique, la physique, la metaphysique et l'ethique* and was written by Scipion Dupleix. I used the Geneva edition of 1636.

132. Cod. 36–110, p. 89; Acton, *A Philosopher's Note Book*, 185–186.
133. Lamm 1915, 183; 2000, 182.
134. Cod. 36–110, p. 8; Acton, *A Philosopher's Note Book*, 15. Translation by Matilda McCarthy.
135. Migne, *Patrologia latina* XL, col. 781–782; Swedenborg, cod. 36–110, p. 9; Acton, *A Philosopher's Note Book*, 20. Translation by Matilda McCarthy.
136. *De inquirenda veritate* III:II:VI, ed. cit., 214; noted in cod. 36–110, p. 197; Acton, *A Philosopher's Note Book*, 408. Translation by Matilda McCarthy.
137. Lamm 1915, 44; 2000, 44-45.
138. *De anima*, 238; *Rational Psychology*, §521, p. 297. Translation by Matilda McCarthy.
139. Cod. 36–110, front cover; Acton, *A Philosopher's Note Book*, 1.
140. Lamm 1915, 172; 2000, 171.
141. October 7–8, 1744, *Swedenborgs drömbok*, 268; *Dream Diary*, 294.
142. Lamm 1915, 153–154; 2000, 152.
143. Dream of October 3–6, 1744: *Swedenborgs drömbok*, 262; *Dream Diary*, 287. See Lamm 1915, 149–150; 2000, 148–149.
144. *An Introduction to the Word Explained*, 104, note 4: "This passage may indeed be regarded as the first of Swedenborg's spiritual Memorabilia."
145. Dream of October 6–7, 1744: *Swedenborgs drömbok*, 266–267; *Dream Diary*, 290, 292. The last word is incomplete.
146. Lamm 1915, 150ff. and 181–185; 2000, 148ff and 180–184. See Stroh's evaluation of the allegorical and dogmatic elements in *The Worship and Love of God*, "Analysis and Review," 61–65.
147. See Toksvig, 218–230, and compare her view of this work as "inspired," 314; English translation, 148–155, on inspiration, 202.
148. Lamm 1915, 191ff.; 2000, 189ff.
149. Lamm 1915, 105–106, 151, and 179; 2000, 105–106, 150, and 178–179.
150. *De la recherche de la verité* (Paris, 712), I: 549; translation cited, 175–176. Translation by Inge Jonsson.
151. Cod. 36–110, 67–68; Acton, *A Philosopher's Note Book*, 132ff.
152. Ibid., 67; English translation, 132. Translation by Matilda McCarthy.
153. Ibid., 63–66; English translation, 120-131. Leibniz's polemics against Bayle shows how close he is to Malebranche: "*ce prétendu* fatum, *qui oblige même la Divinité, n'est autre chose que la propre nature de Dieu, son propre entendement qui fournit les regles à sa sagesse & à sa bonté; c'est une heureuse necessité, sans laquelle il ne seroit ni bon, ni sage*" (this pretended fate, which binds even the Divinity, is nothing else than the proper nature of God, his very judgment which conveys rules to his wisdom and goodness; it is a happy necessity, without which he would be neither good nor wise.) Translation by Inge Jonsson. *Essais de theodicée*, §191; French ed., 233; Latin ed., 903–904; cod. 36–110, 64; Acton, *A Philosopher's Note Book*, 125.
154. Cod. 36–110, 63; Acton, *A Philosopher's Note Book*, 120; the quotation from Kortholtus' ed. (Leipzig, 1738), 67. Translation by Matilda McCarthy. This entire philosophical letter to Hansch (64–70) is of the utmost interest with regard to Leibniz's attitude toward the ancients.
155. *De anima*, 123; *Rational Psychology*, §253, p. 153.
156. See O. Bensow, *Biblisk ordbok* (Biblical Dictionary), 4. ed. (Stockholm: Evan-

geliska Fosterlandsstiftelsens förlag, 1936), VT, 294–295 and 553ff.; NT, 234–235 and 427–428.

157. Cod. 36–110, 181; Acton, *A Philosopher's Note Book*, 386–387. *Essais de théodicée*, French ed., 295ff.; Latin ed., 1041–1046.

158. *Essais de théodicée*, French ed., 295–296; Latin ed., 1043; the Latin quotation comes from the *Aeneid* VII:770–773 (transl. cit., p. 257), in Leibniz's version (*"at"* instead of *"tum,"* see ed. cit., 247). Translation by Inge Jonsson from the French text.

159. Ibid., §273; French ed., 297; Latin ed., 1046.

160. Ibid., §274; French ed., 298; Latin ed., 1047. Translation by Inge Jonsson.

161. Humphries translation, 10–11; Walchius edition, 42ff.; see Magnus edition, 18–19. In notes, the editor of Walchius' version presents a multitude of references to ancient and modern writers (among others, to Genesis) with regard to the end of the world (esp. §§74 and 75, pp. 44–50).

162. A conceivable sentence might be *"Et punit, et amat"* (He both punishes and loves), if you want to emphasize the role of the Father in the drama.

163. *Mundus Symbolicus* I:91–94.

164. Ibid. I, 93; the quote from Ovid comes from *Trist.* lib.IV:VIII:45 (a misprint in Picinelli, IV:VII). Translation by Matilda McCarthy.

165. Ibid. I:351.

166. Praz, 124.

167. Ibid., 131–132.

168. Ibid., 139–140.

169. A reproduction of this picture can be seen in ibid., 149.

170. Ibid., 153.

171. The verb *conterere* is used in the Tremellius-Junius Bible but not in the other Bible editions in the collection of excerpts, *Biblia Sacra ex Sebastiani Castellionis interpretatione* (here quoted in a Leipzig edition from 1778); see *Cat.bibl.*, 4.

172. See cod. 36–110, p. 178; Acton, *A Philosopher's Note Book*, 4.

173. It seems that Swedenborg wanted to fulfill what the author of the Apocalypse had done in Leibniz's view, namely, to *"éclaircir ce que les autres Ecrivains Canoniques avoient laissé dans l'obscurité"* (to clarify what the other canon writers left obscure).

174. Lamm 1915, 189; 2000, 188.

175. John Bunyan, *The Pilgrim's Progress from This World to That Which Is to Come*, ed. J. B. Wharey (Oxford: Clarendon Press, 1928), 144. On the Apollyon episode see, R. M. Frye, *God, Man, and Satan: Patterns of Christian Thought and Life in* Paradise Lost, Pilgrim's Progress, *and the Great Theologians* (Princeton, N.J.: Princeton University Press, 1960), 124ff.

176. Praz (206) has placed a picture from *Cor Iesu amanti sacrum*, mentioned above, together with a passage from *Pilgrim's Progress*: "Then the interpreter took Christian by the hand, and led him into a very large parlour that was full of dust, because never swept; the which, after he had reviewed a little while, the interpreter called for a man to sweep, etc. . . . . The parlour is the heart of a man that was never sanctified by the sweet grace of the Gospel—the dust is his original sin. . . ."

177. Wharey edition, 174.

## Chapter 8

1. Lamm 1915, 187ff.; 2000, 186ff.

2. Oxenstierna points out in his translation of *Paradise Lost* ([Stockholm: 1815], 153) that *"Hennes speglande i vattnet kan vara tagit af Fabeln om Narcissus"* (her looking at herself in the water can be fetched from the fable of Narcissus); see ed. cit., index, II:1336 (Narcissus) and Lamm 1915, 188; 2000, 186.

3. Compare Benz 1948, 279; 2002, 253 *"Sie kommt durch ein Narzissus-Erlebnis zum Bewusstsein ihrer selbst"* (Through an experience like that of Narcissus, she becomes conscious of herself). On the style of the *Metamorphoses,* see L. P. Wilkinson, *Ovid Recalled* (1955; Portway, England: C. Chivers, 1974), especially chapter 7, "Narrative and Description." On a theological interpretation of Eve's Narcissus experience in *Paradise Lost,* see Frye, 46.

4. See, for example, the account of the brain in *Photolith.* VI:75–81; English translation, *The Brain* I:56–64. It was probably easy to combine *mens* and *animus* into one unit with separate levels, since both of them had been located to the cerebrum. On the psychology of the theosophist, see Lamm 1915, 267–277; 2000, 264–274.

5. See, for example, Benz 1948, 426–443; 2002, 388–397.

6. *Opera* I:337: *"Emedan jag wid mitt wistande uti Haag, hade den ähran, at med Högwelb: Hr Envojen communicera twenne mina första dehlar, af Regno Animali, så fodrar min skyldighet, at nu tredie delen deraf tilhanda senda; och derjemte första dehlen af en liten* piece, de Cultu et Amore Dei, *den jag beder Hr Envojen techtes påögna, i synnerhet slutet, som handlar de amore Primogeniti; och i fall Hr Envojen finner nöje deruti, at distribuera de 4 Exemplaris, jag derhos sender, til dem Hr Envojen finner godt; såge helsst om det wore till några scavans af Ministrarna"* (Since at my stay in The Hague I had the honor of communicating with the Hon. Envoy the two first parts of my *Regnum animale,* it is my duty to send you the third part of it, and in addition the first part of a little play, *De cultu et amore Dei,* which I ask you, Mr. Envoy, to peruse, in particular the end, which deals *de amore Primogeniti* [with the love of the firstborn]; and if you, Mr Envoy, take pleasure in it, to distribute the four copies I include to those you, Mr. Envoy, decide; I would prefer if it was to be to some learned men among the ambassadors). Translation by Inge Jonsson. Obviously Swedenborg did not feel disdain for his work at this time; on the contrary, his way of expressing himself indicates expectations of its reception, especially of the psycho-theologically central fifth scene. If the second part had been completed, he would probably have enclosed it.

7. *De civitate Dei* lib. XI, cap. XXX; B. Dombart's edition (Leipzig, 1877), I:504.

8. The Royal Library, Stockholm, collection of autographs Em. Swedenborg; printed in *New Church Life* (1896): 186. Translation by Matilda McCarthy.

9. *Msed. cit.,* 122; translation cited., 192.

10. *Swedenborgs drömbok,* 81; *Dream Diary,* 91.

11. *Regnum animale* I, §186. Translation by Matilda McCarthy.

12. Stroh, "Swedenborg's Contributions to Psychology," 156.

13. Lamm 1915, 36–47; 2000, 37–48.

14. *Photolith.* III:95; English translation in *Scientific and Philosophical Treatises* II:21–22, 23; Lamm 1915, 40–41; 2000, 40–41.

15. Ibid. III: 53, *Resebeskrifningar,* 64: "July 20, 1736: *Såg samma dag Wollfens theologiam naturalem; hwaruti han tycktes något röra mig, men utan namn"* (Saw on the same day *Theologia naturalis* by Wolff, in which he seemed to touch somewhat on me, but without mentioning the name). Translation by Inge Jonsson. This note has been pointed out by Lamm (1915, 48; 2000, 48). The annotation on the day after about his making excerpts from Wolff's

*Ontologia* and *Cosmologia* is interesting as a glimpse of the preparations to *Oeconomia*.

16. These excerpts, which have been published in *Photolith*. III under the heading *"Comparatio Systematum Christiani Wolffii et Swedenborgii"* (Comparison between the Systems of Christian Wolff and Swedenborg), 102–140, have been used above in the section on the doctrine of correspondence in the Acton edition (*Psychologica*).

17. The sketch has been reproduced in *Photolith*. III:108, and in *Psychologica*, 24–25.

18. *Photolith*. III:108; *Psychologica*, 27. Translation by Matilda McCarthy.

19. *Photolith*., 130–131; *Psychologica*, 122–123; on the effect of the Fall, see *Photolith*, 111–112, resp. pp. 38ff.

20. *Photolith*., 124; *Psychologica*, 92–93. Translation by Matilda McCarthy.

21. *Photolith*., 132ff.; *Psychologica*, 102ff.

22. See Clissold's index in his translation of *Oeconomia* II: 360, and the passages listed there; and Wilkinson's "Bibliographical Notices" in his translation of *Regnum animale*, 706–714.

23. *Opera* III:265–268. The quotation appears on page 268.

24. Jonsson, *Swedenborgs korrespondenslära*, 56–58.

25. As always it is an issue of balance. In principle, I am not questioning Lamm's brilliant evaluation of Swedenborg's erudition, but it seems to me that he went to extremes, probably because he wanted to disprove once and for all New Church scholars' attempts to deny that Swedenborg was acquainted with Neoplatonic and mystical ideas; the eulogies on modern science, which have been quoted above, must be taken into account in deciding how Swedenborg viewed his own position and ambition.

26. *Photolith*. VI:265–266; *Psychologica*, 52.

27. *Photolith*. VI: 267ff.; *Psychologica*, 53–56. In connection with an account of Descartes' ideas on an artificial language, Louis Couturat and Louis Leau summarized the characteristics of the philosophical languages as follows: *"l'analogie de toutes les idées avec les notions de nombre; la recherche des idées simples qui forment par leurs combinaisons toutes les autres idées; l'analogie de ces combinaisons avec des opérations arithmétiques, et par suite l'assimilation du raisonnement à un calcul mécanique et infaillible"* (the analogy of all ideas to the concepts of number; the search for simple ideas which form all other ideas through combinations; the analogy of these combinations to the arithmetical operations, and as a consequence the similarity of reasoning with a mechanic and infallible calculus). Translation by Inge Jonsson. Compare also the sections on Dalgarno, Wilkins, and Leibniz, 15–28.

28. Published posthumously as *De fibra*; see chapter IV, note 44.

29. Swedenborg himself has made such statements on several occasions, for example, in *Oeconomia* I, §18; compare M. Ramström's article in *Uppsala läkareförenings förhandlingar*, NF bd XVI 1910–1911.

30. *Oeconomia* II, §116. Translation by Matilda McCarthy.

31. Compare *The Worship and Love of God* §41, notes a and b.

32. *Oeconomia* II, §222; *Photolith*. VI:265; trans. cit., 52–53; *Opuscula*, 38 and 48; *Psychological Transactions*, 79 and 91–92.

33. See, for example, the essay *"De sanguine rubro"* (On red blood) in *Opuscula*, 25–26; *Psychological Transactions*, 105–106.

34. *The Worship and Love of God*, §§95–98; *fluidum spirituosum* becomes the transport instrument of the inflow of life into the different degrees of the se-

ries, but it is not an immediate inflow as in the influx doctrine or in occasionalism; compare *Oeconomia* I, §579 and §§633–638.

35. *De fibra*, 25ff. (§§118–121); *Economy of the Animal Kingdom*, III:43ff.
36. *De fibra*, 34 (§128); *Economy of the Animal Kingdom*, III:54ff.
37. *De fibra*, 45ff. (§142); *Economy of the Animal Kingdom*, III:73–79; compare cod. 36–110, p. 2; Acton, *A Philosopher's Note Book*, 7 (also pp. 135 and 291, referring to *De fibra* in the Engl. ed.). Compare the prologue to *Oeconomia*.
38. *De fibra*, 72 (§190); *Economy of the Animal Kingdom*, III:114. Translation by Matilda McCarthy.
39. *De fibra*, 114–138 (§§261–273); *Economy of the Animal Kingdom*, III:171–203. The author refers to *Principia* in several places (for example, 122–123), which emphasizes the connection between macrocosm and microcosm.
40. The clearest description is given in *Oeconomia* I, §§579-587.
41. *Opuscula*, 16; *Psychological Transactions,* 94. Translation by Matilda McCarthy.
42. *Opuscula*, 27 (chap. XV); *Psychological Transactions*, 107–108. Swedenborg's way of expressing himself indicates his ambition to unite empiricism and rationalism, as well as the connection of the doctrine of forms to a universal language.
43. Cod. 36–110, pp. 255 and 265; Acton, *A Philosopher's Note Book*, 483–484 and 494. Previous plans for the *Oeconomia* include also a doctrine of forms; see cod 36–110, p. 263; *A Philosopher's Note Book*, 491.
44. *Oeconomia* I, §297; II, §252. Translation by Matilda McCarthy. It is obvious that already here Swedenborg has distanced himself from the brisk rationalistic optimism of *De Infinito*; compare, for example, pp. 23–26; *The Infinite Cause of Creation*, 18ff.
45. Quoted in cod. 36–110, pp. 160, 200–201, and 236; Acton, *A Philosopher's Note Book,* 345, 416, and 457.
46. Cod. 36–110, p. 120; *A Philosopher's Note Book*, 243.
47. Benz 1948, 60–61; 2002, 54. Malebranche was one of the most famous members of this order, and Lelong was an intimate friend of his; see Gouhier, 4ff.
48. Aspelin, II:71. Translation by Inge Jonsson.
49. Cod. 36–110, pp. 200–201; Acton, *A Philosopher's Note Book,* 415–416.
50. Cod. 36–110, p. 201; *A Philosopher's Note Book*, 416; *De inquirenda veritate*, Illustrationes seu explicationes ad lib. II:88–89.
51. Cod. 36–110, p. 174; *A Philosopher's Note Book*, 374; for Swedenborg the theosophist, however, Paul does not hold the same authoritative position; see Benz 1948, 497ff.; 2002, 458–459.
52. Gouhier, 39. Translation by Inge Jonsson.
53. Compare the extract from Malebranche in cod. 36–110, p. 124, and the Leibniz excerpts, p. 152; Acton, *A Philosopher's Note Book,* 257ff., and 330.
54. *De anima*, 243–254; *Rational Psychology*, §§533–560, pp. 303–317.
55. *De anima*, 252; *Rational Psychology*, §555, p. 314.
56. *De anima*, 254; *Rational Psychology*, §559, p. 316. Translation by Matilda McCarthy. Compare *Essais de theodicée*, §82, French ed., 126–127; Latin ed., 695ff.; noted in cod. 36–110, p. 64; Acton, *A Philosopher's Note Book*, 123–124.
57. See, for example, *Summaria expositio doctrinae novae ecclesiae* (Amsterdam: 1769), §64ff.; phototyp. ed. (Basel: Swedenborg Institut, 1955), 30–31.
58. Lamm 1915, 176; 2000, 175.
59. Gouhier, *Traité de la nature et de la grâce*, 100. Translation by Inge Jonsson.

60. Ibid., 103; the hymn "*O felix culpa*" is quoted here. Translation by Inge Jonsson.
61. Lamm 1915, 265ff.; 2000, 262ff.
62. *Oeconomia* II, §299. Translation by Matilda McCarthy. Compare *De anima*, 149–150 (§§8, 9); *Rational Psychology*, 187–188, §§312–313.
63. After the intelligences have been separated from the soul, the first-born is called "*non jam infans sed adolescentulus*" (no longer a child but a youth) (§52).
64. Acton regards §78 with its account of the battle between good and evil as evidence that the drama of creation is not "the story of an individual man but of the mind of the whole human race, here set forth by Swedenborg after the pattern of spiritual representations" (*An Introduction to the Word Explained*, 111, note 6). His conclusion is correct to the extent that the drama, like all hexaemera, aims at presenting the fate of the human race and its preconditions. Nevertheless, Swedenborg's psychological Golden Age ideas have inherent difficulty in combining an individualizing portrayal with a universal message.
65. See Lamm 1915, 74–75; 2000, 74–75.
66. *Photolith.* III:141.
67. Acton, *Psychological Transactions*, xxx–xxxi.
68. *Oeconomia* II, §348. Translation by Matilda McCarthy. See also *Oeconomia* II, §366.
69. *De anima*, 243–247; *Rational Psychology*, 303–308 (esp. §§538–542).
70. Lamm 1915, 94; 2000, 93–94.
71. See Jacobsson, 28ff.
72. Forssell, 145ff. On Leibniz's syncretism, see, for example, P. Hazard, *La crise de la conscience européenne* (Paris: Gallimard, 1935), I:290ff.
73. On Leibniz's evaluation of Knorr von Rosenroth's *Cabbala denudata*, see Benz 1958, 24–25.
74. *The Worship and Love of God*, §2; Lamm 1915, 257ff.; 2000, 256ff.
75. *De anima*, 245; *Rational Psychology*, 305–306, §538. Translation by Matilda McCarthy. The importance of this *varietas harmonica* is also illustrated by concrete examples, *De anima*, 253–254; *Rational Psychology*, 316 (esp. §558).
76. *De anima*, 245–246; *Rational Psychology*, 305–306, §§538–539.
77. *De anima*, 247ff.; *Rational Psychology*, 308–322, §§543–548; 308–311 (esp. §547).
78. Diestel, 700–708. See also the extensive account of the doctrine of spirits in Benz 1948, 422–443; 2002, 326–347.
79. *De fibra*, 101; *Economy of the Animal Kingdom*, III:153–154. Translation by Matilda McCarthy. Immediately after the quotation, Swedenborg refers to Wolff's *Cosmologia* for support.
80. See primarily book VIII with its combination of constitutions and types of character; transl. by B. Jowett, *The Great Books* (Chicago: Encyclopaedia Britannica, 1952), 7:401–416.
81. Cod. 36–110, p. 263; Acton, *A Philosopher's Note Book*, 492. Translation by Matilda McCarthy.
82. Cod. 36–110, p. 270; Acton, *A Philosopher's Note Book*, 499–500. In his interpretation of the Lord's Prayer, Swedenborg emphasizes the eschatological aspect in a way that comes very close to Malebranche.
83. *Clavis hieroglyphica, msed. cit.*, 123; Acton, *Psych.trans.*, 193; cod. 36–110, pp. 239–240; Acton, *A Philosopher's Note Book*, 462ff.

84. Cod. 36–110, pp. 239 and 144; Acton, *A Philosopher's Note Book*, 463 and 314.
85. See Benz 1948, 414–415; 2002, 376–377. Paul's text (1Cor. 15:40–47) is noted in cod. 36–110, p. 190; Acton, *A Philosopher's Note Book,* 398.
86. Lamm 1915, 244–261; 2000, 245–262. The rather absurd effects of this idea in literary application can be studied in Carl Jonas Love Almqvist, esp. in *Murnis*, ed. E. Gamby (Uppsala, Sweden: Bokgillet, 1960), 85–96. On similar concepts in Böhme and his English followers—as well as on the problem of Böhme's alleged influence on Swedenborg—see S. Hutin, *Les disciples anglais de Jacob Böhme aux XVIIe et XVIIIe siècles* (Paris: Edition Denoël, 1960), esp. 128–143.
87. For instance lib. I:XVIII; edition cited, 48–49.

## Chapter Nine

1. See the sketch of the section on the senses in *Regnum animale* (*De sensibus*), 202 and 164: *"vidi muscam. Illa abiit, recessi"* (I saw a fly; it went away and disappeared); *The Five Senses*, 252 and 206. Acton combined these notes with *The Dream Diary* and presented a speculative interpretation in *An Introduction to The Word Explained*, 86ff. The account of the senses exists only as a sketch; Swedenborg might have made notes of spiritual experiences here without letting them influence the final shape of the work. Still, it is interesting to catch a glimpse of how the occult experiences intrude upon the author and how he hesitates to interpret them, still another illustration of the personal background to the drama of creation and of the author's ability to transform it into a symbolic fable.
2. Curtius, 146–152; *Lefwernes Beskrifning*, 473; *Resebeskrifningar*, 74, 75, 85.
3. The problem of Kant's relations to Swedenborg falls outside the scope of this study, and I will only refer to a few representative examples in the extensive literature on this issue: H. Hoppe, "Die Kosmogonie Emanuel Swedenborgs und die Kantsche und Laplacesche Theorie," *Archiv für Geschichte der Philosophie* Bd XXV:NF XVIII (1912): 53–68; Benz 1947, 233–285; 2002, 216–267; A. Nyman, *Utflykter i idévärlden* (Excursions in the World of Ideas) (Malmö, Sweden: Bernces förlag, 1956), 61–79: here the similarities between Kant and Swedenborg are seen as a result of a common reading of Leibniz, which seems to be a very probable conclusion; Crasta, 222–224, 255–257, 271–273; *Kant on Swedenborg*: Dreams of a Spirit-Seer *and Other Writings*, translated by Gregory R. Johnson and Glenn Alexander Magee, edited by Gregory R. Johnson (West Chester, Pa.: The Swedenborg Foundation, 2003).

## Appendix

1. Acton, *A Philosopher's Note Book,* xiv.
2. Stroh and Ekelöf, *Kronologisk förteckning*, 31.
3. Acton, *A Philosopher's Note Book*, vii.
4. Ibid., viii; Acton writes "pp. 261–263," which is a mistake since page 261 is empty.
5. Ibid., xi.
6. I thank my late friend, Assoc. Prof. Carl Reinhold Smedmark, for suggesting this interpretation; I had the privilege of discussing these manuscript problems with him, as well as other issues during my studies.
7. An exhaustive account can be found in Acton's preface to *Psychological Transactions*, xx–xxviii.

8. *Documents* III:927–928; Lamm 1915, 95; 2000, 95.
9. Evidently Swedenborg did not identify his doctrine of correspondence with the philosophical language of universals but looked upon it only as a substitute for that, a short cut to the goal; see *De anima*, 256ff.; *Rational Psychology,* 319ff, §§563–567; and *Clavis hieroglyphica, msed. cit.*, 115; Acton, *Psych.trans.*, 184.
10. See the reference to "*paragraphus de voluntate*" (*msed. cit.*, 89), the request "*vide libertate*" (ibid., 96), the mention of "*mathesis universalium*" (ibid., 100), and others; Acton, *Psych.trans.*, 157, 164, and 168 (the note as well in which Acton has observed that we are close to *De anima*).
11. As Acton pointed out, Swedenborg later added the word "*allegorica*" to the headline of the category *Correspondentia parabolica* in cod. 36–110, a term used for this type in *Clavis*. See cod. 36–110, p. 220; Acton, *A Philosopher's Note Book*, 431, and Acton's preface, xiii; *Clavis hieroglyphica, msed.*, 123; Acton, *Psych.trans.*, 192–193.
12. Cod. 36–110, pp. 263 and 268, respectively; pp. 255, 265, and 269; Acton, *A Philosopher's Note Book*, 483, 491, 494, 496, and 498.

# BIBLIOGRAPHY

## Primary Sources

### Manuscripts

*The Library of the Royal Swedish Academy of Sciences, Stockholm, Swedenborg Collection*
Cod. 36–110 (Varia Philosophica, Theologica, Mathematica, etc.)
Cod. 37–90 (Index Variorum Philosophicorum)
Cod. 86–53 (Geometrica et Algebraica)
Cod. 88–93 (Varia Philosophica, Anatomica et Itineraria).

*The Royal Library, Stockholm:*
Autograph collection: Notes on the third part of *The Worship and Love of God.*
*Emanuelis Swedenborgii Autographa: editio phototypica* vol. XVIII (Miscellanea Theologica, Stockholm 1916).
Deleen, C. Copy of *The Memoirs of Carl Robsahm* (Biogr. Swedenborg I, 55).
Johansén, Ch. Translation of §§ 1–28 of *The Worship and Love of God.* (Teol. Swedenb. No A 616).
Tafel, R. L., ed. *Emanuelis Swedenborgii Autographa: editio photolithographica* vol. III (Itineraria et Philosophica, Stockholm 1870), vol. VI (Miscellanea Anatomica et Philosophica sive Supplementum Regni Animalis, Stockholm 1869), and vol. VII (Opusculum de Cultu et Amore Dei, Stockholm 1870).

### Works by Swedenborg

Acton, A., trans. *Psychologica, Being Notes and Observations on Christian Wolff's* Psychologia Empirica *by Emanuel Swedenborg.* Philadelphia: Swedenborg Scientific Association, 1923.

————. *A Philosopher's Note Book.. Excerpts from Philosophical Writers and from the Sacred Scriptures on a Variety of Philosophical Subjects; together with Some Reflections, and Sundry Notes and Memoranda by Emanuel Swedenborg.* Philadelphia: Swedenborg Scientific Association, 1931.

*Clavis hieroglyphica arcanorum naturalium & spiritualium, per viam repraesentationum et correspondentiarum ab Emanuele Swedenborg.* Ed. by R. Hindmarsh. London, 1784.

—English translation in Acton, A., ed. and trans. *Psychological Transactions and Other Posthumous Tracts, 1734–1744.* 1920, repr. Philadelphia: Swedenborg Scientific Association, 1955.

*Daedalus Hyperboreus.* Upsala, 1716–1718.

*Emanuel Swedenborg: Religiösa skrifter i urval.* Swedish translation by H. Bergstedt, with a preface by M. Lamm. Stockholm: Hugo Gebers förlag, 1925.

*Emanuelis Swedenborgii Adversaria in libros Veteris Testamenti.* 6 vols. Ed. by I. Tafel. Tübingen and London, 1847–1854.

—*The Word of the Old Testament Explained.* 8 vols. Trans. by A. Acton. Bryn Athyn, Pa.: Academy of the New Church, 1928–1948.

*Emanuelis Swedenborgii Oeconomia regni animalis in transactiones divisa* III. Ed. by J.J.G.Wilkinson. London, 1847.

—Acton, A. *The Fibre.* Philadelphia: Swedenborg Scientific Association, 1918.

—*Three Transactions on the Cerebrum: A Posthumous Work by Emanuel Swedenborg.* 2 vols. Philadelphia: Swedenborg Scientific Association, 1938, 1940.

—Tafel, R. L., ed. and trans. *The Brain Considered Anatomically, Physiologically and Philosophically by Emanuel Swedenborg.* 2 vols. London: James Speirs, 1882, 1887.

*Emanuelis Swedenborgii Opera poetica,* publ. by Swedenborg Society, London. Uppsala: Typis Academicis, 1910.

—Helander, H., ed. and trans. *Festivus applausus in Caroli XII in Pomeraniam suam adventum.* Uppsala: Acta Universitatis Upsaliensis, 1985.

—*Camena Borea.* Uppsala: Acta Universitatis Upsaliensis, 1988.

—*Ludus Heliconius and other Latin poems.* Uppsala: Acta Universitatis Upsaliensis, 1995.

*Emanuelis Swedenborgii Opuscula quaedam argumenti philosophici.* Ed. by J.J.G. Wilkinson. London: W. Newbery, 1846.

—English translation in Acton, A., ed and trans. *Psychological Trans-actions and Other Posthumous Tracts, 1734–1744.* 1920, repr. Philadelphia: Swedenborg Scientific Association, 1955.

*Emanuelis Swedenborgii Principia rerum naturalium sive novorum tenta-minum phaenomena mundi elementaris philosophice explicandi.* Dresden & Leipzig, 1734.

—Phototyp. edition. Basel, Switzerland: Swedenborg Institut, 1954.

—Clissold, A., trans. *The Principia.* 2 vols. London: W. Newbery, 1845–1846.

*Emanuelis Swedenborgii Prodromus philosophiae ratiocinantis de infinito, et causa finali creationis: deque mechanismo operationis animae et corporis.* Dresden & Leipzig, 1734.

—Wilkinson, J.J.G., trans. *The Infinite and Final Cause of Creation.* New edition. London: Swedenborg Society, 1908.

*Emanuelis Swedenborgii Regnum animale anatomice, physice et philosophice perlustratum.* I–II. The Hague, 1744; III. London, 1745.

—Wilkinson, J.J.G., trans. *The Animal Kingdom Considered Anatomically, Physically and Philosophically by Emanuel Swedenborg.* 1843–1844; repr. Bryn Athyn, Pa.: Swedenborg Scientific Association, 1960.

*Emanuelis Swedenborgii Regnum animale anatomice, physice et philosophice perlustratum, ejus pars septima de Anima agit.* Ed. by I. Tafel. Tübingen and London, 1849.

—Acton, A., and Rogers, N.H. trans. *Rational Psychology.* Philadelphia: Swedenborg Scientific Association, 1950.

*Emanuelis Swedenborgii Regnum subterraneum sive minerale de cupro et orichalco.*Vol.III. Dresden and Leipzig, 1734.

*Experientiae spirituales.* 4 vols. Ed. by J.D. Odhner. Bryn Athyn, Pa.:Academy of the New Church, 1983–1993.

*Första delen av Gudsdyrkan och kärleken till Gud, hvarest handlas om jordens uppkomst, paradiset och lefvande varelsers boning, äfvensom den förstföddes eller Adams födelse, barndom och kärlek,* af Emanuel Swedenborg. Swedish translation by J. Boyesen and A. H. Stroh. Nya kyrkans härold, 1902–1903.

—*The Worship and Love of God.* Trans. by F. Sewall and A. H. Stroh, London 1914; repr. West Chester and London: The Swedenborg Foundation and Swedenborg Society, 1996.

—*Emanuel Swedenborg: Om Guds dyrkan och kärleken till Gud.* Swedish translation by Ritva Jonsson. 1961; repr. Stockholm: Natur och Kultur, 1988.

—*The Worship and Love of God.* Trans. by S. S. Shotwell. West Chester, Pa.: The Swedenborg Foundation, forthcoming.

"L. Annaei Senecae & Pub. Syr. Mimi forsan & aliorum selectae sententiae cum annotationibus Erasmi & graeca versione Jos. Scaligeri." Ph.D. diss., University of Uppsala, 1709.

*Miscellanea observata circa res naturales & praesertim circa mineralia, ignem & montium strata.* Leipzig, 1722; repr. in *Opera quaedam aut inedita aut obsoleta de rebus naturalibus,* 3 vols., I. Stockholm: The Royal Swedish Academy of Sciences, 1907.

*Oeconomia regni animalis in transactiones divisa* I–II. London and Amsterdam, 1740–1741.

—Clissold, A., trans. *The Economy of the Animal Kingdom.* 2 vols. London: W. Newbery & H. Ballière, 1845–1846.

*Om Jordenes och Planeternas Gång och Stånd.* Skara, 1718; repr. in *Opera quaedam aut inedita aut obsoleta de rebus naturalibus,* 3 vols., III. Stockholm: The Royal Swedish Academy of Sciences, 1911.

*Regnum animale,* pars quarta. Ed. by I. Tafel. Tübingen and London, 1848.

—Price, E. S., trans. *The Five Senses.* Philadelphia: Swedenborg Scientific Association, 1914.

*Regnum animale,* pars quinta. Ed. by I. Tafel. Tübingen and London, 1848.

—Acton, A., trans. *The Animal Kingdom . . . , parts 4 and 5.* 2nd ed. Bryn Athyn: Swedenborg Scientific Association, 1928.

*Resebeskrifningar af Emanuel Swedenborg under åren 1710–1739* (Travel notes). Uppsala: The Royal Swedish Academy of Sciences, 1911.

—*The Letters and Memorials of Emanuel Swedenborg.* Ed. and trans. by A. Acton. Bryn Athyn, Pa.: Swedenborg Scientific Association, 1948–1955.

*Scientific and Philosophical Treatises by Emanuel Swedenborg.* Ed. and trans. by A.H. Stroh. Vol. II, *On Anatomy, Physiology, Psychology, and Philosophy.* Bryn Athyn, Pa.: Swedenborg Scientific Association, 1905.

*Summaria expositio doctrinae Novae Ecclesiae, quae per Novam Hierosolymam in Apocalypsi intelligitur.* Amsterdam, 1769.

—*A Brief Exposition of the Doctrine of the New Church.* In *Miscellaneous Theological Works.* Trans. by J. Whitehead. 2nd ed. West Chester, Pa.: The Swedenborg Foundation, 1996.

*Swedenborgs Drömmar 1744 jemte andra hans anteckningar* (Sweden-borg's Dream Diary). Ed. by G. Klemming. Stockholm: P.A. Norstedt & Söners förlag 1860.

—*Swedenborgs Drömbok: Glädjen och det stora kvalet.* Ed. by L. Bergquist. Stockholm: Norstedts, 1988.

—*Swedenborg's Dream Diary.* Ed. by L. Bergquist. Trans. by A. Hallengren. West Chester, Pa.: The Swedenborg Foundation, 2001.

## Secondary Sources

Acta Eruditorum, *anno MDCCXXXV publicata.* Leipzig, 1735.

Acton, Alfred. *An Introduction to The Word Explained. A Study of the Means by Which Swedenborg the Scientist and Philosopher Became the Theologian and Revelator.* Bryn Athyn, Pa.: Academy of the New Church, 1927.

Adams, Robert M. Ikon. *John Milton and the Modern Critics.* Ithaca, New York:Cornell University Press, 1955.

Almquist, Carl Jonas Love. *Murnis.* Ed. by Erik Gamby. Uppsala: Bokgillet, 1960.

Andrae, Tor. *Mystikens psykologi: Besatthet och inspiration.* Stockholm: Sveriges kristliga studentrörelses förlag, 1926.

Annerstedt, Claes. *Upsala universitets historia.* II:1. Uppsala: University of Uppsala, 1908.

Aristophanes. *The Birds.* Trans. by Dudley Fitts. New York: Harcourt, Brace & World Inc., 1936, 1960.

[Aristoteles]. *Libri quatuordecim qui Aristotelis esse dicuntur, De secretiore parte divinae sapientiae secundum Aegyptios.* Ed. by J. Carpenter. Paris, 1572.

—German translation by F. Dieterici, *Die sogenannte Theologie des Aristoteles.* Leipzig, 1883.

Arrhenius, Svante. *Människan inför världsgåtan.* Stockholm: Hugo Gebers förlag, 1907.

—"Emanuel Swedenborg as a Cosmologist." In *Opera quaedam aut inedita aut obsoleta de rebus naturalibus,* 3 vols., II. Stockholm: The Royal Swedish Academy of Sciences, 1908.

Aspelin, Gunnar. *Tankens vägar: En översikt av filosofiens utveckling.* 2 vols. Stockholm: Almqvist & Wiksell, 1958.

Atterbom, Per Daniel Amadeus. *Svenska siare och skalder.* Vol. I. Uppsala, 1841.

Augustinus. *Confessiones*. Ed. by P. de Labriolle, *Saint Augustin: Confessions Livres* I–XIII, tome I–II. Paris: Desclée de Brouwer, 1947.

———*De civitate Dei*. Ed. by B. Dombart, *Sancti Aurelii Augustini episcopi De civitate Dei libri* XXII, vol. I–II. Leipzig, 1877, 1892.

———*De Genesi ad Litteram*. Ed. by J.- P. Migne, *S. Aurelii Augustini Hipponensis episcopi De Genesi ad Litteram libri duodecim*. Patrologia latina, tom. XXXIV. Paris, 1887.

[Augustinus]. *De spiritu et anima*. Ed. by J.- P. Migne. Patrologia latina, tom. XL. Paris, 1887.

Avitus. *Alcimi Ecdicii Aviti Viennensis episcopi Poematum*. Libri VI.I: *De initio mundi*. Ed. by R. Peiper. Monumenta Germaniae Historica. VI:2. Berlin, 1883.

Bacon, Francis. *The Works of Francis Bacon*. Ed. by James Spedding, Robert Leslie Ellis, and Douglas Denon Heath. Vols. III, V, VI. London, 1887–1890.

[Baker, Thomas]. *Reflections upon Learning, Wherein is Shewn the Insufficiency Thereof, in Its Several Particulars: in Order to Evince the Usefulness and Necessity of Revelation, by a Gentleman*. 4th ed. London, 1708.

Ballet, Gilbert. *Swedenborg. Histoire d'un visionnaire au XVIIIe siècle*. Paris, 1899.

Bauerreiss, Romuald. *Arbor vitae: Der 'Lebensbaum' und seine Verwendung in Liturgie, Kunst und Brauchtum des Abendlandes*. München: Bayerische Benediktinerakademie, 1938.

Baumann. Hermann. *Das doppelte Geschlecht. Ethnologische Studien zur Bisexualität in Ritus und Mythos*. Berlin: Reimer, 1955.

Bensow, Oscar. *Biblisk ordbok*. 4th ed. Stockholm: Evangeliska Fosterlandsstiftelsens förlag, 1936.

Benz, Ernst. *Die christliche Kabbala: Ein Stiefkind der Theologie*. Zürich: Rhein- Verlag, 1958.

———. *Emanuel Swedenborg. Naturforscher und Seher*. München: Hermann Rinn, 1948.

———.*Emanuel Swedenborg: Visionary Savant in the Age of Reason*. Trans. by Nicholas Goodrick-Clarke. West Chester, Pa.: The Swedenborg Foundation, 2002.

———. *Swedenborg in Deutschland. F.C. Oetingers und Immanuel Kants Auseinandersetzung mit der Person und Lehre Emanuel Swedenborgs nach neuen Quellen bearbeitet*. Frankfurt am Main: Vittorio Klostermann, 1947.

Bergquist, Lars. *Swedenborgs hemlighet*. Stockholm: Natur och Kultur, 1999.

Beskow, Bernhard von. *Minne öfver Assessoren i Bergs-kollegium Emanuel Swedenborg*. Svenska Akademiens handlingar 31. Stockholm: P.A. Norstedt & Söners förlag, 1859.

*Bibliothèque raisonnée des ouvrages des savans de l'Europe*. Vol. XXXIV. Amsterdam, 1745.

Bilfinger, Georg Bernhard. *De harmonia animi et corporis humani, maxime praestabilita, ex mente illustris Leibnitii, commentatio hypothetica*. Frankfurt & Leipzig, 1723.

*Biographiskt lexicon öfver namnkunnige svenska män*. Vol. 16. Uppsala, 1849.

Björkhem, John. "Antoinette Bourignon. Till den svärmiska religiositetens historia och psykologi." Ph.D. diss., University of Lund, 1940.

Boëthius, Bertil. "Gustaf Johan Billberg." *Svenskt biografiskt lexikon* (SBL). Vol. IV. Stockholm: Albert Bonniers förlag, 1924.

Bogg, J.Stuart. *A Glossary or the Meaning of Specific Terms and Phrases Used by Swedenborg in His Theological Writings, Given in His Own Words*. London: Swedenborg Society, 1915.

Boll, Franz. *Aus der Offenbarung Johannis. Hellenistische Studien zum Weltbild der Apokalypse*. Leipzig & Berlin: Teubner, 1914.

Bring, Samuel Ebbe. *Bidrag till Christopher Polhems lefnadsteckning*. Stockholm: Svenska teknologföreningen, 1911.

Broadbent, J.B. *Some Graver Subject: An Essay on Paradise Lost*. London: Chatto & Windus, 1960.

Bunyan, John. *The Pilgrim's Progress from This World to That Which Is to Come*. Ed. by J.B. Wharey. Oxford: Clarendon Press, 1928.

Burnet, Thomas. *Archaeologiae philosophicae: sive doctrina antiqua de rerum originibus libri duo*. 2nd ed. London, 1728.

———. *The Sacred Theory of the Earth: Containing an Account of the Original of the Earth, and of All the General Changes which it Hath Already Undergone, or Is to Undergo, till the Consummation of All Things*. 2 vols. 6th ed. London, 1726.

———. *Telluris Theoria Sacra: orbis nostri originem & mutationes generales,quas aut jam subiit, aut olim subiturus est, complectens, libri duo priores de diluvio & paradiso*. London, 1681. *Telluris Theoria Sacra: orbis nostri . . . , libri duo priores de diluvio & paradiso; posteriores duo de conflagratione mundi & meliori rerum statu*. Frankfurt am Main, 1691.

Cassirer, Ernst. *Descartes. Lehre—Persönlichkeit—Wirkung.* Stockholm: Bermann- Fischer, 1939.

————. *Die platonische Renaissance in England und die Schule von Cambridge.* Studien der Bibliothek Warburg. Vol. XXIV. London: Cassell & Co., 1932.

[Castellio]. *Biblia sacra ex Sebastiani Castellionis interpretatione ejusque postrema recognitione praecipue in usum studiosae iuventutis denuo evulgata.* Leipzig, 1778.

Cayré, F. *Dieu présent dans la vie de l'esprit.* Bruges & Paris: Desclée de Brouwer, 1951.

Cicero. *De natura deorum.* Ed. by H. Rackham. The Loeb Classical Library 268.London: Harvard University Press, 1933.

Collier, Katherine B. *Cosmogonies of Our Fathers: Some Theories of the Seventeenth and Eighteenth Centuries.* New York: Columbia University Press, 1934.

Collijn, Isak. *Sveriges Bibliografi, 1600-talet.* Vol. II. Uppsala: Svenska litteratursällskapet, 1944.

Conklin, G.N. *Biblical Criticism and Heresy in Milton.* New York: King's Crown Press, 1949.

Courcelle, Pierre. *Recherches sur les Confessions de Saint Augustin.* Paris: Boccard, 1950.

Couturat, Louis, and Louis Leau. *Histoire de la langue universelle.* Paris: Hachette, 1903.

Crasta, Francesca Maria. *La filosofia della natura di Emanuel Swedenborg.* Milan: Franco Angeli, 1999.

Creutzer, Friedrich. *Symbolik und Mythologie der alten Völker.* Vol. III. Leipzig & Darmstadt, 1823.

Cudworth, Ralph. *The True Intellectual System of the Universe: the First Part; Wherein All the Reason and Philosophy of Atheism Is Confuted; and Its Impossibility Demonstrated.* London, 1678.

Curtius, Ernst Robert. *Europäische Literatur und lateinisches Mittelalter.* Bern: Francke Verlag, 1948.

Descartes, René. *Opera philosophica.* Frankfurt am Main, 1692.

Dickinson, E. *Physica vetus et vera: sive tractatus de naturali veritate Hexaemeri Mosaici.* Hamburg, 1705.

*Dictionary of National Biography.* Vol. III. London: Smith, Elder & Co., 1908.

Diestel, L. *Geschichte des Alten Testamentes in der christlichen Kirche.* Jena, 1869.

Dieterici, F. *Ueber die sogenannte Theologie des Aristoteles bei den*

*Arabern.* Abhandlungen und Vorträge des fünften internationalen Orientalisten- Congresses. Berlin, 1882.

Dole, George, and Kirven, Robert. *A Scientist Explores Spirit.* West Chester, Pa.: Chrysalis Books, 1997.

Du Bartas, Guillaume de Salluste. *La Sepmaine.* Ed. by Urban T. Holmes, John C. Lyons, and Robert W. Linker. Vol. II–III. Chapel Hill, N.C.: University of North Carolina Press, 1938–1940.

Eby, S.C. *The Story of the Swedenborg Manuscripts.* New York: The New Church Press, 1926.

Ekenvall, Asta. "Eric Benzelius d.y. och G.W. von Leibniz." *Linköpings biblioteks handlingar* 4:3 (1953): 5–64.

Emerson, Ralph Waldo. *Representative Men.* Boston, 1850.

Engelmann, W., and E. Preuss, eds. *Bibliotheca scriptorum classicorum.* Vol. II. 8th ed. Leipzig, 1882.

Eusebios. *Preparatio evangelica.* Ed. by F. Vigerus. Paris, 1628.

Evander, Sven. *Londonsvenskarnas kyrka genom 250 år.* Lund: Berlingska Boktryckeriet, 1960.

Falk, Wendla. *Bergsrådinnans dagbok: Kulturbilder från svenskt sjuttonhundratal.* Stockholm: Diakonistyrelsens förlag, 1957.

Fletcher, H.F. *Milton's Rabbinical Readings.* Urbana, Ill.: University of Illinois Press, 1930.

Forssell, Hans. *Minne af Erkebiskopen doktor Erik Benzelius den yngre.* Svenska Akademiens handlingar 58. Stockholm: P.A. Norstedt & Söners förlag, 1883.

Fredén, Gustaf. *Orpheus and the Goddess of Nature.* Göteborgs universitets Årsskrift LXIV:6. Göteborg, 1958.

Frey, Torsten S:son. "Paranoiska-paranoida syndrom." *Nytt och nyttigt,* medicinsk tidskrift utgiven av Hässle no 2 (1960):1-10.

Friberg, Axel. "Den svenske Herkules. Studier i Stiernhielms diktning." Ph.D. diss., University of Stockholm, 1945.

Frye, R.M. *God, Man, and Satan: Patterns of Christian Thought and Life in* Paradise Lost, Pilgrim's Progress, *and the Great Theologians.* Princeton, N.J.: Princeton University Press, 1960.

Fryxell, Anders. *Berättelser ur svenska historien* 43. Stockholm, 1875.

Frängsmyr, Tore. *Wolffianismens genombrott i Uppsala.* Uppsala: Acta Universitatis Upsaliensis, 1972.

Galling, K., ed. *Die Religion in Geschichte und Gegenwart. Handwörterbuch für Theologie und Religionswissenschaft.* 3 vols. 3rd ed. Tübingen: J.C.B. Mohr, 1957, 1958.

Garmann, Ch. *Homo ex ovo.* Chemnitz, 1672.

————. *Oologia curiosa duabus partibus absoluta, ortum corporum naturalium ex ovo demonstrans.* Zwickau s.a.

Gautruche, P. *L'histoire poétique.* 3rd ed. Paris, 1695.

George, Karl Ernst. *Ausführliches latein-deutsches Handwörterbuch.* Vol. II. 8th ed. Hannover & Leipzig: Hahn'sche Verlagsbuchhandlung, 1918.

Gilson, Etienne. *Introduction à l'étude de Saint Augustin.* Etudes de philosophie médiévale XI. Paris: J. Vrin, 1929.

Gouhier, H. *La philosophie de Malebranche et son expérience religieuse.* Bibliothèque d'histoire de la Philosophie. 2nd ed. Paris: J. Vrin, 1948.

————. *La vocation de Malebranche.* Bibliothèque d'histoire de la philosophie. Paris: J. Vrin, 1926.

Gordh, T.Jr and Sourander, P. "Swedenborg, Linné och hjärnforskningen." *Nordisk medicinhistorisk årsbok* (1990): 97–117.

Gradin, Arvid. *A Short History of the Bohemian-Moravian Protestant Church of the United Brethren.* London, 1743.

Grotius, Hugo. De *veritate religionis christianae.* New ed. Amsterdam, 1669.

Gruhle, H.W. "Swedenborgs Träume: Ein Beitrag zur Phänomenologie seiner Mystik." *Psychologische Forschung.* Band 5. Berlin: Springer Verlag, 1924.

Gruppe, Otto. *Die griechischen Culte und Mythen in ihren Beziehungen zu den orientalischen Religionen.* Vol. I. Leipzig, 1887.

————. *Geschichte der klassischen Mythologie und Religionsgeschichte während des Mittelalters im Abendland und während der Neuzeit.* (Supplement to Roscher's Ausführliches Lexikon der griechischen und römischen Mythologie.) Leipzig: Teubner, 1921.

Guthrie, W.K.C. *Orpheus and Greek Religion: A Study of the Orphic Movement.* 2nd ed. London: Methuen, 1952.

Görres, Joseph. *Emanuel Swedenborg, seine Visionen, und sein Verhältnis zur Kirche.* Strassburg, 1827.

Hagberg, Knut. "Linnaeus, Swedenborg och barocken." *Svenska Dagbladet,* February 18, 1961.

Hallengren, Anders. "The Code of Concord: Emerson's Search for Universal Laws." Ph.D. diss., Stockholm University, 1994.

————. *Gallery of Mirrors: Reflections of Swedenborgian Thought.* West Chester, Pa.: Swedenborg Foundation, 1998.

Harnack, Adolf von. *Lehrbuch der Dogmengeschichte.* Vol. I. 4th ed. Tübingen: Mohr, 1909.

Harris, Victor. *All Coherence Gone*. Chicago: University of Chicago Press, 1949.

Haskins, Charles Homer. *The Renaissance of the Twelfth Century*. 4th impression. Cambridge, Mass.: Harvard University Press, 1939.

Hazard, Paul. *La crise de la conscience européenne*. Vol. I. Paris: Gallimard, 1935.

Hedin, Greta. "Manhemsförbundet. Ett bidrag till göticismens och den yngre romantikens historia." Ph.D. diss., University of Göteborg, 1928.

Helmont, Jan Baptista van. *Opera omnia*. Frankfurt, 1707.

Henning, K.F.S. "Johan Conrad Dippels vistelse i Sverige samt dippelianismen i Stockholm 1727–1741." Ph.D.diss., University of Uppsala, 1881.

Herrlin, Olle. "Religionsproblemet hos Thorild." Ph.D.diss., University of Uppsala, 1947.

Hesiod. *Erga kai hemerai*. Swedish translation by Elof Hellquist. Lund: Gleerups, 1923.

———. *Theogonia*. Swedish translation by Elof Hellquist. Lund: Gleerups, 1924.

———. *Theogonin och Verk och dagar*. Swedish translation by Ingvar Björkeson. Stockholm: Natur och Kultur, 2003.

Hitschmann, Eduard. "Swedenborgs Paranoia.." *Zentralblatt für Psychoanalyse* III, no.1 (1913): 32–36.

Hobart, Nathaniel. *Life of Emanuel Swedenborg*. Boston: Allen and Goddard, 1831.

Hocke, Gustav. *Lukrez in Frankreich von der Renaissance bis zur Revolution*. Köln: Kerschgens, 1935.

Hofsten, Nils von. *Skapelsetro och uralstringshypoteser före Darwin*. Uppsala: Uppsala universitets årsskrift, 1928.

Holberg, Ludvig. *Jödiske Historie fra Verdens Begyndelse, fortsatt til disse Tider, deelt udi tvende Parter*. Tom. I. Köpenhamn, 1742.

Holmberg, U. *Der Baum des Lebens*. Annales Academiae Scientiarum Fennicae. Ser.B.Tom. XVI. Helsinki, 1922–1923.

Holmquist, Hjalmar. "Ur Swedenborgsforskningens historia." *Kyrklig tidskrift* 15 (1909): 97–132.

Hoppe, H. "Die Kosmogonie Emanuel Swedenborgs und die Kantsche und Laplacesche Theorie." *Archiv für Geschichte der Philosophie* XXV:NF XVIII (1912): 53–68.

Horatius. *Horatius Flaccus Oden und Epoden*. Ed. by Adolf Kiessling and Richard Heinze. 7th ed. Berlin: Weidmannsche Buchhandel, 1930.

Huber, Kurt. *Leibniz*. München: Oldenbourg, 1951.

Hutin, Serge. *Les disciples anglais de Jacob Boehme aux XVIIe et XVIIIe siècles*. Paris: Edition Denoël, 1960.

Jacobsson, Nils. "Den svenska herrnhutismens uppkomst. Bidrag till de religiösa rörelsernas historia i Sverige under 1700-talet." Ph.D.diss., University of Uppsala, 1908.

Jaspers, Karl. *Strindberg und van Gogh: Versuch einer pathographischen Analyse unter vergleichender Heranziehung von Swedenborg und Hölderlin*. 2nd ed. Berlin: Springer Verlag, 1926.

Jonsson, Inge. "Emanuel Swedenborg och Yttersta domen. Ett litterärt tvåhundraårsminne." *Ord och Bild* 67 no 6 (1958): 417–424.

――――. "Köpenhamn-Amsterdam-Paris: Swedenborgs resa 1736–38." *Lychnos* 1967–1968: 30–76. Uppsala: Almqvist & Wiksell, 1969.

――――. *Swedenborgs korrespondenslära*. Acta Universitatis Stockholmiensis. Stockholm: Almqvist & Wiksell International, 1969.

――――. *Visionary Scientist: The Effects of Science and Philosophy on Swedenborg's Cosmology*. Translated by Catherine Djurklou. West Chester, Pa.: The Swedenborg Foundation, 1999.

――――. Review of F.M. Crasta, *La filosofia della natura di Emanuel Swedenborg*. *ISIS* 93, no. 2 (2002): 312-313.

Josefson, Ruben. "Emanuel Swedenborg: En konturteckning till 250-årsminnet." *Ny Kyrklig Tidskrift* 1 (1938):1-13.

Jung, Carl Gustav. *Psychologie und Alchimie*. Zürich: Rascher, 1944.

(Kant, Immanuel.) *Kant on Swedenborg: Dreams of a Spirit-Seer and Other Writings*. Trans. by Gregory R. Johnson and Glenn Alexander Magee. Ed. by Gregory R. Johnson. West Chester, Pa.: The Swedenborg Foundation, 2003.

Kleen, Emil A.G. *Swedenborg: En lefnadsskildring*. 2 vols. Stockholm: Sandbergs, 1917, 1920.

Koch, H. "Anders Sunesen." *Dansk Biografisk Leksikon* (DBL). XXIII. Köpenhamn: Gyldendal, 1942.

Lagerborg, Rolf. *Fallet Swedenborg i belysning av nyare undersökningar*. Stockholm: Hugo Gebers förlag, 1924.

Lamm, Martin. *Swedenborg: En studie öfver hans utveckling till mystiker och andeskådare*. Stockholm: Hugo Gebers förlag, 1915: New ed. Stockholm: Hammarström & Åberg, 1987.

――――. *Emanuel Swedenborg: The Development of His Thought*. Trans. by Tomas Spiers and Anders Hallengren. West Chester, Pa.: The Swedenborg Foundation, 2000.

――――. *Upplysningstidens romantik: Den mystiskt sentimentala strömnin-*

*gen i svensk litteratur.* 2 vols. Stockholm: Hugo Gebers förlag, 1918, 1920. New ed. Stockholm: Hammarström & Åberg, 1981.

Lanson, G. *Manuel bibliographique de la littérature franc,aise moderne.* New.ed. Paris: Hachette, 1925.

Laurentius Paulinus Gothus. *Historiae arctoae libri tres.* Strängnäs, 1636.

Leeuwenhoek, Antony van. *Arcana naturae detecta.* Vol. I. Leyden, 1722.

Lehmann, Alfred. *Overtro og Trolddom fra de aeldste Tider til vore Dage.* Vol. III. Köpenhamn, 1894.

Leibniz, Gottfried Wilhelm von. *Essais de theodicée sur la bonté de Dieu, la liberté de l'homme et l'origine du mal.* Amsterdam, 1720. Latin trans. G.G. *Leibnitii Tentamina Theodicaeae de bonitate Dei, libertate hominis et origine mali.* Frankfurt & Leipzig, 1739. G.G. *Leibnitii Epistolae ad diversos.* Ed. by Ch. Kortholt. Vols. III–IV. Leipzig, 1738–1742.

———. *Oeuvres philosophiques de Leibniz.* Ed. by P. Janet. Vol. II. Paris, 1866.

Lenhammar, Harry. "Tolerans och bekännelsetvång. Studier i den svenska swedenborgianismen 1765–1795." Ph.D.diss., University of Uppsala, 1966.

Liedgren, Emil. "Jacob Arrhenius." *Svenskt Biografiskt Lexikon* II. Stockholm: Albert Bonniers förlag, 1920.

———. *Svensk psalm och andlig visa.* Stockholm: Diakonistyrelsens förlag, 1926.

Lindborg, Rolf. "Descartes i Uppsala. Striderna om 'nya filosofien' 1663–1689." Ph.D. diss., University of Uppsala, 1965.

Linderholm, Emanuel. *Sven Rosén.* Stockholm: Almqvist & Wiksell, 1911.

Lindqvist, Svante. "Technology on Trial: The Introduction of Steam Power Technology into Sweden, 1715–1736." Ph.D. diss., University of Uppsala, 1984.

Lindroth, Sten. "Emanuel Swedenborg." *Ny illustrerad svensk litteraturhistoria.* Vol.II, 177–199. Stockholm: Natur och Kultur, 1956.

———. "Paracelsismen i Sverige till 1600–talets mitt." Ph.D.diss., University of Uppsala, 1943.

———. "Uralstringen: Ett kapitel ur biologiens äldre historia." *Lychnos* (1939):159-192.

Lippmann, Eduard von. *Urzeugung und Lebenskraft: Zur Geschichte dieser Probleme von den ältesten Zeiten an bis zu den Anfängen des 20. Jahrhunderts.* Berlin: Julius Springer, 1933.

Lowes, John Livingstone. *The Road to Xanadu: A Study in the Ways of the Imagination.* 2nd ed. London: Constable, 1951.

Lucretius. *On the Nature of Things*. Trans. by H.A.J. Munro. Great Books of the Western World. Vol. 12. Chicago: Encyclopedia Britannica, 1952.

————. *Titi Lucreti Cari De rerum natura libri sex*. Ed. by C. Bailey. Vol. I. Oxford: Oxford University Press, 1947.

Lundgaard Simonsen, V. *Kildehistoriske studier i Anders Arrebos forfatterskab*. Köpenhamn: Munksgaard, 1955.

Maass, E. "Untersuchungen zu Properz und seinen griechischen Vorbildern." *Hermes* 31 (1896):375–434.

Macrobius. *Aur. Theodosii Macrobii Opera*. New ed. by I. Pontanus., J. Meursius, and J. Gronovius. London, 1694.

Malebranche, Nicolas de. *De inquirenda veritate libri sex. In quibus mentis humanae Natura disquiritur, & quomodo variis illius facultatibus, ut in scientiis error vitetur, utendum sit, demonstratur*. Genève, 1685.

————. *De la recherche de la verité, où l'on traite de la nature de l'esprit de l'homme, & de l'usage qu'il en doit faire pour éviter l'erreur dans les sciences*. 6th ed. 4 vols. Paris, 1712.

————. *Entretiens sur la metaphysique & sur la religion*. Rotterdam, 1688. *Oeuvres complètes de Malebranche*. Tome I, *De la recherche de la vérité*. Ed.by D. Roustan. Paris: Boivin, 1938.

Matter, Jacques. *Emmanuel de Swedenborg, sa vie, ses écrits et sa doctrine*. Paris, 1863.

Mersennus, F.M. *Quaestiones celeberrimae in Genesim*. Paris, 1623.

Migne, J.- P. *Admonitio in librum De spiritu et anima*. Patrologia latina. Vol. XL. Paris, 1887.

Milton, John. *Paradise Lost*. Great Books of the Western World. Vol. 32. Chicago: Encyclopedia Britannica, 1952.

————. *Det förlorade paradiset. Poem i tolf sånger af Milton*. Trans. into Swedish by Johan Gabriel Oxenstierna. Stockholm, 1815.

More, Henry. *Henrici Mori Cantabrigiensis scriptorum philosophicorum*. Tom. II. London, 1679.

Mornet, Daniel. *Molière*. 4th ed. Paris: Hatier, 1943.

Mouy, P. *Le développement de la physique cartésienne 1646–1712*. Bibliothèque d'histoire de la philosophie. Paris: J. Vrin, 1934.

Needham, John. *A History of Embryology*. Cambridge: The University Press, 1934.

Nelson, Axel. "Eric Benzelius d.y:s eftermäle: Några anteckningar." *Donum Grapeanum: Studier tillägnade Anders Grape: 77–94*. Uppsala: Almqvist & Wiksell, 1945.

*Neue Zeitungen von Gelehrten Sachen auf das Jahr MDCCXLV.* Leipzig, 1745.

Nilsson, Martin P:son. *Geschichte der griechischen Religion.* Vol. I. München: Beck, 1941.

Nordenmark, Nils V.E. "Swedenborg som astronom." *Arkiv för matematik, astronomi och fysik* 23 A, no. 13 (The Royal Swedish Academy of Sciences, 1933): 1–102.

Nordenskiöld, Erik. *Biologins historia: En överblick.* 3 vols. Helsingfors: Björck & Börjesson, 1920–1924.

Nordström, Johan. "Georg Stiernhielm: Filosofiska fragment I." Ph.D.diss., University of Uppsala, 1924.

Nyman, Alf. *Själsbegreppets förvandlingar: Fyra allmänfattliga kapitel jämte ett inlägg om växtbesjälning.* Stockholm: Hugo Gebers förlag, 1943.

———. *Utflykter i idévärlden: Från Sokrates till Korzybski.* Malmö: Bernces, 1956.

Odhner, Claes Teodor. "The Worship and Love of God." *New Church Life* 34 (1914): 329–334.

Odhner, Hugo Lj. *Swedenborg's Epic of Paradise and Its Literary Sources.* Bryn Athyn, Pa.: Academy of the New Church, 1945.

Olsson, Henry. "C.J.L. Almquist före Törnrosens bok." Ph.D.diss., University of Stockholm, 1927.

———. "Den svenska romantikens litteraturforskning." *Finsk tidskrift* CXII (1932):51–75.

Ovid. *Metamorphoses.* Trans. by Rolfe Humphries. Bloomington & Indianapolis: Indiana University Press, 1955.

———. *Ovidii Metamorphoser öfversatte af Gudmund Adlerbeth.* New ed. by Jacob Adlerbeth, repr. Örebro,1862.

———. P. *Ovidi Nasonis Metamorphoseon.* Libri XV. Ed. by H. Magnus. Leipzig: E. Rohmkopf, 1914.

———. *Publii Ovidii Nasonis Metamorphoseon.* Libri XV. Ed. by G. Walchius. Leipzig, 1731.

[Palmblad, Wilhelm Fredrik.] *Samtidens märkvärdigaste personer.* Biographisk tidskrift I. Uppsala, 1820.

Paracelsus, Theophrast. *Das Buch Paragranum.* Ed. by Franz Strunz. Leipzig: E. Diederichs, 1903.

———. *Sämtliche Werke.* Ed. by Karl Sudhoff. Vols. 13 and 14. München & Berlin:Oldenbourg, 1931.

Pareus, D. *Operum theologicorum exegeticorum.* Tom. I:1. Frankfurt, 1647.

Pauly, A.- Wissowa, G. *Real-Encyklopädie der classischen Altertumswissenschaft.* Bd VI, Halbbd 36:1. Stuttgart: J.B.Metzler, 1909, 1942.

Pernetty, Antoine Joseph. *Granskning af Emanuel Swedenborgs lefnad och lära.* Stockholm, 1820.

Petavius, D. *Uranologion sive systema variorum authorum.* Paris, 1630.

Peter, J. *A Critique of Paradise Lost.* New York: Columbia University Press, 1960.

Philo Judaeus. *Philonis Judaei Opera.* Ed. by Th. Mangey. Vol. I. London, 1742.

Picinelli,Fillipo. *Mundus symbolicus, in emblematum universitate formatus, explicatus, et tam sacris, quam profanis eruditionibus ac sententiis illustratus.* 2 vols. Köln, 1695.

Pico della Mirandola, Ioannes. *Opera quae extant omnia.* Vol. II. Basel, 1601.

Pintard, René. *Le libertinage érudit.* 2 vols. Paris: Boivin, 1943.

Plato. *Timaeus.* Ed. by R.G. Bury. In *Plato.* The Loeb Classical Library, vol. VII. London: Harvard University Press, 1952.

———. *The Republic.* Trans. by Benjamin Jowett. Great Books of the Western World, vol. 7. Chicago: Encyclopedia Britannica, 1952.

Pleijel, Henning. *Karolinsk kyrkofromhet, pietism och herrnhutism 1680–1772.* Svenska kyrkans historia V. Stockholm & Uppsala: Diakonistyrelsens förlag, 1935.

Plutarch. *Vermischte Schriften.* Ed. by H. Conrad. Vol. I. München & Leipzig: Georg Müller, 1911.

Praz, Mario. *Studies in Seventeenth-Century Imagery.* Vol. I. Studies of The Warburg Institute 3. London: The Warburg Institute, 1939.

Ramström, Martin. "Emanuel Swedenborg as an Anatomist." *British Medical Journal* (Oct. 15, 1910):1153–1155.

———. "Hvarpå grundar sig Swedenborgs åsikt om hjärnans funktion, och särskildt om hjärnbarken som själsverksamhetens säte?" *Upsala Läkareförenings förhandlingar* XVI (1910):1-54.

———. "Om Corpora striata's och Thalami funktion enligt Swedenborg och nutida forskning." *Kungl. Sv. Vetenskapsakademiens handlingar* 49, no 9 (1912):1–52.

Robbins, F.E. *The Hexaemeral Literature: A Study of the Greek and Latin Commentaries on Genesis.* Chicago: University of Chicago Press, 1912.

Robsahm, Carl. *Anteckningar om Swedenborg.* Ed. by Anders Hallengren. Stockholm: Föreningen Swedenborgs Minne, 1989.

(Roscher, W.) Ausführliches *Lexikon der griechischen und römischen Mythologie.* 6 vols. Leipzig & Berlin: Teubner, 1884–1925.

(Rosén, Sven.) *Sven Roséns dagbok.* Ed. by N. Odenvik. Stockholm: Filadelfiaförlaget, 1948.

Rudberg, Gunnar. "Antika urtidsteorier." *Samtiden* 23 (1921):89–104.

Rudwin, M. *The Devil in Legend and Literature.* Chicago & London: The Open Court Publishing Company, 1931.

Russell, Bertrand. *A Critical Exposition of the Philosophy of Leibniz.* 2$^{nd}$ ed. London: George Allen & Unwin, Ltd., 1949.

Rydberg, Sven. "Svenska studieresor till England under frihetstiden." Ph.D. diss., University of Uppsala, 1951.

Rydberg, Viktor. *Undersökningar i germanisk mytologi.* Vol. II. Stockholm: Albert Bonniers förlag, 1889.

Rydelius, Andreas. *Anmerkningar öfver then så kallade Christiani Democriti Demonstratio evangelica.* Linköping , 1736.

———. *Nödiga Förnufts-Öfningar, at lära känna thet sundas wägar och thet osundas felsteg.* 2$^{nd}$ ed. Linköping, 1737.

Scheuchzer, J.J. *Kupfer-Bibel.* Augsburg & Ulm, 1731.

Schlieper, Hans. "Emanuel Swedenborgs System der Naturphilosophie, besonders in seiner Beziehung zu Goethe-Herderschen Anschauungen." Ph.D. diss., University of Berlin, 1901.

Scholem, Gershom. *Les grands courants de la mystique juive.* Paris: Payot, 1950.

———. *Major Trends in Jewish Mysticism.* New York: Schocken Books, 1946.

Schück, Henrik. *Från det forna Upsala: Några kulturbilder.* Stockholm: Hugo Gebers förlag, 1917.

Sennert, Daniel. *De chymicorum cum Aristotelicis et Galenicis consensu ac dissensu* lib. I. Wittenberg, 1619.

Sewall, Frank. "A Drama of Creation." *The New-Church Review* 3 (October 1882): 167–195.

———. *Swedenborg and the* "Sapientia angelica." London: Constable, 1910.

———. "The Only-Begotten in Swedenborg's Cosmology and Theology." *The New Philosophy* 17 (1914):89–103.

Sigstedt, Cyriel O. *The Swedenborg Epic: The Life and Works of Emanuel Swedenborg.* 1952. London: Swedenborg Society, 1981.

*The Spectator 1711.* London, 1797.

Spegel, Haquin. *Guds Werk och Hwila.* Stockholm, 1685. New ed. by

Bernt Olsson and Barbro Nilsson. Stockholm: Svenska Vitterhetssamfundet, 1998.

Statius, P. *Papini Stati Thebais*. Ed. by A. Klotz. Leipzig: Teubner, 1908.

Stolpe, Sven. "Från stoicism till mystik. Studier i drottning Kristinas maximer." Ph.D.diss., University of Uppsala, 1959.

Stroh, Alfred H. "Analysis and Review of 'The Worship and Love of God.'" *The New Philosophy* 5 (1902):33–75.

―――, ed. *Catalogus bibliothecae Emanuelis Swedenborgii*. Stockholm: 1907.

―――. "The Sources of Swedenborg's Early Philosophy of Nature." In *Opera quaedam aut inedita aut obsoleta de rebus naturalibus, nunc edita sub auspiciis Regiae Academiae Scientiarum Suecicae*, 3 vols., III. Stockholm: The Royal Swedish Academy of Sciences, 1911.

―――. "Swedenborg's Contributions to Psychology." In *Transactions of the International Swedenborg Congress* 1910:151–164. London: Swedenborg Society, 1911.

―――. "Swedenborg's Early Life, Scientific Works, and Philosophy." *The New-Church Magazine* 34 (1915):172–179, 204–210, 262–269, 354–359, 396–403, 440–445, 490–498, and 540–547.

Stroh, Alfred H., and Ekelöf, Greta. *Kronologisk förteckning öfver Emanuel* Stockholm: Diakonistyrelsens förlag, 1959.

Sundelin, Robert. *Swedenborgianismens historia i Sverige under förra århundradet*. Uppsala, 1886.

Sundén, Hjalmar. *Religionen och rollerna: Ett psykologiskt studium av fromheten*. Stockholm: Diakonistyrelsens förlag, 1959.

Swedberg, Jesper. *Lefwernes Beskrifning*. I. Ed. by G. Wetterberg. Publications of Kungl. Vetenskapssocieteten i Lund 25:1. Lund, 1941.

Svendsen, Paulus. *Gullalderdröm og utviklingstro: En idéhistorisk undersökelse*. Oslo: Gyldendal Norsk Forlag, 1940.

Tafel, Rudolf L. *Documents concerning the Life and Character of Emanuel Swedenborg*. Trans. and ed. by R.L. Tafel. 3 vols. London: Swedenborg Society, 1875–1890.

Taylor, G.C. *Milton's Use of Du Bartas*. Cambridge, Mass.: Harvard University Press, 1934.

*Thesaurus linguae latinae*. I. Leipzig: Teubner, 1900.

Thibaut de Maisières, M. *Les poèmes inspirés du début de la Genèse à l'époque de la renaissance*. Louvain: Université de Louvain, 1931.

Tigerstedt, E.N. *Svensk litteraturhistoria*. 3d ed. Stockholm: Natur och Kultur, 1960.

350 ✸ Bibliography

Toksvig, Signe. *Emanuel Swedenborg, Scientist and Mystic.* 1948; repr. New York: The Swedenborg Foundation, 1983.

Tottie, H.W. "Jesper Swedbergs lif och verksamhet. Bidrag till svenska kyrkans historia I–II." Ph.D. diss., University of Uppsala, 1885–1886.

(Tremellius, I., and Junius, F.) *Testamenti veteris Biblia sacra.* Frankfurt, 1579.

———. *Biblia sacra, sive Testamentum vetus, ab Im. Tremellio et Fr. Junio ex hebraeo latinè redditum, et Testamentum novum, à Theod. Beza è greco in latinum versum.* Amsterdam, 1648.

Wahlström, Bengt. "Swedberg och änglarna." In *Psalm och sång: Studier tillägnade Emil Liedgren.* Lund: Gleerup, 1959.

Walden, Frederik Hermann von. Asessor Svedenborgs Levnet. Köpenhamn: s.a.

Walli, G. "Gabriel Andersson Beyer." *Svenskt Biografiskt Lexikon* 4. Stockholm: Albert Bonniers förlag, 1924.

Warren, Samuel M. *A Compendium of the Theological Writings of Emanuel Swedenborg.* 1875; repr. New York: The Swedenborg Foundation, 1979.

Varro. *M. Terentii Varronis De lingua latina libri qui supersunt.* 2 vols. Zweibrücken, 1788.

Wedberg, Anders. *Filosofins historia.* II. Stockholm: Albert Bonniers förlag, 1959.

Vergilius. *P. Vergili Maronis Aeneidos.* 12 books. Ed. by R. Sabbadini and L. Castiglioni. Torino, Italy: G.B. Paravia & C., 1958.

———. *The Aeneid.* Trans. by J. Rhoades. Great Books of the Western World 13. Chicago: Encyclopedia Britannica, 1952.

Whiston, William. *A New Theory of the Earth, from Its Original to the Consummation of All Things.* 5th ed. London, 1737.

White, William. *Swedenborg: His Life and Writings.* London, 1856.

———. *Emanuel Swedenborg: His Life and Writings.* 2 vols. London: Simpkin, Marshall, 1867.

Whiting, G.W. *Milton's Literary Milieu.* Chapel Hill, N.C.: University of North Carolina Press, 1939.

Widengren, Geo. "Gnostikern Stagnelius." *Samlaren,* new series 25 (1944), 115–178.

Wijkmark, Henning. *Wolffs filosofi och svensk teologi: Strövtåg i 1700-talets disputationslitteratur.* Bilaga till Nya Elementarskolans årsredogörelse 1914–1915. Stockholm, 1915.

Wilkinson, J.J.G. *Emanuel Swedenborg: A Biographical Sketch.* 2nd ed. London: James Speirs, 1886.

Wilkinson, L.P. *Ovid Recalled.* 1955; repr. Portway: C. Chivers, 1974.

Villars, N. de. *Comte de Gabalis, ou Entretiens sur les sciences secretes.* Amsterdam, 1715.

Willey, Basil. *The Eighteenth-Century Background.* London: Chatto & Windus, 1940.

Williams, A. *Commentaries on Genesis as a Basis for Hexaemeral Material in the Literature of the Late Renaissance.* Studies in Philology 34. Chapel Hill, N.C.: University of North Carolina Press, 1937.

Wolff, Christian von. *Philosophia prima, sive Ontologia, methodo scientifica pertractata, qua omnis cognitionis humanae principia continentur.* Frankfurt & Leipzig, 1730.

————. *Psychologia empirica methodo scientifica pertractata, qua ea, quae de anima humana indubia experientiae fide constant, continentur et ad solidam universae philosophiae practicae ac theologiae naturalis tractationem via sternitur.* Frankfurt & Leipzig, 1732.

————. *Psychologia rationalis methodo scientifica pertractata, qua ea, quae de anima humana indubia experientiae fide innotescunt, per essentiam et naturam animae explicantur, et ad intimiorem naturae ejusque autoris cognitionem profutura proponuntur.* Frankfurt & Leipzig, 1734.

Worcester, Benjamin. *The Life and Mission of Emanuel Swedenborg.* Boston: Roberts Brothers, 1883.

Voss, Gerhard Johannes. *De theologia gentili, et physiologia christiana; sive de origine ac progressu idololatriae, ad veterum gesta, ac rerum naturam, reductae; deque naturae mirandis, quibus homo adducitur ad Deum.* Liber I et II. Amsterdam, 1642.

Zöckler, D. *Geschichte der Beziehungen zwischen Theologie und Naturwissenschaft.* 2 Vols. Gütersloh, 1877, 1879.

# INDEX OF NAMES

**Inge Jonsson** was born in 1928 in Stockholm. He received his Ph.D. from Stockholm University in 1961 and became assistant professor at the university in the same year. In 1973 he was appointed full professor of Comparative Literature at the university, a position he maintained until his retirement in1994. For the last six years prior to his retirement, he also served as rector of the university. His bibliography contains four books on various aspects of Swedenborg's thinking, two books on the history of literary theory, and a large number of articles on research policy and university administration problems. Dr. Jonsson has also written a book on the history of the Royal Swedish Academy of Letters, History, and Antiquities, of which he was president from 1993 to 2001. As emeritus, he has participated in many university evaluation programs, nationally and internationally.

**Matilda McCarthy** was born in 1971 in Stockholm. She has a degree in Comparative Literature with English from Stockholm University. She currently works for Academic Books in Stockholm.

## Swedenborg Studies

is a scholarly series published by the Swedenborg Foundation.
The primary purpose of the series is to make materials available for understanding
the life and thought of Emanuel Swedenborg (1688–1772) and the impact his
thought has had on others. The Foundation undertakes to publish original studies
and English translations and to republish primary sources that are otherwise
difficult to access. Currently available in the series are:

315-0   *A Drama of Creation: Sources and Influences in Swedenborg's* Worship
and Love of God *by Inge Jonsson, trans. M. McCarthy, pb, $19.95

314-2   *The Covert Enlightenment: Eighteenth-Century Counterculture and Its
Aftermarth* by Alfred Gabay, pb, $19.95

310-X   *Kant on Swedenborg:* Dreams of a Spirit-Seer *and Other Writings* by
Immanuel Kant, trans. G. Johnson/A. Magee, pb, $19.95

301-0   *Swedenborg Explorer's Guidebook: A Research Manual* by W. F. Woofenden,
hc, $29.95

198-0   *Swedenborg's Dream Diary* by Lars Bergquist, trans. A. Hallengren, hc, $24.95
199-9   *Swedenborg's Dream Diary,* pb, $17.95

197-2   *Epic of the Afterlife: A Literary Approach to Swedenborg* by Olof Lagercrantz,
trans. A. Hallengren, hc, $21.95
248-0   *Epic of the Afterlife,* pb, $16.95

195-6   *Emanuel Swedenborg: Visionary Savant in the Age of Reason* by Ernst Benz,
trans. N. Goodrick-Clarke, hc, $24.95

194-8   *Emanuel Swedenborg: The Development of His Thought* by Martin Lamm,
trans. T. Spiers/A. Hallengren, pb, $18.95

192-1   *Visionary Scientist: The Effects of Science and Philosophy on Swedenborg's
Cosmology* by Inge Jonsson, trans. C. Djurklou, hc, $24.95

191-3   *Visionary Scientist,* pb, $17.95

188-3   *Gallery of Mirrors: Reflections of Swedenborgian Thought* by Anders
Hallengren, hc, $24.95
189-1   *Gallery of Mirrors,* pb, $16.95

187-5   *Schelling and Swedenborg: Mysticism and German Idealism* by Friedemann
Horn, trans. G. Dole, hc, $17.95
186-7   *Schelling and Swedenborg,* pb, $13.95

184-0   *Swedenborg: Buddha of the North* by D. T. Suzuki, trans. A. Bernstein, pb,
$13.95

183-2   *Swedenborg and Esoteric Islam* by Henri Corbin, trans. L. Fox, pb, $14.95

182-4   *With Absolute Respect: The Swedenborgian Theology of Charles Carroll Bonney*
by George Dole, pb, $6.95

181-6   *Swedenborg and Kant: . . . Mystical View of Mankind and the Dual Nature of
Humankind . . .* by Gottlieb Florschütz, trans. G. Dole, pb, $6.95

180-8   *Sampson Reed: Primary Source Material for Emerson Studies* by George Dole,
pb, $6.95

The Swedenborg Foundation Publishers
320 N. Church Street
West Chester, PA 19380
Tel: 610-430-3222, ext. 10 • Fax: 610-430-7982
customerservice@swedenborg.com
www.swedenborg.com

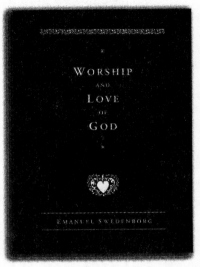